L. F.

Legislative Behavior

A READER IN THEORY AND RESEARCH

Legislative Behavior

A READER IN THEORY AND RESEARCH

EDITED BY

John C. Wahlke VANDERBILT UNIVERSITY

Heinz Eulau STANFORD UNIVERSITY

THE FREE PRESS OF GLENCOE, ILLINOIS

Contents—An Overview

Contents

Section III—THE SOCIAL AND PSYCHOLOGICAL BASES
OF LEGISLATIVE BEHAVIOR

Contributors

Benjamin Akzin
Hebrew University, Jerusalem

Charles A. Beard

Samuel H. Beer
Harvard University

George M. Belknap
University of California
(Berkeley)

Eric C. Bellquist
University of California
(Berkeley)

Dean R. Brimhall

William Buchanan
University of Southern California

Peter Campbell
University of Manchester

David R. Derge
Indiana University

Leon D. Epstein
University of Wisconsin

Heinz Eulau
Stanford University

David G. Farrelly
University of California
(Los Angeles)

Charles D. Farris
University of Florida

LeRoy C. Ferguson
Michigan State University

Herman Finer
University of Chicago

J. Leiper Freeman
Vanderbilt University

Oliver Garceau
Bennington College

H. R. G. Greaves
*London School of Economics
and Political Science*

Ivan Hinderaker
University of California
(Los Angeles)

Alice M. Holden

Ralph K. Huitt
University of Wisconsin

Charles S. Hyneman
Indiana University

Malcolm E. Jewell
University of Kentucky

Otto Kirchheimer
New School for Social Research

John D. Lewis
Oberlin College

Duane Lockard
Connecticut College

R. Duncan Luce
Harvard University

John B. McConaughy
University of South Carolina

W. J. M. Mackenzie
University of Manchester

Duncan MacRae, Jr.
University of Chicago

Allan W. Martin
*New South Wales
University of Technology*

Fritz Morstein Marx
U. S. Bureau of the Budget

John H. Millett
University of Rochester

Richard E. Neustadt
Columbia University

Arthur S. Otis

Stuart A. Rice

William H. Riker
Lawrence College

Arnold Rogow
Haverford College

James N. Rosenau
Rutgers University

Lloyd S. Shapley
The Rand Corporation

Edward A. Shils
University of Chicago

Martin Shubik
General Electric Company

Howard E. Shuman
Office of Senator Paul Douglas

Corinne Silverman
Inter-University Case Program

David B. Truman
Columbia University

John C. Wahlke
Vanderbilt University

Legislative Behavior

A READER IN THEORY AND RESEARCH

Introduction

OF ALL POLITICAL INSTITUTIONS, none is more vital to the process of linking governors and governed in relationships of authority, responsibility, and legitimacy, than the modern legislature. Without some understanding of its character and functioning one can have only very partial understanding of the process of government and its place in society.

Understanding of the legislature calls for more than merely a grasp of the mechanics of parliamentary rules and procedures, the detailed facts about length of session, size of chamber or structure of legislative offices, or the legal technicalities of bill-drafting, engrossment, and executive veto. Legal rules and procedures and environmental facts undoubtedly describe much of the activity of legislatures by prescribing some actions and proscribing others for legislators. But legislators engage in many actions not accounted for in simple formal or legal description of the legislature as an institution. In particular, the choices they make (of which the choice to vote "aye" or "nay" is no doubt the chief one) are left wholly unexplained by formal and legal study. Explanation of such choices is essential to explanation of the decisions made by the legislature as an institutionalized group of persons. And it is this latter explanation that is of concern to students of politics. Indeed, students of politics are interested in parliamentary mechanics and legal formalities only insofar as these will help them understand legislative decisions. The student of politics, therefore, must of necessity seek to understand the behavior of legislators if he is to gain that kind of knowledge about the structure and functioning of the legislature as an institution which is requisite to understanding the larger political system. For the legislature as an institution exists physically only in the persons called "legislators." As an institution, it is never more nor less than, nor different from, the patterns or uniformities in the actions of legislators. What the legislature decides and how it decides it can never be divorced from the behavior of legislators.

Political science as a discipline has only recently come to recognize the place of political behavior study in the study of government. For some, the term "political behavior" is even today more polemical than analytical. It is a principal assumption of this volume that behavioral analysis and institutional analysis are not mutually exclusive categories, not alternative fields of study, but rather are mutually interdependent approaches to the central problems of political inquiry. Without questions about institutional functions and structure as a guide, behavioral analyses obtain no theoretical focus relevant to the study of politics; without behavioral analyses to explain the conduct of human actors, institutional analyses remain wholly speculative.

We have therefore included in Section I of this volume, a number of selections dealing directly with conceptual and theoretical problems familiar to students of legislative institutions. Some of the reasons for studying the behavior of legislators are suggested in the discussions presented in this section, as are some basic terms and concepts for that study.

In this volume, we are using the term "legislature" in a somewhat restricted sense, to refer only to those elected bodies in political systems of the Western culture that engage in the functions of proposing, deliberating, and deciding about public policy. The legislatures of the Soviet Union and its satellites do not fall within this frame of reference, since their essential functions within their respective political systems are quite different. Likewise, many representative bodies of other times and places—for example, the Areopagus of classical Athens or the Concilium Plebis of latter-day Rome—are not included within our definition of "legislature" since their functions, too, were considerably different from the functions of, say, the American Congress or the British Parliament today. Comparative analysis of the functions of the many types of collectivity sometimes connoted by the term "legislature" is no doubt urgently needed by political science, and historical analysis of the evolution and development of modern legislatures from earlier crypto- or pseudo-legislatures would no doubt illuminate legislative study. But such analyses could not be included within the limits of this volume.

Our aim has been to present, in compact and convenient form, some significant theoretical and research contributions dealing with the most important problems concerning the behavior of legislatures and legislators. We should expect such a volume to be especially useful to students of the legislative process as a specialized topic in political science. But we hope, beyond this, that it will be useful to others in helping them place the study of legislatures in the broader context of political inquiry. We hope it will prove useful in relating the study of legislative behavior to the study of legislatures as institutions, in suggesting ways of approaching the study of political behavior in other institutional contexts—judicial, administrative or voting behavior, for example—and in suggesting relationships among the various institutions and behaviors that ultimately make up the process of government.

Obviously we cannot in this limited space offer a truly comprehensive treatment covering all details and every work in the field of legislative behavior. We have had perforce to omit many works of signal merit and to leave unmentioned many significant problems relevant to the main one. In making our selections, we have sought first of all what seem to us particularly important contributions to the understanding of legislative behavior. Some of these are the products of insightful speculation, based on conceptual imagination or on personal legislative experiences; others, the products of carefully delimited empirical research into particular, narrowly defined aspects of the problem. Some of them offer summary analyses of whole stretches of the field; others, more detailed consideration of lesser parts of it.

In general, we have utilized works appearing in various professional journals and omitted familiar works more readily available in most libraries. At the same time, we have tried to broaden conceptions of the legislative process by including discussions focused on many different legislatures rather than limiting ourselves to only a single political system. Very few of the selections attempt comparative analysis of problems of legislative behavior, and we do not suggest that the analyses of the various particular legislatures presented here can be immediately used for such purposes. But we do think that consideration of

the various problems in the light of discussions focused on many different systems will help promote that broad view of the legislative process which, in turn, will eventually lead to genuinely comparative analyses of legislative behavior.

We have not attempted to provide summary bibliographical suggestions. The literature generally relevant to the subject is so vast as to deserve a separate work merely to treat it adequately for bibliographical purposes. More important, however, the student who wishes to pursue more closely any of the topics covered here will find a wealth of bibliographical suggestions in the footnotes to the individual articles dealing with those topics. Any listing of the materials which directly treat problems of legislative behavior as such would merely duplicate, to a large extent, information available in the footnotes.

The utility and the feasibility of a volume such as this were first brought to our attention in the course of theoretical explorations for research into the role orientations of American state legislators, undertaken with the aid of research grants from the Committee on Political Behavior of the Social Science Research Council. Further encouragement and aid, as well as valuable suggestions and ideas, were given by our colleagues in the research project, William Buchanan of the University of Southern California and LeRoy C. Ferguson of Michigan State University. We wish to express our gratitude and appreciation to the Committee members and to our research colleagues, without, of course, implicating any of them in any way in the substance of this work. We are also indebted to the Center for Advanced Study in the Behavioral Sciences whose superb facilities made our task both easier and more pleasurable.

John C. Wahlke
Heinz Eulau

Stanford, California

SECTION I

The Historical and Institutional Context
of Legislative Behavior

INTRODUCTORY NOTE

IF LEGISLATIVE BEHAVIOR is to be distinguished from other forms of political behavior, such as administrative or judicial conduct, account must be taken of the institutional context in which it occurs. For it is the legislature as an institution which sets boundaries within which legislative action takes place, and by which the behavior of legislators is circumscribed. By legislative behavior is meant not only conduct in the performance of the legislative role, but also those attitudes and perceptions which relate to the process and substance of legislation. The institutional objective of law-making, as well as the institutional procedures designed to achieve the objective, may be considered parameters of legislative behavior.

As a legislature is an institution whose existence transcends the individual legislator's incumbency, legislative behavior may also be patterned by past as well as current configurations in the power structure of the political system. As institutions, legislatures are phenomena in time, with human memories going beyond the limitations of time. These memories are transmitted from generation to generation and come to develop an existence of their own which, consciously or unconsciously, shapes current legislative behavior.

The making of laws—legislation—is the oldest, and continues to be the central, objective of legislative bodies. But, as Benjamin Akzin shows in "The Nature of Law and Legislation," the specification of law-making as the peculiar province of assemblies, though recognized and institutionalized in ancient Rome, had to await the emergence of the modern state, and, in particular, of the democratic state. As long as custom, nature, divinity or king were accepted as the highest authorities, representative bodies were severely limited in their law-making capacity. Only gradually did their participation in legislation change from petition and consent to formulation and promulgation. In this development, both the conception of law and of legislation underwent a process of secularization coinciding with the growth of representative bodies and changes in their social composition.

Yet, paradoxically, the increasing representational character of popular assemblies tended to make legislative behavior less relevant to legislative output than one should expect if legislation were the only objective of legislatures. The representational function and the legislative function could readily conflict. Moreover, once the technical development of society reached a scale where expert knowledge rather than lay enlightenment became a condition of effective government, the formulation of public policy tended to be either a function of the executive, with its corps of expert civil servants, or policy suggestions came from well-informed, interested groups outside the formal governmental apparatus. Under these conditions, a legislator's pre-occupations will be less with the facts relevant to law-making —facts which "are seldom at hand when the legislator needs them"—than with the climate of opinion as it relates to the decisions confronting him. Legislation, T. V. Smith has said, is "the way in which gossip transforms the suggested into the customary."

Indeed, because they are preeminently representative institutions, modern legislatures are more sensitive barometers of public moods and feelings than either administrative or judicial institutions. The notion that a legislature has the objective of articulating expressions of popular sentiments, either in favor of or in opposition to governmental policies, is widely held by legislators themselves. In fact, many more proposed laws die in legislative committees or on legislative floors than are passed. So it comes about that the legislature may be an instrument of social change, or an instrument of social obstruction, and these conditions, stemming from its representative character, are just as likely to mold legislative behavior as the law-making task as such.

Representation is, of course, one of the great engineering feats of man in the governance of men. Yet, it has proved frustrating because, more often than not, the attempt was made to solve its attendant problems by definition in speculative and normative terms. Should the representative be a free agent, or should he be bound by instructions? This formulation of the problem has tended to obfuscate, rather than clarify, the key questions by removing representation from its historical setting, structural context and polemical frame of reference. More insight has come from historical descriptions of the emergence and development of representative institutions. In particular, historical research has been cumulatively corrective of many false impressions, such as that representation was unknown in antiquity, or that it originated in the forests of Germany. Unfortunately, some of these studies, exemplified by the article of Charles A. Beard and John D. Lewis on "Representative Government in Evolution," are possessed by an evolutionary bias which tends to identify representation with particular representative institutions, instead of maintaining a distinction which seems desirable for theoretical clarity. Or historical study, though lucid in distinguishing between unconditional and mandatory representation, is limited by the singular nature of the situations under investigation, as appears from Alice M. Holden's "The Imperative Mandate in the Spanish Cortes of the Middle Ages."

On the other hand, once representation is seen as a functional problem, from the point of view of the political system as a whole, inquiry need no longer be directed towards discovering or specifying the "nature" or "essence" of the representative process, but rather towards the conditions or circumstances under which the political system assumes representational forms. Moreover, the functional approach deals with repre-

sentation as a means rather than as an end. For instance, if responsibility is postulated as an appropriate end, the problem of the relationship between representative and represented can be reformulated. The problem becomes one of stating the conditions under which representation can guarantee the responsibility of the governors to the governed. The classical, normative question —whether the representative should be bound by a mandate, or whether he should follow his own best judgment—becomes largely irrelevant. The problem is now to discover under what conditions the representative can afford to disregard the wishes of his constituents and still hope to maintain their confidence, or under what conditions the demands of constituents do, in fact, become mandatory.

Two major types of representative government have long been recognized as constitutional alternatives of democratic political systems—parliamentary government and presidential or congressional government. Both are concerned with representation from the point of view of insuring political responsibility, and in the construction of these constitutional types the relationship between the legislature and the executive in regard to the organization of power is the crucial variable. As Eric C. Bellquist indicates in a far-ranging and informed review of theoretical formulations and historical developments, both types of government allow for a multiplicity of empirical variations. Of course, a constitutional typology is not the end, but only the beginning of political inquiry. While Bellquist does not concern himself with the problem of just what behavior members of legislative bodies in differing constitutional types can be expected to exhibit, it may be assumed that—ignoring other factors such as the character of the party system or electoral methods —constitutional differences set significant institutional parameters for legislative behavior. But comparative behavioral research in this area has not as yet been undertaken, and one can only speculate about the legislator's role as a lawmaker and representative in different types of constitutional government.

Constitutional limitations are, of course, both determinants and consequences of political behavior. Constitutional arrangements, though more permanent than other institutional features of government, are never static, but subject to continuing changes which themselves are behavioral responses to the exigencies of public policy and transformations in the social and psychological bases of political systems. For instance, the institutionalization of the Opposition in the British system has profoundly changed the behavioral alternatives available to members of Parliament. Less well known, but even more interesting from the point of view of its effect on legislative behavior, is the post-war Austrian system where the two major parties are permanently aligned in forming the government, yet compete uninterruptedly between themselves. Otto Kirchheimer, in a brilliant diagnosis of "The Waning of Opposition in Parliamentary Regimes," shows how the classical parliamentary system comes to assume new institutional devices under the impact of internal and external conditions which were absent at the time of its genesis. The article is, in many respects, a masterpiece of political analysis, sensitive to the sociological, psychological and institutional problems of government in a changing historical context.

If Kirchheimer's analysis stresses developmental patterns, as they emerge from and are likely to influence legislative behavior in parliamentary systems, Fritz Morstein Marx, in "Party Responsibility and Legislative Program," deals with the consequences of the constitutional separation of powers in the American presidential system—not all consequences, of course, but those which seem to be crucial for legislative policy-making. In some respects, the separation of powers has been a convenient point of attack for those who deplore its dysfunctional effects on national policy-planning. But more relevant, probably, from the point of view of legislative behavior, has been the enormous influence of localism in American legislative bodies, both on the federal and state levels. This influence is, of course, institutionalized in the representational structure of American legislatures, with its emphasis not only on the single-member district (which is also found in parliamentary England), but also on the requirement that a representative must be a resident of the locality where he stands for election. If, as Marx points out, the parties could succeed in supplying a counter-pull to this excessive localism, many of the differences between the parliamentary and presidential regimes would disappear. Of course, such a change would fundamentally affect the role of the American legislator in making him even more a register rather than a creator of public policy than he presently is.

Yet, even severe constitutional arrangements, such as the separation of powers in the presidential system, have a way of allowing for functional alternatives which may be disguised and rationalized in terms of traditional political lore, but which, in reality, tend to make the consequences of behavior in different constitutional systems more similar than divergent, at least from a functional rather than structural point of view. In the American system, for instance, the parties may have failed so far to provide for the integration of legislative and executive policy-making, but the requirement of such integration has been satisfied, at least partially, by institutional arrangements on the executive side of the relationship. As Richard Neustadt describes it in "Presidency and Legislation: The Growth of Central Clearance," Budget Bureau review of administrative proposals for legislation was originally designed to meet the need for policy coordination in the executive establishment alone, but became an important mechanism of executive participation in the legislative process, more significant, perhaps, if less sensational, than the Presidential veto. Moreover, it has had the effect of not only strengthening the role of the executive in legislation, but, as Neustadt points out, of also benefitting Congress as well. If what one may consider the "professionalization of policy-making" continues as an important aspect of the presidential-congressional system, it is likely to have far-reaching consequences for legislative behavior.

Constitutional prescriptions and limitations are "external" parameters of legislative behavior; the rules and procedures of legislative chambers may be considered "internal" boundaries. It would, of course, be a mistake to expect, as much of the older literature did, that legislative behavior is what the formal rules say it should be. But it would be equally mistaken to assume that legislators act without reference to the procedural requirements. It was the genius of Jeremy Bentham to recognize, as H. R. G. Greaves makes explicit in "Bentham on the Functioning of Legislatures," that parliamentary rules are not simply prescriptions of routine operations which one may take for granted, or which make little difference in actual behavior. On the contrary, very definite needs underlie most legislative rules, and certain rather than other consequences are likely to follow from particular rules. As a theorist, therefore, Bentham was a "functionalist," and while normative-ideological considerations undoubtedly influenced his theorizing, he was especially sensitive to the political antecedents and consequences of legislative procedures.

Bentham recognized that the rules of debate are relevant not only for orderly conduct, but also for the substance of legislation. Howard E. Shuman, in a meticulous study of the debates concerning the first civil rights bill, "Procedural Rules and the Substance of Policy," makes it clear that rules not only set limits to legislative behavior, but that they can be effectively manipulated in shaping and modifying the substance of legislation. Moreover, rules are not only manipulable, but may even occasion irrational conduct. For instance, the order of voting on amendments as prescribed by the rules may create more problems than it solves. As William H. Riker, using the logic of mathematics, shows, in "Voting Methods and Irrationality in Legislative Decisions," the rules may place legislators in a position where their behavior, from the point of view of legislative objectives, becomes unconsciously irrational. Both studies exemplify the importance of institutional parameters in legislative behavior.

In so far as the provisions of legislative apportionment—how seats are to be distributed among geographical areas—are part of the institutional

context of legislative behavior, particular arrangements have significant consequences for legislative action. Farrelly and Hinderaker, in "Legislative Apportionment and Political Power," demonstrate how some of the most important factors in the power relations of American Congressmen are functions of the political impact of population changes as these affect the apportionment of legislative offices. Apportionment, they show, is crucial not only in determining the socio-economic composition of the House of Representatives, but also the character of the party system, the influence of particular delegations, and, in connection with the seniority principle, the power position of particular Congressmen.

A. Problems of Legislation and Representation

1. THE NATURE OF LAW AND LEGISLATION

Benjamin Akzin

THE LITERAL MEANING of *legislation* is "law-bringing," "law-making."[1] It is thus intimately connected with the concept of law. Before mankind began to differentiate systematically between various kinds of rules governing human conduct, the terms used were not confined to one specific meaning. Of the two relevant expressions in early Hebrew, *mishpat* meant a law as well as a judicial decision or judicial proceedings, while *khukka* was a generic term which denoted any type of command by an acknowledged authority. The Greek *nomos* comes nearer to our modern term and is mostly used in the sense of a written rule laid down by the authority of a state, but occasionally it is used also to denote any rule or principle of right or equity or morality. The absence of a clear-cut concept of the difference between various kinds of rules, one of which could be characterized today as a *law*, is the result of two causes: (1) the insufficient differentiation between the sources of authority from which various rules derive their binding force; and (2) the insufficient division of functions between various agencies of society. Indeed, the concept of *a law* presupposes the existence of an organized state in which various agencies are authorized to enact rules of a varying degree of authority. Beginnings were made in this respect in pre-Roman times, but they never progressed far enough. The difference between Divine and state law, between written and customary law, even between an individual judgment or order and a general rule were perceived, but these differences were not firmly adhered to, and so neither a clear concept of varying rules, nor a corresponding terminology could be developed.

The Latin *lex* appears really as the first specific term denoting a particular juristic rule, namely one expressly enacted on behalf of the state in a certain formal manner by a high authority, and tending toward general application. This the definition of Papinianus:[2]

Reprinted from *Iowa Law Review*, Vol. 21 (1936), pp. 713-50, where it appeared under the title, "The Concept of Legislation," by permission of the author and the publisher.

"A *lex* is a command of general application, a resolution on the part of learned men, a restraint of offences, committed either voluntarily or in ignorance, a general covenant on the part of the state."

Historically, the Roman concept of *a law* was essentially connected with a specific agency which would alone be competent to enact laws. The agency originally competent to enact these rules consisted of the assembled citizens of Rome, organized in *comitia*. According to classical Roman theory, the people of Rome possessed the highest authority within the state. Consequently, the *leges,* the rules enacted by the people, appeared as possessing the highest degree of authority among all other rules of the civil law of Rome. The growth of the state made it difficult to keep the *comitia* active as legislative agencies; on the other hand, a growing tide of aristocracy saw with disfavor the pre-eminent part of the essentially democratic *comitia*. Under the influence of these two factors, the senate displaced gradually the *comitia* as supreme law-making agency, and the *senatus-consultum* became the recognized procedural form for the creation of a written rule of highest authority. Still later, imperial edicts acquired the position of a highest type of written rule and became thus the equivalent of the *lex* and of the *senatus-consultum*. This evolution is clearly shown in the Institutes of Justinian:[3]

"4. A *lex* is an enactment of the Roman people, which it used to make on the motion of a senatorial magistrate, as for instance, a consul. . . .

"5. A *senatusconsult* is a command and ordinance of the senate, for when the Roman people had been so increased that it was difficult to assemble it together for the purpose of enacting *leges,* it seemed right that the senate should be consulted instead of the people.

"6. Again, what the Emperor determines has the force of a *lex,* the people having conferred on him all their authority and power by the *lex regia,* which was passed concerning his office and authority. Consequently, whatever the Emperor settles by rescript, or decides in his judicial capacity, or ordains by edicts, is clearly a *lex*: and these are what are called constitutions. Some of these of course are personal, and not to be followed as precedents, since this is not the Emperor's will; for a favor bestowed on individual merit, or a penalty inflicted for individual wrongdoing, or relief given without a precedent, do not go beyond the particular person: though others are general, and bind all beyond a doubt."[4]

The quoted passages indicate clearly the outstanding features of the *lex* and of its equivalents —its high authority resulting from its derivation from the highest juristic agency of the state. The context of the passage in the Institutes establishes, in addition, all other elements of the concept *lex*. It is one of *jus civile*—an expression meaning in this connection municipal law—as distinct from *jus naturale* and from *jus gentium*. It is, further, one of *jus scriptum*—written law—as distinct from *jus sine scripto*—unwritten law.[5] Furthermore, there can be detected in the texts a tendency to ascribe to the *lex* a general character, though the codifiers have to admit that some rules considered as *leges*, particularly among the *constitutiones* of the Emperors, have a validity restricted to given persons or to specific cases only.[6]

It must be admitted that the characterization given to *lex* in the *Corpus Juris Civilis* impresses one as being highly up-to-date. The *lex* is emphatically defined as a rule of high juridical authority, enacted by a specific agency held in great esteem. Almost equally emphatic is the affirmation that the *lex* is an expressly enacted rule of municipal law, and should be confused neither with the law of nature and of nations nor with customary law. In addition, the theoretically inclined Roman jurists obviously try to emphasize the general character of a *lex*, but their efforts cannot overcome the undeniable fact that many rules traditionally considered as *leges* lack the criterion of generality. All these features are equally present in any modern discussion of *laws* and legislation in the positive systems of the twentieth century.

It appears that, aside from its more or less established technical meaning, the term *lex* was widely used in the Roman Empire in a less discriminating manner. It has been seen already that the Institutes and the Digest themselves are not quite certain about the criterion of generality. Similar imprecisions seem to have been current with regard to the criterion of the enacting authority and of the manner of enactment. Expressions such as *lex mancipi* and *lex commissoria* are frequent in the technical language of Roman law, and show that *lex* must have been already as overworked a term as *law* has become in the English language.

If we depart from strictly technical language and go into the general literature of the period,

we find that *lex* has become even broader in its scope. Even the essay *de legibus* written by a professional lawyer, Cicero, is extremely vague in its use of the term. Other works of the period are even more generous in their use of *lex*, applying this term to almost any kind of rule, whatever its origin, manner of enactment, scope of application, nature and extent of binding force. *Lex* has obviously become a highly popular word, and its indiscriminate use in every-day life has influenced its more cautious technical usage. It does not seem that the purity of the technical term *lex*, such as we find it in the Institutes, was observed in Rome before Justinian, and it is certain that the insertion of the technical definition in the Institutes did not succeed in maintaining this definition as prevailing in the years and centuries to come.

In the ensuing period, beginning with the fall of the Roman Empire and until the modern state begins to free itself, in the thirteenth century, from the ties of feudalism, the concept of a general rule of conduct expressly enacted by the highest authority within the state and denoted by the term *lex* loses much of its former importance. Several factors contribute to this situation.

The predominant part played by theology in the juristic theory of the period tends to unite the three systems of *jus naturale*, of *jus gentium* and of *jus civile* which the Romans were at such pains to keep distinct. With the disintegration of the state unit, the specifically municipal rule loses its characteristics, and the expression *lex* is applied to a rule of any system. Not merely an enacted or customary rule of municipal law, but also asserted principles of *jus gentium* or of *jus naturale*, and rules claiming none but Divine authority are now occasionally described as *leges*. The term, thus extended, loses its value as denoting a certain type of municipal law.

Another important factor is that of the lack of well-delimited spheres of jurisdiction within the state. Feudalism represents a device by means of which social organization may be maintained in the face of a weakened central power. No specific function is certain to be preserved under the feudal system as sole prerogative of the central power. Everything may become a feudal right to be exercised by the vassal. The term *law* as denoting a particular rule emanating from the highest authority nearly loses its meaning, as the highest authority—the Emperor or the Pope— may have forgone its right to enact a general rule in favor of a vassal. The whole procedure of enacting general rules became dissolved in the maze of specific rights and privileges of various feudal lords.[7] The concept of *a law* as a particular kind of a rule and that of legislation as a particular function could not well be maintained in those conditions.[8] The vagueness extended in those times to all elements of the term: to the procedure of its creation; to the scope of the human conduct which it intends to govern; to the authority from which it derives its binding force; to the agency which formulates its contents; to the sanction guaranteeing its observance; to the degree of social effectivity which it is able to maintain. Religious precepts, accepted or advocated moral standards, customary rules antedating a given political organization, express enactments by established state authorities, principles considered deriving their force from *jus gentium*, from *jus naturale*, from *jus divinum*, are frequently thrown together. General rules purporting to govern future relations, administrative orders relating to a special case, judicial decisions settling a concrete litigation, contractual rights and duties created by private persons, appear indiscriminately. Not that there was no consciousness of the varying character of their binding force, or of the heterogeneity of their sources of authority. But the centuries of feudalism never went so far as to develop a clear-cut and generally accepted legal terminology which would do justice to these differences.

On the other hand, *lex* is extended now beyond the particular rule and embraces a whole body of rules, being used in this sense concurrently with *jus*. *Lex Salica, lex Romana*, became current technical expressions in which *lex* stands for *jus*.[9] The plural, too, is used in the same sense: *leges Alemannorum, leges Langobardorum, leges Francorum*, and at a later period, *leges Anglorum* do not denote the sum of those rules in force among these peoples which, as distinct from other rules in force among them, are described as *leges;* they denote the whole of the juristic rules respectively in force. This despite the occasional use of the form *leges et consuetudines* which would tend to show a certain survival of the idea that the term *lex* ought to be confined to the sphere of written rules.

The terminology of private international law, largely dating back to that period, bears testimony to this expansion of the term *lex*. In all such expressions as *lex fori, lex situs rei, lex contractus, lex* stands for the whole of the law applicable, not for a certain rule or a certain type of rules of this law, and would have been translated in classical Latin by *jus*.

The English language retained the use of the term *law* in this largest sense acquired during the early middle ages. *A law* is used in the sense of *lex* in classical Latin, denoting a particular rule of a certain kind; *the law* is used to denote a body of rules such as *law of the land, common law, criminal law, Divine law*, even the etymological paradox of *customary law*. Other modern European languages have reverted to the original Latin use of the terms. When speaking of a body of rules constituting a system, the expression used on the European continent is *droit criminal, diritto penale, Strafrecht, ugolovnoie pravo, derecho criminal*. The term *loi, legge, Gesetz, zakon, ley*, is usually reserved to a particular rule of a certain kind.[10]

On the whole, however, it may be said that the use of the English term *law* in the sense of the Latin *jus*, though at first confusing, is so clearly different from its use in the sense of the classical *lex*, that once one is aware of the difference, there is no difficulty in ascertaining the particular meaning.

The revival of the study of Roman law at the Italian universities between the eleventh and the thirteenth centuries led gradually to the creation, all over Western Europe, of a new school of jurists. Guided by the systematic divisions typical of Roman law, they attempt to introduce some order in the maze of contemporary rules. In this spirit, they approach the civil and canon law, the *coutumes* of France, customs of England and Germany, feudal principles, and express enactments of princes and of autonomous institutions, and become increasingly aware of the diversified character of rules governing human relations. They not only differentiate clearly between rules the maintenance of which is a function of the existing political organization—the state—and those which the state does not feel itself called upon to maintain by its authority; they go further and distinguish within the first group—the law of the state—the rules emanating from the action of various agencies and differing in their scope and in the degree of their binding force. Despite the remaining elements of confusion, a technical terminology begins to develop, differentiating between written and unwritten law, between general rules of conduct, particular rules applying only to a given situation, judicial decisions and executory actions, between rules enacted by virtue of superior authority and those resulting from the agreement of parties meeting on a basis of equality, and the like. Their attention is drawn to the utility of reserving a particular term to the most binding form of a general rule which may be enacted on behalf of the state, and they revert accordingly to the use of *lex* as defined in the Institutes of Justinian. *Lex*, followed by *loi, Gesetz*, becomes more specifically used to denote a rule of general character, expressly enacted by high political authority within the state, binding upon all persons subject to this authority unless exempt from its provisions, and establishing standards for their future conduct. In this sense, *law* becomes the antithesis of an administrative decree, of a judicial decision, of a customary norm, of a ruling made by an inferior authority, of an agreement between parties, of a mere authoritative pronouncement not creating binding standards for future conduct, and, more generally, the antithesis of all rules which may not be attributed to the state, but derive their force from some other authoritative system.[11]

An interesting development in this connection is the frequent differentiation between *lex* and that other much-abused term of medieval juristic language—*statutum*. There is a general tendency to use *lex* predominantly in the sense of a general and common rule made by a supreme authority,[12] while the term *statute* becomes increasingly used in the more general sense of "jus proprium, quod quilibet sibi populus constituit in scriptis redigendum, & per hoc separatur a consuetudine".[13] In keeping with this distinction of substance, jurists of that period attempt to differentiate between the *potestas legis ferendi* attributed only to those who wield supreme and underived authority,[14] and the *potestas statuendi*, which may be exercised by any authority having general jurisdiction over a given domain.[15] *Legislator* makes its appearance in this scheme as the authority competent to formulate laws, and—a somewhat later abstraction—legislation, as the process of enacting them or, in another sense, as the body of rules thus enacted.

In order to understand fully the influence which this school of jurists acquired in theory and in practice, one must realize that it coincided with the beginning of the renaissanse of the state as a distinct organization differing both from the church-dominated society and from the net of feudal relations. In both directions, the state begins to develop signs of growing independence. Its machinery, its rules, its methods of assuring obedience, become distinct.

Within the state, a certain differentiation of functions begins to develop, gradually confining the feudal lords to the enactment of individual rules, and leaving the enactment of general rules to the state. The conception also gains ground that the feudal lord holds all his rights (and not merely the fief as such) from the state and subject to its law, and that the lord is himself subject to the law of the state, and not merely a vassal owing to his over-lord the traditional duties of fealty in respect of his fief. Thus does the conviction develop that general rules of superior

binding force permeate the whole domain of a state, and that the enactment of such rules is a monopoly of the state, unless delegated by the state to an inferior body subject to its authority. The specific function of *legislation* comes thus to be noticed.[16]

The evolution of the term *law* for the next few centuries is intimately connected with the gradual differentiation between the functions of various state agencies. Indeed, while the prince, whether sovereign or not, exercises the function of enacting both general rules determining future conduct and particular orders relating to one particular case, there is considerable difficulty in drawing a formal distinction between the two kinds of enactments. The same form, frequently that of a *decree,* an *edict,* an *ordonnance,* a *constitution,* is used to enact both, but even if forms of enactments vary with the types of provisions[17] this does not really matter so long as the principle prevails of *quod principi placet, legis habet vigorem.* With identity of origin and with equality of binding force, all rules emanating from the prince seem to occupy a similar place in the legal system. No doubt certain restrictions were considered binding upon the princes of continental Europe of that period, calling in theory for the consent of representative assemblies to some acts. However, as far as actual practice was concerned, these representative assemblies lost their powers over most of continental Europe and the absolute power of the princes became prevalent, sweeping away before its uniform authority all distinctions between basic and subordinated rules.

Among those countries in which the representative factor continued powerful as part of the law-making machinery, the most important were the Netherlands, Poland, and the republican commonwealths, such as Venice, Genoa, the Hanseatic cities, and the Swiss cantons. In these countries, indeed, did the differentiation between the agencies called upon to enact rules make for an early realization of the difference between the resulting sets of rules. A rule which can be made only with the consent of the representative assembly and which can be modified only in the same way, appears there as "higher law" than that enacted by the mere "executive authority."

In monarchical countries such as the Netherlands and Poland, this clear-cut conception was somewhat confused owing to the concept of the prince's "own right" or of his "prerogative" which constitutes a rival system of "higher law" impenetrable to the powers of the representative body. Still, despite these claims of the prerogative powers, the rules enacted by consent of representative bodies emerged slowly as rules of higher authority, both in the consciousness of the population and in juristic practice. In those countries in which representative bodies participated actively in the enactment of certain rules, the technical term *law* or its local equivalent became increasingly reserved to the rules enacted with such participation.

Another field in which a differentiation of rules according to the manner of their enactment has early started is that of local units within a state. While many states in the medieval period were governed autocratically without the intervention of representative bodies, smaller units within them, such as provinces and particularly towns, had evolved certain rudiments of self-government exercised by means of a representative body.[18] This circumstance facilitated the conception of a specific difference between rules enacted within such unit by action of the representative body and those enacted by the executive authority. The term *statute* rather than *lex* was applied to rules of such local units, but the conception of a higher authority of the rules thus enacted has remained and became of importance in view of later developments.[19]

The most important development in the direction of promoting the modern conception of *a law* as a rule enacted in a certain manner and therefore possessing a certain distinct character occurred in England.

In the formative period of English law, there was already a clear conception of two great divisions of rules binding within the realm—written rules enacted by express authority, and unwritten rules created by long usage. Scholars were aware that the two kinds of rules should be properly distinguished from one another and identified respectively as *leges* and as *consuetudines*. Obviously under the influence of Italian glossators, both Glanvill and Bracton adopt an apologetic tone in trying to justify what appears to be a somewhat daring departure from the acknowledged terminology, namely, the inclusion of unwritten rules in the term *leges*. Thus Glanvill:[20]

"For the English Laws, although not written, may as it should seem, and that without any absurdity, be terms Laws, since that itself is a Law—that which pleases the Prince has the force of Law, I mean, those Laws which it is evident were promulgated by the advice of the Nobles and the authority of the Prince, concerning doubts to be settled in their Assembly. For, if from the mere want of writing only, they should not be considered as Laws, then, unquestionably, writing would seem to confer more authority upon Laws themselves than either the Equity of the persons constituting, or the reason of those framing, them. But to reduce in every in-

stance the Laws and Constitutions of the Realm into writing would be, in our times, absolutely impossible, as well on account of the ignorance of writers, as of the confused multiplicity of the Laws."

The same note is struck by Bracton:[21]

"Whereas in almost all countries they use laws and written right, England alone uses within her boundaries unwritten right and custom. . . . But it will not be absurd to call the English laws, although they are unwritten, by the name of Laws, for everything has the force of Law, whatever has been rightfully defined and approved by the counsel and consent of the magnates, with the common warrant of the body politic, the authority of the king or the prince preceding."

Even then, Bracton is careful not to call every custom a law, but to reserve this name, and the binding force attached to it, to those customs only which can be shown to have been "defined and approved by the counsel and consent of the magnates, with the common warrant of the body politic, the authority of the king or the prince preceding."

Out of such considerations, it was found necessary to evolve a broader conception of *a law* which would include some ascertained customs in addition to written rules. Thus, the Bractonian definition, closely reminiscent of that of the Digest:[22]

". . . it is to be known that law is the common precept of prudent men in council, the coercion of offences, which are committed either voluntarily or through ignorance, and the common warrant of the body politic . . . although in the widest sense of the term, everything which may be read is law, nevertheless, in the special sense, it signifies a rightful warrant, enjoining what is honest, forbidding the contrary.

"Custom, also, is sometimes observed for law in parts, where it has been approved by habitual usage, and it fills the place of law, for the authority of long usage and custom is not slight."

In this definition, the written character of the rule retreats, and every rule, even of customary origin, is entitled to be considered a law provided that its binding force, based on the *sponsio rei publicae communis*, is sufficiently ascertained. It becomes then a synonym of any such rule containing *sanctionem justam, jubentem honesta, prohibentem contraria*.

Since the times of Glanvill and Bracton, the situation had materially changed. Unwritten "laws," developed mainly by judicial decisions, became so overwhelmingly important in the juristic system of England that they almost superseded written laws as rules possessing the highest authority within the realm.[23]

Several factors contributed to the growth of this conception. One of the most important appears to have been the close control which the Crown maintained over the enactment of written rules. For a long time, the King's power of enacting executive orders was not clearly distinguished from the procedure of enacting acts of Parliament. Later, the Kings still used their prerogative powers to issue proclamations dispensing with and generally suspending acts of Parliament. The requirement of parliamentary co-operation in enacting and repealing written rules was thus a disputed subject, and the whole sphere of written legislation became suspect as a possible source of arbitrariness and abuse. No exception was made even in the case of acts of Parliament, which appears justifiable in view of the control which the Crown had at times over the Houses of Parliament. As against these rules enacted by the Prince with or without parliamentary co-operation, the courts of justice and the learned jurists preferred to rely upon the more predictable and stable precepts of the customary law of England, which, besides, was more in conformity with the juristic convictions of the population. It was out of this spirit of subjecting the prince to the laws,[24] that the English jurists proclaimed the superiority of unwritten over written laws. Hence Coke:

"And it appears in our books, that in many cases, the common law will controul acts of Parliament, and sometimes adjudge them to be utterly void: for when an act of Parliament is against common right and reason, or repugnant, or impossible to be performed, the common law will controul it, and adjudge such act to be void."[25]

After the Revolution, this danger largely disappeared. It became established doctrine that written rules in their most general and binding form require parliamentary sanction, and, on the other hand, the influence of the Crown over the Houses of Parliament diminished appreciably. However, the attitude of distrust toward written law subsisted for some time, and so did a certain unwillingness to acknowledge the superior binding force of acts of Parliament. Occasional pronouncements are found therefore even after the Revolution placing common law, the law of nature or the law of nations above acts of Parliament and holding it to be the duty of the courts to refrain from applying the latter when inconsistent with the former.[26] On the whole, however, it has become the accepted doctrine since the Revolution that an act of Parliament is at the top of the juristic system in England[27] and is clearly superior to the common law.[28] With the disappearance of the cause of distrust in written laws—their use as instruments of the prince's fancy—the distrust vanishes too, at least in as much as the formal acknowledgment of their superiority is concerned,[29] and today no one questions that the Act of Parliament constitutes the peak of the hierarchy of English law.

Thus did the clear attribution of the legislative function to a specific agency—the King in Parliament—lead to the acknowledgment of the proper place of legislation in the law of England.

The United States seceded from England at a time when a distinct procedure had already evolved, thus identifying legislation and distinguishing it from other forms of written and unwritten law. There was no difficulty therefore in taking over the concept of legislation as a specific function within the legal system and of *laws* properly speaking as a distinct group of written rules.

The doctrine of parliamentary supremacy and of the supremacy of the acts of Parliament, on the other hand, was not yet unchallenged even in England. The insurgent colonists, finding themselves opposed to some items of parliamentary legislation, and generally less attached to the tradition of Parliament because of their lack of representation, were particularly prone to question the privileged position of legislation. The United States never did depart from this initial position, and never arrived at the acknowledgment of the supremacy of written legislation.[30] Certain rules of customary law were put on a higher level—that of equality with the constitution, and courts as well as the whole legal profession have since acted on the assumption that written laws have to be applied subject to its provisions. Though ordinary rules of the common law might be superseded by legislation, an important body of received common law principles was read into the constitution and thus put beyond the reach of legislative changes. The concept of reasonableness and constitutional provisions such as "due process of law" became particularly rich receptacles for common law tucked away safely on the constitutional shelf.[31] Under these conditions, the juristic authority of legislative acts is considered both in theory and practice of the United States to be a distinctly subordinate one, in federal as well as in state law.

It has been seen that the concept of legislation in England has grown to be closely connected with a certain procedure of enacting an express rule, the procedure, namely, of putting behind the rule the sanction of the King in Parliament. The expression *law* having become, in the English language, of very broad and therefore very vague application, it ceased to be used as a specific term denoting the products of "legislation." Such a term was found, in special application to England and later to the United Kingdom, in "act of Parliament." As a generic term, applied to the results of legislation in other countries as well, the expression "statute" became of general use in the English language.

In the United States, the identical term "statute" is used to denote the rule emanating from the process of legislation. The difference between an English and an American statute, as far as their place within the respective legal systems is concerned, is so enormous that it almost may be said that their only common feature is one of procedure: both are enacted with the consent of a representative body.[32] It will be clearly seen, in the instance of the United Kingdom and of the United States, that after a history in which the concept of a written *lex* has always been closely connected with a specific procedure, we have arrived at a stage in which the decisive test of a *lex* lies precisely in the procedure of its enactment. *Legislation* as a term is younger than *lex,* yet a *lex* in the modern sense is nothing but a rule resulting from *legislation.* In the Anglo-American world, this specific procedure is one arrived at with the participation of an institution considered representative of the people.

In other States, this evolution is less pronounced. The term *lex* as applied to the positive law in force would be frequently used in a very broad sense indeed, and, the efforts of legal purists notwithstanding, its exclusive use in the sense of a rule emanating from a given authority did not develop until comparatively recently. The republics and parliamentary monarchies of Europe were the first on the Continent to restrict thus the use of the term. Hungary seems to have been among the earliest.[33] In the Netherlands, an evolution in this sense, not yet completed, may be found in Grotius.[34] In Poland, the practice of the sixteenth and following centuries appears largely built on the assumption of *laws* being rules enacted with parliamentary consent, though theoretically the term is used in a broader sense even in the middle of the eighteenth century.[35] In those other countries, where most fundamental functions in connection with law-making were concentrated in the person of the prince, the concept of *laws* and of *legislation* remained highly vague and controversial.[36]

The parallel development of the concepts of a distinct legislative function and of direct or indirect expression of popular will is truly remarkable. It is because of the essentially democratic ideologies of republics and of parliamentary monarchies that we find there the first crystallization of modern ideas on laws and legislation. It is true that the democracy of the Italian and of the German republics was limited to certain groups of the population only and that such was also the case of the Netherland provinces. No doubt, the Polish Sejm and the Hungarian Parliament were as little representative of the whole population as were early British parliaments. In all three cases, it was the nobility that was mainly represented, with a mere sprinkling of other groups. Still, these institutions, even if moved by selfish group-interests, embodied the idea of the participation of broad groups of the population in determining the law of the land. What followed was merely a gradual widening of the groups thus represented, a process extending throughout the nineteenth century.

The clear differentiation between *laws* and other rules, between legislation and other functions, over most of continental Europe is a phenomenon of the nineteenth century: It begins with the adoption of the modern constitutions of limited monarchical or republican states, and is only made possible by the distribution of functions among various and distinct agencies. In one form or in another, these constitutions define as legislation the enactment of rules participated in by representative bodies or by popular vote.[37]

It may be interesting to note that the recent trend to diminish the role of representative institutions has cut across the distinctions resulting from this evolution and has served to efface the difference between laws and other rules. The growth of "delegated" or "subordinated legislation" in England,[38] the practice of "décrets-lois" in France,[39] the rapid development in Germany of delegated legislation in 1930-1933,[40] and the growth everywhere of ministerial powers, have served largely to rob the distinction between *laws* and other rules of much of its meaning. When we come to the instances of Germany since 1933 and Austria since 1934, where, whatever the theory, *legislation* and administration are concentrated largely in the same agency,[41] we come back to the state of affairs prevalent over most of Europe previous to the nineteenth century.

Fundamentally, it is not an inevitable trait of *legislation* that it be enacted with the participation of a representative body. Viewed in a strictly formal light, it is sufficient for the adequate identification of legislation that it be exercised by way of a specific procedure. History has shown, however, that the specific nature of a given procedure tends to be disregarded unless it represents the action of a distinct agency. That this agency tends to become one representing the whole population or at least some influential groups of the population is merely a result of the apparently irreducible influence of democratic ideas at all times.

Indeed, whatever the formal structure of a political regime, whether seeking to derive its authority from Divinity or from some other principle of leadership—elements of democracy can always be detected. Dictatorships may plead the principle of leadership and violently denounce democracy—they will resort to referenda and to popular election. Oligarchies may restrict the exercise of the vote to certain groups of the population only, and provide for voting conditions which will prejudice its result —but in some form they will seek to rely on popular support. This trend may be noted even in those oriental regimes of which we know anything. The very theocratic regime of ancient Jews still shows elements of democracy: witness the essentially democratic regime of the judges, the establishment of the Kingdome of Saul as a result of popular demand, the revolution with popular support of Jeroboam, and the like. Greece, Carthage, Rome, were at all times containing some elements of democracy, if only confined to certain groups of fully qualified citizens.

But when we come to the later middle ages, at which time the term *lex* begins to assume its modern significance, the situation is even more clearly defined: in theory and in practice, the idea of popular sovereignty has never since ceased to be a vital factor of political and juristic evolution. This was clear in England, in the European republics, in Poland (where it assumed the peculiar form of the *liberum veto* of all nobles). At a critical moment, such as 1613, it became decisive even in Russia. In Germany and in Spain it found refuge in local self-government.

Of course, the force of the democratic factor was very unequal. And so was the degree of differentiation between *laws* and other rules. If we search for a substantive and non-procedural definition of *laws* applicable to almost any situation it would be that of expressly enacted rules of a particularly strong binding force. This conception would therefore be usually attached to the rules enacted by the authority considered the most important. The old Jews ascribed such a position to the enactments of God revealed in the Pentatuch; the Romans—to the decisions of the people and, later, of the Senate. At a time when absolutism or feudalism reigned unchecked, any enactment by the monarch assumed this position. This is why the maxim of the Digest, *quod principi placet legis habet vigorem,* played so important a part down to the French Revolution, resulting in effacing the difference between *laws* and minor rules. With the emergence of the principle of popular sovereignty, it became customary to consider these rules as having a higher authority—that is, as *laws*—which are enacted with the consent of the people or of its representatives.

Other characteristics have been suggested from time to time as determining the nature of *a law* as distinct from other kinds of juristic rules. Among these characteristics, a frequently recurring one is that of generality. *A law,* according to this view, is essentially a rule laying down the standards of conduct intended for general application. This view has been traditionally popular in the theoretical literature[42] and has been recently enunciated with particular emphasis by Kelsen.[43]

This attitude may appear theoretically satisfactory. It would indeed facilitate the classification of rules according to a most important objective: that of setting up standards for application in any future case, and that of setting up a solution for a concrete given case. Unfortunately, the test of generality, attractive and convenient though it might have been, will not serve any useful purpose in analyzing the historically developed concept of *a law* because it had been very consistently neglected throughout the known practice. The very definition of *lex* in the Institutes of Justinian[44] hesitates on this point and notes that some laws are *personales, quae nec ad exemplum trahuntur.* That *leges speciales* have played a major part throughout the process of legislation and were considered as laws properly speaking along with *leges generales,* is well-known.[45]

In no modern country in which the term laws is authoritatively determined, does the official definition contain the element of generality. The definition is rather confined, in the modern state, to the element of procedure. A rule enacted by a "legislative" agency acting as such is *a law,* whatever its intended scope of application. As a matter of fact, a great part of the legislative output in many states represents rules which in no way lay down abstract and general standards of conduct, but simply contain decisions affecting a given situation. In some countries, it is even openly acknowledged that such acts are an intrinsic part of the legislative output, and *laws* (or statutes) are officially sub-divided into general and particular ones. Notable in this respect is the instance of the United Kingdom,[46] where parliamentary bills are divided into public and private ones, and where the Acts of Parliament are divided into public, general, local, and personal ones.[47]

In the United States, an equal recognition of the two variations of the statutes exists, though to a lesser extent.[48] Some states of the union do not take cognizance of the division of statutes on the ground of their generality or particularity, but this does not by any means indicate that private bills and statutes confined to specific cases are not dealt with under the general legislative procedure. It merely means that these states accept without questioning or doubt the fact that both general rules and special decisions may be enacted as statutes.

The extent to which particular rules may play a part in the legislative output of a modern state is shown by the survey made by Reinsch on the legislation of Maryland for 1902 and 1904:[49]

	1902	1904
Local Acts	45%	56%
Special Acts	35	29
General Acts	20	15

The Roman conception makes legislation a function of the sovereign, or at least of the highest agency through which the will of the sovereign may be expressed. Not all commands of the highest state agency need be necessarily *laws,* but no rule would be considered *a law,* unless it emanates from this agency. *A law,* in this sense, is a rule of conduct laid down by the supreme authority of a political society and binding upon its subjects.[50]

This conception received a strong blow during the middle ages, when the absence of a clear political hierarchy transformed legislation, as it was currently understood, into a subjective right or a privilege which may be exercised by any duly authorized person or institution.[51]

The influence of absolutism in continental Europe and of growing parliamentary supremacy in England, allied with that of the civilians, seemed to overcome this blow, and to reintroduce the concept of *legislation* as the process of enacting rules of the highest authority and emanating from the highest political agency in the state. The classical expressions of this view are found in the writings of Bodin[52] and Blackstone.[53] But a new complication arose in the eighteenth century with the conception of the formal supremacy of the constitution, first accepted in the United States, and then adopted all over continental Europe in the form of the French theory of a *pouvoir constituant.* Written constitutions became the rule of the day in the predominant majority of the states of the world. The function of legislation, the legislative agency, and its product—the statute—all fell from their sovereign heights.[54] According to contemporary theory in almost any state (Great Britain being the only notable exception), there is nothing that makes it imperative to reserve the legislative function to the highest political authority. As a matter of practical convenience, it may be exercised by this agency immediately, but then it may be delegated to various subordinate agencies. Equally, the supreme binding force of legislative law became less of an unquestioned premise: some states adopted the practice of the United States in denying at all this character of legislation, and of opening all statutes to judicial review. Other states still adhere to the doctrine of the unchallengeable binding force of statutory law enacted with the participation of Parliament and the Head of State, *i. e.,* with the concurrence of the two institutions which, taken together, are currently considered as the highest political agency of a modern state, or enacted in the process of plebiscite, while "legislation" enacted by subordinate autonomous or delegated institutions is sometimes open to such review. Still, in some countries all acts considered as "legislative," whether emanating from the highest legislative agencies or enacted by a process of delegation, are accorded a status of supreme law of the land without permitting judicial review as to their constitutionality on the merits. Great Britain is a pertinent instance of the latter trend, and the same attitude is increasingly adopted in those continental states of Europe in which the executive gains a firmer hold. As a result of this rather varied evolution, no conclusion may be offered as to the identification of legislation either with rules emanating directly from a sovereign agency or from the highest agency in a given state, nor can it be identified with the body of rules possessing a legal force which may not be challenged except on formal grounds. The truth is that, in both these respects, no definite criterion has become definitely established, and the term legislation is officially and currently applied to various kinds of rules.

Modern continental theory has devoted considerable attention to the problem of determining an objective criterion of legislation, and has come to the conclusion that the term is used in two different meanings, one being the substantive, the other being the formal.[55]

The definitions of *a law* and of *legislation* in the substantive sense, have frequently varied. As has been seen in the preceding pages, emphasis would be placed at various times on the scope of the human conduct sought to be regulated, on the source of authority, on the degree of binding force, or on combinations of these characteristics.[56] *A law* in the formal sense is any rule enacted in accordance with the "legislative" procedure in force.[57]

Both these definitions are somewhat artificial

devices aiming at a more precise determination of the sense of our terms. They demonstrate the impossibility of clearly defining our concepts so as to include all asserted characteristics and all relevant features. If both the formal and the substantive characteristics of legislation are to be present, we would arrive at a definition so narrow as to be manifestly inconsistent with its prevailing use in the theory and the practice of states. By sacrificing either the formal or the substantive characteristics, it is possible to offer a definition more in accord with actual use. It will be noted, of course, that such sacrifice involves a lack of completeness in the result. Besides, the rules conforming to the formal characteristics will not necessarily show the substantive characteristics required, and *vice versa*. The results of applying to a rule either the formal or the substantive test will be frequently contradictory. This makes the matter of choice between the two a very serious one indeed.

Fundamentally, it would seem that a substantive analysis of the term is the more scientific approach. In most preceding sections of this study it has been attempted to deal with substantive analysis. It has been seen that the results are highly unsatisfactory. The variations in the type of rules which, at various times and by various authorities, have been designated as *laws,* were and continue to be so wide that no conclusive result can be attained. It would be easy to follow some variation which would appeal to the present writer as being the most plausible one. But this would place the whole subsequent discussion on a basis which any critic might reject as being essentially arbitrary. Indeed, the matter under consideration represents simply one of terminology. No arguments relating to terminology may be satisfactorily solved except on the basis of prevailing use. As to the substantive characteristics of our term, the use has been so varied and inconclusive that, left in this sphere, the argument would appear incapable of solution. The preceding sections have shown that, in this sense, legislation has been variously defined as comprising rules of general scope, rules attributed to a sovereign authority with a power of command over the parties made subject thereto, rules with a particularly strong measure of binding force, rules establishing abstract standards of conduct, rules creating rights and obligations, rules enacting law substantively different from that previously in force—or combinations of these elements.

The appreciation of this impossibility of arriving at a satisfactory scientific definition of the term, logically adequate and consistent with the facts, has led many writers to turn increasingly toward a purely formal definition. Essentially, this acceptance of a purely formal definition of legislation means nothing else than the abdication by jurisprudence and political theory of their prerogative of independent investigation and conclusion in favor of whatever happens to be the use of the term by the states of the world. Instead of attempting to influence the terminology applied to state policies, theory, in respect of the definition of legislation, submitted to official usage. It refers to the existence within the state of a particular kind of rules officially known as *laws,* or *statutes.* These rules, in the modern state, are determined by the existence of a certain agency authorized to enact rules and officially considered as the *legislative power.* Whatever rule is enacted by the *legislative power* in its specific capacity is *legislation* or legislative law in the eyes of the State, and this view is also accepted by the theory in as much as it seeks to determine legislation in a formal sense.

In the contemporary literature on municipal law and general legal theory, less and less emphasis is put on a substantive definition of legislation. This field, so extensively explored in former days, is now increasingly left to the discretion of the state.[58] Now and then, one still finds the vigorous assertion that legislation has to be defined materially, that a formal definition is insufficient.[59] But in most cases, continental treatises, having once declared that the term may be used in a double meaning, and having indicated the particular "substantive" definition attractive to the particular author, turn to legislation in the formal sense and in the following pages deal almost exclusively with the latter. In the United States, frequent attempts have been made by judicial tribunals to arrive at a substantive concept of legislation. The criterion mainly proposed during these attempts was that of generality of the rule enacted,[60] or that of its applying to future situations,[61] or a combination of both.[62] It must be admitted that the prohibitions contained in the Federal and in the State Constitutions against the enactment of bills of attainder and of *ex post facto* laws make the second criterion applicable indeed as a limitation on the concept of legislation as established in this country. But the efforts to restrict the "legislative" output to general rules have remained utterly unsuccessful, as has been shown already.[63]

As for Anglo-American doctrine, it is less conscious of the whole problem,[64] but, as a matter of practice, its analysis of positive law is predominantly influenced by an unchallenged acceptance of the terms as they are determined officially on the basis of formal considerations.[65]

Still, American and English writers characteristically ignore the large output of private, special, and local acts, and assume implicitly that only general acts are properly legislative.

The preceding considerations, while unable to furnish us with a clear-cut *definition* of legislation, may give us sufficient insight to permit an adequate *description* of the subject. This insight will be based mainly upon the understanding that in dealing with this matter, we are faced with a concept which results from a long process of historical evolution, and which can be explained only with reference to its historical background. In this sense, we may look for a description of those rules which, throughout legal history, have incited a trend to put them in a class apart and which have been, at various times during the history of European civilization, designated more particularly as laws or legislation.

This description will run somewhat as follows: in a society which tends to exercise effective control of the conduct of its members, there will be a trend to exercise this control through a concrete agency. This agency will not find it possible to stay within the limits of traditional precepts, but will find itself induced to formulate expressly additional written rules. The rules enacted by this agency will tend to assert themselves with all the powers of the organized society behind them, and will consequently assume a greater measure of binding force than mere agreements of members of the society *inter se*. For reasons of convenience, this law-making agency will develop a technique of enacting general rules of conduct as well as rules meant to apply to a particular case only. A trend will appear to separate those agencies competent to enact general rules from those competent merely to enact particular rules, and to make the latter rules subject to those of a general character.

As soon as the agencies of a society and the rules enacted by them have attained a degree of organization sufficient to perceive the trends toward a gradation in the hierarchy of rules, making some rules a mere "application" of other, more basic, ones, we will be faced with a nascent conception of laws and legislation. With the continuing differentiation of functions and of rules, a stage will be achieved at which a given agency, with the powers and authority of the political organization behind it, will be conceived as the legislative agency, and rules enacted by it will be considered as laws.

Notes

1. The Latin term *legis lator* has been used since Roman times. See Codex of Justinian I, 14, 5. It is not certain that it denoted anything in the nature of the modern concept of a legislator. See 1 Savigny, Geschichte des Römischen Rechts im Mittelalter (2d ed. 1834) 427 *et seq.* The term appears in French, with approximately the modern meaning, in the 14th century. See Littré's dictionary: *"législation."* In English, it has been in constant use ever since the beginning of the 17th century. See New Oxford Dictionary: "legislation." For a systematic bibliography on legislation, see Pound, Outlines of a Course in Legislation (1934).

2. (140-212 A.D.) Digest of Justinian I, III, 1. "Lex est commune praeceptum, virorum prudentium consultum, delictorum quae sponte vel ignorantia contrahuntur coercitio, communis rei publicae sponsio." Monro's translation is used in the text.

3. Institutes I, II. "4. Lex est, quod populus Romanus senatorio magistratu interrogante, veluti consule, constituebat. . . .

"5. Senatus-consultum est, quod senatus jubet, atque constituit. Nam cum auctus esset populus Romanus in eum modum, ut difficile esset in unum eum convocari legis sanciendae causa: aequum visum est, senatum vice populi consuli.

"6. Sed et quod principi placuit, legis habet vigorem: quum lege Regia, quae de ejus imperio lata est, populus ei et in eum omne imperium suum et potestatem concedat. Quodcunque ergo imperator per epistolam constituit, vel cognoscens decrevit, vel edicto praecepit, legem esse constat. Haec sunt, quae constitutiones appellantur. Plane ex his quaedam sunt personales, quae nec ad exemplum trahuntur; quoniam non hoc princeps vult. Nam quod alicui ob meritum indulsit, vel si quam poenam irrogavit, vel si cui sine exemplo subvenit, personam non transgreditur. Aliae autem, quum generales sint, omnes proculdubio tenent."

4. Moyle's translation is followed here, except for the substitution of the original term *lex* for his "statute."

Much of the text quoted is taken from the Institutes of Gaius (middle of 2nd century) I, 3-5, and from the Institutes of Ulpianus (170-228 A.D.), see Digest I, 4.

5. Institutes I, II, 9: "Sine scripto jus venit, quod usus approvabit: nam diuturni mores consensu utentium comprobati, legem imitantur." Moyle's translation reads: "The unwritten law is that which usage has approved: for ancient customs, when approved by consent of those who follow them, are like a *lex*."

The text of the Institutes is much more careful in placing *leges* within the category of written law than the Greek source quoted in Institutes I, II, 3.

6. On generality as criterion of *leges*, see also Digest I, III, and Codex I, 14, 3.

7. See 2 Schaeffner, Geschichte der Rechtsverfassung Frankreichs (1849) 169 *et seq.*

8. See 3 Flach, Les Origines de l'ancienne France (1904) 329 *et seq.*; Schröder-Künnsberg, Lehrbuch der Deutschen Rechtsgeschichte (7th ed. 1932) 708; and particularly 3-8 Waitz, Deutsche Verfassungsgeschichte (1860-1878) *passim.*

9. See 1 Savigny, Geschichte des Römischen Rechts (2d ed. 1834) 131 *et seq.*; Waitz, *loc. cit. supra* note 8.

10. It is important to note this difference of attitude maintained in modern languages. In all these languages, there are but two words seeking to denote three ideas: that of a subjective right, that of an objective rule, and that of a body of objective rules. The English language uses the word "right" to denote the first idea, and the word "law" to denote the two others. Other languages use *loi* or its equivalent to denote the second idea, and *droit* or its equivalent to denote the first and the third idea. In either case a source of possible confusion is created. On the various meanings in which the term *law* is used, see Pound, More About the Nature of Law, in: Legal Essays in Tribute to Orrin Kip McMurray (1935) 513.

Of even more direct bearing on our subject is the inevitable difference in interpreting the term *legislation* as law-making, in various languages. Does *legislation* mean the making of *the law* in the English sense, or does it mean the making of that particular kind of a rule called *a law* (in modern English: a statute)? It may be stated that even in the English language, *legislation* is referred to predominantly as the function of enacting laws in the sense of statutes.

11. While the term *lex* begins to be used less profusely with reference to rules of the law of nature, divine rules of a general character are still considered laws, whether they be rules laid down or implied in the Holy Scripture, or whether they be church laws. In this case, we are faced by another system of rules, possessing a clear hierarchy of authorities, and presenting many features analogous to the structure of the state. The use of *laws* in connection with *church laws* remains current in the technical language until our days, in Catholic as well as in Protestant countries. A good exposition of the relation between state and religious *laws* is given in Suarez' classical treatise, *De Legibus ac Deo Legislatore*, written in 1612. In this treatise, we find one of the first thorough treatments of the problem of legislation in its various aspects.

For a general survey of the relevant juristic theories of the middle ages, see 3 Gierke, Deutsches Genossenschaftsrecht (1881) *passim*.

12. Thus Albericus a Rosate, Commentarii de Statutis, I, III and I, IX, 53. Published in the great collection of medieval juristic learning, Tractatus Universi Iuris (1584) t. 2; and in the collection Tractatus de Statutis (1606).

13. *Id.* at I, I, 1. Other indications of this trend will be found throughout the volumes of the Tractatus Universi Iuris, under *leges* and *statuta*, and in the Tractatus de Statutis.

14. Thus Franciscinus Curtius Junior, De Feudis: "Auctoritas legis condendae dicitur est de reservatis principi, in signum supremae potestatis" (Tractatus Universi Iuris, t. X, pt. 2, fol. 43, Questio prima, no. 5). Another jurist of the period, Petrus Albinianus, attempts in his study *De Pontificia Potestate* to go further into the idea that legislation is an attribute of supreme authority only. Even the Emperor is said by him to possess only derived authority, conferred upon him by the people. As for the people, it never possessed original law-making powers (An interesting change of position in his arguments: he accepts the Roman law theory as to the derived status of the Emperor, but chooses to ignore the Roman law theory as to the original law-making power of the people!). Consequently, the Pope, as the Vicar of Christ and as successor to Moses the law-giver, emerges in his opinion as the only one possessing legislative power (Tractatus Universi Iuris, t. XIII, pt. 1, fol. 137, nos. 100-103).

15. See particularly, Paridis de Puteo, De Sindicatu (Tractatus Universi Iuris, t. VII, fol. 230, no. 23).

16. At first, the Italian school finds itself involved in the struggle between the Emperor claiming political supremacy and the emerging states claiming independence, and adopts an attitude favorable to the Emperor. Hence the distinction between the *potestas legis ferendi* and the *potestas statuendi*. With the growth of the states and the expansion of the new school of jurists to places other than Italy, this attitude is largely abandoned.

17. See 3 Schaeffner, Geschichte der Rechtsverfassung Frankreichs (1850) 152.

18. See Schröder-Künnsberg, Lehrbuch der deutschen Rechtsgeschichte (7th ed. 1932) 672 *et seq.*; 1 Gierke, Deutsches Genossenschaftsrecht (1868) 249-332, and 2 *id.* (1873) 573-828.

19. Autonomous legislation of subordinate units within a state has become nowadays an important feature. In the United States, *"legislative"* activities by municipalities are an acknowledged phenomenon. *Cf.* the cases cited *infra* note 60.

20. Glanvill, De Legibus et Consuetudinibus Regni Angliae (Woodbine ed. 1932, p. 24): "Leges namque

Anglicanas licet non scriptas leges appellari non videatur absurdum, cum hoc ipsum lex sit, quod principi placet legis habet vigorem, eas scilicet quas super dubiis in concilio definiendis, procerum quidem consilio et principis accedente auctoritate constat esse promulgatas. Si enim ob scripturae solummodo defectum leges minime censerentur, maioris procul dubio auctoritatis robur ipsis legibus videretur accomodare scriptura, quam decernentium aequitas aut ratio statuentis. Leges autem et iura regni scripto universaliter concludi nostris temporibus quidem omnino impossibile est, tum propter scribentium ignorantiam tum propter earum multitudinem confusam."

Beames' translation is given in the text.

21. Bracton, De Legibus et Consuetudinibus Angliae, I, I, 2: "Cum autem fere in omnibus regionibus utantur legibus et jure scripto, sola Anglia usa est in suis finibus jure non scripto et consuetudine. . . . Sed absurdum non erit leges Anglicanas (licet non scriptas) leges appellare, cum leges vigorem habeat, quicquid de consilio et de consensu magnatum et rei publicae communi sponsione, autoritate regis sive principis praecedente, juste fuerit definitum et approbatum."

Bracton's statement as to the absence in other countries of an unwritten and customary law is obviously incorrect. He must have paid attention, as far as the continent of Europe was concerned, to Roman law only. The translation given in the text is from Twiss' edition (1878) c. 1, p. 2.

22. Bracton, *supra* note 21 at I, III, 13: ". . . sciendum, quod lex est commune praeceptum virorum prudentum consultam, delictorumque quae sponte vel ignorantia contrahuntur coertio, rei publicae sponsio comunis . . . et licet largissime dicatur lex omne quod legitur, tamen specialiter significat sanctionem justam, jubentem honesta, prohibentem contraria.

"Consuetudo vero quandoque pro lege observatur in partibus, ubi fuerit more utentium approbata, et vicem legis obtinet, longaevi enim temporis usus et consuetudinis non est vilis autoritas."

The translation given in the text is from Twiss' edition (1878) c. 3, p. 13.

23. On the following, *cf.* Allen, Law in the Making (2d ed. 1930) 248-277; Stimson, Popular Law-Making (1910) c. 1-6.

24. *Cf.* 12 Co. Rep. 65.

25. 8 Co. Rep. 118.

26. *Cf.* Lord Mansfield, in Heathfield v. Chilton, 4 Burr. 2015, 2016 (K. B. 1767).

27. See 1 Bl. Comm. 49.

28. See Hale, History and Analysis of the Common Law (1713) 27.

29. The dislike of statutory law by the legal profession in England still survives. This dislike continues to play a major part in the process of applying and interpreting statutes in actual court litigation. See Pound, Common Law and Legislation (1908) 21 Harv. L. Rev. 383.

30. See Jones, Statute Law-Making in the United States (1912). On the doctrine of constitutional supremacy and its implications, see Section XV, *infra*.

31. See Willoughby, Constitutional Law in the United States (1910) cc. 2, 46; Haines, The Revival of Natural Law Concepts (1930); Wright, American Interpretations of Natural Law (1931); Corwin, The "Higher Law" Background of American Constitutional Law (1928-29) 42 Harv. L. Rev. 149, 365.

32. The scope of the population actually represented in Parliament has varied. The extension of suffrage to the whole of the adult population is a very recent innovation. Yet the idea that Parliament is called to represent somehow the people as a whole has been firmly established for a long time.

33. On Hungary, see Rado-Rothfeld, Die Ungarische Verfassung (1898) 100-109, and Law XII of 1790-1791, *id.* at 181.

34. Grotius, The Jurisprudence of Holland (Lee's ed. 1926) I, II, particularly §§ 17-20.

35. On Poland, see 1 Lengnich, Jus publicum Regni Poloni (1775-1776) 3-11; 2 id. at 589-897.

36. See Esmein, Cours élémentaire d'histoire du droit français (14th ed. 1921) 464-527; Ulbrich, Das oesterreichische Staatsrecht (Das offentliche Recht der Gegenwart, Vol. 10) (1909) 235; Luschin v. Ebengreuth, Oesterreichische Reichsgeschichte (1896) § 43 et seq., particularly pp. 355-357.

37. Cf. the relevant provisions of European and South American constitutions, as well as those of some Asiatic States, beginning with the French Constitutional Law of October 1, 1789. See, for the various constitutions in force at present or at any time during the last century: Dufau, Duvergier, Gaudet, Collections des Constitutions (1821-1830); Dareste, Delpech, Laferrière, Les Constitutions Modernes (1928-1934).

The constitutional provisions dealing with law and legislative power are drafted so as to imply a pre-existing concept of *laws* and *legislation*, and as if they did simply assign agencies to fulfill functions falling into this sphere. In fact, however, the concept of laws and legislation, previous to its positive assignment to a specific agency, is so vague as to be of very little value. Under these conditions, the nature of laws and legislation, instead of explaining the scope of the activity of the "legislative" agencies, ends by being explained and determined by the latter. This, provided that the judicial agencies are not given the power to hold the legislative agencies down to the "proper" sphere of legislation. A simple power of reviewing the constitutionality of legislation according to formal tests still leaves the legislative agency master over the scope of legislation. But when the judiciary goes so far as to decide that a certain matter is or is not "properly" within the domain of "legislation," as is the case in the United States, the critical stage is reached. We do not contemplate in this connection the veto-functions of agencies such as the Head of State, the French Imperial Senate or the Russian Imperial Senate, which may refuse consent; these, indeed, must be considered an integral part of the legislative machinery.

38. Allen, Law in the Making (1930) c. 7.

39. Barthélemy et Duez, Traité de droit constitutionnel (nouv. ed. 1930) 779 et seq. The authors of this work go far beyond a formal criterion and consider as legislative acts all general rules, whether enacted by the *pouvoir constituant* (constitution), by Parliament (laws), or by governmental or administrative agencies (*règlements*). Id. at 723 et seq., 772 et seq.

40. See Medicus, Reichsverwaltung (1932) 20 Jahrbuch des offentlichen Rechts 9-14; Poetzsch-Heffter, Vom Staatsleben unter der Weimarer Verfassung (1933-34) 21 id. at 184.

41. See Poetzsch-Heffter, Vom deutschen Staatsleben (1935) 22 id. at 257-264.

42. Aristotle, Politics, III, 15; Rousseau, Contrat Social, II, VI; Pütter-Häberlin, Handbuch des Deutschen Staatsrechts (1797) II, 159 et seq.; Austin, Lectures on Jurisprudence, Lecture I; Bluntschli, Allgemeines Staatsrecht (5th ed. 1876) 8.

43. Kelsen, Allgemeine Staatslehre (1925) § 33. While previous authors consider the generality of a rule only one of many symptoms of *a law*, Kelsen considers it to be the only decisive test.

44. See *supra*.

45. See 2 Zachariä, Deutsches Staats- und Bundesrecht (3d ed. 1867) 140, 187 et seq.; Jellinek, Gesetz und Verordnung (1887) passim, particularly 238 et seq.

46. The British dominions have adopted the same classification of statutes. See 1 Keith, Responsible Government in the Dominions (2d ed. 1928) 389.

47. Sir E. May, Parliamentary Practice (12th ed. 1917) 595-612, 802 et seq.; Sir C. Ilbert, Mechanics of Law-Making (1914) 11, 132-134; Williams, Private Bill Legis-

lation (1927); Craies, Treatise on Statute Law (3d ed. 1923) 57-59, 465-497.

48. Rules of the U. S. Senate, Rule XV, 3; Rules of the U. S. House of Representatives, Rule XIII, 1; Jones, Statute Law-Making in the United States (1912) 32-43, 52-54; Binney, Restrictions upon Local and Special Legislation in State Constitutions (1894); Freund, Legislative Regulation (1932) 28-44; Sanderson, Validity of Statutes in Pennsylvania (1898) pt. 3; Reinsch, American Legislatures and Legislative Methods (1913) 300 et seq.

49. Reinsch, *op. cit. supra* note 48 at 302.

50. See *supra*.

51. See *supra*.

52. Bodinus, De Republica Libri Sex III, V (Frankfort ed. 1622, p. 466): "*Verbum legis aliud nihil est, quam summae potestatis iussum.*"

53. 1 Bl. Comm. (Cooley's ed.) 46, 49 et seq.

54. This difference in judging the position of the legislature is dramatically expressed in the contradiction, in Cooley's edition, between the text of 1 Bl. Comm. pp. 44, 49 et seq., and the editor's notes to that text.

55. See Jellinek, Gesetz und Verordnung (1887) 226-261; Kelsen, Allgemeine Staatslehre (1925) passim, particularly at 182, 192, 231 et seq.; 1 Carré de Malberg, Théorie générale de l'Etat (1920-1922) passim, particularly at 273-377.

56. *Supra*.

57. *Supra*.

58. In case this apparent doubt as to the value of an official use of the term seems strange to those readers who believe that an official use of the term should be conclusive, the problem might be illustrated by citing the instance of sovereignty. Legal theory does not attach much importance to official documents designating certain units as "independent" or "sovereign." The Swiss Federal Constitution speaks of "sovereign" Cantons; several constitutions of individual states of the Union, adopted after the Constitution of the United States, speak of their states as "independent." The agreement between Great Britain and Johore of Dec. 11, 1885 (76 British and Foreign State Papers 92) speaks of the "Independent State of Johore," and a letter from a British Executive Department certifies that the Sultan of Johore is a "sovereign ruler," Mighell v. Sultan of Johore [1894] 1 Q. B. 149, 150. Courts of justice may have to consider themselves bound by the language of official documents, as did Lord Esher and Kay, L. J., in this latter case, id. at 158, 160, 161. But legal theory adheres to the notion of sovereignty and independence as "*civitates quae superiorem non recognoscunt*" and applies this test as conclusive. It is, as Kelsen says, a matter for *Rechtserkenntnis*, not for *Rechtssatzung*, for legal theory, not for legal practice. Such critical attitude, based on theoretical considerations rather than on strict interpretation of official documents, has been occasionally adopted by courts of justice, Penhallow v. Doane, 3 U. S. 54, 80 (1795); Cherokee Nation v. Southern Kansas Railroad Co., 33 Fed. 900, 906 (W. D. Ark. 1888); State ex rel. Mills v. Dixon, 66 Mont. 76, 86, 213 Pac. 227, 230 (1923). This should certainly be the attitude of theoretical jurists. The same ought to be true of the concept of legislation. It will be noted that constitutional texts do not explain authoritatively the use of the term. They employ it in a sense which theory should work out in accord with traditional standards. Judicial tribunals in the United States proceed frequently on the assumption that they are able to detect a definite traditional meaning of legislation and legislative power, but the correctness of this assumption is rather doubtful. See Mr. Justice Baldwin, in Rhode Island v. Massachusetts, 37 U. S. 657 (1838). At any rate, as a matter of comparative law, a theoretical concept of legislation has not been found, and contemporary theory has retreated to a "formal" consideration of the subject. Thus, particularly, 1 Carré de Malberg, Théorie Générale, 369 et seq.

59. Barthélemy-Duez, Traité de droit constitutionnel (nouv. ed. 1933) 724 et seq.

60. People v. Sturtevant, 9 N. Y. 263, 273 (1853); Wagner v. State, 173 Ind. 603, 607 (1909); Hile v. City of Cleveland, 107 Ohio St. 144, 148, 141 N. E. 35, 36 (1923).

61. Union Pacific Railroad Co. v. United States, 99 U. S. 700, 761 (1878).

62. Smith v. Strother, 68 Cal. 194, 197 (1885).

63. *Supra.*

64. A good instance of the unconsciousness of Anglo-American theory of this problem is Allen, Law in the Making (1930) which does not contain the slightest mention of it. As clearly shown by a perusal of pp. 255 *et seq.*, the author has in mind merely statutory legislation in the formal sense, though in other passages the author seems to enquire after the material characteristics usually associated with statutes. See also Salmond, Jurisprudence (8th ed. 1930) § 49.

65. One of the authors least conscious of the whole problem is Holland, Elements of Jurisprudence (13th ed. 1924). He deals with law as *jus*, and with law as "a rule of action," but fails to pay any attention to the law in the sense of *loi*.

2. REPRESENTATIVE GOVERNMENT IN EVOLUTION

Charles A. Beard and John D. Lewis

REPRESENTIVE GOVERNMENT on a national scale did not originate in the psychology of primitive Teutons, as English historians long contended;[1] nor is it a mere bourgeois institution of passing significance, designed to delude the masses, as Fascists and Bolsheviks have alleged. Its vast historical complications conform to no such simple thesis. On the contrary, representative government began its career as an instrument of political power, in a given complex of social and economic circumstances, to serve the purposes of ruling monarchs; and it has played a bewildering role, in form, spirit, and authority, for more than five hundred years. Flexibility has been its prime characteristic. As a means, not an end in itself, it has served an infinite variety of causes, and has displayed both adaptability and survival power. In form, it has not been a political stereotype. Rather, it has been amazingly variable. In spirit, in the ideas associated with its evolution, and in the uses to which it may be put, representative government is subtle and adaptable, offering to statesmen who have imagination and manipulative capacity a tool of inexhaustible utility. Hence a wide historical view of representative government in evolution is indispensable to any understanding of its nature or its possible place in the future government of mankind.

It is fitting to inquire at the outset rather narrowly into the concept, or idea, of representation—a term that is used freely in political literature as if the thing for which it stands were an objective reality, the same always and everywhere. Unfortunately, this is a difficult task.

If the idea of representation could be caught on the wing, transfixed, and dissected at a given moment, the troubles of the searcher would not be at an end. Every political idea is in process of continuous evolution. It changes from time to time as its possessors give new content to it out of inquiry and experience. And at a particular moment it may mean one thing to the logically competent and something else to the more or less obfuscated generality. To this rule, the conception of representation offers no exception. It evolves in structure and spirit, precisely as the institution itself is confronted by new tasks thrown up by the social and economic development of the society in which it functions.

For these reasons, and many others, it is appropriate to ask first of all: What realities are covered by the word "representation"? The term has come into the English language through French derivatives from the Latin *repraesentare*, meaning, quite literally, "to bring before one, to bring back, to exhibit, to show, to manifest, to display." In classical Latin, it was not a political term, but was applied primarily to concrete objects, in a very realistic fashion. When it appeared in England, after a sojourn in France, transformed through *représentation*, its original meaning still clung to it. In fourteenth-century English, it meant "to symbolise, to serve as a visible and concrete embodiment of;" as, for example, in Wycliffe: "Ymages that representen pompe and glorie of the worlde."

No illustrations of its use in a political sense appear before the sixteenth century, at least in the record of the Oxford Dictionary. By that time, it had come to mean to take or fill the place of another in some capacity or for some purpose; to be a substitute in some capacity for another person or body; to act for another by deputed

Reprinted from *American Political Science Review,* Vol. 26 (April, 1932), pp. 223-40, by permission of Professor Lewis and the publisher.

right. "Our Generall," runs a quotation from about 1595, "sent Cap. Jobson, repraesenting his person with his authority, as his Leiftenante Generall." Speaking strictly, of course, this is not a political usage, but it implies agency, deputation, and authorization, and hence marks an easy transition to the purely political terminology employed by such writers as Coke, Hobbes, and Locke. Doubtless the English transformation was facilitated by the fact that during the early Middle Ages *repraesentare* had acquired, in the hands of Latin writers, a political meaning akin to its present sense. However this may be, representation had come into general use in England by the opening of the seventeenth century to describe the system of deputation that had grown up with the development of Parliament.

But in time the term took on more mystic implications. Near the close of the sixteenth century, Sir Thomas Smith could write that the Parliament of England "representeth and hath the power of the whole realme both the head and the bodie. For everie Englishman is entended to be there present, either by person or by procuration and attornies, of whatever preheminence, state, dignitie, or qualities soever he be, from the Prince (be he King or Queen) to the lowest person of England, and the consent of Parliament is taken to be everie man's consent."[2] This concept Burke carried another step: "The value, spirit, and essence of the House of Commons consists in its being the express image of the feelings of the nation." In other words, the idea of representation has in it the concept of bare agency, the substitution of one for many, but it is more: the supreme representative body is supposed to mirror the whole movement of social and economic forces within the nation, to express the nation's will and its sentiments. Correctly conceived, it involves a philosophy of history.

Although representative government now carries with it such democratic implications, it has not always been democratic in conception. Some of the mediaeval writers looked upon the absolute monarch as *representing* the community. According to John of Salisbury, "the prince is first of all to make a thorough survey of himself, and diligently study the condition of the whole body of the commonwealth of which he is the representative, and in whose place he stands. . . ."[3] Again: "Wherefore in the ordinances of princes or the promulgations of magistrates the plural number is used by prolemsis to the end that every ordinance and other kind of promulgation may be seen to be the act not so much of the officer personally as of the corporate community. . . ."[4] In John's political theory, the prince is the repre-

sentative of the community—in other words, stands in the place of the community. Owing to his representative character, the acts of the prince are to be deemed acts of the community. Yet while he acts for the generality, he is not responsible to the commonweath for what he does. As Dickinson puts it, "the prince is responsible *for* the commonwealth, but not *to* it."[5] Since he holds his office from God rather than the people, he is responsible only to God or to God's representatives.[6] Later mediaeval writers make use of a similar concept of representation; and the controversies over conflicting authority are often expressed in terms of rival representative capacities.[7]

If we leave speculative writers for concrete realities, we also find representation often disassociated from democratic notions. A representative body may speak for a narrow class, as did the English parliament for about six hundred years. Neither does it carry with it republican implications; England has retained her monarchy through all the vicissitudes of parliamentary development, save for a brief period in the seventeenth century. There are additional limitations on the doctrine in practice. The Fathers of the American Constitution believed in representative and republican government, but they feared the populace as they feared original sin. One of their fundamental purposes in shaping the form of the federal government was to break the force of majority rule at its source in elections and in the operation of the government itself. In itself, therefore, representative government need not be republican or democratic. It may be monarchical, or aristocratic, or so designed as to prevent the kind of popular government which operates through simple majorities.

Yet, despite these difficulties of definition, we may say, for the sake of convenience, that the modern idea of representation can be broken into three component parts: (1) a representative person or group has power to act for, or in place of, another person or group; (2) the representative is elected by those for whom he is to act; (3) the representative is responsible for his acts to those whom he represents.

But this analysis is not at bottom as simple as it seems on the surface, and should not be allowed to stand without a caveat. What is this power which resides in the constituency or body politic and is transferred in whole or in part to the representative? At best, it is an elusive fluid. What methods of nomination and election are established by law to govern choice by the voters, and how do they operate in practice? What is responsibility in essence, and how is it to be enforced? Obviously, the representative is more than an agent in the private law sense of the term. He helps to make the ideas and wills which he represents. Often he has to deal with issues which his constituents have scarcely considered, if at all—issues on which they have expressed no will. Hence, when we define representative government in simple terms, as above, we arbitrarily lay out a little land of rational certainty and speak in the language of anatomy. This is not enough, for representative government is merely one phase of the whole process of civilization, and those who speak of it as if it were a Victorian bustle, to be put on or entirely discarded at will, display a woeful ignorance of its history and nature.

From what has been said about the history of the word representation, it may readily be imagined that the philosophy of representative government was unknown to the ancients and but dimly foreshadowed by the writers of the Middle Ages. During the thousands of years which we call antiquity, monarchies, despotisms, dictatorships, tyrannies, democracies, and aristocracies, with numerous variants, rose, flourished, and fell; but nowhere, at no time, did representative institutions appear, at least on any impressive scale. Aristotle, the father of political science, does, indeed, refer once to the fact that democracies, such as existed at Mantinea, did exercise the power of electing magistrates, and thus acted "through representatives elected in turn out of the whole people;" but this reference is casual, and is made in a tone which suggests that the case is exceptional.[8] A modern writer on political philosophy, Jellinek, while claiming that Greek magistrates were regarded as representatives in the execution of policies adopted by popular assemblies, admits that the Greeks had no notion of representation as applied to the creation of legislative assemblies.[9] Even if his first point be conceded, namely, that Greek magistrates were representative in character, it is significant to note that Aristotle lays no great stress on the conception.

In Roman, as well as in Greek, thinking, the idea of representation in government appears only in shadowy forms. Polybius, it is true, speaks of the responsibility of the consuls to the senate and to the people, of the responsibility of the senate to the people, and of the responsibility of the tribunes to the people.[10] Certain passages in Roman law have also been interpreted to imply that the senate was representative in character, that is, spoke for others who were not members of that body.[11] But Polybius does not look upon the Roman officers of state as agents or representatives of the people; nor does the actual composition of the Roman senate lend any color to the view that it was representative in any

modern sense, or indeed any strict sense, of the word.

This does not mean, of course, that the theory and practice of agency was unknown to the ancients. "The city," says Ernest Barker, "was not devoid of representative institutions, nor unacquainted with the political machinery which is connected with those institutions."[12] He cites the Athenian council as an example of an elected representative assembly, but admits that it did not have "representative authority," that is, authority "to deliberate and decide as the exponent of the general will within its sphere." Again, the synod of the Boeotian League "consisted of 660 members, elected in equal numbers from the eleven electoral divisions of the League;"[13] but that was more of a diplomatic assembly than a legislature in the modern sense. While it would not be correct to say, therefore, that representation was utterly foreign to Greek and Roman politics, practical illustrations of it were few and must be strained to make any case worthy of serious attention. At all events, modern legislative bodies have no historic connections with Greek and Roman representative agencies.

The starting point of representative government on a national scale, then, is the Middle Ages in time, and the place is Europe. It did not spring up because people suddenly decided to govern themselves, displayed the capacity, and set up parliaments. It was called into being by mediaeval monarchs who had established or maintained by the sword political power over wide territorial areas containing a large population socially aggregated into classes and groups and communities. The monarchs who first called representatives of communities or estates to grant money and give counsel were not thinking of democracy; they were concerned primarily with the conservation of the peace, the administration of lucrative justice, and the replenishment of their royal treasuries.[14] Even the most despotic mediaeval monarch could not tax and exploit his subjects without limits; as a matter of expediency also, he had to consider ways and means. The estates and classes that composed the social order under him had interests and sentiments which he could not ignore, save at great peril to himself; and a certain degree of coöperation with them offered the most effective method of gaining his immediate ends. Beyond that he could not see, for practical men are adjusters, not prophets.

The rest of the record is equally clear. Although the several phases are familiar to students of constitutional history, it seems fitting to set down here, in summary form, for purposes of illustration, the principal stages in the development of representative government in England.

1. The first parliaments were called by monarchs primarily for the purpose of voting taxes for the royal treasury. The original parliament did not represent people—free and equal heads—as such, but the estates of the realm (the nobility, clergy, landed gentry, and burgesses of the towns); in a strict economic sense, two estates, i.e., land and commerce.[15] In the early assemblies, there was some talking about ways and means of raising revenues (hence the term "parliament"); but discussion was an incident, not a prime end.

2. In time, the tax-voting body became a law-making body by gradual steps. The members of the estates who were being consulted and taxed had grievances of a practical sort. Sometimes the king laid on too heavily. Sometimes his officers, without his knowledge and against his desires, acted in an arbitrary fashion, extorting extra money from his subjects, imprisoning or fining them in an irregular manner, and otherwise laying exactions, burdens, and inconveniences upon them or depriving them of concrete rights which they had hitherto enjoyed by immemorial custom. Nothing was more natural than that the representatives of the estates, when assembled for purposes of voting taxes, should consider their grievances and come to agreement about them. Hence parliaments soon began to list their protests in the form of petitions to the king for redress. If he approved a petition, it became a law, binding on his officers and subjects. Since the parliament held the purse strings, it could often compel the king to consent, even though it pained him to do so. In due time, the petition was dropped for the bill—a proposed measure drafted in and passed by the parliament. Thus the tax-voting body became a legislature of large powers —everything depending on the character of the monarch and the willfulness of the parliament.

3. The third stage was reached by a gradual process culminating in the revolutions of the seventeenth century. At last, the king was substantially deprived of law-making and tax-voting powers, and his civil and military administration was confined within the limits laid down in constitutional measures. In other words, the estates summoned in the beginning to supply the royal treasury became conscious of their potential powers and transformed themselves into a sovereign body. Their crowning act was to compel the king to choose his chief officers of state, his cabinet or inner council, from the party that had a majority in Parliament. Although an elaborate ideology was developed in the course of this struggle, the operation itself involved a concern with very practical matters, largely economic in char-

acter, rather than a moral straining after a general ideal or the best of all possible worlds. When once the ruling classes represented in Parliament gained their ends, they settled down to the enjoyment of the spoils of office in the fashion meticulously described by L. B. Namier in *The Structure of Politics at the Accession of George III.*[16]

4. The economic estates that made themselves sovereign through representative institutions had not long enjoyed the fruits of their labors when rumblings were heard below, among the nameless and unhonored masses that had not shared in the process—serfs who, though rightless in the Middle Ages, had now become freeholders or agricultural laborers, craftsmen in towns, and other persons from whom the suffrage had been withheld. Indeed, these rumblings had been heard early—in the time of the Peasants' Revolt during the Middle Ages, and especially in the tempestuous age when Cromwell was upsetting the throne.[17] But they were turned into a loud roar by the French Revolution, whose prophet, Rousseau, declared that all men were equal, and that each one was entitled to an equal share in governing.[18] This, of course, was flatly contradictory to the system of English classes, but in time it prevailed—with the gradual extension of the suffrage until in our own time all adult men and women, as such, without regard to property are included within the political pale. And this extraordinary outcome, entirely unforeseen by the founders of representative institutions, was largely the result of a movement of economic, intellectual, and educational forces outside the sphere of legislation and administration.

It was by these stages, speaking cursorily, that we got down to the modern conception of representative government, which may be summarized in the following fashion. Speaking politically, all adult heads are equal and alike, each having an equal share of governing power (whatever that may be). The sovereign power of government is exercised either by constitutional conventions or parliaments composed of deputies elected by the voters. Logically applied, this principle means that the representatives shall be distributed among districts containing substantially the same number of inhabitants, and shall be chosen by majority or plurality vote. Duly assembled, the delegates shall organize themselves and proceed to the exercise of their authority by majority rule. In other words, the political assembly no longer represents estates, classes, or orders as such, but free and equal heads—abstract political persons.

Although there were variations in the theory and many deviations in practice, this conception seemed in a fair way to conquer the world at the opening of the twentieth century. Even China, after living under despotic government for five thousand years, "off and on," as a philosopher once put it, arose from her slumbers and tried the parliamentary experiment—with disastrous results. And during the world conflict that broke out in 1914, the most popular slogan was "Make the world safe for democracy." It is true that President Wilson had said in his *Congressional Government* (p. 227), written in 1888, that "the British government is perfect in proportion as it is unmonarchical, and ours safe in proportion as it is undemocratic;" but that was forgotten during the turmoil of battle. All the world was to go over to representative democracy; and for a time, it seemed almost axiomatic in politics.

Yet long before "the great crusade" began, this Euclidian theory of representative democracy had been vigorously challenged in many quarters. Monarchs and landed aristocracies, real and vestigial, from the Baltic to the Mediterranean, resisted its onward march with all the powers of police and ideology as a matter of course. But there were doubts also in countries that had accepted and applied the doctrine with more or less completeness. Conservatives were disgruntled with representative democracy because it seemed to be growing radical, imposing heavy burdens of taxes on large fortunes, and assuming "improper" functions in the nature of social services. Some of their spokesmen—Prins, Benoist, and others—suggested a revision of the canonical creed and the substitution of the representation of economic classes or groups for the representation of free and equal heads.[19] And so zealously did they push their agitation that they produced quite a furor among the theorists, particularly in the academic world.

At the other end of the scale, syndicalists and radical socialists made war on representative democracy. They insisted that heads were not, and could not be, free and equal as long as there were great discrepancies in wealth, that elections and campaigns were farcical since the press and schools were on the side of the heaviest economic battalions, and that the mass of the people suffered from poverty and unemployment under the representative scheme of perfection as under all other systems. The social reforms which conservatives denounced as dangerous, socialists and syndicalists condemned as paltry or insufficient, going on to demand yet more revolutionary installments. Despairing of winning adequate majorities to their cause by the ordinary processes of agitation, they began to demand government by economic parliaments—assemblies composed of members representing the proletariat alone, the

proletariat organized at the bottom as workers' councils in factories. After the close of the World War, encouraged by the Soviet experiment in Russia, they renewed their onslaught on representative democracy of the type that had become almost traditional.[20] So at the very moment when this institutional device seemed about to sweep the world, it was rudely challenged; its adequacy for the economic tasks of the technological age was questioned in quarters high and low; and the theory that once looked as sound as the multiplication table was everywhere subjected to critical examination.

From this brief and sweeping survey, certain conclusions seem to emerge. Representative government originated in an agricultural age as an instrument of central authority, dictatorial in substance if monarchical in form, to secure the obedient coöperation of classes as yet only dimly conscious of any urge to the exercise of authority. It spread discipline over these classes, drew them into functions not of their own deliberate designing, gave them knowledge and experience in the field of government, and awakened in them a sense of power. At the same time, amazing instrumentalities for the distribution of political information facilitated the transfer of expertness and comprehension from the monopolists at the center to the very edges of the social periphery. In this way, arbitrary government under royal direction was transformed into parliamentary government resting on a broad popular base. Thus monarchy, which began as a kind of military dictatorship, created for its own uses an agency that ultimately deprived it of sovereignty. Meanwhile, vast masses had become literate and conscious of powers and potentialities. Men who were not by nature political animals were made such by parliamentary discipline. Apparently, by a similar process, illiterate and unconscious masses in other portions of the world may also be transformed into political animals. But, unless there is a general decay of civilization, it is doubtful whether the operation can be reversed, and those once awakened can again be reduced to cogs in an automatic machine deriving its momentum from the center—at all events, for long periods of time as measured by historical standards.

Doubts on this score are accentuated by the course of economic evolution. Since the origin of representative government, the technological revolution has intervened. For various reasons, economic institutions have become highly centralized in the most advanced industrial nations, and governmental activities have multiplied in response to new forces. Conceivably, political functions, confined largely to police and finance, could remain centralized and despotic for a long period in an agricultural society in which economy is localized and self-sufficient, assuming astute management at the center. But when both economy and politics are centralized and cannot proceed effectively without coöperation from top to bottom—wise consideration for popular welfare at the top and loyal coöperation at the bottom—then it becomes doubly doubtful whether it is possible to keep the organism long in motion from heat generated merely at the center. Again we return to a consideration of representative government in evolution as one aspect of the movement of civilization.

Speaking philosophically, the issue before us is not one of attack or defense, but of understanding, as far as our limited intelligence will permit. Speaking practically, the question is one of convenience and utility. Is representative government in any form competent for the tasks of modern society? Is it possible to settle all social conflicts within the limits of law and rationality by discussion and public resolution? Can a great society, confronting difficult technological problems, retain the loyalty of its people without drawing them into intimate coöperative relations with its government and national economy? Can any kind of a dictatorship, no matter how benevolent, deal effectively, in the long run, with collective requirements? And finally, in last analysis, will it be found necessary to make modifications in the structure and operation of representative government with a view to reaching a higher technical proficiency? If so, what is to be the nature of those modifications?[21]

Notes

1. Cf. Charles A. Beard, "The Teutonic Origins of Representative Government," *American Political Science Review*, Vol. 26 (February, 1932).

2. *De Republica Anglorum*, 1583 (Ed. Alston, 1906, Cambridge Press), p. 49.

3. *Policraticus*, 1159 (tr. Dickinson, N. Y., 1927, v. 2, p. 64).

4. *Ibid.*, v. 4, p. 74.

5. *Ibid.*, p. XLIV.

6. However chosen, the prince derives his authority from God. "He is placed by the divine governance at the apex of the commonwealth, and preferred above all others, sometimes through the secret ministry of God's providence, sometimes by the decision of his priests, and again it is the vote of the whole people which concur to place the ruler in authority" (*ibid.*, v. 6, p. 83). "The place of the head in the body of the commonwealth is filled by the prince, who is subject only to God and to those who exercise his office and represent him on earth" (*ibid.*, v. 2, p. 65).

7. As in John's writings, the prince is considered as representing the whole community of his subjects. Cf. especially the following passages: *Princeps repraesentat illum populum et ille populus imperium etiam mortuo*

principe . . ., Baldus, 1391, Gierke, *Political Theories of the Middle Ages,* tr. Maitland, 1900, note 216. The emperor *"in loco ipsorum populorum"* represents the whole Christian people, *"cum in eum translata sit iurisdictio et potestas universi orbis,"* Zarbarella, c. 1406, Gierke, note 192; *Ordinare autem aliquid in bonum commune est vel totius multitudinis vel alicuis gerentis vicem totius multitudinis; et ideo condere legem vel pertinet ad personam publicam quae totius multitudinis curam habet,* Thos. Aquinas (Gierke, note 217). In like manner, the pope is considered the representative of the universal Church and the lesser prelates the representatives of local church units (Gierke, note 213). Many writers considered this representative character of the ruler or prelate as complete or "absorptive" (cf. Gierke, notes 121, 122). Such claims to a complete representative character, and therefore unlimited authority, were confronted by the mediaeval doctrine of a fundamental law binding upon ruler as well as subject (cf. Bracton, *De Legibus et Consuetudinibus Angliae,* 1250-1267, ed. Twiss, 1871, folio 5b, I, p. 38; John of Salisbury, *op. cit.,* IV, c. 1), and by vaguely recognized rights of the communities represented. The Civilians, following certain sections of the *Digest,* insisted that the Roman emperor had received his power as a grant from the Roman people, and that the basis of political power was still the consent of the *populus* or *universitas* (cf. especially the famous *lex regia,* L.I. *Dig.* 1, 4: *Quod principi placuit legis habet vigorem; utpote cum lege regia, quae de imperio eius lata est, populus ei et in eum omne suum imperium et potestatem conferat.* This is a doctrine which could easily be taken over by the constitutional writers. "Ever since the days of the Glossators [the twelfth century], the universally accepted doctrine was that an act of alienation performed by the people in the Lex Regia was for Positive Law the basis of the modern, as well as of the ancient, Empire" (Gierke, p. 39; cf. A. J. Carlyle, *A History of Mediaeval Political Theory,* II, ch. 7). A new ruler, or a new line, therefore, could be instituted only through election by the whole *populus,* or by delegates representing the whole *populus.* It was taken for granted that the rights of a community could be delegated as well to a representative assembly, which then stood in the stead of the represented community and exercised all of its powers (Gierke, p. 65). The electors in the Empire were capable of choosing the emperor because there was delegated to them as representatives a right belonging to the whole *populus* (Gierke, note 240). The General Council could act on behalf of all Christendom because it represented all Christendom. The cardinals, when choosing a pope, acted as representatives of the universal Christian community (Gierke, note 194). The fact that individual members of the communities represented had no voice in the choice of their representatives was of no consequence to the writers. During this controversial period, the democratic implications of the doctrine of representation seem to have been buried under this imposing series of fictions. In the radical doctrines of Marsilius, William of Occam, and Nicholas Cusanus, we begin to find some recognition of the democratic implications of representation; but these three are hardly typical of their period. They are prophets of another age which is still centuries off (cf. Emerton, *The Defensor Pacis of Marsiglio of Padua,* Harv. Theol. Studies, VIII, 1920, pp. 23-32; Dunning, *Political Theories,* I, at 239, 241; Gierke, notes 233, 215, 235, 238).

8. *Politics,* VI, 4, 4 (tr. Jowett).

9. G. Jellinek, *Das Recht des modernen Staates,* I, pp. 519-520.

10. F. W. Coker, *Readings in Political Theory,* p. 116.

11. Gierke, *op. cit.,* note 236.

12. *Greek Political Theory; Plato and His Predecessors,* p. 33.

13. *Ibid.,* pp. 34-35.

14. The *witenagemot* and the later *commune concilium* could be considered representative only in the same sense that electoral colleges and assemblies on the Continent

were representative (cf. note 7 above, and W. Stubbs, *Select Charters*, 8th Oxford ed., 1905, p. 36). During the thirteenth century, there was injected into this entirely feudal assembly two new elements representative of rising economic interests. The knights, increasing in number and in influence in the local communities, were separating out of the feudal organization and being gradually transformed into the landed gentry which later acquired such a powerful vested interest in Parliament. The town burgesses, also increasing in size, affluence, and influence with the expansion of trade, was also separating out of the feudal system and increasing their independence through charter privileges and special "liberties" (cf. G. B. Adams, *Const. Hist. of England*, 1921, pp. 169-170). To align these new economic forces with the monarchy was obviously a matter of necessity and convenience to the king in his dealings with his subjects. "It was the king who imposed upon his subjects the duty of sending him their representatives. Edward I changed an occasional expedient into a regular custom, not in order to associate the whole nation with himself in the work of government, but in order to strengthen the royal power. . . . If in the end he made a practice of summoning them [the Commons] almost regularly, this was because he perceived that the previous consent of the knights and burgesses greatly facilitated the collection of aides and even enabled the government to collect more than would otherwise have been possible" (D. Pasquet, *Origins of the House of Commons*, tr. Laffan, Cambridge, 1925, pp. 225-226. Cf. also Professor Ford's thesis that representative government developed early in England because of the strength of the monarchy. *Representative Government*, 1924).

15. The device of representation introduced into Parliament in the thirteenth century was, of course, not novel in England. It was a device already in use in the local courts, where service was an obligation to which all were liable, but from which tenants might be excused by the attendance of their lord or another representative. "Representation was not the offspring of democratic theory, but an incident of the feudal system. Suit and service were due from all; but we are told in the *Leges Henrici Primi* if the lord or his steward will go to the county court, his presence will 'acquit' the tenant on his domain. If neither lord nor steward is present, there must come the priest and reeve, and four best men in the township on behalf of their fellows. The boon of representation is not in the election to serve, but in the license to stay away . . ." (A. F. Pollard, *The Evolution of Parliament*, 1925, p. 109). The representatives to the county courts, then, were not popularly elected, but attendance was an obligation of their position rather than a matter of choice. Those eligible (or, more correctly, obligated) to jury service later became electors of the delegates to Parliament. After 1430, this eligibility was determined in the shire by the possession of a forty-shilling freehold. The "best men" of the shire were apparently those with substantial property holdings (cf. Pollard, pp. 153-154; Adams, *op. cit.*, pp. 174-175). Only when it was finally realized that attendance at Parliament could be utilized to impose upon the king and the rest of the country a recognition of group interests did the liability of serving become a privilege (cf. Pollard, pp. 158-159). It is interesting to note that even as late as the seventeenth century Coke considered it necessary to state that the king could not exempt a knight, citizen, or burgess from attendance at Parliament, since such attendance "is for the service of the whole realme" (*Institutes*, 1642, ed. 1797, IV, pp. 48-49).

16. London, 1929.

17. The sixteenth and early seventeenth century writers seemed to feel that Parliament, however the members might have been chosen, was, in some mysterious fashion, representative of every citizen of the realm. Sir Thomas Smith speaks of "the parliament of Englande, which representeth and hath the power of the whole realme. . . .

For everie Englishman is entended to be there present, either by person or by procuration and attornies . . . and the consent of the parliament is taken to be everie man's consent" (*De Republica Anglorum*, 1583, ed. Alston, 1906, p. 49; cf. also intro., XXXVI). On the eve of the Civil War, Sir Edward Coke speaks in similar terms: "For the parliament concerning making or enacting of lawes consisteth of the king, the lords spirituall and temporall, and the commons; and it is no act of parliament, unless it be made by the king, the lords and the commons. And where it is said, by all the commonalty, all the commons of the realme are represented in parliament by the kights, citizens and burgesses. . . . Commons are in legal understanding taken for the frank tenants or freeholders of the counties. And whosoever is not a lord of parliament and of the lord's house, is of the house of commons either in person, or by representation . . ." (*Institutes*, IV, p. 1; cf. also pp. 5, 14, 26). This is the conventional point of view taken by the Puritans and expressed in the resolution of January 4, 1649, in the House of Commons (cf. Adams, *op. cit.*, 321). But to this statement of the supremacy of Parliament as representative of the people the more radical Levellers added two further strikingly modern propositions. They contended (1) that representation in Parliament should be reapportioned on a widened franchise; (2) that all government officials (including representatives in parliament) were subject to *definite* limitations of power for which they might be held responsible by their electors. The *Agreement of the People*, drawn up in 1648 and laid before the Commons in 1649, presents the political theory as well as the immediate demands of the Levellers. Had it gone into effect, it would have set up a limited parliamentary system with manhood suffrage (cf. Gardiner, *Constitutional Documents of the Puritan Revolution, 1625-1660*, 3rd ed., 1906, pp. 359-369). In the debate over manhood suffrage, the Levellers supported their demand by appealing to the "law of God and of Nature"—that is, to the natural right of individuals to equal privileges. The following comes from a speech from Rainborow: "I doe heare nothing att all that can convince mee why any man that is borne in England ought nott to have his voice in Election of Burgesses. . . . I doe nott finde anything in the law of God, that a lord shall chuse 20 Burgesses, and a Gentlemann butt two, or a poore man shall chuse none. I finde noe such things in the law of nature, nor in the law of nations" (*Clarke Papers*, I, pp. 304-306; cited by Shepard, *Theory of the Nature of the Suffrage, 7 Am. Pol. Science Rev.*, Supp., at p. 120). "We judge that all inhabitants who have not lost their birthright should have an equal voice in elections," insisted another of the radicals. And to this Rainborow added that no man was bound to a government under which he had not placed himself (quoted from Pettus, in Gooch and Laski, *English Democratic Ideas in the Seventeenth Century*, 2nd ed., 1927, pp. 130, 138). In answer to the demand for manhood suffrage, Cromwell replied: "The consequences of this rule tend to anarchy, must end in anarchy. For where is there any bound or limit set if men that have but the interest of breathing shall have voices in elections?" (*Clarke Papers*, I, pp. 309, Gooch and Laski, *op. cit.*, p. 194). Ireton insisted that, in the interest of stability, the franchise had to be restricted to property holders (*Clarke Papers*, I, 301, 302, cited by Shepard, *op. cit.*, p. 121). The opinion of Cromwell and Ireton naturally prevailed. The *Instrument of Government* provided that the suffrage should be restricted to those possessing property to the value of £200, providing that they were "persons of known integrity" and had not opposed the parliamentary party (*Instrument of Government*, 1653, secs. XVIII, XV, VII; Gardiner, pp. 401-411).

18. Rousseau maintained that sovereign power can reside *only* in the people themselves or a majority of them. It cannot be delegated to representatives. Legislation, being an expression of the *volonté général*, can come only from the sovereign people; that which has not been

accepted by a majority of the people themselves cannot be considered law (cf. *Social Contract*, Everyman ed., p. 83). Willing to admit the logical conclusions of his thesis, Rousseau finds that true democracy is possible only in a political unit small enough to permit of legislation by a primary assembly, and that very few modern nations actually have laws (*ibid.*, p. 84). He recognizes the difficulty of applying this city-state theory to modern European countries, and speaks in one place of reconciling theory and fact by the device of *federalism* (*ibid.*, p. 85 and note 1). But he does not attempt to develop this idea. The importance of Rousseau and Paine (cf. *Common Sense*, 1776, and *Rights of Man*, 1791) is amply demonstrated by a comparison of their writings with the *Declaration of the Rights of Man* and the later revolutionary constitutions. All assert that sovereignty resides in the whole people, and that every citizen must have the right of concurring in the making of law. But, departing from Rousseau, all concede that this right may be exercised through representatives. Cf. the statement on sovereignty in the constitution of 1791, which is practically a quotation from Rousseau (*Const. du 3 Sept., 1791*, Tit. III, art. 1; Duguit et Monnier, *Les constitutions de la France*, 1925, p. 7; cf. also *Declaration des Droits de L'Homme . . .*, art. 6, *ibid.*, p. 2; *Const. 1791*, Tit. III, art. 2, *ibid.*, p. 7; *Const. Girondine de 1793*, arts. 26, 27, 28, *ibid.*, p. 37; *Const. du 24 Juin 1793*, arts. 25, 26, 27, *ibid.*, p. 69; *Const. 5 Fructidor An III*, arts. 17-20, *ibid.*, pp. 79-80).

19. The modern movement for "professional representation" has been popularized, particularly in France, during the last quarter-century by a considerable group of writers. As early as 1896, Benoist argued the fallacy of the doctrine of national sovereignty based upon the traditional system of representation, and urged the election of deputies by voters grouped according to professions (cf. *L'Organisation du Suffrage universel*, 1896; *Les Sophismes politiques de ce Temps*, 1893). More recently, the eminent constitutional jurist Duguit has staunchly defended the doctrine of professional representation. An assembly elected by proportional representation according to numerical party strength must be supplemented, he maintains, by an assembly representing professional groups. "The establishment of proportional representation is not a sufficient electoral reform. The assembly elected according to that system represents only individuals, and all or most of the individuals in political or social parties. But it is not individuals and parties that form a nation; there are other elements that form the inner structure of the social edifice. They are groups founded upon community of interests and of occupation, the professional groups, to use that term in its widest meaning. If one wishes to approach the ideal that all political representation should tend to realize, one must insure the presence in parliament of all the elements of national life; it is necessary to find a place for an assembly elected by the professional groups in addition to the assembly elected by individuals. . . ." In answer to Esmein's objection that the principle of national sovereignty excludes representation of interests because it would necessitate a division of sovereignty (*Droit Constitutionnel*, 7th ed., I, pp. 312-313), Duguit replies that, far from being in contradiction to the dogma of national sovereignty, professional representation is its logical consequence. "A parliament cannot be representative of the state unless it includes the two elements which constitute the state: the individual element and the collective element. . . ." (*Droit Constitutionnel*, 2nd ed., 1911, II, pp. 596-598).

20. The most outspoken of this group are to be found among the English guild socialists, whose general point of view and specific proposals are stated most thoroughly and consistently by G. D. H. Cole and S. G. Hobson. Society, as Cole views it, is a complex of associations, each one of which is formed by "a group pursuing a common purpose or system of purposes, by a course of coöperative action. . . ." Each association, therefore, expresses a particular need, and exists for the performance of a particular function. Each individual's loyalty and interests are divided among a number of such associations, since no one of them can cover the whole sphere of his activity— not even the state, whose claim to "sovereignty" the guild socialists thus attack (*Social Theory*, 1920, probably the most valuable contribution which the guild socialists have made to political thought). Upon this theoretical basis, Cole elaborates a program for the organization of industries into integrated, self-governing guilds (*Self Government in Industry*, 1919, especially pp. 205-227; cf. also *Guild Socialism*, 1920). A system of local, regional, and national communes made up of representatives from the various functional groups would take the place of present governmental structures. While the national commune in its rôle as a "supreme coördinating body" would exercise functions of the present national Parliament, its composition would be closer to that of the Russian Congress of Soviets (*Guild Socialism*, p. 121). Hobson outlines a similar system of nationally organized, self-governing guilds centered in a functionally-chosen guild congress. Parliament, supposedly elected as at present, would be relieved of economic functions. Conflicts of authority between the economic guild congress and the political parliament would be settled by joint committees (*National Guilds, An Inquiry into the Wage System and the Way Out*, 1914; cf. the Webbs', *A Constitution for the Socialist Commonwealth of Great Britain*, 1920). Outside the circle of the guild socialists, Professor Laski has been one of the most persuasive of the "pluralists" who have attacked, along with the doctrine of state sovereignty, the accepted view of representation. Authority, Laski insists repeatedly, must be based upon consent (*Grammar of Politics*, 1925, pp. 29, 62). And this demand for consent cannot be satisfied by the Hegelian assumption that the state embodies the "real will" of its citizens. Popular sovereignty and majority rule, both based upon a monistic view of the state and an Hegelian belief in real will, are untenable concepts (cf. *ibid.*, pp. 29 ff.; *Foundations of Sovereignty*, 1921, pp. 213-214). The only way of securing consent from the welter of conflicting wills which exist in society is by decentralization and federalism—functionally as well as geographically (cf. *Grammar*, pp. 32, 34-35, 263; *Foundations*, p. 242). Provisions must be made for the representation of the functional or associational interests of the individual, as well as for the representation of the individual as an individual (*Authority in the Modern State*, 1919, p. 65; *Grammar*, p. 67). But functional representative bodies will apparently remain advisory or consultative organs (*Grammar*, pp. 72-73, 84, 133, 140, 488 ff., 508 ff.).

21. While we cannot discern with certainty the exact direction in which representation is moving at present, we can notice a distinct tendency toward the path indicated by some of the pluralists. Economic and social interests have never been content to trust to the omniscience of the representative assembly for recognition of their particular problems. And, as the tangle of conflicting interests has been further complicated in a world of highly mechanized and highly specialized activities, organizations of interest groups outside the representative assembly have become more persistent and effective in pressing their claims (cf. E. P. Herring, *Group Representation Before Congress*, 1927; Peter H. Odegard, *Pressure Politics*, 1928). There has been a noticeable tendency in recent years to bring the lobbyists into the chamber, or to recognize interest groups in at least a consultative capacity. In accordance with Fascist theory of the "corporate state," members of the Italian Chamber are chosen to represent, not individuals, but functional or cultural interests (law of May 17, 1928; cf. C. Haider, *Capitalism and Labor Under Fascism*, 1930). Representatives to the local soviets in Russia come from functional rather than geographic units (cf. W. Batsell, *Soviet Rule in Russia*, 1929). The German Reichstag is supplemented by the National Economic Council, with advisory powers, standing at the apex of a system which,

when completed, will form a hierarchy of functional councils (Weimar Const., art. 165; cf. H. Finer, *Representative Government and a Parliament of Industry*, 1923; Prelot, *La Représentation professionnelle dans l'Allemagne*, 1924; L. Lorwin, *Advisory Economic Councils*, 1931). In France, there has been in existence since 1925 a National Economic Council similar in a general way to the German Economic Council (cf. C. Lautaud, *La Représentation professionnelle*, 1927; Lorwin, *op. cit.*; *ibid.*, "A Federal Economic Council," *New Republic*, April 29, 1931; Léon Jouhaux, "The Economic Labour Council in France," *International Labour Review*, February, 1921). There are at present fourteen countries in which economic councils

have been set up or are provided for. These economic councils have assumed a new importance to American individuals and groups who have recently hit upon the idea of economic planning as a way out of industrial chaos. From such divergent sources as the *New Republic* and the National Chamber of Commerce have come proposals for an integration of productive forces through a central economic council representing functional groups (cf. *Report of Subcommittee of the Committee on Manufactures, U. S. Senate, s. 6215—A Bill to Establish a National Economic Council, 1932*; C. A. Beard, *America Faces the Future*, 1932).

3. THE IMPERATIVE MANDATE IN THE SPANISH CORTES OF THE MIDDLE AGES

Alice M. Holden

A STUDY of the beginnings of national representation inevitably brings to the surface details which in their time were part or parcel of mediaeval practices. One cannot expect that these usages, even as connected with representative institutions, can be of concern in our more complex modern circumstances, since the Middle Ages had comparatively few and simple problems for legislative solution. In those days the questions of relationship between the administrative and the legislative, and between the local and the central or national, had not emerged clearly. Nevertheless, such details and questions are interesting as examples of mediaeval theory and efficiency, and, moreover, some of them are not entirely devoid of connection with present-day difficulties.

The custom of making in advance a decision which was imposed by the electors upon their chosen representative, a custom known as the imperative mandate, was an important factor in early representative government. It was sound in legal theory,[1] and some of its practice will be seen in the pages which follow. Also, its connection is with that early stage in popular government in which the development of representative institutions corresponded somewhat to one phase of the present. I refer to what is apparently a need to ask from the electors themselves their opinion on large, general questions of principle —for example, in our time, the referendum in Germany on the adoption of the Young Plan.

There is, I take it, no serious criticism nowadays of the theory of representative institutions,

nor adverse comparison of its advantages with those of direct democratic participation in popular government (in spite of numerous deviations in practice), although confidence in the representatives chosen has often been shown to have been misplaced. The following account of the imperative mandate need have no bearing on modern times, although it may conceivably possess some interest as an example of mediaeval efficiency in dealing with the simple exigencies of the period.[2]

When the electors impose upon their representative a decision fixed in advance,[3] it is called an imperative mandate, and the person elected is rather a delegate, or an agent, who votes as instructed than a representative of his constituents who acts in accordance with his own best judgment. It will be remembered that Burke condemned this kind of "representation" in his famous speech to the electors of Bristol in 1774[4] on the ground that it would result in sacrificing the "unbiased opinion," "mature judgment," and "enlightened conscience" of the representative if he had to carry out blindly "authoritative instructions," especially when the latter were "contrary to the clearest conviction of his judgment and conscience." On the other hand, Burke emphasized the need of the representative's living "in the strictest union, the closest correspondence, and the most unreserved communication with his constituents." The imperative mandate of the Middle Ages met Burke's objections by providing him that essential constant communion, and by supplying, in place of his undeveloped individual inclination and opinion, the concerted reason and judgment of the community, which, through hav-

Reprinted from *American Political Science Review*, Vol. 24 (November, 1930), pp. 886-912, by permission of the publisher.

ing its interests to conserve, really existed in a degree unknown today. But an agent or delegate, and not a free representative, he certainly was.

A modern objection to the mandated representative is derived from the fact that the program of the present-day legislature is too complex for its issues to be covered by instructions, and that unforeseen contingencies always arise and have to be met. Hence, no set of instructions in advance could possibly be adequate. Yet it is true that in all probability every election is preceded by pledges, platforms, and professions of faith and belief by candidates and parties, although such pre-election promises fall short of the actual issues presented in a session. Such sketchiness is made inevitable by lack of time, interest, and foresight. The pre-election statements of the modern candidate might, nevertheless, be considered as an imperative mandate upon him, one which is imposed directly by himself or by his party, and to which he is morally bound. For promises unfulfilled and duties neglected beyond reason, the modern answer is a recall device or direct legislation, neither of which is a highly satisfactory check upon ill-behavior. The imperative mandate would be impracticable today, but as used in Catalonia it has some current interest and possibly a suggestion for the present.

Again, the collective vote or decision of a legislature usually represents a compromise of positions, which often has worth as a process of "give and take." Such a decision, valuable in itself, could not be provided in advance; an imperative mandate could only hinder. None the less, legislatures the world over do at present act occasionally upon some great, single question of national interest, and for these fundamental matters, the imperative mandate of the past may well afford an answer as satisfactory as does the present-day popular referendum. The imperative mandate is thus not inconsistent with representative government; it was a help to development in Spain, and its safeguards might still be usable under special conditions in modern representative government.

Since the instructed delegate acted far more as a local agent than as a representative of the nation as a whole, the conception of national representation as distinct from sectional was lacking in the mandate. National representation in the modern sense did not exist in mediaeval Spain, for at none of the assemblies of the Cortes were present representatives of anything like all of the cities; nor were all of the nobles or clergy convoked. The addition of the third estate to the nobles and the clergy brought an approximation to representative government. But it must be admitted that each procurator represented only the municipality which granted him his mandate and that he certainly did not feel himself a spokesman for more than his own community. The imperative mandate, therefore, as has been suggested, may not have greatly added to the true understanding of representation and of national legislative power, which were undoubtedly present in germ; but at the same time it did not retard their development.

The advent of the third estate in the determination of national affairs probably took place at an earlier date in Spain than elsewhere. There is evidence that the people of the Spanish cities were summoned by their rulers, for consultation if not for deliberation, during the second half of the twelfth century in Leon. This was due, first, to the king's need for other aid than that given him by the nobles in freeing the country from the Moors and, later, to the flourishing circumstances of the Spanish cities, which required recognition. The imperative mandate as given by these cities to their representatives varied in degree and in conditions: in Castile and Leon it was explicit and almost unchangeable; in Aragon, it was general and more easily modified; and in Catalonia it was as binding as in Castile, but more flexible in its provisions for constant consultation and advice. Accurate generalization always presents difficulties. This is peculiarly true in connection with mediaeval Spain, for Spain was divided into separate and individualistic states; moreover, there was diversity as well even among the localities within each state; and circumstances and conditions produced great variety in Spanish institutions. Nevertheless, some general observations should be attempted before considering the specialized development in the three principal regions.

Perhaps the greatest single fact underlying the situation was that feudalism had a slighter hold in Spain than elsewhere in western Europe. There was lacking the complicated network of fiefs, or complete hierarchy from the lowest to the highest, that characterized a feudal state. Several essentials were not present—notably that relation between suzerain and vassal that meant thoroughly reciprocal duties and ties binding through the land as well as through the person. In Spain, these duties were chiefly personal. Hence, ownership of land did not carry with it dominant authority over the inhabitants, and this exemption became important in the Reconquest, when the king rewarded his helpers with grants of territory but did not, as a rule, include personal dominion over the inhabitants thereof. In other words, partial, or even complete, freedom from ties (other than to the king) was a familiar condition. This slight hindrance to fluidity of population influenced the building up of cities, especially in the regions that had to be restored after the devastations caused by Moorish occupation and later dispossession. But there were other important factors. Agriculture on barren and wasted land had become distasteful; concentration in towns had the further attraction of offering comparative safety from raids; lands reconquered from the Moors had to be peopled and cultivated under some protection and inducements in the way of privileges. Consequently, while the kings made many grants to the nobles who had aided them in recovering the lands, they kept the greater part within their own royal domain and founded on this territory free and independent cities, to be inhabited by all who would share in the new work, whether urged to it by mere restlessness, by zeal for greater activity and profit, or by the desire to escape from their feudal lords. The very act of coming to one of the cities on the king's domain was rewarded by freedom and greater rights, as well as by enfranchisement from feudal tributes and services.[5] The royal cities thus became collections of free men who were vassals of no other lord than the king; *fueros* were granted to them;[6] and as they grew and acquired sufficient importance to care for and defend their own borders and interests, their charters gave them more authority—in fact, all the privileges of internal government and administration.[7] In this constant progression toward organization and autonomy, the kings frequently aided by granting to the cities renewed confirmations of former privileges and additions of new powers as reward for support against the powerful nobility.

The eleventh century brought the rise of the municipality in Castile and Leon; the period of its regular and powerful development came in the second half of the twelfth; and from the beginning of the fourteenth century the prelude to its decline was evident in decreasing simplicity and democracy. In Aragon, the cities matured later. The thirteenth century found them increasingly prosperous, and in the middle of the fourteenth the third estate came into its own when the nobles had definitely to yield to the king. The founding of the *real villa* in Catalonia took place early in the twelfth century.[8]

When the cities in Spain had acquired enough autonomy and prosperity to enable them to constitute collectively a potential force, they were summoned to the assemblies of the king, nobles, and clergy, first for consultation and before long for deliberation. Admission to the Cortes gave them assured position as lever or balance in national affairs. Their decline showed itself in the choice of municipal officers. This was in effect a vicious circle in which autonomous cities, of greater prosperity because of the admission of their deputies to the national assembly, in turn caused the Cortes to become by their presence so real a power in national affairs that the king did not scruple to exert his wiles to gain control over it by meddling in the internal affairs of the cities themselves, and more particularly in the appointment of their deputies to the Cortes. The city then lost its importance, and the Cortes declined with it. The Castilian Cortes of the thirteenth and fourteenth centuries has been called the sum of all the *concejos*. Its prerogatives were secured both by means of and to the enrichment of the third estate, and the diminishing of the advantages of the one would bring down, *pari passu,* those of the other. Even the device of the imperative mandate, which attempted to keep constant the will of the *concejo* in the assembly of all, could no longer block the domination of centralizing royalty.[9]

To the king belonged the right of assembling the Cortes. The letters of convocation designated the time and place of meeting, and, ordinarily, the purposes underlying the meeting. Between the imperative mandate and a convocation which stated why a Cortes was to meet there is an evident connection, and, furthermore, periodicity of assembling is concerned. When the electors were notified in advance of matters upon which their representatives were to consult or to deliberate, the latter could be directed how to act, and their powers could be limited and defined with greater or less precision. On the other hand, when meetings of the assembly became the expected procedure, to be followed with some regularity because, for the most part, occasions were similar and needed similar action, the letters of convocation were naturally less explicit regarding the objects of the meeting. In the latter circumstances, the powers given had to be broader and more general, since the procurators sent by the municipalities could be less restrained by previous orders and thus would be more free to act unless the giving and receiving of instructions could be carried on contemporaneously with the sessions of the Cortes. In Castile and Leon there was no provision for fixed meetings. The Cortes assembled when, in general, the presence of the nation was necessary for its authority or consent, especially in the imposition of new taxes or services.[10] But in Aragon and in Catalonia, by the end of the thirteenth century, there was periodicity, if not regularity, in the meetings of the Cortes.[11] The corresponding differences in the mandates given will be noticeable.

The use of the imperative mandate also affected the election of procurators. When the representative's power of decision and action was controlled by the municipality through the mandate given to him—that is, when the municipality was present at the Cortes in all but actuality—his person was of slight importance. It mattered comparatively little who was chosen, or by what method, merely in order to carry the municipality's decision to the Cortes. Elections were characterized by the same lack of uniformity that existed in the organization of the cities and towns and in their representation at the national legislature. The method of choosing deputies depended upon the individual locality, since each might follow its particular customs. For the most part, democratic practices prevailed until the fifteenth century. After that, the royal power interfered often, at first only to influence the choice by gifts and promises, but, finally, by the actual naming of the procurators or by their coincidence with the royal officers in the cities. One may say that in general the procedure in the various communities differed (1) as to the mode, whether by lot, election, or turn (succession); (2) as to the number of degrees, either proceeding directly or by two, and even three, steps; (3) as to the participants, whether the electors were the male inhabitants, the citizens, the heads of families, the governing body, or still others; (4) as to the choice of persons elected, whether or not confined to the official body.[12] These details depended upon the laws and customs, and upon the degree of independence enjoyed by the community. If there was one practice more usual than another, it seems to have been that of representation by officers of the *concejo,* chosen by lot from among all the eligible names, or selected by their colleagues.[13]

Just as the beginnings of representative institutions vary widely in the principal regions of Spain, so we find similar differences in respect to the imperative mandate: it was almost constantly used in Leon and Castile; it was only exceptionally employed in Aragon; in Catalonia, the device of the Vintiquatrena de Cort (in Barcelona, and what corresponded to it in the other cities) was regularly followed and made strictly binding upon the deputies.

Only by these means could the deputies in Spain, and, indeed, in France of the same period, resist the will of the monarch; that is, by shielding themselves behind the unavoidable obligation of adjusting their vote to the instructions which they had received. In time, complexity of national business, as well as the more simple autocracy of the monarch, would be bound to modify such a system. Questions are raised inevitably. What is representation in any case? And what are the irreducible conditions necessary for its appearance in the Middle Ages? In other words, when did the third estate appear as such in national legislatures?

Notes

1. According to ancient law, with its formalist character, judicial acts had to be performed by the interested person himself; but later the influence of certain cases in which it was possible to get away from strict formalism (for example, consensual contracts, such as marriage by proxy) made representation possible in law, and everyone could make his will known not only by a letter or a *nuncius* (a speaking letter), but also by a mandatory furnished with powers and instructions ample enough to qualify him as more than a simple *porte-parole.* By fiction, the mandatory was likened to a mere messenger, and his acts were regarded as those of the mandated person. The practice of representation, however, made its way slowly, and it was not unusual to doubt the validity of the act of the representative and to insist upon its being confirmed by the person represented. The necessity for this fiction was always likely to be present, and a remedy had to be found. When this principle was applied to a deputy to the assembly, he was regarded only as a *porte-parole* of his electors, with no powers of his own and under strict obligation to conform to the will of his constituents. J. Brissaud, *Manuel d'histoire de droit français,* 803, 1442-1443 (1903).

2. This study has been made from secondary materials and neither unprinted documents nor archives generally have been examined. Nevertheless, it is offered in the hope that the collection and presentation of its subject-matter in English may be not without value.

3. M. Block, *Dictionnaire général de la politique,* II, 255 (1867).

4. *Works* (London, 1823), III, 18 ff.

5. James the Conqueror's words in founding the royal city of Figueras were: "*Quien quiera que entrare a establecerse en Figueras sea libre y no deba redimirse del domino feudal.*" Cited by J. Pella y Forgas, *Historia del Ampurdán* (1883), 630.

6. Briefly defined, the *fuero* was a general or a municipal charter, usually based on custom or common law.

7. Some of the lay and ecclesiastical seigneurs also gave charters to populations on their lands which freed the people concerned from their feudal dominion. The royal cities were far more numerous and tended to have a unifying effect, whereas the seigneurial cities were diverse, as emanating from many lords.

8. The third estate was at first of slight importance in Catalonia, but through the extraordinary development of commerce and industry it came to have preponderating influence. Barcelona very early was a sort of democratic republic which, from its geographical position, naturally turned to commerce, navigation, and industry, and its influence over the rest of Catalonia was great. Hence it led and guided all the other cities in matters of government as well as of economics, and this leadership made for unity and centralization in Catalonia. Pella y Forgas, *Historia del Ampurdán,* 634.

9. I shall limit the explanation of terms to the municipality of Castile, but that will sufficiently make clear also the *universidad* of Aragon and of Catalonia. The word *concejo* is of very old use in Spain, and occurs synonymously and indiscriminately with the other words, *villa* and *ciudad,* but more for personifying the city, as comprised of its territory and inhabitants. The individuals

forming the *concejo*, in turn, became the *vecinos* (inhabitants) of the city or town. In explaining the homage due to the king, the Second Partida stated that each *villa* should assemble its *concejo* "*á pregon ferido*" to choose men to swear for all, great and small, "*varones et mujeres, nacidos y por nacer.*" For the text, see *Las Siete Partidas* (Madrid, 1807), pt. 2, tit. xv, ley 5 (37). From this, Señor Gregorio Lopez, the editor, concluded that those who formed this assembly of inhabitants were only the *varones mayores*, fourteen years of age. Hence, the *concejo* at the end of the thirteenth century would comprise all the inhabitants fourteen years old who had full civil rights. So constituted, the *concejo* had a single entity of its own (*sola entitad*); it was a corporation aggregate. Eduardo de Hinojosa, *Estudios sobre la historia del derecho español, passim,* especially pp. 65-70 (1903).

Señor Colmeiro defined the *ayuntamiento* as "*la junta de vecinos presidios por el estado de la justicia para ordenar el gobierno de la ciudad*"; that is, the governing body. It made the municipal ordinances, based on custom and on the privileges granted to the *concejo* by the *fueros* and charters, and it usually named the officers of the *regimiento*, or administrative board, whose individual members were the *regidores*. The disorganizing change in these communities thus took place through the gradual dislocation in the *regimiento* of the proportion of persons not of their own choice. In general, see M. Colmeiro, *De la constitución y del gobierno de los reinos de Leon y Castillo* (1855), and particularly II, 164-171, for a statement of the usual municipal officers in Castile.

10. It was at least customary that the Cortes should assemble at the death of one monarch to swear fidelity to the new ruler and for his coronation, to concur in the guardianship of a minor, and to consult in all serious and difficult circumstances of the kingdom. Colmeiro stated that the only legal limit to the absence of the Cortes in Castile was the need of paying every seven years the *moneda forera,* so that no more than five years could elapse before the voting of the necessary funds was required (*Curso,* I, 349). The Cortes of Palencia in 1313 imposed during the minority of Alfonso XI the obligation to call a Cortes at least once in two years. A. Sacristan y Martinez, *Municipalidades de Castilla y Leon,* 305 (1877).

11. It is probable that before 1283 there was no fixed rule as to periodicity. The provision for annual meetings in the General Privilege of 1283 and in the Privileges of the Union was modified in 1307 for biennial meetings, and again renewed in 1348 and 1381. M. de Bofarull y Romaña, *Las antiguas Cortes,* 46 (1912). In Catalonia was granted in 1283 the right of regular assembling of the Cortes every year at whatever time seemed best, provided no just reason prevented it. This was reiterated in 1292, and in 1300 a definite day for assembling was appointed, the first Sunday in Lent. The following year, however, the rule was again changed, to provide for meetings only every three years, except in case of emergency. V. Belaguer, *Estudios historicos y politicos,* 284-285 (1876); J. Coroleu y J. Pella y Forgas, *Las Cortes Catalanas,* 35 (1876), *Los Fueros de Cataluña,* 524, 529 (1876).

12. See, for example, V. Piskorskii, *Kastil'skie Kortes . . . .* 34-35 (1897); Bofarull y Romaña, 37; T. Marina, *Teoría de las cortes ó grandes juntas nacionales de los reinos de Leon y Castilla,* I, 197 (1813).

13. Although there was variation in the number of procurators sent by each community, two was the usual number; but in no case did a city have more than one vote. Zaragoza in Aragon and Barcelona in Catalonia always sent larger delegations. In Catalonia, moreover, the votes were weighed and not counted. See Piskorskii, 38-39; Colmeiro, *Curso de derecho politico,* I, 325 (1873); Coroleu y Pella y Forgas, *Las Cortes catalanas,* 61; A. Marichalar y C. Manrique, *Historia de la legislación y recitationes del derecho civil en España,* VII, 200-201 (1862).

B. The Constitutional Framework

4. CONGRESSIONALISM AND PARLIAMENTARISM

Eric C. Bellquist

MODERN CONSTITUTIONAL GOVERNMENT presents two sharply distinguished and opposed types: congressionalism—or presidentialism, as it is often called, which is found in the United States, many of the other American Republics, and the Philippines; and parliamentarism—commonly although somewhat erroneously termed cabinet government, which obtains in Great Britain, the other members of the Commonwealth, and in free Europe generally. As the government of the United States is the best example of the congressional type and has served as the pattern for the other governments which have adopted this form, so the government of Great Britain is the outstanding example of parliamentarism and has constituted the model which has influenced the Dominions, most of Europe, and many other countries. Parliamentarism is today the more widely accepted system. None of the many constitutions coming out of World Wars I and II incorporated congressionalism, all of them preferring responsible government. While our system of federalism has commended itself to some other states, modern constitution-makers have valued separation of powers less highly.

These two types embody fundamentally antithetical political theories with regard to the relationship between the executive and the legislature, and it is the distribution of authority between these two branches of the government that determines whether we have congressionalism or parliamentarism. The former is based upon the doctrine of the separation of powers and operates through an elaborate scheme of checks and balances. Parliamentarism, on the other hand, has as its chief characteristic the fusion or union of executive and legislative powers. Authority is concentrated under strict control. The government shapes the program of legislation which is submitted to the legislature; and from it emanate the broad and general public policies with respect to both domestic and foreign affairs. We need

Reprinted from *The NUEA Manual*, Vol. 27 (1953), pp. 13-29, by permission of the author and the publisher.

not here be concerned with the judicial power. While in the United States much is made of the tri-partite distribution of authority, when the European thinks of separation of powers he takes for granted the independence of the judiciary. It is appointed, even as in the United States, by the executive, but on terms which render it fully as independent as in our own country. In England the independence of the judiciary was established by the Act of Settlement, 1701, and in all constitutional states this is now accepted. Our concern is rather the executive-legislative relationship. On that, as already stated, depends what type of government prevails. On that, moreover, depends what type of parliamentarism we find where that system is practised.

The principle of parliamentarism implies that the legislature, and the there prevailing dominant opinion, is the determining factor in the formation of the government and its tenure of office. The government, while exercising supreme direction over both law-making and administration, must for the execution of its responsibilities possess the confidence of the legislature or, at least, be tolerated by it. The ministry is collectively responsible immediately to the legislative body, particularly to its more popular branch, and ultimately to the electorate. Upon a vote of lack of confidence, the defeat of an important governmental measure, or a setback in an election the government resigns and gives place to one drawn from the opposition. Ministerial tenure thus depends upon the maintenance of a majority in the legislature. There should therefore be a close relationship, preferably complete understanding and agreement, between the majority of the representative body and the executive. To insure such confidence it has become customary for the executive to be well anchored in the legislature, by selecting the members of the cabinet wholly or largely from the parliament or recruiting other active political leaders from the outside. Ministers are as a rule members of the parliament and leaders of the party or parties in the majority.

Parliamentary control of the ministry is balanced by ministerial leadership and control of parliament. In this system the head of the state occupies a position of dignity and may be a symbol of great importance. While the chief of state under parliamentarism does not necessarily have to be a "figurehead," usually nearly all authority, nominally vested in him, is in effect exercised by the ministry—which assumes full responsibility for acts performed in his name. The unity and collective responsibility of the cabinet are achieved through the prime minister, so often described as the keystone of the cabinet arch. Considered in this light parliamentarism is part of the democratic process, although there is not necessarily any indissoluble tie between democracy and parliamentarism. Parliamentarism in England antedated the great Reform Bill of 1832 and existed in Sweden during much of the eighteenth century, long before the coming of democracy. We have democracy in the United States without parliamentarism.

For the roots of parliamentarism it is necessary to go far back in English history. As early as the fourteenth century impeachment was invented as a means to enforce responsibility upon royal advisers. Other methods to control the ministers included frequent attempts to secure approved ministers by election or nomination and it has been said that from 1404 to 1437 the king's council was not merely dependent upon parliament but was actually nominated by it. In 1679 a pretentious scheme was attempted to reconcile incompatibles, combining in the council with the king's men leaders of all factions in parliament. For the real origins, however, we have to look at the period from 1660 to 1835 and in the final analysis the successful reconciling of the legislature and the executive came from the king who resorted to a procedure which led directly to the real enforcement of ministerial responsibility, and not from parliamentary innovation or domination over the king. As H. M. Clokie has well brought out, from the first years when parliament had been firmly established in its rights it had been increasingly evident that the conduct of government rested ultimately upon the monarch's ability to carry through the necessary measures respecting finance and legislation. This meant that the ministers of the day must have behind them, with a fair degree of regularity, a majority of votes in both houses. Gradually, therefore, it became the practice of shrewd monarchs to choose as advisers men who, in addition to having the confidence of the throne, were influential in the legislature. As political parties developed, moreover, the ministries were adapted to the party complexion of parliament. This, of course, was important. The responsibility of ministers, the confidence of the House of Commons, and the methods of getting a majority are intelligible only in the light of party divisions.

The essentials of parliamentarism were thus present in England by the end of the seventeenth century. During the eighteenth they became more firmly rooted in constitutional practice and ultimately it became impossible for a cabinet to continue in office if it was unacceptable to the House of Commons. Sir Robert Walpole's resignation in 1741 was the first instance of a prime minister's going out of office because of a defeat in Commons. In 1782, when the whole cabinet of Lord North resigned in consequence of having lost the confidence of the House of Commons, the principle of ministerial solidarity was acknowledged. Parliamentarism may be said to have been fully established in England by 1835, when the Conservative ministry of Sir Robert Peel, although still enjoying the confidence of the King and the House of Lords, resigned office because "in conformity with the constitution, a government ought not to persist in carrying on public affairs, after a fair trial, against the decided opinion of the majority of the House of Commons." Since Peel's resignation in 1835 parliamentarism has prevailed in England. To be sure, classic *cabinet* government of the type pictured in the textbooks, responsible government resting upon the majority of the lower house, the power of the throne eliminated, majority single party basis of the government, solidarity of the cabinet, government and opposition playing the game according to the well-established rules, and other leading characteristics of British parliamentarism, do not fully arrive until the Victoria-Disraeli-Gladstone days, but the pattern had been fully established. As A. Lawrence Lowell wrote in 1890,

The system which had been devised in order that the king might control the House of Commons became the means by which the House of Commons, through its leaders, controlled the king, and thus all the power of the House of Commons became vested in the same men, who guided legislation and took charge of administration at the same time.

In essence the British Constitution, and parliamentarism in Britain, rests upon the fact that the King-in-Parliament is supreme. In this sense it is proper to speak of Cabinet Government in England. The Queen's assent is a mere formality. Parliament is the supreme governing body, but as the powers of the House of Lords are strictly limited both by tradition and law the House of Commons is the ruler of Great Britain. Yet Parliament no longer has an important function as the initiator of legislation. It is the Cabinet which is responsible for the general policy and administration. It is the Cabinet which initiates legislation, ninety per cent of all the laws enacted by Parliament having been introduced by members of the Government and no private member's bill having any chance of being passed without at least the benevolent neutrality of the Government. In all matters dealing with finance, furthermore, the Government has exclusive legislative power. As Sir Maurice Amos has put it: "All financial business, whether directed to the raising or to the spending of money, is originated by the Crown alone; all money is granted to the Crown, at the request of the Crown, to be spent by the Crown." Moreover, as Lloyd-George declared in 1932, and this is even truer now than it was then, "Parliament has really no control over the Executive; it is pure fiction." Under modern conditions all Governments are able within their five-year term even to choose for themselves the order and timing of their going. None of these facts, however, means that Parliament has now ceased to have any real importance. As Francis Williams has underlined, its importance rests in the circumstance that it provides a sounding-board for public opinion. This so far from diminishing has increased. Its function is to serve as a place in which policy can be publicly debated and questions asked, to keep the public informed of what the Government is doing and why. It faces the Government with a lively body of active and intelligent critics in close touch with what ordinary men and women are thinking. While the Government thus is the creature of the legislature and leads, nay, drives its creator, there is a direct link between the people, legislature, and executive; and as a rule they act in general unison, moved by the same tide of political feeling. Herman Finer states it this way: "The legislature is responsible to the people; the cabinet is responsible to the legislature and to the people. They are one body at different stages of leadership but in the straight line of ascent from the people." In the United States, on the other hand, "popular sovereignty operates by bifurcation and even trifurcation: it divides into channels which run parallel to each other but do not fully meet or mingle, but are connected by draw-bridges."

While Earl Grey in 1858 was the first English writer to postulate the theory of parliamentarism as one of united powers and Walter Bagehot nine years later presented the classic interpretation of British government, in France and Germany the true nature of the English constitution was discovered earlier and a theory of parliamentarism formulated for the direct purpose of introducing the parliamentary system to the continent. Tendencies toward responsible government may be noted in some of the French revolutionary constitutions and changes in the composition of the Committee of Public Safety followed lack of confidence votes in the National Assembly. In 1814-15 Benjamin Constant initiated the discussions of parliamentarism centering around the organic law of the Restoration and other French writers also presented a more accurate picture of the way in which the English system of government was developing than that seen through the eyes of Montesquieu, Blackstone, and De Lolme. The principles of constitutionalism and Parliamentarism expounded by Constant, Chateaubriand, Guizot, and others found much support and parliamentary theory remained an integral part of French constitutional thought throughout the nineteenth century. It was given impetus by the July Revolution, was expressed in Thiers' formula that "the king reigns and does not govern," and partially applied in the Dutch and Belgian constitutions of 1830 and 1831—influential in later constitution-making on the continent. The stream soon entered south German political thought and while parliamentarism was not to be realized in Germany until the October reforms of 1918 the principle was generally understood by the framers of the Frankfurt constitution of 1849, among whom was its leading exponent, Robert von Mohl. By that time it was fully operative in Belgium and in 1848 had been accepted in the Netherlands and in the Italian octroyed *Statuto*. In France the ministerial responsibility begun under Louis XVIII and Charles X was finally established by the founders of the Third Republic. In Norway parliamentarism broke through in 1884, in Denmark in 1901, and in Sweden the dualism of the constitution of 1809 had gradually developed into parliamentarism by 1905. At the outbreak of the first World War all of the constitutional states of Europe were operating under parliamentarism, except the German and Austro-Hungarian empires and Switzerland.

In 1917, as Finland declared its independence, the draft constitution of this former Russian Grand Duchy was the first organic law explicitly to put provisions for parliamentarism into the text of a written constitution. Following the example of Germany at Weimar, some thirteen monarchies and as many republics accepted parliamentarism of one kind or another after World War I—most of them also incorporating this type of government into their new written constitutions. In some instances, as in Finland and Germany, there was an attempt to combine parliamentarism with a degree of presidentialism and in other constitutions various devices were provided in detail to insure the responsibility of ministers. Constitutions adopted between the two World Wars likewise normally included provisions for responsible government and this was true of the organic laws coming out of World War II. The new French and Italian constitutions, the Bonn Basic Law, and the Danish constitution of 1953, for example, all spell out parliamentarism to an extent that had not previously been true of the organic laws of these states.

Meanwhile responsible government had been achieved in the British Dominions, in Canada in the years following the rebellion in 1837 and before the Confederation in 1867; in New Zealand in 1856; in five of the Australian states in the 1850's, West Australia in 1890, and in the Commonwealth in 1901; and in South Africa through a gradual development both before and after the Boer War. The Indian constitution of 1949 confirmed the practice of parliamentarism which had been developing over many years and a year earlier Ceylon graduated to this status by way of the usual forms of crown colony government. Similar practice prevails in the component parts of what may become the British Caribbean and Central African federations. In Southern Rhodesia, for example, the Legislative Council as early as 1920 passed a resolution praying that responsible government should be established and this was done four years later. In the older Dominions the essentials of British parliamentarism are largely intact: the combination of strong executive leadership with parliamentary and popular influence, the intimate relations between executive and legislature through the agency of a majority party, the close control by the executive of legislation and expenditure, the secondary position of the upper house, the importance of the Opposition, and other characteristics of cabinet government. At the same time, the essentials of the inheritance have often been profoundly modified in the new environment.

This is even more true of parliamentarism on the continent of Europe which, because of historical and social circumstances, seldom approximates *cabinet* government and instead often rests upon the concept of *gouvernement d'assemblée* —with the cabinets subservient to the parliaments and their groups, factions, and committees. We find parliamentarism, responsible government, but hardly the effective executive leadership which is the crux of executive power and which typifies the British system. The legislative branch remains the seat of real power; and it, rather than the ministry, is the core of the government. The executive branch, the cabinet, constitutes but its

agency, responsible at all times to it for the manner in which it performs its duties. While there is a fusion of powers, that union is in the hands of the legislature rather than the executive and it is the legislature which, in the last analysis, determines legislative action and controls the exercise of the executive function by the ministry. Whereas in England *cabinet* government normally prevails, on the continent it is more correct to speak of *parliamentary* government. Emphasis upon parliamentary sovereignty, traditional suspicion of executive power, the multiplicity of parties, powerful committee systems, regionalism and confessionalism, attempts to combine parliamentarism, presidentialism, and direct democracy, the electoral systems, the absence of sufficient political traditions, deeper cleavages of public opinion, and, more recently, the rise of extremist parties of the Right and Left, have created different types of parliamentarism from that best known to us through the British model. These and other reasons have made more difficult the "facility for compromise" and, as Lord Balfour pointed out, the whole system of cabinet government is based on the assumption that the *possibility* of compromise exists.

A French premier once stated that the government could govern only when the Chamber of Deputies was on vacation and in 1926 the late Will Rogers wrote that he had watched the change of guard at St. James Palace in London and had gone to France to witness another daily spectacle, the change of premier. During the Third Republic France had no less than 108 ministries, with an average life of about seven months. Lebrun, its last president, had nineteen cabinets during his six years in office. Under the Fourth Republic this situation has deteriorated rather than improved, government tenure averaging less than six months and without the power to issue *decret-lois* in financial and economic matters which at times enabled pre-World War II ministries to exercise real leadership. But few changes were made in key posts from the outgoing governments. This, of course, is what enables French government to continue to function—plus the fact that permanent under-secretaries conduct business as usual. On the 25th anniversary of his first ministerial post Aristide Briand had occupied a total of thirty-six ministerial posts. He had been a member of twenty-five governments and served as premier eleven times and foreign minister sixteen times. Since World War II a half-dozen men have served in fifteen governments and more than a score in ten. As Maurice Duverger has written, ministries change, but the members are largely the same; they perpetuate themselves in office, and general policy is little affected by the changes. Under such circumstances, however, governments can hardly exercise any real leadership.

Elsewhere on the continent there has been much the same situation. From 1919 to 1933 Germany had twenty-one governments. The Reichstag was segmented into parties, none of which approached a majority. Five elections did no more than shift the balance of power and permit a choice among three coalitions. As in France, cabinet changes meant a new deal of the same cards rather than a different deck. Gessler was minister of defense fourteen times, Braun headed the Labor Department twelve times, and Stresemann was a member of nine governments and died in harness. Efforts to give stability to the government by protecting it against the Reichstag were ineffectual. Caretaker governments were utilized at times to tide over a political crisis, as was true in the Baltic States, Finland, and on two occasions in Sweden. Even such governments, of course, are responsible, can be voted out of office, and represent another variation of parliamentarism. Responsible government in some of the succession states presented an even more confused picture, as might be expected in view of their limited political experience and the attempt to transplant alien institutions not easily rooted in native soil. Northern Europe furnishes yet another variety, with minority governments the normal pattern during much of the between-the-wars period. When the Germans occupied Norway in 1940 the Nygaardsvold cabinet had been in office for more than four years, the longest tenure of any Norwegian ministry since 1920. It was a minority government, as was true of the other eleven cabinets during these two decades. Finland had twenty-two governments between 1917 and the Russian attack in November, 1939, with greater stability towards the end of this period as there were only three from December, 1932, to the formation of the national coalition seven years later. In Sweden there were twelve governments between 1917 and the outbreak of the war, only two of which had a majority in the *Riksdag*. In Denmark minority government was less characteristic and the ministries more stable, the Stauning Social Democratic-Radical coalition enjoying the support of a majority from 1929 to the Nazi occupation in 1940, when it was expanded to include the Conservatives and Liberals in a national ministry. Denmark, however, despite its multi-party system, has really operated under what in effect is a two-party system —with Government and Opposition—differing from her neighbors in that respect. More recently the situation in Scandinavia has changed, as the Social Democratic or Labor parties have obtained majorities or, in any case, greatly outnumbered their rivals. Norway has thus had a Labor government since November 5, 1945, while in Sweden the Social Democrats have governed since August of the same year—although they took out some life insurance by including the Agrarians in 1951. Whereas three and even two decades ago the Swedes were complaining about the "governing *Riksdag*" and seeking ways to strengthen the executive, the Opposition now criticizes parliament's having become a "mere trucking company," obediently delivering what the government requests. Real cabinet government may therefore be said to prevail in Sweden, despite the fact that the chief of state is not a complete figurehead, proportional representation and a multi-party system prevail, the two houses are constitutionally and in practice equal, and administrative power to a considerable degree is separated from the executive power. Much the same is true of Norway under its unicameral system.

Post-war Italy, on the other hand, now again more closely coincides with the French pattern of parliamentarism. To be sure, Dr. Alcide De Gasperi first became Premier of Italy in December, 1945, and for almost eight years he kept his country on a moderate course, tying it firmly to the West, making domestic reforms, and fighting off attacks from both the Communists and the extreme right. Italy has enjoyed remarkable political stability since the war, despite her large Communist minority. For this reason she has received less attention than France, which has passed from one government crisis to another and found each one more difficult to solve. As Anne O'Hare McCormick has pointed out in the *New York Times,* however, Italy is less able than France to weather political storms. Whether or not republican Italy's parliamentary system has the political wherewithal to continue to operate successfully is an open question.

As indicated at the beginning of this essay, parliamentarism is in striking contrast to congressional or presidential government which separates the executive from the legislature and makes each independent of the other. Separation of powers was constitutionalized in the United States in 1787 as a result of Montesquieu's failure to understand the real nature of the British political system during a transitional period, the distrust of the executive power due to the colonial experience, the reaction to a brief experiment with legislative supremacy in some of the states which had led to majority tyranny, fear of a strong executive at the *national* level in view of the strong belief in states' rights, constitutional provisions in and experience under the state organic laws, and the desire to accomplish the immediately practical task of safeguarding liberty and property. Whatever the respective weights of these and other influences, the American constitution consciously and elaborately incorporated this basic tenet and the United States is today the most important country in the world which operates upon this principle.

No idea is probably more firmly held by the mass of the American people than that the most fundamental principle upon which their government is based is that of a separation of powers. As the Supreme Court held in Kilbourn v. Thompson (1881), "It is believed to be one of the chief merits of the American system of written constitutional law, that all the powers intrusted to government . . . are divided into the three grand departments, the executive, the legislative, and the judicial. . . ." In O'Donoghue v. United States (1933) Mr. Justice Sutherland stated: "This separation is not merely a matter of convenience or of governmental mechanism. Its object is basic and vital: namely to preclude a commingling of these essentially different powers of government in the same hands. . . ." The courts have repeatedly stressed this "fundamental tenet" and in the Steel Case in 1952 President Truman was reminded that "The Founders of this Nation entrusted the law-making power to the Congress alone in both good and bad times." To be sure, the Court's minority observed that this imposed a "messenger-boy concept" on the Presidency that, if maintained, would prevent him from carrying out the obligations of his office, but the decision was popular and in the 1952 campaign General Eisenhower promised to show "respect . . . for the great functions of the Legislature," which, he said, "is, after all, the United States and speaks for the population." As President he has shown deep respect for the tripartite nature of our government and believes that he can share the leadership of the nation on a coordinate basis with the Congress, that the Congress and the Executive are "coequal partners under the Constitution." He thus seems to be in agreement with the views expressed by the Supreme Court in the Humphrey case (1935) where, after referring to the "essential coequality" of the three branches of the government, the tribunal declared: "The sound application of a principle that makes one master in his own house precludes him from imposing his control in the house of another who is master there. James Wilson, one of the framers of the Constitution and a former Justice of this Court, said that the independence of each department required that its proceedings 'should be free from the remotest influence, direct or indirect, of either of the other two powers. . . .'"

Despite law or theory, however, so strict a separation is not feasible. Even Montesquieu realized that this would "bring about a state of repose or inactivity. But since, by the necessary movement of things, they are obliged to move, they will be forced to move in concert." In *The Federalist* James Madison explained that the theory of separation of powers "does not require that the legislative, executive, and judiciary departments should be wholly unconnected with each other" and stated that "unless these three departments be so far connected and blended as to give each a constitutional control over the others, the degree of separation which the maxim requires as essential to a free government can never in practice be duly maintained." So far as that goes, once having provided for the separate organs of government the framers of the constitution refused to vest in them the exclusive exercise of the powers to which they correspond. On the contrary, they so defined the powers of each and so distributed the exercise of the three powers among them that no one can act independently in his own field. This is particularly true of the administrative power, where there was the greatest failure to locate authority and responsibility in a single organ. The Congress is the ultimate directing, supervising, and controlling authority in respect to matters administrative and yet we normally think of the President as head of the administration. Too often we emphasize the separation, without examining the checks and balances. The framers appear to have been more interested in the latter, in preventing abuses and forestalling possible dangers rather than in establishing an efficient governmental system. Like Montesquieu they failed to appreciate exactly how the harmony among the powers, admittedly so necessary, will be produced. Madison at least stated the problem, "the defect must be supplied, by so contriving the interior structure of the government as that its several constituent parts may by their mutual relations, be the means of keeping each other in their proper place." The defect was met by something not foreseen by the framers, our political parties. The movement in concert, hardly obtainable within the constitution, had to be obtained by something outside it, whether with complete or partial success. The indispensable institution was found in the party system which redistributed the authority divided by the constitution—reassembling those powers informally and helping them to become a working team. The party system is the unwritten constitution which helps to make the written constitution work, which brings the ends of Pennsylvania Avenue together. Only from this point of view can its illogicalities be explained, and its strength be appreciated. Moreover, political practice has shown that the influence actually exerted by a department of the government depends not so much upon the legal authority which it enjoys in law or theory as upon the great interests which function through it in reality. The people holding office and the time during which office is held greatly determine the amount of power exercised. The amount of power exercised by whom determines whether we have congressionalism, presidentialism, or the coequal partnership announced by President Eisenhower.

While the terms are often used synonymously, congressionalism implies the predominance of the legislature—as, for example, during the reconstruction period following the Civil War, when the Congress dominated the executive, overrode the exercise of his veto power, and through various devices and measures gathered into its hands almost the entire domain of federal authority. It was at the close of this period that Woodrow Wilson wrote his *Congressional Government,* properly naming and correctly describing what we had at the time. In that book he showed more clearly than had any previous writer the difference between the theory of the constitution and the reality of the government. For the first time, also, he stressed the point that congressional government means committee government. In 1885 he stated: "I know not how better to describe our form of government than by calling it a government by the chairmen of the Standing Committees of Congress." He went on to say that "this disintegrate ministry, as it figures on the floor of the House . . . has many peculiarities." That this may be as true today as it was sixty-eight years ago recent examples illustrate. In this sense, moreover, congressional government—despite its basic differences—may more closely resemble continental parliamentarism than it does presidentialism and cabinet government. As Dorothy Thompson has written, "If the usurpation by Congress of the executive's function continues and accelerates we shall approach the condition of political impotency which is the mortal disease of France." This was demonstrated in the first session of the Eighty-Third Congress when, even though the President of his own party, the floor leaders and a majority of his branch of Congress and of his committee called for action, a committee chairman could successfully prevent it. To a considerable extent, this is due to our party system: save for presidential elections, where the two-party system operates, our politics can be more akin to those of France than of Britain. The course of government may be largely determined by sectional viewpoints that represent a minority in the party that has just won the presidency by espousing a contrary viewpoint.

The only effective balance at the Capitol is and always has been tough presidential leadership. This is the key to presidentialism and, again, Woodrow Wilson put it better than had been done before and has therefore been quoted ever since. In 1908 while president of Princeton, and before becoming governor of New Jersey and president of the United States, he delivered some lectures at Columbia University on *Constitutional Government in the United States.* By that time Grover Cleveland had reestablished the independence of the executive, William McKinley had proven himself "a statesman singularly gifted to unite the discordant forces of government," and Theodore Roosevelt "showed the singular primitive quality that belongs to ultimate matter—the quality that medieval theologians assigned to God—he was pure act." Under the circumstances Wilson could say:

Greatly as the practice and influence of Presidents has varied, there can be no mistaking the fact that we have grown more and more inclined from generation to generation to look to the President as the unifying force in our complex system, the leader both of his party and of the nation. . . . The nation as a whole has chosen him, and is conscious that it has no other political spokesman. His is the only national voice in affairs. Let him once win the admiration and confidence of the country, and no other single force can withstand him, no combination of forces will easily overpower him. His position takes the imagination of the country. He is the representative of no constituency, but of the whole people. . . . If he rightly interpret the national thought and boldly insist upon it, he is irresistible; and the country never feels the zest of action so much as when its President is of such insight and calibre. . . . A President whom it trusts can not only lead it, but form it to his own wishes.

His office is anything he has the sagacity and force to make it. . . . His is the vital place of action in the system, whether he accept it as such or not, and the office is the measure of the man, of his wisdom as well as of his force.

The American President is *sui generis.* No other elected official occupies a comparable place or plays a similar role. He was originally the head of the government, commander-in-chief of its army and navy, its representative in the conduct of foreign relations. He was, too, the head of a coordinate branch of the government, dependent upon the other branches, with executive powers broad but indeterminate. He became chief of a political party. He emerged, finally, as the peculiar representative of the whole people—the voice and the symbol of national unity. The story of the American Presidency is one of intermittent but progressive enhancement of prestige and aggrandizement of power.

This development came about only with the passage of time, yet it was not time but circumstances that brought the development. And what were these circumstances that created the modern institution of the American Presidency, that concentrated in him actual and potential, formal and informal powers not anticipated in the constitution? They were, to state them broadly, the ambiguity of the constitution, the rise of political parties, the breakdown of federalism, the growth of national unity, and the evolution of democracy. As Henry Steele Commager has explained, it was in response to these developments that the modern American presidency emerged. And it emerged through a succession of strong presidents—men who willingly used all the powers available to them, who pushed the limits of the executive authority to the straining point, who regarded themselves as the direct and complete representatives of the people. And it is suggestive that, with the single exception of Polk, all the strong Presidents were great presidents, and all the great presidents were strong presidents. Whatever may be the theory of the American constitutional system or the official attitude of party spokesmen, the fact remains that no weak president has ever recommended himself permanently to the affection of the American people.

That the American system of government worked at all and weathered the storms of a civil war, economic crises and two world wars is one of the major miracles of constitutional history. Slow-moving and cumbrous, heavy-footed and, as Bryce says, destined rather for safety than for speed, it has provided, with the alternation of parties over long periods, a remarkable degree of political stability. To no small extent, the explanation for this may be found in the development of presidentialism. Executive leadership has at all times been essential to the success of government and this is particularly true in this extraordinary era marked by a vast extension of the range of government and the enormous growth in public business. Constitutionalism and more especially constitutional democracy have been confronted with a most delicate task: how to discover institutional patterns which would provide vigorous and effective action, without allowing those who were called upon to take such action to turn into irresponsible despots. It is Great Britain and the United States who have most successfully met this task. These two systems, while starting poles apart as regards the principle supposed to govern in respect to the

distribution of governmental powers functionally, and still having this difference from the technical standpoint of constitutional law, have tended constantly to approach each other in respect to the manner in which they operate. The most striking illustration of the English approach to the American system has to do with the manner of selection, terms of office, and independence of power of the executive. In both cases, the chief executive officer gets his real mandate to act from the electorate, and in both cases can exercise his powers largely in independence of legislative direction and control. The American system, in a no less striking way, has tended to approach the English system in respect to the relationship that the executive bears toward the legislature. The formulation of a work program to guide the legislature in the performance of its duties is a prime requisite of an effective political system. This requisite is fully met in England. No such automatic provision for leadership and program-making exists in the government of personal separation of powers of the United States, but this major defect has been in the process of correction through the steadily growing movement for the American people to look to their chief executives, the president and governors of the States, to play much the same role as the English prime minister in the way of formulating programs for legislative action and using the powers of his office to have such programs adopted. No more important change has ever taken place in the practical workings of our political system. If the American president has not always the success of the English premier, this is due primarily to the fact that the party system in the United States has not as yet developed the principle of collective responsibility that characterizes the English party system.

Just as there are more than superficial resemblances between congressionalism and continental parliamentarism, so there are fundamental similarities between cabinet government and presidentialism. As a result of long experience and much experimenting, the English-speaking peoples have become convinced of the necessity of a strong executive—one to which the people can look for the formulation of political policies and which can give leadership to the legislative branch in the consideration of its proposals. It is instructive, finally, to remember that no strong American or British executive has yet impaired the fundamentals of the respective constitutional systems or of democracy. Liberty, democracy, what we may call the American and British ways of life, have not only survived the growth of executive power but have flourished under it.

5. THE WANING OF OPPOSITION IN PARLIAMENTARY REGIMES

Otto Kirchheimer

POLITICAL OPPOSITION is an eternal paradox. It postulates the principle that impediments to political action may be wholesome and are therefore to be protected. But what is the chance of institutionalizing such limitations? The parliamentary regime, and the favorable climate it created for the rise of the political party as a vehicle for the exercise of both governmental and opposition functions, has been one of the more felicitous inventions in the limited field of political institutions. But contemporary parliamentary institutions, working as they do in the framework of mass democracy, obey different laws and pressures from those governing their predecessors half a century or a century ago.

Reinvestigation of the meaning of opposition under the conditions of the present age may be in order. For the sake of preciseness these remarks will be restricted to European parliamentary regimes, omitting the role of opposition under presidential regimes, which obey somewhat different political and, as the case may be, social considerations.

I should like to put up three models, two of which pertain to the forms of political opposition. First is the "classical opposition" under the parliamentary form of government, developed from the practices of eighteenth-century England. Second is what might be styled "opposition of principle," bent not only on wrenching power from the government of today but on ending once and for all the system on which that government rests. The third is a counter-concept to the other two; it relates to government under various forms of cartel arrangements among political organizations operating within the framework of parliamentary institutions.

If we look only at definitions we might regard Messrs. Eden in 1946 and Gaitskell in 1956 as the linear descendants of Edmund Burke and Charles Fox. Burke's 1770 formula,[1] describing a party as a body of men united for promoting the national interest, by their joint endeavors, on the basis of some particular principle on which

we all agree, seems quite acceptable as a definition for the minimum of coherence needed to carry through an effective opposition. But we should not claim more for Burke or for Bolingbroke, his predecessor in the field of manufacturing political ideologies, than is due to them. For both of them, the Archimedean point of party was still "connexion, affection, and friendship" in the face of possible political adversity.[2] It needed the injection of a less savory character, John Wilkes, into the placid waters of eighteenth-century aristocratic politics to start the enlarging of faction to party and the assertion of more than evanescent group interest. But it is important to recall that this transition from the aristocratic parliament of the eighteenth century via the alternation of conservative-liberal governments of the nineteenth century, with their restricted basis of urban middle-class and landowning strata, to the present-day mass-democracy dichotomy of conservatives and labor has taken place in the framework of parliamentary institutions and their game of government opposition.

What are the bases for this game of alternation? John Morley, the Victorian, considered the right of the defeated group to publicly maintain its principles after they were rejected by the majority to be the foundation of the opposition's functioning.[3] By the end of the 1850s, however, Walter Bagehot had already shown that this continuous right of vindicating solutions rejected by the electorate presupposes that the participants in the political game consist of moderate elements. "An ultra-democratic parliament" could not preserve such a state of affairs. There each class would speak its own language, unintelligible to the others, and an "immoderate ministry" and "violent laws" would be the consequence.[4] John Stuart Mill applied similar considerations specifically to the conditions of a society resting on well organized groups. Competition must be a competition of ideas as well as of interests, because without a competition of ideas and the duty to listen to them the victory of the momentarily more powerful group would always be a foregone conclusion.[5]

To this day the British system and the practices

Reprinted from *Social Research,* Vol. 24 (Summer, 1957), pp. 127-56, by permission of the author and the publisher.

of most of the Dominions of English stock are well within the range of these considerations. On the social and economic level there is continued agreement either on major objectives or, at least, on the mutually permissible range of change. If this agreement no longer existed, it would be rather doubtful whether parliamentary government could be maintained along traditional lines. This would raise questions to which, as a contemporary Australian author puts it, "the current focus of politics hardly suggests an answer."[6] But the experience of the last decades seems not to have confirmed Harold Laski's well known notions on "the bridgeable abyss" between Conservatives and Labour, on which he laid so much stress in his analysis of the British parliamentary system in the 1930s.[7]

In an age when foreign policy may determine the very existence of a nation, parliamentary government also presupposes a high amount of opposition confidence in the government's sense of direction in reacting to situations that have to be handled without prior parliamentary discussion; at a minimum it presupposes a complete and unfaltering belief in the majority's sincerity, if it decides to make grave (but in its own mind unavoidable) changes. The Conservative attitude toward the Labour Party's abandonment of India may in this connection be compared with the sea of hatred and mutual recrimination recently produced in comparable circumstances in France. The government-opposition game further presupposes conditions in the army and the civil service which make for firm control and responsiveness to the civilian government. Both army and civil service must leave behind them the idea of forming social-political blocs of their own, warring and coalescing at will with other forces, thus upsetting and falsifying the delicate balance of forces between opposition and government.

If all these conditions are met the respective roles of government and opposition become both clearly defined and constitutionally sacrosanct. As a ceaseless critic, the opposition will try both to wring concessions from the government and to force changes of policies. As the alternative government, it will try to focus public opinion on the possibility and desirability of a speedy change via the electoral process. On the other hand, it is the government's duty to give the opposition full opportunity to carry through its function. To exercise their correlative rights and duties, both majority and opposition are therefore equipped with prerogatives, weapons, and sanctions. The official and salaried position of the leader of the opposition, the practice of informing and conferring with him,[8] the opposition's right to debate topics chosen

by itself, the differentiation between the normal function of opposition and obstruction, and the majority's right to use cloture and guillotine to break such obstruction mark the different phases in the institutionalization of opposition.[9]

The government-opposition duel, moreover, does not interrupt the government's relations with the social and professional groups that by tradition and inclination belong to what one may call the clientele of the opposition party. Acceptance of the claims of the opposition's clientele may be limited both by policy considerations and by prior incompatible obligations toward groups closer to the heart of the government. Within these limits, however, the test of the political skill of a new cabinet may often be found in its dexterity in dealing with and acquiring the confidence of the social strata belonging traditionally to the other flock. This is of the utmost importance as each party competes for the support of voters among the strata that are to a large extent among the opposition's traditional clientele.

The more skillful (or simply lucky) the government, the greater the opposition's quandary in developing what would amount to a policy alternative, and the more intensively must the opposition rely on purely tactical attitudes, taking its cues from the frequent boners that any far-flung administration is bound to commit at one time or another. Like its predecessors of former centuries, it will often pursue opposition for opposition's sake, but its scope of action is now many times enlarged, commensurate with the infinitely larger and more complex administration on which it can focus and pounce for criticism. But though the opposition's writ now extends further, its rewards may be as subject to caprice as those of its predecessors. No longer does caprice take the form of a king's whims and the accompanying reshuffling of party connections, which within the lifetime of a single parliament could bring victory to the opposition. Now, more often than not, the opposition has to wait for the decision of the sovereign electorate, possibly some years distant, to get another chance at power. Even then, the electorate may simply react to momentary situations or persevere in following long-standing social images, neither necessarily connected with the labors of the opposition, real or inconsequential as they may have been. This strong factor of chance, the difficulty in foreseeing which element in a given situation will determine the voters' choice, is inherent in the game of political competition and strengthens the camaraderie of all those participating actively in the political lottery.

While the players are the parliamentary leaders, the game is no longer played for the parliamentary

of them, the attem
Doumergue's endeavou
transparent endeavor and
cal realignment of the nation?
goodwill of the nation?

theater alone, but for the quite different audience of mass democracy—the wholesale consumers, or the interest groups, and the retail public, the individual voter. The stage acting is essential only to get the show before the mass audience, the voter. In such circumstances resoluteness and energy are needed to prevent opposition from degenerating into mere routine, and to relate it to the lives and expectations of a political clientele. The energetic inclinations of the opposition leader are the weaker the more he has come by habit, or just occupational disease, to react as part of the overall governmental machine. He may fall easy prey to the comfortable belief that his political chances increase by minimizing rather than by magnifying the policy differences between opposition and government.

If this should happen, the opposition that exists within every opposition is what becomes the moving force of the country's political machinery. The irregulars rather than the official leadership will strive to inquire into the deeper reasons for the party's last defeat, clamor for the overdue great inquest, shout for reformulations of principles and goals, and redraw the battle lines between government and opposition. The local party worker may be uninformed, the voter inarticulate; yet such gadflies may force on the recalcitrant party leadership a sharper differentiation between official opposition and governmental policies. They may, at times, run ahead of both leaders and voters, or sometimes even run amok. Their attitudes may lead the whole organization into the political wilderness, but that danger may be no greater than the disorganization threatening from total surrender to the government.[10] For every Stafford Cripps there is always an aspirant for the position of the 1931 Ramsay MacDonald. If the opposition may be called the auxiliary motor of the government, the irregulars—whether in the ranks of the opposition or of the government party—may well appear to future generations as the conscience of the public enterprise.

The government-opposition relation as it has unfolded since Disraeli's times presupposes that the government designated by the popularly decided interparty contest remains the final arbiter of the political fate of the nation. This primacy has not gone unchallenged. British history at the turn of the century presents a series of challenges of this supremacy. Charles Parnell and Tom Mann, Sir Edward Carson and the warlords of the first world war, all opposed this leadership claim, and each was in turn defeated by the political leadership of the nation.

Why did not the government-opposition pattern of parliamentary government implant itself more firmly into the mores of the major continental countries of Europe? One decisive reason is that the monopoly of final political decision so long remained beyond the grasp of political parties. Until the middle of the nineteenth century, and often much longer, opposition remained "institutional opposition." To some extent parliament as a corporate entity formed the opposition to the government. In such circumstances parliament had to fight for recognition of strictly limited influence against the representatives of more traditional powers, arrayed against it under the cloak of the crown.[11] And even after this system ended —in France in 1869, in Italy in 1871, and in Germany in 1917—political decisions often remained subject to what one may call an *avis préalable,* or a veto exercised, as the case might be, by the army, the upper bureaucracy, or central-bank institutions.[12] With parliament bereft of decisive power and unable to concentrate political decisions in its own hands, strata of the people which had little chance to make their voices heard through other channels turned toward groups that promised remedial action by supplanting the political system as a whole. Hence arose what I should like to call the "opposition of principle."

Speaking of the opposition of principle, one thinks mostly of the last decades' totalitarian parties, and is inclined to forget that European socialism of the 1880s, 1890s, and the 1900s posed similar, though less insoluble, problems. The opposition of principle assumes that realization of its program requires full political power—or at least its intentionally or unintentionally ambiguous statements may be interpreted by its more moderate competitors in this fashion. At times the opposition of principle may be insignificant, and it may never have the chance to seize political power except with the help and as an instrument of foreign backers. At other times it may loom large enough to deflect competition partially or completely from the rules of the parliamentary game, and may force the parliamentary parties into a kind of compulsory cartel and even abdication of their powers into the hands of other institutions—the army, the police, the bureaucracy. In a sense, therefore, the opposition of principle makes its own analysis and prophecy come true. By postulating the uselessness of the whole parliamentary game it may, by its very existence, threaten the parliamentary parties enough to force them into abandoning many of the rules of the parliamentary game.

In these circumstances the meaning of both government and opposition deviates markedly from the classical model. Parliamentary opposition in its classical sense presupposes both the possibility and the preparedness to form an alternative government willing and able to grant its presumptive successor in the opposition the same privileges it enjoyed itself. The very character and goals of an opposition of principle limit its parliamentary chances. It threatens the existence of the other parties, and forces its competitors into preventive and defensive measures. New and discriminatory differentiations between loyal and disloyal opposition are introduced into the parliamentary game. There may be discriminatory constitutional changes, but even outside the sphere of explicit derogation from constitutional rules, new differentiations may be introduced.[13] The votes of the opposition of principle, though counted correctly according to constitutional rules, may be weighed differently in counting votes of confidence or no-confidence. Special rules and usages may be adopted to exclude the members of such an opposition from partaking in parliamentary functions and administrative positions.

Whatever the justifications for these precautions, they inevitably distort political reality by denying adequate representation to those who, for better or worse, insist on giving these parties their confidence. Parliament may continue to provide the basis for the exercise of governmental functions, and not be paralyzed into inaction as in the classic case of pre-Hitler Germany. But its representative function and its possibility of giving expression to the various currents of opinion are bound to suffer.

Thus one test of a democratic political system is the degree to which such opposition of principle, if it has reached some magnitude, may eventually be integrated into the existing political order without forcibly dissolving it or liquidating it or substantially weakening the pursuit of the legitimate interests it represents. Such integration is the more difficult the more elections and parliament are visualized from a purely instrumental viewpoint as a possible, but by no means exclusive, field of political manoeuvre. European experience in the first half of this century contains numerous examples of both alternatives. Each case of failure or half failure has left the parliamentary system of the country weaker and less able to form the basis for the exercise of political leadership.

We come now to the third model: the elimination of major political opposition through government by party cartel. What I have in mind here are not the national or national-unity governments of war and crisis vintage.[14] By their very definition they are exceptional occurrences. Moreover, two of them, the MacDonald government of 1931 and Doumergue's attempt in 1934, were nothing but transparent endeavors to hide an attempt at political realignment and to cash in on the possible goodwill of the national-unity label. Rather, I have

in mind the more than temporary abandonment of the government-opposition relation in contemporary Austria.

Between the end of World War I and the 1934 civil war Austria had a record of bitter and incessant struggle between two major parties, both resting on an amalgamation of social class, political creed, and religious conviction, with a third party too small and inconsequential to play a balancing role. After a relatively short period of coalition between the two major parties immediately subsequent to World War I, the Christian Social Party entrenched itself firmly in the saddle of national government. For over a decade its socialist competitor hovered uneasily between the position of a parliamentary opposition and that of an opposition of principle. After World War II approximately the same party constellation emerged, with the two major parties dividing more than eighty per cent of the total vote almost evenly between themselves. In view of the difficult situation of Austria, occupied by both Eastern and Western powers, and the republic's historical record of political frustration and abiding suspicion, the parties decided on a carefully prearranged system of collaboration.[15]

Renewed after the 1956 election, this system has outlasted the occupation. Neither party has been willing to leave the conduct of public affairs in the hands of its competitor or of a civil service working exclusively under its competitor's direction.[16] The two parties proceeded with a detailed parceling out, among their adherents, of all cabinet posts and the majority of the significant administrative positions. This involved explicit understandings on many issues, on appointments, on the filling of regional, local, and semi-governmental jobs, and on the elaboration of legislative programs.[17]

This procedure has led to significant changes in the function of parliamentary institutions in Austria. The inconsequential right-wing and left-wing opposition parties have kept their freedom of parliamentary action. But the members of the two big parties can exercise their normal parliamentary prerogatives—what is now called "acting within the coalition-free area"—only with the permission of the partner party. It would jeopardize the functioning of the cartel agreement to allow party caucuses or individual backbenchers to oppose bills proposed by the government or to introduce motions themselves without previous clearance with the cartel. The area free of the binding rule of the coalition government is predetermined neither by general criteria nor by preestablished subject matter. In each case the parties' possibility of taking back their freedom of action rests on a particular agreement between the coalition partners.[18]

Major parliamentary criticism is thus relegated to the status of opposition by joint license.

What have been the consequences of this cartel arrangement? Curiously enough, the restricted exercise of parliamentary opposition has not dried up the competition between the two major parties for the votes of the new voters, of potential switchers from each, and of the declining reservoir of third-party voters.[19] In effecting this competition in face of the stringent rules of the cartel agreement, both partners have been quite ingenious in discovering and profiting from any opportunity for competition. A minister may utilize the key position assigned to him under the coalition pact in order to carry through some controversial policy by administrative fiat, thus trying to create a fait accompli in favor of his own party. On the other hand, if a party has to agree to a compromise particularly distasteful to its clientele, it will be allowed to make enough parliamentary and extraparliamentary noises to convince its clientele of the intensity of its reluctance. This then leads to a new kind of built-in opposition which the Austrians themselves have baptized *Bereichsopposition,* meaning opposition to what is happening under the agreed-upon jurisdiction of the other party.[20] The Socialists may fight verbal battles against a monetary policy of the Ministry of Finance, controlled by the Christian People's Party. The latter may pay back in vehement extraparliamentary and measured parliamentary criticism of the conduct of the Socialist ministry responsible for transport, electricity, and—until the jurisdictional changes of last summer—nationalized enterprises.

Although Austria has come close to being a two-party state, the election does not decide which party will form the government and which will be relegated to the opposition. Nevertheless, as the 1956 election has convincingly shown, the electoral process retains a clear-cut meaning. The shift of votes decides the conditions of collaboration. Administrative and legislative determination of the issues that are controversial between the parties is heavily influenced by the verdict of the voters. But it takes place by agreement and compromise worked out on the basis of election results rather than by majority fiat.

What about the compatibility of the different social-economic orientations of the partners of a coalition government? How are the views of the proponents of extensive state intervention and of an important planned sector made compatible with the endeavors of those who want a so-called free-market economy? The problem looks more formidable in theory than it is in practice. All governments operate within the limits and necessities of their period, which rarely allow either a consistent interventionist or a consistent free-market pattern. The most arduous adherents of a free-market economy have steadfastly followed a policy of protection and interventionism in the agricultural sector, with the Austrian government assuredly no exception to this rule. Everything is therefore a matter of degree and compromise; and these compromises have to be carried out irrespective of whether they are forced on a classic one-party alternation government, by the needs of multifarious political clienteles, or on a coalition government, where the various currents are represented by distinct parties.[21] Changes rarely spring Minerva-like from Zeus's head at the prompting of program builders who got the ear of the public at election time. More often than not it is the imperative requirement of a new societal situation which makes such programs sprout and be adopted by all those who want either to stay or to get a fresh start in the political business. What at first looks like a clear-cut dichotomy is mostly in point of fact a continuum.

A more fundamental objection to the Austrian-type cartel agreement, and one that has been voiced against similar tendencies of some present-day German state governments, rests on the resulting absence of the opposition's control function. Each party may have an interest in covering up the inefficiency, waste, and corruption of its partner. Hence arise all the problems of institutionalized reinsurance practices. Neither public opinion, to the extent that such an animal exists independently of interest groups closely tied in with the major parties, nor the small opposition of principle represented in parliament has enough breadth of action, inside knowledge of the administration, or authority with the public at large to compensate for the absence of a major parliamentary opposition group.[22] Control is mutual control in the matrix of a government acting within the confines of the coalition agreement; the party and parliamentary discussion sets the frame for the compromise effected inside the government. And the contours of this discussion are doubtless more skimpy than those indicated by the classical distinction between opposition and obstruction. In any case the voters, by increasingly concentrating their votes on the two major parties, have decided that from their viewpoint the two parties' right to participate jointly in government and administration is of greater social and political consequence than the traditional opposition function, and has preference over it.[23]

One might argue that the Austrian case constitutes an extreme procedure responding to the particularities of a very difficult local situation in a weak nation. But while the Austrian arrangement may differ considerably from other European coalition governments, they all to a greater or lesser extent depart from the principle of concentrated responsibility and alternative government inherent in the classical formula. The deviation may be small when the main governmental coalition partner, as at present in Sweden[24] or in the Federal Republic of Germany,[25] or the major opposition party, as in Belgium, is so strong that the system in some respects, though by no means in all, operates as if there were a clear-cut government-opposition dichotomy. The deviation is bound to become much more accentuated in France—at least until the disappearance of a unified Gaullist party—and in Italy, where the existence of a substantial opposition of principle forces the traditional parliamentary parties into a kind of compulsory cartel, irrespective of whether they form part of the government. If the regime is assailed by a substantial bloc of non-cooperators on both the right and the left flanks, or if cooperation can be bought only at unacceptable terms, opposition and opposition of principle may become almost identical.

In France, despite the presence of a substantial opposition of principle, either the working of the election system—especially tailored for that purpose in 1951—or, in the present assembly, the availability of blocs of overseas deputies for a variety of governmental combinations has left a certain margin within which individual political figures may whip varying party combinations into line. But from the viewpoint of the public at large the major difference between parliamentary groups and extra-parliamentary mass movements operating within parliament as an opposition of principle tends to blot out more subtle distinctions. The French elections of January 1956 gave evidence that in the voter's mind the major decision lies between the traditional parliamentary groups and the opposition of principle. Transfer of votes to and from the opposition of principle is of greater importance than the internal transfer of votes among the various parliamentary groups. Acting in this fashion, however, the voter largely abdicates the role assigned to him under the classical government-opposition scheme, namely, to participate in the arbitration of conflicting leadership claims among parties operating within the framework of the regime. Thus the vote determines at best the margin that the groups loyal to the regime retain to form and reform their ephemeral alliances, and influences to a lesser degree the process of cabinet forming.[26] This insensitivity of government formation toward popular currents allows the opposition of principle to contest the moral title of the government to represent the country, thus confronting the *pays légal* with the *pays réel*.

There may be neither abiding suspicion, leading to a watertight voluntary cartel, nor crisis of the regime, leading to a compulsory or near-compulsory cartel arrangement: coalition government may be simply a consequence of a well established multiparty system, as in present-day Holland, Weimar Germany, or interwar Czechoslovakia. But whatever the reason for the coalition arrangements, their establishment and practices are all bound to lead to deviations from the classical norm. The major government party may be concerned mainly with dislodging one partner or switching coalition partners. The opposition parties too may fight on various fronts; without the possibility of setting up a government of their own, they may concentrate energy on improving tactical chances of government participation.[27] This purpose may involve subtle modulations of policy in regard to various governmental or other opposition parties. The possible variations and combinations are of great variety. Neither of the constellations is conducive to a sharp differentiation between government and opposition policies. The tortuous ways of the multiparty government and of multi-opposition tactics are the province of the political professional. The public at large looks at the results, while the more loyal party public may judge also by intentions.

Nevertheless, a multiparty coalition government need not be congenitally weak, nor need a divided opposition be impotent. Everything depends on the character of the various participants and their leadership, and on the temper of national political discourse and action. The maxim "where all govern, nobody governs" does not correctly describe all relevant factual situations.[28] Prewar Czech and postwar Dutch governments, though they were difficult to assemble, show a reasonable record of stability and efficiency.[29] On the other hand, multiparty government in the larger countries has more often than not been weak. The difficulty in bringing together various factions, the limited minimum program to which the coalition partners are willing to subscribe, and the concomitant attempts to restrict the mandate given to the parties' representatives in the cabinets inevitably provoke sharp counter-thrusts. Each cabinet minister will try to assert his maximum independence of his group, emphasize the dignity and independence of his office, and make the most of his assertion that he is His Majesty's or the nation's representative. He will therefore fall in most eagerly with the higher ranks of the bureaucracy who might liberate him from the embraces and demands of his party.

Such "liberation tendencies" are not restricted to representatives of multiparty coalition governments. But the fact of having been carried to power by a strong party, whether within the frame of the classic two-party system or as participant of a strong and stable coalition, enhances the chance that a minister will be willing and able to implant his party's value scale and program. Ministers of a weak coalition government are more predisposed to become instruments in the hands of their official advisers. It is in such cases that the always latent nineteenth-century antinomy, with parliament opposing the administration as an intrinsically inimical institution—so well known from the practice of presidential regimes—has a tendency to become universal. But unless the parties want to be relegated to the role of political prayer mills, this can be only a transitional and, from the viewpoint of the parliamentary regime, uncomfortable solution.

Political opposition as a continuing function presupposes the existence of a yardstick for governmental performance. The opposition on principle need not bother to unearth such a yardstick, as the very existence of the government is sufficient proof of its wickedness. In contrast, opposition within the confines of the parliamentary system presupposes some semblance of coherence if at least some vestige of a rational alternative to the government's policy is to be preserved.

This coherence may have its roots in program, ideology, and tradition. To be sure, coherence is always threatened, if for no other reason than the fact that in our day and age both government and opposition are always faced with unforeseen and unforeseeable situations requiring immediate action without their catechism offering satisfactory or, indeed, any answers. Gone are the days when a man could make up a program at the outset of his career to last all his life.[30] But coherence is more likely with a party that has a tradition and some hold over its clientele, and therefore can afford the luxury of convictions, than with a marginal group whose survival, depending on the outcome of the next election, requires that it make its decisions on exclusively tactical grounds. The freedom of movement of the first is principally determined by the objective requirements of the situation it encounters when it comes to power; the latter is subjected to all the additional impediments stemming from its uneasy and always imperiled relations with its more comfortable competitors. To the extent that coalition government and multifarious opposition rest on quickly shifting and purely tactical alignments, they provide only an indistinct focus for the exercise of governmental responsibility and the complementary function of parliamentary opposition.

The question arises whether this desiccation of the opposition function that has here been followed through a number of variations can be attributed to more or less technical factors, and hence could be reversed by technical changes in election procedures or parliamentary rules. Can it be maintained, for example, that the voluntary cartel system of Austria, the erosion of the opposition function under the semi-compulsory cartels of France and Italy, the abuses of some multiparty coalition governments—all detrimental to the exercise of the classic opposition function—could be changed by the introduction of more suitable electoral systems or by different practices governing rules of no-confidence, dissolution, and the setting up of new governments? It seems unlikely. There is no meaningful connection between the form of the electoral system, the practices and malpractices of government formation, and the crisis of the concept of political opposition. It may be more rewarding to look into the incongruities between continental party systems and the social realities of the twentieth century.

Continental European parties are the remnants of intellectual and social movements of the nineteenth century. They have remained glued to the spots where the ebbing energy of such movements deposited them some decades ago. The more violent twentieth-century eruptions, fascism and communism, have surged much further, but in flowing back have petrified rather than envigorated the existing system. Postwar attempts at rationalization have produced some new variations, but have not eliminated the basic heritage of the parties. They were built around combinations of nineteenth-century class, occupational, and religious, or, as the case might be, anti-religious interests. How does this heritage relate to the most important stages of twentieth-century transformation?

From the viewpoint of political dynamics, the most important change is probably the emergence of a substantial new middle class of skilled workers, the middle ranks of white-collar people, and civil servants. All their work is done under instruction from superiors. Similarities of situation, thought processes, and expectations outweigh still existing traditional distinctions. Their consumption expectations, resting on the concept of increasing prosperity, as well as the demands they address to the community at large for sufficient protection against institutional and personal hazards of life, are identical. The cleavage that separates them from the more successful elements of the older independent middle classes—the artisans and peasants of medium-size holdings, both with enough capital equipment to profit from technological progress—is diminishing. The technological revolution is changing the outlook of these tradition-bound and conservative groups at the same time that it reduces their size. Increasingly enmeshed in the fortunes of the national economy, they now raise claims, identical with those of the new middle class, for guaranteed real-income levels and participation in social-insurance schemes. To this extent the struggle between the independent old middle class and the employed new middle class is more a struggle for similar goals than a clash of incompatible programs.

To the extent that all major parliamentary parties are permeated by the opinions and attitudes of these groups, strategic on account of both their size and the compactness of their professional organizations, one may justifiably say that diminished social polarization and diminished political polarization are going hand in hand. As Beatrice Webb expressed this particular phenomenon forty-odd years ago, "the landslide in England towards Social Democracy proceeds steadily, but it is the whole nation which is sliding, not the one class of manual workers."[31] We are faced with a somewhat languishing system of interparty competition which in many cases is even overshadowed by intraparty competition, the attempt of the various interest groups represented in one party to have an official party stand adopted that is maximally favorable to them.[32] The parliamentary party has thus become in a double sense a harmonizing agency. It harmonizes first the conflicting claims within its ranks, and on this basis participates in interparty adjustments on the governmental level.[33]

The same harmonizing tendencies are potently reenforced by the contemporary opinion-forming process. The rise of the nineteenth-century party was inseparably linked with the growth of newspapers as vehicles for the creation and expression of public opinion. The newspapers, being politically oriented, and helping aspirants for political power to obtain recognition and spread their doctrine, were the handmaidens of emerging parliamentary government.[34] Twentieth-century media of communication are not primarily politically oriented. They are business enterprises bent on maximizing profits from huge investments by catering to the inclinations and aspirations of a presumed near totality of readers and listeners, rather than appealing to an educated elite. They interlace the consumption expectations of their readers and listeners with the interests of their backers and advertisers. In order to fulfill this dual mission they preserve a maximum of neutrality, not only between the possibly conflicting interests of the various advertisers but also between the prejudices of the various strata of their readers and listeners. Resting on a presupposed harmony of interests among advertisers, financial backers,

readers, and listeners, they are using the Hays-office technique of neutralizing and playing down divisive elements or transferring elements of conflict from the domestic to the international scene.[35] The rise of consumer-oriented public-opinion formation has been one of the most powerful elements in the reduction of the political element to the semi-entertainment level.[36]

Thus objective factors of social development and conscious efforts join in breaking down barriers between some strata of society and in creating what has been rather prematurely styled a unified middle-class society. This theme of a unified middle-class society has been pressed most consistently in postwar Germany; one author has recently gone so far as to approximate present-day conditions with the classless society, alluding in this context to the well known slogan of the transformation of the state into an organ for day-to-day administrative concerns.[37] It is open to question to what extent such utterances both overstress and generalize from some particular aspect of German postwar experiences. At any rate, analogous, if not always so pronounced, social and economic changes in other continental European countries have not been followed to the same degree by tendencies toward privatization which allow, as it were, for the transformation of political problems into administrative and technical routine; the persistence of a large opposition of principle in France and Italy is inevitably leading to an emphasis on the repressive function of the state.

Moreover, the same process that has created a new middle class and lessened the distance between the old and new elements has everywhere uprooted diverse other social strata, and has so far failed to assign them a satisfactory position within the new society. The main victims of this process of transformation have been older people whose income has not kept pace with inflation, small peasant holders, small artisans and retailers without the capital to modernize their shops, and white-collar elements, economically outflanked by many groups of manual workers and unable to acquire a new feeling of "belonging" to compensate for the meagerness of their occupational existence. These changes, too, have indelibly marked the present party system. These strata form a steady source, even in present favorable economic circumstances, for a predominantly but not exclusively right-wing opposition of principle. By the same token, they are an element in the petrification of the traditional parliamentary parties.

To compete with the opposition of principle for this substantial vote, the parliamentary parties find it useful to fall back on their nineteenth-century heritage. This heritage may vary widely: with the socialists it may mean an occasional harking back to the class basis of political structure and its promise of a classless society; with the vaguely Christian catch-all parties, in vogue after the war, it may mean the concept of spiritual brotherhood or a specific religious appeal, transcending the cleavages of the day; and with the liberal or radical socialist parties it may refer to the autonomy claim of the non-collectivized individual, raised against both church and state. What we are here concerned with, however, is not the content of the often interchangeable doctrines but their survival as an element in keeping together or bringing again together the various elements of formerly unified groups, now torn asunder in the process of social transformation, employing here the unity of the working classes or there the image of a self-reliant independent middle class.

To be sure, not all—or even most—members of status-threatened disadvantaged and dissatisfied groups join the ranks of the opposition of principle. But this is probably less significant as indicating the continuing attraction of the parliamentary party than as emphasizing the fact that the primarily consumption-oriented thought process of their more fortunate brethren has become for them a natural habit. They momentarily accept the parliamentary party not because it struggles to uphold a lien on their grandfathers' social vision, but because they grant some advance credit to its promise to give a high priority to their material claims.[38] Mistrustful of the more remote if all-embracing solutions of the opposition of principle, they accept the parliamentary party's arbitration regarding the extent to which their claims can at present be honored without conflicting with other weighty claims. But some claims have to be honored here and now if their loyalty to the parliamentary party is to last.

In the final analysis it is this urgency of group claims which militates against the parliamentary party's breathing for any length of time outside the precincts of government. It has greatly weakened the party's desire to don the robes of parliamentary opposition, as this would lessen its effectiveness in the adjudication of group claims, which in our time has become its raison d'être. If a party chooses voluntarily to go into opposition —which happens under conditions of a multiparty state—it does so for purely tactical reasons, in order to fasten the burden of unpopular policies on some political competitor, or in order to be free to outbid the opposition of principle by espousing some manifestly inflated group claims.

The rise of the consumption-oriented individual of mass society thus sets the stage for the shrinking of the ideologically oriented nineteenth-century party. After the unlimited extension of the party concept, first in the traditional *Weltanschauungs* party and more recently in the totalitarian movement, its recent reduction to a rationally conceived vehicle of interest representation becomes noticeable.[39] By and large, European parliamentary parties are reducing their special ideological and material offerings.[40] Instead, they substitute a demand for a wide variety of ever expanding community services, open on a basis of equality to whole categories of citizens. Unlike the totalitarian movements they are not equipped to overrun the state machine; at best they aspire to participate in the rewards and premiums it offers. In reminiscence of tradition,[41] or more likely as a planned investment in a public career, individuals may still become party workers. But the tendency for the party to exercise a brokerage function for specific interest groups is present, and is likely to become more accentuated as time goes on. Thus the non-professional in politics is destined to be relegated to a back seat. The interest group, however, as distinct from the individual party member, manifests a loyalty that is limited and contingent. Not only may this loyalty be transferred to more useful political groups, but support may be given simultaneously to groups competing in the political arena.

The modern party is thus forced to think more and more in terms of profit and loss. To it, opposition scarcely relates to the sum total of style, philosophy, and conduct of government, but concentrates on some concrete measure where the government decision may reflect a balance of forces disadvantageous to the interests the party represents. This does not mean that in other instances the balance may not be more favorable, or, even more important, that participation in administrative implementation could not redress the balance in its favor. In such circumstances government participation becomes a matter of necessity; the party would consider it an unmitigated evil if it were excluded for any length of time. But it is also worth while to look at the other side of the coin. While government participation furthers the claims of the party's backers, it also allows the party to assert its own authority over them. The radiation of state authority involved in the party's moving from the brokerage stage to the position of an arbitrator removes the party from many suffocating embraces and carries it beyond the confines of its interest configurations.

The party's alertness in first pursuing and then arbitrating the claims of its clientele is not necessarily related to an equally clear-cut vision of the processes of history at large. The modern party man knows where he has to take his stand if the roll call concerns a question of taxation of consumer cooperatives or an increase in maternity benefits. There are few guideposts to enlighten him as to the best course on EDC or the recognition of Communist China. A roll call of contemporary politicians of many countries and parties would show only a tiny minority who could meaningfully relate the broad canvas of international politics to their domestic objectives.[42] In addition, the more freedom of decision in the realm of foreign policy has narrowed down in the last decade, as a consequence of international developments, the more difficult becomes the offering of foreign-policy alternatives. No parliamentary opposition in Great Britain, France, Italy, or Germany can, without evoking the specter of incalculable and frightening consequences, propagandize a reversing of alliances as a goal and consequence of its coming to power. This lack of realistic alternative solutions leads to a certain sterility and artificiality in the foreign-policy arguments of parliamentary opposition parties, which for better or worse are tied to the geographic location, to the prevailing social system, and consequently also to the international engagements of their countries.

Differences within the precincts of parliamentary politics thus narrow down to squabbles over the most advantageous arrangements and courses of action within the concert of Western powers. Such differences, as the French battle over the ratification of EDC showed, do not necessarily set one parliamentary party against another, but may cut across party lines. Only the opposition of principle, which does not have to face the likelihood of its coming to power in the near future, may envisage and even risk its very existence on a revolutionary foreign-policy program, its opposition becoming the more irreconcilable the more its policy outlook as a whole is determined by its foreign-policy affinities. The present international situation need not last. The imminent loss of the major powers' monopoly of atomic weapons, and the consequent likelihood of a loosening up of the bipolar international system, may create new areas of foreign-policy choice. But as long as the present bipolarity lasts, it contributes both to widening the gulf between parliamentary parties and the opposition of principle and to shrinking the sphere of the truly parliamentary opposition.

This transition from the ideologically oriented continental party of earlier times to the more limited congeries of interest-oriented groups is one of the elements behind the erosion of the classic opposition. But the demise of the opposition is not tantamount to the complete dismantling of the European party, relegating it to some form of procedural device to be used for every comer to fight particular and eternally changing issues, as the stereotype of the political party in the United States would have it.[43] Other factors still favor some measure of party cohesion. One is the existence of an opposition of principle, threatening the continuation of present political patterns. Another is the fact that there are fairly constant elements—slurred and overlapping though they may be—determining which type of interest a party may pick up.[44]

Thus the parliamentary party may continue as a relatively stable entity. But the unifying and leveling element of the mass media and a certain lessening of social polarization mark a definite stage in the decline of this delicate part of our political heritage, the classic parliamentary opposition. It is in this sense that the Austrian practice of coalition pacts with built-in opposition devices commands interest. It presents a limited survival and revival of the opposition concept at a time when opposition ideologies either have come to serve as handmaidens of total and revolutionary social and political change or are becoming downgraded to the role of relatively meaningless etiquettes and advertisement slogans within the framework of interest representation.

Notes

1. Edmund Burke, "Thoughts on the Causes of the Present Discontents," in *Works*, World's Classics ed., vol. 2, p. 82.

2. To cite but one out of many, see H. Butterfield, *George III, Lord North and the People* (London 1949).

3. See John Morley, *On Compromise*, 2nd ed. (London 1877) p. 209.

4. Walter Bagehot, *Works and Life*, vol. 5, p. 269.

5. John Stuart Mill, *Representative Government*, Chapter 5; see also G. Burdeau, *Traité de science politique*, vol. 3 (Paris 1950) p. 327.

6. L. F. Crisp, *The Parliamentary Government of the Commonwealth of Australia*, 2nd ed. (London 1952) p. 121.

7. Harold Laski, *Parliamentary Government in England* (New York 1938).

8. There may be, however, self-imposed limits to the right of information. The leader of the opposition may find it inconvenient to burden his freedom of action by access to special-privileged knowledge. See *New Statesman and Nation*, vol. 52, September 1, 1956, p. 234.

9. In the individual instance it may become difficult to draw the dividing line between opposition and obstruction. Herbert Morrison, the parliamentary veteran of the Labour Party, has even doubted whether the opposition has the right to suggest the absence of a quorum; see his *Government and Parliament* (London 1954) p. 157. On the guillotine resolution to close the debate by compartments and allot a certain amount of time to the discussion of specific sections of a bill—and its democratic indispensability—see Lord Campion, ed., *Parliament, A Survey* (London 1952) Chapters 1 and 7, and J. Jennings, *Parliament* (London 1939) p. 240.

10. This quintessence of a long political career is drawn by L. S. Amery, *My Political Life*, vol. 1 (London 1953) p. 416.

11. See F. Guizot, *Du gouvernement representatif et de l'état actuel de la France* (Paris 1816) pp. 25 ff. Nearly a century and a half later we read in a posthumously published article by one of the martyrs of the Weimar Republic, "In imperial Germany the government is in the hands of the top of the bureaucracy; the bureaucracy is not dominated by politics; on the contrary, to a large degree it determines policy. On the other hand, in Western Europe the bureaucracy has much less independence of the political hierarchy, the really and immediately governing parliament": Rudolf Hilferding, "Das historische Problem," in *Die Zukunft* (March 1956) p. 83. See also Thomas Ellwein, *Das Erbe der deutschen Monarchie in der Staatskrise* (Munich 1954); Ellwein (p. 126) characterizes popular representation as "only a limiting element in public life."

12. On the role of the Bank of France under the Third Republic see Otto Kirchheimer, "Political Compromise," in *Studies in Philosophy and Social Science,* vol. 9, no. 1 (1941).

13. See George Berlia, "La revision constitutionelle," in *Revue du droit public,* vol. 61 (1955) p. 164, and Roy Macridis, "A Note on the Revision of the Constitution of the Fourth Republic," in *American Political Science Review,* vol. 50 (1956) pp. 1011-22.

14. See Dolf Sternberger, *Lebendige Verfassung* (Gleisenheim 1956) p. 107.

15. See Bruno Pittermann, "Oesterreichs Innenpolitik nach dem Staatsvertrag," in *Die Zukunft* (July 1955) p. 88.

16. To quote Pittermann (*ibid.*): "The party that governs alone dominates not only the state apparatus but practically a great part of the economy. In such circumstances not only the employees of the administration of the federal enterprise come under its knuckle, but directly or indirectly also hundreds of thousands of independents and wage earners in the economy. To leave the government is tantamount to losing influence on both political and economic administrative hierarchies."

17. After the wording of the 1949 and 1953 coalition pacts had become known piecemeal from parliamentary and newspaper discussions and polemics, the participants decided to publish the June 1956 agreement in its entirety, together with the special agreements on the new delimitation of administrative jurisdictions. The main agreement, as translated from *Arbeiterzeitung* of June 27, 1956, is as follows: "1) The Austrian People's Party and the Socialist Party of Austria form a government to the exclusion of third parties; they obligate themselves to take over together the responsibility for governmental policy. 2) The relation of strength between the two parties is in principle determined by the results obtained in the elections of May 13, 1956. This proportion is to be applied to proposals for the top positions of the socialized enterprises. The same proportion applies for positions on the boards of directors and in the management of the state-managed banks. The federal government decides appointments as well as changes of the statutes and rules for the banks. 3) The collaboration of the two parties extends over the duration of the parliamentary period. Before the end of its term new elections can be ordered only through the agreement of both parties. The next elections will be carried through by the cabinet as formed by both parties. 4) A coalition committee, consisting of five representatives from each party, is formed in order to guarantee smooth collaboration. It should convene regularly, and in any case in the event that differences arise between the parties. The federal Chancellor will preside; his deputy is the Vice Chancellor. The two chairmen of the parliamentary clubs are members of the coalition committee. 5) If the two parties represented in the government have unanimously agreed on government bills, as to both substance and form, the bills become binding for the two coalition partners in the national council. Amendments of principle need the consent of the coalition committee. If the government in presenting a bill decides to give the parties a free hand for its legislative stage, the parties regain their freedom of action in the national council. 6) In regard to all other bills and postulates both parties will decide on the modus of voting and, if the case should arise, on reestablishing the freedom of voting for their members. 7) As before, currency problems will be a common responsibility of the two parties. For this reason public statements on currency measures, above all by members of the government, may be made only with the agreement of the Chancellor and the Vice Chancellor."

18. This interpretation, based on the earlier coalition agreement, is confirmed by Bruno Pittermann, the speaker of the socialist faction and more recently Vice Chancellor, though he expresses some regrets as to the emasculation of parliamentary functions which is thereby implied. See his "Aschenbrödel Parlament," in *Die Zukunft* (February 1955) p. 33.

19. The relevant election results—taken from Hans Müller, "Die Wahlen im Spiegel der Statistik," in *Die Zukunft* (May-June 1956) p. 136—are as follows:

	1945	1949	1953	1956
Registered voters	3,449,000	4,391,000	4,586,000	4,614,000
Election participation in % of reg. voters	95%	96.8%	95.8%	95.9%
Per cent of valid vote received by:				
Christian People's Party (OVP)	49.8	44.4	41.26	45.96
Socialist Party (SPO)	44.6	38.7	42.1	43.04
Independents (Freedom Party 1956)	...	11.68	10.59	6.52
Communist Party (KPO)	5.41	5.08	5.28	4.44

20. In the words of Friedrich Scheu, "Die Kritik der Demokratie," in *Die Zukunft* (February 1956) p. 36, "Austria succeeded in inventing a political system in which two parties are permanently in coalition with each other and nevertheless continue to compete uninterruptedly between themselves. Each of them is simultaneously government party and opposition party, because each of them is opposition within the governmental jurisdiction of the other party." The same viewpoint is expressed by the spokesman of the Austrian People's Party; see Alfred Maletta, "Wahlausgang, Regierungsbildung und künftiges Programm," in *Oesterreichische Monatshefte* (May 1953) p. 258. Representatives of the rightist opposition, excluded by these agreements from political influence, characterize the situation disparagingly as *Reserveopposition;* see Kraus in Nationalrat, 3rd Session, 63rd Meeting, March 1, 1955, *Stenographische Berichte,* p. 2937.

21. See, however, Henri Bartoli, "Rôle et exigences d'une planification socialiste," in *Esprit* (May 1956) pp. 749, 755, who denies that a mixed economy could be feasible for any length of time.

22. The postmortem discussion concerning the U. S.-controlled radio broadcasting station Red White Red, with its popular Watschenmann broadcasts, illustrates the difficulties of independent criticism under a coalition-party government. Scheu (cited above, note 20) p. 38, remarks about this station: "It was a creation of the American occupation powers, and as such responsible to nobody in Austria. Aside from U. S. propaganda, it needed to consider nobody and to pursue nobody's interests. But its existence was a paradox, and this paradox terminated necessarily with the occupation. An Austrian office cannot be so irresponsible, it cannot risk besmirching citizens by assertions which might turn out to be wrong." Scheu goes on to emphasize how desirable it would be if certain broadcasts could be made within the "party-free area," though he hastens to admit how difficult it would be to create independent organs for criticism. The usual difficulties with media run by public authorities are compounded in this case by the fact that the authority is

bipartite and that extreme care has to be taken lest the media create the slightest disturbance in the delicate inter-party equilibrium.

23. The East German bloc system, which forces artificially created parties into collaboration with the State Party, has little similarity with the voluntary cartel described here, or, for that matter, with any of the other forms of coalition government. In order to protect the State Party and the other admitted political organizations from unfair competition, the DDR prevents the rise of any non-participating organization. Its government thus becomes a full-fledged compulsory cartel, dominated by one of its members, the State Party, with the latter allocating tidbits of power to the other participants, strictly according to its own devices. Moreover, any element of competition among the cartel participants themselves is excluded by the device of common electoral lists, with prearranged quotas of seats allocated to each participant. Steiniger, the theoretician of the system, referred to it—before he was forced into abandoning his somewhat too cynical exegesis—as "the maximum of artificial homogeneity which may be obtained by political technique," but he hastened to add that even this degree of homogeneity, in what he considered still a heterogeneous society, presupposes for its functioning some changes in the social order. See Alfons Steiniger, *Das Blocksystem* (Berlin 1949) pp. 20, 21.

24. The permanent hegemony of the Social Democratic Party in Sweden, and the consequent permanent opposition in which the conservative and liberal parties find themselves, has led to a demand for a national coalition of all "constitutional parties"; see D. A. Rüstow, *The Politics of Compromise* (Princeton 1956) pp. 219 ff. Such proposals seem to have little chance, in spite of the favorable echoes they have found. Nobody seems to press them too hard, as there exists a high amount of mutual confidence among all parties and the actual administration is separated well enough from purely administrative positions to minimize the disadvantages of those who are not represented in the government.

25. For an exhaustive discussion of the character of the federal government in Germany see Sternberger (cited above, note 14) p. 128. His acute observations and interesting formulations suffer, however, from a tendency to shove off sociological party analysis as unproductive for his constructs and then proceed on a somewhat problematic basis to proclaim the classic government-opposition relation both as norm and as desirable goal; see especially p. 147.

26. Some of these problems are discussed in R. A. Aron, "Electeurs, partis et élus," in *Revue française des sciences politiques* (April-June 1955) p. 304, and in Philip Williams, *Politics in Post War France* (London 1954), especially p. 358.

27. On this point see S. Landshut, "Formen und Funktionen der parlamentarischen Opposition," in *Wirtschafts und Kultursystem*, Festgabe für A. Rüstow (Winterthur 1945) p. 223.

28. See M. F., "Vom Fug und Unfug der Koalitionen," in *Gegenwart*, May 19, 1956, pp. 303, 305, underlining the statement by Sternberger (cited above, note 14) that the rise and acknowledgment of opposition is one of the most significant deeds in the history of democracy. While the historical truth of this statement is uncontestable, it has to be read in the light of all the modifications that have marked the fate of opposition in the last decades.

29. On the Dutch experience see H. Daalder, "Parties and Politics in the Netherlands," in *Political Studies*, vol. 3, no. 1 (1955) p. 1.

30. See the instructive remarks of D. Ostrogorsky in *Democracy and Political Parties*, vol. 1 (New York 1902) p. 22.

31. Beatrice Webb, *Diaries, 1912-1924* (London 1952) p. 18.

32. These trends appeared earliest and in the most suc-

cinct form in Sweden. See Herbert Tingsten, "Stability and Vitality in Swedish Democracy," in *Political Quarterly*, vol. 26 (1955) pp. 140-51: "As the general standard of values is so commonly accepted, the function of the state becomes so technical as to make politics appear as a kind of applied statistics." See also his statements (p. 148) on the nature of political parties.

33. Compare the formula utilized by Fritz Erler, a leading contemporary German politician, in "Die Sozialdemokratische Partei—Eine Partei unter Vielen," in *Neue Gesellschaft* (1956) pp. 200, 203: "The SPD even in its own concepts needs to harmonize the various group interests, in order to obtain in this fashion the total interest of a libertarian-democratic society."

34. "A political party needs a newspaper for its propagandistic purposes. In order to keep the newspaper going one needs a literary section (*feuilleton*); therefore the author of a serial story must press the ideas of his party chief and his newspaper": A. Thiers, as quoted by A. Vagts, "Heinrich Börnstein, Ex and Repatriate," in Missouri Historical Society, *Bulletin* (January 1956) p. 112.

35. For a partial analysis see Jacques Kayser, *Mort d'une liberté* (Paris 1955). S. Diamond, *The Reputation of the American Businessman* (Cambridge, Mass., 1955), brings out very well the importance of mass communication for the maintenance of consensus in the functioning of society.

36. The role of the "lowest common denominator" in the news presentations of the movie industry is forcefully analyzed in H. M. Enzensberger, "Die Anatomie einer Wochenschau," in *Frankfurter Hefte* (1957) vol. 12, pp. 265-78.

37. The extreme formulation is that of S. Landshut, "Die Auflösung der Klassengesellschaft," in *Gewerkschaftliche Monatshefte*, vol. 7 (1956) p. 451; in the same direction is H. Schelsky's speech, "Haben Wir heute noch eine Klassengesellschaft?" reprinted in *Das Parlament*, February 29, 1956.

38. Thorough post-electoral inquiries into voters' motivations and preferences, recently carried through in the first electoral district of Paris, contain much material reinforcing this thesis as to voters' motivations in preferring parliamentary parties; see Jean Stoetzel and Pierre Hassner, "Resultats d'un sondage dans le premier secteur de la Seine," in *Les elections du 2 janvier 1956*, Cahiers de la Fondation Nationale des Sciences Politiques, vol. 82 (Paris 1957) pp. 199-248, especially 228-30.

39. Of course, there are exceptions. Israel, with its odd mixture of avant-garde and arrière-garde elements, responds to a conscious transfer of traditional European institutional patterns and the pressing material needs of the moment. Its parties are conceived of both as ideological entities and as vehicles for special party-connected customer services. An intensive party life results. See Benjamin Akzin, "The Role of Parties in Israeli Democracy," in *Journal of Politics*, vol. 17 (1955) p. 507; but note especially his remark on page 519, visualizing the possibility of a receding of direct intervention of parties into social matters in the foreseeable future.

40. Carlo Schmid's speech, "Die Sozialdemokratische Partei Deutschlands vor der geistigen Situation dieser Zeit," before the 1950 SPD convention in Hamburg, is characteristic of this tendency toward a sharp reduction of party functions.

41. Heinz Meyer, "Struktur der deutschen Sozialdemokratie," in *Zeitschrift für Politik* (1955) pp. 348, 354, reveals that only one of nineteen functionaries on whom the inquiry centered did not have a background of "family party tradition."

42. Gerhard Lütkens, "Die parlamentarische Aussenpolitik in der Opposition," in *Aussenpolitik*, vol. 2 (1951) p. 398, makes a somewhat tormented attempt to vindicate this dualism as more than technical in character. A more realistic German appraisal may be found in Wilhelm Hennis, "Parlamentarische Opposition und Industriegesell-

schaft," in *Gesellschaft-Staat-Enziehung* (1957) pp. 205-22.

44. Interesting material for comparisons between reality and stereotype can be found in L. D. Epstein, "British Mass Parties in Comparison with American Parties," in *Political Science Quarterly*, vol. 71 (1956) p. 97.

44. Problems of "interest coloration" of political parties

are discussed by R. Breitling, *Die Verbände in der Bundesrepublik* (Meisenheim 1955), and by M. L. Lange in the postscript to *Parteien in der Bundesrepublik* (Stuttgart and Düsseldorf 1955) pp. 507 ff. On the predominance of the interest motive in what is officially dubbed a *Weltanschauungspartei* see the interesting discussion by G. Schulz, "Die CDU," *ibid.*, pp. 3, 146.

6. PARTY RESPONSIBILITY AND LEGISLATIVE PROGRAM

Fritz Morstein Marx

LAWMAKING IS a vital function of modern government. But the legislative process does not operate in a political vacuum, nor is it everywhere the same. The theory and practice of legislation in the United States, as in any other country, has been deeply influenced by the party system. . . .

Given the local basis of representation, especially in the single-member constituency, the pull toward things local is the most immediate and the most continuous influence to which the representative is exposed. A parallel pull, allied in many ways with the local, arises from the competitive advantages which the special interest enjoys over the general. By comparison with matters of general importance, the special interest is favored by its single-mindedness as well as by its bread-and-butter persistence, and both together are usually able to support a superior organization. It is a rare feat for the representative singly to be equal to these constant pulls and thus qualify himself for consideration of the common good, for a strong and steady countervailing pull is needed to free him for an active share in drawing up and carrying out a program of legislation designed to serve the people at large.

Capacity for supplying such a countervailing pull is the fundamental condition which determines capacity for government. There is no institutional mechanism to supply this pull other than the great political parties. But parties, with effective national organizations, must be so organized as to accomplish commitment and decision with relative ease.

Neither of our major parties has supplied this pull. To quote a student of American legislation, "In a very real sense there is no such thing as

a national political party. The National Committee of each party which presumably heads such an organization is merely a conference of ambassadors from the party organizations in the various states and territories; it meets quadrennially to fix the time and place of the National Convention, to determine the basis of representation in the convention, to select its temporary officers, to call upon the state organizations to choose the number of delegates assigned to them, and after the convention is over to reorganize, raise the necessary funds, and conduct the presidential campaign. The election over, the National Committee goes into hibernation until another presidential year. Some effort has been made in recent years to establish a full-time secretariat for the National Committees which would function between campaigns, but without much success."[1] What still aggravates the effects of such dormancy on the national level is the degree to which state and local party structure relies upon informal organization, making responsibility for party policy a highly elusive thing.[2]

With national party organization in such a lowly state, its inability to generate a vigorous pull toward the general interest can hardly occasion surprise. This condition releases a whole chain of reactions with a direct effect upon the legislative process. In the first place, victory at the polls does not give the winning party the potential benefits of party government; the party is said to be in power, but in its use of power it is severely limited by its inconclusive performance in achieving political identity. Such identity could derive only from an interrelated set of avowed goals—meant to be accomplished, not just to adorn a keynote speech. But, as a second point, without a national organ to secure sanction for a program and to have it acted upon, both the political identity of the party and the direction of its course are bound to remain vague; the party's legislative agenda may always turn into a free-for-all. Since

Reprinted from *Columbia Law Review*, Vol. 50 (March, 1950), pp. 281-99, by permission of the author and the publisher.

so much enticement is offered for interest groups to enter the scramble at any time, a third result is grievous fragmentation of the legislative product. And fourth, because neither major party is prepared to assume responsibility for program development in the sense of providing general guidance for the total effort of government, the American presidency is made single-handedly to attend to what is in considerable part the job of Congress.

How is it possible for the party that is said to be in power to make so little of it? An informed critic answers as follows: "The greatest shortcoming of the party system results from *the failure of the system to convert party politics into party government*. This deficiency is related in turn to the whole problem of the locus of power in the party system . . . the parties do badly the one thing that they might be expected to do with perfection: *they fail to organize the nominees they have elected to office into an effective, cohesive team for the control of the government. Nearly all of the conflict and confusion in American government can be traced to the failure of the parties at this point.*"[3] Much of the governing, in brief, is being done by individual elements of the machinery of government in varying degrees of independence from the supporting party.

There is no good reason to assume that it is poisonous for either of our major parties to have a political identity. On the contrary, if a party attains unity through full acceptance of a distinctive program, it stands to reap large gains. "One incalculable advantage at the disposal of a united party is that it is able to make a consistent record throughout the government. A record of this kind, deliberately established in the public mind, and well exploited in public discussion, ought to give either of the major parties a great competitive advantage. The assumption is that the performance of the parties in the government *in the interval between elections* has an immeasurably greater influence on public opinion than party platforms and campaign propaganda. Speeches become persuasive in relation to the actual record made by the party . . . nothing recommends a party so well as evidence that it knows its own mind, is able to mobilize its full legitimate strength in the government, is capable of governing and seriously intends to do so."[4] Unblushing admission by a party of its political identity may prove to be the party's most successful propaganda.

Perhaps worst of all, the ambiguities surrounding the program of each major party have had "one result that might easily have been anticipated —an enormous overdevelopment of pressure politics, because pressure groups feed upon their suc-

cesses. The political system has tended, therefore, to give excessive recognition to the claims of the special interests; and the whole policy and condition of the government reflect this fact."[5] Interestingly, one of the weakest points in this respect is the House of Representatives, the legislative body which theoretically is supposed to be closest to the people.

It is no longer a secret that the lower house of Congress is easily subjected to imprudent pressures. Two reasons have been advanced to explain this phenomenon.[6] The first of these has to do with the general composition of the House. Because of the inordinate delay of many state legislatures in recasting congressional districts, rural areas have long enjoyed an advantage over metropolitan centers that are deprived of the representatives which their rapidly increasing population justifies. The second reason relates to the pattern of House leadership which rests in the Speaker, the floor leaders, the members of the Rules Committee, and the chairmen of the standing committees. These leaders attain their positions by seniority, and this in turn means that those districts where one party habitually wins and which often are predominantly rural, provide that small group of leaders, regardless of which party is nominally in power. Naturally these "safe" districts, by and large, breed a conservative point of view.

The leaders of the House and rural representatives in general have tended to see eye to eye on many questions and hence have formed a fairly homogeneous body. "Business has found this a convenient and usually compliant group for achieving its purposes. The two major parties are more often quite evenly divided in metropolitan congressional districts and the competition there results in frequent shifts of power from one to the other of the major parties. As a consequence these metropolitan Congressmen seldom acquire the seniority so necessary to give them places of influence in the organization of the House. So metropolitan interest groups are relatively impotent in Congress."[7] The greater influence of rural elements in the House of Representatives thus gives larger play to pressures from business interests.

Finally, in view of the diffusion of power which weak national organization of the parties carries into Congress, it unavoidably falls to the president to step into the breach. This corollary is recognized even by those who think that our party system is excellent in its present form. Followers of this school of thought welcome such presidential efforts to keep the legislature on the course of a general program on the theory that the president is the only officer elected by all the people. They admit, however, that this situation leads inevitably to frequent conflicts between Congress and the chief executive.[8] Of course, the story does not end there. If the premise be granted, certain inferences become compelling. "Today we have come to recognize that this conflict is one of the most important obligations of the Presidency. No really strong executive tries to avoid it—he accepts it as an essential part of his job. If he simply tries to placate the pressure groups which speak through Congress, history writes him down as a failure. For it is his duty to enlist the support of many minorities for measures rooted in the national interest, reaching beyond their own immediate concern—and, if necessary, to stand up against the ravening minorities for the interest of the whole."[9] The only question is whether the prescription works as a *generally* effective formula of government. . . .

Demanding too much of the presidency amounts to a disservice to American government, for the representative assembly cannot safely shift its essential functions to any other place. This is true more than ever in a critical era such as the one ushered in by the outcome of World War II. Congress occupies a crucial position in a period of uncertainty. It is all too plain, therefore, that "the greatest single contribution our Congress could make to our security would be to show itself strong, efficient, and clear-cut so that its actions would yield neither ammunition to our enemies nor confusion to our friends."[10] A strong Congress means a Congress under conditions of party responsibility.

None of the great powers of government exists for small purposes. None is well exercised when it is frittered away. None is fully brought to bear on public business save when its exercise is planned. This, in simplest outline, is the case for program in government, and in particular for program in legislation.

The case for program is as old as government, but modern government has made this case progressively cogent. The challenge to pressure politics arises ultimately from the growing need for program, for the "notion that public policy can ever be the mere resultant of the blind pressures of a multitude of special interests each working for its selfish advantage is fantastic."[11] Public policy today must seek to shape the drive of diversified interests in such a way that advance is achieved over a single front involving many different governmental agencies.

In large measure, the mounting emphasis on comprehensive and coherent public programs is merely the reverse side of "big government." A piecemeal approach leads to defeat when coordi-

nation of a wide range of efforts is of the essence. But more is involved than "big government" as such. The American economy itself insists upon answers to its problems in the large. That is why the leaders of industry, labor, and agriculture are finding it necessary to define their own position, not in splendid isolation, but in relation to all of the basic interests affected. As one might expect, the political impact of our industrial evolution has not escaped attention. Over the decades, class politics has tended to outflank sectional politics,[12] but the slowest to capitalize on this tendency have been the two major parties.

In the day of "full employment" at home and uneasy political balance abroad, it is particularly evident that "there must be reasonable continuity and coherence of legislative policies if domestic programs and foreign relations are not to be jeopardized."[13] As a matter of fact, "the political problems which dominate our national life today, foreign policy and industrial policy, are precisely the problems which interest and pressure-group compromise is least equipped to handle."[14] Who, then, is to handle them? Can anyone propose an alternative to the one political agency marked for the task by its very purpose? The choice is between the majority party acting on a program and nothing. . . .

Because certain contemporaries feel stung by a common-use word like "plan," it seems equally possible to read more than one meaning into the word "program." A somewhat offensive implication of the word is suggested, for instance, in the assertion that "the American party has no permanent program and no fixed aim, except to win elections. Its one purpose is to unite the largest possible number of divergent interest groups in the pursuit of power. Its unity is one of compromise, not of dogma."[15] Here program is equated with dogma, absence of program with compromise.

This kind of differentiation has recently gained some cover behind the name of one of the most original minds in American political theory, John C. Calhoun. With program and compromise placed at opposite poles, Calhoun is made to emerge as the great formative influence in our national affairs. He is given much credit for the fact that "organization on the basis of sectional and interest compromise is both the distinctly American form of political organization and the cornerstone of practically all major political institutions of the modern United States."[16] . . .

One might guess that beneath the claims to unlimited political bargaining and the suspicions about any kind of program there is a feeling that program is somehow linked with principle, principle with faith, and faith with ideology. Ideology, it is felt in turn, should never be made the basis of party, because ideologically charged parties are bad for our health, gravitating toward extremes and dividing us too deeply. . . .

Nothing is clearer, however, than the fact that the difference between "polarized" parties and others does not lie in the presence or absence of a program. The decisive point is what constitutes the program. In other words, as a convenience of laying out goals of varying magnitudes and priority in an orderly relation to one another, program can render good service all the way from the trivial up to the momentous. Moreover, if the formation of "polarized" parties is to be prevented by deliberate design, one prerequisite is to make our existing parties fit for a superior showing. If they flounder for lack of program, by all means let the condition be repaired. We should not close our ears when a veteran campaigner says that the present condition of our party system "breeds immense popular cynicism concerning politics."[17] The fact that strong feeling, not cynicism, prevailed in the opening phase of the New Deal demonstrated how positive—though quite unideological—was the bond of program.[18]

Nor is it correct to say that the program formulated by his *party* would merely help to advance the estate of the president by aiding him to bully into line every member of his party in Congress. On the contrary, the biggest incentive toward executive dominance is a party *without* a program, for then the *president* must get the program from his own conviction or from somewhere else, usually jointly from an amalgamation of interest groups and the career bureaucracy. . . .

As a last point, it should perhaps be made explicit that precisely as there is flexibility under a constitution, so there is leeway under a program. No party needs literally to kill itself over its program. Nor is the party program the single statement of goal; from it must be forged the detailed legislative program in its specific application to each session. The particulars of the legislative agenda, including the timing of individual policy measures, are to a high degree matters of political judgment rather than matters of party program.

It is a remarkable fact that for nearly an entire generation American government has gone ahead in its steadfast quest of forms and means of program-making, while party organization has remained blissfully aloof from these moves. One must consider it unlikely that further adjustments to the needs of the twentieth century on the side of formal government alone will lead us significantly beyond the current stage. What is now most urgently necessary is appropriate action to effect a realignment of the party system with the structure of government as it operates in our day. It is the party system that has lagged behind.

Recognition of the need of government for viewing its sprawling activities as one tremendous but integrated enterprise dates back at least to the beginning of our century. The decisive step, however, was not taken until 1921 with the passage, after several years of unusually penetrating debate, of the Budget and Accounting Act.[19] This act made it the duty of the president annually to submit to Congress a comprehensive work plan for the government as a whole—the federal budget. It was felt that this should be the duty of the president because he had command of the full informational resources of the administration system and therefore access to the required facts and figures in proper detail; and, still more pertinently, because as head of his party the president alone could be charged politically with his budget proposal.[20] Of course, there would have been no point in charging him politically save for the fact that a thing like the annual work plan of the government called for *political* accounting. The president's willingness to be charged politically for it in fact meant a commitment by his party. . . .

Government made another step forward in the Employment Act of 1946,[21] the eventual outcome of legislative proposals to insure "full employment." The most important of these proposals had aimed at a full-scale annual debate in Congress of a formulated economic program to be written into law.[22] In the Employment Act this idea was modified by provision for a yearly economic report to Congress by the president, to be studied by a new joint committee; the committee, in turn, was directed to make early recommendations for the guidance of the standing committees in either house. Such guidance, of course, is apt to be feeble, and its reception by the other committees inhospitable, if the program assumptions of the majority of the Joint Committee on the Economic Report are not underpinned by an adequate party program, which then is taken as common coin by the members of the party on each committee.[23] As to the president, just as he gets his budget in shape with the assistance of the Budget Bureau, his economic report and similar policy recommendations are prepared with the help of a three-man Council of Economic Advisers as a source of high-grade professional judgment.[24] As part of the President's Executive Office, the Council looks to economic policy as a whole above the concerns of individual departments. But it gets its cue in policy matters from the president.

The latest move to increase the capacity of

American government for dealing with broad problems was the Legislative Reorganization Act,[25] brought under roof in the closing days of the Seventy-Ninth Congress. In a considerable number of ways, much to the surprise of the skeptics, this act has succeeded in tidying up both congressional organization and legislative procedure. But, measured against its original purposes,[26] it did not make enough headway in pushing responsibility upon the parties. The initially proposed pattern of party policy committees, together with legislative-executive arrangements to bridge the gap between the two main branches of government, never truly came about. Thus another chance was passed up for a workable scheme under which "party positions would be crystallized and clearly set forth."[27] . . .

It has been said that as to Congress we rely on "institutions which were not devised for the needs of a complicated economy."[28] But who is to contend that these institutions block all attempts at improvement? A major shortcoming in the present scheme is the lack of party responsibility, but the only obstacle to a national vitalization of our major parties lies in the ordinary inertia of a condition sanctioned by time, around which a thousand interests short of the general interest have wrapped their tentacles. The weight of inertia is not removed by mere pronouncement. It does dissolve, however, when exposed to the force of widespread understanding of the need for change. In welding this force for the common good, thoughtful citizens and public leaders inside and outside the political parties are able to make a telling contribution.

Notes

1. Walker, *The Legislative Process* 89 (1948).
2. In the case of each major party, "the organization as it appears on paper has little or no relation to the organization as it actually functions. For aid in campaigning, the national chairman may depend on state leaders, who occupy no position of importance in the state's formal party organization, and he may recognize them in the distribution of patronage. In turn, the state central committee and its chairman may exist largely on paper. The 'real' chairman may be someone other than the titular chairman. Within each party factional leaders of state-wide importance may have their county managers and leaders, loyal to them but not necessarily occupying positions in the formal party hierarchy. The machine that a national chairman, a state chairman, or a county chairman forms tends to be hierarchical, with lines of influence and authority binding it into a closely knit unit. Yet the hierarchy in fact often does not coincide in many respects with the formal organization as outlined in the laws and regulations." Key, *Politics, Parties, and Pressure Groups* 288-89 (rev. ed. 1947).
3. Schattschneider, *The Struggle for Party Government* 29-30 (1948) (italics in original).

4. *Id.* at 33 (italics in original).
5. Schattschneider, *Pressure Groups Versus Political Parties,* 259 Annals 17, 19 (1948).
6. Binkley, *The Party of Business,* 39 Fortune, No. 1, at 98, 106 (1949).
7. *Ibid.*
8. Fischer, *Unwritten Rules of American Politics,* 197 Harper's, No. 1182, at 27, 34 (1948).
9. *Ibid.*
10. Coyle, *Reorganizing Congress,* 24 Va. Q. Rev. 13, 14 (1948).
11. Schattschneider, *supra* note 13, at 19.
12. "The passing of the frontier and the growth of urban industry have shaken the foundations of the old party system in national politics. The old sectional interests are changing and the old sectional alliances are breaking down. . . . There will be less sectional politics and more class politics." Holcombe, *The New Party Politics* 11 (1933).
13. Galloway, *Congress at the Crossroads* 335 (1946).
14. Drucker, *supra* note 2, at 412. In the author's elaboration ". . . no foreign policy can be evolved by the compromise of sectional interests or economic pressures. . . . An industrial society cannot function without an organ able to superimpose the national interest on economic or class interests." *Id.* at 422-23. See also Morstein Marx (ed.), *Formulating the Federal Government's Economic Program: A Symposium,* 42 Am. Pol. Sci. Rev. 272 (1948).
15. Fischer, *supra* note 16, at 32-33.
16. Drucker, *supra* note 2, at 412.
17. Thomas, *supra* note 18, at 24.
18. The "Roosevelt charm" rested in good measure upon a tough willingness to undertake program commitments, and thus to draw together various sources of support. This is conceded even by an observer who is generally inclined to plead for "party politics as usual," as the following statement shows: "The classic alliance of this sort was formed in the early days of the New Deal, when most of the Roosevelt legislation was shoved onto the statute books by a temporary coalition of the farm bloc and urban labor, occasionally reinforced by such minor allies as the public power group and spokesmen for the northern Negroes. Mr. Roosevelt's political genius rested largely on his ability to put together a program which would offer something to each of these groups without fatally antagonizing any of them, and then to time the presentation of each bill so that he would always retain enough bargaining power to line up a Congressional majority." Fischer, *supra* note 16, at 31.
19. 42 Stat. 20 (1921), 31 U.S.C. § 1 *et seq.* (1946).
20. The history of the Budget and Accounting Act is traced in Morstein Marx, *The Bureau of the Budget: Its Evolution and Present Role I,* 39 Am. Pol. Sci. Rev. 653 (1945).
21. 60 Stat. 23 (1946), 15 U.S.C. §§ 1021-1024 (1946).
22. For an exposition of this proposal and its underlying motives, see Murray, *A Practical Approach,* in *Maintaining High-Level Production and Employment: A Symposium,* 39 Am. Pol. Sci. Rev. 1119 (1945).
23. An incisive discussion of the problems faced by the joint committee may be found in Flanders, *Administering the Employment Act—The First Year,* 7 Pub. Adm. Rev. 221 (1947).
24. For an authoritative analysis of this new agency, see Nourse and Gross, *The Role of the Council of Economic Advisers,* 42 Am. Pol. Sci. Rev. 283 (1948).
25. 60 Stat. 812 (1946).
26. For an informative review, see La Follette, *Systematizing Congressional Control,* 41 Am. Pol. Sci. Rev. 58 (1947).
27. *Id.* at 63. A comprehensive appraisal of the organizational and procedural condition of Congress is presented by Galloway, *op. cit. supra* note 25.
28. Young, *This Is Congress* 267 (1943).

7. PRESIDENCY AND LEGISLATION:
THE GROWTH OF CENTRAL CLEARANCE

Richard E. Neustadt

TEN MONTHS AFTER President Eisenhower's inaugural, an article in *Fortune* extolled a presidential aide in terms which would have seemed familiar ten months before;[1] the picture of his role in Eisenhower's entourage might easily have been drawn in President Truman's time. The subject of this piece was Roger W. Jones, an Assistant Director of the Bureau of the Budget and chief of its Office of Legislative Reference. In *Fortune's* terms, here was a confidential, if "non-political," member of the White House circle performing tasks of great importance to the President, trusted, respected, and relied upon by all of his associates. As an analysis of governmental functions and relationships, this testimonial was scarcely definitive, but its mere publication testifies to the continuation of the Budget Bureau's so-called legislative clearance operations, handily surviving the Great Transition of 1953.

What are these clearance operations? Essentially they amount to central coordination and review of stands taken by the various federal agencies at three successive stages of the legislative process.

Large numbers of the public measures introduced in Congress are formally proposed by agencies of the executive branch; departmental drafts officially en route to Congress first have to clear the Bureau of the Budget for interagency coordination and approval on the President's behalf. Once bills are introduced, regardless of their source, congressional committees ordinarily solicit views from interested agencies; official agency responses—in whatever form, to whomever addressed—first channel through the Budget Bureau for coordination and advice on each bill's relation to the President's program. When enrolled enactments come from Congress to the President for signature or veto, the Budget Bureau, as his agent, obtains, coordinates, and summarizes agency opinion on the merits, preparing in each case a presidential dossier complete with covering recommendation. These are the components of "legislative clear-

ance" as the term is normally employed.[2] In practice, these operations are much more complex and a good deal less absolute than this simple recital would indicate. But generally speaking, central clearance has proceeded along these lines for many years.

In 1953, despite the change of Administration, 380 agency drafts, 3,571 agency reports on pending bills, and 525 enrolled enactments were processed by the Budget Bureau.[3] In 1954, the Bureau's Office of Legislative Reference, control center for clearance operations, is handling an even larger volume—with President Eisenhower and Budget Director Hughes earnestly supporting clearance regulations in effect since 1948, signed by a Budget Director long out of office, issued "by direction" of the President whose term expired January 20, 1953.[4]

Here is presidential machinery to coordinate a vital aspect of executive policy development; machinery to control, in some degree at least, the means by which the diverse elements of the executive express and implement their own designs. In Truman's time this mechanism was, as one observer put it, "the only clearing house that operates regularly between the multitudinous departments and bureaus . . . sometimes the only possible way to get government agencies working together. . . ."[5] In the present Administration, it may well be that legislative clearance is losing this particular distinction. Elsewhere in the Executive Office of the President, new life has been breathed into the National Security Council, as an apparatus of policy coordination and control. Even the Council of Economic Advisers, with its revised chairmanship and interdepartmental advisory board, shows signs of institutional advance in these directions. So, indeed, does the Cabinet—though history suggests this may not last.

But if legislative clearance is no longer unique, it is by far the oldest, best intrenched, most thoroughly institutionalized of the President's coordinative instruments—always excepting the budget itself—receiving new stability and new significance by virtue of its demonstrated power to adapt and

Reprinted from *American Political Science Review*, Vol. 48 (September, 1954), pp. 641-71, by permission of the author and the publisher.

to survive. And this power is not something suddenly achieved and first displayed in 1953. The central clearance system has surmounted every governmental transition since the 1920's, preserving into Eisenhower's term not only the accretions of two Democratic decades, but even the inheritance from Harding, Coolidge, and Hoover.

What is the nature of this mechanism? How has it adapted? Why has it survived? These are the questions to which this paper is addressed.[6]

I. Financial Clearance in the Twenties. When President Harding approved the Budget and Accounting Act on June 10, 1921, the federal agencies lost their historic freedom to decide for themselves what appropriations they should ask of Congress; now the President, alone, was to decide and to request, with a new staff agency, the Budget Bureau, to help him do it. Moreover, in accordance with the Act's intent, but one committee in each House of Congress was to receive and review appropriation requests.[7] Here, prescribed in law, was a new restrictive way of handling the life-and-death concerns of every agency—and most congressmen. And here were new organizations with a tremendous institutional stake in the successful assertion of that new way: the presidential Bureau of the Budget and the congressional Committees on Appropriations. Furthermore, these organizations had a clear mutuality of interest in closing off, as nearly as might be, all avenues to action on appropriations save their own. Substantive congressional committees, no less than executive agencies, were potential conspirators against the exclusive jurisdictions conferred by the new budget system. Facing common dangers, the system's beneficiaries made common cause. Central legislative clearance was a principal result.

It is significant of this community of interest that the original proposal for some form of central clearance came not from the new Budget Bureau, but from the House Appropriations Committee. In November, 1921, less than a month before the first presidential budget went to Congress, the Committee Chairman voiced to the Budget Director his concern about two minor measures—introduced at an agency's request and referred to a substantive committee—which authorized diversion of appropriated funds from the purposes originally specified. In the Chairman's view, ". . . matters of this character should come through the Bureau of the Budget . . . I have called them to your attention in order that you may take . . . steps . . . to include [such] requests . . . in the control which the Bureau has over direct estimates."[8] It was this congressional observation which precipitated the first presidential effort to assert central control over agency views on proposed and pending legislation, an effort embodied in Budget Circular 49, issued December 19, 1921, "by direction of the President," after clearance with the House Committee.

This first approach to legislative clearance was a rather curious affair. The language of the Budget Circular was very sweeping, requiring—in accordance with the "spirit" of the Budget and Accounting Act—that all agency proposals for legislation or expressions of views on pending legislation "the effect of which would be to create a charge upon the public treasury or commit the government to obligations which would later require appropriations," be submitted to the Budget Bureau before presentation to Congress. The Bureau was to make recommendations to the President, ascertain the "relationship of the legislation to the President's financial program," and advise the agencies accordingly. Agency proposals for legislation were to go forward only if approved by the President; agency views on pending legislation, when presented to Congress, were to include a statement of the advice received from the Budget Bureau.[9]

Here, at least on paper, was a new assertion of presidential control over the agencies, a new form of continuing staff intervention between President and department heads, conceptually a radical departure in American administration matched only by the new budget process. Yet the official sponsors of Circular 49 avowed no such intent. There is nothing in the record prior to the order's issuance to show that either the Budget Director or the President grasped these implications in the language they approved.[10] But there is plenty in the record demonstrating that the members of the Cabinet did not leave them long in ignorance, once the order had gone out. The subsequent course of legislative clearance in Harding's time is mainly a matter of apologies, concessions, limitations tacitly approved or self-applied, to soften agency reactions against Circular 49.

The agencies were aroused both by the Circular's potential coverage—broadly interpreted, its criteria reached virtually all subjects of legislation—and by interposition of the Budget Bureau between them and the President on such a range of measures. In beating his retreat, at the President's behest, Dawes did not try to find fixed subject-matter limits for his procedure; instead he let it be known that matters of importance could be cleared with the President directly. Only on routine affairs would the Budget act as agent.[11] In practice, Dawes went even farther, leaving interpretation and compliance to departmental discretion. The Budget Bureau neither guided nor protested; the agencies proceeded accordingly.

For two years Circular 49 remained in limbo.

Then a new Administration seized on this empty order and within it built a strong and well enforced, if narrowly defined accessory to central budgeting. The forms of financial clearance are traceable to Harding's time. The actuality begins with Coolidge.

By early 1924, the presidential budget system was a going concern, veteran of three "budget seasons." The Budget Bureau had been staffed and organized, routines established, procedures set. The Bureau's leadership had passed from Dawes to his hand-picked successor, General Lord, a zealot for the small economy.[12] And the presidency had passed to perhaps the most determined economizer ever to hold the office. "I am for economy and after that I am for more economy," so Coolidge put it, conceiving economy not merely as a matter of politics or economics, but as an exercise in personal morality, an ethical principle, a constitutional requirement, an end in itself.[13] In the Coolidge Administration the theme of budget policy was reduction: reduction of expenditures, of taxes, and of the public debt, with presidential budgeting mainly a means of cutting back on current outlays and avoiding new commitments. It is in this context that legislative clearance was revived.

Early in 1924, the Budget Bureau, with presidential support, began a vigorous campaign to activate Circular 49. For nearly two years, Lord peppered key departments with letters of warning, abjuration, and complaint, backed by a considerable amount of Budget staff investigation and analysis.[14] By 1926, he was able to report that agency compliance had become "practically universal."[15] Of course, the Coolidge clearance system, thus successfully asserted, was carried on within a very narrow frame of reference. Cabinet officers were constrained to accept Budget Bureau placement between them and the President, but only on proposals clearly costing money, and only with respect to cost, not substance. The Bureau's task of ascertaining the relationship of agency proposals to presidential program was rendered relatively safe and sure by virtue of the program's identification with recorded budget policies and estimates.

The purpose of the exercise is clear from Budget's rules of thumb for processing what came its way. An adverse agency report on a pending measure was usually taken as conclusive. An affirmative report resulted in careful scrutiny of relationship to the current budget and implications for future years. It was common practice to hold favorable agency reports "in conflict" with the President's financial program. Frequently, legislation was held "in conflict" unless the money authorization were reduced. This negative advice also applied wherever a semblance of prior legislative authority could be found to render the current proposal "unnecessary."[16] When the Bureau was confronted with opposing views from two departments, its normal procedure was to endorse the negative position. If this were not feasible, an independent staff analysis was sometimes made the basis for decision. Changes in drafting were sometimes suggested to the agencies, but always as a Budget idea, not as the result of any effort at coordination. Occasionally, the Bureau would attempt to mediate major differences of opinion, but it never undertook to seek them out.

The Coolidge clearance system, then, was quite straightforward in its negative endeavor to buttress the President's control over his budget policies and his—or the Budget Bureau's—forward financial plans. In no sense did the system operate as a coordinative or developmental mechanism in areas of substantive policy. And what was true in Coolidge's Administration was also true in his successor's term. President Hoover not only inherited and applied this form of central clearance, he even refined its terms of reference, emphasizing more than ever its budgetary association and its negative cast.

Shortly after his inauguration, Hoover suggested that the Budget Bureau take no action on agency requests for clearance unless and until it received a clear intimation of congressional interest. The President intended personally to approve all clearance actions and saw no point in bothering with measures which were not going to receive action.[17] A further refinement followed late in 1929, when Hoover sanctioned a formal amendment to Circular 49 exempting from clearance all agency reports on private bills and all *unfavorable* reports on public bills.[18]

These minor changes simply put finishing touches on the edifice of Coolidge clearance; within these limits, the character of clearance actions remained unchanged through Hoover's term. His budgetary problems became immeasurably more difficult than Coolidge's had been. As the economic decline worsened after 1929 and federal revenues fell steadily, enormous pressures built up for increased federal spending. But the Hoover Administration remained unalterably opposed to deliberate deficit financing, and in its clearance operations the Budget Bureau tried harder than ever to ward off all possible legislative authorizations for unbudgeted expenditure.[19] Of course, after the mid-term elections of 1930 the President was unable either to develop a coherent budget policy and make it stick, or to avoid the opposition's criticism for his failure to do so. And in that painful situation, financial clearance became the least of remedies.

II. The Roosevelt Revolution and Policy Clearance. President Franklin D. Roosevelt's inaugural in 1933 was accompanied by a clean sweep topside in all the departments, after twelve years of continuity under the Republicans. The procedures for financial clearance had grown up in those years and concern about them, or even understanding of them, seems to have been carried off with the outgoing Administration. The succeeding regime was enormously busy and very new.[20] Only the President himself was really familiar with governmental administration. His cabinet members were novices at it.[21] Moreover, they were moving at much too fast a pace to stop for the niceties of an auxiliary budget procedure.

They moved fast; they moved the federal government into unprecedented ventures, into new spheres of action on many different fronts. The first years of the New Deal released a torrent of measures for reform, and these were mingled with a host of shifting, often contradictory improvisations in the fight against depression. Roosevelt had pledged financial stringency in the 1932 campaign, attacking Hoover on home grounds. During the next two years "sound money" and "economy in government" remained on-again-off-again themes, but sounding ever fainter as the New Deal gathered impetus, their principal adherents mostly out of office before the end of 1934.[22]

The motives which led Coolidge's Administration to stress financial clearance were scarcely in the forefront of the new regime's concerns. Not until January, 1934, did the Budget Bureau take any steps to remind department heads of their continuing obligations under the old circulars. And then the Bureau's action was muted, almost apologetic. Taken by the staff, not the Director, it was a bureaucratic restoration of routines, not in any sense a presidentially-inspired campaign for compliance.[23]

Roosevelt's contribution to central clearance was of quite another order. Nearly a year after this Budget Bureau "restoration" of financial clearance, the President took the initiative in launching a different kind of clearance: clearance of all agency proposals for legislation, "policy" clearance in substantive terms.

Roosevelt brought the matter up on his own motion at a National Emergency Council Meeting in December, 1934, shortly before the convening of the 74th Congress. He told the assembled officials he had decided to stop the practice of uncoordinated agency requests for legislation. At the preceding session of Congress he had been "quite horrified—not once but half a dozen times

—by reading in the paper that some department or agency was after this, that, or the other without my knowledge."[24] He wanted no more of that. In the future, agency officials should come to him with their proposals before taking them to Congress.

One Cabinet officer observed that the departments were already clearing through the Budget Bureau. Roosevelt brushed this aside. "That," he said, "was for appropriations. What I am talking about is legislation. . . . Coming down to legislation there has never been any clearing house . . . and, I think in the last analysis that has got to be tied in and go through the National Emergency Council . . . and up to me if necessary. In all probability it will come to me."[25]

On December 13, 1934, the secretariat of the Emergency Council followed up the President's remarks with a memorandum to all members, signed by Donald Richberg, then NEC's Executive Director. This instructed the agencies that at the forthcoming Congress all proposals for appropriations and all bills "carrying appropriations measures" should be cleared with the President through the Bureau of the Budget. All "other proposed legislation" was to be cleared through the Council's Executive Director, or in certain cases with special-purpose NEC committees.

While this directive referred to proposals only and contained a caveat on appropriation matters, its language was far from precise. The result was wide-spread confusion over the relationship between the new procedure and the old Budget circulars. In April, 1935, the Acting Budget Director, Daniel Bell, protested to Richberg; the problem was raised at an Emergency Council meeting on April 23 and the President decided that clarifying instructions should go out.[26] These took the form of a new Budget Circular 336, issued "by direction of the President" on December 21, 1935.[27]

Circular 336 brought together and superseded outstanding NEC directives, as well as previous Budget circulars. It provided that all agency proposals for legislation and all reports on pending legislation should clear through the Budget Bureau "for consideration by the President," before submission to Congress; as before, private relief bills were exempted. Agency proposals or reports when subsequently sent to Congress were to include a statement as to "whether proposed legislation was or was not in accord with the President's program." This was also to apply to oral testimony before congressional committees.

Procedurally, the circular provided that the Budget Bureau was to check directly with the President on legislation "solely concerning fiscal matters." Legislation "solely concerning policy matters" was to be referred to the President through the Emergency Council staff. The two organizations were to clear with him jointly on legislation involving both "fiscal" and "policy" matters. The Council was to inform the Bureau of clearances which it obtained from the President independently; the Bureau was to inform the agencies in all instances.

In print—and in practice—these procedures had a very clumsy look; for obvious reasons they proved cumbersome and somewhat unrealistic. Two years later they were superseded. But while the mechanics were transitional, the basic requirements have remained in force, without essential change, for nineteen years.

The Roosevelt clearance system, thus established, incorporated its financial precursor but was no mere extension of the budget process.[28] On the contrary, in form and fact and terms of reference this was Roosevelt's creation, intended to protect not just his budget, but his prerogatives, his freedom of action, and his choice of policies, in an era of fast-growing government and of determined presidential leadership.

Roosevelt's statements make it plain that he sought to protect both President from agencies and agencies from one another. In the first place, he wanted the Administration's stand made known on agency proposals, not only in his own defense but for the sake of everyone concerned, including the congressional leaders. Of these proposals he remarked:

They fall into three categories: first, the kind of legislation that, administratively, I could not give approval to—[clearance] will eliminate that; secondly, the type of legislation which we are perfectly willing to have the department or agency press for, but at the same time we do not want to put it in the [third] category of major Administration bills. Obviously I have to confine myself to what the newspapers called last year "the comparatively small list of *must* legislation." If I make every bill that the Government is interested in *must* legislation, it is going to complicate things . . . very much; and where I clear legislation with a notation that says "no objection" that means you are at perfect liberty to try to get the thing through, but I am not going to send a special message for it. It is all your trouble, not mine.[29]

In the second place, it was good business to have ideas and information contributed by all agencies concerned, not just the originating departments. Having bills cleared through a central agency would, in Roosevelt's words, "give somebody else outside the department itself the opportunity to have happy thoughts."[30] Moreover, such exchanges in advance would prevent crossed wires within the Administration. The President did not want the agencies "stepping on each others' toes"

and he definitely did not want them "stepping on mine . . . :"

Just the other day a resolution was passed through Congress—a House resolution that did not even have to come to me—asking for a certain report on a very important matter from one of the departments. It was a policy matter. The department was asked to send the report up to the Committee and nobody outside the department knew about it. We happened to catch it. If the report had gone up in the form in which it was prepared, it would have been absolutely contrary to the policy of the Government.[31]

On pending bills which the Administration had not sponsored, he wanted the departments to keep out of each others' way:

In all our testimony before Congress and in all our answers to questions, let us stick to our own last and let us be factual about it. This is one of the most important things that has been said for a long time . . . let us say the Secretary of Agriculture goes up there and he doesn't know much about the bill, but he knows that he is going to be asked about it. It might . . . [relate] . . . not only to Agriculture but to Interior and some other departments as well and he ought to in some way find out what the general attitude is through some kind of clearing house. . . .[32]

Thus Roosevelt expressed the purpose of his new clearance system: by and large a negative purpose, even as Coolidge's had been. An opportunity for "happy thoughts" apart, the system's new coordinative elements, no less than broadened clearances, were seen primarily as means to keep the many-voiced executive from shouting itself down in the legislative process.

Granting Roosevelt's purpose, what, in fact, did he obtain? Initially, not very much:

Clearance as practiced in the 74th Congress [1935-6] was restricted almost entirely to minor departmental bills . . . nearly all of the really important bills and many minor measures originating in the Executive Branch, did not pass through this machinery. . . . Matters discussed with the President in person by a department head were not submitted for clearance, except in a few cases . . . the President's approval, orally given or read into his statements was deemed sufficient . . . nearly all of the measures about which the President sent messages to the Congress [the major administration bills] . . . [were] . . . exempt from clearance . . . many lesser matters also escaped such checking.[33]

This appraisal was based on a study utilizing only Emergency Council records. A later survey of the period, based on Budget Bureau files, concluded that there was "less evidence of deliberate agency failure to comply . . . than of Bureau failure to follow the prescribed procedure in the clearance of policy matters."[34] Perhaps so—but there is nothing in print or on file to controvert the general tenor of the earlier view.

Yet by 1939 the Budget Director was talking confidently before Congress of the scope and general coverage of central clearance.[35] In 1943, an acute and experienced observer could write that Budget clearance was "frequently commanding," the Bureau's influence "very great."[36] For this changed appraisal at least four things were responsible: the demise of NEC, the Budget Bureau's great expansion, the slowing down of New Deal creativity, and the formal marriage of central clearance to the veto power.

The Emergency Council was dying on the vine by 1936, commanding little presidential interest, or agency respect. Its diminished status and potential were accurately reflected in the Brownlow Committee's recommendation that the Council be abolished, and its staff activities discarded or dispersed.[37] Undoubtedly the Council's relative and growing weakness had much to do with the lax attitude of agencies and Budget Bureau toward the Executive Director's prerogatives under Circular 336. Had he been the sole institutional peg for "policy" clearance, that process might well have gone under also, retrievable with difficulty, if at all. But behind him stood the Budget. When he vanished, it inherited. This happened, actually, as a matter of course, a detail of administrative tidying, a minor item among all the major changes in the Bureau's status, role, and outlook envisaged by and following upon the Brownlow Committee Report of January, 1937.[38]

In the two years after publication of the Report, the Bureau moved, as never since the twenties, to strengthen and consolidate its clearance operations. In the spring of 1937, Director Bell loosed a stream of correspondence on the agencies, reminiscent of Lord's effort thirteen years before.[39] In December, 1937, Circular 336 was formally re-issued—renumbered 344—as a means of removing reference to the Emergency Council in official clearance instructions.[40] Henceforth, the Bureau was to be in form and fact the President's sole institutional clearance agent, on matters of substance no less than finance. Internally, also, the Bureau acted—Brownlow Report in hand—to put new life and strength into the job. In 1938, Bell increased the staff assigned specifically to clearance work, reorganized it as a separate, full-time, undertaking and gave it status as a major Bureau function, autonomously organized in a Division of Coordination, precursor of the present Office of Legislative Reference.[41]

During 1939, in the first session of the 76th Congress, the Budget Bureau processed agency reports on 2,448 pending public bills. Four years before, in the days of financial clearance, only 300 pending measures had been covered by submissions to the Bureau. Again, in 1939 the Bureau handled 438 drafts of proposed legislation; this compares with 170 proposals sent by the agencies to NEC under the procedure of 1935, or 162 proposals sent to NEC and Budget both, under the procedure of 1936.[42] These figures are illustrative of the rise in clearance coverage after 1937, though nothing can be more elusive than the search for such objective measurements, nor anything more misleading than raw data of this type.[43] But there are other evidences also, in Budget Bureau files of agency and White House correspondence, and in transcripts of legislative hearings and debate, to demonstrate that central clearance was now reaching wider than before.[44]

The climate of the times, perhaps, contributed to this no less than did improved organization and procedure. The main thrust of New Deal innovation was long past by 1939. The emergency had lost its cutting edge; emergency agencies had either disappeared or dug roots into routine. In Europe and in Asia world war threatened. In Congress, the anti-New Deal coalition had become a formidable fact of life. In the executive, sails were trimmed accordingly. Real legislative ambitions for most agencies were now measured largely by consolidation and amendment—goals much more easily contained in clearance channels than the great, unprecedented ventures once hurried before relatively complaisant Congresses.

And one thing more: in 1938, the Budget Bureau gained a new sanction, and an unassailable rationale, for its clearance of proposed and pending measures. That year, the Bureau came into control of agency communications to the President on signature or veto of enrolled bills. Henceforth, Roosevelt's clearance agency was also his chief institutional advisor on the generality of measures passed by Congress. Within this combination lay real power, and the Bureau made the most of it.

III. Policy Clearance and the Veto Power. Traditionally, Presidents have sought advice from their department heads on disposition of enrolled enactments. Until the thirties, though, this custom had some drastic built-in limitations. When an enrolled bill reached the White House, the President's Secretary or Executive Clerk would hazard a quick guess at the agencies concerned; the bill itself would then be passed by hand to each in turn—a document of state, handled with care—and their replies, filtering back, one by one, would get such correlation as hard-pressed White House aides might manage. All this went on during the ten days within which the President could veto. Frequently he was but poorly served, receiving very late, for fast decision, an ill-digested mountain of material.[45]

From its establishment in 1921, the Budget Bureau had been asked for views on each enrolled appropriations bill. In 1934, Roosevelt told his staff to get Bureau reactions on all private relief bills involving an expenditure of funds. His aides went one step further, urging—as a measure for their own relief—that on such bills the Bureau also seek and summarize the views of other agencies concerned. This worked, and presently, without fanfare, the White House staff began to send across the street all manner of substantive public bills as well, asking the Bureau to circularize agencies and correlate views. By 1938 almost all enrolled bills were going to the Bureau for this handling. That year, the few exceptions followed no clear line of demarcation; after 1939, there were no more exceptions. This process of pragmatic delegation took but five years, from start to finish.

So long as the original enrollments had to be handed around, the Budget Bureau was as helpless as the White House staff had been to make of this anything but a thankless, mainly ministerial performance. In 1938, however, the Public Printer was persuaded to prepare facsimile copies of each enrolled bill; these went directly to the Bureau at the same time the original went back to Congress for signature by Speaker and Vice President. Armed with these copies, the Bureau could put an official text before each agency simultaneously, hours or even days before the bill itself could reach the White House and the President's time began to run.

This was a simple, mechanical improvement, but what it gave was time, and time spelled opportunity. On January 19, 1939, the Bureau issued "by direction of the President" Circular 346, defining agency obligations under the new procedure. For the first time Budget was identified officially as presidential agent on all enrolled enactments. Bureau requests for agency opinions were to receive an absolute priority; agency replies were to be forthcoming within forty-eight hours, and were to include in each case a specific recommendation, backed by as much factual information as possible. Any recommendation against presidential signature was to be accompanied by a draft veto message or memorandum of disapproval (for use with pocket vetoes). In these terms Circular 346 formalized previous practice, giving it a mandatory application beyond anything remotely possible in absence of facsimile procedure.[46]

Within the Budget Bureau, corresponding steps were taken. The chores of asking agencies for views, pressuring the dilatory, correlating replies, reworking message drafts, were all put on a centralized and systematic basis. Summaries and covering recommendations to the President were now developed uniformly, carefully, and in much greater detail than before. All this took organization, specialization, and somebody's time and effort; by 1939, the Bureau had these at hand in its Division of Coordination. There full responsibility for enrolled bills was vested.

This new function quickly became the key element in central clearance. The Budget Bureau's work on agency proposals and reports built up a general, comprehensive record, unmatched elsewhere in government, to buttress its consideration of enrolled bills. At the same time, its mandate on enrolled enactments now lent special point and purpose to clearances of measures in proposed and pending stages.[47]

The veto power's potency in this connection depends, of course, upon its use, and Roosevelt was a constant user. "If the decision is close," he once remarked to his department heads, "I want to veto."[48] In 1939, he chose to veto sixteen bills despite approval by the Budget Bureau, remarking to an aide, "The Budget is getting too soft; tell them to stiffen up."[49] Indeed, he was prone to call occasionally for "something I can veto," as a "reminder" to department heads and congressmen alike.[50] This was not frivolity; to FDR the veto power was among the presidency's greatest attributes, an independent and responsible act of participation in the legislative process, and a means of enforcing congressional and agency respect for presidential preferences or programs.[51]

From the beginning, Roosevelt placed a great deal of reliance on the Budget Bureau's weighing and sifting of bureaucratic opinion. On the generality of measures he inclined to discount Cabinet, congressional, and interest group advices which found their joint and several ways directly to the White House. But he took care that there should be, between him and the Budget, some White House staff review to check the institutional approach against the personal, to balance off the presidency with the President. In 1943, that task went to Judge Rosenman, in his new post as Special Counsel to the President; there, with temporary lapses, it has remained, assumed by each of Rosenman's successors in Truman's time and Eisenhower's.[52]

The Budget Bureau took its staff work on enrolled enactments as seriously as Roosevelt did his veto power. Here, unchallengeably in the Budget's hands, was all-important preparation for decisive acts of state, exclusively in presidential jurisdiction. Of course, on the great, controversial measures, the White House could expect appraisals and advice from many other sources and through many other channels. But usually on the general run of bills enrolled at every session, particularly the private bills, the Budget file was the "works." Within the Bureau, priorities were set accordingly.

In Roosevelt's later years, no other element of central clearance received half the attention, time, and effort which Bureau staff gave to enrolled enactments, especially to lesser issues where its word weighed the most. From 1940 on, coordination of proposed and pending bills was routinized increasingly, with stress on negative, protective aspects only, and great reliance on the written word. Rarely were agencies called in for face-to-face discussion; rarely were efforts made to conform clearance actions with the exigencies of the legislative timetable. If agencies and committees wanted such advantages as clearance offered at the pending stage, they could ask and wait their turn; if not, they took their chances when the bills became enrolled.

IV. From Roosevelt to Truman. The coming of World War II confirmed this Budget Bureau tendency to concentrate on enrolled bills, its inescapable job, while energy, interest, and opportunity were diverted from staff work on proposed and pending measures. The war itself made operating policies and administrative actions the pivotal affairs of government. Congress lost the center of the stage; the legislative process ceased to be either the Administration's chief concern, or the nation's main measure of governmental progress.

"Dr. New Deal" was succeeded by "Dr. Win-the-War." The new physician prescribed far less than the old in the way of urgent home-front legislation—and most of this in war-related fields, now the concern of new emergency agencies. This was not the stuff, nor these the agencies, to stay confined in peacetime clearance channels. And once their operating conflicts forced establishment of an effective wartime instrument for mediation and control—the Office of War Mobilization—their legislative conflicts and ambitions gravitated toward the War Mobilizer, not the Budget Director.[53] The result, of course, was to down-grade all previous coordinators on the governmental stage—not least the Budget Bureau's clearance mechanism. OWM action in the legislative field was limited, deliberately, to matters of the highest policy or greatest urgency. But by the war's end, its successor's interests were proliferating through the government. Most Budget staff accepted, without much demur, OWM's wartime over-shadowing of their coordinating role; they took with far less grace OWMR's widening postwar interventions on the legislative front.

Meanwhile, Truman suddenly succeeded to the presidency. With this the Budget Bureau's role was shaken mightily amidst pangs of transition unmatched since 1933. The two years after Roosevelt's death were doubly transitional: the government was entangled in a complex shift from war to peace and back again to something in-between; the presidency was in process of adjustment from the old to a new personality, and to new work methods and interpersonal relationships. It was a complex, clouded, often contradictory time, climaxed by the congressional overturn of November, 1946. To the great alterations in the executive, there were now added many changes in personalities and power on Capitol Hill, profoundly affecting relationships and atmosphere at both ends of the Avenue.

In all this swirl, the Budget Bureau stumbled badly, its prestige and position challenged as rarely before or since. Most of the services Roosevelt had charged it to perform were little understood, at first, by the new President and his new team of close associates; legislative clearance least of all. "I simply do not see," allegedly remarked one high-placed Truman aide, "why [legislative] *policy* is any business of the *Budget* Bureau."[54] Truman's three successive OWMR Directors—Vinson, Snyder, and Steelman—were all, in varying degree, much closer to the President than were the holdover Budget leaders, Smith and Appleby. And in the months after V-J day, it was to OWMR, not Budget, that Truman and his White House aides looked mainly for help on policy problems, legislative and other.

By mid-summer, 1946, the Budget Bureau's status in the presidential orbit had reached its lowest point. OWMR seemed superficially to be assured a strong, perhaps a permanent position. A new staff agency of unknown policy potential, the Council of Economic Advisers, had just been authorized by statute.[55] Between these two, the Budget's future role, particularly in the legislative sphere, appeared attenuated and uncertain.

Yet scarcely two years later the Bureau was entrenched as the prime source of presidential staff work on the Administration's legislative program, its clearance tasks, especially at proposed and pending stages, more actively developed and more central to the President's concerns than ever in their history. Three things, mainly, lay behind this change: reappearance of the legislative process as the key government preoccupation; attrition or demise of other institutional staff facilities; and the personality of James E. Webb, Truman's new Director of the Budget.

The first Truman term, be it remembered, was a time of executive retrenchment, of climbing down from wartime peaks. The early Fair Deal blueprinted many a large-scale peacetime venture in administration, but save for atomic energy and foreign aid—and the short-lived emergency housing program—these remained largely on paper. For this was a time, also, of congressional stalemate in home affairs, and these new ventures needed legislation. Numerous issues of domestic policy confronting the regime were, therefore, first cast up in legislative guise, then frozen in that status by an unresponsive Congress.[56] The operating tasks, which in their magnitude had called forth OWM, were finished; nothing comparable took their place. Presidential messages to Congress became the central focus for policymaking; legislative drafts the major means for translating policy into coordinated action. With Congress formally in opposition after 1946, the object of the game—save in the foreign field—turned into record-building, pure and simple. But more than mere demands were needed in the record; for someday there might be response, if not from the current Congress, then the next. Serious proposals had to be specific; specifics meaningful—and viable.

This called for central staff work, continuous effort on a large scale. Where could it be obtained? The OWMR staff had been dispersed, abruptly, at the end of 1946; Steelman, its last Director, had returned to the White House in the new post of Assistant to the President.[57] The Economic Council was then untried, preoccupied, and short on staff, its product showing from the first the strains imposed by step-child status and divergent membership.[58] The White House Staff—the President's Assistant, Special Counsel, and the rest—could guide, review, and interject, but scarcely could engage in all the detailed and continuous endeavors these legislative tasks required.

This left only the Budget Bureau, or some new creation. And at the crucial moment the new Budget Director managed to reorient the Bureau's role anent the Truman White House, thereby giving the President the staff work he required.

By early 1947, Webb had become a principal adviser to the President, a full-fledged member of the Truman team. This built the Budget's entree and Webb made much of it, selling staff services as he sold himself. He broke precedent by making his subordinates freely available to White House aides, on their terms, for their purposes.[59] He cheerfully acceded to several full-time transfers of Budget staff to White House assistantships, thus building bridges which were bound to last.[60] Above all, Webb turned to his machinery for legislative clearance as a prime means of focussing staff efforts to help meet the President's needs. The clearance of proposals and reports had not

been sensitive to congressional schedules; it was to become so. The emphasis of central clearance had been negative; it was to be made positive. It had interpreted policies and programs where it found them; it was to help create them. It had relied on Bureau staff resources; it was to draw, instead, on the expanding Executive Office as a whole.

Those were the goals Webb set for central clearance in Truman's time. To implement them he relied on a reconstituted Legislative Reference organization, now given status as a sort of institutional Executive Office secretariat for legislative policy development, formally within the Budget Bureau but serving, in effect, as back-up staff to Truman's Special Counsel, then chief White House officer in fields of forward policy.[61] Webb did not delegate all responsibility, nor abdicate all interest, but as a practical matter, Legislative Reference's White House ties became both real and generally respected.

V. The Character of Clearance in Truman's Time. All this involved great changes in the character of clearance at proposed and pending stages. After 1947, the Budget Bureau's war-encouraged passive attitude gave way, perforce, to much activity. A first step was the campaign begun early in 1948 to mesh these clearance actions with congressional requirements, and this despite the opposition character of the then Congress:

We had found in the immediate post-war years that there were a great many situations in which the . . . clearance process was an annoyance to the Congress and properly so. . . . Consequently . . . [in 1948] . . . Webb . . . specifically charged me with responsibility of talking with the staff directors and clerks of . . . major committees to see if our . . . process could be tied more closely into the committees' desires for the scheduling of items to come before them. On the other side of the coin, I was to acquaint the committees with the issues and items which . . . were being advanced in priority by the President, or . . . major departments. . . .

With the . . . cooperation of the Public Works Committees it was possible for us to work out . . . almost a precise schedule of what [they] wanted . . . and when . . . and . . . then go back and hasten our clearance process.

From the Public Works Committees this same kind of cooperative effort was extended to other . . . committees.[62]

Indeed, this operation steadily expanded; by 1950, the Budget was regularly and informally in touch with both majority and minority staffs of most major legislative committees, having by then a record of successful relations with committee chairmen of both parties.

In 1948, the Bureau also embarked on a wholly

new approach to the coordinative aspects of its clearance tasks, subordinating negative protection of President and agencies to positive development and drafting of Administration measures. Executive Office "working teams" came into being with "leadership" assigned to the White House, Budget, or the Economic Council, as the case might be, while Legislative Reference served as secretariat and stimulator of them all. Each unit of the presidential staff contributed its experts and its points of view; all agencies concerned were called on to confer.[63] A high proportion of the Fair Deal's later measures were worked out in detailed form through this new application of "coordination"; for example, the Housing Act of 1949, and the Social Security Act Amendments of 1950.[64] On many lesser proposals, involving fewer agency and private interests, or interests lower in importance to the President, the Budget's Legislative Reference staff led similar excursions on its own, sometimes merely tinkering with agency submissions, sometimes redoing the whole drafting job around the conference table.

This new technique—new, anyway, as an adjunct of central clearance—developed alongside and, in part, grew out of efforts to provide fixed meaning, concrete form, and better advance planning for the President's own legislative program. Toward that end, White House and Budget legislative staffs worked in close combination, after 1947, developing relationships which lent both strength and informality to team play on particulars.

Coinciding with these various endeavors came an external change which gave the clearance system a new dimension and new opportunity. In 1947, congressional committees began to ask Budget for its views on pending bills, at the same time that requests for views were sent to the agencies. These so-called "direct referrals" were an 80th Congress innovation; a means whereby Republican committee chairmen could gauge the intentions of the Democratic Administration. Whatever the initial motive, the practice became increasingly popular with the committees in each succeeding Congress, regardless of party coloration. During the 80th Congress there were 370 of these direct referrals; during the 81st, 974; during the 82nd, 1,102. In the 83rd Congress, there were 889 for the first session alone. Of course, this volume has not stemmed equally from all committees of each House in every Congress. For example, since 1947 the Senate Labor and Welfare Committee has referred nearly all bills to the Budget; not so its House counterpart.[65] Variations have their roots in diverse compounds of committee composition, jurisdiction, clientele. But while they keep the practice less than universal, this has not altered one significant result: the Budget's growing opportunity to register a presidential view directly on a high proportion of the bills considered actively by both houses.

Moreover, since 1949 other direct channels have opened to the Bureau, further enhancing this opportunity. For example, during Truman's second term the Majority Leader of the House and the Democratic chairmen of several Senate and House committees—including the House Rules Committee—acquired the habit of checking with White House or Budget staff (sometimes both), by telephone or special note, for the current Administration stand on bills nearing the reporting stage.[66] Wherever addressed, these inquiries almost always passed through Budget hands; responses, however conveyed, afforded vital supplements to clearance actions and formal reports. While these particulars and others have altered since Eisenhower's accession, comparable avenues continue to link the clearance system not only with congressional committees but with the leadership as well.

Here are alternatives to the traditional approach of central clearance, wholly independent of agency action, and compensating for deficiencies in agency compliance, while naturally increasing the incentive to comply. Progressively, the Bureau has inclined to concentrate its energies upon its own responses and those it readies for White House staff use; these rather than agency reports become the key documents of clearance action at the pending stage. Of course, there have been instances —no doubt there will be more—where Budget's direct answers have reflected its own institutional concerns more nearly than the President's personal designs.[67] But Bureau advice via agency reports has been no less susceptible to such confusions. That problem is generic.

The new spirit of Truman's clearance system affected not only proposed and pending stages, but also operations on enrolled enactments. From 1947 on, the technique of the working team was frequently applied, with varying degrees of informality, to staff evaluation of the major measures passed by Congress and to preparation for the President's own action, especially where vetoes were involved. From time to time, this teamwork at the enrolled stage proved useful in the development of new proposals: alternatives to measures vetoed and additions to bills signed with reservations.[68] In this respect, a positive note was injected into the review of enrolled bills, equivalent in purpose, if not scale, to the new ventures in coordination of proposals and reports.

In Truman's time, work on enrolled enactments came to contribute in another way to policy development. On certain classes of enactments, the

President found it possible to make consistency in signature or veto a potent instrument for setting and enforcing general policies. On veterans benefits, his vetoes drew and held a general line; on private immigration bills, his signatures held one last entryway wide open. These things were done despite unceasing protest from affected agencies, a testimonial not only to the President's determination, but to the Budget's constancy in finding counter-arguments to justify his action.

From 1947 to 1950, central clearance progressed vigorously in these various directions. New Budget circulars, while adding nothing to the substance of the old, provided literary—and official—recognition of the changed pace and emphasis.[69] Then in June, 1950, came Korea, and in November, full-scale Chinese intervention. Thereafter, throughout Truman's last two years, the Administration's crucial policy preoccupations were operational, no less than congressional, the legislative focus narrowing, meanwhile, from Fair Deal to defense.

Partial mobilization and limited war had an immediate impact on clearance operations, though the effect was less decisive than in the all-out conflict nine years earlier. During 1951 and 1952, central clearance did not lose its mandate, nor greatly shift its goals; it simply ceased to grow, mirroring thereby the "half-way" character of changes in the governmental climate. With the new Office of Defense Mobilization—nearest equivalent of the old OWMR—the Budget Bureau managed peaceful collaboration in the legislative field, easily adapting pre-existing patterns to the special case of economic controls. Here, by common consent, ODM took the Executive Office "lead," organizing and directing efforts to develop an Administration product, serving thereby as acknowledged "agent" of the central clearance system, and utilizing Budget clearance channels to fortify its interagency coordination.[70]

Aside from "defense production," only "mutual security"—consolidated, defense-packaging of foreign aid—emerged in Truman's final years as a major, new legislative venture requiring sustained developmental staff work. And here the Bureau worked out arrangements with the Director for Mutual Security similar to those established with ODM. The Harriman Office took the lead, while Budget staff manipulated clearance channels on its behalf.[71] Otherwise, the Budget's clearance system carried on much as before, though with less emphasis on positive coordination, because there was less presidential need; relying heavily, by way of substitute, upon the store of plans worked out and positions clarified in pre-Korean years. The patterns of staff action and relationship which had emerged by 1950 were, in the main, consolidated

during 1951 and 1952. But there was little new adventuring in the high policy arena.

Korea and its consequences were not the only factors responsible for this; there was, as well, the President's acute awareness that the presidency would soon change hands. In 1951, Truman appointed as Budget Director a top Bureau careerist, Frederick J. Lawton, charging him specifically, though not publicly, to batten down the institution, readying it for the transition ahead.[72] There was to be no more expansion in politically-charged directions. The Bureau's reputation for "non-political" expertise, its institutional respectability, were to be guarded at all costs, thereby preserving its utility to the next President.[73]

VI. The First Year Under Eisenhower. On January 20, 1953, the new President took office, his inauguration marking the first complete party turnover in twenty years. Superficially, this had a sweeping impact throughout the government. But paradoxically, perhaps, the Budget clearance system was affected less this time than in the previous transition years of 1945 and 1933; reasserting, not in years but in months, its old role in the new regime.

Why did this occur, and how? Why not the fall into drawn-out obscurity, the slow revival, that characterized both previous occasions? There seem to be three reasons: some relatively careful pre-inauguration planning on both sides; some vital accidents of personal relationship; and, underlying everything, a very real continuum in the outlook for government.

In November, 1952, immediately after Eisenhower's election, Truman took a number of specific steps toward the goal of orderly transition, among them an invitation to the President-elect to have his representative participate as an observer in final preparation of the forthcoming (Truman) budget. During the nine weeks before inauguration, Eisenhower's Budget Director-designate, Joseph M. Dodge, worked full time in the Budget Bureau, conducting himself with great discretion, watching the staff at work, learning their problems and routines, winning their confidence as they gained his respect.[74]

Once installed in office, Dodge emerged as a strong member of the new inner circle. His influence, the value of his services, and his ability to act were enhanced, no doubt, by his acceptance, hence effective leadership, of the established staff at his disposal. This set the stage for firm and confident assertion of Budget Bureau functions in the new regime, central clearance no less than the rest. Even before Inauguration Day, most of the Cabinet members-designate were called into the Bureau for Dodge-sponsored indoctrination lectures on its prerogatives and their responsibilities. Clearance regulations received attention at that time. And after the inaugural, Dodge made a point of picking up initial failures to comply, taking a strong line with department heads, reminiscent of Lord's language thirty years before.

The new Budget Director did one thing more for central clearance: to his hold-over chief of Legislative Reference he gave the backing of his own unqualified endorsement, and a total delegation of authority surpassing anything experienced in Truman's time. Between these two men, Dodge and Jones, evolved a personal relationship of greatest moment for clearance's survival. Dodge used his own prestige unsparingly to break a path for Jones into the Eisenhower White House, overcoming tendencies to treat careerists with extreme reserve. He then cut Legislative Reference entirely loose to seek its lead from presidential staff, thus extending under Eisenhower an innovation Webb had introduced in Truman's first term.

It was one thing to open an acquaintance between White House and Legislative Reference; quite another to establish adequate patterns of staff interaction. The Budget's clearance operations were dependent, now more than ever, on guidance from the President and access to him, by and through his White House aides. All the well-worn Truman channels were erased; they had to be rebuilt from scratch around another President, new aides, new methods. That this was done in less than six month's time, as *Fortune* attests, is tribute partly to the sheer inescapability of so much of the matter grinding through the clearance mill. And partly it is tribute to the personality equation, once again: to Jones' success in working with the three key legislative policy officials in Eisenhower's entourage—Adams, Persons, and Shanley.[75]

Reinforcing these relationships were some deep strains of continuity in government's most basic problems. Only on the surface was transition sharp and sudden. There was neither 1945's dramatic plunge from total war to general peace, nor 1933's wholesale experimenting with new rules for the governmental game. True, by 1953 the emergency impacts of Korea were diminishing, economically, psychologically, militarily. The cold war was entering a new phase, the atomic arms race a new dimension, the American economy a new adjustment. But these remained the underlying problems, whatever their changed aspects, with the new President, no less than the old, pledged to collective security and full employment as goals of governmental action. And as the operating crisis faded, policy-making tended to resume its pre-Korean cast.

The new regime brought many alterations of detail, quick shifts of attitude, emphasis, approach, which in the longer course of time may prove profound. But in 1953, at least, the real conditions and commitments—and dilemmas—overhanging from the past left little room for sweeping change, save on the planes of people and "psychology." Particularly was this the case for a regime so "new" as Eisenhower's. The President was new to national politics and civil government, his Cabinet members mostly newer still, his congressional colleagues wholly unused to a Republican Executive. His campaign for election had been influenced by concepts and illusions bred of opposition; some basic a-b-c's had to be learned anew.

Combined with this inexperience, the continuity of problems confronted the new White House with two needs, sharply felt: the need for facts about the past to help project decisions for the future, and the need for caution in commitments until homework had been done. The Budget clearance system proved a handy instrument in both instances. Once the ice was broken, the White House staff, however much mistrusting bureaucrats in general—holdovers schooled for twenty years in Democratic policies—could turn to Budget's, in particular, to tap resources of careerist expertise through clearance channels everywhere in government.[76] Simultaneously, the White House could obtain from central clearance a series of continuing protections for presidential freedom to withhold decision. The congressional session of 1953 was a time for ducking and dodging on a wide range of legislative issues, while study groups studied and administrators felt their way.[77] As legislative clearance had once helped protect FDR's own choice of action, it now helped safeguard Eisenhower's choices of inaction.

The gathering of background facts, the sidestepping of new commitments, were the services commending central clearance to the White House staff in early 1953; initially the clearance system's *raison d'être* in the new regime. The fact that budget-cutting was one measure *not* deferred that year, soon gave the system added opportunities for service, harking back to purposes three decades old. And when, in August, 1953, the Eisenhower White House faced its first end-of-session flood of enrolled bills, its dependence on Budget aid—and Budget staff's dependability—was demonstrated forcefully, with due effect.

Thus, by midsummer, 1953, it was quite evident that legislative clearance would survive, remaining a close institutional adjunct of the White House staff, retaining a real role in the presidential orbit. But what kind of role, of what significance? The scope and character of Truman's clearance system evolved out of the drive to build a comprehensive legislative program, buttressed by specific measures bearing an Administration label. Nothing of the sort occurred while Congress was in session during 1953. And though the Truman forms remained, the substance of the clearance job, that session, bore less resemblance to postwar operations than to the narrower, more limited approach of Roosevelt's early years—or even, in some aspects, Coolidge's. "The key to this whole operation," remarked a Budget aide, "is whether Ike decides to have a legislative program. We can't interpret, much less help develop, something that isn't there."

In the event, that decision was emphatically affirmative, as demonstrated by the stream of presidential messages when Congress reconvened in January, 1954, and by the prompt introduction of Administration bills to carry out most Eisenhower proposals.[78] Thereby central clearance gained the last element required for a new start on its postwar course.

This did not bring full restoration of all Truman methods; naturally, there have been adaptations as to ways and means. However, most of the changes made in 1953 and early 1954 relate to a phenomenon which may prove transitory: the imperfect acquaintance, trust, relationship between the new principals and old staffs. No two departments are alike in this, but its effects are widespread still. Hence, much of the informal, day-by-day coordination once carried on through departmental bureaucrats is being handled by the Budget now—no less informally—through "little cabinet" officers or department heads themselves. Much of the developmental effort on main measures, once farmed out to staff-level working teams, now turns on full-dress departmental presentations to the Cabinet, dry-run for White House and Budget staffs well in advance; with essentials of agreement at the Cabinet table providing, then, the base for formal interagency accord through clearance channels. Even where something like a "Truman" working team has been employed—as with Taft-Hartley changes, for example—its membership has comprised principals rather than staff, save at the White House level.

It is too soon, of course, to be definitive about the Eisenhower pattern. As this is written—in the spring of 1954—many things remain unsettled and unsure. To cite just one example, there has not been, so far, a single Eisenhower veto of the disciplinary, attention-calling kind which lent its sting to clearances in Roosevelt's time and Truman's.[79] But if one thing is certain, it is this: the pre-existing patterns show a hardy tendency to reassert themselves in Eisenhower's present circumstances.

VII. The Circumstances of Survival. For more than thirty years now, central clearance has persisted, its history marked by a long series of "accidental," unforeseen accretions. Nothing once absorbed has been wholly displaced; each new element somehow encompasses the old. There have been periods of relative stability, if not stagnation; times of obscurity, even decline. But overall, here is a record of great growth, successful adaptation—this under six successive Presidents, through every variation in national and governmental circumstances since Harding's term of office.

What contributes to this continuity? What explains this institutional survival and advance, particularly in the years since F.D.R. cut clearance loose from its "financial" moorings? There is no answer in the statute books; no law prescribes this system. There is no guide in partisan commitments; one finds no platform planks or campaign speeches, pro or con. As for old presidential orders on the subject, the signatures of Roosevelt, Truman, Smith, and Webb are not, *per se*, coin of the realm today. The explanation lies in many things, but in these least of all.

Part of the answer can be drawn directly from events recorded in this paper. Note the impact of personalities, among them Roosevelt himself, Webb, Dodge, Bailey, Jones. Their interactions helped to mold—and to sustain—the modern clearance system. Note also the close correspondence of that system's varied fortunes, since 1933, to shifting presidential policy preoccupations in an era of "big government," successive national emergencies, and changeable White House political prestige. It is not sheer happenstance that central clearance was but temporarily obscured by operational crises in depression and war; or that its greatest institutional expansions followed the political events of 1938 and 1946; or that its postwar growth, while checked by the Korean outbreak, seems to be resuming in Korea's aftermath, despite the change of Administration.

Note, finally, the clearance system's formal locale in the Budget Bureau, a fact of real significance for continuity and for survival. Here is the oldest, toughest organism in the presidential orbit. The making of the budget is still the prime general-purpose, decision-and-action-forcing process yet institutionalized in the executive. The budget process, as it stands, is so firmly a fact of governmental life, so thoroughly assimilated in legislative and administrative practice and expectation, that its continuation goes unquestioned; its institutional embodiment, "The Budget," commanding everywhere a healthy measure of respect, if not always regard. Perhaps, as students now are fond of pointing out, the Bureau is by no means the ideal locale—not, anyway, in theory—for policy staff work on the substantive side.[80] And yet, in practice, nothing is so vulnerable as the high policy performer dangling loose, a ready target and potential sacrifice at every turn in presidential circumstance (e.g., NEC, OWMR). The more immediate the clearance system's policy involvement, the more advantageous, at least for survival, its impersonal exterior, its undescriptive designation, its "budgetary" context.

Theoretically, perhaps, the combination of effective personal relationships, continuing White House requirements, and stable staff resources should suffice to explain survival of a presidential mechanism aimed at administrative agencies. So might it be, were Presidents, in fact, "administrators" of some neatly unified executive. But they are not; instead, the White House looks out on:

. . . a protean agglomeration of feudalities that overlap and crisscross in an almost continual succession of changes. Some of the lines of control . . . terminate in the Presidency, some in . . . the legislature and some . . . 'outside' the government; a few lie in the hands of 'subordinate' executives; many more involve all of these in collegial arrangements so informal as to be but dimly recognized even by the chief participants.[81]

This is the context in which "central" clearance actually operates; its very terminology a contradiction of the feudal order. How then does it survive?

It lasts because most of the wielders of real power in this wilderness find in it net advantage to themselves. Of course, the agency secure in a strong "horizontal" power complex—buttressed by potent clientele and purposeful congressional committees—may have but little tolerance for clearance of its pet proposals. But every agency is not a Corps of Engineers; few, if any, are so "favorably" situated all the time. Most measures of most agencies face an uncertain future in the legislative process. Whatever clearance brings by way of support, even acquiescence, from President and Budget Bureau, from other agencies and, implicitly, their clientele, may help to reduce hazards, strengthen prospects in the Congress. Of course, advance accommodation is the purchase price. Whether to pay or not to pay involves a complex, variable estimate of cost and return, power and position, which bureaucrats must calculate afresh in every case. This does not produce absolute adherence to either the form or the spirit of clearance regulations; it does, at least, give most agency officials a real, long-term stake in the system's survival. And that is reinforced, for every agency, by virtue of the chances clearance brings to sit in judgment on the other fellow's viewpoints and designs.

As for senators and congressmen, they may show small concern for clearance niceties when potent sponsors or committees seize hold of an issue strongly backed by tough and vocal interests stimulating wide support. One thinks of Taft-Hartley, for example, or the McCarran Acts, or the Bricker Amendment. But Congress moves, perforce, on many measures of a very different character: on those the President stakes out for his own, and on a host of others which are neither "musts" for Presidents nor irresistibly appealing to members *en masse*. On the bulk of this business, overburdened legislators, in committee and out, need a handy criterion for choice of measures to take up, especially when faced with technical alternatives in which they have but little vested interest. They need, as well, an inkling of Administration attitude toward the outcome: how much, if at all, does the President care? What will he stand for when the bill comes down? What will he do thereafter, by way of budgetary follow-through? And save when they themselves choose otherwise, congressional committees need some measure of defense against time-wasting or discreditable cat-and-dog fights on their premises among the agencies concerned in pending bills. These services the clearance system can provide; that Congress wants them as a matter of practical self-interest is demonstrated by committee and leadership initiation of the direct referrals and other links to Budget now so integral a part of clearance operations.[82]

Naturally congressmen, like bureaucrats, incline to weigh the relative advantages of heeding or ignoring clearance actions, case by case. Particular results have varied greatly from issue to issue, from committee to committee, and even among personalities and between the Houses. But there can be few members who have not found some clearance actions to their taste, few legislative leaders or committee chairmen who have not seen some disregarded clearance warning rise to haunt them in a veto message or a bobtailed budget. Again, this does not make for uniform responses to the terms of clearance; it is productive, though, of genuine concern for the system's survival.

For all these reasons, the "feudalities" at both ends of the Avenue have found that it pays to tolerate the clearance system. They have, indeed, found it quite possible to do so without yielding to the President their underlying freedom to maneuver. Yet simultaneously the President, while also husbanding his liberty to move, has found in clearance means to make these gentry heedful of his powers when they exercise their own. The vitality of central clearance lies in the fact that it can satisfy, at once, both these conditions. The President as he may choose, gains ample opportunities to make known his desires. But Congress and the agencies are not compelled to notice. And he, meanwhile, retains the right to alter course, or change his mind. The voice that speaks is not the President's; it is the Budget Bureau's. And when need be, the Budget serves as whipping-boy.

This is a neat arrangement; it helps preserve the enterprise. But it can do that only so long as the distinction remains more fiction than fact. Were there to be a demonstration, generally and over time, that Budget really spoke not for the President but for itself alone, then the whole game would lose its point and the participants soon cease to play. Here one is brought to a new set of questions: What is the "program of the President" that Budget claims to interpret in clearance actions? Does such a thing exist and if so how is it constructed, and by whom? These questions lie outside the scope of this paper, but they can serve, perhaps, as curtain-raisers for another study.[83]

Notes

1. Katherine Hammill, "This is a Bureaucrat," *Fortune*, Vol. 48, pp. 156 ff. (Nov., 1953).
2. Agency proposals for executive orders, proclamations, and certain other formal presidential actions are also coordinated and cleared through the Bureau of the Budget, as are feasibility reports on proposed public works requiring congressional action.
3. Source: Office of Legislative Reference, Bureau of the Budget. In addition, there were 889 "direct referrals" from congressional sources asking Budget for views on pending bills.
4. Budget Circular A-19, Revised, dated October 25, 1948, sets forth coordination and clearance procedures and requirements concerning proposed and pending bills. Budget Circular A-9, Revised, issued at the same time, deals with enrolled enactments. Both circulars codified and brought up to date earlier usage and regulations.
5. Bertram M. Gross, *The Legislative Struggle* (New York, 1953), p. 169.
6. This article deals with legislative coordination and review centering in the Bureau of the Budget. At a later date the author hopes to deal with a related process, planning the President's own legislative program: a process but newly and incompletely institutionalized, centering more nearly in the White House than the Budget Bureau, yet also exhibiting a high degree of continuity from Truman's time to Eisenhower's.
7. As an integral part of the budget reform, the House of Representatives changed its rules in 1920, at the second session of the 66th Congress, to reduce from eight to one the number of committees authorized to deal with appropriations. The Senate followed suit two years later, at the second session of the 67th Congress.
8. Letter from Chairman Madden of the House Appropriations Committee to Budget Director Dawes, November 17, 1921. Budget Bureau central files; 1921-38: *Legislation No. 1*. The measures in question were Senate Joint Resolutions of very limited significance, affecting War Department obligating authority. Madden's concern was clearly not with these specifics, but with their procedural implications.
9. In contrast with the asserted presidential veto over agency proposals volunteered to Congress, this circular

and its successors have carefully refrained from claiming any right to stop or alter agency responses to congressional requests for views on pending bills. Formally speaking, the only requirement has been that the President's position, as expressed by Budget, be stated in an agency report along with the agency's own views. Furthermore, by long custom now acknowledged in current regulations, an agency's response to congressional requests for "technical drafting service" is exempt from clearance so long as it carries no official endorsement. Thus has the Budget tried to duck the charge of "interference" with congressional access to agency opinion or expertise. In practice, this means non-interference with agency calculation of the risks involved, if any, in holding to views which do not square with those of the Executive Office.
10. Dawes obtained Harding's approval in advance, sending him the proposed circular on December 3, 1921, with the notation that it "needs no argument," being intended "simply to insure that all estimates and requests for appropriations [are] presented in the manner provided in the Budget and Accounting Act." Dawes may have said less than he believed, but there is no hint of this either in the official files or in his published memoirs, *The First Year of the Budget* (New York, 1923).
11. This modification was suggested by Harding himself at a conference with Dawes in January, 1922. A formal amendment to Circular 49 was actually drafted along these lines but was never issued; an oral clarification in Cabinet meeting appears to have been substituted, supplemented by explicit waivers of jurisdiction in Budget Bureau correspondence with particular departments. Budget Bureau, central files; 1921-38: *Legislation No. 1*. For detailed discussion of this and other aspects of the subject, see Richard E. Neustadt, "Presidential Clearance of Legislation," unpub. diss. (Harvard, 1950), pp. 28 ff.
12. Herbert Lord, an army careerist and wartime associate of Dawes, served as Budget Director from 1922 to 1929. It was his custom, in the search for economy, to inspect his subordinates' desk drawers after office hours, confiscating extra pencils, paper clips, and pads of paper. Note that the total full-time Bureau staff numbered less than thirty in 1924. Ten years later the total was still under forty.
13. *Addresses of The President of the United States and the Director of the Bureau of the Budget at the Seventh Regular Meeting of the Business Organization of the Government* (Washington, G.P.O., 1924), p. 6. See also the corresponding releases for the ninth meeting (1925), and the eleventh meeting (1926). The Business Organization of the Government, including all department heads and bureau chiefs, met semi-annually from 1922 to 1929 for purposes of presidential exhortation on, and departmental oaths of fealty to, economy in government. Coolidge's addresses on these occasions are classics of their kind. A Dawes innovation, becoming more ritualistic with each passing year, these meetings were abruptly terminated by Herbert Hoover when he assumed the presidency after years of attendance as Secretary of Commerce.
14. For a detailed review of these efforts, see Donald A. Hansen, "Legislative Clearance by the Bureau of the Budget," unpub. staff monograph (Budget Bureau, 1940), pp. 10-19. For Lord's correspondence with departments, see Budget Bureau central files; 1921-38: *Legislation No. 1*.
15. Bureau of the Budget, *Third Annual Report of the Director of the Bureau of the Budget to the President of the United States* (Washington, G.P.O., 1926), p. 28. Within his limited frame of reference, Lord's claim for compliance appears reasonably accurate. Apparently he was afforded the opportunity to see in advance those legislative reports and proposals that he and the President really wanted. See Hansen, *op. cit.*, pp. 19 ff.
16. Hansen, *op. cit.*, especially pp. 17-20. See also Budget Bureau central files; 1921-38: *Legislation No. 1* for a variety of typical clearance letters in this period.
17. Budget Bureau central files; 1921-38: *Legislation*

No. 1, Budget Director's Memorandum to the files, May 17, 1929. Hoover actually did review and initial virtually every Budget Bureau clearance letter issued during his term of office, an interesting commentary on the presidency of twenty-five years ago. The documentation behind such letters was relatively haphazard in those days, frequently lacking in summaries of the issues, or of agency positions, or even of the bills themselves. The President must often have had to plow through the legislative language to reach an understanding of the subject at hand.

18. Budget Circular 273, issued December 20, 1929. The Budget Bureau shortly found it expedient to issue supplementary instructions requiring that to qualify for the exemption, reports on public bills must be definitely unfavorable, not merely non-committal. This amplifying note was contained in a "Memorandum to the Heads of all Departments and Establishments," issued April 10, 1930, "by direction of the President." In Coolidge's regime, these types of reports had received almost automatic clearance from the Budget Bureau, usually without referral to the President.

19. This theme appears strongly in Hoover's last three Budget messages. For example: ". . . we cannot afford to embark on any new or enlarged ventures. . . . There will be before the Congress many legislative matters involving additions to our estimated expenditures. . . . The plea of unemployment will be advanced . . . but Congress [should] give full due to our financial outlook. . . . In the absence of further legislation . . . we can close [the] year with a balanced budget." *Message of the President of the United States Transmitting the Budget for the Fiscal Year Ending June 30, 1932* (Washington, G.P.O., 1930), p. XIX.

20. For sidelights on the "newness" of the incoming Cabinet see Frances Perkins, *The Roosevelt I Knew* (New York, 1946), pp. 228-30. See also Harold Ickes, *The First Thousand Days* (New York, 1953).

21. Roosevelt's really extraordinary grasp of the tempo and politics of departmental administration comes clear in the meetings of the National Emergency Council, an enlarged Cabinet group which met under his chairmanship from 1933 to 1936. The verbatim transcripts of these meetings, available in the National Archives, preserve intact his "lectures" to his department heads on such subjects as how to manage bureau chiefs, congressional committees, and the press.

22. Notably Roosevelt's first Budget Director, Lewis Douglas, and his first Undersecretary of the Treasury, Dean Acheson. Both returned to government with the coming of World War II.

23. The Bureau's reminder was contained in a memorandum from the Budget Director's career assistant to the heads of all major agencies, January 22, 1934. It was a gently phrased affair and while most of the agencies replied in kind, the Bureau's records indicate that they were slow to take their duties very seriously. See Budget Bureau central files; 1921-38: *Legislation No. 1*. Budget Director Douglas seems to have had no part in this proceeding, nor much interest in the outcome. Two weeks later, when queried by a Cabinet member, he expressed himself as unfamiliar with the "old orders," and uncertain of their scope. See National Emergency Council, *Proceedings of the Fourth Meeting* (February 6, 1934), pp. 21 ff.

24. National Emergency Council, *Proceedings of the Nineteenth Meeting* (December 11, 1934), p. 7.

25. *Ibid.*

26. National Emergency Council, *Proceedings of the Twenty-sixth Meeting* (April 23, 1935), p. 8. Bell, at the time a senior career official in the Treasury Department, had taken the Budget Directorship on an acting basis after Douglas' departure. He held the job in addition to his duties as a special assistant to Secretary Morgenthau and this "temporary" arrangement was continued for nearly five years, until Harold Smith relieved him in 1939.

27. This new order was discussed by the Emergency Council before issuance and the President then went to great lengths to emphasize his personal approval. See National Emergency Council, *Proceedings of the Twenty-eighth Meeting* (December 17, 1935), pp. 14-23.

28. In 1937, when a revision of Circular 336 was under discussion, F. J. Bailey—soon to become the first Assistant Budget Director for Legislative Reference—wrote an undated memorandum pointing out that "there is no authority whatever in the Budget and Accounting Act for our procedure with respect to reports on legislation. And I would not try to make believe that there is. The authority we have over [these] reports comes from Executive authority and *not* from any Act of Congress." Budget Bureau central files; 1921-38: *Legislation No. 2*.

29. National Emergency Council, *Proceedings of the Twenty-second Meeting* (January 22, 1935), p. 2.

30. *Ibid.*, p. 3.

31. National Emergency Council, *Proceedings of the Twenty-eighth Meeting* (December 17, 1935), p. 17.

32. *Ibid.*, pp. 19-21.

33. Edwin E. Witte, "The Preparation of Proposed Legislative Measures by Administrative Departments," *Studies on Administrative Management in the Government of the United States for the President's Committee on Administrative Management* (Washington: G.P.O., 1937), p. 56.

34. Hansen, "Legislative Clearance by the Bureau of the Budget" (cited in note 14), p. 34.

35. Testimony by Daniel W. Bell, Acting Director of the Budget, before the Treasury Subcommittee of the House Committee on Appropriations, *Hearings on the Treasury Department Appropriation Bill for 1940*, 76th Cong., 1st sess. (Washington, G.P.O., 1939), p. 936.

36. Roland Young, *This is Congress* (New York, 1943), p. 59.

37. See President's Committee on Administrative Management, *Report with Special Studies* (Washington, G.P.O., 1937), pp. 15-21.

38. *Ibid.* The Report recommended essentially that the Budget Bureau become the President's chief staff agent for "administrative management," enlarged, revitalized, and formally made part of the President's own office. In passing, the report endorsed a staff proposal that NEC clearance functions devolve upon the Bureau, with Circular 336 simplified accordingly and then generally enforced. In so urging, the Committee simply followed the logic of events, which fitted neatly enough into its major theme: building up the Budget Bureau.

39. See Budget Bureau central files; 1921-38: *Legislation No. 2*, especially entries between March and May, 1937.

40. Circular 344—virtually identical in its terms with 336, save for deletion of NEC's participation—was drafted in May, 1937, but for various reasons, mechanical and other, was not released to the agencies until December 17, 1937. Circular 344 was later renumbered A-19.

41. In 1938, the President obtained from Congress a supplemental appropriation enabling the Budget Bureau to start tooling up for the new or redefined tasks envisaged in the Brownlow Report. For details on the ensuing reorganization and restaffing see Bell's testimony, *Hearings* (cited in note 35), pp. 936-55. This preceded by a year the Bureau's formal transfer from the Treasury to the Executive Office of the President (Reorganization Plan I and Executive Order 8,248 of 1939). Before Bell's reorganization, clearance work had been handled almost entirely by the Bureau's estimates examiners as an adjunct of their other duties. The new Division of Coordination was conceived, both in the Brownlow studies and by its Bureau sponsors, as a small, full-time unit to guide and coordinate, but not supplant, the contribution of all other Bureau staff to legislative analysis and review. This has remained the concept, though since World War II not just the Bureau but the whole growing Executive Office has become the field from which staff contributions have been sought. By 1939, the Coordination Division's professional staff for legislation numbered five; in the fifteen

years since, the comparable figure has never risen above nine. The unit's changes in title have had no substantive purpose or effect.

42. Source of Budget figures: Office of Legislative Reference, Bureau of the Budget. For NEC figures see Witte, *op. cit.*, p. 53.

43. To illustrate: In the 1939 session some 5,000 public bills were introduced in the two Houses of Congress; of these, 452 were passed by both Houses and enrolled that year. But only an item-by-item comparison—which no one has ever made—would show the relationship between the 2,400-odd bills cleared and the 5,000 introduced, or between the 438 drafts cleared and the 452 bills passed. To complicate the issue further, the figures on drafts cleared and on bills enrolled represent separate subjects in virtually all cases; not so the figures on bills introduced, where substantial duplications within or between the two Houses may run as high as forty per cent in the average first session. This is an estimate; firm data are not available.

44. For examples see Hansen, *op. cit.*, pp. 81-84.

45. There were other hazards too: ". . . one enrolled bill was lost and once when we called up one of the new [New Deal] agencies and asked where the bill was, they said they had put it in the files." Testimony of Frederick J. Bailey, Assistant Director for Legislative Reference, Bureau of the Budget, before the House Committee on the Civil Service, 78th Congress, 1st sess., *Hearings Pursuant to H. Res. 16.*, Part 2 (Washington, G.P.O., 1943), p. 361. The writer is indebted to Bailey; to the late Maurice Latta, former White House Executive Clerk, whose tenure in subordinate capacities began with McKinley; to William J. Hopkins, Latta's successor as Executive Clerk; and to James H. Rowe, Jr., a Roosevelt Administrative Assistant, for data on the evolution of enrolled bill procedure. Information here provided is drawn from their recollections, from Roosevelt's enrolled bill files (now at Hyde Park), and from contemporary Budget Bureau records.

46. "This is a splendid contribution," wrote Rudolph Forster, then White House Executive Clerk, "we could never have got half as far before." Budget Bureau central files; 1921-38: *Enrolled Bills No. 1,* undated memorandum from Forster to F. J. Bailey.

47. In order to build up back-ground files for use on enrollments, private bills were brought back under clearance at the pending stage by Budget Circular 390, June 1, 1942.

48. National Emergency Council, *Proceedings of the Twenty-eighth Meeting* (December 17, 1935), p. 17.

49. Budget Bureau central files; 1921-38: *Enrolled Bills No. 1,* undated memorandum from Rudolph Forster to F. J. Bailey.

50. See note 45.

51. All Roosevelt aides consulted by the writer have been emphatically agreed on his conscious adherence to these views and his consistent application of them.

52. Review of Budget Bureau submissions on enrolled bills first became a distinct White House assignment in 1939, shortly after the Bureau's formal assumption of responsibility for their handling. Initially, this assignment went to James H. Rowe, Jr., one of the original Administrative Assistants to the President appointed under the Reorganization Act of 1939. Rowe had left the White House by the time Samuel I. Rosenman was appointed Special Counsel in 1943; this work then gravitated naturally to Rosenman, who had performed a similar service for F.D.R. in Albany, a decade earlier. Rosenman was succeeded as Special Counsel by Clark M. Clifford in 1946; Clifford by Charles S. Murphy in 1950; Murphy by Bernard Shanley, the present incumbent, who took office with the Eisenhower Administration.

53. The Office of War Mobilization (OWM) was established by Executive Order 9347, May 27, 1943. It was transformed into a statutory Office of War Mobilization and Reconversion (OWMR) by the War Mobilization and Reconversion Act of 1944. For an admirable summary of OWM-OWMR history, see Herman M. Somers, *Presidential Agency* (Cambridge, Mass., 1950), pp. 47-108.

54. A comment dating from the early spring of 1946, made by the then OWMR Director to a member of his staff and relayed by the latter to the writer.

55. The Employment Act of 1946 was approved February 20, 1946. The Council did not begin to function until the following September.

56. For a survey of Truman's domestic legislative program and the character of congressional response, see Richard E. Neustadt, "Congress and the Fair Deal: A Legislative Balance Sheet," in the forthcoming Vol. 5 of *Public Policy*, eds. Carl J. Friedrich and J. Kenneth Galbraith (Cambridge, Mass.).

57. OWMR was terminated by presidential action through Executive Order 9809 of December 17, 1946. Some of the factors leading to its demise are discussed in Somers, *op. cit.*, pp. 100-1. Steelman's principal lieutenants had planned to move the core of the whole organization to the White House with him, but they reckoned without his sensitivity to Cabinet and congressional resentment over late-coming, subordinate "empires" in the President's own office, especially after the 1946 election.

58. Quite apart from the so-called "Nourse-Keyserling dispute," Budget, Treasury, and OWMR each had hoped and planned to assume the staff responsibilities ultimately conferred on the Council. Only the mutual jealousy of these three agencies stalemated executive opposition to the Council's creation. Their grievances did not yield, all at once, to the accomplished fact; and an uncertain performance on the first Economic Report did not enhance the Council's standing with its sister agencies, their heirs and assigns.

59. The 1947 veto of Taft-Hartley, for example, was preceded by a special White House appraisal undertaken by the Special Counsel at the President's behest, with the full-time assistance of three Budget staff members whom Webb turned loose entirely, requiring from them neither consultation nor report.

60. A residual reflection of the then dependence on the Budget, which Webb so strongly aided and abetted in 1947-48, is found in the fact that in 1953 fully a third of the outgoing Truman assistants had come to the White House staff from the career service in the Budget Bureau.

61. F. J. Bailey retired as Assistant Director of the Budget for Legislative Reference after the first session of the 80th Congress in 1947. His place was taken by Elmer B. Staats; in 1949, Staats was succeeded by Roger W. Jones, the present incumbent.

62. Testimony of Roger W. Jones before the House Select Committee on Lobbying Activities, 81st Congress, 2nd sess., *Hearings Pursuant to H. Res. 298*, Part 10 (Washington, G.P.O., 1950). Note that the current version of Circular A-19 is printed with Jones' testimony.

63. After 1949, NSRB, ODM, and DMS staff, and occasionally NSC staff, were also drawn into or given leadership of such Executive Office teams.

64. Of course, not all proposals were prepared in this way. For example, the so-called "Brannan Plan" was first set forth informally in the shape of "suggestions for study" put to congressional committees in testimony by the then Secretary of Agriculture. Truman's health insurance proposals were never translated into Administration-approved specifics; nor did the Administration ever commit itself to the details of bills introduced in Congress. As for revenue measures, their preparation, for the most part, was—and still is—dominated by the Treasury.

65. Currently, the committees which engage most frequently in direct referrals are: Senate Interior, Labor, Public Works, Finance, Banking, Commerce, Civil Service, Government Operations; House Agriculture, Commerce, Merchant Marine, Public Works, Government Operations, Civil Service. Source: Office of Legislative Reference, Bureau of the Budget. Note that the early adherence of the Senate Labor Committee reflects Senator

Taft's own view of the need for a formal channel between President and committees on current measures.

66. Also in 1949, the Senate Majority Leader arranged to have the Budget report to him the number of each bill cleared and the nature of the clearance given, week by week. These data were then tabulated by his staff for ready reference to Administration stands on the general run of pending bills. So routinized a transmittal of so much information proved of limited utility. After 1950, the practice was curtailed.

67. A classic example is provided by Budget reports to the Senate Labor Committee on S. 614, the Hospital Construction Act Amendments of 1949. For details see Budget Bureau central files; Enacted Legislation, 81st Congress, *Hospital Construction*, R6-15/48.3.

68. See, for example, Truman's message to Congress, July 13, 1951, announcing the signature of S. 984, a bill to aid recruitment of Mexican migrant workers, of which the President remarked: "I could not have given my approval had I not been assured . . . that supplementary [measures] would receive prompt attention." Truman then recommended a three-point supplementing program, produced by a staff team after the bill's passage.

69. See note 4.

70. The Office of Defense Mobilization was established by Executive Order 10193 on December 15, 1950, within the Executive Office of the President, to exercise direction and control over all aspects of the post-Korean mobilization program. ODM received permanent status through Reorganization Plan 2 of 1953, absorbing the war mobilization planning functions of the National Security Resources Board under the National Security Act of 1947.

71. In June, 1950, Averell Harriman was appointed Special Assistant to the President to coordinate various overseas affairs. Under the Mutual Security Act of 1951, his post was transformed into an Office of the Director for Mutual Security (DMS), within the Executive Office of the President. DMS was abolished by Reorganization Plan 7 of 1953 and its functions transferred to the Foreign Operations Administration.

72. Lawton had been a senior Bureau official since 1935, number-three man under Webb, number-two man under Webb's successor, Frank Pace, Jr. He is serving presently as a member of the Civil Service Commission.

73. It is an interesting sidelight on the longevity of Truman's concern for a smooth transition that a number of the preparatory actions Lawton took, both before and after the 1952 election, corresponded with arrangements planned by Webb on a "contingent" basis during the summer of 1948.

74. Dodge was not precisely a newcomer to government, having organized War Department renegotiation activities in World War II and having carried out significant overseas assignments for the occupation authorities of both Germany and Japan. His attitude toward his new role was very healthy for the institution he would head, fairly free of the suspicion and uncertainty which plagued so many Eisenhower appointees and their career subordinates. Dodge resigned as Budget Director, April 15, 1954, and was succeeded by his deputy, Rowland Hughes. For information on this and other aspects of the 1953 transition, the writer is indebted to the many officials throughout the Executive Office who have answered his inquiries with candor and good will.

75. Under Eisenhower, Sherman Adams, the Assistant to the President, has a formal, though not always operative, role in the coordination and direction of all White House staff undertakings. Wilton B. Persons, now Adams' deputy, had major responsibility for congressional liaison during Eisenhower's first year and is still heavily involved in legislative affairs. Bernard Shanley, Special Counsel to the President, acquired during 1953 a good share of his predecessors' tasks in policy development, especially on the legislative side, resuming, among other things, the Counsel's old role as regular channel between Budget and President on enrolled enactments and other clearance actions.

76. The legislative clearance system was not, of course, the only means employed. The National Security Council Staff—especially the old Senior Staff reconstituted as the Planning Board—contributed importantly in some major areas. Certain of the presidential and agency study groups, among the many operating in 1953, helped also to build effective links between the new regime and its inherited experts; notably in the government organization, psychological warfare, social security, and housing fields.

77. Note that Eisenhower's inaugural marked the first change of party in the executive under the so-called "Lame Duck" Amendment; the new President was inaugurated only ten weeks after his election; the new Congress was in regular session two weeks before Inauguration Day.

78. It has been the custom during 1954 for the White House to disavow Administration "sponsorship" of measures introduced by committee chairmen or other senior members after congressional receipt of presidential recommendations. But in the great majority of cases, as almost any *New York Times* account will show, these bills actually represent departmental drafts, conveyed with the Administration's blessing to competent authorities in Congress. This is the same route previously taken by most Truman "must" measures, which seldom traveled straight from White House to Congress. In all such cases, denials of Administration sponsorship are merely exercises in semantics, sometimes accepted at face value by the press, rarely, if ever, by congressmen, though giving all concerned a useful "out" for future reference.

79. This is not to say that the President subscribes to a Whig theory of the veto power. Staff aides contend otherwise and the evidence is not yet in.

80. For examples, see Somers, *op. cit.*, pp. 213 ff., Norton Long, "Popular Support for Economic Programs," *American Political Science Review*, Vol. 42, pp. 326-36 (April, 1948); Arthur Maass, "In Accord with the Program of the President?" in *Public Policy*, eds. Carl J. Friedrich and J. Kenneth Galbraith (Cambridge, Mass., 1953), Vol. 4, pp. 77-93.

81. David B. Truman, *The Governmental Process* (New York, 1951), pp. 437-38.

82. Another service merits passing mention: favorable clearance gives a sponsor opportunities to wrap his project in the "presidential" mantle; unfavorable clearance lets him rise to defend Congress and the public interest—and his bill—against executive blundering or "interference." Each tactic has its uses in the legislative struggle; each may bring members and their measures within reach of the publicity inherent in the presidential office. For a recent illustration, see the press treatment of sponsors' complaints against an apparently adverse Budget report on several House bills depriving Alger Hiss of retirement benefits. *New York Times*, June 23-25, 1954.

83. See Richard E. Neustadt, "Presidency and Legislation: Planning the President's Program," *American Political Science Review*, Vol. 49 (December, 1955), pp. 980-1021.

C. Procedures and Practices

8. BENTHAM ON THE FUNCTIONING OF LEGISLATURES

H. R. G. Greaves

BENTHAM WAS NOT SATISFIED with providing for a popular assembly. It was not enough that it should have supreme lawmaking power, unshared with a second chamber, nor that it should be elected directly and by universal suffrage. Although this proposal was made a century before it was carried out, Bentham was not content to stop there. He wanted to be sure that the assembly would be properly organised inside. With this object he made a full study of the procedure of Parliament in England and of the provincial *parlements* in France. He is the only theorist on this subject produced by Britain, although British practical experience has been the foundation of procedure in nearly every legislative chamber in the world. Being the sole interpreter to other countries, Bentham naturally had an immense influence upon them. Others, such as Hatsell in Bentham's time, Sir Erskine May later, and Sir Courtenay Ilbert in our own day, may have described the development of rules of procedure at Westminster; but no one of these three distinguished clerks of the House of Commons undertook a theoretical analysis of the needs underlying those rules or the advantages resulting from them, or regarded political tactics as a science in itself. Bentham did each of these things. . . .

In order to decide how an assembly should go about its work Bentham had to answer three broad questions. He must regulate the relations between members and the House. He must prepare the rules of debate. He must deal with the initiation of laws.

Bentham insisted tediously on the presence of every member at every session of his assembly. But his insistence is to be explained by the prevalence of absenteeism in the unreformed House of Commons. . . . According to Bentham nonattendance makes possible the passing of surprise measures against the real will of the assembly. It also encourages a member to avoid voting against

Reprinted from "Bentham on Legislative Procedure," *Economica*, No. 33 (August, 1931), pp. 308-27, by permission of the author and the publisher.

a bill which he secretly disapproves, out of deference to some powerful interest; it opens the door to corruption. So important was this attendance, therefore, in his view, that drastic measures should be taken to enforce it. For every day of absence a member must be fined by the retention of his salary or of a deposit made for the purpose. Bentham's proposals, however, proved of small practical value. The remedy, in fact, came not from ensuring that there should be no hidden doors or devious ways of exit, but from the growth of a powerful public opinion. Bentham's apparent mistake lay in failing to allow for this; but had a public interest failed to develop some sort of measure for encouraging attendance might well have been needed. His real mistake lay rather in his characteristic failure to remember that the dragooning of live men has a glorious habit of defeating its own purpose. . . . But Bentham also was right when he urged that so long as members regarded their functions as quite secondary and a mere amusement at the best, such a desire was impossible.[1]

But "non-attendance," Bentham added, "is not the only cause of frustration and retardation in the provision for public exigencies. Another is the want of a supply for the involuntary deficiency created by death or sickness."[2] So anxious is he to destroy inattendance for corrupt causes that he is even ready to allow the member to appoint a substitute—a still worse evil. At first sight that would seem to open the way to irresponsibility on the part of the member. But Bentham was careful to explain that every act of the substitute should be deemed an act of the member, who would remain entirely responsible. One of Bentham's chief reasons for demanding reform was the member's lack of interest in his parliamentary duties, his tendency to consider the functions of his position of much less importance than its prestige, and it seems clear that such an important failing would have been strengthened by leaving him quite free to delegate his obligations to a secretary or a lackey. In such circumstances the vital quality of personal contact and responsibility would be lost, because the acting member was neither responsible to the electors nor necessarily in touch with them. The importance of the personal factor in politics was overlooked by Bentham here as elsewhere because he was ever anxious to create an exact science impervious to human variations. His one psychological maxim, the dominating power of self-interest, was here inadequate. He was unable, therefore, to see the value in a group of men of maintaining personal contact between those responsible, in order to promote the growth of a corporate spirit. . . .

But Bentham was inconsistent. He was in agreement with Burke's famous plea for the member's independence and free judgment: "you choose a member indeed; but when you have chosen him he is not a member of Bristol, but he is a member of Parliament." "Paramount to his duty to a part," said Bentham, "is, on every occasion, his duty to the whole."[3] Yet he was willing to penalise the member for thus disregarding a local interest and considering himself a guardian of the nation as a whole, by making him removable at any time at the will of his electors. Here again, had his recommendations been applied, they would seriously have impaired that very corporate sense which he was trying by his procedural code to secure, and which Dumont claimed as one of the chief reasons for the survival of the British Parliament.[4]

* * *

About the control of members through a speaker, or president as he prefers to call it, Bentham has the most enlightening remarks to make. To one brought up in knowledge of the high traditions of impartiality of the Speaker's office it seems unnecessary to explain why he should be impartial. But different experiences in other countries have shown the value of such an analysis. By no means every parliament follows the practice of Westminster, and even there the disinterestedness of the Speaker has only been perfected in comparatively recent times. At Washington the Speaker is one of the leaders of his party; in Holland and Sweden the president is appointed for each session by the Crown.[5] Those are fundamental contradictions of the principle on which the office is founded in England. The best analysis of that principle and the best presentation of the case for it is Bentham's. The president, according to him, is partly a judge and partly an agent. He has to judge in disputes between members, and to apply the rules which the assembly upholds. In both functions he is subordinate, and subject to appeal to the assembly. His duty is not to try to impose his own will, for he is not permitted one, but to discover and translate that

of the assembly. It is "the duty and art of the accoucheur . . . to assist nature, and not to force her—to soothe, upon occasion, the pangs of parturition—to produce, in the shortest time, the genuine offspring; but never to stifle it, much less to substitute a changeling in its room."[6] The president should be chosen freely by the assembly itself. "The president ought to be permanent," Bentham explained in an unanswerable way, "not only that the embarrassment arising from multiplied elections may be avoided, but especially for the good of his office. If permanent, he will possess more experience, he will know the assembly better, he will be more conversant with business, and will feel more interested in managing its work. . . . The permanent president, who will only lose his office if he discharge it ill, has an additional motive for performing all his duties well."[7] Bentham was surely right. It was by just this union of permanency with subordination that the tradition of complete disinterestedness was enabled to develop. And it was that removal of one member from the passions of debate that contributed most of all to the spirit of fair-play, the consideration for minorities, and the general orderliness of the procedure at Westminster.

So much for the regulation of relations between members. On the actual conduct of debate, the order and forms of speaking, moving, amending, and voting, Bentham had much to say. Many of the conclusions seem axiomatic to an English reader. To discuss them might appear to him, therefore, to be profitless. That is probably why it has been so seldom done. But, in reality, to explore their foundations may be all the more valuable for being rare. The best way to explore them to-day, as it was a century ago, is to read Bentham's *Essay on Political Tactics*.

* * *

The main advantages of publicity, according to Bentham, are three. It enables the governors to know the wish of the governed, and to benefit from any special information that may be possessed by members of the public. As a result of the free discussion of proposed laws it is possible to sound the opinion of the electorate. Since it is impossible to govern for any length of time against the general opinion, the consequence of publicity is to make for government by popular consent, and for stability. Bentham is a disciple of Locke in his desire for rule by consent. Open discussion on alternatives increases the confidence of the people in their rulers. That is the second advantage. "The government is much more assured of the general success of a measure, and of the public approbation, after it has been discussed by two parties, whilst the whole nation has been spectators." "Objections have been refuted—false reports confounded." "Calumny will lose its force; it collects its venom in the caverns of obscurity, but it is destroyed by the light of day." "Let it be impossible that anything should be done which is unknown to the nation—prove to it that you neither intend to deceive nor to surprise—you take away all the weapons of discontent." In his treatment of publicity Bentham accounts strikingly for the fact, still more frequently demonstrated since Bentham's day than it was before, that, given distrust, moderate reform from above leads often to violent revolution from below. When government is conducted secretly, and when, he says, "odious imputations exist; the explanations which are given of necessity, are considered as the acknowledgments of weaknesses. Hence improvement itself produces a shock, when improperly introduced, and when it is opposed to the inclinations of the people. The history of the Emperor Joseph II would furnish a multitude of examples."

But Bentham's chief argument for publicity is that it forces the members of the assembly to do their duty. That is, presumably, to govern in the interests of the greatest number. No possible body is a better means of keeping the assembly to its duty than the public to which it is answerable and by which it is elected. For a lively public opinion there is no substitute whatever. But when it is present there is a sure guarantee of good government. It keeps each member continuously alive to his responsibility, and the better informed it is the keener and wiser must he be. It is for this reason that voting in the assembly ought to be open and not secret.[8] Of the supreme importance of public opinion Bentham has much that is admirable to say. "The public compose a tribunal which is more powerful than all the other tribunals together. An individual may pretend to disregard its decrees—to represent them as formed of fluctuating and opposite opinions, which destroy one another; but everyone feels, that though this tribunal may err, it is incorruptible; that it usually tends to become enlightened; that it unites all the wisdom and all the justice of the nation; that it always decides the destiny of public men; and that the punishments which it pronounces are inevitable. Those who complain of its judgment only appeal to itself." These arguments were of the utmost value when Bentham was writing. At that time a large proportion of the people were illiterate; there were but one or two news-sheets, expensive and scantily distributed; communications, though much improved, were still bad; and the first railway had yet to be built. In such conditions what public opinion there might be was

neither widely based nor much scattered and divided. To realise its potency and emphasise its importance even when only an extremely small section of the public had the right to translate its opinion into votes, was an indication of deep insight. To-day the enfranchised public has multiplied a thousandfold. Public opinion means something much less simple than it did to Bentham. It is not one but legion. We are aware of its complexity and of some of the devious ways in which it is formed. We know, for instance, that the influence on it of wealth—with its instruments, the press, the church, the social hierarchy—is overwhelming. In view of this it is not possible to be as sure as was Bentham that public opinion is incorruptible, nor that it continually tends to become enlightened. Yet Bentham's analysis at least reminds us how completely we rely upon these assumptions for the whole justification of our political system, and should they be found to be untrue then that system will indeed have lost its firmest foundations, and perhaps with them its future.

There ought, Bentham argues secondly, to be no fixed places for members.[9] Those holding similar views may then sit together and concert action. The practice of giving to each town or district a fixed seat makes for disputes over precedence. He might have added that it encourages parochialism. When the assembly is numerous, however, Bentham thinks that for reasons of acoustics speeches should be made from a rostrum,[10] although he is ready to allow a short explanation, answer, or question, to be delivered from the body of the hall. He acknowledges that the British parliament has no tribune, and that "no great inconvenience results from the want." In any case, wherever members speak from, they are never to be allowed to read a written speech. That rule should be most strictly observed.[11]

Somewhat on the lines of the House of Commons distinction between meeting as the House and as a Committee, Bentham claims that a valuable division can be made between strict and free debate. The former is more necessary when the assembly is large. Then it may be useful to allocate the right to speak to certain speakers either by agreement that they are representative or by casting lots. With the one exception of the opener of the debate, no member should be permitted to reply or speak a second time. The free method of debate, however, has tremendous advantages. "In an argument between two persons, the discussion is better followed—the reasoning is more connected than when many persons are engaged." Each reply tends to increase the information received . . . every step taken leads on to the conclusion."[12] There should be liberty of reply because "the reply will go at once to the point without losing time in set phrases, exordiums, and apologies, as is done by each new orator."[13] There should not, therefore, in free debate be a predetermined order of speaking.[14] On an important subject there should be both types of debate at different stages.[15]

Bentham's view that there ought to be a time for ending debate was original. Nothing of the sort was practised in the House of Commons until much later. The twelve o'clock rule was adopted only about half a century afterwards. It took sixty years, the investigations of seven committees on procedure, and the organised obstruction of the Parnellites to induce the House to accept change. Bentham's proposal, though it is suggestive, shows that he by no means foresaw the essentials of future development. Obstruction, he thought, would not be resorted to because "the individual who should speak merely to consume time, would do too much injury to himself."[16] To do so would demand "a rare degree of impudence." In ordinary times Bentham was not without reason. The cause of the most drastic curtailment of debate, however, has been not obstruction but the enormous increase of legislation, which also Bentham failed to envisage. But, given the necessity for some sort of limit, the guillotine itself, and still more the closure by compartments, is based on the view, as he put it, "that there is no other method of securing to each subject a degree of discussion proportioned to its importance."

The form of a Bill or project of law Bentham considered to be vital to a good conduct of debate. In dealing elsewhere with the initiation of these he had much that was important to propose as to the substance and drafting, but he considered that an ordered discussion could not be organised except on an ordered Bill. It must be printed previously to the debate, as also should amendments. This is a means of allowing for reflection and obviating the danger of surprise. Its clauses must be numbered, each dealing with a single point, briefly, simply, but nevertheless completely. By this means alone is it possible to preserve that unity of debate without which no good results can accrue.[17] There must always be only one motion before the assembly at a time. Voting on it must remove it from further discussion. He felt it particularly necessary to urge this because French practice seemed to disregard it.[18]

* * *

It was probably for similar reasons that Bentham was ready to accept and approve the well-established English practice of giving three read-ings to a Bill. Ordinarily these would be taken on different days, and a considerable time would generally separate the first stage from the last. In the interval there was an opportunity to reflect; passions and the mere transports of eloquence would subside; public opinion could make itself known; new light could be shed on the question by experts. When we are told, however, that the House of Commons rule that readings be taken on different days may be, and has been, suspended in emergency so that a project has passed through all its stages in both houses in one day, it becomes clear of what small effect any sort of procedural rules will be in preventing a rash assembly from being rash. But all these considerations are expressed by Dumont alone. Bentham's treatment of this subject was only incidental. He never gave it specific discussion. What is to be found on it in the *Essay* is the work of Dumont,[19] who, however, here seems to have been giving much the views of "the master."

Finally, there are certain other observations drawn from British method.[20] These are of less importance, but nevertheless of value. "The former were dictated by necessity, these by prudence." No member should be allowed to doubt the sincerity of another, nor in any way to impugn his motives. Partly this is mere courtesy and a proper humility, but it is also demanded by expediency. "All who have watched political assemblies know that improper expressions are the sources of the most tumultuous incidents and of the most obstinate wanderings." In the same way, in order to obviate personalities, it is better to refrain from naming a member by his proper name.[21] By calling him "the honourable member" "it is as though an abstraction were made of the individual that he might be considered only in his political character." To address the president, instead of the assembly, also promotes the purpose of making debate objective, because it is then less easy to fall into personalities. The practice is natural because it is the president who must judge of the regularity of the speech. Words addressed to him will also be "more grave and temperate." "An excited individual addressing himself to an impartial magistrate, to a respected president, will feel the necessity of measuring his expressions, and repressing the movements of his indignation and wrath." Having dealt with the important subject of personalities, Bentham insists—obviously thinking of safeguards against a tyrannous executive—that nothing shall be used as evidence in debate which is not open to the examination of members.

Of Committees Bentham makes a short but admirable analysis.[22] In a mere three or four hundred words he manages to summarise the most important points. If art be "what oft was thought but ne'er so well expressed" then the jurist here, at least, is an artist. "The more numerous an assembly is," he says, "the less is it fitted for certain labours. By dividing itself into committees, it multiplies itself. . . . The labour is distributed—progress is accelerated—a degree of attention may be given to all the details of each new project of which a large assembly would be incapable."

Bentham foreshadowed three different developments of the committee system in legislation. He showed the value of multiplying the assembly by forming standing committees or bureaux for general purposes. Two such standing committees were formed in the House of Commons in 1882, and stabilised in 1888.[23] He recommended the setting up of permanent committees for certain subjects, such as finance, commerce, economics, because "there will be in a permanent committee greater coherency in their proceedings, more experience and special knowledge." This is a proposal which has been widely carried out abroad—and on the whole with satisfactory results where Bentham's warning has been remembered that the assembly, which is to say in modern conditions the majority government, should remain master. It has since been repeatedly suggested in England, and seems not unlikely eventually to be applied. Lastly, Bentham demonstrated the usefulness of occasional committees. The members of these, "having made the object in question their particular study, may be considered as better acquainted with it; and . . . as they are only charged with a single operation, may give more application to it."

* * *

The process of making law does not consist only in discussion and decision. The law must also be prepared. It is when Bentham deals with the initiation of law that his proposals are most striking. He considers, first, the drafting of new projects and their co-ordination with the existing law. The value of carrying on half-finished legislation from one session to another seems to him, secondly, to require special implementing. And lastly, he has suggestions to make upon the preparation of the substance of new law.

1. Bentham was always the enemy of the confusion, inconsistency and clumsiness of statute law. Like Dickens he saw that this and the consequent tediousness of litigation survived largely because they increased the fees of lawyers. In Bentham's State there was to be no use for the lawyer. So clear would be the law that he would have nothing to do. In the "pannomion," or the whole body of law, everything would be clearly defined and classified. But since the law must develop and change as the result of motions from

all sorts of people, it could not retain its ordered form or its clarity unless there were an official specially charged with its supervision. Bentham's "Legislation Minister" was to perform this function. Any proposal, before being moved in the House, was to be submitted first to the minister who would be most closely concerned if it became law. The Legislation Minister was then to be consulted "as to the bearing of the proposed ordinance on those already in existence, and thence, as to the form in which, on its introduction, the proposed ordinance may most conveniently stand expressed."[24]

Bentham, it is hardly necessary to say, was thinking of a legislative chamber where, as in the House of Commons of his own time,[25] the main initiative of new laws came from the private member. It was not the government's duty to have a policy for home affairs that should require legislative enactment. The government's task was executive and administrative, but by no means to make law. What is particularly striking is that Bentham should have foreseen the necessity of government coordination of the process of making law, as well as of the law in its ultimate form, so long before it became the regular practice. He insisted that when a Bill was proposed the Minister should have "to receive it and to attend to it: and so throughout its progress until it is either adopted or rejected." If Bentham did not give to his recommendations the form taken by subsequent practice, he yet saw the need underlying that later development. He failed, however, to carry his reasoning far enough to show him that when a group of ministers is given such powers—or even when the need for the exertion of such powers is already present—it will irresistibly seek means of gaining control over the whole process.

* * *

2. Bentham's parliaments were to be annual. He therefore felt it necessary to arrange that legislative measures not completed in one session should not thereby be lost. In the British system no Bill could then, or can to-day, be carried forward from one parliament to the next. If it is not passed into law in one, it must go through all its stages again when it is reintroduced. In 1848 and again in 1869, it is true, a Bill was brought forward in the House of Lords to change this, but on both occasions it was rejected.[26] To obviate the waste of time and of good measures Bentham had an original idea to propose. He urged the creation of what he called a Continuation Committee.[27]

"Each Legislature, antecedently to its outgoing, will elect a Committee, the members of which—to the number of from seven to twenty-one or more—will, under the name of the Continuation Committee, under the direction of the Legislature, apply their endeavours, collectively or individually, in the next succeeding legislature, to the carrying on of the designs and proceedings of the then next preceding Legislature, in an unbroken thread." Any member of the assembly or the Continuation Committee might be elected to serve in the next Committee. Thus a member might serve for any length of time. If, however, he were not re-elected to parliament he would not have the right to vote in it, although he would always have the power to speak or to propose a motion in it.

Any value that such a committee might have for the purposes for which Bentham intended it has been destroyed for modern conditions. The Cabinet now fulfills its functions. But it has present relevance in two other ways. The argument which Bentham put forward that it is a method of prolonging the service of specially valuable members of parliament who have not been re-elected, or who have not sought re-election, is, perhaps, the only valid argument for a second chamber .

* * *

3. When he comes to deal with the preparation of the substance of new law, Bentham has some equally interesting suggestions to make. For any legislative act to have value it must be founded on "correspondingly extensive information, or say evidence." "What can we reason," he quotes, "but from what we know?"[28] "As soon as a law is proposed . . . the information possessed by the different parties in the kingdom ought to be collected concerning it."[29] Otherwise an important part of the relevant facts may be concealed by the legislators for "their own particular and sinister purposes," and the statute be based on substantial falsehood. The House of Commons has been rightly called the Grand Inquest of the Nation, because its duty is to investigate and judge before it enacts the result.[30] The gaining of the necessary information is exactly the same function as the eliciting of evidence by a judge in a court of law. For this reason Bentham calls the instrument he creates for the purpose a "Legislation Inquiry Judicatory." Just the same judicial rules of evidence which he elsewhere urged[31] ought to be applied to its method of conducting inquiry. It should have the same power of compelling attendance, and where necessary it might confront the representative of one interest with that of another and allow them to contend. The departmental official was one of the most important means both of eliciting and of supplying the needed information, and he, therefore, would be one of the most valuable witnesses called before the inquiry committee of the legislature.

For Bentham's "Legislation Inquiry Judicatory"[32] was to be, wherever possible, a committee of the legislative assembly. It was to consist of one or more members, and to have as much authority as the legislature should determine, according to the needs of each particular case.

While Bentham had the royal commission in mind when he made these proposals, he differed from that most valuable system of preparing new law in the closeness with which he linked the "Inquiry Judicatory" with the legislature. The peculiar significance of this view is emphasised if it be coupled with his earlier argument, when dealing with committees of the House, that they are "absolutely necessary for the collection of documents—for engaging in those preparatory researches which require that a great number of persons should be heard—for the verification of accounts—etc."[33] The Legislation Inquiry Judicatory was only one type of these committees. Bentham did not lay stress on its permanence in any one form; on the contrary, he seems to have thought of it as existing for particular and temporary objects. The really significant feature of it, however—as of Bentham's other proposals for committees of the legislative assembly—is that it was to call witnesses. It would act, therefore, as a strong link between the private member of the assembly and the outside world. It would connect him with the department because the official was one of the most important witnesses; it would bring him openly into touch with the conflicting interests, since they would be called in evidence; above all, he would get in this way that free and impartial knowledge of the facts without which his function as a judge of the fitness of a proposed legislative act could not be properly or fairly exercised.

The importance of his having this information is the consistent underlying doctrine of Bentham on the subject. And it is precisely that principle which is being remembered at the present time, when congestion of business in the British House of Commons has combined with party discipline to remove the private member very largely from all opportunity of judging the fitness of measures or from adequately discovering the facts on which they are based. To bring him into contact, to gain his assistance in what is essentially his function, various schemes have been proposed. They all embody one or other of the committees suggested by Bentham. As early as 1832 a pamphlet was published, which proposed the creation of ten permanent committees of the House, of fifty members each, corresponding roughly with departments.[34] . . .

In the preparation of law, therefore, still more than in dealing with discussion on it, Bentham's suggestions have value. Some of them have been applied, with good results. Others yet appear, after a century fraught with change, to indicate valid methods of meeting modern difficulties. In his consideration of the rules of debate so profound is his analysis that the politician, and still more the organiser of the new international deliberating bodies, has much to learn from it. And finally, out of Bentham's study of the relations between members and the House there emerges, not merely a picture of intense historic interest, but a defence of the permanence and impartiality of the Chair, which he would not have been the last to-day to urge upon his admired "Anglo-American United States." It does not seem too much to say, then, that the spirit of Jeremy Bentham has presided over a century of parliaments, returning at strange moments to strike awe into conservative and innovator alike, nor to claim that even to-day it walks the corridors of the House of Commons.

Notes

1. Bentham, *Plan of Parliamentary Reform* (1817), p. 246.

2. Bentham, *Works*, IX, 165.
3. *Works*, IX, 160.
4. *Op. cit.*, I, 11.
5. Reginald Dickinson, *Summary of the Constitution and Procedure of Foreign Parliaments*, pp. 229, 242.
6. *Works*, II, 330.
7. II, 328.
8. II, 367.
9. II, 321.
10. II, 322.
11. II, 361.
12. II, 359.
13. II, 360.
14. II, 346.
15. II, 373.
16. II, 323.
17. II, 341.
18. II, 343.
19. II, 360, *note*, but compare with II, 373.
20. II, 362 *et seq.*
21. For the present practice in the British Parliament see Erskine May, *Law and Usage of Parliament* (eleventh edition, 1906), p. 333.
22. II, 372.
23. Redlich, *op. cit.*, I, 184.
24. IX, 191.
25. Ilbert, *Parliament*, p. 52.
26. Redlich, *op. cit.*, I, 105.
27. *Works*, IX, 170.
28. IX, 260.
29. II, 353.
30. IX, 184.
31. See *Principles of Judicial Procedure*, II, 57-62; also Vols. VI and VII.
32. IX, 181 *et seq.*
33. II, 372.
34. A. Symonds, *Practical Suggestions for the Internal Reform of the House of Commons*.

9. PROCEDURAL RULES AND THE SUBSTANCE OF POLICY

Howard E. Shuman

THE RULES of the Senate of the United States are only 40 in number and comprise only 49 of the 832 pages of the *Senate Manual*. Yet, when literally invoked they can bring Senate business to a standstill. They are most often ignored or circumvented by unanimous consent in order that the Senate may operate conveniently as a deliberative and parliamentary body. To pass legislation when they are invoked is a formidable enterprise.

Just as the law is said to be no better than the procedures by which it is carried out, so the substance of legislation is shaped and modified by the procedures that may be required under

Reprinted from *American Political Science Review*, Vol. 51 (1957), pp. 955-75, where it appeared under the title, "Senate Rules and the Civil Rights Bill," by permission of the author and the publisher.

the Senate rules, or by the mere threat to invoke those procedures, for they are compelling. The procedures preceding and surrounding the passage of the first civil rights bill in over 80 years illumine and illustrate the effect of the rules on the substance of legislation as have few other legislative controversies in recent years.

The Senate rules are the product of sectionalism. They were designed to prevent action unacceptable to a sectional minority. Among the more important specific rules with this design are: sections 2 and 3 of Rule XXII—the filibuster rule; section 1 of Rule XXII, which makes a tabling motion not debatable and which, therefore, acts as a "negative" form of majority cloture for, if successful, it can stop talk and kill a bill or amendment without a vote on the merits;[1] Rule

XXVI, which requires that all reports and motions to discharge a committee of a bill must lie over one legislative day—in practice this can mean several weeks if the Senate recesses from day to day rather than adjourns; Rule XL which requires one (legislative) day's notice to suspend the rules; Rule VII, which requires that a petition to discharge a committee be filed in the so-called morning hour, except by unanimous consent; and the same Rule VII which when literally followed requires the reading of the Journal in full, the presentation of messages from the President and reports and communications from executive departments, and numerous other time-consuming procedures in the morning hour, and so may preclude the opportunity for discharge petitions to be reached, for at the close of that hour the Senate must proceed to the unfinished or pending business; and two unwritten rules, first, of seniority, and second, the rule of recognition under which the chair recognizes either the Majority or Minority Leader as against other Senators who are seeking recognition. This can prevent a Senator from making a timely motion or point of order to which the leadership is opposed and so helps give the leadership command of the parliamentary situation.

How these rules affected the course of the civil rights debate and the strategy of both sides in the 1956 and 1957 sessions is now to be shown.

I. The Abortive Civil Rights Bill of 1956. With only a few days of the 84th Congress remaining in July, 1956, the House of Representatives, by a margin of 279 to 126, passed H.R. 627, a bill substantially the same as H.R. 6127 of the 85th Congress, part of which is now the law of the land. A small band composed of Senators Hennings, Douglas, and Lehman and finally supported by Senators Langer, Ives, and Bender, attempted to gain Senate action on the bill when it came from the House. This move was made notwithstanding the determined opposition of both Majority and Minority Leaders which, in the end, proved crushing.

Senator Douglas was guarding the Senate floor as the House passed the bill, and left his seat to go to the House chamber to escort H.R. 627 through the long corridor from the Speaker's to the Vice President's desk. As he was walking to the House he was passed, unknowing, by a messenger carrying the bill to the Senate. With Senator Douglas outside the Senate chamber and with Senator Hill of Alabama in the chair, the bill, with jet-age speed, was read a first and second time and referred to the Senate Judiciary Committee where its Senate counterparts had languished for two years.

This action took place by unanimous consent and so by-passed the specific provisions of Rule XIV, which require three readings of a bill prior to passage, "which [readings] shall be on three different days," but state that bills from the House of Representatives ". . . shall be read once, and may be read twice, on the same day, if not objected to, for reference. . . ."

An attempt was then made under Rule XXVI, section 2, to file a petition to discharge the Judiciary Committee from the further consideration of H.R. 627. Except by unanimous consent the petition must be introduced in the morning hour.

On the same calendar day the bill came from the House a unanimous consent request to file the petition was blocked by a motion of the Majority Leader to recess overnight. At the beginning of the next day's session, in what would ordinarily have been the morning hour, the Senator from Georgia, Mr. George, ruled that the petition could not be filed, except by unanimous consent, for the Senate had recessed the previous evening and, in fact, had not adjourned since the evening of July 13, *i.e.,* 10 days previously. Although the date was then July 24, the legislative day was July 16, and thus technically there was no morning hour for the routine business of filing bills, reports, petitions, etc. Individual Senators then objected to further unanimous consent requests to file the petition. The Senate recessed that day and did not adjourn overnight until July 26, the evening before adjournment *sine die.* In the meantime a motion by Senator Douglas to adjourn for five minutes, in order to bring a new legislative day and a morning hour, was defeated by the crushing vote of 76 to 6.

In the morning hour on the last day of the session, the discharge petition was finally filed. But a discharge petition, under section 2 of Rule XXVI, must lie over one further "legislative" day. If consideration of the petition is not reached or is not concluded in the morning hour or before 2 o'clock on the next "legislative" day, it goes to the calendar. Then the motion to proceed to its consideration and the motion on passage of the petition are both subject to unlimited debate, unless cloture is applied to each. Such action, even if successful, would only result in placing the bill itself on the calendar, where it in turn must lie for another "legislative" day. The motion to proceed to its consideration and the motion on final passage are also both subject to unlimited debate, unless cloture is applied. Thus the filing of the petition came too late to bring action in the 84th Congress. Even if commenced at the beginning of a session, and even if 64 votes were obtainable for cloture on each of the four occasions when they are potentially necessary, the process of discharging a committee can be drawn out over several weeks, and even months, if the rules of the Senate are literally invoked.

Although this attempt was abortive the experience was useful to the civil rights proponents in 1957. It brought a familiarity with the rules of the Senate which can only be gained from step-by-step proceedings under them; from it they concluded that action must begin very early in the session if it were to be successful; they saw that the route of discharging a committee meant meeting countless roadblocks, which could only be stormed and surmounted by determined efforts and with overwhelming bi-partisan support; and they concluded that a fight to change Rule XXII was essential because the inadequacy of cloture had either killed previous civil rights bills or brought their death by the mere threat of a filibuster.[2]

II. The Fight to Change Rule XXII. The effort to change Rule XXII was made at the opening of the 85th Congress in January, 1957. In the past Rule XXII has been the gravedigger in the Senate graveyard for civil rights bills. Section 2 of Rule XXII requires 64 affirmative votes to limit debate and section 3 provides that on a motion to proceed to the consideration of a change in the rules there can be no limit on debate of any kind. The rules of the Senate have carried over from Congress to Congress and changes in them have been made only after a unanimous consent agreement has been reached narrowly limiting the language and amendments which could come before the Senate.

Because of section 3, the only chance of success seemed to lie in a move at the beginning of a Congress that the Senate proceed to adopt new rules, relying on Article I, Section 5 of the Constitution which provides that ". . . each House may determine the rules of its proceedings." Such a motion was made in 1953 and was defeated by a vote of 70 to 21. Its opponents argued then that a civil rights bill would be passed, and that the rules should be changed only by ordinary processes of piecemeal amendment.

In 1957 the vote to table the motion to proceed to the consideration of new rules was carried, 55 to 38. Three absentees, Senators Neely and Wiley, and Javits, who had not yet taken his seat, opposed tabling and so brought to 41 the total who favored adopting new rules. Thus a shift of seven votes, plus a Vice President's favorable vote or ruling, was all that was now required to change Rule XXII. This was a major gain over 1953, for these 41 votes were obtained over the concerted objections of the leadership of both parties.

The size of the vote and its near success caught Southern Senators on the horns of a dilemma. They knew that any actual and organized use of the filibuster would ultimately bring an end to Rule XXII, and they also knew that if they did not use the filibuster Congress would most likely pass a civil rights bill. The fight to change Rule XXII thereby produced a climate in which not only a meaningful bill could pass but, it can be persuasively argued, a bill much stronger than that which was actually passed. The arguments and the parliamentary strategy involved in the Rule XXII fight were therefore crucial.

The opponents of the change relied basically on a single argument, namely, that the Senate was a continuing body, and as two-thirds of its members carry over from Congress to Congress, its rules should therefore also carry over from Congress to Congress as they have in the past.

The proponents argued that whatever the Senate had done in the past it had explicit constitutional power to adopt its rules at the beginning of a new Congress. Unlike their course in 1953, when the attempt to adopt new rules was hastily devised, the proponents did not meet the continuing body argument head on, but argued instead that it was immaterial whether the Senate was a continuing body or not. Acceptance of the continuing body argument did not deny to a majority of the Senate the right to adopt its own rules. Proponents also argued that proceedings on all bills and resolutions, as well as on treaties, begin again in a new Congress; that the Senate is newly organized and new committees are appointed; and that the newly elected one-third, even though only one-third, could alter the party alignment and thus provide a new majority and a new mandate which it had the right to carry out.

A second argument by the opponents, less used but probably more telling than the first, was that until the adoption of new rules the Senate would be in a parliamentary "jungle." Senator Russell combined with this argument a threat to proceed to rewrite each of the 40 rules of the Senate.

In rejoinder the proponents argued that the House of Representatives entered and left the parliamentary "jungle" in a very few minutes at each new Congress. They proposed that until the rules were adopted the Senate should proceed under general parliamentary rules including the motion for the previous question under which debate could be shut off by a simple majority. The proponents also relied on the precedents of the Senate to support the contention that majority cloture could be applied, for it was shown that the previous question rule was a part of the Senate rules from 1789 to 1806 and was used to bring debate to a close on several occasions.

The potential parliamentary moves were extremely involved, but basically the proponents sought to gain a ruling from the Vice President that their motion to proceed to the immediate consideration of the adoption of new rules was in order. This was their strongest position but, in the end, it was not gained.

It was their strongest position for a variety of reasons. To succeed, strong bi-partisan support was needed. The Democratic Party, by its nature, was split on the issue and could not provide a majority of votes. This was true even though the Democrats have traditionally supplied more votes on procedural issues in support of civil rights, and occasionally more on substantive civil rights issues, than the Republicans. In 1953, of the 21 votes for the adoption of new rules, 15 were Democratic. Only 5 Republicans and Wayne Morse, then an independent, voted for the change. That year Vice President Barkley let it be known that he would rule such a motion in order. But he had no opportunity to do so for Senator Taft gained the floor and gave immediate and pre-arranged notice that he would move to table the motion and thus shut off argument after a short debate. In 1957 with a Republican Vice President and with Republican votes needed to win, it was obvious that the strongest position would follow from a favorable ruling by the Vice President, and on the vote to uphold or overturn his ruling. The Democrats could provide no more than half of their numbers in support of such a favorable ruling. But the Republicans could provide, potentially, almost all of their votes if the issue were one of supporting their own Vice President.

In 1953 it mattered little whether the motion to proceed to the adoption of new rules were tabled, or whether a point of order were made and a ruling sought, for there would still have been a limit to the number of potential Democratic votes on this issue in support of a Democratic Vice President. The Republicans were obviously under no political pressure to support the ruling of a Democratic Vice President who was to leave office in a very few days.

In 1957 it was a different matter. Whether the vote came on a motion to table or on an appeal from the ruling of the Chair was critically important. If a Republican Vice President now ruled favorably, he would no doubt be supported by more than a majority of his own party which, combined with the Democratic support, could provide the winning margin. The proponent group

knew that they would make gains over 1953 however the Vice President ruled, but if he ruled for them there was an opportunity for spectacular gains and perhaps a victory.

The strategy was therefore devised that the mover of the motion to proceed to the consideration of new rules for the Senate should also couple with his motion a parliamentary request for a ruling from the Chair that the motion was in order. If this were not done a motion to table would no doubt be made, thereby cutting off debate and bringing an immediate vote. The proponents of a change in Rule XXII not only had more to gain from a ruling from the Chair but also felt that time for debate, which could educate and arouse public opinion, was necessary to the success of the effort. A steering committee representing those who favored adoption of the new rules therefore met with the Vice President to advise him of their proposed course of action. They did not seek nor did they receive the Vice President's opinion as to the merits of their proposal.

They were advised, however, that the Majority Leader had informed the Vice President that immediately following the motion to proceed to the consideration of new rules he would seek recognition for the purpose of tabling that motion. The Vice President then gave his opinion that under the precedents of the Senate a point of order could not be coupled with the substantive motion, and that under the unwritten rule of recognition he must recognize the Majority Leader as against some other Senator seeking the floor. This meant, of course, that once the motion was made the Majority Leader would be recognized to move to table that motion and thereby shut off debate before any other Senator, including the mover of the motion, could raise a point of order.

The unwritten rule of recognition thus brought the vote on the issue of Rule XXII on the least advantageous grounds for the proponents of new rules and an end to the filibuster. It was, however, very ironic that the proponents of unlimited debate should immediately move to shut off debate on the question of changing Senate Rule XXII which, in effect, provides for unlimited debate. Recognition of this anomaly led to a unanimous consent agreement which fixed a limited time for debate on the tabling motion. When the motion to proceed to the consideration of new rules was made, consequently, and was sent to the desk and read by the clerk, the Majority Leader sought and gained recognition. He proposed to table the motion which, but for the unanimous consent agreement, would have cut off debate immediately; as it was, debate was limited and the issue came to a vote as had been planned.

In the course of these events the Vice President gave it as his informal opinion, though not as a formal ruling, (1) that a majority of the Senate could adopt new rules at the beginning of a new Congress if it wished; (2) that Section 3 of Rule XXII was unconstitutional for it allowed a previous Senate to bind a majority of a future Senate;[3] and (3) that until such time as the Senate either adopted new rules or by some action, such as the tabling motion, acquiesced in the old rules, the Senate would proceed under its previous rules except for those which could deny a majority of the Senate the right or opportunity to adopt new ones, or, in short, sections 2 and 3 of Rule XXII.

Thus, the unwritten rule of recognition and the use of the tabling motion as a negative form of majority cloture, not available to the proponents of a motion, bill, or amendment, were decisive parliamentary weapons in the fight over Rule XXII and the filibuster.

Although the fight was lost it nevertheless brought several clear gains to the proponents of the civil rights bill and of majority rule, apart from the dilemma of the Southern Senators over their future use of the filibuster. First, rhetorically, it foreshadowed the end of the effectiveness of the argument that the Senate is a continuing body with necessarily continuing rules. The debate showed it to be irrelevant as well as circuitous to argue that the rules carry over because the Senate is a continuing body, and that the Senate is a continuing body because the rules carry over. Second, substantively, the episode brought clear bi-partisan gains over 1953; the Democratic vote increased from 15 to 21, and the Republican from 5 to 17. While the press was predicting an overwhelming defeat for the 1957 effort those close to the scene estimated quite accurately that approximately 40 would support the motion to proceed to the adoption of new rules. Third, tactically, this fight gave a political urgency to civil rights legislation which it might not otherwise have had, and improved immeasurably the chances for a meaningful bill.

III. Filibuster by Committee. H.R. 6127 passed the House on June 18, 1957. In the Senate its companion bill, as well as some 15 other civil rights bills, still had not been acted on by the Judiciary Committee.

This inaction followed precedent. In the 83d Congress four civil rights bills were reported from the Subcommittee on Constitutional Rights to the full Judiciary Committee, where they died.

In the 84th Congress, the Constitutional Rights Subcommittee reported three bills on February 23, 1956, and a fourth bill on March 4, 1956, to the full Judiciary Committee; but they too died following 10 days of hearings by the full committee spread over the 11-week period from April 24 to July 13. In the 85th Congress, after every legitimate attempt by Senator Hennings and his colleagues to gain action on the bills, not one was reported to the Senate during the entire session. A chronology of the efforts to report a bill to the Senate will show how filibuster by committee takes place.

A number of civil rights bills were introduced during the first days of the session. On January 22, Senator Hennings moved in committee that February 18 be set as the deadline for ending hearings on them and that a vote on the legislation and the reporting of a bill to the Senate should not be delayed beyond one further week. This motion was not acted on.

Four days later, on January 26, the 14 bills by then in committee were referred to the Constitutional Rights Subcommittee.

On January 30 Senator Hennings, the chairman, presented an omnibus bill to the subcommittee and moved that it be reported to the full committee. The motion was defeated.

The subcommittee then agreed to hold hearings and Senator Hennings moved that these should begin on February 12 and be limited to two weeks, after which the subcommittee should act on the bills immediately. This motion was defeated.

Hearings by the subcommittee did begin on February 14 and ended after three weeks on March 5. On March 19, the subcommittee approved S. 83 and reported it, along with majority and minority views, to the full committee.

On March 21, Senator Hennings introduced S. 1658; its language was identical with that of H.R. 6127.

On April 1, in the full committee, Senator Hennings moved that the Judiciary Committee dispose of civil rights legislation by April 15. He was unable to obtain a vote on this motion.

On April 8, Senator Hennings intended to renew his motion, but there was no meeting of the committee owing to the absence of a quorum.

On April 15, Senator Hennings moved that S. 83 be voted on by May 6. The committee took no action.

On May 13, at the next meeting, Senator Hennings desired to move that the committee meet every morning and all day, when the rules of the Senate permitted, and in the evenings if necessary, so that a vote on the bill could be taken by May

16. He was unable to obtain recognition to make this motion.

On June 3, the committee added the sweeping "jury trial" amendment to the bill.

On June 10 and June 17, Senator Hennings was unable to gain recognition during committee meetings.

On June 18 the House passed H.R. 6127 and it was sent to the Senate.

How was it possible for the Judiciary Committee, which contained only a minority of Southern Senators, to delay action on civil rights for such a lengthy period of time? Under Section 134 (c) of the Legislative Reorganization Act, "No standing committee of the Senate . . . shall sit, without special leave, while the Senate . . . is in session." Under Section 133 (a) of the same Act, each standing committee is required to fix a regular day on which to meet. The regular meeting day of the Senate Judiciary Committee is Monday. While the Senate is often in recess on other days of the week, it is invariably in session on Monday, because that day is set for the call of the calendar of unobjected-to bills, and because the Constitution provides that neither House may adjourn for more than three days without the consent of the other. Consequently, when the hour of 12 noon arrives or when, as in the later stages of the session the Senate meets at an earlier hour, any member of the Judiciary Committee may make a point of order that the Committee may no longer sit. This was done, and was one means of postponing action.

In addition, by the chairman's power to recognize an opponent first, and by his power to hold off a vote on a motion until such a member has concluded his remarks on it, it was easy for the chairman either to prevent a motion from being offered or to prevent action on a specific bill during the Committee's normal two-hour meeting. Further, the unwritten rule of seniority has generally placed a Southern Senator in the chair when the Democratic Party controls Congress. While Rule XXIV reads that ". . . the Senate, unless otherwise ordered, shall proceed by ballot to appoint severally the chairman of each committee. . . ," this rule was not enforced either when Senator Eastland was first appointed chairman, on the death of Senator Kilgore, or at the beginning of the 85th Congress when he was reappointed. There was neither a ballot nor a motion to "order otherwise." Finally, on several Mondays it was impossible to muster a quorum.

IV. Placing H.R. 6127 on the Senate Calendar. Faced with this situation, a small group of pro-civil-rights Democratic Senators met a few days prior to the passage of H.R. 6127 by the House of Representatives, to determine on a course of action when that bill arrived in the Senate.

Several possibilities were canvassed. These included: (1) moving to send H.R. 6127 to the Judiciary Committee with instructions to report it to the Senate on a specific date; (2) allowing H.R. 6127 to go to Committee but moving to discharge the Judiciary Committee from further consideration either of that bill or of one of several of the Senate bills; (3) moving to suspend the rules under Rule XL in order to place H.R. 6127 on the calendar; and (4) moving to place the bill on the calendar under Rule XIV.

After consultation with the Senate Parliamentarian the group ruled out the first possibility, of sending the bill to committee with instructions to report it to the Senate on a day certain. Such instructions may be added to a motion to refer or to commit only when the bill itself has been motioned up and is actually before the Senate. Before the bill could come before the Senate it had first to be placed on the calendar, and then to be motioned up. Such a motion is subject to unlimited debate unless cloture is applied. This procedure was therefore evidently impossible, notwithstanding later statements by Senator Morse who, in justifying his opposition to placing the bill directly on the calendar, asserted that instructions to report the bill on a day certain could have been added after the second reading.

Similarly, as we have already seen, the method of discharging a committee is lengthy, and was probably impossible for legislation as controversial as a civil rights bill. More specifically, the steps involved in this procedure include:

1. Filing a discharge petition during the morning hour.
2. A successful motion to adjourn so that a new legislative day may arrive.
3. Reaching the petition during the morning hour, in which case it would go to the foot of the calendar if debate were not concluded in two hours; or, if it was not reached in the morning hour, motioning it up at a later stage.
4. Moving to proceed to consideration of the petition, after it has reached the calendar, and after one legislative day has elapsed (which requires an intervening adjournment), when such a motion becomes in order.
5. Securing a vote on this motion, which is debatable and requires either unanimous consent or cloture and 64 affirmative votes to bring the debate to an end. Passage of this procedural motion requires only a simple majority.
6. Securing a vote on the next motion, to agree to the petition to discharge the committee.

This motion too is debatable and requires cloture.

7. Placing the bill, now discharged from committee, at the foot of the Rule VIII calendar, which follows automatically if the previous steps are successful. It must remain there for another legislative day, which requires another successful motion to adjourn in order to reach a new legislative day.

8. Moving to proceed to consideration of the bill and securing a vote on this motion, which is by now in order, is debatable, requires cloture to end debate, and a simple majority for passage.

9. Moving to agree to the bill and securing a vote on it, after all amendments have been dealt with; this again is debatable and requires cloture.

In the face of determined opposition, and without the help of the party leadership, the procedures outlined here would take a minimum of five to eight weeks even if there were 64 votes in support of action at every stage, which was by no means certain. The group therefore determined that the route of discharging the Judiciary Committee was impractical; indeed, that the votes and physical endurance necessary to break four successive potential filibusters made it impossible.

Suspending the rules of the Senate in order to place the House-passed bill on the calendar was also considered. This procedure is no near cousin of the method of moving to suspend the rules and pass the bill, which is a short-cut frequently used in the House of Representatives and common in state legislatures, where with the backing of the party leadership and a disciplined two-thirds vote at hand an opposition minority can be steamrollered. In the Senate version it has the advantage merely of reducing from four to three the number of potential filibusters and cloture motions to be met.[4] On the other hand, in comparison with the discharge procedure, it has two immediate drawbacks. First, because the tradition that all matters, unless by unanimous consent, should go to a committee before floor action is rightly very strong, suspension of the rules is open to the charge of by-passing the committee; the discharge procedure at least makes a gesture of giving the committee a chance to act. Second, because the suspension procedure has been so rarely used, it is open also to the charge of novelty in procedure—an unorthodox means of gaining an unorthodox end. The steering group of civil rights senators therefore discarded this alternative, and in fact concluded that if a choice had to be made between the two, the discharge route was preferable.

Finally, the possibility of placing the House-passed bill on the calendar under Rule XIV was canvassed. The relevant parts of Rule XIV read as follows:

No bill or joint resolution shall be committed or amended until it shall have been twice read, after which it *may* be referred to a committee; bills and joint resolutions introduced on leave, and bills and joint resolutions from the House of Representatives, shall be read once, and may be read twice, on the same day, if not objected to, for reference, but shall not be considered on that day nor debated, except for reference, unless by unanimous consent. (Section 3, emphasis added.)

Every bill and joint resolution reported from a committee, not having previously been read, shall be read once, and twice, if not objected to, on the same day, and placed on the Calendar in the order in which the same may be reported; and every bill and joint resolution introduced on leave, *and every bill and joint resolution of the House of Representatives which shall have received a first and second reading without being referred to a committee, shall, if objection be made to further proceeding thereon, be placed on the Calendar.* (Section 4, emphasis added.)

Although infrequently used, this seemed to be a relatively simple and direct method of placing the House-passed bill on the calendar. If it could be attacked for by-passing the committee, it was nevertheless a well settled part of the rules of the Senate; and, compared with many rules, its meaning appeared to be crystal clear. On that count it was therefore preferable to suspending the rules. And although perhaps less orthodox than discharging the committee, it reduced the potential number of filibusters in finally passing the bill from four to two. It was decided, therefore, that this method had the best, and perhaps the only, chance of success.

On June 14, following press reports that a group of Republican senators, including their leadership, were also considering using Rule XIV to place the bill on the calendar, a group of 15 Democratic liberals issued a statement in which they (1) urged the Judiciary Committee to report out a bill promptly, (2) stated that, while they preferred to act on a Senate bill, if a Senate bill were not reported they would join and cooperate with any other senator or groups of senators on either side of the aisle who wished to place the House bill on the calendar under Rule XIV, (3) gave formal notice of their intention to do so to the leadership and whips on both sides of the aisle, to the Parliamentarian, and to all other Senators, and (4) gave notice that they would not give unanimous consent to any motion to refer the House-passed bill to committee and formally requested that they be notified before the bill was laid before the Senate or referred, so that they might be in their places to ask certain parliamentary questions or to make certain motions. This last request grew out of the experience in 1956, when the House-passed bill was referred to committee while interested Senators were not on the floor. A further important reason for giving notice was that bills from the House as well as bills introduced in the Senate are ordinarily, for the convenience of all, read perfunctorily, not actually laid down by the presiding officer, and automatically referred to committee. Even when a bill is actually laid before the Senate, this can be done at any time and while the floor is unguarded, for under section 7 of Rule VII,

The Presiding Officer may at any time lay, and it shall be in order at any time for a Senator to move to lay, before the Senate, any bill or other matter sent to the Senate by the President or the House of Representatives, and any question pending at that time shall be suspended for this purpose. Any motion so made shall be determined without debate.

Thus with a senator who opposed civil rights in the chair, another senator could move to, or the chair without a motion could, lay the House bill before the Senate and have it referred before another senator could gain recognition to object.

Certain precautionary steps were therefore taken. The first was to try to make certain that a senator in sympathy with the move to place the bill on the calendar, or the Vice President, would be in the chair when the bill arrived at the desk. Teams of senators were organized to guard the floor at all times. Arrangements were made with House members to notify key senators of the step-by-step actions on the bill in the House. Further, it was publicly pointed out that when the bill arrived the Senate would be in executive session considering the Atomic Energy Treaty, and hence that the bill would remain in limbo at the desk until the Senate moved back into legislative session. As the Senate can move back and forth from legislative to executive session by a simple unanimous consent request, attention was called to this fact so that senators would not lower their guard and stay off the floor during executive sessions under the mistaken impression that no action on the bill could be taken. Sheets of instructions were issued to the Democratic senators in sympathy with the move, in which parliamentary details were outlined; these instructed them to object to any attempt to read the bill a second time or to refer it, and to call for a quorum when in doubt. As a result, the rights of individual senators were protected as they had not been in 1956. Agreements were entered into at almost every stage for a specific time when action would take place and motions would be made, so that the rights of each senator could be asserted.

H.R. 6127 was laid before the Senate on June 19. It was read a first time, after which Senator Russell asked unanimous consent that it be read a second time on that day. Objections were heard from Senators Knowland and Douglas.

At this time Senator Russell argued that Rule XXV took precedence over Rule XIV. He claimed that following the procedures under Rule XIV would ". . . throw out the window the laws, the rules, and the Constitution in order to get at 'these infernal southerners' in a hurry." His major argument rested on the premise that the changes made in the rules by the Legislative Reorganization Act of 1946 superseded other rules with which they were inconsistent. In his view the language of Rule XXV, which enumerates the subject matter over which specific committees have jurisdiction, was in conflict with Rule XIV and therefore took precedence over that rule. He quoted Section 101 (a) of the Reorganization Act which reads, in part, ". . . such rules shall supersede other rules only to the extent that they are inconsistent therewith," and Section (k) of Rule XXV which reads:

Committee on the Judiciary, to consist of fifteen Senators, to which *shall be referred* all proposed legislation, messages, petitions, memorials, and other matters relating to the following subjects. (Emphasis added.)

A list of subjects then follows, including "civil liberties." Senator Russell urged specifically that the phrase "shall be referred" is mandatory and superseded sections 3 and 4 of Rule XIV.

The proponents of the move argued that nothing could be clearer than the language of Rule XIV; that Rule XXV was not mandatory concerning referral but merely a specification of the subject matter over which each committee had jurisdiction; that the history of the Legislative Reorganization Act showed this to be true; that there were numerous examples of House bills going directly to the calendar both by precedent and under Rule XIV; and that the phrase "shall be referred," should not now be construed as mandatory when it had not been so on hundreds of other occasions.[5]

Development of the argument brought out examples of House-passed bills which were automatically placed on the Senate calendar when a Senate companion bill was already on the Senate calendar, and examples of a House-passed bill placed on the calendar prior to the Senate bill being placed there, when it was known that a Senate bill would soon be reported. Further, although this point was not made on the floor, it is well known that, especially on the last day of a session, numerous House-passed bills are motioned up on the floor of the Senate when there are no Senate companion bills. There have even been examples of the bill clerk officially referring a bill to a committee and entering that referral in the Journal, only to find that the House bill is motioned up and passed in the last few hours before adjournment. In such cases the Journal has been corrected after the fact to show that the bill was sent to the calendar, in order to be there legitimately when motioned up. These examples added considerable weight to the argument that the phrase "shall be referred" in Rule XXV was by no means mandatory. Since these bills were sent to the calendar by a private decision of the Vice President or his agent, it was argued that what one man could do *in camera* under the precedents a majority of the Senate could do openly under the provisions of a specific rule.

On June 20, Senator Knowland objected to the "further proceeding thereon" immediately after H.R. 6127 was read a second time. Senator Russell raised the point of order that Rule XXV took precedence; and debate on this point, which is not debatable except at the pleasure of the Chair, took place for several hours. One problem concerning the use of Rule XIV bothered some Senators, namely, that a "single" Senator, by objection, could prevent a bill going to committee. The proponents of the move argued that while such a case might theoretically arise, there would no doubt, on an issue of such importance as a civil rights bill, be a point of order, such as Senator Russell raised; and that a majority of the Senate would, in fact, decide whether the bill should go to the calendar or to the committee.

Senator Case of New Jersey was particularly concerned about a single Senator's objection sending the bill to the calendar, and felt that greater support for the move could be obtained if some method were found to decide the issue more directly by majority vote. He proposed that, after the second reading, a motion rather than an objection should be made, to send the bill to the calendar. He had numerous discussions with the Vice President on this point and prepared a detailed memorandum outlining his views. The Vice President's opinion on the Russell point of order reflects, to a considerable extent, these original views of Senator Case.

The leaders of the liberal Democratic group, while sympathizing with Senator Case's position, believed that if a specific motion were made to place the bill on the calendar following the second reading, rather than an objection by a single Senator under Rule XIV, such a motion would be debatable and hence would require 64 affirmative votes and cloture to end debate. If this were true then the attempt to place the bill on the calendar could not succeed.

This point was overcome by the opinion of the Vice President, who stated (1) that Rule XXV did not require a mandatory referral to committee; (2) that if objection were made under Rule XIV and no point of order were raised the bill would go directly to the calendar; but (3) that if a point of order were raised the effect of it would be to put the substantive question, "Shall the bill be referred," in which case the issue would be decided by a majority vote. A filibuster at this stage was precluded when the Vice President went on to state that a motion to table could lie against the point of order. A simple majority, therefore, could end debate by moving to table the point of order. No such tabling motion was made, but the fact that it could be made allowed the Senate to vote on the substantive issue, "Shall the bill be referred?" The vote was 35 to sustain Senator Russell's point of order and 45 who opposed; and the bill went to the calendar.

Major Results of the Maneuver. There were at least three major, and perhaps historic, results of this action. In the first place it was probably the only method by which a civil rights bill could have been placed in a position to come before the Senate. Without it the civil rights bill would no doubt have languished again in the Senate Judiciary Committee until the end of the Congress. This procedural move was a major and essential step towards the final passage of the bill.

Secondly, for the first important occasion since 1938, the coalition of Southern Democrats and conservative Republicans was shattered. The *quid pro quo* of that coalition has long been that Southern Democrats would provide enough votes to defeat liberal social and economic legislation while the conservative Republicans provided the votes to defeat civil rights moves. Now, for the first time, a coalition of Northern Republicans and liberal Northern Democrats had acted together on a procedural issue to further the progress of a civil rights bill. This was all the more significant for, in the past, the conservative Republicans had furnished their votes in support of the South mainly on procedural rather than substantive issues, such as the 1949 appeal from the decision of the chair and amendment to Rule XXII which made it even more difficult than before, to shut off debate. They provided just enough votes or absentees so that cloture could not be applied to previous civil rights bills. They opposed and defeated the 1953 and 1957 attempts to adopt new rules of the Senate at the beginning of a new Congress. In that way the Republicans hoped to avoid the charge of opposing civil rights, for they professed their willingness to support, at least in part, the bills themselves on which, in almost every case, they prevented action. This was playing both sides of an issue and, because procedural niceties are little understood by the public and even more difficult to explain, they avoided condemnation for opposing civil rights which was the real effect of their actions.

In place of this coalition two new coalitions emerged. One was the Knowland-Douglas Axis, as Senator Russell referred to it, on the civil rights issue. This coalition is probably limited to civil rights and was more the result of public opinion, of the Republican gains in the Negro districts in 1956, possibly of the personal Presidential ambitions of individual Senators, and of the effective filibuster by committee, than the basis for any agreement or tacit arrangement for mutual support on other issues.

The other coalition was a revival of cooperation between the Southern and Western Democrats together with the remaining hard core of the Republican right wing. In many respects this coalition was not new for it has operated for years on such economic issues common to both areas as legislation on sugar cane and sugar beets, rivers and harbors and reclamation projects, the wool tariff, the silver subsidy, aid to the Western mining industry, and similar matters. As the course of the civil rights debate continued, this combination became dominant and civil rights, apparently, was added as a part of the bargain.

A third and most important effect of the vote was that for the first time in many years the Senate asserted a disciplinary jurisdiction over one of its committees. In theory, at least, committees of the Senate should be the servants of the Senate as a whole. Notoriously, in practice this has not been so. Examples include the unwillingness of the Senate to deal with the excesses of investigating committees; the tacit arrangement whereby the leadership, committee chairmen, and those Senators who are within or who are seeking admittance to the "inner circle" join to provide 52 to 55 votes to defeat motions and amendments on the floor when offered by individual Senators who are not members of the committee; and the unwritten rule of the Senate leadership that it supports the substance of committee action without regard to opposition by what may be even

a majority of the party. In this respect, placing the civil rights bill on the calendar was unique and precedent setting. Although committees will no doubt continue to operate substantially as they have in the past, the possibility or threat of similar action may well serve to allow action by the full Senate on controversial bills of great importance for which there is overwhelming support and which otherwise would die in a committee stacked against them.

V. The Debate on H.R. 6127. Although the vote to take up the bill was 71 to 18, the new Southern-Western coalition proved powerful enough to effect major changes in the bill itself. They forced the deletion of Section III of the bill and they added a jury trial amendment to the voting section which, as it passed the Senate, would have made the bill least effective in those areas of the Deep South where it was most needed.

Apart from the coalition, two other major factors operated towards weakening the bill. The first was the press conference statement of the President on Section III, saying that it was not his intention that the Attorney General should have the power to initiate civil rights suits under that Section and the 14th Amendment. The second was the fact that the press centered its coverage almost wholly on the contest—the strategy and maneuverings in connection with the bill—and avoided, almost completely, the moral and substantive grounds for supporting it in the first place. For example, Senator Douglas placed in the Record a detailed legal brief on the jury trial amendment and contempt proceedings, showing that no "right" to trial by jury was being denied by the provisions of the bill. This was ignored by the press. County-by-county figures on Negro registration in the South were also detailed, as were the various subtle methods by which Negroes are denied the franchise; and these too were largely, although not entirely, ignored. Further, Senator Javits and others made lengthy and even brilliant rebuttals of the attack on Section III of the bill which were little reported and went almost unnoticed even by such papers as the *Washington Post* and the *New York Times*.

On three further occasions after the bill was taken up the rules of the Senate, together with other internal and external factors, affected the substance of the bill materially. These include the abortive attempt on the part of the Knowland-Douglas forces to modify Section III when it was clear, following the President's press conference, that it would otherwise be stricken; the various revisions of the jury-trial amendment; and the successful use of the unanimous consent device to bring a third reading and deny the possibility of further amendments at the late stages in the debate.

Striking Out Section III. Once the bill was before the Senate, Senators Anderson and Aiken moved to strike out Section III. This section would have permitted the Attorney General to seek injunctive remedies under the equal rights provisions of the 14th Amendment in cases affecting the use of schools, busses, public parks, etc., either on his own initiative, or at the request of an aggrieved party, or at the request of local public authorities which, in practice, would generally have meant school boards. Despite repeated claims to the contrary during the course of debate, the bill gave him no power to issue court orders or to decide how fast school integration must proceed. The remedies sought were milder in form, though easier, it was hoped, to obtain, than the criminal penalties now available against those who deny rights guaranteed under the Constitution; they were to supplement, not supplant, these penalties. The Little Rock, Arkansas, case has since shown something of the potential effectiveness of the injunctive remedies. But the Attorney General was able to act in that case only because the original court order was sought by the Little Rock School Board, and because the court then invited him to intervene. Section III would have given the Attorney General the right to take the initiative.

When it was clear, after the President's press conference, that Section III would be deleted, the Knowland-Douglas forces sought to reach agreement on some substitute which could gain majority support. The Knowland position was that such an amendment should allow the Attorney General to intervene only when he was requested to do so by the local school boards or officials. The Douglas group's position was that the amendment should enable the Attorney General to intervene in these cases and also when an aggrieved party sought his intervention. Both versions abandoned the provision for the Attorney General to initiate action on his own and without specific request.

The parliamentary situation was that the amendment to strike out Section III could only be decided after perfecting amendments to the section in its original form had been offered and voted on. Under the rules even though the motion to strike out was offered first its priority for purposes of voting was last. The Knowland forces were unable to agree to the Douglas amendment, largely because they felt they could not push beyond the President's position; but the two groups tried to work out a strategy whereby they would fall back step by step, attempting

to pick up strength as they did so. They decided that Senator Knowland should first offer his amendment, and that Senator Douglas would then move to substitute his own amendment for it. In this way they hoped that the liberal Democrats and other supporters of the stronger position could vote for the Douglas motion and when defeated, as they no doubt would have been, they could join the Knowland position as the next defensive move.

Because of the rules and precedents of the Senate this strategy had eventually to be abandoned. The supporters of the Douglas position were willing to fall back a step at a time, but could not agree to support a weaker provision when it was presented against a stronger position. They could vote for the Douglas motion as against the Knowland motion. They could vote for the Douglas or the Knowland motion as against the Anderson-Aiken motion to strike out Section III. They could not vote for the Douglas or the Knowland motion if either were to lie against Section III.

The parliamentary situation made it impossible to carry out their strategy. Once the Douglas motion was defeated there was no way in which the Knowland motion could be made to lie against the Anderson motion to strike Section III. The issue would have been between the Knowland motion and Section III, in which case the liberal Democrats and some Republicans would have felt compelled to vote against the Knowland motion. This was true because of the precedent that a motion to strike is only voted on after the perfecting amendments to the basic provisions of a section have been disposed of. Efforts to substitute a weaker provision for the existing Section III were therefore abandoned at this stage. It was decided to let the vote come on the Anderson motion to strike, and to offer a revised Section III at a later stage, preferably following a victory on some substantive issue.

The Moving Target. Yet another example of the effect of the rules of the Senate on the substance of legislation may be seen in the successive revisions of the jury trial amendment. It is a cardinal principle of most parliamentary procedures that once a motion is offered it belongs to the full body and not to the mover. The parliamentary body determines what action should be taken, *i.e.*, to amend, commit, refer, etc. This is not true of the Senate of the United States. An amendment, even after it is offered, belongs to the mover of the amendment and until such time as the yeas and nays have been ordered, he may amend it, revise it, or change it as he sees fit. In this fashion the jury trial amendment was changed almost from day to day, not by any vote of the Senate but by the offering or acceptance of revisions on the part of its mover, Senator O'Mahoney. As Senator Douglas said on the floor, the opponents of the jury trial amendment were "shooting at a moving target." The initial point at issue was the definition of the criminal contempts to which a jury trial would be made applicable—an exceedingly intricate technical question.

The first version met strenuous objection. The distinction it drew between civil and criminal contempt was whether or not questions of fact were at issue. As any good defense lawyer could raise a question of fact, the effect of this version was to allow a jury trial in all contempt cases.

The second version attempted to distinguish between civil and criminal contempt on the basis of whether or not the act committed was a crime. The traditional distinction between the two types of contempt, often hard to draw in practice, turns on whether the action of the court is for the purpose of compelling compliance with a previous court order, or for the purpose of punishment for failure to carry out the order. Thus in a voting case, a local registrar could be held in contempt for failing to carry out the court's order, but so long as he could remove that contempt by compliance with the order it would be civil contempt. Once the day for election had arrived and passed, and the defendant was no longer able to remove his contempt by compliance, then the contempt would be criminal, for the court could send him to jail or impose a fine only for the purpose of punishment. Since almost all obstructive actions connected with voting in federal elections are criminal, the effect of the second version was to grant a jury trial in contempt cases arising from interferences with voting.

In the third version of the O'Mahoney amendment the orthodox distinction was finally drawn between civil and criminal contempt. In an attempt to gain more widespread support for it, however, the amendment was broadened to apply not only to voting cases but to all contempt actions under federal law. At least 40 other statutes were affected, but primarily this revision was aimed at gaining labor support, particularly from the Railroad Brotherhoods and the United Mine Workers who were sensitive about past abuses of labor injunctions and who, in turn, influenced a number of key votes in the Senate. This provision was a most radical departure from existing procedures. Like the second version, it was merely accepted on the floor by Senator O'Mahoney, and no vote was taken on the question of substituting it for the previous version.

At this stage the question of passage of a jury trial amendment was touch and go. Those opposed to it still appeared to be in the majority. Finally, a fourth version was offered to meet the complaints over the absence of Negroes from Southern juries, and so to pick up a few more votes. Federal law sets certain standards for service on Federal juries, but also provides that no one may serve on a federal jury who is incompetent to serve on the grand or petit jury under the laws of his state. As one must be a voter or qualified elector in Texas, Arkansas, Mississippi, South Carolina, and the Parish of New Orleans in order to be eligible to serve on a local grand or petit jury, and as Negroes are largely excluded from voting in these states, this means that by law Negroes are also excluded from federal jury service there. The fourth version, offered by Senator Church, repealed the provisions of the United States Code which excluded those from federal jury service who could not meet state qualifications. The effect of this final version was to provide the margin of strength to pass the jury trial amendment. However, as Negroes are excluded from jury service in other Southern states, in practice and by other means, it is doubtful that this change will have much practical effect.

The right to revise and modify an amendment at the will of its sponsor played a large part in attaching a jury trial amendment to the bill, for had the vote come on the first, second, or possibly the third version, it appears fairly certain that the amendment would have been defeated; and that, once defeated, the forces favoring it could not have recovered enough strength to pass even a greatly modified new amendment.

Unanimous Consent. The final instance in which parliamentary practice affected the substance of the bill occurred following the jury trial amendment vote and prior to the vote on the remaining amendments. Senator Russell referred to it in a speech on August 30, after the bill had passed, in which he justified and explained the failure of Southern Senators to filibuster the bill and took great credit for watering it down. He had this to say on the floor:

When we had arrived at this particular stage of the proceedings in the Senate I happened to learn that a determined effort would be made to revive some of the provisions of Part III that had been stricken from the bill. The new amendment appeared harmless on its face, but if it had been adopted it would have placed the stamp of congressional approval on the erroneous, if not infamous, decision of the Supreme Court requiring the mixing of the children in the public schools without regard to the wishes of the parents of either race. We, therefore, quickly closed the bill to amendments in order to assure that none of the victories that we had gained would be snatched from us.[6]

What happened was that a bi-partisan group determined to try to revive a part of the Section III previously stricken. Before they could offer their amendment a unanimous consent agreement was reached, at a time when there was general commotion on the floor, limiting further proceedings to those amendments which had already been offered and printed and confining the time for debate to 30 minutes on each amendment. Senator Douglas was within minutes of offering the revised Section III amendment and was prevented from doing so by Senator Johnson's unanimous consent request which was made and agreed to at a time of confusion when his request could not be heard in the chamber. Apparently a gentlemen's agreement had also been reached that all further amendments would be voted down by voice vote and without a roll call.

VI. The Filibuster: A Paper Tiger? One final point should be made concerning the effect of the rules of the Senate on the substance of the civil rights bill. A number of highly competent journalists who were not close to the debate, or who have since been misled by the interpretations placed on it by some, have asserted that the absence of a filibuster at any stage in the proceedings on the floor represented a willingness on the part of the Southern opponents to accommodate themselves at least to the voting rights provisions of the bill. A closer view leads to the opposite conclusion, that the passage of the bill represents no compromise or accommodation on the part of the Deep South Senators at all. Rather, the failure to filibuster may be regarded as a carefully calculated decision to avoid consequences which would have been worse, from the Southern point of view, than those of the bill as it passed the Senate.

Throughout the debate, and preceding the votes on Section III and the jury trial amendment, the threat of a filibuster was used to gain support for both these amendments. Senator Russell has since frankly admitted what many on the inside felt sure of at the time, namely, that the South would not filibuster and that the threat of doing so was more effective than the reality would have been. Notwithstanding the arguments made earlier in the year, that no meaningful civil rights bill could be passed unless Rule XXII was changed, the filibuster, after the Rule XXII fight and after the bill was placed on the calendar, became a paper tiger. In retrospect it seems clear that the Southerners did not dare to use it because they feared the results would be the loss of Rule XXII and the passage of a much stronger bill than was

passed. They were sufficiently convinced that a filibuster would so outrage the country and the Senate that they had more to lose than to gain by its use. This accounts for the severe condemnation of Senator Thurmond by his Southern colleagues following his 24-hour "talkathon."

The Southern group decided, instead, to attempt to filibuster the bill to death in committee. In this they were successful; they could have kept it throttled there indefinitely. However, as a result of the great increase in votes for a change in Rule XXII and the vote to place the bill on the calendar, they knew they could not successfully transfer that filibuster to the floor. In Senator Russell's words:

In years gone by, it has been a great source of pride to me that our group was able to defeat bills of this nature when they were forced to the consideration of the Senate. In the case of H.R. 6127 we were from the outset faced with greater odds than ever before . . .[7]

There was not a man among us who was not willing to speak against this iniquitous bill until he dropped in his tracks. We would have done so, but for the conviction, growing out of our knowledge of the Senate and the experience of many years in this body, that a filibuster was certain to make a bad bill infinitely worse . . .[8]

Our group held numerous meetings and the wisdom of launching a filibuster was often discussed. All members of the group were living with the problem from day to day, defending the things dearest to our heart while under heavy fire. At no time did any member of our group declare in any of our meetings that it was his belief that a filibuster was advisable, much less that one could be successfully waged. The contrary view was expressed on innumerable occasions . . .[9]

They therefore decided to avoid a filibuster while using the threat of it to gain their points. They decided also to keep debate relevant, and with one or two very glaring exceptions this was done. With the wholehearted support of Senator Johnson, the Democratic leader, they then pressed for the two basic amendments which, from their point of view, would gain the least offensive result. In this, too, they were successful. They took this course not from any desire for accommodation or willingness to compromise but because a different course would, from the Southern position, "make a bad bill infinitely worse."

Although the filibuster was not used, the existence of Rule XXII made it still possible for Senator Russell to claim that:

. . . the fact that we were able to confine the Federal activities to the field of voting and keep the withering hand of the Federal Government out of our schools and social order is to me, as I look back over the years, the sweetest victory of my 25 years as a Senator from the State of Georgia.[10]

Because of the filibuster rule, the unwillingness of some professed supporters of civil rights to see that the South dared not filibuster at this time, the consequent surrender to the mere threat of its use, and the skillful tactics of Senators Russell and Johnson, the bill as passed by the Senate was largely a victory for the forces of segregation. As civil rights proponents saw it, all their sweat and struggle to overcome the parliamentary obstacles had led to a bill which, except for a few minor gains, was almost form without substance. They took what consolation they could in watching the House revise it enough to make it a modest forward step.

Notes

1. The Senate has no similar form of "majority" cloture which could end debate and bring a vote on the substance of a bill or an amendment.

2. Since 1917, or for 40 years, cloture has been successful on only four of twenty-two attempts and never on a civil rights bill. Sixty-four votes have been forthcoming only three times, all in the period 1917 to 1927. Thus, no cloture motion has successfully prevailed in the last 30 years.

3. It has been asked why, if the Vice President believed section 3 was unconstitutional, Senators did not press the issue later in the session. The anwer is that the Vice President's position was that it was unconstitutional to the extent that it bound one Senate by the actions of a previous Senate. However, if the new Senate agreed to be bound, *i.e.,* acquiesced in the old rules as it did when the tabling motion was successful, section 3 would remain in effect throughout the 85th Congress.

4. The steps involved in suspending the rules in order to place the bill on the calendar run as follows: (1) When the bill arrives from the House, either a motion that it be laid before the Senate, or a wait until the presiding officer laid it before the Senate in order to object to the second reading of the bill on the same day. (2) Simultaneously giving notice of an intention to move to suspend the rules, and reading or placing in the *Record* the terms of the motion. (3) Gaining an adjournment

to bring a new legislative day. (4) On the new legislative day and after the reading of the Journal, either calling up the motion to suspend the rules, or waiting until the presiding officer laid the bill before the Senate for a second reading. At this time, and prior to the customary referral to committee, gaining recognition to prevent such a reference by calling up the motion to suspend the rules. Since no motion to proceed to the consideration of that motion would be necessary, one potential filibuster is avoided at this point. (5) Securing a vote on the motion to suspend the rules, which is debatable and would require cloture to stop a filibuster. An affirmative two-thirds vote of those present and voting on this motion would send the bill to the calendar. (6) From this stage on the procedure is the same as with the discharge method—an adjournment to bring a new legislative day, when a motion to proceed to the consideration of the bill would be in order; a vote on this motion, which is debatable and would require cloture; disposition of amendments and a vote on final passage, which again is debatable and would require cloture.

5. There were only a few examples of a bill going to the calendar under Rule XIV prior to 1946. Since then procedures under this rule were followed once on May 3, 1948, when Senator Downey of California objected after second reading to further proceedings on the Tidelands Oil bill, which then went directly to the calendar. Immediately following that action and on the same day Senator Fulbright attempted to do the same thing to the oleomargarine tax repeal bill. However, the chair (then the President pro-tempore, Mr. Vandenberg) had first recognized Senator Wherry, who raised the issue of committee jurisdiction before Senator Fulbright made his objection. In a series of parliamentary questions and votes the bill eventually went to committee, but it is quite clear from a thorough reading of that incident that it did not conflict with Senator Downey's action. Senator Vandenberg stated not only that it did not conflict but that the issue turned finally ". . . upon the pure question as to who is first recognized by the Chair to assert his rights under these conflicting rules." He said specifically:

There is no collusion whatever between the precedent of yesterday and the precedent of today. . . . It is the view of the Chair that the question of precedence in a case of this character depends entirely on who raises the point first. Since the question of jurisdiction has been raised first it is the view of the Chair that the question of jurisdiction takes priority.

6. *Congressional Record,* August 30, 1957, p. 15171 (daily ed.).

7. *Ibid.,* p. 15172.

8. *Ibid.,* p. 15171.

9. *Ibid.,* p. 15171-2.

10. *Ibid.,* p. 15172.

10. VOTING METHODS AND IRRATIONALITY IN LEGISLATIVE DECISIONS

William H. Riker

WRITERS ON PARLIAMENTARY LAW frequently begin their essays by citing with approval Hatsell's famous observation that ". . . it is more material

Reprinted from *The American Political Science Review,* Vol. 52 (1958), pp. 349-66, where it appeared under the title, "The Paradox of Voting And Congressional Rules for Voting on Amendments," by permission of the author and the publisher.

that there should be a rule to go by than what that rule is. . . ."[1] So generally is this notion accepted that it probably ought to be regarded as a fundamental premise of parliamentary law. Indeed the whole structure of this branch of law rests on the assumption that form is more important than content. Its literature consists almost entirely of the compilation of precedents, and, further-more, parliamentarians have seldom been concerned to justify the decisions they compile. This indifference to rationalization clearly follows from Hatsell's premise: if one believes that form alone is important, one appropriately concentrates on the form of rules, largely ignoring questions of whether or not their substance is efficient, or fair, or reasonable.

In some respects the emphasis on form has had beneficial effects; *e.g.,* it has encouraged precision of statement in an area where precise rules are especially necessary for quick decision by presiding officers. But in other respects the emphasis has been unfortunate. Thus, it has inhibited criticism of content, thereby obscuring the possibility that the rules may lead to unsatisfactory results. Indeed, despite Hatsell's premise, there may be circumstances in which one can justifiably say: "Better no rules at all than rules that have this particular effect." It is the purpose of this essay to describe in detail one such set of circumstances in the United States Congress and thus to suggest to parliamentarians that criticism is as important as the collection of precedents. More immediately, the purpose is to suggest a desirable revision of the rules of both houses of Congress in respect to the order of voting on amendments.

A significant circumstance in which one might say "Better no rules at all than these" arises when the rules of a legislature lead to irrational behavior. Although it might seem that a group of presumably rational men following long prescribed rules of behavior could not possibly act irrationally, it is nevertheless true that, under its present rules of procedure, Congress may act irrationally and in fact probably does so occasionally. This essay is intended to explain just how this can occur. As a preliminary, it is necessary to define precisely what is here meant by rational and irrational behavior.

While the notion of rationality has been variously defined, one minimum element which most definitions include (at least implicitly) is the ability to order preferences transitively. Transitivity, which is a generalization of the notion of syllogistic inference, is formally defined thus: Given three elements, a, b, c, and a relation, R, between pairs of them, R is transitive when the following inference is true: if aRb and bRc, then aRc. When such an inference is not true, R is said to be intransitive. An example of a transitive relation is the mathematical notion of equality. One validly writes: if a = b and b = c, then a = c. On the other hand, the relation of fatherhood is intransitive. One cannot validly write: if a is the

father of b and b is the father of c, then a is the father of c. Assuming that the relation of preference is defined as transitive, then it is intuitively justifiable to insist that rational behavior includes at least the ability to order preferences transitively. Thus, a citizen who approaches the voting booth certain that he prefers the Democratic candidate to the Socialist and the Socialist to the Republican, is regarded as rational if he actually votes for the Democrat. If, with the same ordering of preferences, he votes for the Republican, he is regarded as irrational.

Several scholars have lately doubted that rational behavior should be defined in terms of the transitivity of preferences. They have adduced impressive experimental evidence to indicate that in certain kinds of events men who in vulgar usage would be described as rational do not in fact order preferences transitively.[2] But these experiments are hardly sufficient to justify abandoning the traditional definition of rationality. They do, of course, demonstrate that the area of irrational behavior is somewhat larger than might at first be supposed. And they are extraordinarily valuable in that they have permitted an explanation of why irrational behavior happens to occur as frequently and insensibly as it does. But a proof that people are often confused should not lead us to abandon the standard of what constitutes confusion.

A more incisive attack on the use of transitivity of preference as a standard of rationality is Kenneth May's argument that the definition of preference does not imply transitivity. His argument is applicable, however, only to those events in which the chooser is successively confronted with only two choices in overlapping but non-identical sets.[3] In those more frequent events where the chooser is simultaneously confronted with more than two choices, the notion of preference does imply transitivity. The latter, rather than the former, is the kind of event customarily met with in economic and political choices and we are in most instances justified, therefore, in continuing to regard consistency of choice as a standard of rational behavior.

If we do so regard it and if we assume that most members of Congress are sufficiently sophisticated and thoughtful to be able to arrange their preferences transitively, it might seem to follow that any decision taken by this group would also be rational. Such, however, is not the case. Whenever the so-called paradox of voting occurs, the sum of the preferences of members is intransitive, even though each member's preferences are themselves transitively ordered. For an example of the simplest possible instance of the paradox, assume a three-member legislature with three motions simultaneously before it. Designating the members by "A," "B," and "C," the motions by "m_1," "m_2," and "m_3," and the relation of preference by P, assume that the members' preferences are ordered thus:

A: m_1Pm_2, m_2Pm_3, and hence, by the transitivity of P, m_1Pm_3.

B: m_2Pm_3, m_3Pm_1, and hence, m_2Pm_1.

C: m_3Pm_1, m_1Pm_2, and hence, m_3Pm_2.

A majority of this legislature (A and B) prefers m_1 to m_2 and another majority (A and C) prefers m_2 to m_3. If the sum of the preferences in this model were transitive, it should be validly inferred that a majority prefers m_1 to m_3. In fact, however, only A (a minority) prefers m_1 to m_3 and a majority (B and C) prefers m_3 to m_1. Hence the social, as distinct from the individual, ordering of preferences is intransitive.

The paradox of voting has recently been subjected to considerable scholarly scrutiny, especially in the work of Kenneth Arrow, *Social Choice and Individual Value*.[4] In this notable volume, Arrow demonstrated by mathematical methods that, if there are three or more choices and three or more choosers, then the possibility is ineradicable that the paradox may occur.[5] Inasmuch as legislative rules all over the world permit at least three choices to face legislators simultaneously, the possibility of the occurrence of the paradox exists in every legislature.

The mere development of an instance of the paradox in an actual legislature is not, however, by itself a cause for concern. An intransitivity in the social ordering of preferences is not in itself irrational behavior. Rather, behavior becomes irrational only when one of the choices in an intransitively ordered set is enacted into law. Fortunately, it is often possible to discover the existence of an intransitivity and, under the rules of some legislatures, to prevent action when the intransitivity exists. Duncan Black has shown that one of the characteristics of an intransitive ordering of the preferences of a legislature is the fact that no one of the intransitively ordered motions can defeat each of the alternatives to it.[6] In the example of a three member legislature just given:

m_1 defeats m_2, but loses to m_3
m_2 defeats m_3, but loses to m_1
m_3 defeats m_1, but loses to m_2.

If each of these motions is pitted against each of the others, each motion will lose once. If the rules of this model legislature require for the passage of a motion that it defeat each alternative to it, then no action can be taken. Hence the paradox results in a stalemate, in which, with no decision whatsoever, it is impossible to decide irrationally.

The rules of many legislatures require that, when there are three simultaneous motions, each one be pitted against each of the others in a vote. But, so far as I know, no set of rules in actual use requires such round robin voting when there are more than three simultaneous motions. (When there are three motions, the round robin necessitates only three votes; but when there are four motions it necessitates six; when there are five motions it necessitates ten; and, in general, if n is the number of motions, and if r is the number of votes in a round robin, $r = n[n-1]/2$.)[7] Hence the sheer difficulty of repeated voting prevents the full exposure of an existing paradox. But by a remarkable extension of his observation, Black also proved that the existence of a paradox is always revealed if there are as many votes taken as there are motions to be voted upon.[8] In effect, he showed that, if an intransitivity exists and if the legislature votes as many times as there are simultaneous motions, then no motion is able to pass. Hence a stalemate results in which irrational behavior cannot occur simply because action is not completed.

It is apparent from these researches that a large loophole exists for irrational behavior by legislatures. If, as Arrow showed, the possibility of the occurrence of the paradox is ineradicable when three or more choosers face three or more simultaneous choices, and if, as Black showed, the existence of the paradox cannot be revealed unless the legislature votes at least as many times as there are simultaneous motions, then a legislature may behave irrationally when its rules allow it (a) to consider three or more motions simultaneously and (b) to vote fewer times than there are motions. The rules of many natural legislatures provide just these conditions. But, for the sake of brevity, I shall limit the ensuing discussion to the possibilities in the rules of the United States Congress.[9]

In both houses of Congress, it is permissible to consider simultaneously as many as four amending motions to a bill or resolution. Hence, Congressmen may be faced with five choices at the same time, in which circumstance, the paradox of voting may, of course, arise. When the original matter and the amendments are simple motions (*e.g.*, a motion for adjournment, with perhaps two or more amendments offering alternative dates for re-assembly), the existence of an intransitivity is easily discovered. The body soon votes as many times as there are choices and, if an intransitivity exists, the final vote carries in the negative. Thus, there is no decision and no irrational decision. When, however, the original matter is an elaborate bill, it is quite possible that the existence of an intransitivity will not be discovered and that the House or Senate, unaware of the paradox, will irrationally adopt clauses that are supported only by a minority. This result is most likely to occur when Congress is amending details of a complex bill. It can be illustrated from the process of amendment in the Committee of the Whole in the House of Representatives. Classifying the situations according to the number of choices, the following events can occur:[10]

Case 1: If, after the reading of a paragraph or section, no amendments are offered, the Committee of the Whole passes on to the next paragraph or section without voting on the one just read. (In the Senate this procedure is so formalized that the only parts of bills considered on the floor at the time of a committee report are those parts to which amendments are offered.) The assumption behind this procedure is, of course, that, if no amendments are offered, the paragraph is unopposed. While this assumption may not be invariably valid, still the omission of the vote is in effect a form of consent procedure and as such is fully justified as a means of saving time. Nevertheless, in legislatures far more pressed for time than the House of Representatives (*e.g.,* the House of Commons in Great Britain and the National Assembly in France) it is customary to vote on every paragraph of a bill, whether or not amendments are offered. This is doubtless a precaution against adopting words opposed by a taciturn majority. American procedure differs in that it forces all opposition to become vocal if it wishes to be effective.

Case 2: If, after the reading of a paragraph, only one amendment is offered to particular words, the Committee votes on the amendment; and, both when the amendment passes and when it fails, then passes immediately to the next business. If the amendment has the effect of negativing the motion, there are in effect only two choices. If there are only two choices, irrational decision is impossible, for two choices cannot be ordered intransitively.[11] If, however, the amendment does not negative the motion, there are in effect three choices, *i.e.,* for the unamended motion, for the amended motion, and against the motion whether amended or not. This latter case should be regarded as a case 3 event.

Case 3: If, however, more than one amendment is offered to the same words in a paragraph, the situation is altered drastically and the House runs the risk of adopting the preference of a minority.

When the Committee has before it a paragraph, an amendment to the paragraph, and an amendment to the amendment, it votes first on the amendments. If the amendment to the paragraph (whether amended or not) passes, it takes the place of the original words without further vote, *i.e.,* the House does not vote on the paragraph as amended. Thus, while the Committee has three choices, it votes only twice, which is not sufficient to discover an existing intransitivity. The House does, however, decide, and if the House's uncanvassed preferences are actually intransitive it unconsciously but necessarily decides irrationally.

The House may be saved from this consequence only in one way: if, when the Committee reports to the House and the Speaker puts the question on the engrossment of amendments, a Member demands and secures a separate vote on a particular amendment adopted in Committee, there are then as many votes as there are choices. Thus the House may discover an intransitivity. But since the rejection of an adopted amendment simply results in the incorporation of the original words in the bill, and since the original words may also be favored only by a minority, the intransitivity is merely discovered, not resolved, and the House still behaves irrationally. Although the discovery of intransitive preferences depends in this case on a request for a separate vote at the time of engrossment, such requests are in fact rare. When they do occur, they are usually prompted by a desire for a roll-call vote (which is not permitted in the Committee of the Whole) rather than by a desire to reveal an intransitivity.

Case 4: If two or more amendments to the same words are offered and if none of them pass, the original words remain in the bill without a vote on their adoption. Thus the House may adopt a provision favored only by a minority without any opportunity to discover this fact. Theoretically, an amendment to a paragraph, even one of the amendments rejected in Committee, might be offered before the vote on engrossment. But in practice, this never occurs; and, if a special rule providing for the previous question to final passage governs the procedure on a bill, then it is not even possible to offer an amendment at the report stage.

The House, of course, votes several times on the whole bill (as distinct from particular sections), that is, on third reading and engrossment, on recommittal, on final passage, and on reconsideration. But if a putative intransitivity has arisen over a single paragraph, the majority opposing that paragraph may not wish to vote against the whole bill in order to win its point. The majority that has opposed, for example, one item in an appropriation bill containing hundreds of items may not wish to bring the whole government of the United States to a standstill simply to change the funds of one bureau. Hence, one cannot assume that votes on the whole bill discover or resolve an intransitivity arising around one paragraph of it.[12]

Irrational action of the sort described in Cases 3 and 4 is probably fairly frequent. Although it is difficult to estimate empirically the frequency with which this paradox of voting occurs in nature, one may estimate it theoretically as follows: If there are three choices and three choosers, intransitivities occur in two out of a possible twenty combinations of three orderings. In general, the frequency of intransitivities increases as the number of choices and choosers increases.[13] Since the House and Senate frequently consider three to five alternatives at once, it is not unreasonable to assume that intransitivities occur in actual practice more than ten per cent of the time when two or more amendments are offered.

A typical example of an event occurring in a Case 4 situation, an example chosen almost at random from the proceedings of the Committee of the Whole, illustrates just what risks the Congress runs:[14] In the consideration of the Agricultural Appropriation Act of 1953 the most significant and controversial subject was the amount of money for the Soil Conservation Service. The Committee on Appropriations had reported a bill providing $250,000,000 for the Service. Many Democrats supported this proposal (hereafter called the original amount), but some from wholly urban districts opposed it. These defectors were apparently sufficient in number to forestall a partisan majority for the original proposal. Almost all Republicans opposed this figure, although in varying degrees. Some wanted only a small cut; others a large one. Representative Javits of New York City, a Republican, offered the first amendment which, in the form it was ultimately voted upon, provided for the deletion of $250,000,000 and the insertion of $142,410,000. This was a serious amendment, intended to cut out entirely the activity of the Service in supplying fertilizer. Subsequently, Representative O'Toole of New York City, a Democrat, moved to amend the Javits amendment by deleting $142,410,000 and inserting $100,000,000, a provision on its face intended to destroy the Service; perhaps it was designed to establish a trading position for its backers. While O'Toole's amendment was frivolous in effect, it was seriously offered and the pique displayed in its offering symbolized the breakdown of the urban-rural coalition in the Democratic party. The stringent economy of the Javits amendment well expressed the Republican opposition (at that time) to a high budget; but of course it was unpalatable to Republicans from rural constituencies. Perhaps a few rural Republicans supported the original proposal; but most of them doubtless supported a substitute amendment offered by Representative Andersen of Minnesota, a Republican and the ranking minority member of the Subcommittee on Agriculture of the Committee on Appropriations. Mr. Andersen's amendment cut the amount from $250,000,000 to $200,000,000, thereby presumably satisfying the Republican desire for economy, but still providing substantial funds for the Service. As soon as the Andersen substitute was offered, Representative Whitten of Mississippi, a Democrat, offered an amendment to the substitute providing for $225,000,000 instead of $200,000,000. Since Mr. Whitten was chairman of the Subcommittee on Agriculture and as such was the author of the $250,000,000 figure, and since he was the floor manager of the bill in the House, one can assume that his amendment was a compromise intended to rally some Democrats who opposed the original figure but who might support a token cut.

The Committee of the Whole thus had before it five proposals of varying amounts of money: (1) the original proposal for $250,000,000; (2) the Javits amendment for $142,410,000; (3) the O'Toole amendment to the Javits amendment for $100,000,000; (4) the Andersen substitute for $200,000,000; and (5) the Whitten amendment to the Andersen substitute, for $225,000,000. This is the maximum number of choices that by Rule XIX the House may have before it at one time.

In such circumstances, the House votes first on the amendment to the amendment, then on the amendment to the substitute, then on the substitute, and finally on the amendment; a total of four votes. The rationale of this order of voting is that, before voting on either the amendment or its substitute, the Committee should first perfect what is proposed to be struck out and then perfect what it is proposed to be struck out with. As far as it goes, this is eminently reasonable. However, the House does not go on to a final vote on the adoption of the proposal, even if all the amendments fail.

In this instance, the House voted first on the O'Toole amendment, which failed by a voice vote. The Whitten amendment, voted upon next, failed by a division of 74 to 139. Then the Andersen substitute, the crucial choice, failed by a teller vote of 126 to 131. Finally, the Javits amendment failed by a division of 35 to 220. Since roll calls are not taken in the Committee of the Whole, names and party affiliations on these votes are not available.

From the fact that all amendments failed one

might infer that a majority favored the original proposal. Nevertheless, one awkward fact casts doubt on this inference: although the largest amount stayed in the bill, the third largest amount (Andersen) beat the second largest amount (Whitten). From this fact one may reasonably suspect an intransitivity here, for if the largest amount were really favored over all others, and the amount was the dominant criterion, then logically the second largest sum should have defeated the third largest.

When, as in this case, there are fewer votes than choices, it is impossible to decide whether or not the preferences of the House were transitively ordered. Nevertheless, by carefully reconstructing the situation on the basis of all information available, it is possible to postulate a set of orderings of preferences, and from them to discuss the probability that the House took irrational action. On the best informed guesses, it seems likely that the House did just that to the extent of at least $25,000,000 in this instance. I cannot demonstrate that an intransitivity occurred; but I do assert that from the circumstances a genuine case of the paradox of voting may well have happened.[15]

Let us number the choices in the order in which they were presented to the House: "1" for the original paragraph; "2" for the Javits amendment; "3" for the Andersen substitute; "4" for the Whitten amendment; and "5" for the O'Toole amendment. We will write "1P2" to signify that the original paragraph is preferred to the Javits amendment.

It is, I believe, fairly obvious that the members who preferred the O'Toole amendment ($100,-000,000) above all others probably arranged their preferences inversely to size so that the smallest amount stood first and the largest last: O'Toole, Javits, Andersen, Whitten, original; or 5P2, 2P3, 3P4, 4P1. (Those who so ordered their preferences will be called "O'Toole supporters"; and similarly other groups will be designated by their first preference.) Since the Javits supporters favored a cut only slightly less drastic than the O'Toole supporters, the Javits group probably ordered their preferences thus: Javits, O'Toole, Andersen, Whitten, original; or 2P5, 5P3, 3P4, 4P1. Those who supported the Andersen substitute above all else certainly favored some cut, but were opposed to cuts so deep as the Javits or O'Toole proposals. It seems reasonable to assume that their preferences were arranged: Andersen, Whitten, original, Javits, O'Toole; or 3P4, 4P1, 1P2, 2P5. Although possibly for some of them the ordering may have run 3P4, 4P2, 2P1, 1P5, it is not necessary to choose between these two guesses for both orderings lead to the same result in the summation of preferences of the whole House.

The supporters of the original paragraph were probably divided into two groups. Most of them doubtless ordered their preferences from the largest to the smallest amount, i.e., original, Whitten, Andersen, Javits, O'Toole; or 1P4, 4P3, 3P2, 2P5. But some of them followed a highly contrived strategy in voting and necessarily reordered their preferences accordingly. Assuming that the original paragraph could defeat the Andersen substitute but not the Whitten amendment, they voted first against the latter and then, safely, for the former. Hence they ordered their preferences thus: original, Andersen, Whitten, Javits, O'Toole; or 1P3, 3P4, 4P2, 2P5. (The former group will hereafter be called Original-Whitten supporters, and the latter Original-Andersen supporters.)

The Whitten supporters present a special problem. Since they favored only a token cut, clearly they least preferred the Javits and O'Toole alternatives. But one can only guess about whether they placed the Andersen or the original amount second. Presumably Whitten moved his amendment to attract Andersen supporters. Hence, if his maneuver succeeded, the Whitten supporters' preferences were ordered: Whitten, Andersen, original, Javits, O'Toole; or 4P3, 3P1, 1P2, 2P5. But if his maneuver failed, if it merely attracted some supporters of the original, then their preferences were: Whitten, original, Andersen, Javits, O'Toole; or 4P1, 1P3, 3P2, 2P5. There is good reason to believe that, in fact, all of Whitten's supporters were drawn, as he was himself, from the supporters of the original. On the crucial vote, although the Andersen substitute was formally pitted against the Javits amendment, the members clearly assumed that the substitute lay against the original. Since the Javits, O'Toole and Andersen supporters all preferred the substitute to the original, the 126 who voted for the substitute must include these. If this 126 also includes the Whitten supporters, then the supporters of the original are the only ones on the other side; and it must be concluded that the original paragraph had a clear majority over all other choices. Quite possibly such was the situation; yet this detailed investigation was undertaken simply because there was reason to suspect an irrationality. For the sake, therefore, of reconstructing a possible intransitive ordering of preferences, we shall assume that Whitten's maneuver failed, that he simply attracted support from the original paragraph, and that his supporters ordered their preferences thus: 4P1, 1P3, 3P2, 2P5.

Guesses about the number of members who held each set of preferences are much less defensible than guesses about the orderings themselves; but an estimate of numbers is essential for a reconstruction of the event and, with some trepidation, I offer the following: Although the number of members voting varied among the four votes, in the best attended and crucial vote 257 members participated. Assuming that all of these had one or another of the six orderings of preferences derived above, the number 257 will serve as the total. On the last vote 35 members voted for the Javits amendment as against the original paragraph. Only the Javits and O'Toole supporters can be assumed to have had this preference, so the maximum number of both together is 35. Since the O'Toole amendment was defeated in a voice vote, it is impossible to say with assurance how these 35 were divided. But assuming that the Javits amendment, which was a carefully planned attack on soil conservation, attracted more supporters than the O'Toole amendment, which was somewhat frivolous, I have arbitrarily divided these 35 into five O'Toole supporters and 30 Javits supporters. (Either figure could be varied from zero to 35 without affecting the outcome of the subsequent calculations.)

On the third vote, 126 members voted for the Andersen substitute. It has already been indicated that in this vote the Javits, O'Toole and Andersen supporters stood together against the supporters of the Whitten amendment and the original proposal. Subtracting 35 for the Javits and O'Toole groups from the 126 on the losing side, the Andersen supporters must number 91. From this same vote we know that the supporters of the Whitten amendment and the original proposal total 131. When the Whitten amendment was voted on just previously (as against the Andersen substitute), however, it had been defeated 74-139. Presumably all those who voted in the negative preferred Andersen's amount to Whitten's. But if the Andersen, Javits, and O'Toole supporters number at most 126, where did these additional 13 come from? Since the Whitten supporters are necessarily among the affirmative minority of 74, the only possible source of additional votes for the negative majority is the supporters of the original. Hence the Original-Andersen group must number at least 13 and possibly more.

The maximum number of supporters of the original and of the Whitten amendment is 131. Since the Original-Andersen supporters are 13 and, if we arbitrarily assume that the Whitten supporters total ten, then there must be something like 108 Original-Whitten supporters.

In summary, the reconstruction of the ordering of preferences is:

108 Original-Whitten supporters: 1P4, 4P3, 3P2, 2P5, from which it is inferred that 1P3, 1P2, 1P5, 4P2, 4P5, 3P5.

13 Original-Andersen supporters: 1P3, 3P4, 4P2, 2P5, and hence, 1P4, 1P2, 1P5, 3P2, 3P5, 4P5.

30 Javits supporters: 2P5, 5P3, 3P4, 4P1, and hence, 2P3, 2P4, 2P1, 5P4, 5P1, 3P1.

91 Andersen supporters: 3P4, 4P1, 1P2, 2P5, and hence 3P1, 3P2, 3P5, 4P3, 4P5, 1P5.

10 Whitten supporters: 4P1, 1P3, 3P2, 2P5, and hence 4P3, 4P2, 4P5, 1P2, 1P5, 3P5.

5 O'Toole supporters: 5P2, 2P3, 3P4, 4P1, and hence, 5P3, 5P4, 5P1, 2P4, 2P1, 3P1.

The result of adding these preferences (*i.e.,* of pitting each choice against each other one) can be set forth in matrix form:

*Figure 1—Matrix of Outcomes of Preference Additions**

	1 Original	2 Javits	3 Andersen	4 Whitten	5 O'Toole
1. Original	—	+187	+5	—15	+187
2. Javits	—187	—	—187	—187	+247
3. Andersen	—5	+187	—	+21	+187
4. Whitten	+15	+187	—21	—	+187
5. O'Toole	—187	—247	—187	—187	—

* Read this matrix by rows, so that a positive number in a box indicates a victory for the choice in that row and a defeat for the choice in that column; conversely a negative number in a box is a defeat for the choice of that row and a victory for the choice of that column. Thus "+15" in the fourth row and first column means that the Whitten amendment defeats the original paragraph by 136 — 121 = 15.

Examination of this matrix quickly reveals an intransitive ordering, (*i.e.,* no one alternative can defeat each of the other four; or, stated another way, in no row are all the numbers positive). It is possible to order the sum of the preferences in several ways, but each of these involves an intransitivity, for example:

1P3, 3P4, 4P2, 2P5, from which one infers, *inter alia,* 1P4, although in fact 4P1 by a margin of 15. By the House rules, under which the votes are taken in the order 4, 5, 3, 2, this is the result that will occur from preferences arranged as in Figure 1.

4P1, 1P3, 3P2, 2P5, from which one infers 4P3, although in fact 3P4 by a margin of 21. This is the result that would occur if the motions were voted upon in the order 5, 3, 1, 4.

3P4, 4P1, 1P2, 2P5, from which one infers 3P1, although in fact 1P3 by a margin of 5. This is the result that would occur if the motions were voted upon in the order 5, 1, 4, 3.

This reconstruction clearly reveals the possibility that the action of the House may have been irrational. Certainly, if a situation substantially similar to that in Figure 1 actually existed, then the preferences of the whole House were necessarily intransitive.

In the argument so far several more or less arbitrary assumptions have been made. The reader may therefore doubt the likelihood of the occurrence of this particular intransitivity. Still, even with other guesses, undesirable results appear in most possible situations:

1. If the Whitten supporters number two or less, then the social ordering is transitive and the original paragraph wins. This is the only alternative assumption that guarantees a rational result.
2. If there are three or more Whitten supporters, and
   a. if they are drawn from supporters of the original paragraph and order their preferences 4P1, 1P3, 1P2, 2P5, and
      (1) if an Original-Andersen group exists, then the ordering of preferences in the whole House is intransitive (this is the situation here examined in detail); or
      (2) if an Original-Andersen group does not exist, then the ordering is transitive, but the Whitten amendment will win instead of the original paragraph which actually won; or
   b. if they are drawn from the Andersen supporters and order their preferences 4P3, 3P1, 1P2, 2P5, then, whether or not an Original-Andersen group exists, the ordering is transitive, but the Andersen substitute will win instead of the original paragraph.

Of these four situations, which are, I believe, the ones most likely to have existed, only one involves a transitive ordering in which the original paragraph wins. The others involve either an intransitivity or a clear majority for a motion that in fact lost. Inasmuch as there must be at least as many votes as there are motions in order to reveal an intransitivity, and inasmuch as in this event there were fewer votes than motions, we cannot possibly determine which one of these five situations existed. We are, however, well justified in suspecting that the actual behavior was irrational.

This procedure, through which the House—and in a similar way, the Senate—risks irrational action, probably developed by an accident of history. The House of Commons, when considering a bill in Committee of the Whole, votes not only on amendments but on the paragraph (amended or unamended) as well. So far as I can discover, this has always been the English procedure. It was also the procedure in the United States in 1789; but sometime in the first half of the nineteenth century this detail was dropped without notice of the consequences of the omission. With the consequences exposed, it may be that Congress will wish to change its Rules in order to avoid the risk of behaving irrationally.

Of course, Congress may prefer its present procedure for, along with the risk, the present Rules allow a skilled minority to defeat an unsophisticated majority; or, to put it differently, a committee chairman to control House action. In the instance here discussed, Mr. Whitten, not certain of his majority, introduced an amendment which both brought about a possible intransitivity and ensured victory for the original paragraph which he was managing through the House. And perhaps the Congress wishes to give this kind of advantage to those skilled in parliamentary contrivance. If, however, the Congress as a whole is disturbed by the danger of passing motions favored only by a minority, some revision of the Rules is necessary. Hence, it seems appropriate to consider how to discover and eliminate intransitivities.

One superficially attractive revision of the Rules is a provision permitting consideration of only one amendment at a time. Since intransitivities cannot occur when there are only two alternatives (*i.e.,* an original paragraph and one amendment), this provision might be supposed to ensure that each successful motion had a clear majority over its alternative. Actually, however, it would ensure no such thing. If a subsequent amendment were offered to the same words, the legislature would then in effect be faced with three choices, entailing the danger of an intransitivity. With at most two votes on three choices, there would be no more opportunity than at present to discover it. This is substantially the procedure in the National Assembly in France, where the likelihood of intransitivities is about as great as in the Congress of the United States.

This latter difficulty might be formally surmounted by permitting no more than one amendment to any set of words. Such a limitation would prevent the possibility of intransitivities; but it might be undesirable for other reasons. It might tend to drive all the opponents of a paragraph together, and so work toward tightening party discipline. In a legislature with only two rigorously disciplined parties, one amendment might sufficiently express the range of opinion. In the English House of Commons, for example, it is quite rare for more than one amendment to be offered to the same words—and this fact explains why intransitivities rarely appear there, even though its procedure provides for discovering them. But in the United States Congress, with its many intra-party and inter-party factions, a limit to one amendment might unduly restrict the free play of opinion: if a race to preempt the right to offer that one amendment were precipitated, and the presiding officers continued the practice of recognizing the floor leaders ahead of the others seeking recognition, the opportunities to offer dissident amendments might be foreclosed. Hence while a limit of this sort would undoubtedly circumvent intransitivities, it might also eventually change the character of the Congress.

A more feasible revision of the rules is a requirement that the original paragraph, whether amended or not, be voted upon. This would guarantee that the Congress take as many votes as there are choices before it. But it would also often waste time—in modern legislatures a precious commodity. If no amendments or only one amendment is offered, no vote on the paragraph itself is needed. Hence the requirement of a vote on the original or amended paragraph might be limited to those occasions in which three or more choices exist. Even on very complex and controversial bills, this would probably mean at most three or four more votes, not an excessive amount of time to spend on discovering intransitivities.

Even if both houses were to provide this method of discovery, they would still need a procedure for resolving the intransitivities discovered. For example, in the event here described, if a vote on the original paragraph were to have carried in the negative, the Soil Conservation Service would have been completely eliminated, a contingency no one except the O'Toole supporters desired.

Students of proportional representation have tried (unsuccessfully) to resolve intransitivities by altering the method by which votes are counted. But, as Arrow has shown, an intransitivity, once in existence, cannot be eliminated simply by juggling the techniques of counting. It might be thought that intransitivities could be resolved by successively eliminating the least popular alternatives. But this too is an illusory solution. If the supporters of three choices are divided into equal factions, there can be no "least popular" choice to eliminate. Even if the factions are unequally divided, successive elimination can not guarantee a rational decision, for one minority faction may, by voting partially against its own preferences, bring about an irrational result favorable to the conspirators as the Figures 2, 3 and 4 show.[16] Hence, what Congress needs to resolve intransitivities is a method that involves at most only one more vote than there are choices and that guarantees that a paragraph favored only by a minority will not win. With proper diffidence, I suggest the

following rule for the House and an analogous one for the Senate:

Figure 2—Matrix of Outcomes with O'Toole Amendment Eliminated

	1 Original	2 Javits	3 Andersen	4 Whitten
1. Original	—	+187	+5	−15
2. Javits	−187	—	−187	−187
3. Andersen	−5	+187	—	+21
4. Whitten	+15	+187	−21	—

Figure 3—Matrix of Outcomes with O'Toole and Javits Amendments Eliminated

	1 Original	3 Andersen	4 Whitten	Row Sum
1. Original	—	+5	−15	−10
3. Andersen	−5	—	+21	+16
4. Whitten	+15	−21	—	−6

Figure 4—Matrix of Outcomes when Whitten Supporters Falsify Their Preferences

	1 Original	3 Andersen	4 Whitten
1. Original	—	+5	+5
3. Andersen	−5	—	−21
4. Whitten	−5	−21	—

(1) *When a bill or resolution or conference report is read for amendment and when two or more amending motions are offered to the same words, the presiding officer shall put the question on such motions as are before the House in the following order: first, on the amendment to the amendment; second, on the amendment to the substitute; third, on the substitute (amended or not, as the case may be); fourth, on the amendment (amended or not, substituted or not, as the case may be); fifth, on the original matter (amended or not, as the case may be). Whereupon:*

(2) *If the last question of section (1) carries in the affirmative, no further amendments to the words just adopted shall be in order.*

(3) *If the last question of section (1) carries in the negative, the presiding officer may, if in his opinion one of the defeated motions could pass at this stage, recognize a Member who moved a defeated motion for the purpose of moving it again. No amendments to a motion so moved shall be in order. If the motion passes, it shall stand part of the text adopted and no further amendments to this portion of the text shall be in order. If it fails, it shall not be in order to move at this stage any further motions, to insert words in*

*place of those deleted by the procedure of section
(1) of this rule.*

*(4) If, at some later stage in the progress of
the bill or resolution or conference report, it is in
order to move to insert words in place of those
deleted by the procedure of sections (1) and (3)
of this rule, and if such motion is actually moved,
no amendments to the motion shall be in order.*

This suggested rule is, I realize, a rather heavy-handed elimination of an intransitivity. Indeed, it would operate by allowing the presiding officer to control the range of choice, once an intransitivity has been discovered. Considering that the Speaker and the Chairman of the Committee of the Whole are responsible leaders of the majority party, this does not seem an unreasonable arrangement. Despite its limitations, the rule would accomplish our purpose: either it would allow the discovered paradox to continue to exist and thus prevent all action, or it would resolve the paradox, if the House wished it resolved, without unduly restricting the range of expressible opinion at the beginning of the amending process.

Theoretically the rule has this disadvantage: it might encourage minority factions to create intransitivities (by voting against their own preferences) so that, with the connivance of the presiding officer, they might obtain a final vote on a motion of their own choosing. In bodies as large as the houses of Congress, however, such a maneuver requires more detailed planning than is usually possible.

The suggested rule has one further advantage: it can resolve paradoxes of preference as well as paradoxes of voting. If one person faces only two choices, he cannot be said to choose irrationally even though he may use more than three criteria, no one of which dominates all the others. In the extreme case, if his criteria are ordered in exactly opposite ways with respect to the alternatives, he is, of course, immobilized by a tie, by an inability to choose. Since the result in this extreme case is indifference, not intransitivity, the suggested rule breaks all paradoxes, both paradoxes of preference and paradoxes of voting.

Inasmuch as the suggested rule has immediate advantages of preventing irrational behavior and inasmuch as its main disadvantage is a fairly remote contingency, Congress might well consider adopting it in order to avoid the risk of adopting motions favored only by a minority.

Notes

1. John Hatsell, *Precedents of Proceedings in the House of Commons* (2 vols., London, 1781; I have been able to examine only the four volume edition published

by Luke Hansard in London in 1818 and therefore I cite it), Vol. 2, pp. 207-08. This aphorism has had a long, semi-independent existence. Jefferson quoted it in the second paragraph of his *Manual of Parliamentary Procedure* (written between 1797 and 1801 and reprinted biennially in *The Rules of the House of Representatives*) and recently Eric Taylor quoted it in the beginning of the second chapter of his excellent essay, *The House of Commons at Work* (Harmondsworth, Middlesex, 1951). It might well be pointed out that Hatsell's comment occurs in connection with his discussion of methods of voting, which methods are the subject of the present essay as well. Hatsell further said (II, 208); "If the maxim, *'Stare super vias antiquas'* has ever felt any weight, it is in those matters, where it is not so material, that the rule should be established on the foundation of sound reason and argument, as it is that order, decency, and regularity, should be preserved in a large, a numerous, and consequently sometimes tumultuous assembly." If voting, certainly the central activity in a legislature, need not be established on the "foundation of sound reason and argument," then there is apparently no need whatever for "sound reason" in parliamentary law.

2. Ward Edwards, "Probability Preferences in Gambling," *American Journal of Psychology*, Vol. 66 (1953), pp. 349-64, reports an experiment in which subjects were asked to choose between bets of differing probabilities. The coefficient of consistency, which is

$$1 - \frac{\text{number of inconsistent triads found}}{\text{number of inconsistent triads possible}}$$

was in the beginning of the experiment .76 and .73 but became in the end of the experiment .84 and .82 for different kinds of bets respectively. The improvement can, presumably, be attributed to an attempt by the subjects to rationalize their orderings of preference. The remaining inconsistence (*i.e.*, intransitivity) derived, so Edwards suggested, from the fact that the subjects chose bets by different standards. On the one hand, they tried to maximize their winnings (*i.e.*, to choose the bet with the highest expected value). On the other hand, they clearly displayed a preference for bets with a 4/8 probability as against bets with a 6/8 probability, regardless of the expected value of the paired bets. When these two standards of choice came into conflict, the subjects tended to be inconsistent. Kenneth O. May, "Intransitivity, Utility, and the Aggregation of Preference Patterns," *Econometrica*, Vol. 22 (1953), pp. 1-13, reports an experiment with similar results. He offered subjects choices which they might order by three different standards and found a somewhat greater degree of inconsistency than Edwards. Examining this result with a mathematical analysis, May proved that, if there are three or more things to be chosen and three or more criteria by which they may be chosen, then it is possible for one chooser to order his preferences intransitively unless one criterion dominates all others. From his analysis, one infers that the primary intransitivity is among the criteria of choice rather than among the ordering of things to be chosen. If the criteria for determining preference can be arranged in a transitive order of dominance, then, apart from human error, preference is transitive. But if the criteria cannot be so arranged, then the preferences of an otherwise unerring chooser may be ordered intransitively. Thus, May has discovered an analogue to the paradox of voting, an analogue which, however, is in a single person rather than a group. To distinguish the two paradoxes, the analogue will here be called a paradox of preference. It may be described thus: Let the criteria $a, \beta, \cdots, \nu$, by which a chooser orders his choices be themselves ordered by a relation of dominance, D, such that if aPb with respect to a and if bPa with respect to β and if in fact aPb, then $aD\beta$. So defined, D is a transitive relation, which however, may calculate to an intransitivity if $\nu \geq 3$ in just the same way that the paradox of voting may appear in a group. Unlike the paradox of voting, which, as this essay suggests, can be broken only by the crudest practical measures, the paradox of preference exists inside one person and so is wholly under his control: once brought to his attention, he can break it by an analysis of his own emotions, if he chooses to do so. Hence, although the paradox of preference might appear to demonstrate the ineradicable irrationality of human behavior, an irrationality so pervasive that it calls the whole notion of rationality into question, still the fact that this irrationality may be eradicated when raised to the conscious level encourages us to conclude that we may continue to use the transitivity of preference as a standard of rational behavior. (Further discussion of these and other experiments along with an elaborate bibliography may be found in Ward Edwards, "Theory of Decision Making," *Psychological Bulletin*, Vol. 51 (1954), pp. 380-417. See also Andreas G. Papandreou, "An Experimental Test of an Axiom in the Theory of Choice," *Econometrica*, Vol. 21 (1953), p. 477 (abstract).

3. Kenneth O. May, "Intransitivity, Utility, and the Aggregation of Preference Patterns," *Econometrica*, Vol. 22 (1953), pp. 1-13. May argues that preference, P, ought to be regarded as the probability, p, that one of a pair of alternatives, a and b, will be chosen over the other in a particular set of circumstances, E. Thus, he defines preference:

(1) $aPb \equiv p(a|a, b; E)$.

He then points out that, on the basis of this definition, it is false to write:

(2) for any E, if aPb and if bPc, then aPc.

Statement (2) can be translated into:

(3) for any E, if $p(a|a, b) > p(b|a, b)$ and if $p(b|b, c) > p(c|b, c)$, then $p(a|a, b) > p(c|b, c)$.

and statement (3) may easily be false because $p(a|a, b)$ and $p(c|b, c)$ are calculated with respect to the non-identical sets, $\{a, b\}$ and $\{b, c\}$. But preference may be, and in most circumstances of real life undoubtedly is regarded as a choice of one element of several. So regarded preference is defined, not as in statement (1), but thus:

(4) $aPb \equiv p(a|a, b, \cdots, n; E)$.

Using statement (4) instead of (1), statement (2) is translated into:

(5) for any E, if $p(a|a, b, \cdots, n) > p(b|a, b, \cdots, n)$ and if $p(b|a, b, \cdots, n) > p(c|a, b, \cdots, n)$, then $p(a|a, b, \cdots, n) > p(c|a, b, \cdots, n)$.

And statement (5) is valid by the rule of syllogistic inference. Hence, if the set of possible choices is identical for all the choices in the chain, then P is a transitive relation. May's argument is valid, therefore, only in the case of a series of binary choices and, as has often been observed, truly "either-or" situations seldom arise in real life.

4. (New York, Wiley, for the Cowles Commission, 1951.) See also Kenneth O. May, "A Set of Independent Necessary and Sufficient Conditions for Simple Majority Decision," *Econometrica*, Vol. 20 (1952), pp. 680-84.

5. See also David G. McGarvey, "A Theorem on the Construction of Voting Paradoxes," *Econometrica*, Vol. 21 (1953), pp. 608-10.

6. Duncan Black, "On the Rationale of Group Decision Making," *Journal of Political Economy*, Vol. 56 (1948), pp. 23-34. See also two other important essays by Black on the subject of transitivity of preference: "The Decisions of a Committee Using a Special Majority," *Econometrica*, Vol. 16, (1948), pp. 262-70; and "The Theory of Elections in Single Member Districts," *The Canadian Journal of Economics and Political Science*, Vol. 15 (1948), pp. 158-75.

7. If $m_1, m_2 \cdots, m_n$ motions are ordered in numerical sequence of the subscripts and if each m_i is paired with each m_j that appears after m_i in the sequence, then m_1 appears first in $n-1$ pairs, m_2 is first in $n-2$ pairs, $\cdots$, m_{n-1} is first in one pair. The sum, r, of the pairings is the sum of the terms of an arithmetic progression: $r = 1 + \cdot \ \cdot \ \cdot + (n-2) + (n-1) = \frac{1}{2}(n-1)(1+n-1) = n(n-1)/2$.

8. "On the Rationale of Group Decision Making," *passim*.

9. A note of warning is appropriate here: The kind of irrationality discussed in this essay has nothing whatever to do with the behavior of individual persons. It is, of course, true that individual Congressmen may order their preferences intransitively. A multitude of studies in social psychology and political behavior have long since made us fully aware of the potentialities of unreason in every man. Despite the revelations from the time of Freud onward, we have nevertheless held onto our eighteenth century faith in our ability to create rational institutions. What the paradox of voting so devastatingly reveals, however, is that our institutions of vote counting may have implicit defects. Even if we charitably assume, as I do in this essay, that the preferences of individuals are transitively ordered, still the institutions of voting may bring about intransitive results. Since this is a study of just this aspect of institutions and not a study of persons, it is only concerned with how votes are counted. Specifically, it is not concerned with how people make up their minds. Whether they think carefully to a decision or simply vote on a nod from a leader or lobbyist, or on a trade for other votes on other matters, their internal thoughts are a matter of complete indifference in this analysis, for it is concerned with external behavior, not motives.

10. Although in this classification only events occurring in the Committee of the Whole are considered, an analogous classification can be constructed for events occurring when a bill on the House Calendar is read for amendments, or when the House considers Senate Amendments to a House bill, or when the Senate considers a bill reported from committee, or when it considers House amendments to a Senate bill.

11. Arrow, *op. cit.*, p. 10.

12. It may be argued that there is no irrational behavior if the bill as a whole is accepted in spite of an intransitivity over one clause. Such an argument, however, denies any significance to the whole process of reading for amendment.

13. Black, "On the Rationale of Group Decision Making," p. 33. I have computed, by a method to be reported elsewhere, the proportion of possible results of adding preferences which are transitive or partially transitive. When $n = 3$, 3/4 of the possible outcomes are transitive. When $n = 5$, only 5/16 of the possible outcomes of addition are such that one choice is preferred to all others.

14. See *Congressional Record*, Vol. 98 (1952), pp. 4713-31.

15. Possibly of course, the intransitivity, if it existed, was not a paradox of voting, but several paradoxes of preference. In the ensuing discussion of this section it will be assumed that the members themselves were rational and that this is an instance of the paradox of voting. At the end of section IV, the event will be briefly discussed with this assumption removed.

16. The potentialities of deceit in the method of successive elimination can be visualized from the Soil Conservation incident. Defining the "least popular" choice as the one able to defeat the fewest of the others, we eliminate the O'Toole amendment. Dropping the fifth row and fifth column of Figure 1 results in Figure 2. Since no one motion in Figure 2 can beat all the rest, the Javits amendment next must be eliminated, whereupon the result is Figure 3. This is identical with Figure 2 except that the second row and the second column are eliminated. Since no one motion in Figure 3 can defeat all the rest, it is again necessary to eliminate one. Assuming that the least popular choice in Figure 3 is the one with the smallest sum in its row, then the original paragraph must be eliminated. Then the Andersen amendment wins. But the Whitten supporters, foreseeing this

result, can ensure victory for the original paragraph (their second preference) by voting against themselves at the stage represented by Figure 3. In effect they re-order their preferences thus: 1P4, 4P3, and hence, 1P3. This results in the matrix of preferences of Figure 4. Thus, by falsifying their preferences, they can profitably

change the outcome—assuming, of course, that other factions do not also falsify their preferences.

Similar examples are discussed in Arrow, *op. cit.*, pp. 80-81. This is substantially the maneuver described in Tapas Majundar, "Choice and Revealed Preference," *Econometrica*, Vol. 24 (1956), pp. 71-3.

11. LEGISLATIVE APPORTIONMENT AND POLITICAL POWER

David G. Farrelly and Ivan Hinderaker

SINCE WORLD WAR II there has been much speculation on the economic, social and political impact of population growth and redistribution in the United States. In 1947 the Bureau of the Census published its first estimates of 1950 population, and it projected trends for the decade of the 1940's. These data and the facts now uncovered by the 1950 census reveal a wealth of evidence on economic and social changes that have taken place during the last decade. Observers are sure that the political impact of population changes is equally significant. But here the lines of development are not as clear, nor as easy to trace, as in the socio-economic field.

Our system of government in the United States is not designed to be immediately and completely responsive to population shifts within the country. Once every 10 years heads are counted; only then do we pause to gear our political institutions to population changes. At the national level this is done primarily by reapportioning representation so as to approximate the populations of each of our 48 states.

The political touchstone of the 1950 census returns is congressional reapportionment. Indeed, at only two points—in Congress and in the electoral college—are there any outward political manifestations of population change. The 1951 reapportionment of congressional seats increased the voting strength of 7 state delegations in the United States House of Representatives and decreased the size of 9. Since a state's representation in the electoral college is based on the sum total of its membership in the lower house of Congress plus its 2 United States senators, there has been a resultant and parallel redistribution of presidential-electoral votes. These two changes

Reprinted from *Law and Contemporary Problems*, Vol. 17 (Spring, 1952), pp. 338-9, 351-61, published by the Duke University School of Law, Durham, North Carolina, where it appeared under the title, "Congressional Reapportionment and National Political Power," by permission of the authors and the publisher. (Copyright, 1952, by Duke University.)

may be said to represent constitutional readjustment to the 1950 census.

Certain relatively obvious political effects stem from reapportionment. The basic change in the electoral college will be reflected in state voting power at the national nominating conventions held by the Republican and Democratic parties in 1952, 1956, and 1960. Individual candidacies for presidential and vice-presidential nomination may well be affected. And the ability of some states to gain more high political appointments for their citizens will be enhanced or retarded.

Some of these consequences may be subjected to measurement, but others may not. The number of electoral votes is not the sole determinant of voting power at a national convention, nor does it alone furnish much of a guide to an appraisal of a state's influence. The chances of a "favorite son" capturing the presidential nomination may be advanced by an influx of population into his state, but a full assessment of his possibilities depends upon many other factors. While pivotal states in presidential politics have received a large share of the major fruits of office—Cabinet appointments, Supreme Court justiceships—pivot status is dependent upon more than population statistics.

In the House of Representatives, reapportionment will also produce certain consequences other than the decrease or increase in the size of 16 state delegations. The rank of a delegation should not be measured on the basis of voting strength alone. Does California, with its present 23 seats, rate below Illinois which has 26 representatives? Nominally it does (in actuality it probably does, too), but there are other criteria. The operation of the seniority rule in the legislative process is an important consideration. Can a delegation work as a unit on matters of fundamental interest to its state? What is the partisan composition of the delegation? What relationship exists between the members and the White House? These suggest the complications which arise when one attempts to survey the implications of reapportionment on political power in Congress.

Even if all the factors contributing to national political power were measurable, the changes produced by any one decennial reapportionment of congressional seats are usually slight. Such huge increases as have befallen California in 1931 (9 seats) and in 1951 (7 seats) are unusual. Ordinarily it takes the sum total of several reapportionment shifts before trends become established. The half-century point has now been passed. Therefore, this article is not concerned alone with the congressional reapportionment of 1951, but it attempts to set this latest reapportionment into the context of population and political trends in the United States since 1900.

Fourteen of the 435 seats in the United States House of Representatives were reapportioned in 1951. This change may be compared to 1941 when 9 seats were affected and 1931 when 27 were readjusted. The breakdown of gains and losses for the 1951 reapportionment is as follows:

	GAINERS		
State	Present Seats	New Seats	Change
Calif.	23	30	7
Fla.	6	8	2
Md.	6	7	1
Mich.	17	18	1
Texas	21	22	1
Va.	9	10	1
Wash.	6	7	1
			14

	LOSERS		
State	Present Seats	New Seats	Change
Ark.	7	6	1
Ill.	26	25	1
Ky.	9	8	1
Miss.	7	6	1
Mo.	13	11	2
N. Y.	45	43	2
Okla.	8	6	2
Pa.	33	30	3
Tenn.	10	9	1
			14

The one state that has gained most from reapportionment is California. In 1951, half of the 14 seats went to California. During the years since 1911, when the House membership was frozen at 435, California's net gain has been 19 congressmen. In other words, 50 House seats have been reapportioned since 1911, and California has received 40 per cent of them.

A. The Influence of Seniority. The mere size of a state's delegation does not ensure success in the legislative process. There are many points in congressional procedure at which the seniority of a state's representatives may be even more decisive than the number of votes that might be mustered for or against a particular bill. Chairmen of standing committees wield great power over matters pending before their committees. These chairmen rise to the top by virtue of their membership in the majority party and unbroken seniority in Congress. Ranking minority members on a committee are also important persons; not only are they in line for the chairmanship in the event of a change in party control, but their long experience aids them in acquiring prestige and influence.

In addition to high position on a committee, or in the absence of such status, there are two other attributes of legislative ability: to have good standing with one's colleagues, and to possess a thorough working knowledge of law-making procedure. Other things being equal, these qualities should become more effective with increase in length of service.

The 7 states that gained congressional seats in 1951 do not hold many high positions on the committees. Only Virginia has a chairman of a House standing committee, and at that it is a relatively unimportant body.[1] Only Michigan, of the gaining states, has any ranking minority members; it has 4.[2] On the other hand, the 9 losing states rate high in both committee chairmanships and ranking minority members. Six of these states have committee chairmen; 4 have ranking minority members.[3]

It should be pointed out that the loss of 1 or 2 seats in the House is not going to damage greatly the power of such states as New York, Illinois, and Missouri, despite the disagreeableness and political inconvenience these losses cause. In part, the losing states may offset their losses with seniority power on House standing committees— a kind of power not possessed by the states that have gained representation.

In the Eighty-second Congress, first session, the average House member had served 8.5 years in Congress. The average length of service of the congressmen from 6 of the gaining states falls below the average: California, 7.7; Florida, 5.3; Maryland, 7.7; Michigan, 6.7; Virginia, 8.0; and Washington, 8.0. Only Texas with 11.5 is above the average. Looking at the losing states, 3 fall below the national average: Missouri, 7.1; Oklahoma, 5.8; and Pennsylvania, 7.8. Each of these losers suffers a loss of 2 or 3 congressmen in reapportionment. But 6 of the losing states have a record of congressional service that is higher than the national average: Arkansas, 10.9; Illinois,

9.8; Kentucky, 9.6; Mississippi, 13.1; New York, 9.2; and Tennessee, 11.6.

Assuming that average length of service is an important factor in measuring potential effectiveness of a congressional delegation, the losing states may further offset their losses by their above-average seniority levels in the House. The average seniority of the gaining states is significantly lower, and with each state being certain of at least one first-term congressman in the Eighty-third Congress, the disparity may then be even greater.

A state's congressional power cannot be assessed in the House of Representatives alone. Turning to the Senate, both gaining and losing states rate low in committee chairmanships and in ranking minority members. Of the gaining states only Texas has a chairmanship; only Washington, a ranking minority member.[4] And of the losing states, only Arkansas and Tennessee have committee chairmen; none of the losers has a ranking minority member.[5] Furthermore, both gaining and losing states also have length-of-service records that are below the average of the Senate as a whole. In the Eighty-second Congress, first session, the average Senate member had 6.5 years. Four of the 7 gaining states fell below the average: California, Florida, Maryland, and Michigan. Of the remaining states that gained by reapportionment, Texas and Virginia have 13.0 and 12.5 averages, respectively; Washington's is 7.0. Considering the 9 losing states, 6 fell well below the average length of service in the Senate. The 3 remaining loser states had above-average seniority records: Arkansas, 8.0; Mississippi, 7.0; and Tennessee, with the most senior member of the Senate, Kenneth McKellar, 19.0.

Thus in the Senate the pattern of high position on committees and length of service in the upper house is unlike that found in the House of Representatives. Only Arkansas and Tennessee would appear to be in any way able to counter-balance the loss of seats in the lower house brought about by the 1951 reapportionment.

Statistics on the average length of service in both House and Senate suggest that, with the development of comparative data over longer periods of time, there may be significant correlations between the relative population increase or decrease of a state and the average seniority of its delegations in the House and Senate. The hypothesis for such a study may be stated thus: congressional seniority will tend to be lowest in states which increase most rapidly in population, but will be highest in states with the most stable populations. That this thesis exists for the House of Representatives seems more certain than for the Senate.

B. Character of House Membership. Some general observation may be made about the effect of the 1951 reapportionment on the political complexion of the House of Representatives. Under the federal Automatic Reapportionment Act of 1929, as amended in 1941, states gaining representation in the House have two alternatives. They may either redistrict to provide for the extra seat or seats, or they may choose not to take any action. If they fail to act, the additional congressmen will be elected at large. The legislatures of the 7 states gaining congressmen are not, therefore, under great pressure to redistrict.

The governors and both houses of the state legislatures of 3 gaining states (Florida, Texas, and Virginia) are Democratic. These 3 states have been allotted a total of 4 new congressmen. Whether they reapportion or not, it should be safe to assume the four new representatives will be Democrats.

California is the only one of the 7 gaining states where the governor and both chambers of the legislature are Republican. California is also the only gainer to have reapportioned its congressional districts in 1951. A person unacquainted with California politics, or a partisan Democrat, might predict that all of the state's new congressmen will be Republicans. But a reasonable estimate might give Republican candidates a good opportunity in 2 of the 7 new districts, and a fair fighting chance in 2 or 3 of the others. The rearrangement of boundary lines in 2 existing districts might make it more possible for Republicans to defeat Democratic incumbents. Otherwise, the 1951 redistricting process should produce no foreseeable changes in the party alignment of the congressional delegation.[7]

California's weak political party structure, the close margin in the Assembly between Republicans (45) and Democrats (35), and the heavy predominance of Democratic registration throughout the state, all tended to offset some of the advantages that might have accrued to the Republican party by virtue of its control of the state government.[8]

In the 3 remaining states that gained representatives, two political parties must share in any state redistricting of congressional seats that takes place prior to the 1952 elections. Both houses of the Maryland legislature have Democratic majorities, but its governor is a Republican. The situation is the reverse in Michigan, with the governor Democratic and the legislature Republican. The governor and senate in Washington are Republican while the lower house of the legislature is Democratic. Out of the kind of deadlocks likely to arise from situations such as these, the result will either be a compromise or inaction.

When a state gains congressmen yet fails to redistrict, the added representation must be elected at large. But when a state loses congressmen and fails to redistrict, one of the following alternatives applies.[9] First, if the new number of congressmen is equal to the number of congressional districts, the candidates for Congress will have to run in the districts as they exist.[10] Second, if the number of districts is less than the number of congressmen, one representative will be elected from each district and the remainder will be elected at large. Third, if the number of districts exceeds the total number of congressmen, the entire congressional delegation will have to run at large.

All of the states losing seats in 1951 fall into the third category. The pressure for redistricting in these states is quite strong. Experience such as Minnesota's in 1932 has shown that an unusually large number of incumbent congressmen are defeated when an entire House delegation of significant size is forced to run at large. Although New York, Missouri, and Tennessee are the only losing states that have reapportioned in 1951, it is reasonable to assume that all of the losers will redistrict before the 1952 elections.

Six of the 9 losing states have Democratic governors and legislatures. Of these, Kentucky might attempt to make its 2 Republican congressmen absorb its one district loss. The effect of Missouri's reapportionment might tend to operate against 2 of its 3 Republican incumbents. Oklahoma might try to reapportion both of its 2 Republicans out of office. And Tennessee might attempt to get rid of 1 of its 2 Republicans. Arkansas and Mississippi have no Republicans to offer in sacrifice; their loss of 1 seat each will have to come from the Democratic side.[11]

The governors and legislatures of New York and Pennsylvania are Republican. The readjustment of 43 seats in New York (down from 45) and 30 Pennsylvania seats (down from 33) might be worked to the advantage of the Republican party.[12] Illinois has a Democratic governor and lower house, but a Republican senate. Generalization as to a party redistribution of its 25 seats (down from 26) is impossible.

Assuming that all the gaining and losing states do reapportion their congressional districts, the states with both Democratic governors and legislatures would control the redrawing of 75 district boundaries. Those states with both Republican governors and legislatures will recarve 103 districts. And states with some split combination of party control will remake 57 districts.

In addition to the political character of the House membership, the urban-rural distribution must be noted. Prior to the 1950 census, there were 21 urban and 27 rural states. Using the same standards for determination of an urban state, the population statistics of 1950 put 4 more states into the urban class. These 25 urban states have a total of 312 House seats as against 123 seats for the 23 rural states. Using the Bureau of the Census' new standards for determining urbanization, 29 states are now so classified. On this new basis they would have 333 House seats as compared with 102 seats for 19 rural states.

It is more important to look at the urban-rural character of individual congressional districts rather than states. Arthur N. Holcombe has classified the districts as they presently exist into 130 urban, 125 mixed urban-rural, and 180 rural.[13] It is difficult to predict what the urban-rural distribution of congressional districts will be after the state legislatures have completed reapportioning on the basis of the 1950 census. The trend in the direction of establishing more urban and mixed urban-rural districts is probably apparent, as it is only a reflection of population shifts from the farm to city areas. California's 1951 reapportionment may serve as an example.[14]

Of the 3 congressional districts allocated to Los Angeles county, in addition to the 9 it now has, 2 should be classified as urban and the third as mixed urban-rural. One is located in the booming Lakewood section between downtown Los Angeles and Long Beach; a second combines Hollywood with part of the rapidly growing San Fernando Valley; a third, though it includes much sparsely settled area in the north portion of Los Angeles county, still deserves a mixed urban-rural classification because part of the San Fernando Valley is embraced by the new district boundary.

A fourth new urban district has been established for San Mateo county, immediately to the south of crowded San Francisco. A fifth new mixed district lies along the coast between the Los Angeles metropolitan area and the city of San Diego, and it might be termed suburban to both. The arrangements for the 2 new districts that went to the great Central Valley resulted from an overflow of San Francisco Bay-area population, and from the rapid growth of a whole string of valley cities, the most important of which are Sacramento and Fresno.[15] Both of these latter districts deserve this mixed urban-rural classification. In sum, all 7 districts have been drawn to follow the population in its outward movement from the old urban centers to the new urban and suburban areas.

C. The Influence of the California Delegation. Considering California's large gain in congressional seats during the period from 1900, the effects of the increasing size of the California House delegation deserve further attention. When California entered the Union in 1850 it was entitled to 2 congressmen. Even by 1900 it had only 7 representatives. But two big decades of growth raised the delegation from 11 to 20 members in 1933. The next largest addition, 7 new congressmen in 1953, has brought the total to 30.

It has been noted that California's average seniority in the Eighty-second Congress, first session, was 7.7 years, while the average for all of the states was 8.5. California's seniority rating in the House has never been high. It took 20 years, from the Thirty-first to the Forty-first Congress, before California's average rose as high as 4 years. In fact the average over the entire period of statehood is 5.1 years. Prior to the turn of the century it was 3.2 years; since 1900 it has increased to 7.0 years.

California has had only 6 representatives who served 20 years or more in Congress.[16] In the Eighty-second Congress, its most senior member in the House is serving his eighth term, 2 are serving their seventh, 1 his sixth, and 4 are in their fifth term. Against this record of service is the fact that more than 45 other congressmen are today serving a ninth term or longer, and therefore rank above California's top man. As noted, California has no committee chairmen in the House; nor does it have any ranking minority members on committees. However, 3 Californians have survived long enough to be second on their party's side of their respective committees.[17]

Although California has increased the size of its House delegation more rapidly than any other state, why has its seniority level tended to be low? Fluidity of population must be part of the answer. As one State Assemblyman remarked recently: "Here I have built up my name in my district for years and my father had built it up before me, and then all these new people come in and they never heard of us!" In part, weak parties are a factor, too. Without strong party organization, a premium is placed on individual congressmen to maintain their own bases of support. And this is made more difficult by the distance between Washington, D. C. and California which precludes frequent "fence mending."

Still another consideration is the fact that California's congressional district boundaries have been altered more than those of any other state as a result of repeated reapportionments. Except for the decade of the 1920's, its districts have been reapportioned on the average of every 10 years. On many of those occasions there have

been rather drastic boundary shifts. Congressional district patterns in other states have not in general been subjected to such tampering. It is interesting that, with but one exception, California's seniority average in the House has gone down in the first Congress after each reapportionment. Then it has gradually built up until the next reapportionment, dropped, and then climbed back up again. In other words, the one-hundred year pattern of seniority takes on the appearance of an undulating line.

It is unlikely that there is a single explanation for the effect of reapportionment on these seniority cycles. Part of the answer may be attributed to the immediate aftermath of redistricting operations. Decrease would result, too, from the fact that new congressional seats had been added. Further, there have occasionally been critical political upheavals in elections that immediately followed congressional reapportionment. In 1912, for example, there was the Roosevelt-Taft-Wilson campaign, and in 1932 the New Deal was voted into power.

In general, the seniority rating of California's congressmen has increased since 1901. Seniority of the House delegation was one of the factors recognized and considered by the Assembly Interim Committee on Elections and Reapportionment when it made its recommendations for the congressional districts established in 1951. Assuming a reasonable ability to maintain seniority, there are substantial and long-range advantages for the large delegation. First, it will have the voting power. Second, there are enough Californians to place one on every standing committee. Third, several may serve on a single committee at one time, and this tends to make it more certain that someone from the state will always have high rank on that body. New York is a good example with its 45 representatives strategically placed on the 19 standing committees.

California's delegation of 23 in the Eighty-second Congress is already large enough to operate in the same fashion as New York. Arizona and California are locked in mortal combat over Colorado River water in the Interior and Insular Affairs Committee. Arizona has one great advantage in Congressman John R. Murdock, chairman of the committee. His power, however, is partially held in check, because California has three representatives on Murdock's committee: Congressman Clair Engle, second ranking Democrat; Sam Yorty in the thirteenth Democratic position; and Norris Poulson, fifth ranking Republican. These men combine their talents without regard to party lines when issues of concern to California are at stake before the committee. As the delegation as a whole grows in the future, this multiple representation on committees will become one of the important elements of California's congressional power.[18]

There has been much speculation about the great increase in congressional power that has accrued to the "new West." When Democrats from 11 western states met in San Francisco in the fall of 1949, major consideration was given to the problem of creating an audible voice for the West in national affairs. One speaker went so far as to suggest that the "Solid West" could be compared with the Solid South, and that the former was more important because it was based "on policy and program, not on blind party regularity."[19]

However, the congressional delegations of the western states do not constitute the regional-interest unit that some observers would like. The theme of the 1949 Democratic conference in San Francisco was "Land, Water, and Jobs." There is land and there are jobs aplenty in the West, but there is not enough water in the right places. Although the influx of population swelled the size of California's congressional representation, the increased demand for water by southern California has created political disharmony in Congress and has made relations between neighboring-state delegations in Congress more difficult. To say that water is a barrier to understanding between Arizona and California is an understatement. California has other problems of public relations, too. The Pacific Northwest reacts negatively and defensively to suggestions that southern California could be supplied with water from the great rivers of Oregon and Washington. Water is also a key to California's relationships with the Rocky Mountain states.

Another factor operating to make it more difficult for the California House delegation to secure support from other states is a natural enmity against the state that is growing larger and larger each decade. The states which are losing representation, regardless of their geographical position in the United States, may resent California's taking seats away from them.[20] And they may be happy to join forces with California's neighboring states who may be genuinely afraid that California will use its new power contrary to their interests.[21] At this time, then, California cannot be viewed as a working part of a self-interest bloc of western states in the Congress.

D. The Two Party System. Parts of preceding sections have touched upon the implications of congressional reapportionment on political-party institutions. In the electoral college Republican states have lost votes to doubtful states during the last 40 years. In the national nominating conventions held at Chicago in 1952 the Democrats have not reduced the representation of those states that suffered a loss in congressional seats, but the Republicans have immediately geared their convention to conform to the facts of the 1951 reapportionment.

The rise of California to the status of a pivot state in presidential politics is a significant development growing out of the current reapportionment. The state is large in population and doubtful in election behavior. As to the essential characteristic of doubtfulness, a pivot state must have a political atmosphere in which Democrats and Republicans can compete on equal footing for its electoral votes. California meets this requirement better than any state. But in a national two-party system, a local nonpartisan climate with weak parties operates against the state and prevents it from harvesting all the political fruits it might otherwise receive.

On the surface, the redrawing of congressional district lines within the states would seem to favor the Republican party. If redistricting is carried out in all 16 states affected by reapportionment, Republican legislatures will recarve 103 districts, Democratic legislatures, 75, and split-party states, 57. The Democratic states, however, are the most firmly partisan in this group. They can hardly fail to employ partisan power so that it will work to their advantage in the redistricting process. The 3 largest states (New York, California, and Pennsylvania) will all have reapportioned before the 1952 elections, and each has a Republican governor and legislature. But there are some mitigating factors present in each case that work against any propensity to gerrymander in an indiscriminate fashion.

The trend of electoral votes and House seats to the doubtful type of state at the expense of traditionally Republican states is noteworthy. It means a shift in political power to states where each major party is forced to make a broad appeal for votes, not only to its own followers, but to independents and members of the opposite party. New York, California, and Pennsylvania may have elected their Republican governors and legislatures largely because of the influence of three men of broad appeal—Dewey, Warren, and Duff. Governor Earl Warren has won in California with what is perhaps the most successful nonpartisan appeal in the nation.

States in which a narrow Republican appeal still seems effective are losing electoral votes. The 5 leading corn-producing states (Indiana, Illinois, Iowa, Nebraska, and Minnesota), often the home of Republican standpattism and isolationism, have lost a total of 10 electoral votes from their highest combined strength. And one should perforce subtract 2 electoral votes from the wheat state, Kansas. None of these 6 states has been 100 per cent Republican, but together they have constituted the backbone of the G.O.P. since its birth. The corn belt used to be the key to Republican strategy, and "farmers of this section held a conscious balance of power in the party."[22] With increasing urbanization and the flow of political power to seaboard states where voters are more internationally minded, a narrow sectional appeal may well be fatal.

The Democratic party has not suffered much decline in strength as a result of successive reapportionments. The Solid South retains about as much strength in the electoral college and in the House of Representatives as it has had throughout this century. There are some nascent indications, however, that the 1940 to 1950 population trends may be making inroads into the solidarity of the southern states.

An interesting question emerges when one considers the transfer of northern industry and northern managers and workers to the South. Will migration affect the South's one-party system? It is reasonable to assume that most individuals take their party politics with them as they move from one section of the country to another. Many Republicans have emigrated to the Solid South. It is possible that the overwhelming Democratic strength will absorb this Republican potential. On the other hand, is is also possible that transplanted Republicans will flourish in a southern political climate. This latter speculation is no doubt attractive to those who still eye with hope the possible development of a two-party system in some sections of the South. Forthcoming data on migration from the Bureau of the Census may furnish some interesting facts which could shed light here.

While some Republican influence may be flowing from North to South, a potential Democratic influence is going the other way. In mid-November the Census Bureau announced that 7 southern states had lost a total of 250,000 Negroes during the decade ending in 1950.[23] Some had moved to Florida, but the vast majority had gone North. Others had moved to California.

The movement of the Negro does not mean a loss of Democratic votes in the South, because Negroes are still generally disenfranchised. But it does mean perhaps that he will influence the outcome of elections in doubtful states, or in states that lean toward the Republican party. One writer suggests the Negro already holds the balance of power in national politics by his large

numbers in certain key northern states.[24] Recent census figures may be employed to support this contention about the Negro vote.

The flow of political power to states in the doubtful category is a healthy trend for American democracy. It should put both major parties on their mettle. Population shifts that tend to break the South up into segments less-solidly Democratic are also healthful. It becomes more necessary, then, for the major parties to make broad appeals and campaign in almost all of the states. Campaigning may become more meaningful, and elections more productive of the kind of presidential and congressional leadership needed by the United States in the world of today.

Notes

1. House Administration.
2. Banking and Currency, Expenditures in the Executive Departments, Interior and Insular Affairs, and Public Works.
3. States with committee chairmen: Illinois (Rules, and Expenditures in the Executive Departments); Kentucky (Banking and Currency); Mississippi (Veterans' Affairs); Missouri (Appropriations); New York (Judiciary, and Public Works); Tennessee (Post Office and Civil Service). States with ranking minority members: Illinois (Rules, Judiciary, and District of Columbia); Missouri (Armed Services); New York (Appropriations, and Ways and Means); Pennsylvania (Education and Labor).
4. Texas (Foreign Affairs); Washington (Public Works).
5. Arkansas (Expenditures in the Executive Departments); Tennessee (Post Office and Civil Service).
6. 46 Stat. 26 (1929), 55 Stat. 761 (1941), 2 U. S. C. §2a and 2b (Supp. 1950).
7. Present party alignment of the California House delegation is 13 Republicans and 10 Democrats.
8. The following is the party alignment on the final votes in the California legislature on the 1951 congressional reapportionment: Assembly Democrats for the bill 13, Republicans 36; Senate Democrats for the bill 8, Republicans 23.
9. Pub. L. No. 291, 77th Cong., 1st Sess. (1941), 55 Stat. 761, 2 U. S. C. §2a(c). (Supp. 1950).
10. For example, Connecticut has 5 congressional districts and 6 congressmen, the sixth at large. Had Connecticut lost a seat in 1951, it would have had 5 congressmen, and because it already had 5 congressional districts, it would not be necessary to reapportion.
11. The following shows the present party alignments of the congressional delegations of the gaining and losing states. Gainers: California, 13 Republicans and 10 Democrats; Florida, 6 D; Maryland, 3 R and 3 D; Michigan, 12 R and 5 D; Texas, 21 D; Virginia, 9 D; Washington, 4 R and 2 D. Losers: Arkansas, 7 D; Illinois, 18 R and 8 D; Kentucky, 7 D and 2 R; Mississippi, 7 D; Missouri, 9 D and 3 R; New York, 23 D and 22 R; Oklahoma, 6 D and 2 R; Pennsylvania, 21 R and 12 D; Tennessee, 8 D and 2 R.
12. The New York reapportionment has quite possibly been done at the expense of from two to six Democratic districts. See N. Y. Times, Dec. 9, 1951, §4, p. 2E.
13. Arthur N. Holcombe, "Our More Perfect Union" 130 (1950).
14. California is 67.1 per cent urban by the old census definition and 80.7 by the new definition. "Bureau of the Census, Population of California, April 1, 1950, Advance

Reports Series PC-8," No. 4 (October 14, 1951).

15. See map of California's 1952 congressional districts, in Hinderaker and Waters, "A Case Study in Reapportionment," *Law and Contemporary Problems,* Vol. XVII (Spring, 1952).

16. Julius Kahn (R), 12 terms; Clarence Lea (D), 16; Charles Curry (R), Albert Carter (R), and Harry Englebright (R), 10; and Richard Welch (R), 12.

17. Clair Engle (D), Interior and Insular Affairs; Chet Holifield (D), Expenditures in the Executive Departments; and Carl Hinshaw (R), Interstate and Foreign Commerce.

18. For a discussion of the delegation see Farrelly and Hall, *Californians in Congress,* "The Politics of California" 228 (1951).

19. Neuberger, *The "Solid West,"* 169 "The Nation" 346 (Oct. 8, 1949).

20. Congressman Norris Poulson (R), Los Angeles, has cited this factor when speaking on the effects of the 1951 congressional reapportionment.

21. Neuberger, *The Case for Intertie,* "Frontier," Oct. 1951, p. 13.

22. W. E. Binkley, "American Political Parties: Their Natural History" 285 (1945).

23. *The Negro Moves,* Time, Nov. 19, 1951, p. 26, col. 3.

24. H. L. Moon, "Balance of Power: The Negro Vote" 10 (1948).

SECTION II

The Political Bases of Legislative Behavior

INTRODUCTORY NOTE

The institutional context within which legislators must operate imposes certain parameters on their behavior which can, therefore, not be described or accounted for by a simplistic conception that views legislative decisions as wholly and exclusively individual, rational efforts to promote some objectively defined public interest. Legislators' views of what is the public interest and what are appropriate ways to achieve it are surrounded and conditioned by their notions of what behavior is appropriate in the kind of office that is located in a particular institutional environment. Moreover, variations in that institutional context, by affecting the legislators' behavior, can have varying consequences for the functioning of the legislative system.

Because the modern legislature is above all an agency for representing the general public in the process of government (but not only for that reason), legislators' behavior will also be affected by their relationships to significant political groups in the larger community "outside" the legislature ("the public") as well as to those centered in other political sub-systems. These relationships constitute the political bases of legislative behavior. Like the institutional context, they not only surround and condition the legislator's conception of the goals requiring legislative action and the means by which they can be attained, but also, by affecting legislative behavior, have important consequences for the system's functioning. Indeed, study of the political bases of legislative behavior has most often been undertaken within a framework of curiosity about their functional significance.

As a result, one can get from these studies a much clearer picture of the functional properties of the various political bases than of the behavior of legislators through which such functions must be mediated if they are to be performed at all. This is true with respect to all three types of political group which have occupied the attention of most students of legislative institutions—political parties, pressure groups, and legislators' geographical constituencies.

A very common assumption concerning the place of parties in the legislative process is that they serve to harmonize, or "mesh," the operations of the executive and legislative branches of government. Another common assumption is that the majority party performs the function of propounding policy while the opposition party performs the function of watching and criticizing. Insofar as a majority and an opposition party perform these functions, they are both assumed to contribute toward the party system's ability to relate legislative policy to public opinion.

In the same way, pressure groups are almost universally assumed to perform significant functions relating to the more general one of linking legislative decisions with public views. Not only do they express wishes and describe goals sought by segments of the public, but they frequently originate legislative measures, and still more frequently express judgments about proposed measures originating elsewhere. In performing such functions, pressure groups at the same time serve the function of providing legislators with information and knowledge, both political knowledge about the strength of competing claims and the consequences of alternative decisions on policy issues and technical knowledge defining the content of policy issues.

The almost universal presumption concerning legislators' constituencies has been that "the district" is the chief agency functioning to relate legislative decisions to public opinion. Precisely how, in concrete terms, it performs such a function is not made clear. It is often supposed that the legislator personally embodies qualities or properties characteristic of the population he represents, although such a supposition contradicts practically all available evidence. It is commonly thought, too, that "the district" functions through some process of direct communication between legislator and constituents, but no legislator can really communicate with or receive communications from so vast and amorphous an entity as his "district." He can only communicate with particular individuals and groups. It is also sometimes assumed that the means by which constituents insure that legislators' actions will correspond to public desires is their choices at the polls. But what is known of voters' information and motivations makes it difficult to believe that the electoral device operates in quite so simple and direct a fashion.

Recent investigations have suggested certain significant political bases of legislative behavior in addition to the three principal ones so far mentioned. Various factional alignments within a legislative body which sometimes take the place of party, particularly in one-party or non-partisan legislatures, are one example. David B. Truman shows, in "The State Delegations and Voting Alignments," that a legislator's own delegation in the legislature may, under certain conditions, serve as a political base. Certain broad interest groupings—such as groupings of "urban" and "rural" legislators—have also been frequently pointed out as significant political bases. While the existence of such bases is clear, their origins and their functioning in the legislative system are much less so. They are customarily looked upon as a surrogate or a substitute for one or more of the three principal bases, and therefore analyzed in terms of their functioning (either through or in place of party or pressure groups) to relate public policy to public opinion.

Studies bearing upon the functional significance of the political bases of legislative behavior have, until recently, been less concerned with investigating the actual behavior of legislators than with seeking to measure, without reference to the individuals composing the legislative aggregate, the net influence of one factor or another. This preoccupation is evident in studies of the impact of party on legislative actions. An estimate of such influence in the legislatures they respectively consider is central to all three articles dealing with the topic—those by Malcolm F. Jewell, Leon D. Epstein, and Peter Campbell.

In the case of party, most studies use some concept of "party cohesion" as an index of the influence of party on legislative activities. Wherever the object of investigation is some political base to which the legislator can be hypothetically related by some external criterion like his party label, the concept of "cohesion" is the central tool for measuring the influence of the factor being studied. Such is the case, for example, in David B. Truman's study of the influence of legislators' membership in a state delegation on their legislative activities. It is also the case in David R. Derge's study of the impact of legislators' residence in urban or rural areas on legislative activities, "Urban-Rural Conflict: The Case in Illinois."

But not all political bases of behavior which have interested students of the legislative process are susceptible to treatment in this fashion. It is difficult to operationalize legislators' relationships to pressure groups, or even their relationships to their constituencies in exactly this way. As a result, political scientists have yet to devise concepts or metrics analogous to "party cohesion" for measuring the net influence of pressure groups, constituencies, and other political bases.

However, when one proceeds from simple questions about *how much* influence any given factor might have to the questions of *why* and *under what circumstances,* one is immediately led to analysis of certain factors in legislators' behavior as distinguished from the behavior of legislatures. From answers to questions about how and when different factors play a more or less significant part in the legislative process one may infer propositions about legislators' behavior which must hold true if the connection between circumstances and net influence really exists or if given functions are really to be performed—propositions, that is, which view these factors as genuine bases of legislative behavior. Though these propositions may not be explicitly stated in many of the selections presented in this section, they are clearly implied in all of them.

With respect to party influence, for example, Leon D. Epstein, in "Cohesion of British Parliamentary Parties," argues (without directly researching all the questions) that, at least in the case of the British Parliament, formal structural features of government—in particular the power of dissolution and the formal disciplinary power of party organs—cannot fully account for what party cohesion there is, whereas fusion of governmental powers, the "nationalization" of politics, and a certain kind of ideological division in the electorate may well be circumstances associated with a high degree of party cohesion (which is, of course, an index of net party influence). Malcolm E. Jewell, in "Party Voting in American State Legislatures," considers, as circumstances possibly associated with high party influence on legislative business, the amount of inter-party competition for legislative seats, the role of the executive officer of the government, the urban or rural character of legislative districts, and others.

To take an example concerning pressure group influence, David B. Truman, in "The Dynamics of Access in the Legislative Process," outlines the circumstances affecting the net influence of a group (of which "access" is an index of sorts) as follows: the governmental structure, as it advantages or disadvantages certain groups; the legislators' individual group affiliations and identifications; certain objective characteristics of the group itself (size, resources, prestige in the community, tactics, etc.); and the legislators' own group identifications with each other as co-members of the legislative group and its subgroupings.

In the case of constituency, to offer a final example, Duncan MacRae, in "The Relation Between Roll Call Votes and Constituencies," shows how the varying socio-economic characteristics of a district affect the influence of constituency as compared with the influence of party.

In all these cases, it should be apparent, certain propositions about the behavior of legislators are logically implied by the explanations offered for the influence of whatever factor is being considered. Without attempting to consider these propositions in detail for any particular case, we can suggest some of the more important propositions implied in functional analyses and stated more explicitly in behaviorally-oriented studies.

It is plain, to begin with, that the legislator, in his relationships with any of the so-called political bases of legislative behavior, is not just an inert object whose actions take their direction and momentum altogether from some pressuring or influencing "outside" force. This has been made most clear with respect to pressure groups. The line between the policy wishes and rationalizations of pressure groups and those of legislators is frequently so fine that it is difficult to say when a legislator is voicing the views of a pressure group which he recognizes as such, and when he is voicing personal attitudes which merely happen to coincide with those of some organized group. Oliver Garceau and Corinne Silverman, in "A Pressure Group and the Pressured," find certain

American state legislators so ignorant of even the existence and names of supposedly powerful pressure groups and their lobbyists, not to mention the groups' policy demands, that any conception of legislators automatically reacting to pressure would grossly misrepresent the case.

It would be equally misleading to think of legislators' constituencies as agencies controlling legislators' actions by mechanically pressuring them one way or another. "The district" is not a solid, objective entity which can exert pressure or influence upon a legislator, but a complex collection of many and diverse persons and groups. It is a legal abstraction which the legislator sees in a certain image. His image may include or exclude whole classes of persons, groups and organizations. He could not passively respond to "it" even if he wanted to do so.

An important but frequently overlooked proposition holds that legislators, when they assume legislative office, assume also a whole set of rules of behavior which constitute their recognition of the "structure of government." For whatever reason they accept them, it is acceptance of such rules by legislators which preserves the legislature as an institution and maintains its relationship to other political institutions so that one can talk about a "structure of government." This kind of imperative of behavior undoubtedly takes precedence over others which concern legislators' relationships with party or pressure group or constituency in cases where conflict might occur.

Another important proposition, advanced by Samuel H. Beer, in "Pressure Groups and Parties in Britain," is that legislators share fundamental beliefs concerning the legitimacy of certain goals and certain modes of action which come out of a community's general political culture, and that their approach to or reaction from party and pressure group (and, by inference, any other political base) will be shaped in a significant fashion by their acceptance of such beliefs. Still another proposition, suggested in the article by Garceau and Silverman, is that a legislator's view of pressure groups is itself closely related to his view of party, constituency and other political bases, and that his views of and consequent relationships with any of them is dependent upon some more fundamental element in his whole conception of the nature of politics and the office of legislator. While that outlook may be closely associated with the political culture, and therefore, in some respects, be similar for all legislators, it is in other respects apparently associated with basic attitudes personal to and different for each legislator. How legislators' policy conceptions and manner of defining policy issues are influenced by their varying political conceptions is one important be-havioral consequence described by Garceau and Silverman.

As pointed out by Truman in his analysis of "The Dynamics of Access in the Legislative Proc-ess," a legislator's views of and attitudes toward any pressure group will be vitally affected by the fact that he is also a member of the legislature, sharing with his fellow members group-norms and folk-beliefs which will in many cases prescribe his behavior not only toward pressure groups, but also, one may infer, toward party, constituency and all other political bases. John H. Millett, in "The Role of an Interest Group Leader," describes how, in the case of a member of the British Par-liament who was also an important officer of a pressure group, the legislator's reactions to a pressure group's policy demands was affected in this way. We can assume that personal identifica-tion with the legislature will similarly affect legis-lators' behavior toward party, constituency, and other political groups.

Implied throughout most of the studies which follow are further questions about legislative be-havior which have yet to be examined by behav-ioral research and for which even speculative an-swers seem less clear than do the few propositions outlined above, but which are obviously of central importance for both a general understanding of legislative behavior and an understanding of the functional place of parties, pressure groups, and constituencies in any given legislative system. For example, with respect to party, one might ask, does the behavior of legislators which we label "cohesive" stem from legislators' personal, con-scious agreement with the policy and program views propounded by party leaders? Does it re-flect a belief that party views coincide with the views of a majority or important segments of their constituency? Is legislators' loyalty to party re-lated at all to a belief of either kind, or is it per-haps associated with some deeper motivation of group identification which ignores policy views and constituency wishes altogether? For what kinds of legislators is one or another of these explana-tions the most plausible explanation of cohesive behavior?

It would likewise be useful to know if and when legislators truly see themselves as representing local constituents, and if and when they see them-selves representing somehow or other the entire commonwealth, and just what they think pressure groups have to do with either representative func-tion. One can probably assume that some legis-lators see themselves one way and others another way. But, which ones which way? And why?

Legislative study to date has pointed out such questions with increasing sharpness and clarity. Increasingly, research is being undertaken to be-gin to answer some of them. What is most needed at this stage of development is some unifying the-ory, some model of the legislative actor, which will make it possible to relate to each other the insights from many political base studies in more meaningful fashion than does the concept of net influence of political factors on total legislative activity. What is needed is a viable theory of leg-islative behavior which can comprehend all po-litical bases of legislators' behavior in a common framework.

A. Partisanship in the Legislative Process

1. PARTY VOTING IN AMERICAN STATE LEGISLATURES

Malcolm E. Jewell

. . . THE STUDY that follows is a comparison of the extent of party voting in the legislatures of eight American states that have the basic prerequisite for a significant degree of party influence: a reasonably strong and healthy two-party system. This study points up the wide variety in the extent of party voting and the relatively high level in the larger urban states.

It is obvious that there are many states which have been so dominated by one party in recent years that partisan factors can have no significant influence over legislative voting habits. Into this category would fall the eleven Southern states, and twelve others—five with Democratic and seven with Republican records over at least the past quarter-century. There are two states with nonpartisan legislatures and one, Wisconsin, with a unique blend of Republican and Progressive control over part of the last two decades. It cannot be said that each of the remaining twenty-two states has had a consistently vigorous two-party system, but in none of them has one party controlled both the governorship and the two houses of the legislature for as much as sixteen of the last twenty years. These are the states in which there is more likely to be a reflection of partisan activity in the legislature. The eight states chosen for examination in this study are among these twenty-two having at least a semblance of an effective two-party system.

Methods of Research. This study of the influence of party in legislative voting is limited to sessions in which the party balance in the legislature was reasonably close, for it was assumed that there would be less party voting, even in strong two-party states, during the years of one-sided legislative control. Two legislative sessions have been chosen for study whenever necessary to get a sample large enough for statistical significance.

For each session, every roll call printed in the legislative journals has been examined. In all of the states studied, except Massachusetts, a roll call is required on the final passage of every bill, resulting in a very large total number of roll calls. No record was made of unanimous roll calls or of those in which at least 90 per cent of the Republicans voted on the same side as 90 per cent of the Democrats. The number of nearly or completely unanimous roll calls is very large, but such roll calls prove nothing about the role of parties on issues which provoked disagreement in the legislature.[1] Every other roll call has been included in these calculations, whether on an amendment, final passage of a bill, or any other question, except in a few cases where the number of roll calls on one issue was so large as to distort the total figures.[2] The duplicating vote on emergency clauses in Missouri and Colorado has also been omitted. No attempt has been made to give added weight to bills considered of major importance. No record has been made of independent or third-party voters or of those who abstained from voting on an issue.

The roll-call totals have been translated into the index of cohesion according to the system suggested by Stuart Rice.[3] When all members of a party vote on one side of an issue the index is 100; when they are evenly divided it is 0. All of the roll-call votes of each party have been divided into three classes: those with a party index of cohesion of 80-100 (90-100 per cent of the members on one side), those with an index of 40-79 (70-89 per cent on one side), and those with an index of 0-39 (50-69 per cent on one side).

No simple formula can describe accurately the degree of party voting in the roll calls of a state, but there are certain keys to an understanding of the complex statistics. First, on what percentage of all the roll calls did a majority of the two parties take opposite sides of a question? Obviously this percentage will tend to vary with the degree of party influence. Second, within this group of roll calls, how much unity did each of the parties display? Third, within this group of

Reprinted from *American Political Science Review*, Vol. 49 (1955), pp. 773-791, by permission of the author and the publisher.

roll calls with the parties opposed, how many produced a high level of unity in both parties? For this purpose we have defined as a "party vote" an index of cohesion of 80 in both parties. Fourth, among the roll calls with a majority of both parties on the same side, did either party have a much higher degree of unity than the other?

The eight states studied contain over one-third of the people in this country; most of these states are large and urban. The 2,743 roll calls furnish a representative sample of party voting in the legislatures of strong two-party states during periods of close party competition. The study does not examine the role of party leaders and party factions in committees in bringing bills to a vote or blocking them, a subject on which more research is necessary.

Massachusetts. Massachusetts has had a strongly competitive party system since the start of the New Deal. The two parties have shared the governor's chair equally in the last two decades. Although the legislature, through skillful gerrymandering, has had Republican majorities in nearly all of these years, the margin has been relatively close. In the year under study, 1947, the Republican administration had comfortable, but not one-sided, majorities in both legislative branches. Massachusetts is one of the few states in which every bill introduced must have a committee hearing, be reported out, and be voted on. Since party influence cannot kill a bill in committee, the roll-call study gives a more comprehensive picture of party activity than it does in most states. This is the only state studied which does not require roll calls on final passage of each bill. In Massachusetts, roll calls are demanded only on highly controversial and usually partisan bills. For this reason the percentage of votes with the

parties on opposite sides is very high and is not truly comparable with the percentages in other states. Conversely, there are so few votes with the parties on the same side that differences in party unity in this category cannot be examined.

Within the category of roll calls with the parties on opposite sides, Table I shows a high level of party unity in both branches, particularly among the minority Democrats; only the Pennsylvania parties showed a higher degree of unity in this respect than the Massachusetts Democrats. Over three-quarters of the Democratic Senate votes shown to have a cohesion index of 80 or more represent party unanimity.

Almost one-third of the large number of roll calls on which the Democrats but not the Republicans had a cohesion index of 80 or more were on labor and welfare issues. This may in part reflect the conflicting pressures on Republicans from urban areas in the state. The difference in party unity might be expected to reflect the comfortable majority of the Republican party, but in over one-fifth of the roll calls on which the parties took opposite sides, the minority Democrats gained enough Republican votes to win.[4]

New York. New York has often been cited, by Professor Lowell and other observers, as one of the few states in which parties play a large role in legislative voting. This study shows that, among the eight states, only Pennsylvania outranked it in the overall degree of party voting. The size and diversity of New York's population and its key position in the electoral college have combined to give it a strong two-party system, although the balance of parties has been reflected more in the governorship than in the legislature. The Democrats have had control of one or both houses during only four out of the eight years

Table I—Party Voting in Massachusetts Legislature in 1947*

	PERCENTAGE OF TOTAL ROLL CALLS			
	Senate N = 133		House N = 128	
Parties on Opposite Sides	93%		93%	
Index of Cohesion:				
Both parties 80-100[a]	38%		40%	
Each party 80-100	Rep. 42%	Dem. 74%	Rep. 48%	Dem. 68%
40-79	37	10	30	16
0-39	14	9	15	9
Parties on Same Side	7%		7%	
Index of Cohesion:				
Rep. 0-79 Dem. 80-100	2%		2%	
Rep. 80-100 Dem. 0-79	0		2	
Rep. 0-79 Dem. 0-79	5		3	

* Political composition: Governor—Republican
Senate—24 Republicans—16 Democrats
House—144 Republicans—96 Democrats
a. In these tables, the percentage of roll calls for which the index of both parties was at least 80 is a subtotal of the similar figure given for each of the parties.

Table II—Party Voting in New York Legislature in 1947 and 1949*

	PERCENTAGE OF TOTAL ROLL CALLS			
	Senate N = 146		House N = 184	
Parties on Opposite Sides	62%		61%	
Index of Cohesion:				
Both parties 80-100	32%		34%	
Each party 80-100	Rep. 42%	Dem. 40%	Rep. 44%	Dem. 43%
40-79	12	12	13	10
0-39	8	10	4	8
Parties on Same Side	38%		39%	
Index of Cohesion:				
Rep. 0-79 Dem. 80-100	9%		14%	
Rep. 80-100 Dem. 0-79	23		11	
Rep. 0-79 Dem. 0-79	6		14	

* Political composition: 1947 Governor—Republican
Senate—41 Republicans—14 Democrats
House—109 Republicans—40 Democrats
1949 Governor—Republican
Senate—31 Republicans—25 Democrats
House—87 Republicans—63 Democrats

they have held the governorship in the last two decades, while Republican governors have consistently had a legislative majority.

This study covers the legislative sessions of 1947 and 1949. In each session there was a Republican governor; in 1947 the Republicans had a large majority in the legislature, in 1949 a moderate majority.

Table II shows the high proportion of roll calls on which the parties were opposed; it also reveals a level of unity within this category that was consistently high and remarkably uniform for both parties in both houses. A breakdown of the figures shows little difference between the two sessions in the Senate, although both parties—particularly the Democrats—had slightly higher levels of unity among the votes with the parties opposed in 1947. The figures varied more in the House, mainly be-

cause the percentage of roll calls with the parties opposed dropped from 76 to 46 per cent from 1947 to 1949. Within this category, both parties, but particularly the Democrats, showed greater unity in 1947, when the party balance was more one-sided. This is an exception to the expected rule that closer party competition breeds greater party unity.

On the issues on which a majority of both parties were agreed, the Republicans showed more unity in both sessions of the Senate and in the 1947 House session, as is generally the case with majority parties, but the Democrats were more united in the 1949 House session.

Pennsylvania. Pennsylvania for a long time was one of the strongholds of the Republican party, which kept an unbroken grip on both legislative branches and the governorship for the

Table III—Party Voting in Pennsylvania Legislature in 1945*

	PERCENTAGE OF TOTAL ROLL CALLS			
	Senate N = 151		House N = 147	
Parties on Opposite Sides	64%		81%	
Index of Cohesion:				
Both parties 80-100	52%		56%	
Each party 80-100	Rep. 56%	Dem. 59%	Rep. 64%	Dem. 62%
40-79	3	3	12	10
0-39	5	2	5	9
Parties on Same Side	36%		19%	
Index of Cohesion:				
Rep. 0-79 Dem. 80-100	11%		4%	
Rep. 80-100 Dem. 0-79	21		9	
Rep. 0-79 Dem. 0-79	4		6	

* Political composition: Governor—Republican
Senate—32 Republicans—18 Democrats
House—109 Republicans—99 Democrats

first 34 years of this century. While the Democratic gain since the New Deal has not been as great as in some states, the party has held the governorship for four years and one or both houses for six years since 1934. Moreover, Democratic minorities have become much stronger than they were before the New Deal. The Republican margin over the Democrats averaged about two-to-one in the 1940's but was less in the 1945 session studied here.

This session provides the strongest example of party unity found in this study. The proportion of roll calls with the parties opposed shown in Table III was exceeded only in Massachusetts, where special circumstances have been noted. The level of unity in both parties and in both houses is extremely high. Pennsylvania is the only state where "party votes" (both parties with a cohesion index of 80 or more) were over 50 cent of all the roll calls. An equally remarkable fact, not shown in the table, is that in one-third of the total votes every Democrat voted on one side and every Republican on the other.

The only significant difference between the parties is shown in the group of roll calls where the majority of both parties were agreed. Here, in accord with the general rule, the majority Republican party showed greater unity, having roughly twice as many votes with a cohesion index of 80 or above as did the Democrats.[5]

Ohio. Ohio, like New York, has a key position in the electoral college and a balance of large urban centers and rural areas, which has given it a strong two-party system. In the last twenty years the Democratic party has controlled the governorship for twelve years, but has had a majority in one or both houses only four years. Despite the

close balance of parties, each has at times had one-sided control of the legislature. The governor was Republican in the first year selected for study (1941) and Democratic in the second (1945), but the Republican majority was larger in both branches of the legislature in 1945.

Table IV shows a level of party voting in Ohio which was lower than in some of the other large industrial states studied, but higher than in the smaller rural states. The Senate, with a closer margin between the parties, had a larger proportion of roll calls with the parties in disagreement, particularly in 1941. Within this category both parties showed more unity in the Senate than in the House, and in both chambers the majority Republicans were more unified than the Democrats. Democratic cohesion remained steady during the two sessions, but Republican unity was somewhat greater in 1941, a difference that could have been caused by the closer party margin and the element of Republican gubernatorial leadership in that year.

Among the roll calls on which the parties agreed, the Ohio Republicans showed the expected greater unity in the House, where the figures were quite similar for both sessions. In the Senate, Democratic unity was greater, particularly in the 1945 session.

Illinois. Illinois also has a close balance of large urban and rural areas that has helped to maintain a strong two-party system, particularly since the New Deal period. In the last two decades, the Democratic party has held the governorship ten years and controlled one or both legislative chambers for eight years. The session under study (1949) was the first year of Adlai Stevenson's governorship, after eight Republican years. The

Table IV—Party Voting in Ohio Legislature in 1941 and 1945*

	PERCENTAGE OF TOTAL ROLL CALLS			
	Senate N = 128		House N = 289	
Parties on Opposite Sides	49%		38%	
Index of Cohesion:				
Both parties 80-100	23%		15%	
Each party 80-100	Rep. 37%	Dem. 29%	Rep. 25%	Dem. 19%
40-79	7	9	6	10
0-39	5	11	7	9
Parties on Same Side	51%		62%	
Index of Cohesion:				
Rep. 0-79 Dem. 80-100	27%		11%	
Rep. 80-100 Dem. 0-79	15		34	
Rep. 0-79 Dem. 0-79	9		17	

* Political composition: 1941 Governor—Republican
                Senate—19 Republicans—17 Democrats
                House—78 Republicans—60 Democrats
        1945 Governor—Democrat
                Senate—20 Republicans—13 Democrats
                House—89 Republicans—47 Democrats

Table V—Party Voting in Illinois Legislature in 1949*

	PERCENTAGE OF TOTAL ROLL CALLS			
	Senate N = 207		House N = 155	
Parties on Opposite Sides	53%		54%	
Index of Cohesion:				
Both parties 80-100	15%		17%	
Each party 80-100	Rep. 17%	Dem. 39%	Rep. 20%	Dem. 40%
40-79	24	7	17	8
0-39	12	7	17	6
Parties on Same Side	47%		46%	
Index of Cohesion:				
Rep. 0-79 Dem. 80-100	25%		34%	
Rep. 80-100 Dem. 0-79	11		4	
Rep. 0-79 Dem. 0-79	11		8	

* Political composition: Governor—Democrat
                        Senate—32 Republicans—18 Democrats
                        House—72 Republicans—80 Democrats

Democrats had a narrow grip on the House, but only a respectable minority in the Senate.

This Democratic rebirth may in part explain the outstanding feature in Illinois, the much higher level of party unity among the Democrats than among the Republicans. In general the state ranks close to Ohio in most of the indications of party voting shown in Table V. The proportion of roll calls with the parties opposed is just over half—about average for the eight states. The Democratic level of unity in this group was equally high in both branches of the legislature, with twice as many roll calls with an index of cohesion of at least 80 as in the case of the Republicans.

It is even more striking to compare the number of Senate roll calls where one party had absolute unity—73 for the Democrats and 13 for the Republicans. On more than one-fifth of the Senate roll calls on which the two parties were opposed, the Democratic minority gained enough Republican votes to win. Welfare issues, taxation,

and appropriations made up over half of the bills on which the parties were opposed and only the Democrats had an index of cohesion of at least 80. In the category of roll calls with party agreement, the Democrats showed far more unity, particularly in the House where they had a majority.[6]

Washington. The state of Washington has had a close balance of parties, has supported the winning presidential candidate in nearly every election in this century, and like other states with important urban areas has grown more Democratic since the start of the New Deal. The Democratic party has held the governorship for ten of the last twenty years, and has controlled both houses for fourteen years, with partial control four years. In the session chosen for study (1945), the Democratic party controlled the governorship and had a comfortable majority in both branches of the legislature.

While in general it may be said that the level

Table VI—Party Voting in Washington Legislature in 1945*

	PERCENTAGE OF TOTAL ROLL CALLS			
	Senate N = 190		House N = 133	
Parties on Opposite Sides	71%		51%	
Index of Cohesion:				
Both parties 80-100	9%		9%	
Each party 80-100	Rep. 46%	Dem. 16%	Rep. 23%	Dem. 25%
40-79	12	42	18	19
0-39	13	13	10	7
Parties on Same Side	29%		49%	
Index of Cohesion:				
Rep. 0-79 Dem. 80-100	15%		26%	
Rep. 80-100 Dem. 0-79	8		10	
Rep. 0-79 Dem. 0-79	6		13	

* Political composition: Governor—Democrat
                        Senate—14 Republicans—32 Democrats
                        House—36 Republicans—63 Democrats

of party unity shown in Table VI is above average, it is lower and less consistent in Washington than in larger industrial states studied, mainly because of great differences in party unity in the Senate. In the House the percentage of roll calls with the parties opposed is about average, but both parties have somewhat lower than average levels of unity. The Senate percentage of disagreed votes—71 per cent—is one of the highest, and within this group the Republican party showed much more unity in voting than the Democrats. Only in Massachusetts and Illinois were there such marked differences between the unity levels of the two parties within this category of votes. Washington is the only state in which the Republicans in either house surpassed the Democrats in unity by such a large margin. With regard to those roll calls on which the parties agreed, we find, as we might expect, a higher level of unity in the majority Democratic party.

Missouri. Missouri has had a close balance of parties and since 1904 has supported every winning presidential candidate; in state politics, however, it has been heavily Democratic. In the last two decades the Democratic party has controlled the governorship sixteen years, with the legislature Democratic in ten of these years, Republican in four, and divided in two. During the four years of Republican governorship the legislature was Democratic for two years and divided for the other two. During the session under study, which lasted through 1945 and 1946, the governor was Democratic and the legislature Republican by small margins in both chambers. Missouri, like Massachusetts, requires that all bills be reported out by committees, and hence a study of roll calls provides a particularly good test of total party influence.

Despite the close party competition in the state, and the close balance in this legislative session, Missouri parties exhibited less unity in voting than those in any other state in this survey. The proportion of votes with the parties opposed was the lowest, being less than one out of four in the Senate, as shown in Table VII. In both chambers the majority Republicans displayed more unity than the Democrats in this respect, suggesting that the influence of the Democratic governor over his party's voting was not strong. Contrary to our expectations, both parties displayed less unity in the Senate, where the Republican margin was only four; the Senate Democrats maintained the lowest level of unity discovered in this survey. When the two parties were in agreement, which was rather often, the majority Republican party showed a considerably higher level of unity than the minority Democrats in both chambers.

Colorado. Colorado has long had a close balance of parties. There has been a Republican governor for twelve of the last twenty years, eight with a Republican legislature, four with a divided legislature. During the eight Democratic gubernatorial years, control of the legislature was Democratic in four years, Republican in two, and divided in two. The two years under study are 1941, with a Republican governor and a divided legislature, and 1947, with a Democratic governor and a Republican legislature.

Table VIII shows that the general level of party unity was low. The proportion of roll calls with the parties on opposite sides was low in both sessions and surpassed only that in Missouri. Likewise within that category the level of party unity was the lowest in any state except Missouri. On these roll calls in 1941 both majority parties—the Senate Democrats and the House Republicans—displayed slightly more unity than the minority parties. In 1947, under a Democratic governor, the minority Democrats showed slightly more unity than the Republicans in both branches, and

Table VII—Party Voting in Missouri Legislature in 1945-1946*

	PERCENTAGE OF TOTAL ROLL CALLS			
	Senate N = 123		House N = 284	
Parties on Opposite Sides	23%		36%	
Index of Cohesion:				
Both parties 80-100	1%		9%	
Each party 80-100	Rep. 8%	Dem. 3%	Rep. 17%	Dem. 13%
40-79	5	7	12	11
0-39	10	13	7	12
Parties on Same Side	77%		64%	
Index of Cohesion:				
Rep. 0-79 Dem. 80-100	17%		15%	
Rep. 80-100 Dem. 0-79	33		30	
Rep. 0-79 Dem. 0-79	27		19	

* Political composition: Governor—Democrat
Senate—19 Republicans—15 Democrats
House—81 Republicans—69 Democrats

there was more party unity generally in the House than in the Senate.

In the category of roll calls with the parties on the same side, the general rule of greater unity in the majority party applied only to the 1941 Senate (where the majority was very small) and the 1947 House (where the majority was very large). The opposite result was found in the 1941 House, and the two parties were even in the 1947 Senate.

Summary of Party Voting. Table IX, which summarizes the results of this study, presents no clear picture of consistently higher levels of unity among either majority or minority party, Democratic or Republican, except on roll calls which found the parties in agreement. On these votes we have found a higher level of unity in the majority party, which in many states achieved a cohesion index of at least 80 twice as often as did the minority party. When there is only limited dissent to a bill, concentrated in one party, that party is usually the minority party. The few exceptions shown in Table IX follow no clear pattern. It might be expected that if the minority party ever displayed greater unity on these issues it would be when it controlled the governorship. This would seem to explain the greater Senate Democratic unity in Illinois and in one Ohio session, but certainly not the other examples of minority unity, in New York and Colorado.

Far more interesting and more important is the summary of roll-call voting on questions that led the parties to take opposite sides. Here the legislative bodies with greater majority party and minority party unity almost balance out, as do the examples of greater Democratic and Republican unity. The Republicans are more often united in the majority and the Democrats more often in the minority, but only because the Republicans controlled most of the legislatures examined. In the 1947 Colorado session and the 1949 Illinois session the greater Democratic unity probably reflects loyalty to the Democratic administration, but similar loyalty was notably absent among the Missouri Democrats and the Massachusetts Republicans. In Washington the disunity among the majority Democratic party in the Senate was due to a small bloc of senators who generally voted with the Republicans. The parties shared nearly equally in the high level of unity evident in New York and Pennsylvania.

Table IX shows that the states under study can be divided into three groups according to the level of partisanship in the legislature of each. The highest level is in Pennsylvania, New York, and Massachusetts. There is a lower level in the second group, Ohio, Illinois, and Washington, with wide variations between the parties in the latter two states. The lowest level of unity is found in Colorado and Missouri. These differences suggest that, among states with a relatively vigorous two-party system, a higher degree of party voting does not result primarily from more intense party competition. We must assume that continuing one-party monopoly of the governorship and a large legislative majority diminish the party influence over legislative voting. The three states with the highest levels of party unity, however, are ones with long records of Republican legislative control, with only a few Democratic years, while the Democrats frequently held large legislative minorities and (except in Pennsylvania) won control of the governorship quite often. The balance between the parties in recent years appears to have been closer in Missouri and Colorado, the

Table VIII—Party Voting in Colorado Legislature in 1941 and 1947*

PERCENTAGE OF TOTAL ROLL CALLS

	Senate N = 198		House N = 147	
Parties on Opposite Sides	36%		38%	
Index of Cohesion:				
Both parties 80-100	6%		7%	
Each party 80-100	Rep. 10%	Dem. 14%	Rep. 16%	Dem. 15%
40-79	12	14	11	11
0-39	14	8	11	12
Parties on Same Side	64%		62%	
Index of Cohesion:				
Rep. 0-79 Dem. 80-100	31%		23%	
Rep. 80-100 Dem. 0-79	20		24	
Rep. 0-79 Dem. 0-79	13		15	

* Political composition: 1941 Governor—Republican
Senate—17 Republicans—18 Democrats
House—37 Republicans—28 Democrats
1947 Governor—Democrat
Senate—27 Republicans—8 Democrats
House—46 Republicans—19 Democrats

two states with the lowest levels of unity. Clearly partisan influences are more pronounced in the legislatures of the larger, more urban, and more industrial states, and not so pronounced in states with smaller and less urban populations, such as Missouri and Colorado, and to some extent Washington.[7]

The Urban-Rural Factor in Party Voting. One factor leading to greater party voting in states with a higher urban concentration is that in most of these states party strength follows more consistently an urban-rural division. In the larger urban states the parties represent more clearly defined groups of interests, with the Democrats coming mainly from the largest cities and metropolitan areas, and the Republicans more representative of the smaller cities and rural areas.[8] In the more rural states, such as Washington and particularly Missouri and Colorado, which have less party voting, both Democratic and Republican legislative strength is widely scattered throughout the state, although the Democrats tend to dominate the few larger cities. In these states the parties are less representative of distinct interest groups, and shifting coalitions of sectional interests are likely to have more influence over legislative voting. An examination of the individual states shows a rough correlation between a high level of party voting and a clear urban-rural alignment of the two parties. It also shows that on

many occasions when one party is considerably more homogeneous than the other—whether it is largely urban or rural—it has also more voting cohesion.

The clearest examples of party division along urban-rural lines are found in the three states with highest party voting. In New York, 98 per cent of the Democrats and 34 per cent of the Republicans in both branches of the legislature for the years studied came from New York City and the counties containing four of the largest cities. In Massachusetts, 87 per cent of the Democrats and 36 per cent of the Republicans came from Boston and thirteen of the largest cities. In Pennsylvania, 79 per cent of the Democrats and 41 per cent of the Republicans came from the counties containing Philadelphia, Pittsburgh, and nine of the other largest cities. Despite the extremely high homogeneity of the New York Democrats, the Republicans, split between New York City and upstate, had somewhat greater unity. In contrast the Massachusetts Democrats, largely from big cities, exceeded the geographically divided Republicans in unity. In Pennsylvania, the Democrats were somewhat more homogeneous, but the Republicans equalled them in unity.

Although Ohio lagged well behind the first three states in party voting, it had almost as much party homogeneity. There 75 per cent of the Democrats came from the counties containing Cleveland and

Table IX—Summary of Party Voting in American State Legislatures

STATE LEGISLATURE		% ROLL CALLS OUT OF TOTAL		% ROLL CALLS OF THOSE WITH PARTIES OPPOSED		% ROLL CALLS OF THOSE WITH PARTIES SAME SIDE*	
		Parties Opposed	Parties Opposed Both with 80 Cohesion Index	80 Cohesion Index Majority	Minority	80 Cohesion Index Majority	Minority
Mass.	S	93%	38%	R 45%	D 80%	Negligible	
	H	93	40	R 52	D 73	Negligible	
New York	S	62	32	R 68	D 64	R 72%	D 28%
	H	61	34	R 73	D 70	R 44	D 56
Penna.	S	64	52	R 88	D 91	R 65	D 35
	H	81	56	R 79	D 76	R 68	D 32
Ohio	S	49	23	R 75	D 59	R 36	D 64
	H	38	15	R 65	D 50	R 76	D 24
Illinois	S	53	15	R 33	D 74	R 31	D 69
	H	54	17	D 74	R 36	D 90	R 10
Wash.	S	71	9	D 23	R 65	D 66	R 34
	H	51	9	D 48	R 44	D 73	R 27
Missouri	S	23	1	R 32	D 11	R 66	D 34
	H	36	9	R 49	D 38	R 67	D 33
Col. 1941	S	34	5	D 39	R 30	D 70	R 30
	H	42	5	R 39	D 30	R 43	D 57
1947	S	38	8	R 29	D 37	R 50	D 50
	H	35	11	R 43	D 52	R 61	D 39

* Roll calls on which neither party had a cohesion index of 80 or more are excluded from these two columns.

eleven of the next largest cities but the remainder were well scattered, while 33 per cent of the Republicans came from these big-city areas, none of them from Cleveland. The more homogeneous Republicans had more voting cohesion.

Illinois had as much voting discipline as Ohio, and more in the Democratic party, although the cumulative voting system gave each party at least one of the three members in each representative district in the state. The counties containing Chicago and the next five largest cities included 56 per cent of the Democrats and 39 per cent of the Republicans.

In Washington the Democrats, who were the weaker of the two parties in voting discipline, had half of their representation in the counties containing the three largest cities, where the Republicans had 39 per cent of their strength. The remaining Democrats were widely scattered in the state.

In Colorado and Missouri, states with the lowest voting cohesion, about 40 per cent of the Democratic strength lay in counties containing the two or three largest cities. But the lack of more large cities resulted in the remainder of Democratic legislative strength being widely dissipated, particularly in Missouri, where it was spread among 42 other counties. Only one-fourth of the Colorado Republicans and a negligible proportion of the Missouri Republicans represented these few big-city areas.

Disunity in a party with widely scattered representation would logically be caused by dissenting legislators representing areas where the party is not dominant. Studies of individual voting records on selected issues in Illinois and Washington suggest the extent to which this is true. In Illinois twenty roll calls in the Senate and thirteen in the House, covering a variety of issues, were selected; on these Republican cohesion was considerably lower than Democratic. (Examples of the opposite situation were too few for useful comparison.) Among the Republican Cook County senators and representatives, 54 per cent voted against their party on at least 30 per cent of the roll calls. Of the rest of the Republicans, only 22 per cent showed this degree of independence. Among the downstate Republican dissenters only a few came from big-city districts or predominantly Democratic areas.

In Washington the low level of Democratic cohesion in the Senate was directly attributable to a remarkably tight-knit bloc of nine Democratic senators, generally referred to in the press as the "conservative Democrats." On 16 selected issues, these nine senators each joined the Republican side in 11 or more cases; no other Democratic senator left the fold on more than two of these roll calls. Although Democratic unity was greater in the House, it is possible to distinguish 17 representatives who voted somewhat frequently with the Republican party. Out of this group of 26 senators and representatives, only three were among the 29 Democrats from the cities of Seattle and Tacoma where the party was strongest. The proportion of rebellious Democrats was one-third in the remaining, less urbanized parts of the western section of Washington which the Democrats dominated, and nearly one-half in the Republican-dominated eastern section, which included one large Democratic city.

These two small-scale examples cannot provide any definite rule, nor can the somewhat irregular correlation of voting discipline and party homogeneity provide an absolute formula for party unity. One cannot ignore factors of gubernatorial and other party leadership and the changing pattern of political controversies. However, larger and more urbanized states do appear to have produced a pattern in which parties reflect urban-rural rather than merely sectional divisions and have therefore achieved greater cohesion in legislative voting. This affects both parties although generally only the Democrats have markedly greater homogeneity in the more urbanized states.

This demonstrated effect of the urban-rural division on party cohesion makes imperative a statistical breakdown of the roll calls by the type of issue involved, in order to determine whether in some or all states there is more voting by party on certain types of issues, such as those closely related to the urban-rural conflict of interests.

Party Voting and Issues. Table X shows a breakdown of the roll calls into fourteen categories most often productive of party votes. The number of party votes (the two parties opposed, each with a cohesion index of 80 or more) is shown for each, together with the percentage of party votes out of the total number of votes on the issue. Bills governing elections, labor, appropriations and taxation, and questions of legislative organization and procedure gave rise to the most active party voting. These five issues, with which 29 per cent of all votes in the legislature were concerned, constituted just over 50 per cent of the party votes. Confirmation of appointments, resolutions on national issues, and veterans legislation were issues that seldom came up but commanded a high percentage of party votes. There were many party votes on welfare bills (including those dealing with health and education) but they represented only an average percentage of the large total of bills of this sort.

The higher level of party voting in urban states

could reflect greater party unity on certain types of issues in two ways. The most partisan issues might arise more often in urban states; or party cohesion might be particularly high on these issues in the urban states. Although too detailed analysis would founder on the limited totals available from a few legislative sessions, a breakdown of total votes and party votes by issue and state gives evidence of both of these trends.

In some urban states many election and reapportionment bills were voted on, but there were fewer such bills in other states, including Missouri and Colorado. Most urban states had a high proportion of party votes on these issues, but Missouri and Colorado did not.

Table X—Party Voting on Specific Issues in American State Legislatures

Type of Issue	Number of Party Votes*	% of Party Votes* out of Total Roll Calls on Issue
Elections and Reapportionment	65	44%
Appointments	12	44
National Issues	12	44
Labor	52	41
Appropriations	68	38
Legis. Procedure & Organization	47	37
Taxation	62	29
Veterans Affairs	8	28
Welfare, Health, Education	79	22
Civil Service	28	21
State Administration	16	19
Local Administration	15	14
Judicial and Legal	21	11
Business Regulation	14	6
Other Issues	84	11
Total	583	Average 21%

* Party votes are those on which the parties are opposed and both have an index of cohesion of at least 80.

Taxation and appropriations together gave rise to a large number of votes in all of the states examined except Massachusetts. These issues might be expected to cause a high level of party voting in all states, since they are essential to the prestige and success of any administration. In the four urban states other than Massachusetts these two issues resulted in a high level of party voting, but in Missouri, Colorado, and Washington the number of party votes was negligible—only four out of a total of 150 roll calls on these issues.

Questions of legislative procedure and organization came up fairly regularly in most states. These are questions of narrow party interest, and it is not surprising that the percentage of party votes on them was uniformly high.

There were a substantial number of labor bills voted on in all states except Illinois, Missouri,

and Washington. In the urban states these led to a generally high proportion of party voting, but in rural Colorado, which had more roll calls on labor bills than any other state, only four of the 31 were party votes. Labor bills in the various states resulted in many roll calls with a high level of unity for one of the parties but not both.

Welfare issues (including health and education) came up frequently in every state except Pennsylvania; the proportion of party votes on these issues was moderately high—from 22 to 53 per cent in the five urban states. But in Washington, Colorado, and Missouri party votes averaged only four per cent of the total number of welfare bills. In most of the urban states, particularly Massachusetts and Illinois, this was one of the issues on which the Democrats most frequently displayed greater unity than the Republicans; in Washington the reverse was the case. These are the three states, incidentally, with the greatest difference in unity between the parties.

Appointments, national issues, and veterans affairs came up too infrequently to permit a meaningful breakdown, but both urban and rural states usually showed a relatively high proportion of party votes whenever any of these issues arose several times.

The remaining categories that have been treated separately—state and local administration, legal and judicial affairs, civil service, and business regulation—covered a significant proportion of the total roll calls, each of them being numerous in most states. The level of party voting on these issues was generally low, varying less from state to state than more partisan issues; it was highest, however, in Pennsylvania, Massachusetts, and New York.

We conclude that the more partisan issues did arise somewhat more often in the large urban states. But the higher party voting record in these states was primarily a direct result of much more party cohesion on those very partisan issues.

In general it may be said that the issues most significant for party voting fall into three classifications: those which involve rather narrow party interest—election laws and the legislature; those which involve the basic policy and prestige of the administration and are therefore sensitive to party pressure—appropriations, taxes, and appointments; and those which involve social and economic issues and reflect national liberal-conservative party alignments—labor, welfare, and most national issues.

William J. Keefe has emphasized that the political parties in Pennsylvania and Illinois have quite narrow interests, comparable to those of other pressure groups; these interests occasioned a substantial proportion of the party votes in the legislature, which he estimated at about one-fourth in Pennsylvania.[9] These interests may not always be evident on the surface, but may motivate votes on appointments, local and state administration, and judicial organization, as well as those on elections and legislative organization. Votes on matters as crucial to the administration as taxes and appropriations may reflect party pressure for favors. There needs to be more study of the motivation for high party unity on such issues in the various states.

The highly partisan character of social and economic issues in the larger, urban states suggests that party systems in some of these states not only are strong but reflect to a considerable extent the liberal-conservative, urban-rural alignment of the national parties. It is frequently argued that party voting in the state legislatures is low because "the two major parties are divided mainly on national issues that do not figure greatly in the politics of the states."[10] It is likely that this premise holds true for fewer states than it once did.

We have already noted that in the larger, urban states under study the Democratic legislators were identified with large metropolitan areas and the Republicans with smaller cities and rural areas; this is the familiar pattern of national politics outside of the South. In the Northern industrial states the New Deal not only reinvigorated the two-party system at the state level, but also may have been instrumental in developing a pattern of state party interests similar to that on the national level. The state Democrats, like the national Democrats, probably more often champion pro-labor legislation, larger welfare benefits, and greater control over business. A large proportion of the issues arising at the state level are similar to those which dominate domestic national politics. Although more comprehensive research is necessary on the pattern of state legislative voting and the sources of state party strength, it seems reasonable to conclude that in our larger, more urbanized states the partnership of national and state parties is not so illogical as is often claimed.

Conclusions. 1. In many of the American states with a strong two-party system, during sessions when party balance in the legislature is not one-sided, partisan considerations influence to a significant degree the legislative voting on issues about which there is some measure of disagreement.

2. Among these states with two strong parties, those with the most intense party competition are not necessarily those with the highest levels of party voting.

3. Neither the majority nor minority party, the Republican nor the Democratic, demonstrates consistently higher cohesion than its opponent in voting on issues which find a majority of the two parties opposed to each other.

4. Dissenters in a vote on which the majority of both parties agree are more frequently found in the minority party.

5. Legislative voting records suggest that the effectiveness of the governor in inducing unity in his party varies greatly from state to state.

6. The degree of party voting appears to be significantly higher in those two-party states which are larger and more urban. In these states more than in rural states the Democratic party represents the big-city, metropolitan areas, and the Republican party the smaller cities and rural districts.

7. The most partisan issues in the legislatures of all states, and particularly the large, urban states, involve narrow party interests, the prestige and fiscal program of the administration, and economic and social issues.

8. This record suggests that in the large industrial states, where the two-party system has been invigorated by national political forces which the New Deal unleashed, a high level of party voting in the legislature results from party alignments which have largely followed the liberal-conservative, urban-rural pattern of national politics.

Notes

1. Eliminating these two categories facilitates comparison between the states requiring a roll call on all bills and those (e.g., Massachusetts) that do not. Inclusion of these categories in the studies by other writers has been a major factor leading them to apparently contradictory conclusions about party influence in legislatures of various states.

2. The omitted roll calls were 30 on two issues in the 1945 session of the Washington Senate and 51 on one issue in the 1947 session of the Colorado House.

3. Stuart Rice, *Quantitative Methods in Politics* (New York, 1928), p. 209.

4. In a study of party voting in a similar New England state legislature, Connecticut, for eleven sessions (1931-1951), W. Duane Lockard concluded that "parties, far from being relatively insignificant, play a dominating role." Connecticut, like Massachusetts, does not require roll calls on final passage of all bills and usually has an even lower number of total roll calls per session than does Massachusetts. This figure for Connecticut therefore presumably covers only the most controversial bills. Excluding the small number of unanimous votes (seven per cent in the Senate and three per cent in the House) from Lockard's statistics, we find that the parties took opposite sides in 90 per cent of the Senate votes and 83 per cent of the House votes, slightly less than in Massachusetts.

The Connecticut totals show a high level of unity for both parties, although unfortunately in this category the roll calls on which the parties agreed and disagreed are not separated. The percentage of all roll calls (excluding unanimous ones) on which each party had a cohesion index of 80 or more in the Senate was 59 per cent for the Democrats and 76 per cent for the Republicans, and in the House 83 per cent for the Democrats and 72 per cent for the Republicans. The Republicans controlled the House in all eleven sessions, and the Democrats controlled the Senate in most of the sessions. These figures are similar to the high levels in other urban, industrial states. (Presumably the number of roll calls with 90 per cent of both parties agreed, included by Mr. Lockard, was too small to distort the comparison in a state not requiring roll calls.) See Lockard, "Legislative Politics in Connecticut," *American Political Science Review*, Vol. 48 (1954), pp. 166-173.

5. William J. Keefe reached a different conclusion in a study of the 1951 Pennsylvania legislature, that "the policy decisions which confronted the Pennsylvania legislature were mainly nonpartisan." This is largely because 82 per cent of the Senate roll calls and 70 per cent of those in the House were unanimous. Keefe recognizes that the requirement for a roll call on all bills leads to this high figure. It would seem that the test of party voting should be concentrated on controversial issues that lead to some dispute.

If unanimous votes are excluded, Keefe's figures for 1951 appear to show somewhat less party voting than do those for 1945. In 1951 the percentage of roll calls with the parties on opposite sides was 34 in the Senate and 43 in the House, compared to 64 and 81 in 1945. A large part of the difference is probably accounted for by the inclusion of roll calls with over 90 per cent of both parties in agreement, which in many states are very numerous. The party votes (both parties with an index of cohesion of at least 80) formed a high proportion of all votes on which the parties were opposed in both studies. The House figure for this was 69 per cent in both years, but the Senate figure dropped from 81 per cent in 1945 to 64 per cent in 1951. See Keefe, "Parties, Partisanship and Public Policy in the Pennsylvania Legislature," *American Political Science Review*, Vol. 48 (1954), pp. 450-464. The party vote figures are based on a letter to the writer, January 10, 1955.

6. William J. Keefe, in a study of the Illinois sessions of 1949 and 1951, concluded that parties played a small role in lawmaking. As in his study of Pennsylvania, this resulted largely from the inclusion of unanimous votes, which averaged two-thirds of the total roll calls in the two Illinois sessions. It also resulted from the inclusion of roll calls on which at least 90 per cent of both parties voted on the same side. His figures show that the total of these roll calls exceeded all other non-unanimous roll calls in 1949. Keefe does not list the total number of roll calls on which the parties were opposed and does not compare the unity level of the two parties. These differences in standards make a comparison of the two sessions difficult, but Keefe did find that roll calls in which the parties were opposed and in which both had a high level of unity dropped from 1949 to 1951, particularly in the House. See Keefe, "Party, Government and Lawmaking in the Illinois General Assembly," *Northwestern University Law Review*, Vol. 47 (1952), pp. 55-71. The comparison is also based on the previously-mentioned letter to the writer.

7. By comparison, Professor Lowell's study in 1901, which used virtually the same criteria as this study, showed high party unity in New York, less in Ohio and Illinois, and very little in Massachusetts and Pennsylvania. He noted that only these latter two states had large and consistent Republican majorities.

The parties took opposite sides in about one-half of the roll calls in three states, and in somewhat more than half in Massachusetts and New York. The percentage of party votes (the parties opposed and both with a cohesion index *over* 80, by his standard) was 23 and 45 in the New York Senate and House, 15 and 10 in the Ohio Senate and House, 13 in the Illinois House, and from one to six in the other legislative bodies. The Democrats had much more unity than the Republicans in Massachusetts, somewhat more in New York, Pennsylvania, and Ohio, and less in Illinois. See Lowell, "The Influence of Party upon Legislation in England and America," *Annual Report of the American Historical Society for the Year 1901*, Vol. 1 (1902), pp. 319-542.

8. For the sake of convenience and brevity this "metropolitan and big city versus small city and rural" alignment is described in this paper as urban-rural.

9. See Keefe, "Parties, Partisanship and Public Policy in the Pennsylvania Legislature," and "Party Government and Lawmaking in the Illinois General Assembly."

10. See *American State Legislatures*, pp. 189-92.

2. COHESION OF BRITISH PARLIAMENTARY PARTIES

Leon D. Epstein

IN THE PERSPECTIVE of those political scientists who would reform American parties so as to make them more "responsible," British parties are familiar prototypes. Prominent among the admired qualities is the cohesion displayed in parliamentary voting by the members of each major British party. That this cohesion is greater than that of American legislative parties has been generally observed at least since the work of A.

Reprinted from *American Political Science Review*, Vol. 50 (1956), pp. 360-377, by permission of the author and the publisher.

Lawrence Lowell.[1] And it is common enough, though not universal, to regard British parliamentary solidarity as a virtue particularly because it permits a victorious party, after an election, to enact the program behind which a majority of voters have presumably been rallied.[2] Correspondingly, the relatively low cohesion among Republican and among Democratic congressmen is taken as a defect of American politics.[3]

The purpose of this article, however, is not primarily to discuss value judgments concerning parliamentary cohesion. Rather it is to examine the nature of that cohesion and the ways in which it is maintained. But regardless of the disputed merits of British practice, it is still reasonable to ask after such an examination whether the cohesion of party members in the House of Commons is the product of devices which the United States could adopt, or whether it is the result of underlying factors alien to the American environment. In other words, even if desirable, would parliamentary cohesion of the British type provide a useful parallel for the United States?

Attention is to be focussed on recent developments within the two major parties—that is, within the *parliamentary* parties. For the most part, the mass organizations outside of Parliament are not discussed. Their role, as has been amply demonstrated by recent British scholarship, is not crucial in establishing or enforcing national party policy.[4] Some of the implications for comparative analysis of this limited role of mass memberships are presented elsewhere.[5] Here it is sufficient to say that the cohesion of British parliamentary parties cannot be explained in terms of the pressure of an outside membership.

I. The M.P. and His Parliamentary Party. Since cohesion is unlikely to be spontaneous or automatic in a parliamentary party numbering between 200 and 400, leadership is bound to be of great import. The position particularly of *the* leader is strong because he is either prime minister or a potential prime minister. As such, he bestows the ministerial offices without which an ambitious M.P.'s career is a failure, financially and politically. This is an enviable means for rewarding the faithful and punishing the rebel because the M.P. has no other route, like that of congressional seniority, by which he can achieve power. Yet, in spite of the well-understood potency of the leadership, it must be noted that in the final analysis it is the parliamentary party as a whole which possesses authority. Even if the leadership, especially of a cabinet, ordinarily counts on the parliamentary party's consent, nevertheless the consent of that party (or at least of a majority of it) is essential to the continuity of leadership.[6] Consequently, it is fair to regard the M.P.'s relationship to the majority of his parliamentary party as much the same thing as his relationship to the party's leadership.

The individual representative. In submitting generally to the will of the parliamentary party, the M.P. sacrifices much less of political substance than would an American congressman who similarly subjected himself. The British representative is not expected to trim his legislative votes to the wishes of local interests, whether in the form of local party organizations or economic pressure groups. Therefore, he can afford much more readily than his American counterpart to support his party even if it means overriding the particular desires of his constituents. British custom is such that he need hardly fear strictly local reprisals against his subsequent candidacy.[7]

Although the M.P.'s subordination to national leadership is thus politically feasible, he does make an important sacrifice of his own freedom of action. Since this is contrary to the independence often characteristic of M.P.s until late in the nineteenth century and contrary to the still lively traditions of British liberalism and non-conformism, it is understandable that back-benchers are not always happy about their present status. Few, however, have been so bitter about their lot as Christopher Hollis, an intellectually restive Conservative M.P., who has said flatly: "The member is the obedient servant of the party machine." In Hollis' view, most members, far from making decisions themselves, "must live a life in which it is peculiarly apparent to them that the decisions are taken by other people. The man in the street may think that the ordinary member of Parliament is an important person and has power. The member of Parliament himself cannot possibly think so."[8] At least he cannot think himself important, according to Hollis, as he regularly joins his fellows in trooping in and out of the division lobbies in response to party orders as transmitted by the whips.

The M.P. does, it is true, receive psychological compensation from the question period in the House of Commons. Then the back-bencher has the privilege of trying to embarrass ministers (but not often if they are of his own party) by raising troublesome political and administrative questions. Also the M.P. may be flattered by the attention accorded his occasional debating speech by his audience of fellow-members and, to a lessening extent, by the quality newspapers. Both the debates and the question periods afford opportunities for M.P.s to display their own opinions, and they are also used occasionally to air the grievances of constituents.[9] These seem unsubstantial substitutes for the sense of power and individual responsibility which go with the quasi-independent decisions of American congressmen.

Increasingly British M.P.s are complaining about their humble individual positions. Often what is wanted is a more frequent use of the free vote—which only the leadership has the prerogative to allow.[10] A particularly strong argument against the subordination of the individual member to the whips was made in 1954 when the Conservative Government sought and secured parliamentary approval of the boundary changes recommended by the commission charged with drawing election constituency lines. The changes were opposed by Labor M.P.s in their voting as well as in their thinking, but many Conservatives had also made known their objections without intending to defy the government whips by voting their convictions. These individual Conservative convictions, stemming from historical devotion to old constituencies or from dislike of the frequency and method of boundary changes, were occasionally reinforced by political disadvantages which certain changes caused to incumbent M.P.s. Yet all of these reasons for objection were not enough to cause Conservative M.P.s to refrain from supporting their party's government. It was this which was called "the debasement of the position of the Private Member" by one exasperated Labor opponent—who would undoubtedly have been as debased himself if his party's government had been in an analogous situation. Actually this particular Labor M.P. was candid enough to include his own party in his broad charge against the submergence of individual convictions.[11] However, what is to be discussed here is not whether this submergence is to be deplored, but why M.P.s have permitted it to take place.

Relevance of dissolution. The first and traditional answer of political science is to point to the power of parliamentary dissolution at the disposal of the prime minister. True enough, British constitutional practice does permit the use of this power by a government which wants to establish or strengthen its legislative majority. However, this holds only for the government party. In and of itself, the power of dissolution cannot account for the fact that the opposition is almost as effectively disciplined as are members of the government party.

Indeed, it is doubtful whether the power of dissolution can in any appreciable way account for the cohesion of parliamentary parties. That power, even in the form of threat, is simply not used in order to discipline M.P.s. It was so used in the nineteenth century, when governments lacked the solid majorities which party loyalties provide today, but there is a strong *prima facie* case that dissolution became obsolete as a weapon against M.P.s precisely when they ceased to be independent followers of their leaders. Nowadays dissolution remains the government's weapon, to be sure, but a weapon to be used against the opposition. The fact that the prime minister decides when to call an election is no small party advantage. To maximize its effectiveness, a government may be expected to dissolve Parliament, not when discipline is required because its own ranks are divided, but rather when its supporters can present a united front to the electorate and, if possible, embarrass the opposition should it happen to be disunited at the moment. The dissolution and election of May, 1955, illustrate this neatly.

Nevertheless, the idea that the power of dissolution is a deterrent to revolt by the parliamentary majority remains in the vocabulary of British politics. So experienced a hand as Herbert Morrison mentions it, but adds significantly that the government "must seek to retain the support of a parliamentary majority by persuasion, goodwill, mutual understanding, and, upon occasion, must make concessions, because the consequences to itself and to its electoral support are likely to be damaging if it goes to the country with its ranks divided."[12] In fact, in such a situation it is likely that the party leaders who form the government have more to lose by a dissolution than have many of the back-benchers. If an open division in the parliamentary majority should damage the party's electoral chances, as Morrison suggests, then the most important result would be the loss of enough marginal seats to destroy the party majority which permitted the leadership to hold ministerial positions.

While this result is also serious for individual back-benchers who lose the marginal seats, they often have some chance (though admittedly less than that of the leaders) of obtaining new seats in by-elections. But even without such an opportunity, a defeated back-bencher has lost less by way of salary, power, and prestige than has the former minister (and certainly much less than the former prime minister). Furthermore, it must be emphasized that for the bulk of the M.P.s who occupy safe seats, a general election ordinarily involves no risk at all. Sure of renomination and sure of re-election, many non-ministerial M.P.s can face an election with considerable equanimity. It is hard to believe that they could be seriously threatened by a dissolution. Campaigning is probably a bore and a nuisance, but it is a three-weeks' affair and in these days not always very expensive for the candidate personally. His organization is not a personal one as the American congressman's so often is. The party, or in some cases a trade union, picks up the check and does most of the electioneering. The candidate has to make local speeches and appearances, but it must be assumed that an M.P. has a high tolerance for politicking of this sort or he would have chosen some less extroverted occupation in the first place.

In order for a dissolution to be used effectively for disciplining the majority party, the leadership would have to be willing and able to eliminate its recalcitrant M.P.s during the general election. That is, the national leadership would have to persuade constituency parties to adopt candidates who, if elected, would be more loyal and obedient than some present M.P.s. In extreme cases, individuals have been purged in this way, but only incidental to the general election. Since 1918, at any rate, no party government has called an election principally to replace some of its own M.P.s with a more loyal crop. Nor has any recent party leadership threatened, even implicitly, to operate on such a basis. On the contrary, what happens with a general election in the offing is that the party draws its own dissidents (if they are appreciable in number) closer to the fold so that the opposition may not profit by an appearance of disunity. The relationship of the rebellious Bevanites to the Labor party at both the 1951 and 1955 elections is a case in point. Although the Labor leaders disliked the Bevanites no less at election time, they did not choose to hurt their party, and thereby themselves, by attacking the erstwhile rebels during the campaign. When the Labor government called the 1951 election, it was assuredly not for the purpose of disciplining the Bevanites.

Not only does it seem unrealistic for a party leadership to seek to discipline its followers by threatening to call new elections, but it is doubtful that individual M.P.s would adhere to the party line because of any such threat. This is not to say that the prospect of elections is unimportant in influencing parliamentary parties. Ordinary M.P.s, along with their leaders, do have good political reasons for maintaining their solidarity so long as the electorate regards that solidarity as a virtue. But the unity which flows from a respect for the British belief in the value of a cohesive parliamentary party is very different from a unity inspired by a fear of the leadership's power of dissolution.[13]

Isolated revolts. Freedom of action is not much of an alternative to party loyalty in the British system. No substantial rebellion like that of the Bevanites seeks freedom of action as its end. What the Bevanites as a group want is to convert the Labor party to their policies and their leadership. For this purpose, the Bevanites sometimes find it useful to exercise more freedom than is usual within a British party. On the other hand, an individual M.P. may genuinely prefer to act independently of his party, but he must then be willing to enter a political wilderness. The contemporary British House of Commons has no place either for an independent (completely without formal party affiliation) or for an independent Laborite or an independent Conservative. The parties have a practical monopoly, and their hold is strengthening, not weakening. The inglorious

careers of some postwar independents will illustrate the point.

Best known is the case of the four M.P.s ousted from the Labor party during the 1945-50 Parliament. All four had broken party solidarity by repeated stands in opposition to the foreign policy of the Labor government, and at least three of the four were widely believed to follow the Communist line. Undoubtedly it was the latter belief that made it feasible for the party to resort, as it rarely does, to the formal disciplinary weapon of expulsion. The four lost the official Labor designation, and (together with one earlier rebel) they called themselves "Labour Independents" and as such sought to retain their parliamentary seats in the 1950 election. Defeat was the lot of all the Labor Independents, including one, K. Zilliacus, who was personally popular in his constituency and who by 1950 was no longer accused of following the Communist line.[14] Nevertheless, not too much should be inferred from this very successful example of formal party discipline. Laborites as well as the Conservatives, as will be observed later, are often inhibited from conducting purges by doubts concerning the support of local constituency associations. If the relevant constituency's support is doubtful, the national leadership might want to avoid a full-fledged ouster because the price for its success might be too high in terms of local disaffection. But what the case of the Labor Independents does illustrate is the formidable difficulty which the leadership, in favorable circumstances, can raise for the purged member who tries to get re-elected without major party support.

A different kind of example is that of Ivor Thomas. The Labor party did not expel him; he resigned in 1948 because of his disagreement with the leadership. And this disagreement was related to Thomas' position to the right of the official Labor policy. There may also have been some non-ideological background to the resignation. Thomas, who had been active in the prewar Labor party, was elected to Parliament in 1942 and re-elected by the same constituency (Keighley) in 1945. In the 1945 Labor Government, he first became parliamentary secretary at the ministry of civil aviation and then in 1946 was promoted to the post of parliamentary under-secretary of state for the colonies. Since Thomas was a relatively young man, he seemed to have a bright ministerial future until October of 1947 when, during a cabinet reshuffle, he was dropped entirely from the Government.[15] The cause of this turn for the worse in Thomas' career is by no means clear. Nor, for that matter, is there any certainty about the reasons for Thomas' resignation from the Labor party in the following year.

The first indication Thomas gave of a public break with Labor was in a letter to *The Times* in mid-October, 1948. In that letter he proposed that the Labor Government abandon in the approaching parliamentary session all contentious legislation, meaning the nationalization of steel and the limitation of the delaying power of the House of Lords.[16] No one was surprised that the government ignored this suggestion and showed its intention, at the beginning of Parliament, to introduce the legislation to which Thomas objected. Thomas then took the floor of the House to announce his resignation from the Labor party, to attack its leadership for "a wanton and reckless act," and to declare his general objection to the socialist "concentration of power in the hands of the State."[17] In thus cutting himself off from the Labor party, Thomas was, in effect, surrendering a safe seat in the House of Commons. Or at least he was surrendering the seat as of the next general election. Thomas refused to comply with his constituency Labor party's request that he resign the seat immediately. But he was entirely aware that he held the seat only until the current Parliament was dissolved.[18]

His action in subsequently joining the Conservative party was understandable. He had obviously taken up its policy and its ideological position, and he had no political future in any other direction. As it turned out, neither did Thomas have much of a future with the Conservatives. The best that they did for Thomas was to adopt him as a 1950 candidate at Newport, in Wales, where Labor regularly had a substantial majority.[19] The expected defeat in the 1950 election appears to have ended Thomas' political career. In 1952 he changed his surname to Bulmer-Thomas, and under this name wrote a book on the party system.

"Crossing the aisle," as Bulmer-Thomas did, is not a likely way to political survival in the present stabilized, or perhaps rigid, state of British parties. Even in times past it has been a very risky proposition, and it may have required the quality of a Winston Churchill to pull it off successfully. Today, at any rate, no M.P. concerned with his political future would risk a rebellion on the assumption that he could find a suitable place among his party's opponents. Since 1945 one can point to no instance of an M.P. who has shifted from one major party to the other and then been re-elected to the House.

Another but no more promising course of rebellion was pursued by Sir Richard Acland, also a Labor M.P., in 1955. Disturbed by religious and humanitarian scruples over his party's support of the Conservative Government's decision to manufacture hydrogen bombs in Britain, Sir Richard resigned not only from the Labor party but also from the House of Commons. It was his intention to force a by-election in his constituency of Gravesend and to stand as an Independent candidate on the issue of the hydrogen bomb.[20] Whatever chance he had of winning against the Conservative and the official Labor candidates was lessened by the fact that the general election supervened before a by-election was called. Labor voters could then vote for Acland only if they were willing to split the party's strength and so help elect a Conservative majority in the House of Commons. In fact, less than one-quarter of Labor's normal electorate voted for Acland, but this was more than enough of a break in the previous Labor majority to allow the Conservative to capture the seat. More significant for present purposes, however, is that Acland ran a poor third. Thus the result demonstrated the overwhelming attraction which major party candidacies retain for the British electorate when it is faced, as it always is in a general election, with the choice of alternative governments.

So individualistic and futile a proceeding is possible only for an M.P. who, like Sir Richard, places a higher value on the display of moral righteousness than on the future of his party or his own career in that party. This personality type is rarely successful in the politics of any time or place, and its presence in contemporary British politics seems either accidental or residual. The Acland dash for freedom is hardly indicative of a course which would or could weaken the hold of the parliamentary parties on their members.

Tolerated deviations. Instead of being moved by principles to the point of resigning or of forcing one's party to resort to expulsion, an M.P. may occasionally take individual positions and yet remain within the fold. In the process, he probably stamps himself as unlikely material for ministerial posts and otherwise makes his party relationships difficult. But still both parties do tolerate some deviations or eccentricities. They almost have to make some allowance for an odd quirk here and there. Otherwise party unity would be a good deal more brittle than it is in fact. The Labor party goes so far as to formalize its toleration in a standing order which "recognizes the right of individual Members to abstain from voting on matters of deeply held personal conscientious conviction."[21] In practice, abstention has been allowed on issues touching the pacifism or the alcoholic temperance of Labor members.

Without so explicit a provision, the Conservative party nevertheless tolerates an occasional deviation more complacently than does Labor. Perhaps this is because the Conservatives have less reason to fear open rebellions and because they have fewer habitual or congenital non-conformists in their ranks. One of the most interesting cases is that of Lord Hinchingbrooke. Never the most orthodox of Conservative M.P.s and fortified in his individuality by a distinguished ancestry, Hinchingbrooke openly took issue with his party's government in 1952. For rather special reasons, he announced during the Commons debate on the German peace treaties that he would abstain from voting in support of the German rearmament, to which his Conservative Government and party were committed.[22] However, then and subsequently, Hinchingbrooke remained a loyal member of the Conservative parliamentary party. His personal deviation would have been almost unnoticed except for the fact that the executive council of his constituency association was sufficiently aroused by Hinchingbrooke's defiance of the national party to attempt, unsuccessfully, to initiate a purge.[23]

A more substantial deviation tolerated by the Conservative Government was that of the "Suez group" in 1954. The background for the incident was the widespread unpopularity within the Conservative party of the Government's plan to evacuate Britain's Suez canal base. For many back-benchers the plan represented another detested step in "scuttling the Empire." While the great majority of Conservative M.P.s did finally accept the cabinet's policy, there were about 40 who voiced open objections. Twenty-six of the 40 went so far as to vote against their government when the Suez evacuation agreement was presented to the House of Commons.[24] But except for one M.P. who temporarily resigned from the party, neither the back-benchers concerned nor the party leadership took any overt action. The loss of 26 votes happened to be something which, in the circumstances, the Conservative Government could afford. Although its majority over the opposition was still very narrow in 1954, the government knew that on the Suez issue the 26 Conservative rebels would be voting alone. Labor was thoroughly committed to evacuation and could not reasonably vote against the evacuation agreement. Thus the Suez group of M.P.s could deviate without risk of bringing the government down.

Yet this type of deviation must remain occasional, or even rare, if it is to be tolerated at all. Repeated breaks in party solidarity would give public notice of a disunited party which lacked the capacity to govern. This is the kind of reputation that British parties generally, and their leaders in particular, seek to avoid.

General Perspective. What emerges from this review of some exceptional cases is not just that an individual M.P., or a group of M.P.s, may survive an infrequent deviation from a party position, but more significantly that survival is dependent on remaining within the bounds fixed by the party. Rebel M.P.s have not operated successfully either by asserting a full-fledged independence or by joining the opposing party. Remaining within the fold is all-important, and this requires a course defined by the party. It is not enough for an M.P. merely to declare that he is of a given party and then vote as he pleases. Exactly how far an M.P. can deviate from the line of his parliamentary party and yet remain a member depends on his personality, the particular constituency association, the significance of the issue, and the party to which he belongs. But, in general, there is no doubt that an individual's own convictions are ordinarily expected to yield when at variance with the position of the parliamentary party.

II. The Limitations of Discipline. The power of a parliamentary party to remove a rebellious member from its ranks is real enough, and in the Labor party the procedure for doing so is most specific.[25] But whether the possession of this power is the crucial element in maintaining cohesion is most doubtful. Obviously, expulsion can be effective only insofar as a party values its solidarity enough to countenance such drastic discipline. Therefore, even if expulsion (or threat of expulsion) were to be regarded as the decisive weapon, the explanation for its effectiveness would lie in the nature of the party loyalty which supported its use rather than in the nature of the weapon. The fact is, however, that such drastic discipline is very limited in its applicability. The Conservatives can hardly be said to expel, or threaten to expel, any of their M.P.s. And the recent experience of the Labor party indicates that withdrawal of the parliamentary whip is reserved for isolated and extreme cases involving no more than about a half-dozen M.P.s at a time, and that actual expulsion from the external organization (which prevents campaigning as an official candidate) is even rarer. The limited scope and efficacy of the formal disciplinary weapon is illustrated by two well-publicized breakdowns in Labor unity, one over German rearmament and the other concerning Aneurin Bevan personally.

German rearmament. This issue requires some explanation of its background in Labor party affairs. Before Labor's defeat in the 1951 election, the party's government had indicated its agreement, quite possibly under American pressure, to the proposal to arm West Germany within the framework of European defense. At that time, however, German rearmament had not yet emerged as a prominent subject of controversy. Only after the Conservatives were in office, in mid-1952, was an actual rearmament agreement (the ill-fated European Defense Community) submitted to Parliament. By then Labor's general doubts, plus Bevanite agitation, were sufficient to cause the party leadership to oppose approval of the treaties providing for German rearmament unless certain "conditions," among them another attempt to negotiate with the Russians over Germany, were first fulfilled.[26] Thus any parliamentary revolt within the Labor party was avoided. Neither Bevanite nor non-Bevanite opponents of German rearmament had anything to revolt about on this occasion. The whole party could follow its leadership in voting against German rearmament—even if the leadership's reasons for opposition were different, and less fundamental, than those given by the left wing.

If other European parliaments had moved as rapidly in approving the European Defense Community as did the British Parliament, with its Conservative majority, the Labor party might have been saved a great deal of agony. But with German rearmament unsettled for so many years, Labor could not very well avoid a showdown. Through 1953 the party leadership was able to cover the rift in its ranks on the basis of a conference resolution that "there should be no German rearmament before further efforts have been made to secure the peaceful reunification of Germany."[27] This resolution did not suffice as a compromise after the Berlin meeting of early 1954, when Western ministers actually met with the Russians in the requisite effort "to secure the peaceful reunification of Germany." The failure of that effort caused the Labor leaders to assume, quite logically, that they were now under an obligation to accept German rearmament within a Western defense organization.

The problem was to obtain party support for this position. And on this score, Clement Attlee, as party leader, encountered difficulties at the outset. His resolution in behalf of German rearmament was approved by so narrow a margin (less than 10) in the parliamentary Labor party that it was obviously difficult for Attlee to unite his followers for any vote in the House itself.[28] The Executive Committee of the external Labor organization was also closely divided on the issue.[29] Plainly there was not enough wholehearted Labor support for German rearmament to counter both the outright left-wing opposition and the widespread non-ideological misgivings within the party.

The leadership's difficulty was compounded by the French Parliament's rejection of the European Defense Community and the subsequent development, in 1954, of the Paris Agreement as an alternative means of rearming the Germans. This meant that the issue of German rearmament would again be presented to the British Parliament. While approval by the Conservative majority could be assumed, the parliamentary Labor party would nevertheless be expected to take a united position, which on this issue it found so hard to achieve. Much of the disunion to be expected in the parliamentary party was foreshadowed by the debate at the Labor conference in the early Fall of 1954. Attlee's very conciliatory statement indicating support for German rearmament won the conference's approval by the barest of margins—3,270,000 to 3,022,000.[30] This paralleled the slender majority in favor of German rearmament within the parliamentary ranks, and indicated that the rift was substantial in both organizations.

The anticipated showdown came in November, 1954, when the Conservative Government asked the House to approve the policy of the Paris Agreement (of that October). Until nearly the last moment, it was assumed that the Labor leadership would impose its desire for an affirmative vote on the parliamentary party as a whole. There was no doubt that the top leaders themselves were convinced by the case for German rearmament, and that they were supported by a majority of Labor M.P.s who outvoted 71 opponents in a party meeting which "accepted" the Paris Agreement. However, rather than risk many defections in an open parliamentary division, the leadership decided that Labor should not vote at all in the House of Commons. By making abstention on the Paris Agreement the official party line, Labor would at least save itself the embarrassment of having little more than half of its members in the "Aye" column and some of the others defying the leadership by voting "No." Labor's face could not be fully saved, since its general abstention policy was itself a patent confession of an inability to unite on any positive position. But this would not look so bad, it was calculated, as a split between two division lobbies.

Consequently Attlee, among others, accepted the anomaly of speaking in favor of the Paris Agreement and yet not voting for it. And Aneurin Bevan, for example, spoke against the Agreement and also abstained. But there were seven Labor M.P.s who refused to find unity in abstention.[31] One of these, John McGovern, was a supporter of German rearmament and did the completely unexpected by joining the Conservatives in voting "Aye." He had, as he is supposed to have said, the strength of Mr. Attlee's convictions. The other six rebels were bitter-end opponents of German rearmament, for pacifist or other reasons, and they insisted on voting "No" instead of abstaining. Clearly all seven had exposed themselves to party discipline because, even if motivated by pacifist convictions, they could not claim that such convictions entitled them, under Labor's Standing Orders, to vote against the party's collective decision to abstain. The most that the party conceded to pacifist scruples was the right to refrain from voting altogether when Labor supported an arms program. In the present circumstance, it was hard to see how the parliamentary party could avoid disciplining the seven rebels if its authority to discipline was ever to have significance. And the understandable reluctance to deal with the special case of McGovern became submerged in the political necessity of treating all rebels alike.

The Labor whip was withdrawn from the seven M.P.s almost immediately, but this comparatively mild action was upheld by a parliamentary party vote of only 131 to 93.[32] The sizable opposition to discipline, plus the fact that 70 or so Labor M.P.s did not vote at all in the party meeting, indicated a high degree of sympathy for the six opponents of German rearmament. This sympathy, or agreement with the six, was so great that many Labor M.P.s obviously wanted no discipline at all. Yet the consequences of withdrawing the whip were really not very serious for the rebels. All had already so established themselves as mavericks that they could hardly have been entertaining any ministerial ambitions. And so long as they were not ousted from the external Labor party organization they could be readopted as official party candidates for Parliament. About all they lost because of the withdrawal of the whip were the privileges of attending parliamentary Labor party meetings and of receiving information on how to vote in parliamentary divisions. Two of the rebels also lost their places, as Labor members, on Select Committees of the House, but these places involved only interesting duties and not power.[33]

What seemed really significant about Labor's handling of the seven rebels was the absence of anything like substantial punishment. This cannot be explained entirely as a matter of soft-hearted goodwill on the part of the leadership. The rebels (or at least six of them) represented so popular a point of view that their punishment almost had to be limited. Not only did the six rebels have considerable support within the parliamentary party; they also had the sympathy of a very large section of the external party. At least three of the six opponents of German rearmament received specific assurances of support from their own constituency associations.[34] And there was every reason to believe that the other three did not lack such support. In the face of this, the Labor leadership, even if it wanted to go farther, could hardly manage a successful purge of the rebellious M.P.s without alienating or splitting the local organizations in such a way as to lose the constituencies altogether at a general election. It was manifestly impractical to try to read out of the party those who rebelled for what at least half (and perhaps more) of the rank-and-file zealots regarded as good and sufficient reasons. Therefore, it was understandable that only three months after its disciplinary action, the parliamentary party restored the whip to all seven M.P.s.[35] In effect, then, the Labor party had done no more than lightly slap the wrists of its rebels.

The case of Aneurin Bevan. The frustration of Labor's leadership was even more evident in the abortive effort to discipline Aneurin Bevan in 1955. As the leader of a fairly well-defined faction which had openly disagreed with official party policy off and on since 1951, Bevan had more than once given his right-wing opponents cause to seek his ouster. Finally, during a parliamentary debate on defense in March, 1955, Bevan exposed himself in a way that seemed to afford an especially propitious opportunity for disciplinary action against him. The particular issue concerned the Conservative Government's motion to approve its policy of British manufacture of hydrogen bombs. The parliamentary Labor party had followed its leaders in agreeing in general to this policy and in submitting an amendment which did little more than object to the way in which the Conservatives were administering the defense organization.[36] But it was hardly surprising that Bevan and most of his followers found fault with the position adopted by a majority of their fellow Labor M.P.s. During the debate, Bevan himself showed that he was dissatisfied with both the government statement and the Labor amendment because they failed to make clear that nuclear weapons were to be confined (as he preferred) to retaliation against the kind of aggression which itself employed such nuclear weapons. Also he repeated the familiar Bevanite demand for a policy that emphasized peaceful negotiations with the Soviet Union.[37]

These statements by themselves would not have been enough to expose Bevan to the full wrath of the leadership. He was not alone among Labor M.P.s in raising such objections during the course of the debate. And Bevan did not go so far as the Labor member who was against British manufacture of hydrogen bombs in any circumstances. But Bevan committed a less pardonable act against the party leadership when he openly challenged Clement Attlee during the latter's speech. Bevan addressed Attlee, as though he were questioning a Conservative opponent, to ask—or very nearly demand—that his leader explain whether the official Labor amendment meant support for the use of "thermo-nuclear weapons in circumstances of hostilities, although they were not used against us." Incidentally, Attlee gave no specific answer to the question, and no doubt he thought it odd as well as rude that another Labor M.P. should seek to embarrass him in this way.[38] This was much more flagrant disrespect for party authority than was the behavior of Bevan and 61 other dissidents when they abstained from voting on the Labor amendment.[39] However great the latter offense, it could not effectively be punished anyway. Sixty-two rebels were too many to discipline.

Aneurin Bevan himself seemed to be another matter. His offense against Attlee was singled out for discipline even though it was appreciated that Bevan had spoken the sentiments of his followers and perhaps of some others as well. The apparent objective was to try to separate Bevan from the lesser rebels on the basis that his offense was of a special nature. Within a week of Bevan's "insult" to Attlee, it was known that Labor's shadow cabinet was going to recommend that the parliamentary party withdraw the whip and that this was considered only a prelude to Bevan's eventual ouster from the party at large. The withdrawal of the whip did take place after a week's delay occasioned by Bevan's influenza. However, by this time it was clear that any thoroughgoing discipline of Bevan would be achieved at a very high cost. The parliamentary party voted for withdrawing the whip by the margin of 141 to 122, and defeated a milder substitute resolution of censure by the still narrower vote of 138 to 124. Even these marginal victories might have been impossible if Attlee had not gone so far as to announce that he considered the votes to be questions of confidence in himself as leader.[40]

Attlee now appeared unwilling to push such questions of confidence any further and to be looking for some kind of compromise with Bevan. Indeed, earlier there were rumors that Attlee had been persuaded, against his own inclination, to support the ouster because it was favored by his right-wing lieutenants and by the principal trade unionists. At any rate, when the National Executive of the external Labor party first met to consider what it ought to do about Bevan after the parliamentary party's withdrawal of the whip, Attlee (an *ex officio* member) succeeded in amending the right-wing's expulsion motion so that before any action was taken a special committee would meet with Bevan to seek assurances as to his future conduct. Among other reasons for this conciliatory step, it is significant that Attlee and his supporters "pointed to the effect which his expulsion would have on the constituencies. . . ."[41] This was recognition of the considerable sympathy which had already been aroused in Bevan's behalf by the action initiated against him and of the unpleasant consequence of further alienating large numbers of Labor militants by expelling their champion. That consequence might ordinarily have been accepted, but in the Spring of 1955, with a general election anticipated, there was an urgent political reason to mend party fences. Thus the National Executive, despite its clear anti-Bevanite majority (like that of the parliamentary Labor party), adopted the tactics of conciliation rather than discipline. The great purge of Aneurin Bevan was called off.

All that Bevan had to do was to state to the Executive's special committee that during the intra-party discussion (which he regarded as entirely legitimate) he had not intended to "create difficulties for Mr. Attlee" or cause him "embarrassment in his position as the leader of the party." If, Bevan added, "my actions or speech could lend themselves to the interpretation that such was my motive then I am sincerely sorry and I apologize to Mr. Attlee for any pain I may have caused him. I ask for nothing more than the opportunity to serve our party under his leadership."[42]

This was neither a straightforward confession of wrong-doing nor much of an assurance that Bevan would trim his future conduct to the wishes of the party leadership. Whatever prestige the National Executive could now maintain had to be asserted in its own resolution rather than in anything it obtained from Bevan. Over the opposition of seven Bevanites, or pro-Bevanites, on the Executive, a majority of 16 supported an unusually sharp resolution approving the withdrawal of the whip by the parliamentary party. And the Executive warned that it would take "drastic action against future violations of party discipline."[43] The right-wing might take some comfort from these strong words, but Bevan's supporters had more cause to feel that the triumph was theirs. The Bevanite paper ran its story of the affair under the headline, "The Plot that Failed," and claimed that expulsion was halted because the "protest against this step had been so strong that those who started on this mad manoeuvre have been compelled to beat a retreat."[44]

One does not have to accept the view that expulsion was a "mad manoeuvre" in order to agree that the Labor leadership had beat a retreat. Whether the leadership was compelled to do so is a nice question of language. Certainly Attlee found it expedient to persuade his cohorts to stop short of the expulsion which seemed to have been the original intention. He did not persuade all of the leadership that retreat was necessary, but he secured the requisite majority. The leadership's retreat became complete late in April, when the parliamentary party restored the whip to Bevan. The rebel had suffered no more than a month of partial banishment from Labor councils. No doubt the speed with which Bevan was restored to parliamentary Labor status owed a great deal to the scheduling of the general election for May. Labor meant to present the voters with as much appearance of unity as it could muster.

Implications for Unity. These two instances, involving German rearmament and Aneurin Bevan himself, do not indicate that formal party discipline is altogether useless. Its effectiveness with respect to relatively isolated rebels was previously observed. But it is apparent that the efficacy of discipline is decidedly limited when a party's leadership, though backed by a majority, is faced with parliamentary dissidents representing a substantial body of opinion. This is another way of saying that when there is a real and continuing factional division, the leadership cannot compel obedience. The Labor party has happened to have such a division, and the right-wing majority has lacked the means of bending the left to its will. The nearest thing to a solution—arrived at for the sake of appearances—has resulted not from the use of disciplinary weapons, but rather from statements of policy that make sufficient verbal concessions to the left without abandoning the substance of the leadership's position.

Perhaps the Labor rifts which party discipline has been incapable of resolving may be taken to mean that Labor no longer has the degree of solidarity supposed to characterize a British party. That interpretation, however, seems unwarranted. For one thing, the cases of German rearmament and of Aneurin Bevan are really exceptions, though significant ones, to the day-by-day parliamentary unity which Labor displays on almost all issues. And, secondly, the important breaks in the party's voting have come only during a period of opposition. It should be stressed that the Bevanites, whose policy differences with the Labor leadership were manifested in April, 1951, never voted against their party majority so long as Labor constituted the government. Of course, it is true that parliamentary disunity even in an opposition party is regarded as outside the regular scheme of things. And, most relevant to Labor's situation, disunity openly displayed is considered damaging enough to the party's cause so that the leadership seeks

compromises which the dissidents can accept. Such compromises, it ought to be added, almost have to be sought if Labor is to be counted as an effective political force. Factional voting, by Bevanites no more than by others, can hardly be accepted as normal in the way it so often is by American congressional parties.

III. General Observations. The import of this study is that there appear to be no British party devices which provide a sufficient explanation of parliamentary cohesion. In the absence of such an explanation, it is tempting to turn to general features of the national setting for an understanding of why British parties are more cohesive than American. At least, it is possible to offer some suggestions.

First, there is the nature of the British constitutional system. While parliamentary government has itself been continuously shaped by the parties, the basic conception of executive responsibility to Parliament antedated modern parties and provided the constitutional mold in which these parties have operated. As we now know them, British parties developed around the principle of securing a legislative majority in order to gain control of the executive. Parliamentary parties were not always as cohesive as they are today, but their growing sense of unity in the last century has been conditioned by the desirability of such unity for the maintenance in office of an increasingly important executive authority. The British constitutional system adds to the importance of cohesiveness in a parliamentary party (or as we might say of "party responsibility") in a way that the American Constitution, with its separation of powers, does not. To be sure, there is some political advantage to be gained by an American party, be it a majority or a minority, in maintaining a high degree of solidarity among its legislators, but the stimulus is not nearly as great as it is for a British party, which *must* maintain its solidarity if it is to govern at all, or claim to be able to govern.[45] In this circumstance, it is understandable that cohesion has been made a political virtue.

Another consequence of the British constitutional system which bears on the maintenance of party solidarity is the concentration of power and prestige in ministerial offices. Without the important congressional committee positions which, under the American separation of powers, are awarded independently of executive authority, the British M.P. who is interested in political promotion has to concentrate on obtaining one of the ministerial positions at the disposal of the party leadership when it constitutes the government. This provides a strong personal incentive for some members to demonstrate their party loyalty, although it cannot account for the equally strong loyalty of other M.P.'s who, because of advanced age or temperament, are unambitious for ministerial offices.

Second, some attention ought to be given to the "nationalization" of British politics, and thus to the fact that M.P.s are not expected to vote in response to the pressure of their local constituents. Although conceding that the parties themselves, once established nationally, have played a role in subordinating local issues and interests, it seems more plausible to stress the importance of Britain's relative smallness and homogeneity in facilitating the centralization, not only of governmental authority, but also of political parties. In Britain, party centralization appears to involve the subordination of a less substantial diversity of interests than would be the case in the United States. Parliamentary representatives, in accepting their party's national positions, do not have to run counter to a strong political localism and regionalism which, despite our growingly pervasive industrialism, remain matters of American tradition and habit. And, of course, the British do not have power centers comparable to American states.

The effective freedom of the M.P. from his own constituents may also be facilitated by the fact that British politics have remained largely uninfluenced by the conceptions of direct democracy, whose impact on American parties was so overwhelming in the Jacksonian era and again in the progressive period of the 1900's. Subjecting representatives to the vicissitudes of the direct primary, to take a leading example, has never appealed to the British. Nor have other aspects of American-style direct democracy made much headway against Britain's residual respect for a governing class especially trained for public life. It seems, therefore, that there may be less localism in British parliamentary voting not only for geographic reasons, but also because of a different attitude toward the relationship of the representative to the popular will.

Third, there is the possibility that cohesive parliamentary parties have resulted, in part, from an ideological division which has been assumed, at least until recently, to be much sharper in British politics than in American. If this assumption is warranted, it can be argued that an M.P. would be restrained from joining the parliamentary opposition on any given issue by a loyalty to his party more deep-seated than that felt by an American congressman. For an M.P. to desert his party might seem nearly equivalent to deserting his class. Ordinarily this kind of class-conscious politics is attributed to the rise of the Labor party, and so indirectly to the factors which have produced a large-scale socialist movement in Britain but not in the United States.[46] But it should be noted that British parliamentary parties were already more cohesive than American before Labor became a major political force. The most that might be said is that the solidarity of parliamentary parties has increased since the development of the Labor party.

All three of the above observations, it may be granted, are mainly speculative as to the cause of the relatively high cohesion of British parliamentary parties. Each observation involves general historical and social circumstances about which it is difficult to be definitive. What remains to be pointed out is that insofar as such broad environmental explanations are accepted, there seems little likelihood that American legislative parties can be made to resemble their British counterparts. Unlike devices of party organization, the conditioning factors of constitutional tradition, political history, geography, and socioeconomic background cannot be recommended for another country.

Notes

1. *Government of England,* 2 vols. (New York, 1908), Vol. 2, Ch. 35.

2. A less favorable view of British parliamentary parties has been expressed by J. Roland Pennock, "Responsiveness, Responsibility, and Majority Rule," *American Political Science Review,* Vol. 46, pp. 790-807, at p. 801 (Sept., 1952).

3. However, it has been contended by Julius Turner that the critics of American parties underestimate the degree to which those parties are now "responsible" in the sense of presenting clear alternatives to the voters. "Responsible Parties: A Dissent from the Floor," *American Political Science Review,* Vol. 45, pp. 143-52 (March, 1951).

4. This is the theme of the careful and systematic work by R. T. McKenzie, *British Political Parties* (London, 1955). My own debt to his scholarship is very great.

5. In the author's "British Mass Parties in Comparison with American Parties," *Political Science Quarterly,* Vol. 71, pp. 97-125 (March, 1956).

6. Pressure from M.P.s of the majority party has certainly been known to influence government decisions. A recent instance was provided in 1953 by Conservative back-bench pressure on the Churchill Government to raise the level of pensions provided to retired officers of World War I. For a discussion of the policy-making role of Labor M.P.s, see James M. Burns, "The Parliamentary Labour Party in Great Britain," *American Political Science Review,* Vol. 44, pp. 855-71, at pp. 870-71 (Dec., 1950).

7. This holds for party re-adoption as well as for the election itself. In a rare instance where a constituency association actually sought to reject its sitting M.P. for at least partly local reasons, it is significant that the national party intervened in such a way as to prevent the result. The case was that of Mrs. E. M. Braddock, Labor M.P., whose difficulties with her Liverpool Exchange constituency party were described in *The Times* (London), April 29, 1955, p. 12.

8. Christopher Hollis, *Can Parliament Survive?* (London, 1949), pp. 64, 71.

9. A particularly clear instance of an M.P. addressing the House on behalf of a local interest group may be found in a speech by Barbara Castle concerning the Lancashire cotton industry, 530 *H. C. Deb.* 1743-52 (July 22, 1954).

10. Note the explanation by Herbert Morrison, *Government and Parliament* (London, 1954), p. 163. A free vote was allowed on the question of raising the salaries of M.P.s, 528 *H. C. Deb.* 30-158 (May 24, 1954).

11. Harold Lever, 535 *H. C. Deb.* 1867-71 (Dec. 15, 1954).

12. Morrison, *Government and Parliament*, p. 94.

13. See R. H. S. Crossman's explanation for his vote in favor of the German rearmament agreement which he "passionately" opposed. 533 *H. C. Deb.* 477 (Nov. 17, 1954).

14. H. G. Nicholas, *The British General Election of 1950* (London, 1951), pp. 251-52. Zilliacus was later re-admitted to the Labor party and elected as an M.P. in 1955.

15. *The Times* (London), Oct. 8, 1947, p. 4.

16. *Ibid.*, Oct. 15, 1948, p. 5.

17. 457 *H. C. Deb.* 108-13 (Oct. 27, 1948).

18. *The Times* (London), Oct. 29, 1948, p. 4. Incidentally, the executive council of the Keighley constituency Labor party claimed that it had decided to recommend that Thomas not be re-adopted as a candidate even before his letter to *The Times*.

19. *Ibid.*, Jan. 4, 1949, p. 4.

20. *Ibid.*, March 12, 1955. For an excellent sketch of Sir Richard Acland, see "Bart Errant," *New Statesman and Nation*, Vol. 49, pp. 468-69 (April 2, 1955).

21. *53rd Annual Report of the Labour Conference* (1954), p. 202.

22. 504 *H. C. Deb.* 1905-13 (Aug. 1, 1952).

23. The executive council did adopt a resolution of no-confidence in its M.P., but Hinchingbrooke saved himself by getting a general meeting of the constituency association to overrule the executive council. This was a very considerable achievement, attributable to a unique personality in a largely rural constituency, and it is doubtful whether many other M.P.s could similarly survive after offending both national and local leaders. Hinchingbrooke's constituency troubles were related in *The Times* (London), Oct. 6, 1952, p. 2; Oct. 10, 1952, p. 3; and Oct. 31, 1952, p. 6.

24. 531 *H. C. Deb.* 495-504 (July 28, 1954), 724-822 (July 29, 1954).

25. The Labor party's disciplinary procedure is established in its Standing Orders. The parliamentary party has the power to withdraw the whip. The National Executive Committee (of the external Labor organization) is to be informed of such action and to decide whether expulsion from the party as a whole is appropriate. *53rd Annual Report of the Labour Conference* (1954), p. 202.

26. 504 *H. C. Deb.* 1699-1840 (July 31, 1952) and 1869-1960 (Aug. 1, 1952).

27. *52nd Annual Report of the Labour Conference* (1953), p. 151.

28. *The Times* (London), Feb. 24, 1954, p. 8.

29. *Ibid.*, Feb. 25, 1954, p. 6.

30. *53rd Annual Report of the Labour Conference* (1954), pp. 92-108.

31. 533 *H. C. Deb.* 695-96 (Nov. 18, 1954).

32. *The Times* (London), Nov. 24, 1954, p. 8.

33. Nevertheless, the exclusion of the rebels from essentially non-party posts does illustrate the domination of the parliamentary machinery by the party whips. 536 *H. C. Deb.* 802-54 (Jan. 31, 1955).

34. *The Times* (London) carried stories about favorable constituency resolutions concerning Victor Yates (Nov. 29, 1954, p. 5), Ernest Ferneyhough (Dec. 13, 1954, p. 4), and George Craddock (Dec. 14, 1954, p. 4).

35. *Ibid.*, Feb. 25, 1955, p. 8; March 11, 1955, p. 8.

36. 537 *H. C. Deb.* 2066 (March 2, 1955).

37. *Ibid.*, cols. 2116-22.

38. *Ibid.*, col. 2176. Attlee's discomfiture was indicated by the first sentence of his response: "My right hon. Friend is asking me that question."

39. The number of abstainers is arrived at by noting Labor M.P.s who *did* vote against the government's motion but who did *not* vote for the official Labor amendment. *Ibid.*, cols. 2189-2200. For a refinement introduced into this method of calculation, see the *Manchester Guardian Weekly*, March 10, 1955, p. 5.

40. *The Times* (London), March 17, 1955, p. 6.

41. *Ibid.*, March 24, 1955, p. 8.

42. *Manchester Guardian Weekly*, April 7, 1955, p. 2.

43. *Ibid.*

44. *Tribune*, April 1, 1955, p. 1.

45. Compare the view of American politics expounded by D. W. Brogan. He holds that the United States Constitution is designed to make difficult an effective (that is, a unified) party system. *Politics in America* (New York, 1954), pp. 91-94.

46. The significance of this difference is discussed in the article on British mass parties referred to in note 5.

3. DISCIPLINE AND LOYALTY IN THE FRENCH PARLIAMENT

Peter Campbell

THE INSTABILITY and disunity of French parties are features to which commentators on French politics have long been drawing attention. Since the Liberation a new complaint has been made by some observers, who have discerned a danger-

Originally published under the title, "Discipline and Loyalty in the French Parliament during the Pinay Government," in *Political Studies*, Vol. 1, No. 3, (1953), pp. 247-257, and reprinted here by permission of the author, the editor, and the Clarendon Press, Oxford.

ous excess of party control over the deputies and who have alleged that the old anarchy of the deputies has been replaced by a new tyranny of the parties. Which of these views describes the present position more accurately? This note is an attempt to answer the question by an analysis of the votes in the National Assembly and Council of the Republic during the lifetime of M. Pinay's Government in 1952. That government was the first government of the right-centre to be formed in the second National Assembly; its formation was made possible only by a split in the R.P.F.; during its lifetime the Socialists ceased to be part of the majority giving general support to the government of the day and the M.R.P. had to decide to what extent it was really a party of the left as it had always claimed to be. So the nine and a half months during which M. Pinay held office formed an important phase of the crisis of the majority that has lasted since the general election of 1951.[1]

I. The National Assembly. When M. Pinay came to power in March 1952 the Assembly contained eleven groups, as follows:

Communists—96 deputies

Républicains Progressistes (R.P.)—4 deputies

Socialists—106 deputies

Indépendants d'Outre-mer (I.O.M.)—12 deputies

Mouvement Républicain Populaire (M.R.P.)—88 deputies

Union Démocratique et Socialiste de la Résistance (U.D.S.R.)—23 deputies

Radicals—75 deputies

Républicains Indépendants (R.I.)—55 deputies

Action Paysanne (A.P.)—22 deputies.

Paysans d'Union Sociale (P.U.S.)—23 deputies

Rassemblement du Peuple Français (R.P.F.)—116 deputies

In addition there were a few independent deputies (*non-inscrits*), excluded from this study.

Throughout the Government's life the composition of the Assembly altered slightly from time to time. A few deputies died or resigned from the Assembly, some of their successors belonged to different parties, and occasionally a deputy moved from one group to another, but on balance these minor changes had trivial effects. More important were two changes that occurred in July 1952. First, the two Peasant groups united to form the *Groupe Indépendant Paysan* (G.I.P.), with 46 deputies. Later in the month the R.P.F. was split by the secession of a quarter of its members, who joined with two *non-inscrits* to form the *Action Républicaine et Sociale* (A.R.S.), with 31 deputies, in order to support M. Pinay more continuously than they could within the R.P.F. After this split the R.P.F. was reduced to 87 deputies.

In the ensuing analysis account has been taken of the changes just mentioned. In addition, the members of the Government[2] have not been counted as members of their groups, because they voted as a separate unit.[3] The President of the Assembly—M. Herriot (a Radical), a vice-president actually in the chair, and any deputy recorded as *excusé* or as *absent par congé*[4] or as *N'a pu prendre part au vote*[5] have also been excluded from the count. No distinction has been made be-

Table I—Percentages of the Total Number of Divisions in Which Stated Percentages of the Deputies of each Group Voted Differently from the Largest Section of the Group

GROUP AND MEMBERSHIP[1]		PERCENTAGE OF DEPUTIES VOTING DIFFERENTLY FROM THE LARGEST SECTION OF THE GROUP								
		0	0-5	5-10	10-15	15-25	25-35	35-45	45-55	55-66
Comm.	96	100	—	—	—	—	—	—	—	—
R.P.	4	100	—	—	—	—	—	—	—	—
Soc.	106	99	1	*	—	—	—	—	—	—
I.O.M.	11	98	—	2	*	—	—	—	—	—
M.R.P.	82	57	32	7	2	2	—	*	*	—
U.D.S.R.	21	79	8	3	2	1	4	1	1	*
Rad.	67	63	26	5	1	2	1	1	1	—
R.I.	49	79	14	3	2	*	*	*	*	*
A.P.[2]	19	90	10	—	*	—	—	—	—	—
P.U.S.[2]	22	88	9	1	*	2	—	—	—	—
G.I.P.[3]	42	69	20	7	1	2	1	*	—	—
'A.R.S.'[4]	29	71	18	6	1	3	1	—	—	—
'R.P.F.'[5]	87	76	13	1	1	4	*	2	2	1
R.P.F.[6]	117	62	26	2	*	*	3	4	2	1
A.R.S.[7]	31	80	10	7	1	1	1	*	*	—
R.P.F.[7]	87	67	20	5	3	2	3	—	—	—

　* An asterisk indicates that the stated degree of disunity occurred too rarely to be recorded by a percentage.

　1. These figures relate to membership at 6 March or at the formation of the group concerned in July; they exclude ministers and M. Herriot.

　2. Figures for 257 divisions before the reunion of the Peasant groups.

　3. Figures for 415 divisions after the G.I.P. was formed.

　4. Record for 306 divisions of those R.P.F. deputies who eventually seceded to form the A.R.S.

　5. Record for 306 divisions of those R.P.F. deputies who remained 'orthodox.'

　6. Record for 306 divisions of the whole R.P.F. group before the split.

　7. Figures for 366 divisions after the split.

tween deputies recorded as *n'ont pris part au vote* (except the President or a sitting vice-president) and deputies who *se sont abstenus volontairement;* all are counted as 'abstaining,' although the second rubric indicates a more deliberate refusal to take part in the vote than does the first. Finally, no account has been taken of the *rectifications* which deputies may make for many reasons after the publication of the voting-lists, although effect has been given to the rare *erreurs matérielles* committed by the Assembly's administrative services and subsequently corrected.

During the nine and a half months from M. Pinay's demand for investiture by the Assembly, on 6 March 1952, to the receipt by the Assembly of formal notice of his resignation, on 22 December 1952, there were 673 divisions, of which 1 has been ignored because only deputies who were present in the Assembly were allowed to take part in it.

(*a*) *Discipline.* To what extent did each group vote as a unit, without the defection of any of its members? The answer to this question is given in Table I, which shows the percentage of divisions in which stated proportions of each group voted differently from the largest section of the group. (If none of the deputies votes differently from the others in his group and the group thus votes or abstains unanimously, then 'the largest section' will consist of the entire group; if 33 per cent of the members vote for a motion, 33 per cent against, and 34 per cent abstain, then 66 per cent will have voted differently from 'the largest section.')

From the table it will be seen that discipline was perfect within the Communist and *Républicain Progressiste* groups and that the unanimity of the Socialists was broken only in a few divisions (by an Algerian deputy on motions relating to the ownership of the Algerian press and by several deputies on a Bill relating to the sale of apartments). The groups of the centre were much less disciplined, but those of the right—the *Républicains Indépendants* and the Peasants—showed remarkable unity. At the extreme right discipline again decreased, as the Pinay experiment broke the monolithic unity of the R.P.F. The lack of discipline of most of the smaller groups is more apparent than real, for the defection of a single deputy means the loss of 5 or even 10 per cent of a small group's strength. If this fact is taken into account, and the first two, three, or four percentages (according to the size of the group) are added together, it will be seen how rarely was the discipline of each group violated by more than a very few deputies.

The unity within the groups was to a large measure extended to the major parties formed of two or more associated groups. The Communists and *Républicains Progressistes* always voted together; the largest section of the I.O.M. voted the same way as the largest section of the M.R.P. in 78 per cent of the divisions; the same was true of the U.D.S.R. and Radicals in 83 per cent; of the A.P., the P.U.S., and the R.I. in 93 per cent of the divisions held before the union of the peasant groups in July; of the G.I.P. and the R.I. in 96 per cent of the divisions after that union; of the dissident and orthodox Gaullists in 91 per cent of the divisions before the split in the R.P.F. but in only 71 per cent of the divisions after the split—the A.R.S. deputies now voted as they really wanted on issues of types that had previously seemed not sufficiently important to justify them in violating the unity of the R.P.F. Although the Communists and the Socialists were both in opposition to the Government and to the conservative and Catholic majority that supported it, they voted the same way in only 65 per cent of the divisions.

The topics which caused most of the serious defections from the groups and of the divisions between associated groups were few in number, although they gave rise to many votes. The chief were: the Finance Bills for 1952 and 1953, which caused trouble in all the groups supporting the Government and also in the R.P.F.; the Tunisian problem, which particularly disturbed the internal discipline of the U.D.S.R., Radicals, *Républicains Indépendants,* and Peasants; various routine measures on the education services, which divided both the U.D.S.R. and the Radicals; the amnesty for wartime collaborators, which caused trouble within the R.P.F., Radical, and M.R.P. groups; and the Bill for a sliding scale to connect the minimum wage and the cost of living, which caused trouble in all the governmental groups and in the R.P.F.

(*b*) *Loyalty.* M. Pinay's Government was supported primarily by all the centre groups between the Marxists and the R.P.F. Although it owed its existence to the support of the dissident Gaullists who had voted for M. Pinay's investiture, and although only with their aid could it have a majority over the combined opposition, its working majority normally depended only on the loyalty of the parties represented in it, as the opposition groups rarely combined against it on issues of major importance.

This loyalty can be tested by examining the record of the groups in the 562 divisions in which the Government took part. (The ministers abstained from voting in 110 divisions—16 per cent of the total. Some of these were on issues on which the Government is traditionally neutral, such as changes in the procedure of the Assembly; others were on minor issues about which the Government did not care; and some were on proposals which were not of minor importance but which had so much support in the Assembly that the Government did not wish to record its hostility to them lest it should needlessly arouse the resentment of some of its supporters.)

Table II shows how the groups voted in the remaining 562 divisions. As the Government's position became more difficult after the summer recess, the divisions are considered in two classes —the 235 before the split in the R.P.F. at the end of the summer sittings and the 327 after it; for the Peasant groups the first class includes only the 199 divisions prior to their reunion shortly before the split in the R.P.F. and the second includes all the 363 divisions after it.

Despite minor variations the general pattern is clear. The most loyal supporters of the Government—the groups most satisfied with its policies— were the Radicals, the U.D.S.R., the *Républicains Indépendants,* and the Peasants. They were followed at a little distance by the M.R.P. and at a farther distance by the A.R.S. deputies (both be-

fore and after they formed a separate group) and the I.O.M. Although the orthodox R.P.F. voted with the Government more often than it voted against it or abstained, its support was usually withheld in those critical divisions on important controversial issues when victory was essential to the Government. The Socialists and, above all, the Communists were the parties of sustained opposition, although the Socialists sometimes voted with the Government in critical divisions, such as some of those on the Finance Bill for 1952. Those differences are shown clearly in Table III, dealing with twenty-six divisions of the first importance. Twenty-four of these were on issues on which the Government had posed the question of confidence under Article 49 of the Constitution or which it said it would regard as issues of confidence although for the sake of its timetable it would not pose the formal question; the two remaining divisions were on M. Pinay's demands for investiture and for the indefinite postponement of interpellations on the composition of his newly formed cabinet.

Table II—Percentages of Divisions in which the Largest Section of each Group Voted with the Government, Voted Against It, or Abstained

BEFORE SPLIT IN R.P.F.

Group	With	Against	Abst.
Comm.	12	86	2
R.P.	12	86	2
Soc.	39	55	6
I.O.M.	60	11	29
M.R.P.	82	16	2
U.D.S.R.	87	6	7
Rad.	93	6	1
R.I.	89	9	2
A.P.	89	9	2
P.U.S.	86	12	2
'A.R.S.'	68	20	12
'R.P.F.'	57	23	20
R.P.F.	61	21	18

AFTER SPLIT IN R.P.F.

Group	With	Against	Abst.
Comm.	10	87	3
R.P.	10	87	3
Soc.	24	66	10
I.O.M.	74	13	13
M.R.P.	81	16	3
U.D.S.R.	83	11	6
Rad.	85	11	4
R.I.	85	11	4
G.I.P.	86	12	2
—	—	—	—
A.R.S.	75	19	6
R.P.F.	53	30	17
—	—	—	—

Table III—How the Largest Section of each Group Voted in Twenty-six Critical Divisions

BEFORE SPLIT IN R.P.F.

Group	With	Against	Abst.
Comm.	—	23	—
Rep. Prog.	—	23	—
Soc.	6	16	1
I.O.M.	19	1	3
M.R.P.	20	—	3
U.D.S.R.	23	—	—
Rad.	23	—	—
R.I.	23	—	—
A.P.[1]	22	—	—
P.U.S.[1]	22	—	—
'A.R.S.'	21	—	2
'R.P.F.'	5	2	16
R.P.F.	6	1	16

AFTER SPLIT IN R.P.F.

Group	With	Against	Abst.
Comm.	—	3	—
Rep. Prog.	—	3	—
Soc.	—	3	—
I.O.M.	3	—	—
M.R.P.	3	—	—
U.D.S.R.	3	—	—
Rad.	3	—	—
R.I.	3	—	—
G.I.P.[1]	4	—	—
—	—	—	—
A.R.S.	3	—	—
R.P.F.	—	2	1
—	—	—	—

1. One division took place between the reunion of the Peasant groups and the split in the R.P.F.

Except for the opposition of the I.O.M. to a motion on the clause in the 1952 budget empowering the Government to reduce expenditure by decree, never in these divisions did the largest section of any government group vote against the Government, and abstentions can be recorded only of the I.O.M., the M.R.P., and the dissident Gaullists before they formed the A.R.S.

Although it was rare for the opposition parties to combine, and although after the formation of the A.R.S. the Government was supported by groups commanding an absolute majority of the deputies in the Assembly, the ministers were defeated in 102 divisions—18 per cent of those in which they took part. Usually the defeat was on a relatively unimportant issue, but sometimes it was on an important one, and occasionally the Government would insist that the Assembly should reverse its decision. In sixty divisions the Government was defeated although it received the votes of most of its supporters; in most of these divisions a few at least of the ministerialists abstained or even voted against the Government; in almost a score of them the Government's defeat was due to the hostile votes of ministerialists, as only part of the regular opposition voted against it. In forty-one further divisions the majority of the ministerialists voting cast their votes against the Government. In one division the Government, supported only by the A.R.S., was defeated by the Communists; all the other groups abstained. This was only one of the odd results that occurred. Sometimes the Government found itself supported only by one or more of the opposition groups and would be defeated by the ministerialists and the rest of the opposition. Sometimes the Government, some ministerialists, and part of the opposition would defeat the majority of the ministerialists and the rest of the opposition. Yet eccentric coalitions of this kind were as unimportant as they were unusual, just as the combination of some ministerialists with all or part of the opposition might sometimes provide a *majorité de rencontre* but could never provide a *majorité de remplacement* until either the Socialists or the R.P.F. were prepared to support a new government.

The general picture of the National Assembly that results from this analysis is of a chamber which had rigidly disciplined groups on the left, well-disciplined groups in the centre, and very well-disciplined groups on the right; at the extreme right the unity of the whole R.P.F. before the split was violated as frequently as that of the Radicals and far more seriously; both before and after the split the A.R.S. and the pure R.P.F. showed degrees of discipline intermediate between those of the Radicals and the right-wing groups. The Gov-

ernment could place a fair amount of reliance on all the groups forming its coalition except the I.O.M.; but for victory it needed divisions in the ranks of the opposition, not only to eliminate the absolute majority which the opposition possessed until the formation of the A.R.S., but also to counterbalance the frequent defections of its own supporters. As a result, the Government could never be sure how it would fare in votes on issues that seriously divided both its own groups and the opposition.

II. The Council of the Republic. The composition of the Council during M. Pinay's Government was more complicated than that of the Assembly. At the start in March 1952 there were eight groups, and in June 1952, after the renewal of half the Council, there were eleven, as follows. (The first figure after each name gives the membership of the group in March; the figure in brackets gives the membership in June. The three senators who were ministers—one R.I., two R.G.R.—and the Council's President—R.G.R.—are excluded.)

Communists—18 (17)
Socialists—62 (55)
I.O.M.—nil (11)
M.R.P.—21 (24)
Centre Républicain (C.R.)—nil (3)
Rassemblement des Gauches Républicains (R.G.R.)—78 (71)
Centre Républicain d'Action Rurale et Sociale (C.R.A.R.S.)—16 (19)
Parti Républicain de la Liberté (P.R.L.)—11 (11)
R.I.—46 (46)
R.P.F.—56 (46)
Rassemblement d'Outre-mer (R.O.M.)—nil (8)

The *Centre Républicain* was affiliated to the M.R.P.; the C.R.A.R.S. and P.R.L. were affiliated to the *Républicains Indépendants;* and the R.O.M. was affiliated to the R.P.F. The membership of some groups changed slightly from time to time. There were always a few *non-inscrits.*

In theory, the Government could count on the support of all the groups except the Communists, Socialists, the R.P.F., and the R.O.M. In practice, however, it sometimes had trouble, because its supporters were more conservative than its coalition in the Assembly. There was always the danger that the Council might amend a Bill by an absolute majority which the Government would not be able to override because it lacked the sure support of an absolute majority in the Assembly. As a result, in the division on some Bills, the Government, like its predecessors, found itself in the curious position of wanting the Council to adopt an *avis* that was favourable on the whole, and yet not to do so by too large a majority because of some awkward amendments which the *avis* contained; occasionally this would even cause the three senators who were members of the Government to abstain from voting for a favourable *avis* on one of the Government's own Bills. Divisions in the Council were much less frequent than in the Assembly. Excluding a few divisions in which votes could be cast only by senators who were present, there were no more than 130 divisions during the Government's life; 83 of these took place after the partial renewal of the Council, and it was only in these that the C.R., I.O.M., and R.O.M. took part: the other groups took part in all the divisions.

(*a*) *Discipline.* Discipline in the Council was laxer than in the Assembly—even the unity of the Communists was violated occasionally and that of the Socialists quite frequently. With the exception of the Communists and the I.O.M., all the groups were disunited in more than 20 per cent of the divisions, as can be seen from Table IV, which shows for the Senate what Table I shows for the Assembly.

As in the Assembly, discipline was greatest on the left and right, was least in the centre, and decreased again with the R.P.F., although the divisions in the R.P.F. did not result in any secessions until January 1953, when five members formed an A.R.S. group and one joined the R.I. The indiscipline of the smaller groups is again more apparent than real because a single senator forms several 'per cent' of his group's membership.

The greater degree of disunity in the Senate is shown also in the relations between associated groups. The largest sections of the R.I. and the P.R.L. voted the same way in only 82 per cent of the divisions; for the C.R.A.R.S. and the R.I. the figure is 92 per cent; for each it is less than the figure for the corresponding groups in the

Assembly. In 93 per cent of the divisions after the elections the largest sections of the R.P.F. and the R.O.M. voted the same way; for the M.R.P. and the C.R. the figure is 87 per cent. The Communists and Socialists voted the same way in 66 per cent of the divisions; for their groups in the Assembly the figure is 65 per cent.

(*b*) *Loyalty.* The support the Government received from each group was very like that which it received from the corresponding or similar group in the Assembly. The three ministers abstained in

Table V—Percentages of Divisions in Which the Largest Section of each Group Voted with the Government, Voted Against It, or Abstained

Group	With	Against	Abst.
Communist	14	82	4
Socialist	39	54	7
I.O.M.	60	13	27
C.R.	62	18	20
M.R.P.	71	20	9
R.G.R.	89	8	3
R.I.	88	9	3
C.R.A.R.S.	90	7	3
P.R.L.	80	9	11
R.P.F.	48	32	20
R.O.M.	62	29	9

nineteen divisions—15 per cent of the total. The record of each group in the remaining 111 divisions is shown in Table V. The figures for the I.O.M., the C.R., and the R.O.M. relate to 68 divisions after the elections; those for the other groups relate to all the divisions in which the ministers took part.

The Government was defeated in seventeen divisions—15 per cent of those in which it took part. In five divisions a majority of its own supporters voted against it; in twelve it was defeated by a minority of its supporters voting with opposition

Table IV—Percentages of the Total Number of Divisions in Which Stated Percentages of the Senators of each Group Voted Differently from the Largest Section of the Group

GROUP	PERCENTAGE OF SENATORS VOTING DIFFERENTLY FROM THE LARGEST SECTION OF THE GROUP								
	0	0-5	5-10	10-15	15-25	25-35	35-45	45-55	55-66
Communist	99	—	*	—	*	—	—	—	—
Socialist	67	31	1	1	—	—	—	—	—
I.O.M.	92	—	—	—	—	—	6	2	—
M.R.P.	64	12	7	2	10	2	3	*	—
C.R.	66	—	—	—	—	31	—	—	3
R.G.R.	44	19	8	4	8	12	*	5	—
R.I.	44	38	5	1	3	2	5	1	1
C.R.A.R.S.	73	—	14	2	1	2	4	3	—
P.R.L.	78	—	5	—	5	4	3	5	—
R.P.F.	62	11	5	10	5	3	2	2	—
R.O.M.	63	—	30	—	3	1	3	—	—

* An asterisk indicates that the stated degree of disunity occurred too rarely to be recorded by a percentage.

groups. Most of the defeats were on minor issues. The Constitution makes the Cabinet responsible to the Assembly alone and the Government never declared that it would treat a vote in the Senate as a question of confidence, as M. Marie did once in 1948. Moreover, even some of the major amendments which the Cabinet sought later to have rejected by the Assembly were made by the Council without a vote being recorded. As a result it is not possible to see how the groups in the Council behaved in votes upon issues comparable to those which the Government made into, or treated as, questions of confidence in the Assembly.

The general picture of the Council of the Republic is strikingly similar to that of the National Assembly. The groups in the Council were on the whole only a little less disciplined than the corresponding groups in the Assembly, and they showed about the same degrees of loyalty or hostility to M. Pinay's Government as the latter.

Notes

1. This study is based on the division lists published in the *Journal Officiel, Débats Parlementaires, Assemblée Nationale,* and *Conseil de la République.*

2. At the start 26 members of the Government were deputies (1 I.O.M., 6 M.R.P., 2 U.D.S.R., 7 Radicals, 6 R.I., 3 A.P., and I P.U.S.). In July the four Peasant ministers adhered to the G.I.P.; in September another M.R.P. deputy joined the Government.

3. M. Tony-Révillon, a Radical junior minister, "rectified" his vote in three divisions on the education estimates; he declared he had wished to abstain instead of voting with the other ministers for the maintenance of the special credits opened in 1951 to give public money to Roman Catholic schools. (*J.O., D.P., A.N.,* 1952, pp. 5019, 5020, 5024.)

4. Normally a deputy who is not going to attend a sitting leaves his voting-cards with an officer of his group or with a friend, but sometimes he seeks formal leave of absence and his cards cannot then be cast on his behalf. Socialist and Communist deputies never did this.

5. Such as M. Duclos (Communist) while he was imprisoned during the spring.

B. The Influence of Pressure Groups

4. THE DYNAMICS OF ACCESS IN THE LEGISLATIVE PROCESS

David B. Truman

"EVERY OPINION," Mr. Justice Holmes observed in one of his great dissents, "tends to become a law."[1] In thus adumbrating his conception of the legislative process Holmes pointed to a distinctive feature of modern representative government. Especially in the United States, the legislature, far more than the judiciary or the executive, has been the primary means of effecting changes in the law of the land. In consequence, the legislature traditionally has been the major focus of attention for political interest groups. Though this interest in legislation has not been an exclusive preoccupation, the established importance of group activities in legislatures is reflected in a popular synonym for the political interest group, the word *lobby*. Though for tactical reasons many groups profess slight or no concern with lobbying, legislative activity has been for the layman the distinguishing feature of the political interest group.

It follows that access to the legislature is of crucial importance at one time or another to virtually all such groups. Some groups are far more successful in this pursuit than others. Moreover, access is not a homogeneous commodity. In some forms it provides little more than a chance to be heard; in others it practically assures favorable action. Some groups achieve highly effective access almost automatically, whereas it is denied to others in spite of their most vigorous efforts.

It will be appropriate, therefore, to begin an exploration of the role of groups in the legislative process by examining some of the factors that affect the kind of access that various groups are able to achieve. For the sake of convenience these may be divided into two types: first, a set of formal, structural factors whose importance will be readily apparent; second, a set of informal determinants whose effect is somewhat more subtle but of at least equal significance.

Governmental Structure and Differential Access. The formal institutions of government in the United States do not prescribe all the meanderings of the stream of politics. They do mark some of its limits, however, and designate certain points through which it must flow whatever uncharted courses it may follow between these limits. Such is the character of formal organization in any setting. Although the effect of formal structural arrangements is not always what its designers intended, these formalities are rarely neutral. They handicap some efforts and favor others. Debate over proposals to eliminate such a ritualistic bit of procedure as the electoral college, for example, reveals the fact that, although no one knows the exact consequences that would follow if it were to be abandoned or modified, a change would affect various segments of the community unequally. Such, inevitably, is the influence of formal structure.[2]

Access is one of the advantages unequally distributed by such arrangements; that is, in consequence of the structural peculiarities of our government some groups have better and more varied opportunities to influence key points of decision than do others. Take as an example the provision for equal representation of States in the Senate of the United States. This has allowed agricultural interest groups that are predominant in many thinly populated States more points of access in the Senate than urban groups whose members are concentrated in a few populous States. Thus, were it not for this structural provision, the United States would not have been so solicitous for the sugar beet or silver-mining interests as it has been over the years. It is obvious, moreover, that a group such as the American Farm Bureau Federation, which can cover a great many rural States, can gain readier access than urban groups concerning any matter on which it can achieve a satisfactory measure of cohesion. It is less obvious, but equally important, that an urban group whose interests are such that it can ally with the Farm Bureau derives an advantage in access over another urban group whose claims are such that it cannot effect an alliance of this sort. The Na-

Reprinted from *The Governmental Process* by David B. Truman, by permission of Alfred A. Knopf, Inc. Copyright 1953 by Alfred A. Knopf, Inc.

tional Association of Manufacturers and various trade associations, among others, have been the beneficiaries of such combinations.

Similar advantages, gained from the way in which the boundaries of legislative districts are drawn, whether by legislatures or by constitutions, can be observed throughout the governmental system. They are clearly observable in the House of Representatives, many of whose districts, even in relatively urban States like Illinois, are defined by State legislatures in which rural groups predominate. The State legislatures, of course, show similar patterns.[3]

The existence of the federal system itself is a source of unequal advantage in access. Groups that would be rather obscure or weak under a unitary arrangement may hold advantageous positions in the State governments and will be vigorous in their insistence upon the existing distribution of powers between States and nation. As the advantage of access shifts through time, moreover, groups shift from defenders to critics of the existing balance. At the turn of the century, for example, the insurance companies were active in Washington to get the Federal Government to take over the regulation of insurance, despite the obstacle of an adverse Supreme Court decision handed down shortly after the Civil War. Since the Court in 1944 altered the prevailing doctrine, the insurance companies have been equally vigorous in the opposite direction, at least in so far as they have tried to gain exemption from the Sherman Antitrust Act.[4] A somewhat complicated symptom of a similar state of affairs is suggested by the contrast between argument and behavior in connection with the Tydings-Miller Act of 1937. This legislation, sponsored principally by the National Association of Retail Druggists, exempted from the provisions of the Sherman Act contracts fixing resale prices on goods sold in interstate commerce, provided that they were resold in a State which permitted such contracts. Proponents of the measure argued that it was simply a means of permitting the individual States to regulate their own affairs. When the law was passed, however, the N.A.R.D. set up an unofficial *national* board through which uniform contracts between manufacturers and retailers could be approved and administered. The policy was a national one, but the druggists' access to the States was more effective once the Federal antitrust hurdle was eliminated.[5]

The separation of powers, especially between the legislature and the executive, and the accompanying system of checks and balances mean that effective access to one part of the government, such as the Congress, does not assure access to another, such as the presidency. For the effective constituencies of the executive and the members of the legislature are not necessarily the same, even when both are represented by men nominally of the same party. These constituencies are different, not simply because the president is elected from the whole country rather than from a particular State or congressional district, although this fact has significance under a system characterized by loose party discipline, but rather because within any State or district, for various reasons, the organized, active elements responsible for the election of a senator or representative are not necessarily the same as those which give the State's or district's support to a candidate for president. This situation is accentuated at the national level by the staggered terms of senators, representatives, and president. A senator elected at the same time as a president must face re-election in an "off" year, and vice versa; a representative must "go it alone" at least every four years. In consequence, as Herring has put it, "Most congressmen are still independent political entrepreneurs."[6] The representative, the senator, and the president each must give ear to groups that one or both of the others frequently can ignore.

An admirable illustration of this situation is the fact that four successive presidents—Harding, Coolidge, Hoover, and Franklin Roosevelt—found it possible to veto veterans' bonus legislation passed by the Congress, although on each occasion approximately four fifths of the House of Representatives chose to override the veto. Somewhat the same circumstance is indicated by the periodic group demands that reciprocal trade agreements should be submitted to the Senate for ratification as treaties. Such requests imply less effective access to the executive than to the maximum of thirty-three senators sufficient to reject a treaty.

As the preceding paragraphs suggest, access to points of decision in the government is significantly affected by the structure and cohesion of the political parties considered not just as electioneering devices, but as instruments of governing within the legislature. A single party organization that regularly succeeds in electing an executive and a majority in the legislature will produce one pattern of access to the government. The channels will be predominantly those within the party leadership, and the pattern will be relatively stable and orderly. A quite different pattern will be produced if the party is merely an abstract term referring to an aggregation of relatively independent factions. Then the channels of access will be numerous, and the patterns of influence within the legislature will be diverse, constantly shifting, and more openly in conflict.

Party discipline provides the power to govern because it permits stable control of access to the points of policy determination.

It is no novelty to observe that in the United States political parties, particularly on the national scene, correspond more closely to the diffused than to the disciplined type of structure. Because the legislator's tenure in office depends on no overarching party organization, he is accessible to whatever influences are outstanding in his local constituency almost regardless of more inclusive claims. Whether he carries the label of the majority or the minority party, he finds himself now in the majority and now in the minority on legislative votes. Majorities rarely are composed of the same persons in votes on successive measures. They are likely to be bipartisan or, more accurately, nonpartisan.

The dominant character of access and of influence under the American system is well stated in the remark of a Texas Representative in response to a query concerning his motives in advocating the repeal of Federal taxes on oleomargarine: "If I were from the South and were not interested in a market for my people, I would indeed be unworthy to represent my people. Of course I am interested in the right of the cotton farmer to sell his seed. . . ."[7] Diffusion of access has its ramifications as well. During the struggle over the McNary-Haugen farm "relief" bill from 1924 through 1928 President Coolidge was hostile both to the measure and to its principal group sponsor, the American Farm Bureau Federation. Vice-President Dawes, however, gave "support and assistance," to quote the words of the group's president, that were "of the utmost importance."[8]

Advantages of access are likely to go to the group that can accentuate and exploit the local preoccupations of the legislator. Many corporations and trade associations have long made use of this tactic although the exact forms have been various. Railroad companies have worked through lawyers and doctors retained in the States and counties in which they practice to reach influential supporters of State and national legislators, as have other corporate enterprises. The Association of Railway Executives, predecessor of the Association of American Railroads, organized such a device in a rather complete form. As outlined by one of its officials:

I had it in mind putting into effect a plan whereby we would be advised as to who are the influential men behind the several Congressmen, and the further thought that we might be able through personal contact or by the careful distribution of literature to influence in a perfectly proper way the judgment of the men upon whom the several Congressmen rely for support and advice.[9]

Such a system has never been more completely organized than it has been by the Iowa Farm Bureau Federation. Although the group does not openly endorse candidates for election, after the election it sets up committees of five members in each legislative district, whose function it is to capitalize upon local support. The qualifications of the members of these committees, according to Kile, are four in number: (1) they must be "willing to put Farm Bureau policies ahead of any personal interest;" (2) they must be from the same party as the successful candidate; (3) they must be men who "individually helped get the candidate elected;" and (4) they must be "politically potent in the district."[10] A very similar plan of organization to exert local influence has been employed by, among others, the National Association of Retail Druggists. The Federal Trade Commission has described it as "the most important device" used by the association in its efforts to secure passage of desired legislation.[11]

Such is the effect of our disintegrated national party structure upon access. Although this structure may be in process of gradual change in the direction of greater integration and central control, as some competent observers believe,[12] conclusive evidence of this shift is not at hand. We can be sure, however, that an altered party structure will be reflected in an altered pattern of group access to the Congress.

The effects of party structure upon group access to many of the State legislatures are similar to its effects upon access to Congress. The channels of approach for various groups are numerous and varied, as in Congress, except in those cases where an individual party leader or faction has been able to impose a high degree of discipline upon the rank and file. In the heyday of Boss Platt, access to the legislature of New York was available primarily through him, usually at a price.[13] When in 1935 the Governor of Florida established temporary dominance over the State legislature, the Association of Life Insurance Presidents found that it could not even gain admission to legislative committee hearings until it had persuaded the Governor of its point of view.[14] Other States, such as New York and New Jersey, have quite consistently shown a pattern of party government quite different from that at the national level.[15] Where the party structure is integrated and the legislators are under discipline, access is channeled and is more available to those groups upon which the party as a whole, rather than the individual legislator, is dependent.

Once it has established access, by whatever means, a group will exert tremendous efforts to retain the structural arrangements that have given it advantage. An illustration is afforded by the struggle over the adoption of the Twenty-first Amendment repealing the Eighteenth. When the prohibition amendment was submitted, the Anti-Saloon League favored the method of ratification by the State legislatures, since it had built up its access to most of those bodies and could be sure that the weapons at its disposal would assure favorable action by the required number of States. When the repeal proposal was passed by the Congress in 1933, however, the method of ratification by conventions called especially for the purpose was specified for the first time in the history of amendments to the Federal Constitution. This means was employed in order to get around the established access of the league.

All the factors of a structural character that result in the unequal distribution of access among interest groups operating upon a legislature need not be discussed in detail. We must, however, even in this rough sketch, discuss one additional type, closely related to the structure of the party system—the structure of the legislature itself, including legislative procedure and the committee system. Legislative structure and rules of procedure are by no means neutral factors in respect to access. As Schattschneider observed with reference to the Smoot-Hawley Tariff Act of 1930: "Legislation cannot be understood apart from the manner in which it is made."[16]

No legislative assembly of whatever size can, of course, carry on its activities without some internal division of labor, without methods of setting the order of business, or without means of regulating the process of deliberation. The procedures for selecting those to whom the leadership of an assembly is entrusted, for example, have a direct bearing upon the kind of access to the legislature that various groups may be able to achieve. Thus the practice in Congress and most of the States of assigning committee memberships and designating their chairmen on the basis of seniority gives a special advantage to groups having access to members from "safe" constituencies who are likely to look with hostility on the demands of the less established groups. Organizations whose membership is concentrated in "close" districts, where the incidence of change and the consequent demands for adjustment are high, are less easily able to establish access to committee chairmen.

Whoever sets the timetable of a legislature and determines how long debate on a measure shall continue has a significant control upon access.

This power, of course, is one of the principal means by which the British Cabinet leads the House of Commons. In American State legislatures a unified party leadership, both legislative and executive, may enjoy a similar dominance, and in that case effective access will be through such leadership. In the Congress, and at times in all the State legislatures, control of the timetable lies with a loosely integrated collection of men belonging to the majority party, sometimes acting in consultation with the minority leaders. In the Senate this scheduling function is performed by the floor leader, his aides, and the chairmen of the standing committees. The party Steering Committee and its Policy Committee are nominally a part of this machinery, but their importance is slight. In the House the timetable is set by the Rules Committee, the floor leader, the Speaker, and the chairmen of standing committees.The Steering Committee is of as little functional significance as in the Senate. Depending on the nature of the legislation to be considered and on the skill of the leadership, the legislators who determine the schedule may work in concert, or they may operate at cross purposes. In the latter case the legislative timetable is a compromise or emerges from a test of strength among these various points of power, a process in which the president, if he is of the same party, may play a significant role.[17] Groups with access to parts of this machinery have a privileged influence upon the legislative program, especially if their objective is to obstruct rather than to promote a particular bill.

Both the power to limit debate and the practice of permitting unlimited debate on a measure have significance for the degree of access that various groups achieve. In the House of Representatives where limitation on debate is customary, it usually takes the form of adopting a special rule reported by the Rules Committee. Practically all major legislation in the House is handled under this sort of procedure, which sets both the terms and the duration of debate. The Committee is thus in a position either to block or to expedite action on a bill, and access to its membership is a crucial advantage. Such access is likely to go disproportionately to established groups dominant in "safe" constituencies, since the seniority of all members of this committee is high. For example, in the Seventy-seventh Congress, elected in 1940, no member of the Rules Committee had had less than four consecutive terms of service, and the average number of such terms represented on the Committee was just under seven. Thus most of the members came from districts that had made no change in their representation since before the onset of the New Deal. A similar advantage accrues in the Senate to any defensive group that has access to even a small bloc of members. Under that body's practice of unlimited debate, such a minority can "talk a bill to death" through the filibuster, effectively preventing action by the Senate as a whole. In some cases this result has been achieved by one member alone. Although the Senate has had since 1917 a rule permitting closure of debate, it is rarely applied, and the effective veto power of a Senate minority remains virtually unchallenged.

Finally, the enormously complicated and technical rules under which debate is carried on in legislative chambers have an important influence upon relative access. In the first place, the rules themselves are not neutral; witness the heat frequently generated by an attempt to change them. At the beginning of the Eighty-first Congress in January, 1949, a successful effort was made to modify the House rules so that committee chairmen could call up bills that the Rules Committee failed to report out. The significance of such a modification was indicated both by the activity in the House and by the attention given the amendment in the press.[18] But groups gain advantages in access not just from the substance of such procedural regulations. They may derive tremendous advantage if their representatives, whether in or out of the legislative halls, have a mastery of the ins and outs of parliamentary procedure. Like the technicalities of legal procedure in courts of law, procedural arrangements may be used as often to delay and obstruct action as to facilitate it. Thus the ability to command the services of a skillful parliamentary tactician may be the key to effective access to a legislature.

Reference has already been made to legislative committees. It is necessary to indicate that the place of committees in a legislative body has important effects upon the degree of access that various groups can achieve. It is as accurate today as it was nearly three quarters of a century ago when Woodrow Wilson published his little classic, *Congressional Government,* to say that, although the Congress as a whole formally legislates, the real policy determination takes place in the standing committees.[19] Both because of the volume and the complexity of the problems coming before a modern legislature and because of the size of such bodies, they have had to leave the most important part of the examination, if not the preparation, of legislation to smaller units. Under the British system this function is performed primarily by the Cabinet, which is strictly speaking a committee of the legislature. Relatively minor use is made of other standing committees. In the Congress of the United States the sifting of legislative projects is pre-eminently the function of the committees, primarily the standing committees. Neither house, with rare exception, considers any measure that has not first been acted upon by one of these nominally subordinate bodies. Refusal to report a bill from a committee usually dooms the proposal. But perhaps the most significant feature of the system is that, although many major measures are altered by the Senate or the House after a committee has reported, both houses usually follow closely the recommendations of their committees. Few bills are passed in a form substantially different from that given them at the committee stage.[20]

The effect that this system of committees has upon access stems not only from the relative finality of their actions but also from the comparative independence that they enjoy. These bodies are subject to little or no co-ordinating influence from any source. A committee majority, or even its chairman alone, effectively constitutes a little legislature, especially in so far as it blocks action on a proposal. Therefore access to a committee majority or even to a chairman may give a group effective advantage in the legislature itself, to the virtual exclusion of its competitors.

The role of committees in the State legislatures varies widely. In some their place is roughly similar to that of the congressional committee, whereas in others it is sharply different. One general difference is that, since State legislative sessions are shorter and less frequent and since many State legislators perform their duties on a part-time basis, there is usually less opportunity for prolonged committee consideration in the States. In some States, New Jersey, for instance, the committees are of no significance, except as graveyards for bills, since control by the party leaders is pervasive. Access to the committee under such circumstances is almost meaningless.[21] In other States the committee function appears to be quite similar to that in Congress. Thus a study of several legislative sessions in Maryland and Pennsylvania shows that well over 80 per cent of the committee reports were accepted outright by these legislatures.[22]

This evidence would suggest that committees in Maryland and Pennsylvania were indeed "little legislatures" and that access to them was crucial. Although such undoubtedly was the case in some instances, in these same two States there were other regularities that lay behind the acceptance of committee reports. The legislators followed the committees, to be sure, but the latter were dominated by chairmen who in turn co-operated closely with the governors and other legislative leaders.[23] Similar evidence on the New York legislature indicates that State legislative committees and their chairmen enjoy much less freedom of action than their congressional counterparts. Political management by an informal conference of legislative leaders determines the content of major bills, not the individual committees operating independently.[24] Under such circumstances access to the legislature is not assured merely by establishing relationships with individual committeemen or chairmen. Lines of access tend to be integrated rather than diffused; consequently, the tactics of groups and relative advantage among them can be expected to show a pattern quite different from that characteristic of the Congress.

Aspects of formal structure, therefore, are significant determinants of the channels of access to legislatures, national and State. They afford advantages to some groups and impose handicaps upon the efforts of others to achieve influence in the legislature. Formal structure both reflects and sustains differences in power. It is never neutral.

The Role of Knowledge and the Effects of Overlapping Membership. Governmental structure is not the only factor creating advantages in access to the key points of decision in the legislature. It is the most obvious, but perhaps not the most important. The politician-legislator is not equivalent to the steel ball in a pinball game, bumping passively from post to post down an inclined plane. He is a human being involved in a variety of relationships with other human beings. In his role as legislator his accessibility to various groups is affected by the whole series of relationships that define him as a person.[25] Most of these relationships, however, cannot be identified by viewing the legislator as a creature of the statute book. We need not go into the complicated area of motives to account more fully for differences in accessibility by observing such continuing relationships, remembering that their stability is as important an element in the equilibrium of the individual legislator as are predictable relationships in the well-being of any other human.

One important factor among the informal determinants of access is created by the legislator-politician's need of information and the ability of a group to supply it. Any politician, whether legislator, administrator, or judge, whether elected or appointed, is obliged to make decisions that are guided in part by the relevant knowledge that is available to him. In this deciding, however, the politician is in a position analogous to the late Lord Keynes's stock-exchange investor, whose

knowledge of the factors that will govern the future yield of an investment is necessarily partial or even negligible.[26] The politician also must rely on somewhat conventionalized assessments of trends, corrected by new information about the relevant facts.

The politician is in continuous need of current information because he is at the mercy of the changes as they occur. Like a college president, a politician, especially an elected politician, is expected to have a judgment on all matters ranging from the causes of an outbreak of Bang's disease among the local livestock to the latest strategy of the Kremlin. He must make decisions on many of these questions, decisions on the content of his public statements, on the causes and persons he will champion, on how he will vote on a roll call.

The penalty for numerous or conspicuous decisions made in ignorance or in neglect of relevant available knowledge is disturbance in the politician's established relationships. The disturbance may be minor and temporary or serious and lasting. It may be reflected in a diminution of "reputation" or in a threat to his leadership position in party, faction, or other group. Finally, it may lead to defeat at the polls, a penalty that no elected official can be expected to welcome. Forced to make choices of consequence and to minimize serious disturbances in his established relationships, the legislator is constantly in need of relevant information. Access is likely to be available to groups somewhat in proportion to their ability to meet this need.

For purposes of discussion the knowledge required by the politician may be divided into two types: technical knowledge that defines the content of a policy issue; and political knowledge of the relative strength of competing claims and of the consequences of alternative decisions on a policy issue. Any group may be in a position directly or indirectly to supply information of either type.

Representative of the first sort of knowledge is the specialized information about industry conditions that a trade association can provide for the politician, whether legislator or administrator. Almost any group is likely to regard knowledge of this sort as a major part of its stock-in-trade. Those who are preoccupied with moral judgments of group politics, in fact, normally treat the supplying of such information as a "legitimate" group activity. A measure of access almost inevitably accompanies the ability to provide this type of information. Where competing claims are not present, and where available knowledge of the likely political consequences suggests that the legislator will be little affected whatever decision he makes, technical information may control his decision. The politician who comes from a "safe" district, confronted with an issue of no moment in his constituency, is in a position to act upon what he regards as the "merits" of an issue, to act like what the ward heeler calls a "statesman." Especially where official sources of information are deficient, command of technical knowledge may provide access for groups that can supply the deficiency, especially if other influences are operating in their favor.[27] Thus McKean noted that the absence of a legislative reference library, the impossibility of retaining technical staff on a legislator's salary, and the failure of the State Government to provide such services as information on the progress of pending bills, gave privileged access to groups in New Jersey prepared to perform such functions.[28]

The second type, political information, is of at least equal importance. Many familiar expressions, such as "keeping one's ear to the ground" and "mending fences," testify to this fact. The legislator, as anyone knows who has had even an amateur's brush with politics, can never know enough in this sphere. Who are behind this measure? How well unified are they? What dormant elements in the constituency will be stirred up if the proponents' claims are acceded to? Will there be a later opportunity to pacify them? For questions such as these there is rarely a final answer, but the legislator often must act as if there were. Where the situation remains obscure, his behavior may be ambiguous. Thus he may vote to kill a bill by sending it back to committee, but when that motion is lost, he may change his position and vote for the measure's passage. It may be easier to defend such apparent vacillation than to face the consequences of an unequivocal stand.

In politically ambiguous circumstances, and they are common, a group that can give the legislator an indication of the consequences of supporting or opposing a measure is likely to win his ear at least in some degree. Such "information," of course, is rarely taken at face value, since most groups find it expedient to exaggerate their influence and the cohesion of the rank and file. It is up to the legislator to apply a discount rate that seems appropriate. In some instances his knowledge of his constituency is such that he knows immediately how to evaluate such claims. In others he must be aided by trusted advisers, who may themselves, in consequence, become the objects of petitions from various interest groups. The evaluation of group claims may itself be a puzzling task, although a politician of any skill can often see through assertions that are largely pretense. Yet because pretense and exaggeration are common, a group may gain advantage in access if it is presented by agents who have a reputation for candor and realism. Few elected politicians are in a position requiring no reliable political knowledge.

The desire for information may not be the only informal factor leading the legislator to make himself accessible to particular interest groups. He is not simply a machine for calculating odds and acting on the most favorable ones. When he assumes office he does not cut himself off from all previous connections and divest himself of the attitudes he has acquired up to that time. The prevailing myths may hold that he does so or should do so, but to accept such folklore literally is to fall victim to the institutional fallacy, to look at formalities and to ignore relationships. As John Dewey has put it: "Those concerned in government are still human beings. They retain their share of the ordinary traits of human nature. They still have private interests to serve and interests of special groups, those of the family, clique or class to which they belong."[29] Such was essentially the point argued by Madison in the following passage from *The Federalist, No. 10*:

No man is allowed to be a judge in his own cause, because his interest would certainly bias his judgment, and, not improbably, corrupt his integrity. With equal, nay with greater reason, a body of men are unfit to be both judges and parties at the same time; yet what are many of the most important acts of legislation, but so many judicial determinations, not indeed concerning the rights of single persons, but concerning the rights of large bodies of citizens? And *what are the different classes of legislators but advocates and parties to the causes which they determine?* (Italics added.)

Madison concluded that legislators must inevitably have interest affiliations, and not infrequently we find evidence that members of Congress also assume so. Thus in 1929 the Senate committee investigating tariff lobbying criticized the head of a series of "paper" associations for pretending to an influence that he did not have. After commenting on his lack of technical qualifications, the committee added as further evidence of his fraudulent position: "He is on terms of intimacy with no Member of Congress so far as your committee has been able to learn."[30]

Since an elected representative cannot give up his already existing attitudes and relationships, the legislature and various political interest groups inevitably overlap in membership. Any of the latter that can claim members in the legislature will thus enjoy a measure of privileged access. Other influences aside, the value of this means of access will vary with the number of such members and with the importance that they attach to such affiliation. It is well known, for instance, that the organized bar has had advantages in access to State and national legislatures in consequence of the number of lawyers elected to those bodies. The American Legion usually can list among its membership one third to one half the members of Congress, in addition to Cabinet members and even the President. Not all of these are equally accessible to the Legion, but at least a portion of them are likely to be readily so. Similarly the Chamber of Commerce of the United States constitutes, as one author has put it, "an unofficial functional constituency of the federal legislature" in consequence of having several of its members in the Congress.[31]

Where the claims of a group are or can be made sufficiently central for its members in the legislature, the latter can be formed into a "bloc" that is expected to act as a unit on as many as possible of the issues of concern to the group. At its height such was the "farm bloc" of 1921-2, which included a quarter of the Senators (14 Republicans and 10 Democrats) and a similar but less well defined segment of the House. Though a minority of both houses, it held a balance of power for the better part of four years.[32]

The National Rivers and Harbors Congress, whose membership overlaps with that of a variety of other groups, including Congress, has acquired almost as much influence in the area of its claims. It is made up of contractors and State and local officials, members of Congress, and, ex-officio, officers of the Army Corps of Engineers. The loyalties uniting this group have demonstrated their strength on many occasions. When the Rivers and Harbors Congress announces its opposition to the recommendation of the Hoover Commission that the flood control and rivers and harbors activities of the Corps of Engineers be transferred to the Department of the Interior, it is in effect announcing the opposition of a "bloc" to any effort to implement the suggestion. When Representative William M. Whittington of Mississippi testified in 1945 before a Senate committee in opposition to a proposal to establish a Missouri Valley Authority, he spoke not only as a member of Congress and as chairman of the Flood Control Committee of the House, but as vice-president of the National Rivers and Harbors Congress and vice-president of the related Mississippi Valley Flood Control Association.[33]

The variety of uses to which such multiple memberships can be put is almost infinite. The legislator who is a "member" of an active political interest group may, better than anyone outside the legislature, observe and report on developments within the legislative body and its committees; he may

act as the group's spokesman on the floor; he may attempt to persuade key committee members; he may save the group postage by allowing it the use of his franking privilege; and so on. A few examples will suggest the range of relationships. When the retail druggists and their allies were attempting in the 1930's to secure passage of price-maintenance laws, full use was made of retailer-legislators, according to the manual on the subject issued by the National Association of Retail Druggists. In Iowa the druggists who were members of the legislature met as a group and selected the persons who were to sponsor the measure. In the State of Washington the bill was introduced by a collection of legislators, "several of whom were or had been in the retail business and knew the meaning of predatory price cutting. Such men needed no prodding when it came to arguing the bill on its own merits."[34] Much the same procedures are followed by the veterans' organizations. The Legion distributes among its members in the Congress the responsibility for sponsoring its measures, and it supervises the tactics they employ. During the bonus drive of the 1930's the key member of the Veterans of Foreign Wars in Congress was Representative Wright Patman of Texas. He spearheaded the V.F.W.'s effort to secure immediate cash payment of the bonus.[35] When the tariff revision of 1929-30 was in process, Senator Bingham of Connecticut placed on the payroll of the Senate the assistant to the president of the Connecticut Manufacturers Association. The latter not only advised Senator Bingham, but accompanied him to the meetings of the Senate Finance Committee, which prepared the measure, as an "expert" on tariff matters.[36]

An important possibility to bear in mind in connection with the effect of a legislator's group memberships upon his accessibility is that the willingness to aid a group's claims need not involve any overt act on the part of the group, any "pressure" on the legislator, and it need not involve formal membership in the group. A legislator-politician no less than any other man has, as we pointed out elsewhere, lived his life in a series of environments, largely group-defined. These have given him attitudes, frames of reference, points of view, which make him more receptive to some proposals than to others. As a specialist in politics he may be in possession of information that obliges him to choose between his preferences as a successful upper-middle-class lawyer and the demands of a group of militant workers in his constituency. But in the absence of such conflicts, and even in the face of them, he is likely to be most accessible to groups or proposals that stem from sources comparable to those from which his own attitudes have been derived. Many, if not all, such legislators will insist in all sincerity that they vote as their own consciences dictate. They may even resent any effort from an otherwise acceptable group to force a particular decision from them. This is true; however, whether they are "liberals" or "conservatives," urbanites or country boys, their "consciences" are creatures of the particular environments in which they have lived and of the group affiliations they have formed.

Under such circumstances the notion of group "pressure" has limited value. Bailey makes this point extremely well in his discussion of the attitudes of those members of Congress who were on the joint conference committee that produced the Employment Act of 1946 in its final form. In accounting for the strongly hostile position of Senator Buck of Delaware, Bailey refers to Buck's close connections with the Du Pont family, including his marriage to the daughter of T. Coleman Du Pont. No overt group act was necessary to secure Buck's vote against the measure, for, as Bailey observes, "It was not the pressure of Du Pont *on* Buck but the pressure of Du Pont *in* Buck which was at work."[37] Similarly it is scarcely necessary for an organized interest group to take overt action among members of Congress from the South in order to secure their votes against F.E.P.C. legislation and the like. Access for this point of view is assured in most cases by the attitudes which Southern legislators hold without prompting.

We encounter here again the fact that interest groups operate in a hierarchy of prestige. Some groups, as we have seen previously, enjoy a prestige which makes it unnecessary for them to participate actively in elections. Such high status groups are likely to acquire favorable access to the legislature for the same reasons. A politician need not himself be a member of the Chamber of Commerce of the United States to listen with respect to the testimony of a business leader who is pleading its case. Among the attitudes he is likely to have acquired in the average constituency are ones involving deference toward those groups that enjoy high prestige in the country as a whole. In the legislative process, as in other aspects of politics, groups are affected by their position or status in the society.

In this connection some reference should be made to what is widely referred to as the "social lobby." An informal influence upon access, it provides material for the more lurid exposés of legislative life and lends itself to treatment in eye-catching headlines. Popular impressions to the contrary, there is no reason to revise Herring's judgment that the influence of this device is "de-cidedly secondary."[38] If the minor importance of the "social lobby" is not forgotten, however, examination of the phenomenon will provide instructive illustrations of the informal determinants of relative access.

The "social lobby," a technique rather than a type of group, is a device to create a feeling of obligation on the part of the legislator toward individuals who have established sociable relations with him through entertaining him and his family. It uses social intercourse to develop multiple memberships, on the not unwarranted assumption that in a conflict situation the face-to-face relations of the "social lobby" will be dominant.[39] It is harder to refuse someone who has been kind to you than to turn away a more or less complete stranger.

If the attempted seduction is successful, it probably works best with the new legislator who is just taking up residence in a strange community.[40] Having been a fairly large frog in a comparatively small pond, he suddenly finds the situation reversed. He may be disturbed by the abrupt interruption of his accustomed social relationships and feel the need for adequate substitutes. These may be supplied by the dinner and golf games of a "social set" or by the poker games and other diversions offered by an interest group representative. The implied penalty for sharp political disagreement is ostracism from the friendly group, and the legislator may quite unconsciously find himself avoiding this penalty by conforming. Reinforcement in this direction may come from the legislator's wife and daughters. They too need satisfactory personal relationships in the new community; once established these may involve none of the conflicts which the legislator himself feels, and the sanction then becomes the more unpleasant. Especially if the ladies are "socially ambitious," exclusion from "important" social functions may be acutely painful. The rationale of the device is suggested by the Georgia representatives of the Association of Life Insurance Presidents in a report on the 1933 session of the State legislature. Accounting for their expenditures, they say in part: "This money has been spent in invitations to those of whom we wished to make friends, and seeing that their wives and daughters were looked after properly and courteously. . . ."[41] At its crudest the "social lobby" amounts to simple bribery, as the following case suggests. A new member of the House of Representatives, assigned to a committee considering a power bill, struck up a friendship with a "newspaper correspondent" to whom he had been introduced at a small luncheon. He did not know that the introduction was by prearrangement, nor did he develop suspicions as the men and their wives became quite intimate, the two couples enjoying dinners and week-end excursions together, and the genial "journalist" drawing the congressman and his wife into a new set of friendships. The "reporter" and wife even aided in redecorating the legislator's apartment. After this kind of thing had gone on for some time, the "journalist" one day dropped in at the congressman's office, stated his attitude toward the power bill and his assumption that the legislator also opposed the measure. When the congressman announced that he favored the bill and would not be dissuaded, the pleasant social relations between the two couples ceased completely.[42]

Normally the technique is more subtle, along the lines of the following statement by a former State legislator:

The legislator who remains aloof will find himself, if not quite ostracized, at least not "one of the gang," and will constantly be surprised at an unexpected solidarity on the part of a majority of his colleagues for or against a pending measure. His surprise will be dissipated when he learns that the night before the "gang" were at an entertainment at a downtown hotel, where probably the subject of legislation was not even mentioned, but in some subtle way an understanding was reached as to what was expected of those present as all around "good fellows."[43]

Part of the subtlety in this case, of course, depended upon the clique structure within the legislature itself, to which we shall turn shortly.

Although the "social lobby" illustrates a type of informal overlapping membership, the reasons for its comparative unimportance are fairly obvious. In the first place, the successful politician, like other leaders, is likely to be a person whose pattern of interpersonal relations is fairly flexible and thus not readily subject to the sanction of ostracism. Secondly, since positions of power within the legislature customarily are occupied by experienced legislators rather than by newcomers, the seductive technique must operate in a limited field. The old hand does not need the flattery of the "social lobby" for his personal happiness; he may, in fact, favor a gathering by his presence rather than be favored by an invitation to it. Excepting, therefore, the occasional newcomer and the rare legislator who is undisturbed by bribery, the "social lobby" is at most a means of reinforcing the preferences already held by various members of the legislative body. Even among these it may not prevail over other devices in a legislative situation where opposing influences are present.

An important implication of the various multiple memberships of legislators is that their interactions with interest groups are not just one-way relationships. The popular view is that the political interest group uses the legislator to its ends, induces him to function as its spokesman and to vote as it wishes. As we have already seen, this is not an inaccurate view. But it is incomplete. In most of the examples discussed above the legislators were not subject to overt "pressure." They did not necessarily act in anticipation of group demands but rather behaved as persons in official position whose views of the pending legislation for various reasons approximated those of organized and potential interest groups. When a legislator arouses organized groups in connection with a proposal that he knows will involve them or when he solicits their support for a measure which he is promoting, the relationship becomes reciprocal. Even in connection with the development of a single bill from conception to enactment, the initiative may lie alternately with legislator and with group, including other outside influences.

The Employment Act of 1946 furnishes a good example of such reciprocal relationships, as Bailey's study indicates.[44] Perhaps because this legislation involved few concrete deprivations or indulgences and is, therefore, not entirely typical of many controversial measures, it highlights the use that members of Congress may make of a variety of interest groups. The impetus for the bill came in part, to be sure, from the National Farmers Union. Much of the drive behind the measure, however, was supplied by the most important of the Senate and House sponsors and their aides. These solicited the support of a diversity of groups and welded them into what Bailey dubs the "Lib-Lab Lobby." Some of these interest groups in turn attempted to win over other members of Congress and officials of the executive branch, so that it became difficult to determine who was influencing whom. Certainly, however, it was no simple, one-way pattern of group demands upon legislators. On the opposition side as well, moreover, testimony against the measure was solicited by members of Congress. In particular, Representative Carter Manasco of Alabama, chairman of the House Committee on Expenditures in the Executive Departments, to which the bill was referred, took the initiative in mobilizing opposition witnesses.

Overlapping memberships of legislators, therefore, give privileged access to the interest groups involved, whether the membership is formal or of the "fellow-traveler" variety. Such membership does not mean simply that the legislator is "used" by the groups in a one-way, conditioned-response relationship. As "parties to the causes which they determine," legislators may equally function as leaders of the interest groups with which they identify.

The Group Life of the Legislature. We have seen that formal governmental structure and various informal group-legislator relationships give some groups advantages over others in achieving access to the legislature. These factors are productive of patterns of interaction that affect legislative decisions. A third factor that also regulates access is the pattern of relationships within the legislature itself. We are concerned here more than in the earlier paragraphs with access not merely to the individual legislator, but to the legislature as a unit. Such a body is not properly conceived of as a collection of individual men, unorganized and without internal cohesion. Nor is it any better accounted for exclusively in terms of the formal, legal structure of the legislature. A legislative body has its own group life, sometimes as a unit, perhaps more often as a collection of subgroups or cliques. It has its own operating structure, which may approximate or differ sharply from the formal organization of the chamber. When a man first joins such a body, he enters a new group. Like others, it has its standards and conventions, its largely unwritten system of obligations and privileges. To these the neophyte must conform, at least in some measure, if he hopes to make effective use of his position. The claims and imperatives of his other group attachments must be accommodated and adjusted to those of a new one. This conformity is facilitated by the fact that the new group commands some of the means of satisfying the demands of the outside groups with which the new legislator identifies himself; the adjustment is also strengthened by the morale, the *esprit,* in the legislative body.

The morale of legislative groups is often marked, even when mutual confidence of the members is not productive of the most widely approved results. As one discriminating student of the legislative process has put it: "In general, the *esprit de corps* displayed by legislative bodies, especially the smaller ones, is probably not rivaled by any other formally organized, self-governing body. There seem to be factors inherent in the legislative process which are conducive to the production of good morale."[45] The factors productive of legislative morale are rooted in the continuing interpersonal relationships among the members, which are initially grounded in the common experiences they have had in reaching and holding elective office. Politicians of quite different opinions and of at least nominally opposed political party are likely nevertheless to understand and respect a colleague's fears and triumphs. Like old veterans of a military campaign or like the alumni of a college athletic team, they speak a language which the uninitiated can never quite understand; they have had roughly parallel experiences that set them a little apart from those whose struggles have been of a different order. These commonalities help to support the conforming influences of the legislative group. "Smoke-filled cloakrooms and bars where one can rub elbows with his colleagues who have shared experiences with him and who know what he has been through to get there and stay there, are assimilating and conditioning grounds."[46] The relationships of a legislator with his fellow legislators do much to moderate the conflicts inherent in the legislative process and to facilitate the adjustments without which the process could not go on. Skill in handling such relationships, moreover, generates influence that is reflected in leader-follower patterns within the chamber. Legislative skill, usually acquired only after considerable experience in the law-making body, creates its own following; less experienced or overly busy members will often be guided by the skilled veteran when a vote is called for and in a fashion that cannot be explained simply in terms of party loyalty or of the trading of votes.

The pattern of interpersonal relationships in the legislature may closely approximate the formal structure of floor leaders, whips, and committee chairmen. Whether it does or does not, however, the tyro who reaches the capitol breathing fire after a vigorous campaign soon finds that he can accomplish nothing until he learns how to get along with his colleagues. The acknowledged leaders of the body, whether they are the formal ones or not, can help the newcomer to advance himself and his projects at a modest price in conformity and recognition of reciprocal obligations. The conformity and recognition of obligations, moreover, involve some acceptance of the notion that the ramifications of some of the claims he espouses will, if the claims are unmodified, reach beyond the groups for which the new legislator speaks. The consequences of the demands he voices may affect his colleagues and the legislature as a group. He becomes more or less conscious of the need not to "upset the apple cart." Failure to learn the ways of the legislative group, to "play ball" with his colleagues, is almost certain, especially in a large body like the U.S. House of Representatives, to handicap the proposals in which the freshman legislator is interested and to frustrate his ambitions for personal preferment.[47] The group life of the legislature thus may temper the claims of an interest group, since the legislator-spokesman must reconcile such demands with his role within the chamber. Even the established and skillful legislative leader rarely rides roughshod over his colleagues.

The political interest group whose spokesman "belongs" to the legislative group, who is "one of the boys," enjoys an obvious advantage in access to the legislature, especially if the representative is one of the acknowledged leaders of the chamber. Correspondingly, a group is handicapped if its only connections are with a maverick or a newcomer. It is not enough for the legislator to be a member, in some sense, of the interest group or even to be in a position of formal power. He must "belong" within the legislature as well.

Although the pattern of relationships within the legislature thus affects the access of interest groups, it is important not to assume that these interactions produce an integrated, hierarchical structure. They may, but the life of the legislative group as of others may as easily involve a loosely allied collection of cliques. Where a measure of integration is achieved in one chamber, moreover, it may not extend to the other. The group life of a legislature may bear little or no likeness to cohesive party government. As Woodrow Wilson said of the power of the Rules Committee and the Speaker of the House of Representatives before the 1911 revolt: "It integrates the House alone . . . ; does not unite the two houses in policy. . . . It has only a very remote and partial resemblance to genuine party leadership."[48] Party government is a form of legislative group life, but it is not the only or the most common form in the United States.

The Influence of Office. The influences we have discussed thus far come close to accounting for the relative access of interest groups to the legislature, but they are not complete. Formal structural aspects of government, the legislators' various group "memberships," and what we have called the group life of the legislature do not tell the whole story. In addition to these, the fact of holding public office is itself a significant influence upon the relative access of the groups. Not unrelated to the group life of the legislature, the influence of office is of sufficient importance to deserve separate and extended treatment.

Elsewhere we have had something to say about the positions or statuses that an individual occupies in his society and about norms of perception and behavior that he derives from his experiences in the society. These concepts were treated as determinants of the ways in which an individual knows, interprets, and behaves in his society. Looking more closely at these statuses, we can conceive of a whole society as a system of interrelated positions that people occupy, each individual normally filling a great many. For each recognized status in a society there are norms that prescribe more or less definitely how the occupant is to behave toward persons in related statuses. These prescribed ways of behaving are known as roles. Thus a woman who occupies the status of mother in a given society performs a certain role, that is, she behaves as a mother in prescribed ways toward her children, her husband, her children's grandparents, teachers, friends, and others in related positions.[49]

Public office, including that of a legislator, is such a status. It hardly should be necessary to make this point were it not that its implications are so easily overlooked. When a man enters a legislative position he takes on a new role that is prescribed for him by the society. His success as a legislator depends in large part upon how well he performs that role.

Some parts of the public official's role he has been learning since early childhood, for any youngster early though dimly begins to pick up what it "means" to be a government officer. As he has matured, his understanding of the behavior prescribed for a legislator has been sharpened. He has learned to engage in some of these behaviors in other positions that he has occupied, particularly if he has consciously aspired to be a member of the legislative body. Some requirements he has learned in the course of election campaigns. Others, those toward his colleagues in the legislature, he is likely not to learn until after he has become a member of that body, as the preceding section suggested.

The norms that define a role do not specify all the things that the occupant of a particular status shall do. They require some behaviors and forbid certain others; still others are a matter of the officeholder's discretion; that is, they are permitted under appropriate conditions but are not essential. These required and forbidden behaviors, it is important to bear in mind, are defined by norms that are socially determined; one might call them the standardized expectations of those who are aware of the particular status. Some of these behaviors are, of course, specified in legal enactments, such as corrupt practices legislation and the constitutional right of petition.

As the existence of these formal, legal definitions suggests, these behavioral norms are not neutral. Whether or not they are embodied in statutes and constitutions, they are activities about which many people in the society feel very strongly; that is, these norms are associated with values the violation of which will cause disturbances of varying degrees of seriousness and will be punished in various ways—by impeachment, imprisonment, execution, ridicule, defeat at the polls, insult, lynching, and so on.

Not all behavioral norms are unambiguous. The legislator does not always "know what is expected of him" in a given situation, because in his constituency, unless it is remarkably homogeneous in every respect, various groups—organized and potential—will interpret his behavior in different ways. What is important to one segment may be irrelevant to another; what is bribery to one may be charity to another; some may be able to distinguish between "honest and dishonest graft," and others not; some may be sufficiently organized and cohesive to "remember" his actions for a long time, whereas others are not. Especially if the legislator aspires to move from a smaller to a larger and more heterogeneous constituency—from State legislator to governor, from Representative to United States Senator—what an existing constituency regards as a proper concern for one's supporters may appear to voters in the larger area as narrow parochialism. Hence is derived the importance of the forms and sources of knowledge that we discussed earlier in the chapter.

But many of the norms defining the legislator's role are relatively unambiguous, and these are the ones in which we are primarily interested here. These are included in what have been referred to as the "rules of the game." The legislator is expected to avoid open partiality to the contested claims of a small minority; he must at least appear to be solicitous for the vocal needs of his constituents, but he is expected in some measure to look beyond his constituency; he must defend the orderly procedures of political settlement; he must support the political and civil freedoms involved in a fair trial, in petition, in speech, press, and assembly. These, along with many others, not only define his role but represent the substance of prevailing values without which the political system could not exist. As Kluckhohn has said in a broader context: "A system of beliefs, profoundly felt, is unquestionably necessary to the survival of any society. . . ."[50]

It is, of course, obvious that the "rules of the game" are not invariably adhered to, that they are not accepted universally or with unvarying vigor in all parts of the society at all times. But it does not follow that they are not powerful. The protests of those who denounce "the government" for lapses and deviations, in fact, testify to the power of "the rules." The ability of a small group, speaking in defense of such values, to exercise influence out of all proportion to the size of its paid-up membership has the same significance. These norms, values, expectations, "rules of the game"—call them what you will—largely define the institution of government along with other institutions of the society. For the legislator they set the approximate limits within which his discretionary behavior may take place. Accounting for the observation that "legislation will, on the whole, be more equitable than the legislators are themselves as private individuals," Myrdal puts his finger on this connection between norms and institutions in what we call democracy: "In their institutions they have invested more than their everyday ideas which parallel their actual behavior. They have placed in them their ideals of how the world rightly ought to be. The ideals thereby gain fortifications of power and influence in society."[51] When an individual achieves a widely recognized status such as legislative or other public office, these norms are usually brought to a sharp focus in the rites of oath-taking and investiture. Such ceremonies and rituals serve notice upon the individual and those about him that he has entered upon a new role with new rights and obligations. The norms are reaffirmed and intensified by a variety of devices and situations, including his continued participation in the legislative group. Honorific modes of address, public ceremonies, parliamentary ritual, and imposing public buildings have the function, among others, not only of reaffirming the loyalties of the governed, but also of strengthening and redefining the roles of the governors.[52]

The standards expected of those holding public office, the role of legislator, thus have an important influence upon the relative ease with which political interest groups gain access to points of decision. It does not follow that in every decision he makes the legislator is consciously aware of norms defining his role. It is entirely reasonable to assume, in fact, that the widely recognized norms are given little explicit consideration in daily policy decisions. These decisions constitute the discretionary segment of the legislator's role, and this discretion may be very wide. The existence of the required and the forbidden aspects of the role, however, means that those groups representing the expected or disapproved behaviors will be privileged or disadvantaged, respectively, in the matter of access. Occasional disregard of individual rights, for example, may have little effect upon the legislator's position. Flagrant and continued neglect, however, will provoke demands in the name of the abused norms, demands that are likely to gain privileged access. In the great majority of instances the successful legislator has so learned his role that groups whose demands clearly require the forbidden behaviors will get a cold reception. It is within these limits that the competing demands of political interest groups are given a hearing.

Conclusions. The degree of access to the legislature that a particular group enjoys at a given moment is the result of a composite of influences. These determining factors will include the peculiarities of formal governmental structure and of the political party as a legislative instrument, such informal influences as the knowledge-supplying functions of the group and the character of the legislator's group affiliations, the formal and informal structure of the legislative body, and the influence of the standardized expectations in the community concerning the behavior of a legislator. Depending on the circumstances and the relative importance of these factors in a given situation, some groups will enjoy comparatively effective access, and others will find difficulty in securing even perfunctory treatment. As conditions change, as some of these influences become more and others less potent, the fortunes of group claims upon the legislature will rise or decline.

The most important implication of this multiple-factor conception of the dynamics of access is that the legislature is not just a sounding board or passive registering device for the demands of organized political interest groups. The legislature as a part of the institution of government embodies, albeit incompletely, the expectations, understandings, and values prevailing in the society concerning how the government should operate. These expectations may cover now a wide and now a relatively narrow range of behavior; they may be fairly explicit or highly ambiguous. Although the legislator's role is in part defined by limited expectations and norms prevailing in his constituency and in the interest groups with which he identifies himself, it is also the creation of the norms more widely recognized in the society. Partly because his role as a legislator inevitably gives him a specialized kind of experience from which he learns the limits of his behavior, partly because he has learned some of these norms as a member of the society, he cannot behave simply and completely as a vehicle for organized group demands.

It does not follow from the argument in this chapter that the widespread expectations about the legislature alone account for differences in ease of access or for all features of the legislative product. It is easy enough to identify cases in which the standardized expectations are ignored. The norms of official behavior inevitably partake of the quality of myth, of professed values. On the other hand, they are also operating values that affect all legislative behavior in some measure and that place limits upon both the methods and the content of group demands upon the legislature. In a stable political system the competing demands of organized interest groups are meaningless unless they are viewed in the context of these limiting and defining norms.[53]

A second implication of this conception of the dynamics of access is that "pressure," conceived as bribery or coercion in various forms, is scarcely the distinguishing feature of interest groups in the legislative process. Such coercion is frequently attempted, of course, and it often has an observable effect. "Pressure" of group upon legislator, however, is at most one aspect of technique, one among many different kinds of relationships that exist within the lawmaking body. As indicated by the evidence we have examined, the belief that the relationship between groups and legislators is a one-way, coercive relationship simply does not explain the observed behaviors. The institution of government is not so passive and cannot be understood in such oversimplified terms.

Notes

1. Lochner v. New York, 198 U. S. 45 (1905).
2. Cf. Pendleton Herring: "The Politics of Fiscal Policy," *Yale Law Journal,* Vol. 47, no. 5 (March, 1938), pp. 724-45.
3. Cf. McKean: *Pressures on the Legislature of New Jersey,* chap. 2 and p. 112; C. E. Merriam, S. D. Parratt, and A. Lepawsky: *The Government of the Metropolitan Region of Chicago* (Chicago: University of Chicago Press, 1933), chap. 28.
4. Paul v. Virginia, 8 Wallace 168 (1869). See Edward B. Logan: "Lobbying," supplement to the *Annals,* Vol. 144 (July, 1929), p. 6. U.S. v. South-Eastern Underwriters Association, 322 U.S. 533 (1944).
5. See U. S. Federal Trade Commission: *Report on Resale Price Maintenance* (Washington, D.C.: Government Printing Office, 1945), pp. 62, 145-6, 149.
6. Pendleton Herring: *Presidential Leadership* (New York: Farrar & Rinehart, 1940), p. 27. Copyright by Pendleton Herring and used with the permission of Rinehart & Company, Inc.
7. U.S. House of Representatives, Committee on Agriculture: *Hearings on Repeal of the Oleomargarine Tax,* 80th Cong., 2d Sess. (1948), p. 36.
8. Kile: *The Farm Bureau Through Three Decades,* p. 146.
9. U.S. Senate, Committee on Interstate Commerce: *Senate Report No. 26,* 77th Cong., 1st Sess. (1941), part 2, pp. 51-3. Cf. Danielian: *A. T. & T.: The Story of Industrial Conquest,* pp. 321-5.
10. Kile: *The Farm Bureau Through Three Decades,* pp. 381-2. Copyright 1948 by and used with the permission of Orville M. Kile.
11. U. S. Federal Trade Commission: *Report on Resale Price Maintenance,* pp. 64-6.
12. Cf. E. E. Schattschneider: *The Struggle for Party Government* (College Park, Md.: University of Maryland, 1948), pp. 28-9.
13. Cf. Logan: "Lobbying," p. 5.
14. U.S. Temporary National Economic Committee: *Hearings,* part 10, pp. 4380 and 4758.
15. Cf. McKean: *Pressures on the Legislature of New Jersey,* chap. 2; Warren Moscow: *Politics in the Empire State* (New York: Alfred A. Knopf, Inc., 1948), *passim.*
16. E. E. Schattschneider: *Politics, Pressures and the Tariff,* p. 13. Copyright 1935 by Prentice-Hall, Inc.
17. Cf. Floyd M. Riddick: *The United States Congress: Organization and Procedure* (Manassas, Va.: National Capitol Publishers, Inc., 1949), chap. 6.
18. *Congressional Record,* 81st Cong., 1st Sess., January 3, 1949, pp. 10-11, A. 3-4, A. 6, A. 7 (daily edition).

19. Woodrow Wilson: *Congressional Government* (Boston: Houghton Mifflin Company, 1885), p. 56 and *passim*.

20. Cf. Riddick: *The United States Congress*, pp. 3, 153; Herring: *Group Representation Before Congress*, pp. 250-1; Paul D. Hasbrouck: *Party Government in the House of Representatives* (New York: The Macmillan Company, 1927), pp. 74-5.

21. Cf. McKean: *Pressures on the Legislature of New Jersey*, pp. 47-9.

22. C. I. Winslow: *State Legislative Committees: A Study in Procedure* (Baltimore: The Johns Hopkins Press, 1931), pp. 7, 112 ff., 139.

23. *Ibid.*, pp. 118-21, 137. Cf. Robert Luce: *Legislative Procedure* (Boston: Houghton Mifflin Company, 1922), pp. 493-4.

24. Joseph P. Chamberlain: *Legislative Processes, National and State* (New York: D. Appleton-Century Company, 1936), p. 90.

25. See Newcomb: *Social Psychology*, chap. 10 and *passim*.

26. Keynes: *The General Theory*, pp. 149 ff.

27. Cf. V. O. Key, Jr.: "The Veterans and the House of Representatives," *Journal of Politics*, Vol. 5, no. 1 (February, 1943), pp. 39-40.

28. McKean: *Pressures on the Legislature of New Jersey*, pp. 203-5.

29. Dewey: *The Public and Its Problems*, p. 76. Copyright 1927 by and used with the permission of Henry Holt & Company, Inc.

30. *Senate Report 43*, 72d Cong., 1st Sess., *Congressional Record*, December 20, 1929, p. 994.

31. Cf. Gray: *The Inside Story of the Legion*, p. 99. Paul Studenski: "Chambers of Commerce," *Encyclopaedia of the Social Sciences*.

32. E. Pendleton Herring: "Farm Bloc," *Encyclopaedia of the Social Sciences*, and *Group Representation Before Congress*, pp. 122-4; Kile: *The Farm Bureau Movement*, pp. 188 ff. Not infrequently men have entered the legislature after serving as officials of interest groups. Before he was Governor and Senator, Styles Bridges was the paid secretary of the New Hampshire Farm Bureau Federation (Kile: *The Farm Bureau Through Three Decades*, p. 386).

33. The *New York Times*, April 10, 1949. See U.S. Commission on Organization of the Executive Branch of the Government: *Task Force Report on Natural Resources* (Washington, D.C.: Government Printing Office, 1949), esp. pp. 79-88, 98-9, 149-82; Robert de Roos and Arthur Maass: "The Lobby That Can't Be Licked," *Harper's Magazine* (August, 1949), pp. 21-30. The hearings on the M. V. A. are effectively discussed in James M. Burns: *Congress on Trial* (New York: Harper and Brothers, 1949), pp. 94-7.

34. U. S. Federal Trade Commission: *Report on Resale Price Maintenance*, pp. 52 ff.

35. Cf. Herring: *Group Representation Before Congress*, p. 222. Veterans of Foreign Wars, 35th National Encampment: *Proceedings,* House Document 45, 74th Cong., 1st Sess. (1935); U. S. Senate, Finance Committee: *Hearings on Payment of Adjusted Compensation Certificates*, 74th Cong., 1st Sess. (1935).

36. *Senate Report 43*, part 1, 71st Cong., 1st Sess., *Congressional Record*, October 26, 1929, p. 4922.

37. Bailey: *Congress Makes a Law*, p. 192. Copyright 1950 by and used with the permission of Columbia University Press. See also pp. 148-9, 182.

38. Herring: *Group Representation Before Congress*, p. 40.

39. Cf. Lazarsfeld *et al.*: *The People's Choice*, chap. 16, esp. pp. 153-5.

40. McKean found that the "social lobby" was almost nonexistent in New Jersey because most legislators commute to the capital from their homes (*Pressures on the Legislatures of New Jersey*, p. 192).

41. U.S. Temporary National Economic Committee: *Hearings*, part 10, p. 4770.

42. Reported in Logan: "Lobbying," p. 53.

43. Henry Parkman, Jr.: "Lobbies and Pressure Groups: A Legislator's Point of View," *The Annals*, Vol. 195 (January, 1938), p. 97. Copyright 1938 by and used with the permission of The American Academy of Political and Social Science.

44. Bailey: *Congress Makes a Law*, chaps. 3, 5, 7, and *passim*. For some good examples of this see Burns: *Congress on Trial*, pp. 19-23.

45. Garland C. Routt: "Interpersonal Relationships and the Legislative Process," *Annals*, Vol. 195 (January, 1938), p. 130. A unique study, this article reports on a systematic observation of the Illinois Senate. Cf. Harold F. Gosnell: *Democracy: The Threshold of Freedom* (New York: The Ronald Press, 1948), p. 233; Luce: *Legislative Assemblies*, chaps. 14, 18, 24, and *passim*.

46. Gosnell: *Democracy*, p. 234.

47. Cf. Riddick: *The United States Congress*, pp. 89, 102; and Routt: "Interpersonal Relationships and the Legislative Process," p. 131.

48. Wilson: *Congressional Government*, preface to the 15th edition, p. ix.

49. For a thorough discussion of this point see Newcomb: *Social Psychology*, chap. 8 and *passim*. The material in this section relies heavily on this source.

50. Kluckhohn: *Mirror for Man*, p. 248.

51. Myrdal: *An American Dilemma*, p. 80. Copyright 1944 by and used with the permission of Harper and Brothers.

52. See Charles E. Merriam: *The Making of Citizens* (Chicago: University of Chicago Press, 1931).

53. This is one of the central points in Bentley's argument (cf. *The Process of Government*, pp. 361 and 372), although it is frequently overlooked. MacIver, for example, claims: "To Bentley . . . a legislative act is always the calculable resultant of a struggle between pressure groups, never a decision between opposing conceptions of the national welfare." (*The Web of Government*, p. 220. Copyright 1947 by Robert M. MacIver and used with the permission of The Macmillan Company.) This appears to be an inaccurate and unfair statement of the Bentley position.

5. PRESSURE GROUPS AND PARTIES IN BRITAIN*

Samuel H. Beer

WHEN AN AMERICAN looks at British politics, one of his first questions is likely to be, "Where are your pressure groups?" Since the subject has hardly been studied and most works on British government largely ignore it,[1] he may feel some surprise when he finds that, even if compared with American examples, pressure groups in Britain are numerous, massive, well-organized, and highly effective. In this article I wish in the first place simply to sketch the pattern of pressure group activity in Britain and to illustrate the influence of pressure politics on the policy of British governments in recent years. This cannot be done, however, if the analysis is confined to pressure groups alone. For their aims, methods, and effectiveness are profoundly affected by the context within which they act. We all recognize, for instance, the differences from the American pattern of pressure politics which result from the discipline of British parties and the centralized power of cabinet government. In addition to these elements of structure, I wish to stress the cultural context within which British parties and pressure groups act and which, standing in sharp contrast with that of the American political system, accounts for many of the differences of political behavior between the two countries.

This cultural context of politics, comprising a complex structure of values and ideologies, cannot be explained away, it hardly need be said, in terms of economic development. We distort the facts if we suppose that new values and ideologies arise only as reflections of new patterns of behavior resulting from objective economic development. On the contrary, political values and ideologies profoundly condition the aspirations which may emerge from economic development, determining in no small degree how people group themselves, what they demand as groups, and how they demand it. The culture of a society may provide foci around which political conflict tends to crystallize—for example, the sense of social class in Britain. It may also—and this is particularly important if we are to understand the present convergence of party policies in Britain—provide a consensus on basic social and political values which endures through sharp conflicts of class and party and which may provide the means for their resolution.

Nor should we stress exclusively the merely limiting and "boundary-maintaining" functions of culture. Beyond its function of conditioning those aspirations which emerge from objective development of the economy or of other aspects of the society, the cultural context also has a certain capacity for itself initiating social and political change.[2] In certain respects and at certain times, the culture of a society develops autonomously, producing new forms which are neither a reflection of, nor even a response to, changes in other parts of the social system, but which have arisen spontaneously from the existing culture. In such autonomous cultural developments we may sometimes be obliged to seek the ultimate origins of great revolutions in public policy and of the mutations of the aims and methods of pressure groups.

Without embarking on so difficult an inquiry into social dynamics, however, we can observe the interplay between the cultural context and certain familiar mechanisms of the political system, such as the competition for votes in a two-party system. In this interaction we shall find important clues to understanding the development not only of public policy, but also of the pattern of pressure politics in Britain. The analysis is bound to be complicated. On the one hand, pressure groups have their role—a most important one—in the development of policy. Yet at the same time we cannot understand them unless we also look at the changing context of culture and political structure with which they continually interact.

What is the bearing of these conclusions on the group theory of politics? This depends on what you take that theory to mean. If it means that the political scientist concerned with the origins and formation of policy may confine himself largely

Reprinted from *American Political Science Review*, Vol. 50 (1956), pp. 1-23, by permission of the author and the publisher.

* This article is based on a paper given at the Conference on the Comparative Method in the Study of Politics held under the auspices of the Social Science Research Council at Princeton, N. J., June 2-4, 1955.

or solely to the study of interest groups, then the group theory is not a satisfactory conceptual framework for the study of British politics, or, I should add, American politics. The principal failing of such an approach is that by concentrating on groups and their diverse interests, it fails to direct analysis to the cultural context within which interests emerge and act. In the study of American and British politics, such neglect means passing over important elements of consensus which are shared throughout the political system and which involve not only "rules of the game," but also positive social and political values. Such ideal factors of integration, precisely because they are widely diffused throughout a system, may not strike the eye as sharply as do the differences of contending groups, yet they are indispensable to stable and effective government. Furthermore, not only are forces of integration neglected, but also the function of parties and of the party system may be seriously distorted by concentrating analysis on interest groups. The tendency will be to stress the sense in which a political party is a coalition of interest groups and a mechanism for winning elections, but to neglect the sense in which it may be the bearer of values and ideology and an instrument in their development. Such functions, as we shall see, have been performed by parties and the party system in Britain in the prolonged and complicated process by which the present general acceptance of the welfare state and the controlled economy has emerged.

I. Types of Interest Representation in Britain. If we had some way of measuring political power, we could quite possibly demonstrate that at the present time pressure groups are more powerful in Britain than in the United States. That at any rate is the impression of the present writer after making some preliminary inquiries in this largely uncharted field. Looking at the process of policy-making of the recent Churchill Government, for example, one finds hardly a field of domestic policy in which the effects of organized pressure are not profoundly marked. This is true, for instance, of policy toward agriculture, labor, veterans' pensions, old age pensions, teachers' salaries, equal pay for women, commercial television, and—to bring in an important "sectional" interest—the Lancashire textile industry. Nor have the demands of groups been reflected only in the policy of the Government and the party in power. The Opposition—whether Labor or Conservative—also has been affected and the competition between parties for the votes of the same group is often so intense as to modify profoundly what one might regard as "conservative" or "socialist" principles.

The old age pensioners, for instance, are a large and growing group, whose members, although not as effectively organized as they might be, are nevertheless sharply aware of their interest, of which the competition between the parties continually serves to remind them. If the Tories were to follow what they call their "net and ladder" principle of social policy[3]—i.e., aid for those most in need, the opportunity to rise for the others—they might well prefer to put additional funds into an increase in public assistance, rather than spread them among various types of benefits, some of which are inevitably paid out to persons not greatly in need.[4] They have chosen, however, to meet Labor's promise to restore all benefits to the level of purchasing power which they had in 1948,[5] proposing indeed to make good the rise in prices since 1946.[6] In 1954, as an election year drew near, both party conferences put the raising of old age pensions in the forefront "and," tartly commented the *Manchester Guardian,* "on the domestic side, not much else besides." Opportunely, the Government's increases came into effect only a short time before the General Election of 1955.[7]

At the present time, British parties avoid pitched battles of opposing social philosophies and carry on the political fight through small raids, designed to capture votes from particular interest groups. In general, this tactic, which makes party programs and government policy vulnerable to pressure from organized groups, resembles the present pattern of pressure politics in the United States. And in the past, as in the present, one finds similarities as well as striking differences in the ways in which interests have brought influence to bear on government in the two political systems.

In British history, pressure groups go back at least to the 18th century—witness the various organizations which agitated for parliamentary reform from the 1760's to the 1790's—and the great period of reform in the first half of the 19th century provides many examples of highly effective pressure politics. There was the National Political Union of Francis Place, who, in Bernard Shaw's words, founded "the science of putting pressure on Parliament from outside," Wilberforce's Anti-Slavery Society, Thomas Attwood's political unions, O'Connell's Catholic Association, and that model of successful pressure groups, the Anti-Corn Law League. Yet in Britain as in the United States such organizations, founded primarily for the purpose of putting pressure on government and usually concerned with only a single piece of legislation, need to be distinguished from another type of organization which in both countries in recent generations has become far more important and effective. The latter is best represented by the organizations of the great interest groups of the modern economy—for example, trade unions, trade associations, farmers' groups, and professional associations—although their methods and form of organization may be adopted by other groups, such as war veterans. These organizations commonly have a large dues-paying membership and a considerable private bureaucracy. More important, they normally have other functions than their political ones—for instance, the internal regulation of their members or constituent organizations—and their concern with government policy does not come to an end with the passage of some particular act, but continues and indeed may be heightened as policies favorable to them are adopted. In spite of the earlier development of industrial capitalism in Britain, organizations of this type seem to have come into existence in about the same period in both Britain and the United States, beginning in the latter part of the 19th century.[8] Once the pattern of the permanent bureaucratic organization did emerge in Britain, however, it developed farther than in the United States, British organizations of this type today showing a greater degree of concentration and including a far larger fraction of their potential members.[9]

Pressure groups, whether of the special purpose or the permanent bureaucratic type, have flourished in both Britain and the United States. Going back far into British history, but rarely found in the United States, is another device by which interests have been linked with the political process. This is the M.P. who "represents" a particular interest in the legislature, not covertly or illicitly, but openly and with general acceptance. For in spite of Burke's speech to the electors of Bristol, British custom has always been far more tolerant than American of the legislator who is intimately connected with outside interests. One may doubt that the subsidy for political expenses which Richard Nixon received from his well-to-do supporters would cause much excitement in Britain where not only the M.P.s. sponsored by trade unions but also quite a few others receive help from interested organizations in the form of contributions to election expenses and even to personal income.[10]

The history of the "interested" M.P. has yet to be written. The nature of his connection has ranged through many variations: from sponsorship, which involved subsidies to election expenses or personal income, through office-holding in an association with interests in government policy, to the perhaps less restricting ties of ownership of property and membership in a profession or trade. Under the aristocratic constitution, theory, as well as practice, permitted, indeed institutionalized, such functional representation.[11] Although in the Victorian reaction against placemen and patronage a high valuation was put on the financial independence of M.P.s,[12] they continued to be connected with interests by such ties as property-owning and to act as spokesmen for them in the House.[13] The scores of M.P.s who were railway directors are the best-known examples. Not many degrees removed from this type of connection was the practice of sponsorship, which developed in the latter part of the 19th century. Candidates and M.P.s. subsidized by trade unions became the most numerous of this class. But there were also other examples. For instance, the National Union of Teachers from shortly after its foundation in 1870 has sought out candidates from all major parties who have been willing to advocate its views in the House and who in turn have received a subsidy for election expenses from the organization. Perhaps in recent years the House has become less tolerant of such ties.[14] But there remain many M.P.s who are acknowledged to be spokesmen for outside interest groups and many who receive contributions to election expenses and personal income from non-party organizations. Along with M.P.s who have interests arising from directorships, investments, and the like, the House includes, as Sir Winston Churchill has said, "those people who come to represent particular bodies, particular groups of a nonpolitical character." "We are not supposed to be an assembly of gentlemen who have no interests of any kind and no associations of any kind," he continued. "That is ridiculous. That might happen in Heaven, but not, happily, here."[15]

II. Quasi-corporatism and the Structure of the Welfare State. The M.P. who acts as the acknowledged spokesman for an interest in Parliament has been very important in the past. But although he will still be found today, he has greatly declined in importance as a means of interest representation in comparison with that more modern figure, the private bureaucrat of the permanent, large-scale pressure group. Indeed, when we compare the pattern of interest representation of the Victorian period with that of today, the most significant change is the shift of power from the older to the newer type, from the "interested" M.P. to the private bureaucrat. Yet even in the new pattern there are elements of continuity with the old. In contrast with American theory and practice, the "interested" M.P. was a more "legitimate," a more closely integrated part of the representative system. Similarly, today the massive pressure groups of Britain are, in comparison with the

American pattern, far more intimately linked with the apparatus of government, especially of government administration.

During the war this association was even closer than at present, many trade associations being at least in part virtually embodied in the administration.[16] In spite of the relaxation of control since the war, there remains a system of "quasi-corporatism" which leaves no important organized group without a channel of influence and a real share in the making of decisions. The main substance of this system is continual, day-to-day contacts between public bureaucrats in the government departments and private bureaucrats in the offices of the great pressure groups—the Farmers' Union, the British Legion, the National Union of Teachers, the Federation of British Industries, the British Medical Association, and countless trade unions and trade associations. A great deal can be done at the "civil service" level, especially in view of the opportunities for discretion which must be left to civil servants by the vast network of rules and orders under which Britain's welfare state is run.[17] As an official of one organization put it, "Very much can be done which is in effect policy-making—what you try to do is to create an opinion among officials which is favorable to stretching the regulations."

Sometimes this connection is formalized by the inclusion of representatives of the pressure group in government committees. The Federation of British Industries, for instance, has representatives on some 70 government committees and similar bodies; the Trades Union Congress has representatives on 60 government committees. The old practice of a formal deputation to a minister is also still used, the classic example being the bodies of dignitaries and officials from various pressure groups which call upon the Chancellor of the Exchequer or Financial Secretary in the early months of the year to present their views on what ought to be done in the Budget.

The formal deputation is less important than it once was, but meetings with ministers are, of course, indispensable for major action. (Even then, as one pressure group official pointed out, you are likely to be successful only if you have prepared the way by winning over the permanent secretary of the department and other key officials.) The annual determination of the prices for agricultural products which will be guaranteed by the government provides such occasions.[18] In these prolonged negotiations, on which depend the expenditure of hundreds of millions of pounds, civil servants from the Ministry of Agriculture and certain other departments deal with experts from the National Farmers' Union. The delegation from the N.F.U. will be led by its president, Sir James Turner, who, probably attended by other higher officials of the Union, at critical points will carry the negotiations up to the Minister of Agriculture. At this level, not only the technical arguments—of which Sir James happens to be a master—will be deployed, but also suggestions of electoral retaliation and, so it is said, hints of the withdrawal of farmers' cooperation from certain administrative tasks in which their help is virtually indispensable, in particular the county agricultural committees. Since money is involved, the Chancellor of the Exchequer will at some time be brought in, on which occasion it will make a difference to the outcome if he believes—as a recent Chancellor is reported to have said—that "the farmers are the swing vote."

Confrontations of ministers, however, normally develop out of the immense mass of daily informal contacts at the civil service level. Again and again officials of pressure groups will mention that they continually ring up their "opposite members" in the departments and discuss a problem with them on a first name basis—an informality of contact often made easier by the fact that the private bureaucrat worked with the public bureaucrat in the same ministry during the war. Nor is the initiative confined to the pressure groups. For instance, quite commonly when the Ministry of Education has to draw up a new regulation (which may or may not have ultimately to be submitted to Parliament), it will send its draft of the regulation to the headquarters of the National Union of Teachers to get their comments and criticism. It is understandable that the Union finds it hardly worthwhile any longer to send a formal deputation to the minister, although not many years ago, before it had won its present "recognition," it fought strenuously for the right to such audiences.

A recent summary of certain aspects of the work of the Federation of British Industries by its Director-General in its general outlines also applies to many other pressure groups:

> There are . . . many consultative committees consisting of official and industrial representatives; and almost every day the F.B.I. is approached by one or another Government Department for advice. But consultation is not really effective unless it takes place before rather than after the event. On the Government side, the process may be a nuisance, but it generally saves a lot of trouble in the long run. So we are constantly impressing on Government Departments the need for them to consult and to consult early. . . .
> Of course the great bulk of the work of Government is administration, not policy; and most of what I have called the F.B.I.'s policy work lies in the

field of administration. Let me put it another way. Parliament may decide upon a line of policy. . . . Industry may or may not like the policy; and the F.B.I. will say so on its behalf. But when the issue is decided, it may make a world of difference to industry how the policy is implemented and translated through administration into action.[19]

In the representation of interests, the M.P.'s role has declined, but not disappeared. How old and new methods may be combined is illustrated by the successful campaign by the National Union of Teachers in 1954 to defeat the proposed increase in teachers' contributions to their superannuation fund. Having won a modest victory when the Minister of Education accepted the recommendations for an increase in teachers' salaries presented by an advisory committee—on which the Union has a majority of the teachers' representatives—the Union set out to defeat the Minister's announced intention of raising the superannuation contributions.[20] Possibly, as the Union said, the proposed increase had not been discussed at the committee level, although it hardly seems likely that the teachers' representatives did not know about it. At any rate, being unable to win its point in dealings with the Ministry, the Union turned to more public methods. With 20 M.P.s as members—four of them "sponsored" candidates—the N.U.T. had a fair basis in Parliament to work from. Although all but one of these were on the Labor side, in this instance the Union picked up considerable support from Conservatives, led by a forceful and frequent rebel, Sir Robert Boothby. Within a week or so of the introduction into the House of the bill to raise contributions, branches of the N.U.T. were sending protests to the M.P.s from their constituencies. Within the House of Commons and within the parliamentary parties—the education committees in each party being used—protests were made by M.P.s. Early in February the parliamentary Labor party officially took a stand in opposition to the bill. Later that month the second reading was postponed and after at least two cabinet meetings at which the question was discussed it was put off until autumn. In October the Minister of Education was obliged to resign, and shortly afterwards the new Minister announced the withdrawal of the bill.[21]

Contrasts of this system of "quasi-corporatism" with the relations of pressure groups and government in the United States, if not sharp, are at least suggestive. For obvious reasons, the individual legislator, and the legislature generally, under cabinet government occupy a less important position. While "rebel" groups and party committees from time to time have influence, there are, for instance, no organs, formal or informal, comparable in power with our legislative committees. Not only do interest groups enjoy a greater degree of concentration, but the government with which they deal also is more highly centralized than ours: greater power to exert pressure is linked up with greater power to act. Whether that power to act will be used or not will depend on various factors with which we shall be concerned later on. Usually—this is the point to stress—if you can bring over the Minister and the Chancellor of the Exchequer you have not much else to worry about. Compare the position of the American pressure group which, if it wants positive action, must win its battle at many different points—committees in both houses, the presidency, the secretary, the bureau chief. It is no wonder that our pressure politics is so much noisier and less tidy than Britain's.

The pattern of pressure group relations with the administration, however, in broad outline is not unfamiliar to an American. There is perhaps better articulation in Britain resulting from the fact that normally only one rather than several major pressure groups represents each interest and that more effective contact with the members of the interest group results from its usually including a larger fraction of its potential membership. Perhaps also relations are to a greater degree formalized and institutionalized in Britain than in the United States, although, of course, our national government is clustered with advisory committees and many pressure groups have continual relations with departments and bureaus.

For many British pressure groups there is a striking contrast in their present relations with departments as compared with their relations in the not too distant past. For these groups—the trade unions are the outstanding example—there was a long period of struggle for "political" recognition. Today not only are trade unions brought into frequent and earnest consultation through such means as the important National Joint Advisory Council to the Minister of Labor, but also no matter what government is in power there is always "access," the doors are open. Replying to the traditional vote of thanks to members of the press at the conclusion of the 1945 T.U.C., the correspondent for the *Times* said:

You have no longer any need to thunder; you have only to whisper and Ministers tremble and Field-Marshals bend their knees. How very far away are those days when a few top-hatted, frock-coated gentlemen made a promenade of the Government offices in Whitehall respectfully carrying resolutions passed by Congress, leaving them at the door, extremely happy if they saw a permanent secretary, and most handsomely flattered if by accident they stumbled across a Minister.[22]

A further principal difference from the American pattern is obvious: it is that the amount of "business" transacted between pressure groups and departments is larger and more important. This results not only from the differences between a unitary and a federal system—compare the importance of educational policy at Westminster and in Washington—but also from the fact that Britain has a welfare state and a controlled economy. Perhaps there was a time when most pressure groups wanted government to stop doing things. But today in Britain as in the United States nearly all want—apart from tax matters—positive action: subsidies, benefit payments, services, favorable regulation such as tariffs.[23] The more positive the state, the larger the amount of business transacted between government and pressure groups is likely to be. Quite naturally, it has been the programs of the welfare state and of the controlled economy around which pressure activity has tended to cluster, giving rise to the system of "quasi-corporatism."

The structure of centralized parties and cabinet government is part of the framework within which British pressure groups operate. Such structures will tend to concentrate pressure on the ministerial level, but they do not determine whether the means of exerting that pressure shall be the M.P. or the private bureaucrat. This depends upon other factors, principally the rise of permanent, bureaucratic pressure organizations, a development which itself may be connected with not only the extension of the franchise, but also the decline of the governing class. As many English observers hasten to point out, what has happened in this regard is that old elites have simply been supplanted by new ones. In the previous social situation, interests could express themselves through traditional channels with little or no need for organization. Social class, the country house, the "Old Boy network" sufficed as channels of influence.[24] From that day the members of the House of Commons have not declined in virtue or ability. What they clearly have in lesser degree is the social prestige of the members of Victorian or Edwardian days. On the other hand, the new elites, if they do not enjoy the "deference" accorded the old, nevertheless have effective authority in relation to their organizations and clienteles—a striking example was the remarkable power of trade union leaders to restrain their members from making wage demands during the austerity drive from 1948 to 1950.

Whatever the reasons for the rise of such pressure organizations, they have been drawn to and ever more closely linked up with the bureaucracy by the expansion of the scope of policy and the delegation of power to ministers and, in effect, to civil servants which has been consequent upon that expansion. In addition to the party and constitutional structures, the structure of the welfare state and controlled economy also constitutes part of the framework within which pressure groups operate.

III. Convergence of Party Policy: Effect on Pressure Groups and Parties. A more diffuse, but no less important element of context is suggested by the acceptance by both major parties of the welfare state code and certain basic economic controls. On this topic we need first to say something to substantiate it; then we can examine some of its effects before turning to the most interesting problem of how to explain the reasons for it.

The substance of the first point is that the Tories have moved over to an acceptance of the welfare state as developed by Labor after the war, while Labor has very largely receded from its old doctrinaire position on nationalization and economic planning.[25] Recent Tory budgets from 1951 to 1955 continued the steady increase in the amounts spent on the social services, housing, and education, and retained the heavy taxation of the well-to-do by which Labor financed the welfare state. With regard to economic controls, both parties accept certain basic forms, viz., those necessary to maintain full employment, protect the balance of payments, and encourage productivity. As a result, while significant differences remain, British parties today are in closer agreement on "fundamentals" than they have been for many years.

What are the effects on the activity of pressure groups? One is that they are not obliged to defend the basic legislation or policy on which depend the benefits they receive. Any government, they can be sure, will follow the same favorable policy toward them and their clientele. Also, to a very great extent pressure groups themselves demand no further major changes in policy or legislation. There is, for instance, no thorny question between government and labor such as that presented by the Taft-Hartley Act. And indeed when the trade unions want a piece of legislation, such as the night baking or pneumoconiosis acts of 1954, they need hardly do more than suggest their desires to the government and action is taken. Even when there is a change of policy, as has occurred in the sphere of agriculture under the Tory Government, the basic pledges of the Act of 1947 of "guaranteed prices and assured markets" are upheld. Given this agreement on the basic code, the activity of each pressure group is mainly a matter of getting "more." Corresponding to this tactic of the pressure group is the tactic of the parties, which, as has been mentioned before, is essentially one of attempting to win marginal segments of voters by concessions of "more."

On the side of party tactics, then, we often see the parties making advances to groups toward which they have been unsympathetic or even hostile in the past. This may involve something like a "reversal of alliances," as leaders, taking for granted the votes of traditional supporters, sacrifice or skimp the interests of these for the sake of winning votes normally attached to the other party. More than a trace of this appears in the Conservative policy toward trade unions, as is suggested by complaints on the Tory right wing that for a Conservative Government they have been exceedingly free with employers' money in their attitude toward wage claims. But the relations of Labor with the farmers are an even better example. Here we have a capitalist class— indeed, if we follow Marx, the first of the capitalist classes to emerge in England—to whom, according to E. G. Gooch, the head of the agricultural workers' union, "Labour in office proved to be their best friend."[26]

Nor was Labor in Opposition ready to turn against the agrarian capitalist, as a parliamentary incident of the Fall of 1953 illustrates. Horticulture was left outside the guarantees of the Act of 1947 and the industry felt itself inadequately protected against foreign imports by the low duties carried over from prewar times and by the system of quotas imposed by the Ministry of Agriculture. In the administration of the quota system, there were the closest relations between the departments and the Central Horticultural Committee and other specialized committees of the Farmers' Union—which, for instance, closely associated the representatives of the producers of tomatoes with the ministry when the pattern of quotas was decided each year and enabled them in time of excessive imports to obtain a total embargo.[27] What was desired, however, was a system of higher duties, but this ran into GATT which prevented Britain from raising duties against foreign imports unless they were also raised against Commonwealth and Empire countries—the "no new preference rule." Asserting the unimportance of horticultural imports from the Commonwealth and Empire, some said there was no good reason for not raising the tariffs against them. But this was not the way that doughty imperialist L. S. Amery and his considerable faction in the party looked at the matter.[28] Hence, the President of the Board of Trade was obliged in the Fall of 1953 to go to Geneva

and get permission to raise these tariffs only against foreigners. Thereupon a Board of Trade order providing for increases upon 18 varieties of imported fruit and vegetables was laid before the House and put down for debate on December 10th.

What would Labor's position be? The main issue it was pressing at the time was the rising cost of living, as might have been expected from a party which found its main support among the less well-to-do urban consumers. On December 8th the Food and Agriculture Committee of the parliamentary party decided by a majority of one vote to oppose the increases. The resistance to this step was led by the chairman of the committee, the former Minister of Agriculture, Tom Williams, who said he would resign if the meeting of the parliamentary party as a whole did not reverse the decision. At that meeting the next day, Williams was strongly supported by E. G. Gooch and also by George Brown, former parliamentary secretary of the Ministry of Agriculture and a representative of the Transport workers, a union which also includes quite a few agricultural workers. The electoral angle was stressed by speakers who echoed Gooch's remark at the conference a couple of months before that "you cannot have a Labour Government again with overwhelming power until you win many rural seats."[29] With only 117 of 294 Labor M.P.s voting, the committee decision was reversed 81-36 and on December 10th in the House the order went through with support from both parties.

The next day the Manchester *Guardian* accused the Government of yielding to "pressure from the National Farmers' Union," deplored Labor's "hypocrisy," and generally lamented "the infinite squeezability of politicians." At the annual meeting of the N.F.U. a few weeks later, Mr. Gardener, chairman of the Central Horticultural Committee, took full credit on behalf of the Union for the change in policy.

The other side of this tendency of parties to "reverse alliances" is the greater independence of pressure groups in relation to parties. It is sometimes thought that a distinction between American and British pressure groups is that the American are more independent of party, while the British are more likely to be closely attached to or even embodied in a party. This distinction would accord with a division in the electorate running more along the lines of economic class. But just as the division of the electorate between the two major parties today in Britain in terms of economic class is not greatly different from that between American parties outside the South, so also are some major pressure groups probably as independent of party as the American and certainly more independent than was the case in Britain during the interwar period.

Some stray elements of big business prefer Labor—two directors of Unilever are socialists—and there are not a few very rich men sitting as Labor M.P.s. It remains, however, that business and its organizations must strongly favor the Conservatives, now as in the past. With the trade unions, there has been a change. Not only have they, like business, lost many of their previous terrors of the party of the opposite class, but they also have received solid benefits and friendly treatment from the Tory Government. The extraordinary ease with which the railway workers succeeded in getting what they wanted in 1953 and 1954 is a case in point. One should not overrate the importance of the man or the seriousness of his intent, but at the Labor conference of 1953, the then chairman of the General Council of the T.U.C. advocated in an interview that the trade unions should withdraw from the Labor party and the T.U.C. should divest itself of its present political activities. A principal advantage, he claimed, would be that thereby the T.U.C. would be less embarrassed in its dealing with a Tory Government and with industrialists.[30]

The most marked change, however, has occurred with regard to the farmers. Before World War II, the National Farmers' Union, then having only about half its present membership, was substantially a pressure group within the Tory party. According to Jennings, its support was extremely useful to Tory candidates in rural areas, while both Laborites and Liberals were very hostile to it.[31] Like the trade unions, it had a political fund which it used to sponsor candidates, invariably Tories. During and since the war, its membership has doubled; its expert staff has been greatly enlarged; it has acquired for the first time a full-time president, who has held office since 1948; and in recent elections it has not sponsored candidates, instead encouraging its members to join the party of their choice and then try to get on the party selection committees which choose parliamentary candidates. No one has any accurate idea of how British farmers vote, but it is not unlikely that as nationalization of land drops out of Labor's policy statements, quite a few—in some districts perhaps as many as 25 per cent—vote Labor. Many others are sufficiently independent to mean it when they threaten to abstain, if the government is not more considerate of their demands.

How are we to account for this convergence of party policies? Its effects today we have noted: as compared with the American pattern, the structure of the welfare state and the controlled economy associates pressure groups more closely with the administration and makes pressure groups more concerned with the decisions made at the administrative level. The agreement between parties frees pressure groups from the need to defend the basic policies favorable to them and enables them to be more independent of party. Furthermore, and this is perhaps the most important effect, the consensus on the values of the welfare state and controlled economy—e.g., the high importance of "security"—provides a favorable context within which pressure groups can urge their demands. But how did this convergence of party policy develop? Can we explain it, in turn, in terms of the operations of interest groups and their organizations or need we look at the problem on a different level of analysis from that of interest and group activity?

IV. Effect of Values and Ideology upon Interest. One of the compulsions tending to produce this convergence of policy proceeds from the balance of social forces which has emerged in Britain in recent years. By this I mean that today many groups in the society hold what is almost a veto over public policy in their power to refuse their work, their talents, their capital, or simply their willing cooperation in carrying out public policy. John Strachey squarely stated the problem for a future Labor Government when he observed that if such a Government came to power pledged to a radical redistributionist policy, there might well be a flight of capital.[32] But the threatening possibilities are not all on one side. An equally serious disturbance would face any Tory Government which attacked the welfare state. Trade unions as well as financiers and managers have a veto power, and in the years before 1951 the chances of widespread industrial unrest if a Tory Government came to power were held up as a warning to voters. In fact, these dangers did not materialize simply because the Tories yielded all along the line, even to the point of dropping the demands of their 1950 manifesto that "a final settlement" be arranged concerning "contracting out" and compulsory unionism. We can expect a future Labor Government to show a similar respect for realities.

In a more individualist society, where groups are less highly organized and less aware of their interests, it is more likely that important reforms can be put through even though enjoying the support of only a majority. But in Britain today the extent of group power, nurtured by the welfare state and the quasi-corporatism of the relations of government and the economy, means that the country has come close to the point at which a society must move with near unanimity or not at all. The idea of a balance among social forces seems attractive. Yet there is a real danger that instead of promoting agreement and a convergence of policies, such a balance may produce the "pluralistic stagnation" of the later years of the Weimar Republic, or the *immobilisme* of France today. We may strongly suspect, therefore, that beyond the balance of social forces there are factors of integration which make this situation in Britain promote agreement rather than stagnation.

A similar conclusion is suggested if we examine the effects of the present electoral situation, in which the voters are not overwhelmingly in favor of one of the parties. Such a division in itself may discourage radicalism or reaction and this effect is heightened when we examine how the situation itself has arisen. The principal development was the reform of Tory policy following upon the smashing defeat of 1945 and the welcome with which the fundamental measures of the welfare state were received by the electorate. In this reform of policy we see a familiar mechanism: the leaders of the party, thinking of the problem of winning votes, bring along the rank and file— against the resistance of some of the militants—in an acceptance of measures proved to be popular by the Opposition. This move—led mainly by Butler, Eden, and Macmillan—began soon after the defeat of 1945, centered even more around the question of accepting the heavy taxation involved by the welfare state than around nationalization, and was clinched by the acceptance of the *Industrial Charter* at the Brighton conference of 1947. Nor did it cease then, but continued on into the period of the Tory Government—as in the numerous concessions to pressure groups since 1951. Labor, perhaps because it had not, until the 1955 General Election, suffered a severe defeat, has made its corresponding movement to the right with less internal agreement in the party. Yet that shift has taken place and again one of the best illustrations is the party's tortuous wooing of the farmers—in spite of the fact that nationalization of land was one of the earliest of the doctrines of the socialism which it espouses.

The mechanism of electoral competition can be clearly observed, but how far does it take us in explaining the present general acceptance of the welfare state and the controlled economy? This competition is carried on within a cultural context which limits and guides what politicians will offer in their bids for votes and what demands groups will assert with expectation of finding support. We need, therefore, to look at the ideological and evaluative factors in the situation and their relationship to interests.[33]

In Britain one of the most important changes on the plane of ideology has been the Keynesian "revolution" in economics. Without entering into the important controversies which concern economists who accept the broad framework of Keynesian thought, we can see that the main principles of Keynesianism have profoundly altered people's ideas of what government can do by way of comprehensive control of the economy. In 1929, when Britain was suffering from the chronic unemployment which had continued from the postwar slump, the then Chancellor of the Exchequer, Winston Churchill, could rest his budgetary policy on "the orthodox Treasury doctrine, which has steadfastly held that, whatever might be the political or social advantages, very little additional employment and no permanent additional employment can, in fact, and as a general rule, be created by State borrowing and State expenditure."[34]

Not only the "Treasury view," but also the ideas of active political circles have been liberated by Keynes from that doctrine. That government can act effectively to maintain economic equilibrium in the form of full, or near-full, employment without inflation is a belief which any government in Britain today will accept. Moreover, this belief in more or less simplified form has penetrated widely throughout the electorate. There is no doubt some very small number of voters who reject the ideology on which it is based: the Marxists, for example, and possibly some few remaining adherents of strict laissez-faire, such as the late Sir Waldron Smithers. Whether every member of the British electorate accepts it, however, is not particularly important. The relevant fact is that it is accepted by people of different parties and various interest groups and constitutes part of the framework of common belief within which they carry on their activities.

Keynesianism is not simply the belief of a group; it is part of the ideology of substantially the whole political community. Within the collectivity defined by its acceptance, it limits and guides what groups will demand of government and provides a commonly accepted standard by which demands of groups can be judged. To a significant extent, for instance, wage earners themselves understand the probability that wage increases will heighten inflation, endanger the balance of payments, and threaten their own and others' economic wellbeing. Such understanding was one factor which made possible the "austerity" policy, the "wage freeze," and the continued budgetary surpluses of today.

"Vulgar" Keynesianism is not the only new

element in the economic ideology of the British political community. To locate the other elements, we should need to go back to the development of a knowledge of economic controls which began with the "neo-mercantilist" economic policy of the National Government,[35] went rapidly forward under the tightly planned economy of the war, and has been added to and modified in the postwar years. The general understanding of what government can do to control foreign exchange, the volume of imports, and capital investment has been immensely expanded since the days when the Labor Government sat by impotently while the Great Depression of 1929 swept over the British economy. It is hard to believe today that one of the most doctrinaire socialists in that Cabinet and its Chancellor of the Exchequer, Philip Snowden, was also a firm believer in the gold standard, a balanced budget, and absolute free trade. With respect to the practices of economic nationalism, British socialism has accepted as much from the Tories as they have accepted from it. The familiar formula that the radical party in Britain leads while the conservatives merely follow along and consolidate, is only a half-truth.

No less important than ideology are the new values which have developed and which support the general consensus on the welfare state and the controlled economy. These are primarily political in that they define the role and goals of government and the rights and obligations of individuals and groups in relation to government. Inseparable from these political values are new moral and appreciative standards. Supporting the welfare state policy of income redistribution, for instance, are moral standards which have redefined the rights and obligations of private property. The new obligations are discharged largely through government, but in some cases—e.g., the relations of employers and wage-earners—they are expressed in direct relations between two groups. In some respects, also, these moral standards ease the obligations of property; in the welfare state, for instance, the charitable activities of voluntary associations are not felt to have the same claim they had formerly.[36]

In accord with these developing political and moral values, appreciative standards show a movement away from the aspirations and standards of success of the era of a more vigorous capitalism. A sociologist friend of mine touched on this point while summarizing the results of a social survey he had just concluded. The working classes generally, he said, as they improve their material conditions, adopt the consumption habits of the lower-middle classes. For instance, they not only leave the tenements of the slums, but also reject

life in so collectivist a habitation as an apartment house, preferring their own "semi-detached villas." They do not, however, adopt the familiar middle-class aspiration to own a shop or business. On the contrary, they prefer to remain wage-earners, rather look down on the small shopkeeper, and use their surplus energies to ensure that they get the maximum possible benefits from the welfare state.

When a British author finds a likeness between the new Britain and the United States except "in the case of personal acquisitiveness,"[37] this is a major exception. In all classes, if my experience is a fair guide, the profit motive is under such a cloud as would be inconceivable in the United States. Along with this decline of interest in capitalistic acquisitiveness, has gone a complementary rise in the evaluation of and concern for "security."

The point to be made here is how this change helps explain certain characteristics of British pressure groups and especially certain significant differences of their behavior from that of pressure groups in the United States. One of the problems in the study of the Farmers' Union, for instance, is how it manages to keep the large and more efficient farmers working in harmony with the small and less efficient farmers. In quite important ways, the policies of the Union seem in the postwar years to have shown a bias toward the small and inefficient and against the large and efficient. Yet it is rare that one finds evidence of disharmony or disagreement—in striking contrast, of course, with American experience.

A particularly puzzling example occurred in the autumn of 1953, when the Union was carrying on its prolonged negotiations with the government over the new arrangements for meat marketing. Without going into the technical details of the Union's proposal, we need note merely that in return for guaranteed prices for their meat, the producers were ready to turn over all profit on sales above those prices to the government.[38] The arrangement would have been clearly unfavorable to the high-quality producer, yet the proposal had been framed and put forward by the Union without significant protest from its branches and its members. When an explanation was asked for, the apparent conflict of interest between large and small producer was recognized, but again and again it was stressed that even the large and efficient producers were more concerned with security than with the opportunity to make large, but risky, profits.

The modification of interest by value is perhaps the most interesting aspect of these developments for the student of pressure groups. For the sake of the stability of the political system, it is fortunate that such a modification has taken place. Otherwise, the strain between new values and old interests might be excessive. But values and ideology, of course, have other functions in this situation. In general, they order interests in the estimation of the members of the political collectivity, excluding some potential demands from public utterance, raising others up from previous exclusion, changing the priorities attached to certain interests, heightening or lowering the intensity with which they may be asserted. It is in the different pattern of these cultural elements that the American senses the profoundly different "atmosphere" of British pressure politics.

The present convergence of party policy expresses this consensus on new values and ideology. Not only does this consensus affect the intrinsic nature of the interests asserted and provide an integrating framework within which the electoral competition and the struggle of pressure groups is carried on; it also has a somewhat similar function with regard to the balance of social forces. "Objectively" considered, the interest groups of Britain today are in many ways similar to those of Weimar Germany. Yet instead of "pluralistic stagnation," we find a highly cooperative society and an effective system of government.

V. The Enduring Consensus of British Politics. Interest groups, far from explaining the present consensus of British politics, have themselves been significantly affected by it. How then are we to explain the cultural development which produced that consensus and through it the present convergence of policy? Obviously the analysis of such a development is complicated. Here one or two angles may be examined which are suggested by the comparative approach.

A part of the underlying mechanism is laid bare when we examine certain of the justifications which were used by Tory leaders when they were leading the way in the reform of party policy after 1945. At the conference of 1947, for instance, in the debate on the motion which the opponents of the new policy had chosen for their principal attack, Mr. Eden wound up for the reformist side. In his peroration, he proclaimed the party's belief in "a property-owning democracy," "the family," and "the Christian virtues." Then came an interesting passage:

> We are not a Party of unbridled, brutal capitalism and never have been. Although we believe in personal responsibility and personal initiative in business, we are not the political children of the laissez-faire school. We opposed them decade after decade. Where did the Tories stand when the greed and squalor of the industrial revolution were darkening

the land? I am content with Keir Hardie's testimony: "As a matter of hard dry fact, from which there can be no getting away, there is more labour legislation standing to the credit account of the Conservative Party on the Statute Book than there is to that of their opponents."[39]

The note which Eden struck was what some call "Tory democracy" and others "Disraelian make-believe." It was not, at any rate, a note one would expect to be sounded by a prominent Republican leader at a party convention—even in the bad, old days of Democratic majorities. Yet in the postwar period one finds it running through the programs and pamphlets of the Conservative party and the speeches of its leaders and backbenchers, such as the members of the "One Nation" group. These themes of "Disraelian make-believe" are at least a means of sweetening with "Tory principle" the harsh lessons of electoral defeat. The delegates at a Tory conference are hardly cheered by the thought of heavy taxation of the middle classes. Yet their potential complaints can be converted to silence and even into mild applause by the appeal to these themes[40] which would be received with bewilderment by a Republican partisan gathering.

That these themes are effective with the active members of the party indicates that they have some real part in the operative ideals of the party. Nor does the evidence support the notion that party leaders are not genuinely moved by them. In fact the Tory party does have a long history of social reform and the intimate memoirs, as well as the domestic policies, of leaders such as Baldwin and Neville Chamberlain indicate that their readiness to fight socialism with the weapons of socialism sprang from more than political expediency.[41] In short, there is a real and long-standing difference between British conservatism and American conservatism—in spite of Russell Kirk's efforts in the contrary sense.

Comparison with the operative ideals of American politics, however, suggests an even broader contrast. In his study of the liberal tradition in America, Louis Hartz has elicited important aspects of this contrast.[42] His thesis—to which I can merely refer here—hinges on the fact that the absence of a "feudal" tradition in this country has made the premises of our political action radically different from those of Europe, and so, of course, from those of British politics. Lacking such a tradition and a true aristocracy to embody it, we have not undergone the experience of class conflict between an aristocracy and a bourgeois middle class and have not had the sense of class which such a tradition and such a conflict have perpetuated in Britain. American politics, therefore, lacks the British ideology which defines the political situation in terms of class and guides interests in the direction of class solidarity. Such an hypothesis, for instance, helps us understand why the interests of workingmen could not be satisfied by Lib-Lab reform, but were drawn off into the formation of a party of class. In contrast, American politics, whatever the party, is dominated by a "Lockean liberalism" which greatly impedes the development of a strong socialist movement just as it has excluded a conservatism of the British type. Our politics, therefore, is a politics in which virtually all contending groups accept the premises of "democratic capitalism," while the politics of Britain and Europe tends to center around class conflicts which may bring in question fundamentals of the social order.

Not incompatible with Hartz' analysis is a further point which I should like to suggest. Granting that at times—such as the interwar years—British parties were in this sense more deeply divided than American parties have been in recent generations, it is also possible to discern in their differing positions a certain consensus which stands in contrast with the "Lockean" consensus of American politics. In the Tory tradition, as has often been remarked, there is a strong strain of paternalism and a certain "organic" view of society radically opposed to rugged individualism. Yet, within limits, these operative ideals of government responsibility and social solidarity are, and have been, accepted by British socialists. They too would agree with Burke on that un-American proposition that "government is a contrivance of human wisdom to provide for human wants" and that "men have a right that those wants shall be provided for by this wisdom." The "collectivism" of the late 19th century Herbert Spencer rightly called "the New Toryism." If we may use the names of political philosophers as symbols of these complex attitudes, we may say that both British parties fall within the values and ideology of Hooker rather than those of Locke.

It follows that not only were the interests of workingmen colored by class consciousness, but also the doctrines of the party which they produced provided for wide government responsibility and an enforcement of heavy obligations of individuals to one another. In its elements of class consciousness, the British political tradition provides foci around which sharp cleavages of political doctrine may crystallize. That same tradition, however, also contains certain enduring elements of consensus which may encourage the convergence of these opposing doctrines. In promoting the present consensus on the welfare state and

the controlled economy, this broader consensus seems to have played an important part.

In this process, British parties have been not only coalitions of interest groups, but also bearers of the values of classes and of the collectivity. They have not, however, merely reflected changing values, but have taken an active part in their development and propagation. In the interwar years, for instance, objective economic developments, such as unemployment and Britain's declining international position, were the immediate stimulus to political action. The interests of groups—e.g., the farmers' demands for tariffs or the trade unions' demands that unemployment benefits be maintained—were "data" of the situation facing political leaders. One cannot, however, reduce the policies of the parties to reflections of such interests or mechanical combinations of them. Thought and research did a good deal to give direction and shape to interests which were often in themselves confused and formless. The work of the Fabians is an example; so also is the contribution of the research department of the Conservative party, which Neville Chamberlain set up in 1929 and which he used in developing the "great policy" of protection and imperial preference. Furthermore, the Tory tradition with its emphasis upon nation and Empire served to give direction to policies which party leaders developed in an effort to solve the objective problems and to win and maintain the electoral support of interest groups. The controlled economy of Britain today owes as much to these Tory innovations as to the proposals or experience of Labor.

Often the consequent government action greatly stimulated the growth of pressure groups (as in the case of the Farmers' Union), or even called them into existence (as was often the case with trade associations). In such cases, the initiating influence in policy came from the government, after which the interest group, having been given a definition of its interests and perhaps also a vehicle for expressing them, took up the task of pressing its claims upon government. Important as pressure groups have been in British politics, we cannot think of them as making policy by pushing an inert government or party this way and that. There has been interplay; and again and again government has taken the initiative, thereby crystallizing a latent interest and stirring it into political action. Individual leaders, of whom Lloyd George is an outstanding example, may perform a similar function.

If the Tory emphasis was on the side of foreign economic policy, that of Labor was on the side of internal welfare policy. How the interests of the trade unions combined with the intellectual

socialism of the Fabians and the emotional socialism of the I.L.P. to produce the doctrines of the
welfare state need not be gone into here. The
point is that in the case of Labor doctrine as well
as Tory doctrine there was development. Moreover, the Tories also had a concern with welfare
policy, just as Labor had proposals for a planned
economy. To this extent, therefore, the possibility
was open for each to adopt from the other more
precise policies in fields where it had not fully
elaborated its views. Hence, on the plane of party
doctrine, as well as that of ideology and values,
conditions favoring a convergence of policies existed. Given these favoring elements in the cultural
context, the mechanism of electoral competition
would tend to bring about a convergence of party
policies. Responding to such guidance of public
opinion by party competition, the nature and pattern of interests in the society itself were modified,
in turn providing support for the emerging consensus of the political community.

Again, it must be said that the whole process
was more complicated than this sketch can suggest
and that it has not by any means erased all significant differences between the parties. It is worth
observing in conclusion, however, that during the
past two or three generations British politics, in
dealing with the broad problem of social insecurity,
has framed and solved a great problem in a characteristically British way. The cycle of economic
change—class war—renewed consensus has occurred at least once before in British history. Just
about a hundred years ago, British politics and
British society, after a period of economic revolution and bitter class strife, settled down to what
some historians call "the Victorian compromise."
The present "Elizabethan compromise" has been
achieved through similar political and cultural
mechanisms. It may also introduce a period not
unlike that when Disraeli and Gladstone alternately were victors in a vigorous, but not embit-
tered struggle for the highest political power.

Notes

1. In a recent authoritative article, however, Prof. W.
J. M. Mackenzie of Manchester University has sketched
out the field of inquiry and indicated topics for research.
"Pressure Groups in British Government," *British Journal of Sociology*, Vol. 6, pp. 133-48 (June, 1955).

2. See Talcott Parsons, *The Social System* (Glencoe,
Ill., 1951), Ch. 9, "The Processes of Change of Social
Systems."

3. See "The Ladder and the Queue," from a broadcast by the Rt. Hon. Sir Winston Churchill on Oct. 8,
1951. In *The New Conservatism: An Anthology of Post-
War Thought* (London, 1955), pp. 24-25.

4. See "Pensions in Perspective," *The Economist*, Dec.
11, 1954, pp. 883-88. The article also discusses the "bid-
ding up" of pensions at election time.

5. The Labor Party, *Challenge to Britain: a Programme
for Action* (London, Dec., 1953), p. 25.

6. *The Economist*, July 24, 1954, p. 261.

7. 535 *H. C. Deb*. 146-148 (Dec. 1, 1954) and Cmd.
9338 for the increases and the timetable for their coming into effect.

8. See the discussion of professional associations by
Sidney and Beatrice Webb, who noted the growth of such
organizations in membership and power in the decades
before World War I and the increasing recognition of them
by government. *New Statesman*, Vol. 9, "Special Supplement on Professional Associations," April 21 and 28, 1917,
and Vol. 5, "Special Supplement on English Teachers and
their Professional Organization," Sept. 25 and Oct. 2,
1915. Both were special reports prepared for the Fabian
Research Department at a time when guild socialism
and pluralism were much in vogue.

9. For instance, virtually all trade unions—as compared with our, until recently, three major organizations
—belong to the TUC and the total trade union membership runs not much under 50 per cent of the total
working force—as compared with less than a quarter here.
The National Farmers' Union is the only significant organization of farmers in Britain and it includes about 90
per cent of its potential membership, while here there
are three important organizations, including together probably no more than 30 per cent of all farmers. In Britain
there is only one important veterans' organization—the
British Legion—while we have the Legion, VFW, AM-
VETS, and the AVC. In the field of business organization, the story is rather different. The comprehensive
organizations in Britain are the Federation of British Industries, the National Union of Manufacturers, and the
Association of British Chambers of Commerce. These
three organizations work together smoothly, however, and
one does not get the impression that in political action
British business is more divided than American.

10. An M.P. who wishes to speak in the House on a
matter in which he has a direct pecuniary interest—e.g.,
through the ownership of property—is obliged to "declare
his interest." Sponsorship involving a subsidy, however,
does not entail such a declaration.

11. For the practice, see Sir Lewis Namier's anatomy
of the 18th-century House of Commons in his *Structure
of Politics at the Accession of George III*, 2 vols. (London, 1929). For the theory, see, for example, Sir Robert
Harry Inglis' great speech against the Reform Bill in
1831, when he defended the House as an assembly including representatives of all the great interests of the
country. (2 *H. C. Deb.*, 3rd ser., 1090-1139, esp. at 1109
and 1133 [1 March 1831].)

12. Norman Gash, *Politics in the Age of Peel* (London,
1953), pp. 106-9.

13. Bernard Cracroft, "The Analysis of the House of
Commons, or Indirect Representation," in *Essays on Reform* (London, 1867), pp. 155-90.

14. In 1947 the House resolved that it is a breach of
privilege for a member to enter into a contractual agreement with an outside body "stipulating that he shall
act in any way as the representative of such outside body"
in Parliament. This has not, however, prevented M.P.s
from representing the views of outside organizations in the
House, nor has it prevented outside bodies from continuing their subventions. So long as the "complete independence and freedom of action" of the M.P. is respected,
such arrangements are legitimate. See 440 *H. C. Deb.*
285 and in general the debate on this question, col. 284-
365, and the report from the Committee of Privileges on
which the debate was based (H. C. No. 118, 1946-7).

15. *Report, Committee of Privileges* (H. C. No. 118,
1946-7), Minutes of Evidence, p. 8.

16. At the outbreak of the war, for instance, part of the
organization of the British Iron and Steel Federation
was taken over by the Iron and Steel Control of the
Ministry of Supply and its then president was made the
Iron and Steel Controller. (G. D. N. Worswick, *The Raw
Materials Controls*, Tract No. 257, The Fabian Society;

London, 1944.) The general type of control in the Ministry of Supply was a converted trade association. (*Government and Industry;* Fabian Research Group; Research Series No. 83; London, 1944.)

17. In 1950 the Committee on Intermediaries reported on the relations between government departments and the great bureaucratic pressure groups. It referred to these relations as "organized liaison" concerning not only individual cases, but also "the general formulation and execution of policy" and constituting "an essential and recognised part of the machinery of government." (*Report;* Cmd. 7904; March, 1950, par. 6.)

18. For discussion of the annual price reviews, see the annual reports of the N.F.U.; statements in the House of Commons by ministers; the White Papers normally issued stating the results of the price reviews; comment in farmers' periodicals, especially *The British Farmer, The Farmer's Weekly,* and *The Farmer and Stockbreeder,* as well as the general press, especially *The Times, Manchester Guardian,* and *Economist,* the last of which has the best running comment on agricultural policy.

19. Sir Norman Kipping, *The Federation of British Industries* (London, 1954), p. 6.

20. 522 *H. C. Deb.* 1331 (Jan. 22, 1954) and *Manchester Guardian,* Jan. 22, 1954, p. 14.

21. On the activities of the N.U.T., apart from those invaluable and obvious sources, *The Times* and *Hansard,* see its annual reports and *The Schoolmaster and Woman Teacher's Chronicle,* a weekly periodical published by the Union.

22. Quoted in Allan Flanders, *Trade Unions* (London, 1952), p. 64.

23. The Committee on Intermediaries reported in 1950 that 21 departments of government received some 19,000,-000 applications each year from members of the public for "licenses, permits and various kinds of benefits." "The Departments," it said ". . . have one thing in common. Whatever their particular branch of business, they all have the disposal of something which members of the public want—whether that be a license to acquire material needed for carrying on a business, permission to act in a certain way or the grant of some monetary or other benefit." *Report,* (cited in note 17), par. 6.

24. Writing of the struggle over the Education Act of 1902, Beatrice Webb contrasted "teachers' politics," which was practiced by the N.U.T., with "teachers' diplomacy," which was practiced by the representatives of the "elite" secondary schools. "Teachers' politics" meant lobbying, deputations to ministers and M.P.s, and other forms of public pressure; "teachers' diplomacy" meant informal contacts with persons of influence on the part of secondary school teachers who in general belonged to the same social class. *New Statesman,* Vol. 5, "Special Supplement on English Teachers and their Organization," Sept. 25 and Oct. 2, 1915.

25. For elaboration of this point, see D. E. Butler, "American Myths about British Political Parties," *Virginia Quarterly Review,* Vol. 31, pp. 46-56 (Winter, 1954); and S. H. Beer, "The Future of British Politics: An American View," *Political Quarterly,* Vol. 26, pp. 33-43 (Jan.-Mar., 1955).

26. *Report of the 52nd Annual Conference of the Labour Party* (London, 1953), p. 145.

27. *Annual Report.* National Farmers' Union (London, 1953), *passim* and report of Glasshouse Produce Committee, pp. 78 ff.

28. See his attack on GATT at the Conservative conference of 1953, *Verbatim Report,* p. 63.

29. *Report,* p. 147.

30. *Manchester Guardian,* Oct. 2, 3, 19, and 29, 1953.

31. W. Ivor Jennings, *Parliament* (Cambridge, Eng., 1939), pp. 211-12.

32. "The Powder and the Jam," *New Statesman and Nation,* Vol. 47, pp. 148-49 (Jan. 23, 1954).

33. The terms "value" and "ideology" are used in the senses given them by Talcott Parsons in his *Social System* (Glencoe, 1951), *passim* and esp. at pp. 12 and 349. A value is a standard for selection among the alternatives which are intrinsically open in a situation and may be cognitive, appreciative, or moral. Following Parsons, I distinguish between values and need-dispositions (*ibid.,* pp. 12-13). This distinction is important because values have the function of integrating social action not only directly, but also indirectly by conditioning need-dispositions. Without such integration a stable society would be impossible. Similarly, a principal theme of this article is the integrative function of values in the political system.

The meaning I give to "interest" is based on Parsons' concept of need-disposition. Like a need-disposition, an interest is not simply "appetite," a genetically given need, but is appetite conditioned by social experience. Appreciative values, for instance, will condition the objects in which the ego seeks its gratification—e.g., the profit motive is not inborn—and will be more or less integrated with the developing moral values of a society—e.g., the rise of the moral values of the welfare state will enhance the desire of individuals and groups for economic security. Also, moral values may directly encourage or inhibit the assertion of felt needs. As John Plamenatz has pointed out in a perceptive note, people are not likely to assert demands for the satisfaction of needs unless they believe them to be justifiable. "Interests," *Journal of Political Studies,* Vol. 2, pp. 1-8 (Feb., 1954).

Yet an interest remains a claim for a satisfaction of the individual, or of the smaller collectivity as distinguished from the larger within which the claim is asserted. While, therefore, interests and values are closely related, the interests pursued within a political system must be distinguished from the primary integrative elements of the system, its values.

34. 227 *H. C. Deb.* 54 (April 15, 1929).

35. See Joseph Schumpeter, *Capitalism, Socialism and Democracy,* 2nd ed. (London, 1947), pp. 368-70.

36. For discussion of this and other problems of the voluntary association in the welfare state, see Lord Beveridge, *Voluntary Action* (London, 1948).

37. Donald Chapman, "What Prospect for the Labour Party?," *The Political Quarterly,* Vol. 25, pp. 205-16 (July-Sept., 1954).

38. *Manchester Guardian,* Oct. 16, 1953, p. 12.

39. *Verbatim Report of the Proceedings of the 68th Annual Conference,* Oct. 2-4, 1947. National Union of Conservative and Unionist Associations (London, 1947), pp. 42-43.

40. For example, at the 1953 conference, when a resolution was moved welcoming "the reduction in taxation already made" and urging "further economies in national expenditure," an addendum was offered specifying that this should be done "whilst maintaining and improving the social services." While the supporters of the original resolution were interrupted several times by hearty applause —for example, when asking for cuts in the housing subsidies—those supporting the addendum were heard in silence. Nevertheless, they met with no opposition and were mildly applauded at the end of their speeches; the addendum was accepted by the original movers and the resolution as amended passed unanimously. *Verbatim Report,* pp. 43-49.

41. See Keith Feiling, *Life of Neville Chamberlain* (London, 1947), and on Baldwin, Thomas Jones, *A Diary with Letters, 1931-1950* (London, 1954).

42. *The Liberal Tradition in America* (New York, 1955).

6. A PRESSURE GROUP AND THE PRESSURED:
A CASE REPORT*

Oliver Garceau and Corinne Silverman

THE ORGANIZED INTEREST GROUP does not make the laws of the land. It must devise means for gaining access to and influencing those who are constitutionally empowered to make, administer, or otherwise define the law. This study deals with the efforts of one organized group, the Associated Industries of Vermont, to secure its objectives in the 1951 session of the Vermont legislature. The study is correlatively concerned with the legislator's view of the AIV activities and, more broadly, of the legislative process.

I. The Pressure Group. The Associated Industries of Vermont is a "peak" association; an organized business group which acts as spokesman for many diverse business interests in the state. The membership, which ranges from small manufacturers to the National Life Insurance Company, totaled some 450 concerns in 1951, the year in which the events to be described took place. Membership is by individuals, firms, and a few trade associations. Included were almost all the textile, the granite and marble, and the machine-tool companies in the state—representing three of the state's important industries. A rough estimate of the total payroll of the member concerns was about half of the total payroll of the state. A few retailing and other non-manufacturing members had recently been added.

This study does not attempt to deal with all the events of the 1951 session, nor even with the myriad ways in which business opinion in Vermont gained or failed to gain acceptance on a range of issues. It is concerned primarily with the overall strategy of the staff of the Associated Industries to gain access to the legislature, and with the specific tactics used by the AIV.

Access to the Vermont legislature is always difficult for the Associated Industries. No matter

Reprinted from *American Political Science Review*, Vol. 48 (1954), pp. 672-691, by permission of the authors and the publisher.

* The research, of which this article is one report, was assisted by grants to Bennington College from the Carnegie Corporation of New York and the Rockefeller Foundation.

what the nature of the issues, the AIV is certain to face a legislature more sympathetic to the Farm Bureau than to a business group. Since each township in the state, irrespective of population, is entitled to one representative in the 246-member lower house, the natural preoccupations of the state with agricultural problems are further magnified in the legislature. Although 30.5% of the population live in towns of 5,000 or more, only 5.3% of the members of the lower house represent towns of that size. More than half of the AIV's membership in 1951 were located in towns of more than 5,000 population, which means, of course, that access to legislators through AIV-member-constituents was singularly limited.[1]

Despite these characteristics of the state and the legislature, which continually handicap the Associated Industries in attempts to gain access to the legislators, AIV appeared to be in a strong position when the 1951 session opened. Although it could not appeal to the mass of legislators, the formal leadership of both houses was decidedly receptive to consideration of the AIV point of view. In fact, the formal leaders of the houses were themselves key figures in the formation of the AIV point of view. The Lieutenant-Governor and President of the Senate, Joseph Johnson, was at that time on the Executive Committee of the AIV. He had been a vice-president of the Association, a member of the 1949 AIV Legislative Committee, and had been under consideration for the presidency of the Association until his election as Lieutenant-Governor. In private life he had been vice-president of a large machine-tool company. The Speaker of the House, Wallace M. Fay, was a director and a member of the Executive Committee of AIV. He, too, had been a member of the 1949 AIV Legislative Committee. Fay was vice-president of the Vermont Marble Company. The President Pro Tem of the Senate, and chairman of the Senate Rules Committee, Merrill Harris, who was president of one insurance company and a director of another, was also at that time a director of the AIV.

The chairmen of the standing committees in

the legislature are not designated by virtue of seniority. They are appointed by the Speaker or by the President of the Senate. The AIV was directly influential in the appointments of chairmen and members of the committees considered of probable concern to the business group. The chairman of the House Commerce and Labor Committee, Walter Malmquist, president of a wood products company, had been a member of the 1949 AIV Legislative Committee together with Fay and Johnson. The chairman of the House Social Security Committee, while not a member of the Association, was appointed on the recommendation of Theodore Kane, the Executive Vice-President and manager of the AIV. The two other AIV members of the legislature were appointed chairman of the Senate Finance Committee and chairman of the Senate Commerce and Labor Committee, respectively. However, these two, although members of the AIV, were not as active as Fay, Johnson, Harris, and Malmquist, all of whom had held or were holding positions of responsibility in the formal organization of the group.

The AIV also had reason to suppose that the newly-elected governor, Lee Emerson, would have a readier ear for its opinions than had Governor Ernest Gibson. Although both governors were, inevitably, Republicans, this meant less than the fact that Gibson was associated with one faction of the Republican party in the state, and Emerson was allied with the opposing faction.

The development of the factional split in the Republican party is a major part of the story of the progress of the 1951 session, and is tied in some measure to an understanding of the role of the Proctor family in Vermont politics. This role reaches back to 1878 when Redfield Proctor started on an active political career, serving as governor in 1878, as Secretary of War under Benjamin Harrison, and in 1902 as United States Senator. During this period, the Vermont Marble Company, owned by the Proctor family, became the largest single company in the state. The Proctor family continued throughout the years to take an active interest in the politics of the state; and although the process of gaining office is certainly not a simple one, the history of the Proctors would seem to substantiate the folk tale that as soon as a Proctor reached the proper age he was elected governor of the state. Between 1878, when Redfield Proctor was elected governor, and 1944, when Mortimer Proctor became governor, three other members of the Proctor family served in that position. The Proctors were not and are not today political "bosses" of the state. Although the family might almost be viewed as a fixed pole in Vermont politics, it is fixed not in

terms of ideology but in terms of repeatedly occupying an influential position in the political power structure of the state.

Until the middle 1930's, knowledgeable informants agree, there was no serious or lasting cleavage in the Republican party of an ideological nature. But in 1934 appeared the first glimmer of a split which could be viewed as other than over personalities. In that election the Farm Bureau moved toward a formal endorsement of candidates in the primaries, and successfully backed Charles Smith for the governorship. In 1936 George Aiken was elected governor, again with the support of the Farm Bureau, which also supported his successful campaign for re-election in 1938. In these campaigns, the Farm Bureau in effect opposed Proctor candidates. During the war years Vermont politics quieted down, and Mortimer Proctor was elected in 1944, fully expecting re-election in 1946 for the traditional two terms of office. But in 1946 Ernest Gibson returned from the war and upset the proprieties by defeating Proctor in the primary and gaining the governorship, with the public endorsement of the Farm Bureau.

Gibson's election provoked a split in the Republican party of a type and meaning which remain somewhat enigmatic. Part of his opposition was made up of those who were irritated at the violation of the second term tradition, which would have given Mortimer Proctor a second term in office. To some observers, the split is a "liberal-conservative" one, with Gibson as a "New Deal kind of Republican" opposing the "Old Guard." Yet his program and policies in his two terms of office centered around major points which it would be hard to view as the foundations for a deep ideological cleavage. Gibson opposed the construction of a dam on the Connecticut River on the grounds that it would flood good farm land. This endeared him to the Farm Bureau and solidified the Aiken-Farm Bureau-Gibson combination. It also evoked murmurs of discontent from the private utility companies. The utilities were further incensed when in 1949 Gibson proposed to establish a Vermont Power Authority to negotiate for and distribute electric power produced by the St. Lawrence Seaway developments, if and when such developments occurred. The Farm Bureau backed Gibson fervently on this proposal which was, however, defeated. For Senator Aiken this was one facet of his participation in the struggle for federal endorsement of the Seaway. In Vermont, Gibson's proposal brought cries of "socialism" and established him as something of a radical. Other programs included a Department of Health to administer mobile health units, and a State Police system to augment the local sheriffs. He pressed for additional construction of state institutions, projects which had been ignored during the war years. He created a Development Commission to encourage industrial expansion in the state, to attract new business to the area, and thus to stem the steady outflow of Vermont's younger generation. These policies were viewed by many as radical and involving a wanton expenditure of money. They were acclaimed by others as "progressive" and as sensible investments in the state's health. When, in 1949, Gibson resigned from the governorship to accept a Truman appointment to the federal district court, many felt that the accusations of radicalism were vindicated.

The 1950 campaign was a complicated affair, with candidates for the Republican primaries announcing first for one office and then another in a whirl of indecision. When the merry-go-round slowed down there were three candidates for the Republican nomination for governor. One of them, Peter Bove, was generally regarded as "a Gibson man," but without as broad a backing as Gibson himself had had. The second, J. Harold Stacy, although he had been Gibson's Speaker of the House in the 1949 session, was considered to be nobody's man and a middle-of-the-roader, whatever that might mean in the low temperature politics of the state. Lee Emerson, the third and successful candidate, had been Lieutenant-Governor in Mortimer Proctor's term as governor, although this did not necessarily mean that he was "Proctor's man." The Proctors, in fact, did not appear to take much interest in the 1950 campaign until the last two or three weeks, when, it is often reported, they decided upon Emerson as the least of three evils and it became generally known that he had their backing.

The Associated Industries scrupulously refrained from taking any part in the 1950 campaign. Although the AIV had no direct connection with Governor Emerson, the links were there, and the campaign situation did nothing to weaken the possibility of cooperative relationships between governor, legislative officers, and the business group. At the very least, it was clear that the new governor could expect little support from former Gibson associates. As the new administration began and the legislature convened, the AIV made the explicit assumption that the official climate of opinion in the state government would be more congenial than in recent years and its own problems of effective access much simpler and more direct.

II. The 1951 Legislative Session.[2] The AIV did not concern itself actively with the full range of issues in the 1951 session. Rather, the staff focussed a major portion of its energy on one bill, the proposal of the labor groups to include certain occupational diseases under the Workman's Compensation Act. Theodore Kane, Executive Vice-President of the AIV (and for all practical purposes "the staff"), told the Association's members that this was "the most important legislation affecting industry to come before the 1951 session."

The development of this issue in the 1951 session is a not unrepresentative example of a process of inter-group negotiation characteristic of state legislatures when dealing with issues of something less than first-rank drama and political potential. The nature of such negotiations among interests is often assumed to be characteristically one of mutual hostility. Rather than assuming the legislature to be subject to a barrage of independent and divergent pressures, it may be closer to reality to conceive of a pattern, shifting through time, of alliances of interests which engage in negotiations and compromise outside the legislature. The rather picturesque comment of one member of the Vermont House is suggestive. Commenting on the AIV-labor negotiations on the occupational disease bill, he said that there were too many bills to keep track of in the session, and "if it is satisfactory to them you figure you're not cutting anybody's gut." The example of the occupational disease bill is also a cogent illustration of the role such group negotiations play in broadening access to the legislature for one group or another. The labor groups in Vermont had, with the exception of three or four friendly legislators, little or no opportunity for gaining access *except* through the AIV.

The occupational disease bill story begins in 1947 when the granite workers, concerned about silicosis, sought to have it covered under Workman's Compensation. Procedure followed the pattern prescribed for most legislative proposals of even ordinarily controversial nature: a temporary committee was set up which recommended further study by a five-man commission. The commission was established and reported to the 1949 session, presenting a majority report and a minority report. The AIV, although it preferred the majority report if forced to make a choice, offered still a third course; and the labor groups, although they preferred the minority report if forced to make a choice, came up with a fourth proposal. All four of these proposals reached the floor. The Vermont House normally consists of more than 50% "first-termers" who are unaccustomed for the most part to legislative routine and are traditionally prone to vote "no" on everything when confronted by confusion of amendments, substitutions, and other such sophisticated parliamentary practices. Acting in true form, the 1949 House defeated the majority bill, the minority bill, and labor's proposed substitutions, and passed the AIV's suggestion, which was to authorize the establishment of a Division of Industrial Hygiene in the Department of Health whose function it would be to recommend better methods for preventing occupational diseases.

For the time being, this was doing nothing about workman's compensation. However, the granite industry and the AIV, and most especially Mr. Kane, were well aware of the fact that the labor groups would make another try in the 1951 session. Despite the conservative drift of opinion in state and nation, and the exceptional access to the legislature enjoyed by AIV in 1951, it was never concluded by Mr. Kane that business interests could call the tune, even with relation to labor. This, be it noted, was not because labor was strong, but because business interests remained essentially weak. Farm leaders were characteristically Bull Moose progressive on business issues, disliked bankers for the record, distrusted big business and Wall Street to notable political advantage. Vermont legislative policy had, on a number of issues, been liberal to an exceptional degree, considering the conduct of some of the neighboring states and the very limited per capita wealth of the state. Business endorsement of a policy was considered, in the AIV office, a surety of defeat. This gloomy assessment may well have been an exaggerated projection of the 1930's, but it significantly conditioned the course of the negotiations. Since it was judged doubtful that an occupational disease law could be postponed indefinitely, the better strategy seemed to be for industry itself to take the initiative, present its own bill, and start any negotiations in an offensive rather than defensive position. Although it is not possible to place responsibility for this decision, it is more likely that it was Kane's rather than that of the Barre Granite Association, many of whose members were opposed to the passage of any bill.[3]

In December, just prior to the opening of the 1951 session, a meeting of minds was achieved between the leading members of the Granite Association and Kane, and a bill was drawn up. This bill resembled in its essence the majority bill of 1949, although the form was greatly simplified, especially by the omission of the innumerable "except as hereinafter otherwise provided" clauses to which the minority report had strenuously objected. The bill was taken to the Governor by the AIV and all seemed to be well. Two days later word came from Emerson that there were objections to the proposed bill. Kane would have to reach agreement with labor or there would be trouble in the legislature, trouble in the form of

opposition on the floor by one or another of the handful of legislators friendly to labor. Such objections threatened a repetition of the events of the 1949 session, where the confusion of disagreement on the floor led almost inevitably to legislative disapproval.

The course followed by Kane to secure agreement was to set in motion a series of sessions with the CIO, or as some legislators termed it, "a horse trade." The AIV had planned to introduce in this session three bills aimed at tightening the qualifications for workers claiming benefits under the Unemployment Compensation Law. It is not impossible that these bills were planned as bargaining items, although intrinsically they were compatible with AIV aims. Labor in turn hoped for an increase in the maximum duration of unemployment benefits from 20 weeks to 26 weeks, and for an increase in the maximum weekly payments from $25 to $30.

Kane and the CIO representative went into a determined huddle over who would give up what in return for what. Labor's concern was to get an occupational disease bill on the books in some form or other. The AIV, on the other hand, felt that its legislative position was stronger in this session than it had been for some years and than it might be in sessions to come, and therefore wanted to get an occupational disease law in a form acceptable to business. Labor knew that the most it could hope for in a future legislature would be an increase in the number of "friendly" legislators from the three or four in the 1951 session to a possible five or six. Unless the AIV felt that labor was "cooperative," labor demands might be ignored. It was only through the maintenance of reasonably amicable relations with the Association that labor interests could look for success in the legislature. Labor finally agreed to the occupational disease bill in the form in which the AIV had drawn it, and agreed also to withdraw all its proposals for increasing unemployment benefits and extending the duration of payments. The AIV in turn agreed that it would withhold in this session the bills tightening qualifications for unemployment compensation.

These negotiations were carried on completely outside the legislative halls with only two legislative participants. One, Walter Malmquist, was the AIV-picked chairman of the House Commerce and Labor Committee. However, his role was not that of active negotiator but that of liaison between the AIV and the legislature, a role which he played throughout the session on all AIV issues. He kept Speaker Fay and some of the more important legislators informed on this and all other situations in which the AIV was concerned.

The other legislator present was the representative from Barre Town, Ralph Smith, who was recognized as the principal legislative spokesman for labor. One or two other legislators were involved in some portions of the bargaining process, and although they did not know the details of all that had happened, they knew that, since agreement had been reached, the bill should be approved. The vast majority of the legislators, however, knew only that both Malmquist and Smith rose on the day of debate and announced that both industry and labor thought the bill should pass. They sat down, the vote was taken, and an occupational disease bill passed the House. The Senate, also noting that Malmquist and Smith urged the bill, granted its approval and the bill became law.

The passing of this bill was not accomplished by any visible lobbying. No attempt was made by either of the interested parties, industry or labor, to "buttonhole" members of the legislature and persuade them of the righteousness of the cause. There was no pleading before legislative committees. Rather, the differences of opinion within industry were first resolved and then agreement on the nature of the bill was reached between the representatives of organized industry and labor. Agreement to pass the bill came as a result of swapping and cancelling out objectives announced for the 1951 session. Bargaining was readily achieved by virtue of a long-standing "open-door" policy which existed between Kane and John Mitchell, the representatives of the AIV and CIO, respectively. Success for each of them depended upon maintaining an attitude of willingness to bargain with the other, although this dependence was more keenly felt by the CIO than by the AIV. The bulk of the legislators were more than willing to accept the bill without feeling a need to know what had happened behind the scenes, or if anything had happened. Their attention was caught by the more dramatic bills which had not been so resolved and which thus resulted in a clash of interests on the floor.

These more dramatic clashes, which in 1951 centered about the problem of the Governor's budget and tax policy, illustrate the limitations of the above methods. One factor important to the success of the occupational disease negotiations was that the bargaining and the legislative action came relatively early in the session. The bill was passed by the House in the last days of March and by the Senate in the first week of April. Up to that point the social and political organization of the legislature had been comparatively unstructured, and factional lines had not yet become sharply defined. Less than a week after passage of the occupational disease law,

the entire character of the legislature changed and "the honeymoon was over." If the occupational disease bill had come up any later than it did, Administration support might have proved a liability and the issue might well have become entangled in the struggle which characterized the remainder of the session.

Governor Emerson, in his inaugural address and budget message, proclaimed an era of economy. No state department was to receive funds for additional personnel or new projects; wherever possible duplication was to be eliminated and consolidation of agencies effected. Above all, no new taxes were to be levied, except for a half-cent increase in the gas tax which in Vermont is earmarked for highway development. This program in itself, while perhaps not entirely realistic in an inflationary period, would not have alarmed most members of the state legislature. What did arouse comment, and eventually deep acrimony, was the detail of this program. For the departments and agencies singled out by Emerson as those in which the greatest cuts could be made performed services inaugurated by his predecessor, Ernest Gibson. The Vermont Development Commission was to be virtually eliminated, and the new State Police was to be merged with the Motor Vehicle Department. Savings from these two reorganizations were budgeted as sufficient to avert tax increases. The Governor warned that if his program were not carried out, the burden of balancing the budget would rest upon the members of the legislature.

These two issues were seized upon by those in the legislature who had been Gibson supporters, and by much newspaper opinion, as purely "political" maneuvers, designed only to "undo all Gibson had done." By the time the two bills reached the House in early April they had become regarded as Emerson's "test of strength." In the event, they demonstrated that the Governor could not effectively "control" his legislature, for the House voted $100,000 to the Development Commission instead of the Governor's proposed $20,000, and defeated the proposed State Police-Motor Vehicle Department merger. The Senate restored another $100,000 to the Development Commission, or all but $40,000 of the Commission's original budget request of $240,000.

It was not to the advantage of the AIV to become embroiled in either of these issues. Factions in Vermont do not have the stability of established parties in other situations. Today's opponents may well be tomorrow's political compatriots. The Association managed to stay clear of the merger issue almost entirely. However, the Development Commission battle was more difficult to avoid. When a public hearing was scheduled on the proposed cut, Kane received word from the President of AIV to appear at the hearing and support the Governor's proposal. However, there were pressures in the opposite direction. Among the more determined opponents of the proposed cut were the local chambers of commerce, and the resort and hotel interests. Many of the latter were recent additions to membership. Kane could not afford to alienate one part of his membership in order to satisfy another. Furthermore, perhaps the most determined opponent of the proposal was the Vermont Farm Bureau. Since the Farm Bureau was unquestionably the most powerful organized group in the state, it was never to the advantage of the AIV to appear in direct, certainly not in open, opposition to it, if such a position could be avoided. The day of the hearing found Kane with important matters to attend to elsewhere.

Although the AIV managed to remain nominally neutral in these two issues, the Governor's defeat affected the AIV in the consequent problem of taxation. When both of the Governor's major proposals for economizing were defeated, and when the legislature also passed a bill raising the salaries of state employees, it was clear the budget would not be balanced unless new taxes were levied. As he had promised, Emerson had no tax proposal to offer. The legislators were in this difficulty despite his warnings, and the legislators would have to get out of trouble by themselves.

This interpretation of the role of the executive resulted in something close to chaos in the legislature. No one in the legislative branch considered himself responsible for working out an overall tax program. As one senator pointed out, "it's not very smart politically to introduce tax bills. That's supposed to be the job of the Administration, and everybody was glad to leave it to them." However, a small group of leaders of the Governor's faction attempted to solve the problem by introducing a series of small taxes which became known as the "patchwork taxes." Rather than raise the state income tax, a policy which Emerson had disapproved in his budget message, and rather than leap to the politically unpopular sales tax, this group proposed increases in the taxes on beer, on soft drinks, and on amusements. None of these proposed taxes had the official blessing of the Governor. Contradictory reports about his preferences flowed freely in the legislative corridors. Since the patchwork taxes were being proposed by legislators regarded as "Emerson men," there was some feeling that Emerson was backing the patchwork program;

and in fact Emerson was meeting regularly with this group of legislators to discuss the possible methods of passing these taxes. The patchwork program was speedily defeated.

Kane did not find it appropriate to take the initiative on new taxes. The membership of a business group is not likely to be tolerant of the staff's proposing a more active tax program than those emanating from the executive and legislative branches. Furthermore, over the objections of a number of his members, Kane had actively supported a withholding tax earlier in the session. This was not a "new tax," but a new method of collecting taxes. Since it was to be retroactive, it was to result in an immediate "windfall" of several hundred thousand dollars of revenue. Kane, and the Governor as well, had harbored some hopes that this windfall would lessen the pressure for any further taxes. Having gone beyond his membership in this, Kane was unwilling to approve, in the name of the AIV, any further tax proposals. Finally, though none of the industries presently in the AIV would have been hit by the patchwork taxes, Kane was trying to broaden the base of membership in the Association to include, among others, business at which the taxes were directed. Kane was not prepared to alienate these potential members.

It was now the middle of May. The 1951 legislature had already broken all records for length of session, and a solution to the tax problem was not yet in sight. A sales tax proposal was thrown into the hopper, but did not receive the approval of even 15% of the House. It was generally recognized that a tax of this sort required more preparation than a day or two spent copying a bill currently proposed in New Hampshire.

The legislature finally turned from the confusion to a 15% surtax on the state personal and corporate income tax, a solution proposed and introduced in the House by a legislator readily identified as "a Gibson man." This was the only tax on which the Governor had explicitly taken a stand, stating clearly in his budget message that "I do not favor any change in the existing income tax law at this time." It was the tax which the AIV would logically have wanted to defeat. But the AIV was by this time in a changed position. The Association had, at the outset, enjoyed access to the legislature through the formal leadership of the House and Senate. By the end of the session, the formal leadership did not coincide with the actual leadership. The Governor by his policy throughout the session, and by withdrawing himself from leadership on the whole question of taxes, had precipitated the latent cleavage in the legislature. Two sets of informal leaders had emerged.

It could be argued, no doubt, that the Governor and the AIV had not been wholly realistic in assuming that Emerson's program would be adopted in full and that therefore no tax program would be necessary. It might have been wise to have considered early in January what program would be preferred in the event that some new taxes became necessary. When the major decision of tax policy had to be faced, AIV had neither a policy known and acceptable to its members, nor access to the leadership which had developed in the legislature.

III. The Pressured. After this summary of the 1951 legislative session from the perspective of the Associated Industries, it is appropriate to report how the events of the session looked to some of the members of the legislature. The questions to be explored are how these legislators themselves perceived the legislative process; what they thought was their own role in the process; and what place they attributed to organized group interests and activities. More specifically, what issues stood out for these legislators as "important," and for what reasons? What did they think was the role of organized interest groups in shaping the decisions on these or other issues? How much group activity and what kind of group activity were, in fact, visible to the legislators?[4]

The legislators, who were interviewed from two to four months after the close of the 1951 session, did not tell a uniform story of what had happened during the five-month session. They chose for themselves several different kinds of signposts as guides through the confusion and stress of the session. They had different ways of structuring the experience, different perspectives on the elements of the legislative process.

Among the members of the lower house there appeared to be four different ways of describing the session. One group of House members were distinguished by their reluctance to impose any intellectual scheme or interpretation on the events of the session. All of the many episodes of the session were remembered, often with some difficulty, as so many separate items. There was a striking tendency among these representatives to refer questions about specific issues to the report of the committee which had handled the bill, although this is not to say that they remembered very clearly which committee had indeed handled which of the bills under discussion. Unable to see relationships in the handling of different issues, or relationships among informal groups of legislators, these representatives, making a virtue of necessity, seemed to cut down the confusion

by taking the "safest" course. They argued that the standing committee members ought to have the "right decision" on each bill, and that the committee reports ought to be followed by the legislature. These legislators had not evolved broad standards for judging the issues as matters of social policy. They did not see the legislature as a forum for rival parties, factions, or interests. They did not identify leaders in the legislative process. Their interpretation of events was in terms of a traditional democratic morality. As representatives they were under obligation to their own consciences to do the right thing. The standing committee was to define, from its hearings and special competence, what was right. As observers of the interaction patterns in the 1951 session, they were "non-generalizers," and will be so termed below.

A second group of members of the lower house was sensitive primarily to the factional cleavage among the Republican legislators. Although these representatives could identify some of the more specific issues on which the cleavage had been apparent, they tended to discuss the cleavage as a conflict between rivals seeking advancement and power in state politics. For them a great many of the events of the session had turned on which group of factional leaders was the more effective or persuasive. These representatives will be referred to as the "faction-oriented."

A third group of the legislators added a further dimension to the process. They were aware of the factional clashes. They saw also a relation between the Governor's program and the emergence of factional alignment. Among this group, the Emerson supporters felt that his original message of economy in state programs, to avoid tax increases, had been sound. Although they had doubts of varying degrees about the specific proposals which were to effectuate this program, they cast their lot with the overall aim. Those who developed into "the opposition" had in some cases been Gibson supporters in previous years, and in other cases had been uncommitted. But they agreed that the reorganization and decimation proposals were unacceptable, whatever the merit of economy in general. For these legislators, the session was a struggle between factions emerging out of the Governor's program. They were essentially "program-oriented" in their answers to questions covering the range of legislative activity.

A fourth group of representatives, "policy-oriented," saw the relation between broad program and faction. But their concern was with their own role as active leaders promoting particular policies or seeking to take care of policy in what might be called an issue area. Three were focussed on the interests of labor, and a fourth dealt with education. To these legislators the story of the session was the story of their own activity with relation to these policy matters and their own negotiations with interest groups and legislative factions. To a degree they sought for themselves a limited and special role as factional leaders; but their purpose and their interpretation of events were in terms of particular policies.[5]

IV. Legislative Views of Issues and Groups. The research used a focussed interview. At the outset the legislator was asked what he considered the most important problem of the session. It was mainly from the responses to this question that the varying perspectives emerged.

With one exception, all the "policy-" and "program-oriented" legislators selected as the most important problem of the session the question of the Governor's program and budget, which led them immediately into a discussion of the policy of economy, the State Police merger and the Vermont Development Commission questions, the various tax programs, and the split in the Republican party.

Most of the "faction-oriented" selected the merger, the Vermont Development Commission cut, or one of the tax proposals. The biggest difference between this group and the "policy-" and "program-oriented" groups was the failure of the "faction-oriented" to see the interconnections between any of these issues and the entire range of issues which had made up "the problem" for the first two groups of legislators.

As for the fourth group, the "non-generalizers," almost every representative in this group picked a different issue as "the most important problem in the session." A few chose one or another of the tax proposals, but the range of issues selected was widely scattered. Every issue appearing in the interview with a member of this group was treated by him as a discrete issue with no apparent sense of interconnections.[6]

The most striking fact which emerged from the interviews as a whole was the extremely low level of recognition of interest group activity. Although every representative interviewed knew of the Vermont Farm Bureau, more than a third had never heard of the Associated Industries of Vermont, and only a few more had any notion that the labor interests in Vermont were organized. One third of the representatives had never heard of Arthur Packard, for a generation the president and lobbyist for the Farm Bureau, and about two thirds of them were unable to identify the lobbyists for either the AIV or the

CIO. Even fewer were able to recall more than one issue in which these groups had been interested.

Table 1—Per Cent of Representatives Interviewed Who Were Able to Identify Organized Groups, Their Lobbyists, and Issues in Which the Organized Groups Were Interested (N = 40)

QUESTION	PER CENT ABLE TO RECOGNIZE		
	Farm Bureau	AIV	CIO/AFL*
Group itself	100.0%	62.5%	77.5%
Lobbyist	70.0	40.0	37.5
More than one issue	60.0	30.0	30.0

* Although John Mitchell, the labor lobbyist identified here as the most active during the session, represents officially the CIO, he was considered to have been representing both the CIO and the AFL. The granite quarry workers belong to the CIO and the stone cutters belong to the AFL.

These differentials in the ability of the representatives to recognize organized groups, their lobbyists, and issues in which the groups were interested are closely linked to the different ways the various legislators structured the session. The representatives who made the more complex analysis of the legislative process, the "policy-" and the "program-oriented," saw more organized group activity than did the "faction-oriented." The "non-generalizers" had the lowest level of recall and recognition of organized group activity. Their concept of the legislative process did not require it of them. Or was it that, lacking recognition of interest groups, their concept of process had to build without such elements? The data allow the question to be raised, but do not answer it.

The level of recognition or recall of group activity involved in this analysis is not exacting. It is based on the ability of the legislator to recognize or recall the existence of the organized farm, business, and labor interests; to recognize or recall the name of any of the lobbyists for these groups; and to link either the organized group or its lobbyist to issues which had arisen in the 1951 session. There was far less recognition of inter-group bargaining, techniques of lobbying, and patterns of individual interaction. Only two of the representatives interviewed were fully aware of the inter-group negotiations which had taken place on the occupational disease bill. Two or three others knew that some negotiations had taken place, but did not know that concessions had been made by the two sides. They referred questions about such details to Representatives Ralph Smith or Walter Malmquist, who, it will be recalled, were the two representatives actually involved in the whole range of negotiations. Another two or three representatives knew that business and labor—and they only presumed that it had been Kane and Mitchell —had somehow managed to agree on the occupational disease bill, but had no idea of what the agreement had involved or that it had taken the form of a *quid pro quo*. The remaining representatives could recall the occupational disease bill only dimly, and associated it vaguely with labor, but for the most part did not recall that the AIV or "business" had been concerned with it, and had no knowledge of "business-labor" conferences, negotiations, or compromises.

This less than a dozen representatives who had been aware to varying degree of the protracted and, to the AIV and labor, highly important negotiations, were almost without exception the only ones who were able to discuss in any detail the nature of the membership of the Associated Industries, and it was not clear to all of them how the

Table II—Representatives in Each Category of Perspective on the Session Who Were Able to Identify Organized Interest Groups

LEGISLATIVE PERSPECTIVE	NUMBER	PER CENT ABLE TO RECOGNIZE ORGANIZED INTEREST GROUP		
		Farm Bureau	AIV	CIO/AFL
"Policy-Oriented"	4	100.0%	100.0%	100.0%
"Program-Oriented"	12	100.0	100.0	100.0
"Faction-Oriented"	13	100.0	56.2	76.9
"Non-Generalizers"	11	100.0	45.4	45.4
Totals	40	100.0	62.5	77.5

Table III—Representatives in Each Category of Perspective on the Session Who Were Able to Identify the Lobbyists for Each Group

LEGISLATIVE PERSPECTIVE	NUMBER	PER CENT ABLE TO RECOGNIZE LOBBYIST OF THE GROUP		
		Farm Bureau	AIV	CIO/AFL
"Policy-Oriented"	4	100.0%	100.0%	100.0%
"Program-Oriented"	12	75.0	75.0	41.7
"Faction-Oriented"	13	84.6	23.0	23.1
"Non-Generalizers"	11	36.4	00.0	27.3
Totals	40	70.0	40.0	37.5

Table IV—Representatives in Each Category of Perspective on the Session Who Were Able to Recall More Than One Issue in Which a Group Had Been Interested or Active

LEGISLATIVE PERSPECTIVE	NUMBER	PER CENT ABLE TO RECOGNIZE MORE THAN ONE ISSUE IN WHICH EACH GROUP HAD BEEN ACTIVE		
		Farm Bureau	AIV	CIO/AFL
"Policy-Oriented"	4	75.0%	100.0%	100.0%
"Program-Oriented"	12	83.3	58.3	33.3
"Faction-Oriented"	13	61.5	7.7	23.2
"Non-Generalizers"	11	18.4	9.9	18.4
Totals	40	60.0	30.0	30.0

diversity of membership had influenced Kane's ability to act in the development of the tax program. The other representatives were hardly aware of the existence of the AIV and had no conception of the nature of its membership. All those with the "policy-oriented" perspective and half of those with the "program-oriented" perspective knew that the AIV had a high degree of interest in the various tax alternatives which were being proposed, and they had been watching to see whether the group would, in fact, take a position on tax changes. None of the other representatives (who constitute 75% of the sample of the lower house) had any notion that the AIV was interested in the tax proposals.

The dimensions of a legislator's awareness of group activity do not appear to be related to respondent's affiliation with one faction or another. Faction was also unrelated to the representative's conception of the process in the legislative session. As noted above, however, there was a relationship between the way the legislator structured the events of the session and his ability to report the activity of organized groups. Furthermore, it was not unexpected that the more complex patterns were seen by respondents of longer legislative service, more education, less geographic isolation, and more urban background.

Table V—Relationship Between Perspective on Legislative Session and Socio-economic Variables

LEGISLATIVE PERSPECTIVE	NUMBER	PER CENT OF LEGISLATORS WITHIN EACH CATEGORY		
		From Towns With Pop. of More Than 2,500	With Prev. Leg. Exp.	With Coll. Education
"Policy-Oriented"	4	100.0%	75.0%	100.0%
"Program-Oriented"	12	50.0	66.7	58.3
"Faction-Oriented"	13	15.4	53.8	30.8
"Non-Generalizers"	11	0.0	27.2	9.1

Widely different attitudes and value judgments emerged from the interviews as to the role of interest groups in the decision-making process. A number of the legislators, mostly "policy-oriented" or "program-oriented," recognized the importance of inter-group negotiations in softening the edges of conflict among interests, be they organized or unorganized. Some legislators cited instances when they themselves had urged such negotiations. Others had sought to establish that such inter-group conferences had taken place and that the results were acceptable to the participants. One legislator, for example, discussed the occupational disease bill by saying:

... that was one thing John Mitchell was very interested in. I saw him around and asked him about it, and he told me to vote for it. I asked him if he was satisfied with it, and he said "no," he wasn't, but "go talk to Ted Kane—he isn't satisfied with it either. Or talk to (Ralph) Smith—he isn't satisfied either. None of us are satisfied, but it gets a bill on the books." So it was a compromise bill, and I voted for it.

Then there were the legislators, also among the "policy-" and "program-oriented," who pointed out that unilateral pressure was not ordinarily effective in changing opinions:

Lobbyists are effective only when opinion is not already made up, or when there is a propensity in that direction anyway. I can't think of one instance when an actual switch was brought about by lobbying.

A few others, not so facile with abstractions, confirmed this opinion. One legislator, a farmer himself, told of an attempt made by the Farm Bureau to persuade him to vote against the State Police merger when he himself had been in favor of it:

This was the bill I was most pressured on. The Farm Bureau tried to change my vote. Each county has a Farm Bureau branch, and each branch has a legislative committee of about five people, not themselves legislators. They discuss the issues they think are going to come up and pass resolutions. During the session the local committees meet and talk about bills. The ———— County committee had decided that they were against the merger. After the second reading when they found out that I had voted for the merger they came to me and asked me to change my vote on the third reading. I said I didn't think I would, and I didn't. There was nothing they could do about it.

In another instance a farmer-legislator had been subjected to vigorous argument by the retail grocers, who were working for repeal of laws against the sale of colored oleomargarine: "I guess it will get passed eventually," he said sadly. "More and more seem to be for it; but I couldn't come home and look one of my cows in the eye if I voted for it."

Some of these legislators were anxious to point out that a discussion of interest groups cannot be confined to what is ordinarily termed "lobbying." Said one legislator:

You can't talk about "Farm Bureau" activity on this bill. Farm support or opposition is not always organized. It's the same with any group. For example when this bill came up, or when any bill comes up, the members of the Agricultural Committee sit around for a while in their committee room and discuss the effects of the bill on them as farmers. Sure, they're all farmers and probably all Farm Bureau members. But is this an organized group? Not really. At least not organized in such a way that you can point to direct Farm Bureau influence.

Another legislator talking about the influence of one of the lobbyists who had at one point in his career held state office, had this to say:

It's not so much a question of cornering this one or that in lobbies, . . . had a room on the second floor of the hotel and so did a number of influential legislators. He'd go out about 10 P.M. and get together with a few of them. He's an old guy, very lively and highly respected. They'd pat the man on the back and invite him in. Then he'd say, "you know, about this bill and that. I think this and that." And he'd be listened to. It's much more this kind of thing than actually speaking in hearings, although he did that too.

These were the legislators, too, who considered various organized groups and their lobbyists to be sources of information not only on the actual content of bills, but on attitudes about the bills. A few first-term members reported that they had consulted with the politically experienced lobbyists to get their opinions on techniques of legislative strategy.

In sharp contrast to those who viewed the interest groups as the instruments for softening conflict, defining alternatives, and conveying information, were the legislators who expressed highly negative opinions about the role of interest groups in the legislative process. Some of these fell into the category of "faction-oriented," but most of them were the "non-generalizers." "Lobbying is immoral, indecent, and unnecessary," was a fairly representative statement among this group. "There were lots of lobbyists around, but they knew it wouldn't do any good to talk to me, and I left them alone too," said another. Running through most of such interviews was a concept of an undefined "they." For the most part, unable to fit into their framework of process the activities of organized groups, these legislators could say only that "they killed it," or "they got it passed," but could not identify who "they" actually were, or how "they" had managed to kill or pass the bill.

V. Leadership in the Legislature. At the close of the interview each legislator was asked to nominate the members of the legislature whom it would be most valuable for the research team to visit and question. A noticeable pattern was a pronounced regional division of the state. Legislators from the southern part tended to suggest only other legislators from the south, and northern legislators tended to feel that only other legislators from the north were "worth talking to."[7] In addition, a simple count of the number of times any legislator was recommended revealed an informal structure in the legislature. Certain legislators were recommended many times more frequently than others, and their nomination was independent of respondent's factional preference or geographic residence. Without exception, those nominees appearing in the sample interviewed were "policy-oriented" or "program-oriented" in their own interpretation of the session. Parenthetically and understandably, the "non-generalizers" made the fewest nominations, and made them with the greatest reluctance.

These nominated legislative leaders, who commanded an important position in the informal structure of the legislature, appeared to have played a significant part in interpreting and reporting events for the others. They seem to have defined for the others both the nature of reality and the alternative means for bringing such reality into better adjustment with the legislator's personal preferences. They did not influence to any noticeable degree the final choice among these alternatives for the other legislators, as evidenced by the roll-call votes on crucial issues, and by the factional allegiances of respondent and nominee.[8]

VI. Reviewing the Record. The 1951 session afforded the Associated Industries of Vermont some interesting surprises. On the policy issue defined in advance for action, the strategy of intergroup negotiation worked admirably. The advantage of access gained from the 1950 election was put to immediate use. The substance of the bill was satisfactory to the business members. The timing was right in the legislature. The relations with other groups remained cooperative and available for further issues. The tactical moves were made out of the public eye. The requisite appearance of harmony was sustained; there were no complicated reservations, no outcries of frustration, to precipitate a negative vote.

But the case study suggests forcefully that the business group had interests at stake on many fronts, and was far from free to have its own way. Sure of access to the executive and to both houses of the legislature, convinced that the climate of opinion in the election had been sympathetic to its needs and aspirations, careful to avoid the limelight, aware that the label of business was a handicap to a policy proposal, active to form alliances with labor on social insurance and with agriculture on federal control of inflation, the AIV nonetheless ran into heavy weather. Representatives of business had worked closely with the new governor in preparing the budget message. Economy and no new taxes were the keynotes of the executive program. But an absolute freezing of appropriations was not realistic in a year of inflation. The proposed reorganization of agencies became a symbol of factional rivalry. The informal leadership emerging during the session left the AIV with notably diminished access. The timing on the major

issue of the new taxes turned out to be all wrong. The AIV had not anticipated the problem, and lacked a policy and a strategic plan. The rotten-borough, rural-dominated legislature, with short tenure, afforded little opportunity for AIV to develop a case for business views of fiscal policy. A final irony of the 1951 episode was the 1952 election, in which Governor Emerson, seeking re-election, was widely criticized for the overwhelming surplus in the state treasury, product of these increased personal and corporate income taxes under the stimulus of the Truman boom.

The widely varying conceptions of the legislative process that turned up in the legislative interviews after the session explained much about the cautious approach used by AIV. Kane did not try to be invisible, and there is little to be said for stereotypes of invisible governments and pressure group politics. But, to a political scientist, it is reasonably astonishing to discover how few of the legislators could name the interest groups correctly or associate group executive with group or issue. The amateur legislature, meeting biennially, for nominal compensation, is a remarkably relaxed forum of political behavior. The issues are viewed as postponable. The temperature is kept moderate by this basic technique of resolving conflict. In this case the interest group had to play the game of politics with a legislature that was essentially unorganized until the game was better than half over.

Notes

1. As far as the party division in the legislature is concerned, it should be sufficient to say that the Democrats counted among their members 21 representatives (8.5%) and one senator. On all matters, including that of organization of the House and Senate, a Democrat in the Vermont legislature is indistinguishable by his voting behavior from a Republican.

2. Much of the material presented in this section is based on reports of participant observers who were employed in the offices of the Associated Industries and the Vermont Farm Bureau during the 1951 legislative session.

3. The Barre Granite Association included among its members almost all of the 117 granite companies in the state, and had joined the AIV as an association, paying a lump sum annually as dues.

4. The sample of legislators who were interviewed is not statistically representative of the membership of the 1951 session of the Vermont legislature. Forty members of the 246 representatives were interviewed, and 16 of the 30 senators. Half of the members of the House sample were selected by the participant observers in the Associated Industries and the Farm Bureau as either accessible to the interest groups under study, influential in the legislature, or both accessible and influential. The remaining half of the House sample was selected on a random basis. It was originally planned to interview the entire membership of the Senate, but interviews were completed with only slightly more than half of the senators.
Despite the fact that the entire sample was not chosen on a random basis, the sample as it was drawn is rep-

resentative in certain characteristics considered relevant. The geographic distribution of the members and the party division in the legislature are quite accurately reflected in the sample, as is the distribution by previous legislative experience. The 40 members of the House under-represent slightly the proportion of representatives from the smaller towns, and the proportion of farmer-representatives, and over-represent slightly the proportion of lawyer-representatives.

5. These perspectives and the analyses to follow must of necessity be impressionistic and based on rough qualification. The sample is too small to allow more rigorous validation. The number of representatives who fall into each group should be kept in mind.

Group	Number of Representatives
''Policy-Oriented''	4
''Program-Oriented''	12
''Faction-Oriented''	13
''Non-generalizers''	11
Total	40

The Senate sample is too small to analyze separately. All quantifications are based on the representatives. The findings reported on the representatives appear as tendencies in the Senate. The two samples have not been combined, since the two populations differ in intrinsic characteristics.

6. After the legislator had completed his discourse on "the most important problems," specific issues were introduced unless volunteered by respondent. Since the interest group activity on these issues was available from the participant observers, one purpose of the legislative survey was to complement this story with a picture of how the process appeared to the legislator. Accordingly, it was planned to include discussion of the questions on which the AIV had been most active and interested: the occupational disease and unemployment compensation bills which had been involved in the business-labor negotiations. Each interview was also intended to include a discussion of the Governor's budget, the proposed State Police merger, the proposed cut in the Vermont Development Commission appropriations, the "patchwork" taxes, and the sales-income tax alternatives.

In addition, the interviews were planned to include discussion of two matters on which the Vermont Farm Bureau had been active: a proposal to permit the sale of colored oleomargarine; and two proposals relating to the St. Lawrence Seaway, one memorializing Congress to approve the Seaway, and another establishing an agency in Vermont which would be authorized to negotiate for power resulting from any St. Lawrence development.

The interviews did not follow a prescribed sequence, nor were they confined to these topics. They did not always achieve complete coverage, either because respondent lacked information or interest in the proposed items, or because the interview developed respondent's concepts of party, faction, interest group, executive roles, and issues by other means.

7. This division was a real surprise. Preliminary talks with knowledgeable people had described the political organization of the Republican party as dividing between east and west, with an alternation in office for the two sides of the mountains.

8. Though the data available from the interviews do not bring it into clear focus, there is a further variable related to the informal leadership structure of the legislature. To some members, service in the legislature is a strictly amateur undertaking, pursued for many motives, it is true: out of a sense of civic duty; as an enormously entertaining pastime to relieve the rigor of a northern winter; a varied social occasion; a chance to make business contacts or advance personal status in the home community. To others, it is part of their professional vocation. The professionals may go no further than the legislature, and may not expect to. Or they may be moving rapidly through a series of public offices. They may be freshmen or have many years of experience. In any case, the professional member must bring to his role a different perspective of the process and a different stance in his own activities than does the amateur. Further research is needed to develop the relationships between these roles and the materials analyzed in this case study.

7. THE ROLE OF AN INTEREST GROUP LEADER

John H. Millett

STUDENTS OF POLITICAL BEHAVIOR have long been aware of the phenomenon of conflicting interests centering in the same individual.[1] A person in his interactions with his family may display interests differing from those he expresses in his interactions with his peer group; his interests as a producer may call for public policies counter to those of his interests as a consumer. Many other examples could be given—membership in a religious organization, community association—the possible list is endless.

The purpose of this paper is to survey conflicting interests in the behavior of a particular officer of an organized interest group who is a member of the House of Commons, concentrating on his actions as a member of the Government party. The presence in the House of Commons of a large number of spokesmen for highly particularistic interests may seem a paradox to those impressed with the power of the majority party leadership; indeed, the activities of organized interest groups, much less the expressions of unorganized particularistic interests, have been almost ignored in descriptions of British government.[2] The incredible cohesion of British parties has been well demonstrated since the recent war when the Labour party maintained its majority on all major issues with a majority of no more than six, and the Conservative party did likewise with a slightly larger majority

Reprinted from *Western Political Quarterly*, Vol. 9 (1956), pp. 915-926, where it appeared under the title, "The Role of an Interest Group Leader in the House of Commons," by permission of the author and the publisher.

from October, 1951, to the General Elections of 1955. In spite of dramatic factional groups, such as the "Bevanites" in the Labour party and the "Suez Group" in the Conservative party, the whips have always produced a party majority when needed. What, then, is the role of a lone spokesman of an organized interest group in such an institutional arrangement?

Sir Ian Fraser, M.P., and the British Legion. Sir Ian Fraser, Conservative Member of Parliament for the Morecambe and Lonsdale division of Lancashire, and president of the British Legion since 1947, combines a number of potentially conflicting interests. He has been a Tory M.P. since 1924, with the exception of the periods from 1929 to 1931 and 1937 to 1940. In addition, he is a blinded veteran of World War I, a barrister, a company director, and a citizen of the Union of South Africa. As an M.P. he speaks often for the sectional interests of his constituency, which are primarily two, farming and seaside resorts. Any interests expressed as a war veteran are thus only a small part of the total for which he may wish to speak as an M.P. Yet it is as president of the British Legion that he is probably best known in Parliament today.

The British Legion is the largest and best known of the veterans' organizations in England and Wales. Formed in 1921 from four competing groups under the leadership of Field Marshall the Earl Haig, it is unrivaled as the only organization offering membership to veterans of any service, including women's services, from any date of service. It is best known for its welfare activities and for social clubs which are affiliated with its branches. The English public comes in contact with the group on Remembrance Sunday, the Sunday nearest November 11, and during the preceding week when poppies are sold to collect funds for its welfare activities, the sales annually totaling just under one million pounds.

The Legion's membership is difficult to determine precisely.[3] It reached a peak in 1948 of just under one million; since then a steady decline has set in, its present membership being about 650,000 in 5,200 local branches. In addition to this there is a Women's Section, or auxiliary, composed of wives and daughters of Legion members, perhaps numbering about 250,000.

The top governing body of the Legion is the Annual Conference, a meeting of branch delegates. The Conference is a large and unwieldly body which usually follows the leadership offered by its chairman and the National Executive Council. The Council includes two members chosen by each of several geographic areas, all past chairmen, and the present chairman,

vice chairman, president, and honorary treasurer. Of these officers, the chairman is the most important; he presides at Conferences and Council meetings and, although unpaid, devotes most of his time to Legion affairs. The president is largely a ceremonial officer; he opens the Conference with an inspirational speech and addresses meetings throughout the country, but rarely spends much of his time on Legion business. Probably one of the most important officials is the chief permanent paid officer, the general secretary, whose day-to-day management of Legion affairs and continuous service made him a powerful influence in the affairs of the Council. The present holder of that office has been with the Legion since its formation, first as assistant general secretary and for the past fifteen years as general secretary.

The Legion has from its beginning sought representation in the House of Commons and one or more M.P.'s have always spoken for it. While the Legion goes to great lengths to discourage branches from backing specific candidates for office, it does encourage branches to put the Legion's current position to all candidates and to seek pledges of co-operation from them. Since the recent war less emphasis has been placed upon this type of activity; but whether branches do seek pledges from candidates or not, the Legion has its spokesmen in Parliament, particularly since its President has a safe seat—a majority of over 17,000 in May, 1955.

While strongly proclaiming that it is nonpartisan, the Legion has always claimed to be "political," and proudly points to one of the listed objects in its Royal Charter: "To promote representation of the needs of ex-service men widows and children and dependents to or in Parliament. . . ." For the most part these "needs" have been narrowly interpreted. Rarely has the Legion as an organization announced any views on subjects other than veterans' disability pensions, veterans' employment, and housing. While these subjects may occasionally lead into other matters, such as social security and the nationalized industries, successive Legion pronouncements have been cautious in dealing with any policy which is closely identified with one of the major parties.

During Sir Ian Fraser's presidency, the major claim publicly made upon the Government has been a demand for an increase in the basic rate of veterans' disability pensions. In 1945 this was 40s. per week for a 100 per cent disabled ex-private with no additional allowances for medical treatment, wife or family, or unemployability, a rate identical with that paid since 1919, except for a brief period from 1939 to 1943 when World War II men were temporarily paid at a slightly lower rate. In December, 1945, the basic rate was raised to 45 *s.* per week, bringing it in line with rates just established for civilian disability pensions.

At the 1946 Conference, the National Executive Council submitted a resolution asking for a basic pension rate of 60*s.* a week. Amended from the floor to read 90*s.* a week, this has remained the goal ever since.[4] In view of later criticisms in 1948-49 that the Legion campaign on pension rates was a Tory plot to embarrass the Labour Government, it should be noted that the leadership of the Legion found itself led in this matter by the Conference. Further, in 1948 the leadership of the Legion sponsored a resolution asking for a "substantial increase" in the basic rate. This was again amended from the floor to read 90*s.* a week, although the leadership, including Sir Ian, had asked for moderation.[5] After that the 90*s.* goal was accepted without question by both leadership and rank-and-file.

This was the position of the British Legion when Sir Ian Fraser was chosen president. Previously there had been three presidents, all well-known military leaders who had no connection with any political activities. Apart from the Earl Haig, a founding father of the Legion, Sir Ian is the only president really contributing more than ceremonial service to the Legion.

The circumstances of Sir Ian's election indicate that he was not selected by the Legion leadership, nor selected as part of a preconceived plan to secure Legion representation in Parliament. He was already in the House and already recognized as Legion spokesman there by this organization and by other M.P.'s.[6]

Sir Ian recognized his peculiar position of being a partisan M.P. and Legion president when he told the Conference immediately after his election:

The next thing is to get our minds clear upon politics and I tender to you my very special thanks for the particular confidence you have shown in me in electing a member of a particular Party to be President of a non-party organization. I regard this as a special trust which I will honour, but remember this, that politics is the art of government, that the duty of every citizen is to take his or her part in politics and it is our right as well as our duty to take our hand in politics—not in Party politics, but in guiding and helping the Government of our country in national affairs. Sometimes that requires that we oppose the Government, whatever its Party; sometimes it requires that we support it, but let us make up our minds henceforth, without taking any side in Party politics, that we are going to take a stronger hand in national politics.[7]

The British Legion in the House of Commons. The eight years of Sir Ian's presidency to this time divide neatly into two four-year periods, in the first of which he was a member of the Opposition party in Commons and in the second, a member of the Government party. During the first period (1947-51) his job was to push the Government on Legion issues without permitting the Legion to become identified with the Conservative party, while during the second (1951-55) his function was to push his own party without violating his own party discipline or embarrassing his own Government. Neither proved to be easy to do, particularly as the Legion's first claim on pension rates, amounting to a doubling of the cost of pensions to the Government, came at a time of extreme financial difficulties for Great Britain and had little chance of acceptance in full by any Government.

The opportunities for a private member to express his interests in the House of Commons are limited: debates on the Gracious Speech from the Throne and the Budget; possibilities during finance debates; question time; debates on adjournment; and the rare introduction of private-member bills or motions.[8] Of course Government legislation may touch upon a member's interests; but in the case of the British Legion such legislation is rare.

The Legion has never depended upon only one member to put its point of view. In 1921, Legion friends in the House of Commons organized a "House of Commons Branch" composed of all Legion members in Commons. This is a Legion "Branch" in title only and its members all have membership in a regular branch outside the House. With a membership now of about one hundred, it meets two or three times a year to discuss Legion interests and to urge members to raise Legion policies at every opportunity. Since 1945 the Speaker of the House has served as honorary president of the Branch and has presided at its meetings (both Speakers since 1945 have been veterans and Legion members).[9] The Branch's "officers" are carefully selected to represent all three parties, with the chairmanship alternating among the parties.

The Branch's activities as a branch are severely limited. Questions to be asked ministers at question time are distributed, speeches by Legion officials are heard, and occasionally deputations to ministers are sponsored. But for the most part the Branch merely serves to keep Legion policies before those M.P.'s who are interested. Some M.P.'s utilize Legion membership for their own electioneering purposes, but the Legion cannot utilize the House of Commons Branch to ask M.P.'s to violate party discipline.

The more militant delegates at Legion Conferences annually demonstrate a lack of understanding of the workings of party discipline and regularly complain of lack of activity on the part of the House of Commons Branch. Often, since the formation of the Branch, motions "censuring" it have been put before the Conference. Just as regularly Legion officials attempt to explain the Branch's role to their membership. Typical was Sir Ian Fraser's statement in the Legion *Journal* shortly after he became president—made when he was in opposition and could gain personally from attempts to embarrass the Government:

> Whatever Government is in power the Chancellor of the Exchequer must remain the guardian of the public purse, the national treasurer, and he must be able to rely on the Cabinet and majority in the House or the nation's business cannot go on.
>
> It follows that the ordinary M.P. on the Government side of the House must be willing to give him support, or the Government would cease to exist. This fundamental fact conditions the operation of the Legion's House of Commons Branch, and it is the reason why we cannot use it as a spearhead of attack upon the Government.
>
> On the other hand, it renders a most valuable service to ex-service men and the Legion by creating goodwill for our cause in the House, and in spreading information about our claims.
>
> ... We do not as a Legion take part in party politics, but we ought to exercise our influence in national affairs through our contacts with Members of Parliament, and by our effect on public opinion.[10]

Since World War II, the Legion has developed a highly co-ordinated campaign which has three distinct but related phases. Beginning in about November, a public campaign of posters, leaflets, speeches, letters to the editors, etc., is begun, aimed to hit a climax about a month before the Budget Address. The hope is that branches, individual members, other voluntary organizations and ordinary citizens will fill the mail bags of M.P.'s. Second—and this may well be where genuine bargaining takes place—contacts are maintained with the Ministry of Pensions (now the Ministry of Pensions and National Insurance). Finally, the Legion's friends in the House of Commons step up their questions to the minister and attempt to find opportunities to raise the issue in debate. If the first phase operates well, the number of friends in the House presumably increases. How much Members of Parliament pester their whips and ministers informally is a matter for speculation, but certainly some of that must go on.

Sir Ian Fraser in the House of Commons. As this paper is investigating the possible conflict between particularistic and general interests in the actions of an M.P., Sir Ian Fraser's activities in opposition will be ignored. His own party could

hardly be upset when all the demands the Legion was making would, if not fulfilled, embarrass the Labour party; so few problems with his own whips could occur.

When the General Election of October, 1951, returned a Conservative Government with a majority of seventeen seats, the Legion was preparing an extensive campaign for a pensions increase. The basic rate still stood at 45s. per week and the Legion was still requesting that this be doubled.

The sides were now reversed and loyal Labour party members could join the British Legion in attempting to embarrass a Conservative Government. But what of the Conservative back-bencher who was also the president of the British Legion? A Legion member, at a pensions campaign meeting, asked Sir Ian this very question shortly after the General Election: "If this matter (a Government refusal to increase pensions) came to a division in the House of Commons and the Government put on a three-line whip, how would the President vote?" Sir Ian replied:

> I am not a slave of the whips. The discipline of the whips is a self-imposed one. It is like that of a football team where you play for the side, not for oneself. I would not pledge myself in advance to the whips or the Conservative Party or to the British Legion. I should have to decide the way I vote on a measure on the merits of the case at the time it came up and its wording.
>
> If I vote against the Government, they may be displeased but I am not elected by the Government, I am elected by my constituents. If I go on displeasing the party, they can, at the next election, refuse to endorse my candidature and put up another candidate against me—but that may not happen for five years. On the other hand, the Legion can dismiss me in any one year they please. It is not my custom, either in my private or public life, to let down my friends.[11]

This did not please one Legion member, who wrote to the *Journal*:

> Like many thousands of members must have been, I was very disappointed at the President's "answer" to the question put to him.
>
> Surely it is time that straight answers were given to straight questions, and not "political answers." We have a just cause and it does not need hiding from any political party. If it comes to the question of Service to the Disabled, or to a political party, then it is the duty of the President, or any member of the National Executive who is not fully behind the campaign, to resign. Such holding of office is only giving lip service to a great cause.[12]

Sir Ian's answer to this letter sums up the dilemma of a person in his position:

> I am an avowed advocate of the Legion's Pensions Campaign. No doubt being in Parliament gives me a platform and access to Ministers which may be held

an advantage for any advocate of any cause. The time may come when I may be judge instead of advocate when an issue is voted upon in the House. . . . I will consider the issue when it arises in the circumstances obtaining and use my judgment.

It is by no means certain that on a straight vote whether war pensions should be dealt with separately from other pensions, or whether they should be increased, I might not vote against the Government. But there might be a vote devised for political purposes in which I would support the Government, or a situation arise in which I were convinced that the country could not afford any improvement in any social services because of approaching financial disaster.

Resignation [from the Legion's Presidency] . . . is seldom out of my mind and I often consider whether I could serve the Legion better out of office or in it as an ordinary M.P. The problem is inherent in having a politician as President and can only be avoided by choosing someone who either has no political views, takes no responsibility for the economic affairs of the country, or, if he has a view, keeps it under his hat.[13]

The conflicts for Sir Ian began with the first Budget Address of the new Conservative Government in April, 1952. At this time the basic pensions rate was increased from 45s. to 55s. a week, far short of the Legion's goal. Sir Ian had the job of thanking his own front bench and at the same time pointing out the inadequacy of the improvement.[14] The thanks he expressed on the floor of the House were effusive, but he did state that the increase "did not match even the minimum figures produced to show what compensation is needed to offset the fall in the pound's value."

Labour speakers immediately pointed out that his thanks were too much for the "pittance" granted, and one of the prominent disabled Labourites, a former parliamentary secretary for the Ministry of Pensions, Mr. James Simmons, rubbed in the criticisms by referring to Sir Ian's exchange of remarks on party discipline:

He went out of his way to be nice to his Front Bench after stressing the fact that he was going to make a non-political speech. . . . I am not altogether surprised because . . . he made it clear that what he said as the President of the British Legion would not necessarily influence his action on the floor of the House. . . . [In spite of the Legion's campaign to double pensions rates] hon. Member now comes to the Committee and defends his Front Bench for having given a 10s. increase to meet this grave and aggravated economic situation.[15]

Sir Ian replied that he had balanced his remarks between thanks and criticism. To this Mr. Simmons retorted: "What I am concerned about is what the Legion will think about its President, who in this Committee gives support to these proposals while his demands in the country have been so much in excess of it."

This appeal to the membership of the Legion did indeed reach the Legion rank-and-file. At the 1952 Conference of the Legion, held two months later, the first resolution on the agenda was one of censure of the President, in part for his thanking of the Chancellor of the Exchequer for the 10s. a week raise. The Conference debate, while clearly demonstrating that the membership wanted increased pensions and was far from satisfied with what had happened, did not indicate any lack of confidence in Sir Ian.[16] Sir Ian justified his actions on the ground of tactics and maintained that he always thanks ministers whenever the Legion or the veteran receives favors from the Government, regardless of party affiliations. His speech ended with the Conference voting down the motion of censure 650 to 5. But the very fact of the debate could always be a reminder of the conflicts of interests between the Legion as an organized interest and the Conservative party.

The next two Budgets, in 1953 and 1954, provided no further increases for disabled veterans, although the Legion continued its campaigns with as much vigor as ever. Furthermore, it genuinely seemed to make no difference to Sir Ian that his own party was in power, for when he found opportunity, he continued to raise the issue even when it might be embarrassing. He did attempt a rational justification of the request for a 90s. a week basic pension rate, which was adopted by the 1946 Conference on the impassioned plea of one delegate. By taking 1938 as a parity year, he could demonstrate that 90s. a week was necessary to maintain purchasing power for the disabled. The Government used the year 1919 to justify its stand, while another small but influential group, the British Limbless Ex-Service Men's Association, used 1946 to justify an increase to 62 s. a week. Typical of Sir Ian on this subject was a debate on adjournment just before the 1953 Budget Address, when Sir Ian was gently spoofed by the Minister involved on his method of juggling cost-of-living figures. At this time Sir Ian pressed his case in terminology as vigorous as that he used when in opposition, and even reminded his front bench that they had voted against Labour in 1948 on this very issue.[17]

Budget debates rarely give the individual member any opportunity to vote against his own party on the single clear-cut issue in which he may be interested. Thus at no time while the Conservative party was in power from 1952-54 could Sir Ian pointedly make his case by walking through the Opposition lobby during finance votes. But another opportunity did arise by which he could show his displeasure, vote against his own whips, and win the gratitude of the more militant British legionnaire by demonstrating that he could, when the occasion arose, put the "Legion ahead of his party."

Early in 1953 the Government announced that it planned a reorganization of several departments which involved abolishing the Ministry of Pensions, placing its pensions work with the Ministry of National Insurance and its hospitals with the Ministry of Health. The Legion at first sniffed suspiciously at this proposal and then came out solidly against it at its 1953 Conference.[18]

During the Adjournment Debate which Sir Ian had raised before the 1953 budget, he had suggested that his attitude on the merger might be affected by action taken or not taken on the pensions rate. He said at that time, "However, final judgment on whether the merger is a good thing or not will . . . depend much more upon what Governments do for disabled ex-Service men by way of improving their war pensions."[19] This meant, in context, both that satisfaction in the forthcoming Budget would relieve the real source of discontent and that it would quiet fears that veterans would be forgotten among the long list of other claimants upon the welfare state. For, as Sir Ian brought out clearly when explaining in Commons why he was planning to vote against his own whip on the merger question, he considered the abolition of the Pensions Ministry both as symbolic of the loss of status of veterans compared with other groups such as old-age pensioners, industrial disabled and similar beneficiaries of national insurance, and as a loss of access for veterans to the Treasury. These factors, combined with the fact that the pensions rates were so far below the Legion's request, justified for him his voting against his party. While making clear that he was not voting for the Opposition, he did walk into the Opposition lobby. The Government majority was 14, the vote with a three-line whip being 226-212.[20]

On another occasion the issue of war pensions came up for a direct vote in Commons, but on a Motion of Censure put by the Labour Opposition which covered all types of pensions. This was precisely the sort of situation in which Sir Ian Fraser did not like to find himself. The three-line whip probably troubled him less than the fact that while agreeing with that part of the motion on war pensions, he could not agree to seeing war pensions made a party issue and could not agree that the Labour party had done more for veterans, or would do more for veterans, than did his own party. The choice on this vote was not one of being for or against war pensions, but being for or against the Government.

During this debate Sir Ian spent his time at-

tempting to differentiate between old age pensioners and war disability pensioners to demonstrate why the latter should have preferred place in the queue at the Treasury door, and trying to explain why he was voting with his Government.[21] The latter remarks were clearly directed not at other M.P.'s but at the Legion rank-and-file. In a major portion of his remarks he sought to explain why the Government had put a three-line whip on this vote, a matter one could assume the M.P.'s understood. But at previous Legion Conferences speeches by the rank-and-file indicated clearly that they did not understand why the Government did not permit free votes on such matters as disability pensions.

A motion at the 1955 Legion Conference implying discontent with Sir Ian's activities by asking that the presidency be held by a non-politician was partially caused by Sir Ian's vote against the Labour party motion. In addition, Sir Ian ran into trouble by again thanking his front bench too vigorously. The occasion for this was the announcement on December 1, 1954, that basic pension rates would be increased substantially to 67 s. 6 d. a week. But though the increase was substantial and Sir Ian implied later that he believed it was all the Legion could get at that time, it was still far short of the total Legion demand of 90 s.

Sir Ian's thanks at this time were expressed twice, once with flowery rhetorical questions to the Minister immediately following the announcement, and again in a speech during the debate that followed.[22]

The motion implying censure at the 1955 Conference was withdrawn after no support for it materialized. Only the mover spoke for it amidst shouts from the floor. Sir Ian had no need to speak on his own behalf and consequently did not do so.[23]

Conclusions. No conclusions should be drawn from this brief paper concerning the effectiveness of the British Legion, much less any generalized conclusion concerning particularistic interest effectiveness in Britain. No mention has been made of other Legion claims upon the Government nor upon Government concessions of supplementary pension allowances during this period. A far fuller study involving other competing and supplementary group activity would be needed for such conclusions to have any validity.

This study does indicate certain hypotheses which could be explored in further studies. Particularistic organized interests can be and are active in making claims upon British Governments. If the persons making these claims are often faced with difficult choices between their particularistic interests and a more generalized compromise of interests (represented by a party or a Government), it is not only the institutional arrangement of choices involved in the British decision-making process which brings this about; the same conflict of choices exists within the individual before he ever approaches the decision-makers.

The generalized interests represented by parties in Britain are so inclusive that an organized group seeking to maintain its identity distinct from any one of them has great difficulties. The British Legion attempts this by restricting the scope of its expressed interests and by having its spokesmen make its claims with impartial vigor regardless of the majority party in Commons. But its principal spokesman in Commons must of necessity belong to one of the major parties. That Sir Ian Fraser did succeed in part in maintaining the Legion's identity separate from party identities is a measure of personal skill and integrity plus group strength and cohesion.

This study also suggests that much of an organized interest's representative's time in Parliament is spent in seeking group cohesion among his own followers throughout the nation. Since the decisions are not normally made in Parliament, but in the ministerial and administrative bodies outside Parliament, the activity in Parliament is an outward and visible sign of the inner and invisible negotiations taking place between the group's officials and the ministerial and administrative officials.[24] This seems to serve two purposes for the group: first, as suggested above, to maintain the membership's cohesion and interest in the group—to convince the membership that the group leadership is active in its cause; and second, as an additional means of convincing those making decisions of the group's public support. The fact that Parliamentary activity takes place along with other types of group activity indicates that all of these means of seeking access bolster each other.

Much more could be learned of the political process by further group analysis. The nature of party compromise, and consequently party discipline, the interactions of party, private member, organized and unorganized groups, and those actually making the decisions will probably never be fully illuminated until more is known of the interweaving of particularistic strands of British public opinion.

Notes

1. Cf. John Dewey, *The Public and Its Problems* (New York: Henry Holt & Co., 1927), pp. 188 ff.; Walter Lippmann, *Public Opinion* (New York: The Macmillan Co., 1922), pp. 173 ff.; David Truman, *The Governmental Process* (New York: Alfred A. Knopf, 1951), *passim*.

2. The exception is mention of the presence of trade-union leaders and Labour party members sponsored by unions and Co-operative Societies, as well as a growing literature on trade-unionism and specific unions. The best analysis of these activities is Samuel H. Beer, "Pressure Groups and Parties in Britain," *American Political Science Review*, L (March, 1956), 1-23. As for general works on government, an early brief description is that of A. Lawrence Lowell, *The Government of England* (New York: The Macmillan Co., 1912), Vol. I, chap. xxvi. Sir Ivor Jennings has the most extensive description of such activities in *Parliament* (Cambridge: Cambridge University Press, 1939), chap. vii. The existence of "pressure groups" is briefly noted by Ivor Bulmer-Thomas, *The Party System in Great Britain* (London: Phoenix House, 1953), chap. xviii.

3. The national office of the Legion keeps no membership figures. Its *Annual Reports* give the total "affiliation fees," which may be divided by two shillings, the individual fee, to give a rough figure. But these are uncertain, as branches buy "books" of affiliation fees for use over a period of several years, and then sell them as they acquire members. Further, this does not account for life memberships.

4. *British Legion Journal*, XXVI (July, 1946), 152. Unfortunately this is the only year for which there are no complete verbatim proceedings for the Conference, as the official stenographer became ill at the end of the first day and a replacement was unavailable. References in future Conferences establish beyond doubt the story of how this resolution was passed. British Legion, *Annual Conference Verbatim Report*, 1949, p. 56; and *Annual Conference Verbatim Report*, 1950, p. 87. Hereafter these Reports will be cited: Conf.

5. Conf., 1948, pp. 44-49.

6. Conf., 1947, p. 29. Opposition to Sir Ian had the leadership's blessing. He was apparently elected, according to the brief Conference debate, because of his militant statements on the Legion's behalf in the House of Commons.

7. *Ibid.*

8. The problems of the private member are well discussed by Sir Alan P. Herbert, *The Ayes Have It* (London: Methuen & Co., 1937) and *Independent Member* (New York: Doubleday & Co., 1951). From the beginning of the recent war until 1949 no private-member bills or motions were permitted; and it should be recalled that no private-member bill may authorize the expenditure of money.

9. The propriety of the Speaker so identifying himself with an organization making demands upon the Government was questioned by Mr. Attlee in 1952. The Speaker maintained that he was merely presiding at Branch meetings, keeping order and parliamentary procedure, and that he did not identify himself with Legion claims. H. C. Debs., 496 (5th ser.), cols. 235-37.

10. *British Legion Journal*, XXVII (September, 1947), 200.

11. *Ibid.*, XXXII (January, 1952), 6.

12. *Ibid.*, XXXII (March, 1952), 5.

13. *Ibid.*

14. H.C. Deb., 497 (5th ser.), cols. 1478-82.

15. *Ibid.*, col. 1492.

16. Conf., 1952, pp. 29-32.

17. H.C. Deb., 513 (5th ser.), cols. 1395-1415.

18. Conf., 1953, p. 44.

19. H.C. Deb., 513 (5th ser.), col. 1396.

20. H.C. Deb., 517 (5th ser.), cols. 284-90.

21. H.C. Deb., 530 (5th ser.), cols. 1441-47.

22. H.C. Deb., 535 (5th ser.), cols. 149-50, and 211-12.

23. Conf., 1955. Personal observation of the writer. *Verbatim Report* not published at time of writing.

24. Cf. Samuel H. Beer, "The Future of British Politics," *Political Quarterly*, XXVI (January-March, 1955), 38-39.

C. Constituency Relations and Factional Alignments

8. THE RELATION BETWEEN ROLL CALL VOTES AND CONSTITUENCIES*

Duncan MacRae, Jr.

A MAJOR CONCERN of political theorists has been the definition of the proper role of legislators in relation to their constituencies.[1] Yet relatively little analysis has been made of the uniformities of behavior that actually prevail in these relations. Such uniformities, if they could be found, would bear directly on the theory of the party system, on speculation about the nature of representative government, and on the feasibility of proposals for a reordering of party practices.

It has been shown that the tendencies of Congressmen to vote with their party or to cross party lines are associated with the similarity or dissimilarity between party policy and presumed interest of constituency.[2] One aim of this study is to test the applicability of this proposition to the Massachusetts House of Representatives, by examination of the relation between roll-call votes and constituency characteristics. The evidence indicates that a similar relation exists in this body, and has been present consistently throughout the last two decades.

Over and above this relation, it is also of interest to know whether the state of political competition in a constituency has an influence on a representative's votes. Representatives of similar constituencies do not invariably follow the same voting pattern. These differences in voting may be attributable in part to the differences in the political situations in the constituencies. One way in which political competition might influence a representative's votes is to sensitize him to the wishes of constituents in his quest for support at the next election. The closeness of the vote in a

past election may serve as an index to the problems a representative has had in winning past elections and which he may anticipate in future elections. Operationally, the problem is that of holding constant legislative party affiliation and constituency composition to examine the relation between legislative voting behavior and size of the margin of popular vote in the constituency. This examination is the second principal aim of this study.

The Massachusetts House of Representatives. The Massachusetts House has many advantages for the study of the representative process. Massachusetts at present has a highly competitive two-party system, with parties representing fairly distinct regions and socio-economic groups. This competition has come about through a gradual shift in party strength, the Democrats having won a majority in the House in 1948 after a long period of Republican rule in that body. The House has 240 members, a number sufficient to permit some statistical analysis.

The difference between the Republican and Democratic parties in Massachusetts may be summarized as follows: the Republicans are a suburban and rural, high-status, Protestant party, while the Democrats are an urban, lower-status, Catholic party. This is, of course, an oversimplification, as there are other variables that are also important for political behavior. Nevertheless, such generalizations can be made much more easily within Massachusetts than in the nation as a whole. We shall be concerned with some of these qualifications; others, such as the political affiliations of various ethnic groups, will not be treated here.

One particular variable has been chosen to summarize the various differences between "typically Republican" and "typically Democratic" constituencies: the percentage of owner occupancy of dwelling units in a representative district. This variable was chosen for several reasons. It places on a continuum districts ranging from urban working-class areas to the less densely populated

Reprinted from *American Political Science Review*, Vol. 46 (1952), pp. 1046-1055, where it appeared under the title, "The Relation between Roll Call Votes and Constituencies in the Massachusetts House of Representatives," by permission of the author and the publisher.

* The research here reported was conducted with the assistance of the Laboratory of Social Relations, Harvard University. Special acknowledgment is due to Prof. V. O. Key, Jr., for his advice and guidance in the study.

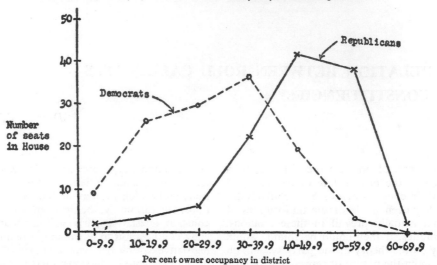

Figure 1—Distributions of Republican and Democratic State Representative Districts in Massachuetts, 1951, by Per Cent Owner Occupancy of Dwelling Units.*

* In this figure and in all succeeding uses of per cent owner occupancy, the source of data is the *Sixteenth Census of the United States, 1940, Housing, Vol. 1, Part 1, Data for Small Areas,* pp. 641 ff.

rural districts. To a high degree it discriminates between Republican and Democratic districts. Its chief drawback appears to be that it groups a few Republican high-status districts, such as Brookline, in the same classification with the solidly Democratic urban districts. This is because per cent owner occupancy is, in Massachusetts, largely a rural-urban variable; for more adequate description of districts a variable measuring average socioeconomic status should also be used.

The difference between Republican and Democratic constituencies in 1951, in terms of per cent owner occupancy of dwelling units, is shown in Figure 1. This figure shows that there is a distinct difference between the types of district that most Democrats and most Republicans represent. There is also an area of overlap, within which most of the competition between parties takes place.

The intensity of competition between parties can be measured by the closeness of elections in various types of districts. If we divide the seats in the House into "sure" and "close" seats, depending on whether or not the representative received as much as 60 per cent of the two-party vote, the distribution of "sure" and "close" seats within the parties is as shown in Table 1. About one-third of the seats held by each party fall in the "close" category.

The way in which "sure" and "close" seats are distributed over the various types of districts, classified by per cent owner occupancy, is shown in Figure 2. In this figure the "close" seats of both parties are grouped together. Figure 2 shows that the close elections in 1950 were largely concentrated in the intermediate range of per cent owner occupancy, while the "sure" Republican and Democratic districts tended to be concentrated at the ends of the scale. These data show that inter-party competition was centered in the intermediate districts. This locus of competition is very similar to what Lubell has called "the urban frontier,"[3] in that a rough dividing point between Democrats and Republicans can be found at a particular level of socio-economic status. A graph similar to Figure 2 for the 1930 election would show a similar picture, with a somewhat less sharp separation of the three curves and a slight shift of the area of party competition back toward the more urban districts. This difference probably reflects the outward push toward the suburbs that has occurred in the last two decades.

Table I—Distribution of "Close" and "Sure" Seats by Parties in Massachusetts House of Representatives, 1951

	"Close" Seats (margin less than 60%)	"Sure" Seats (margin 60% or more)	Total
Democrats	43	81	124
Republicans	41	75	116

In order to examine the relation between election margins and roll-call votes in this body, we shall consider three recent sessions: those of 1931-2, 1941, and 1951. These sessions cover not only the present state of party competition, but also the earlier period of Republican control. They are far enough separated in time so that less than 20 per cent of the membership of one session appears again in the session of a decade later; yet they are close enough so that the use of the 1940 Census as a source of data for all three sessions seems a reasonable approximation.

Data Used in This Study. We wish to study the relation between constituency characteristics and roll-call votes, and the possible effect of electoral contest on this relation. For this purpose we need some measures of election margin, voting behavior, and district characteristics.

a. *Election Margin.* A representative's previous election margin is to be measured by the fraction of the major-party vote he received, with 60 per cent as the cutting point between "close" and "sure" margins. During the sessions studied, there were few candidates outside the major parties. A small number who obtained the nominations of both major parties will be omitted from the tabulations below.

In a number of districts there were two or three seats to be filled at once. To cover these cases, our definition of election margin will be extended as follows: the vote for the candidate in question is to be compared with that for the highest unsuccessful candidate of the opposing party. These two candidates will be treated as if they were the two major-party candidates for a single seat.[4]

b. *Voting Behavior of Representatives.* In an effort to magnify the effect we are concerned with, the roll calls chosen were ones that appeared to reflect socio-economic class differences. For the 1951 session, seven roll calls were chosen by the writer to discriminate Democrats' party regularity. Three were on labor measures, two concerned taxation, and two concerned public expenditures or public works. For the Republicans, eight roll calls were chosen; six dealt with labor legislation, one with old-age assistance, and one with public works. On all these roll calls, majorities of both parties found themselves in opposition. For both parties the choice of roll calls was made so as to maximize the discrimination among party members, along the "social class" dimension, that a scale score would afford. The index used was total number of votes deviating from one's party majority. For convenience in graphical presentation, this was converted into a percentage of the total number of roll calls used in the index. Representatives absent on more than a specified number of these votes were omitted from the analysis.[5]

For the 1941 session, an index tabulated by the Massachusetts Federation of Labor (MFL) was used to measure the deviance of both Democrats and Republicans.[6] The MFL selected seven roll calls taken during this session, which discriminated adequately within both parties.

For the 1931-32 session, separate indices were constructed for Republicans and Democrats. The

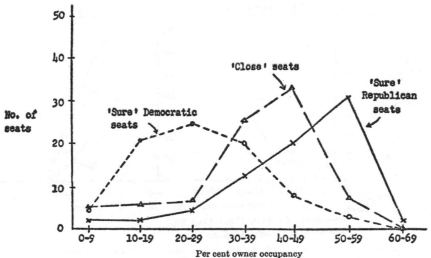

Figure 2—Election Margins (1950) and Per Cent Owner Occupancy of Dwelling Units in District*

* A "close" seat is one for which the winning candidate received less than 60% of the major-party vote. The way in which election margins were calculated will be discussed in more detail in the next section.

Republicans, who showed less party unity than the Democrats in this session, were discriminated by seven roll calls cited in a MFL report. The Democrats, who as a minority party had high cohesion, were discriminated by a set of ten roll calls, mostly on labor issues, selected by the writer.

c. *District characteristics.* The measure of district characteristics used is per cent owner occupancy of dwelling units, which we have discussed above. The basis for calculation is the 1940 Census. Some redistricting occurred in the intervals 1930-1940 and 1940-1950, and this was taken into account in the grouping of data for wards and townships into representative districts.

Findings. The results of tabulation of these data are summarized in Figures 3, 4, and 5. In these figures, the per cent deviation from party is shown for those representatives having close election margins, and for those having wide margins. Each of these groups is represented by two curves. The upper curve of the two shows the most deviant quartile—the extent of party deviation exceeded by only one-fourth of the cases represented by the curve. The lower curve shows the median per cent deviation. Considered together, these two curves give some indication of the dispersion or variability of the data. They are chosen to emphasize the deviant representatives rather than the party regulars; in terms of the voting indices used, the distributions are always skewed toward party regularity. The data have been grouped so that each point represents six or more cases.

Figure 3 shows the results for the 1931-32 session. The following tendencies may be noted in this figure:

1. The extent of party deviation in each party is greatest in districts that are atypical of one's own party, and are most like those of the opposing party. The Democrats from high owner-occupancy districts tend on the average to vote more like Republicans, and the Republicans from low owner-occupancy districts tend to vote more like Democrats.

2. Those representatives with wide election margins (dotted lines) tend more to be party regulars than those with close election margins (solid lines). This effect is especially pronounced for the Republicans in low owner-occupancy districts.

3. The extent of deviation is considerably greater for the Republicans, who had a majority of 141 seats to 99, than for the Democrats. This probably reflects a general tendency for the majority party to be less cohesive than the minority, even though different indices were used for the two parties.[7]

4. There is some evidence that those representatives with close elections were more sensitive to district characteristics than were those with wide elections. This evidence is less conclusive for the Democrats, since there were few Democrats with wide election margins in high owner-occupancy districts.

In order to test these generalizations further we

Figure 3—Party Deviation vs. Per Cent Owner Occupancy, for Wide and Close Election Margins, Massachusetts House 1931-32*

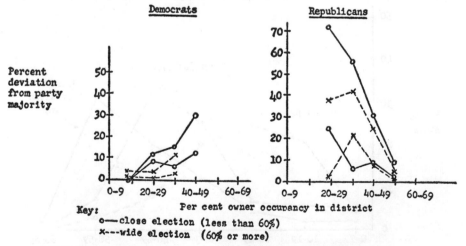

Key:
o—close election (less than 60%)
x---wide election (60% or more)

* Of the four curves in each graph, the pair of solid lines refers to the voting records of representatives with close election margins, and the pair of dotted lines, to that of representatives with wide election margins. The upper line of each pair shows the *most deviant quartile;* only one-fourth of the representatives from a given type of district deviated from their party majority more than this. The lower line of each pair shows the *median* per cent deviation; half the representatives of a given type of district deviated more, and half less, than this value.

must examine other sessions as well. Figure 4 shows the same sort of data for the 1941 session of the Massachusetts House. Again we see that the general tendency of the curves is the same: toward greater deviation in districts less characteristic of the party. The Republican representatives with wide election margins were more "regular"—or recorded more of what the MFL considered "bad votes"—than were those with close margins, especially in atypical districts. The same is true of the Democrats in this session, though to a lesser degree. The Republicans, who had a majority of 143 to 97 in this session, tended more than did the Democrats to cross party lines. The comparison between parties is probably more accurate for this session than for the other two sessions studied, because in this session (1941) the same MFL voting index was used for members of both parties.

Figure 5 shows the same sort of tabulation for the 1951 session. During this session the Democrats had a majority of 124 to 116 in the House. This figure shows some similarities to, and some differences from, the graphs for earlier sessions. As before, the votes of those with close election margins tend to reflect district characteristics to a greater extent than do the votes of those with wide margins. In the 1951 session this is clearly true of Democrats as well as Republicans. With the increasing number of Democratic seats in the House, the Democrats had "wide" election margins in 11 districts of 40 per cent or more owner occupancy. The Republicans retained six seats with "wide" election margins in districts having less than 30 per cent owner occupancy,

but only three seats with "close" margins in similar districts. The seats they held by wide margins in urban areas were mostly in Brookline and Back Bay—both relatively well-to-do areas whose status is not adequately described by their low percentage owner occupancy. For this reason the left-hand points on the dashed curves for Republicans in Figure 5 should be interpreted with caution. Nevertheless the remaining points are in accord with the hypothesis that election margin makes a difference.

The graph for 1951 (Fig. 5) shows some interesting differences from the previous ones. First, the extent of party deviation among the Democrats is roughly the same as that of the Republicans, for the roll calls used. We might expect greater deviation among the Democrats, who are now the majority party. Perhaps this would be observed if other measures of voting behavior were used. The reason for expecting the minority party to be cohesive is probably that no one is strongly motivated to split it; the battle is won if the majority party is held together. But in this case the Republican minority was split for a different reason. Many of the Republican deviations plotted for this session occurred on a roll call on old-age assistance, which passed by a large margin; many Republicans crossed party lines on this roll call, not because their votes affected its passage, but because they wished to go on record as favoring it.

A second new feature appearing in 1951 is the behavior of Democrats with wide election margins. Previously they tended slightly more toward party regularity than did their party colleagues with narrow margins. In 1951 they tended to diverge more

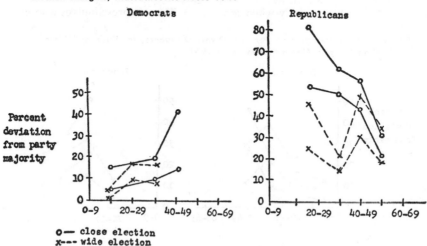

Figure 4—Party Deviation vs. Per Cent Owner Occupancy, for Wide and Close Election Margins, Massachusetts House 1941

o— close election
x--- wide election

Per cent owner occupancy in district

from their party. The voting behavior of the Republicans in this respect did not change. The factors producing this change are of interest, but require further study. Some possible factors that would lead to party regularity are conscientious belief in party principles and the quest for patronage when one's party controls it. A factor that might lead away from party regularity, in addition to one's conscience, is the influence of pressure groups or lobbyists. Some Democrats with wide election margins may have been more susceptible to lobbyists for conservative interests than Republicans in a similar situation were to labor unions. At least this seems a reasonable explanation of the change, for the labor lobbyists could threaten Republicans only with reprisal at the polls, whereas conservative lobbyists may be able to provide other inducements for straying Democrats.

These data may also be used for another purpose: to test Huntington's theory that party differences in liberalism and conservatism are greatest where elections are closest.[8] Figures 3 and 4 show that those representatives having close election margins tended to cross party lines most on issues of interest to the MFL. Figure 5 is inconclusive on this point. Taken together, these data do not indicate any tendency for close elections in themselves, apart from other factors, to accompany ideological divergence between the parties; if anything they indicate the opposite. This emphasizes the fact that Huntington's theory is not concerned with a direct causal relation between closeness of election and ideological divergence between the parties. As he pointed out, where this association exists it is due to underlying cleavages within districts, which may also be accompanied by close elections. The interrelation of these variables can best be clarified by measuring each and examining the effect of each separately while con-

trolling the others. Our data for Massachusetts do not reveal extremely sharp ideological divergences between the parties in "intermediate" districts; rather they show a tendency for the parties to approach one another more closely in those districts where there is a contest between parties. The isolation of these variables on the national scene would be a difficult but enlightening task.

Conclusions. A study of roll-call votes in three sessions of the Massachusetts House of Representatives, in relation to constituency characteristics and election margins, has described in a relatively precise way certain important aspects of the two-party system in Massachusetts. This description applies to one particular type of legislation: that which reflects socio-economic class differences. Generalization of these findings, either to other types of legislation or to other legislative bodies, should be made only with caution. The main findings are as follows:

1. Republican and Democratic districts tend to be differentiated by per cent owner occupancy of dwelling units. This percentage serves as a rough index combining the rural-urban dimension and socio-economic status. The distribution of the two Massachusetts parties with respect to this index is similar to a conventional representation of the national parties; according to this view, both national parties draw support from a wide range of social groups, but they have distinct and separate "centers of gravity."[9]

2. Those representatives who come from districts that are most typical of their parties tend to show highest "party loyalty" on roll calls; those who come from districts atypical of their party tend to cross party lines more often. This agrees with the findings of Turner with regard to Congress.[10]

3. Those representatives whose previous election

Figure 5—Party Deviation vs. Per Cent Owner Occupancy, for Wide and Close Election Margins, Massachusetts House 1951

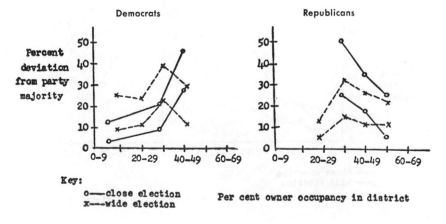

margins were close tend to reflect constituency characteristics in their votes more closely than do those with wider margins. This confirms our original hypothesis and thus may reflect a heightened sensitivity to constituents' wishes resulting from anxiety about reelection. It is also possible, however, that this sensitivity to constituency characteristics results from a general rise in the level of interest in political issues in constituencies where there is a continuing political contest.

4. The tendency of a two-party system to produce moderate parties, at least as it operates in Massachusetts, can be understood in more detail than heretofore. Schattschneider has pointed out that the tendency of each party to be aligned partially with a wide variety of interests leads to this moderation. This study indicates that the moderating influence is most pronounced in those constituencies where political competition prevails—the close districts that are intermediate on the scale of owner-occupancy.

5. Our analysis indicates that there are certain types of representatives who might be approached most effectively by lobbyists and other interested parties. A representative may vote not only in accord with his own conscientious beliefs, but also in accordance with the situation in which he finds himself. Under conditions similar to those studied, those who wish to swing representatives across party lines can probably be most effective by approaching representatives from districts atypical of their party. Those who wish to influence representatives in a direction different from the inclinations of their districts may have most success with those representatives who are in least danger of defeat at the next election. Those who wish to influence representatives toward the inclinations of their districts will probably be most successful with representatives who are in some danger of defeat at the next election. The converse of this suggestion is that party leaders in a legislature who are interested in holding party lines may anticipate in this way where some of the pressures toward party deviation can be exerted, and may prepare to counteract them.

In summary, this study shows something of the way in which the socio-economic characteristics of a constituency influence its politics. But it also indicates that the political contest in a constituency has a distinct effect, over and above socio-economic characteristics.

Notes

1. Doctrines on the question are summarized by Alfred de Grazia, *Public and Republic* (New York, 1951).

2. J. Turner, *Party and Constituency: Pressures on Congress* (Baltimore, 1951).

3. S. Lubell, *The Future of American Politics* (New York, 1952), pp. 58-80.

4. These data were based on the official *Election Statistics* of the Commonwealth of Massachusetts, compiled in the office of the Secretary of the Commonwealth and issued annually as Public Document No. 43 (Boston: 1930, 1940, 1950). The index of "closeness" might be improved in several ways, though it is probably adequate for our purpose. The cutting point 60%, derived from electoral mortality studies of Congress, might be reexamined for Massachusetts. Comparison in multi-member districts might be made with other candidates than the highest unsuccessful one. And, probably most important, other data besides the past election margin might afford a better index of the representative's concern about the wishes of his constituency.

5. Three out of seven for Democrats, and four out of eight for Republicans, were the numbers of absences necessary for exclusion.

6. Massachusetts State Federation of Labor, "Official Labor Record of Senators and Representatives, 1941-1942."

7. This general tendency was noted in the U. S. House of Representatives by Turner, *Party and Constituency*, p. 25n.

8. S. P. Huntington, "A Revised Theory of American Party Politics," *American Political Science Review*, Vol. 44, pp. 669-677 (Sept., 1950).

9. This view is presented, for example, in E. E. Schattschneider, *Party Government* (New York, 1942), pp. 85 ff.

10. Turner, *op. cit.*

9. STATE DELEGATIONS AND VOTING ALIGNMENTS

David B. Truman

RECENT CONTROVERSIES over the degree of responsibility displayed by American parties have underscored at least one feature of voting in the Congress. Whatever the merits of the contending interpretations and demands, the facts adduced on both sides suggest relatively fluid, unstructured voting patterns, especially in the House of Representatives. Although the party label is clearly the single most reliable indicator of congressional voting behavior,[1] it is admittedly somewhat less than perfect. The individual Representative may fairly often dissent from the views of most of his party colleagues, not only on matters of local or minor significance but also on issues of national or even global import.

The Representative's "independence" is most commonly, and in a good many instances accurately, ascribed to peculiarities of his constituency which generate demands for a non-conforming vote or, perhaps more frequently, are expected to be the source of recriminations and penalties if he does not display independence of his party colleagues on certain types of issues. But the Member of Congress is by no means always able to predict the electoral consequences of his choices even though he is sure that they may produce repercussions in his district. This unpredictability contributes to the unstructured character of his position. The political intelligence supplied by interest groups and individual petitioners and advisers, valuable though it may be in helping to resolve doubts, is neither so complete nor so accurate as to eliminate the uncertainties and risks associated with the Representative's response to a call for the "Yeas and Nays."

To the ambiguities of the cues the legislator receives from or perceives in his constituency may be added doubts concerning the preferences and intentions of the formal party leadership on any given vote. On those matters in which the leaders are genuinely interested, means are available for communicating the "party" position to the rank

Reprinted from *American Political Science Review*, Vol. 50 (1956), pp. 1023–1045, where it appeared under the title, "The State Delegations and the Structure of Party Voting in the United States House of Representatives," by permission of the author and the publisher.

and file and even, after a fashion, for enforcing it. But on a number of votes the ordinary Representative, especially if he is a relatively junior member of the House, has no notion of how the party leaders want him to vote.[2] The reasons for this state of affairs may range from a prudent non-feasance to, rarely, a deliberate abdication by the leadership. The stable requirements of the party leader's role in the House may impose his occasional lack of guidance, or it may merely reflect the personality characteristics of the man occupying the role. But, whatever the precise causes, the fact of uncertainty on the part of the rank and file is unmistakable.

In the absence of well-defined, institutionalized, and continuously operative cue-giving mechanisms within the legislative party, one would anticipate that a variety of informal, only partly conscious, but not entirely haphazard devices would be employed by Representatives in arriving at their voting decisions. Moreover, within a body as large as the House or one of the parties in the House these substitute sources of voting-cues would be expected to grow up around familiar associations and relationships serving alternative functions. These would include personal friendships not necessarily political in character, relations of confidence developed through joint service on legislative committees, and even contacts created by the proximity of offices or residences in Washington. They would certainly include the almost ready-made relationships within the state party delegation.

Under certain fairly obvious conditions, voting agreement within the state party delegations is likely to be high. The issues in a given set of roll calls may be of particular importance to organized state-wide interests. They may be of special concern to more localized interests strategically associated with the party organization. Similar voting behavior within the delegation may reflect a tendency of the state party to elect members of Congress from districts roughly similar in socio-economic composition. If the legislative party splits into two opposing regional wings on certain kinds of issues, high intra-state agreement would accompany increased regional solidarity in the House. Finally, if the voting within the legislative party of the House approaches unanimity, it must also do so within most state delegations.

In addition, however, it seems likely that the delegation as a group affects the voting decisions of its members and, under appropriate circumstances, produces marked agreement among them. Some of the factors mentioned in the preceding paragraph, added to the intra-delegation relationships arising from joint concern with matters of legislative party organization or from purely social considerations, make it easy and natural for members of a delegation to consult one another on a variety of legislative questions. The delegation thus tends to constitute a communication structure whose repeated use results in a heightened consensus and similarity of voting among its members. In short, the state party delegation in the House may be a significant alternative cue-giving mechanism within the legislative party, especially on matters whose political implications are ambiguous. Uncertainty is misery and misery loves company.

An opportunity to examine the degree of voting agreement within the state party delegations and some of the conditions of such agreement in a single Congress occurred in connection with a larger study of party voting in the House and Senate in the Eighty-First Congress (1949-50).[3] The basic data are the number of agreements between pairs of Representatives within the two parties on selected roll calls of this Congress. The material suffers from the limitations inherent in a case study, but three features of the procedure somewhat reduce these by introducing elements of recurrence into the analysis. First, comparisons between the two parties are permitted, since they are analyzed independently. Second, limited comparisons in series are possible because the two sessions of the Eighty-First Congress are treated as units rather than jointly. Third, agreements can be compared at three levels of unity within each of the parties, since the roll calls were selected by ranking them according to the Rice Index of Cohesion and choosing them in sets in ascending order of cohesion. This technique produced for each party a set of relatively high and a set of relatively low cohesion votes in the second session and a single set of intermediate cohesiveness in the first session.[4]

There are 74 roll calls in the sets of each party in the first session and in each of the low-cohesion sets of the second. The high-cohesion sets of the second session include 66 Republican votes and 62 Democratic votes. All votes were considered for inclusion except those on private bills and those on which the party was unanimous (cohesion indexes of 100). The characteristics of the cohesion

indexes of the selected sets are given in Table I.

In order to simplify the analysis, ten Republican delegations and thirteen Democratic delegations were selected, representing various regions of the country.[5] For each of the three sets of roll calls the number of agreements between each member of these state delegations and each other member of the same party in the House was computed and tallied by machine procedures, and the resulting

Table I—Distribution of Cohesion Indexes on Six Selected Sets of Roll Calls, House of Representatives, 81st Congress

	Republican	Democratic
First Session		
Intermediate Cohesion Set		
Number of Roll Calls	74	74
Range of Indexes	2.2-87.6	0.4-88.4
Mean of Indexes	51.01	47.6
Median of Indexes	57.05	47.45
Second Session		
High-Cohesion Set		
Number of Roll Calls	66	62
Range of Indexes	73.0-98.7	68.6-99.2
Mean of Indexes	88.5	86.5
Median of Indexes	87.95	89.3
Low-Cohesion Set		
Number of Roll Calls	74	74
Range of Indexes	2.3-73.0	0.0-67.4
Mean of Indexes	43.08	33.3
Median of Indexes	45.05	34.6

scores for each man were ranked in descending order.[6] So arranged, the data show, for example, that on the 74 votes of the first session Representative Bolling agreed with his Missouri colleague, Representative Karsten, on 70, while he agreed with Representative McCormack of Massachusetts on 57 and with Representative Grant of Alabama on only 38. In developing the bloc matrices for these sets of roll calls in the larger study, agreements on fewer than 50 per cent plus one of the votes were ignored. (That is, in the sets of 74 votes, fewer than 38 agreements were not tallied.) This was done in order to keep the analysis within reasonably manageable bounds and to maximize the clarity of the resulting structure. The effect of using the same convention here is to increase the significance of any positive findings. For example, this procedure would ignore the agreements of a New York City representative who spent so much time in Manhattan and was so indifferent about inserting in the *Record* an indication of how he would have voted that he was recorded as agreeing with no member of his party on as many as 38 of the 74 roll calls in the first session. Though he might have indicated his voting preference on

35 roll calls and agreed with seven other New Yorkers on all 35, he would have been treated as if he had not voted at all. Had it been feasible to include such voters in the analysis, the cohesion of such a state delegation would come out higher.

In order to arrive at a rough preliminary indication of the incidence of intra-state agreements and of the relative cohesiveness of the several delegations, it was necessary to determine how nearly the number of agreements within a state delegation approached the number theoretically possible if the group were perfectly cohesive. The first step was to list, for each member of each selected delegation, the number of scores, beginning with the highest, equal to one less than the number of legislators in the delegation. For instance, there were four men in the Democratic delegation from Minnesota, so the three highest scores of each were listed. Representative Wier's three highest agreements on the roll calls of the first session were with Representatives McCarthy of Minnesota, Blatnik of Minnesota, and Jacobs of Indiana. He thus had two intra-delegation scores among his top three. The same procedure was pursued for the other three men in the delegation, and the number of these intra-state scores in the delegation was then totaled for each of the three sets of roll calls. (In counting those from the state, two or more tie scores in the lowest position were counted as only one.) Since the number of scores with others in the same delegation for a perfectly cohesive group would be equal to the number in the delegation times one less than that number, the ratio of the actual number of scores to this theoretically possible number is not only an indicator of the frequency of intra-state agreements but also a rough measure of the group's cohesion.[7] Thus, referring again to the Minnesota Democrats, if the group were perfectly cohesive, the three top scores of each of the four men would be with his three state colleagues, a total of 12 scores. In the first session the actual total of such scores was three, or 25 per cent of the theoretically possible figure. These percentages for all thirteen of the Democratic delegations on the three sets of roll calls are listed in Table II.

Given the variety of factors which might affect the votes of a state party delegation, one would not expect to find perfect consistency in a set of results such as these. Yet a sufficiently stable pattern emerges from the data to provide a reasonably firm basis for speculation and cautious inference. Although there is a good deal of variation from one delegation to another, the ratios in Table II are high enough to give some support to the proposition that the state delegation is an element in the voting process. (It is well, of course, that these ratios fall considerably short of 100 per cent since, if the latter condition existed, it would almost certainly reflect a condition of party disintegration or chaos in the House and in the country, with

Table II—Ratios of Actual to Possible Agreement Scores Within Selected State Democratic Delegations to the House of Representatives, 81st Congress

| STATE | FIRST SESSION | SECOND SESSION | |
	Intermediate Cohesion, 74 Roll Calls (%)	Low Cohesion, 74 Roll Calls (%)	High Cohesion, 62 Roll Calls (%)
Alabama	36.1	18.1	11.1
California	7.8	24.5	4.5
Colorado	33.3	33.3	16.7
Illinois	24.2	24.5	12.7
Massachusetts	6.7	6.7	3.3
Minnesota	25.0	0.0	0.0
Missouri	34.8	15.9	22.7
New York	10.7	26.1	10.9
North Carolina	7.6	7.3	10.0
Ohio	6.8	15.2	4.5
Oklahoma	23.2	37.5	1.8
Pennsylvania	11.0	26.7	15.2
Texas	30.0	26.6	13.5
13 states	18.0	23.1	11.5

each state's representatives functioning as ambassadors to, rather than officials of, a national government.)

More impressive than the incidence of these intra-state agreements, however, or the variations among the delegations, is the pattern indicated by the composite ratios in the bottom line of Table II.[8] These strongly suggest an inverse correlation between the degree of cohesion within the party and that within the state delegations. Again, examination of the figures for each of the state groups reveals that the pattern does not hold for all, yet for twelve of the thirteen delegations, North Carolina being the only exception, the ratios are highest in one of the two sets of votes characterized by relatively low party cohesion. (Note that the mean of the cohesion indexes of the "intermediate cohesion" votes—Table I, above—was nearer that of the low-cohesion set than that of the high-cohesion set.) And in eight of the thirteen delegations the intra-state agreements are highest in the set of votes with the lowest cohesion among the Democrats as a whole, the low-cohesion set of the second session. (The exceptions, in addition to North Carolina, are Alabama, Minnesota, Missouri, and Texas.)

Before attempting to analyze the circumstances of low party cohesion that might account for this pattern it is appropriate to examine the corresponding data for the Republican delegations, for if the same inference cannot be drawn from the votes of the other party, the pattern loses much of its interest and significance. Then one would be forced to conclude that the substance of the particular Democratic votes was responsible for the distribution. But if the pattern holds for both parties, one may legitimately look for more general explanatory factors.[9]

As the figures in Table III reveal, the general tendency noted in connection with the Democratic voting seems to apply equally to the selected Republican delegations. In nine of the ten cases, Oregon being the exception, intra-state agreements occur most frequently in one of two low-cohesion sets. In five of the ten, moreover, the highest intra-

Table III—Ratio of Actual to Possible Agreement Scores Within Selected State Republican Delegations to the House of Representatives, 81st Congress

STATE	FIRST SESSION	SECOND SESSION	
	Intermediate Cohesion, 74 Roll Calls (%)	Low Cohesion, 74 Roll Calls (%)	High Cohesion, 66 Roll Calls (%)
California	15.4	25.0	12.1
Illinois	18.1	15.4	12.8
Iowa	21.4	46.4	1.8
Kansas	26.7	16.7	3.3
Massachusetts	28.6	33.9	12.5
Michigan	15.2	10.6	10.6
New York	7.9	18.9	10.3
Oregon	0.0	0.0	8.3
Pennsylvania	23.5	23.2	16.7
Wisconsin	14.3	23.2	3.6
Ten states	16.1	21.0	11.6

state score occurs on those votes on which the party is most sharply divided. (The exceptions, besides Oregon, are Illinois, Kansas, Michigan, and Pennsylvania. In some of these, especially the last, the difference between the first-session set and the low-cohesion set of the second session is slight.)

When the composite delegation ratios for both parties are arrayed against the median index of

Table IV—Reduced Party Cohesion Accentuates the Cohesion of State Delegations: Median Indexes of Cohesion and Composite Ratios of Actual to Possible Intra-Delegation Agreement Scores on Six Sets of Roll Calls, House of Representatives, 81st Congress

Party and Set	Median Index of Cohesion	Composite Ratios Democrats: 13 delegations Republicans: 10 delegations
Democrats, 81:2, low-cohesion set	34.6	23.1
Republicans, 81:2, low-cohesion set	45.05	21.0
Democrats, 81:1, intermediate set	47.45	18.0
Republicans, 81:1, intermediate set	57.05	16.1
Republicans, 81:2, high-cohesion set	87.95	11.6
Democrats, 81:2, high-cohesion set	89.3	11.5

cohesion for each set of roll calls, as in Table IV, the strength and consistency of the general pattern appears with striking clarity. What this seems to reveal is that a property of lowered cohesion of the legislative party is not merely bi-polarization of the larger group but a fractionation of the party, or a tendency in that direction, out of which the state delegations emerge as one of the elements of residual significance. Clearly they are not the only such elements, nor would one expect them to be. The considerable variations among the states in Tables II and III suggest the influence of factors other than delegation ties. Moreover, the relatively low ratios, even for comparatively cohesive groups such as the Missouri Democrats or the Massachusetts Republicans, testify to the less-than-complete dominance of the state grouping. Yet, pending further analysis, the fact seems tentatively established that the issues which most sharply divide the legislative party in the House of Representatives do not set up comparable cleavages within the state delegations, with the result that the cohesiveness of the latter tends to rise as that of the party declines.

Despite the uniformities just noted, one would be incautious indeed, considering the crudity of these data, not to entertain the possibility that the differences revealed here may be due largely to chance factors. To introduce precise probability calculations into the analysis presents logical and statistical complexities of overwhelming difficulty, yet some further effort to examine these patterns of intra-delegation agreement, taking at least rough account of chance factors, seems imperative.

The simplest appropriate assumption to make is that, if relationships within the state delegations were of no significance, the incidence of intra-state agreements in any sample of scores, such as the number of scores equal to one less than the number of legislators in the delegation, should be no greater than the proportion of the delegation to the legislative party as a whole. Thus, in a legislative party of 100 and a state delegation of ten, it might be expected that on a purely chance basis one (actually .9) of the top nine scores of any member of the delegation would be an intra-state score. Any number of intra-state scores in excess of this, in this example two or more, could be regarded as reflecting the influence of intra-delegation relationships.

For each of the 256 legislators (254 in the second session) in each of the 23 delegations the top scores (equal to the number in the delegation less one) in each of the sets of roll calls were analyzed in this fashion. The results for each delegation were summarized so as to show the number in the delegation, the number having

Table V—Distribution of Intra-State Agreement Scores in Excess of Expected Incidence Within Thirteen Selected Democratic State Delegations to the House of Representatives, 81st Congress

| | FIRST SESSION Intermediate Cohesion, 74 Roll Calls | | | SECOND SESSION | | | | | |
| | | | | Low Cohesion, 74 Roll Calls | | | High Cohesion, 62 Roll Calls | | |
STATE	Number in Delegation	Number with Excess Scores	Mean Excess Scores	Number in Delegation	Number with Excess Scores	Mean Excess Scores	Number in Delegation	Number with Excess Scores	Mean Excess Scores
Alabama	9	8	2.25	9	5	1.2	9	0	0.0
California	10	1	1.0	11	9	1.89	11	1	1.0
Colorado	3	0	0.0	3	0	0.0	3	0	0.0
Illinois	12	9	2.33	11	7	2.86	11	4	1.25
Massachusetts	6	0	0.0	6	0	0.0	6	0	0.0
Minnesota	4	1	1.0	4	0	0.0	4	0	0.0
Missouri	12	11	3.09	12	7	1.43	12	11	1.64
New York	23	10	2.0	24	19	2.89	24	12	1.92
North Carolina	12	3	1.3	11	1	3.0	11	4	1.25
Ohio	12	2	1.0	12	5	1.8	12	1	2.0
Oklahoma	8	4	1.5	8	6	2.3	8	0	0.0
Pennsylvania	15	8	1.5	15	13	2.08	15	10	1.7
Texas	20	17	4.6	19	14	2.8	19	11	2.5
13 States	146	74	2.65	145	86	2.33	145	54	1.83

intra-state scores in excess of expectation, and the average number of such excess scores for those having them within the delegation. In order to develop the data as conservatively as possible, a single intra-state score was never treated as significant, no matter how small the delegation, so that the results understate the situation for delegations no larger than three or four.

In the low-cohesion Democratic votes of the second session, since the bloc matrix revealed, not unexpectedly, a very sharp North-South cleavage, the denominator in the proportion of the state delegation to the party as a whole was reduced. For the Southern delegations this proportion was based on the 137 Democrats from the South and the Border rather than on the 258

Democrats in the House.[10] For the Northern delegations and the two from the border states it was based on the 158 Democrats from outside the eleven states of the South.[11] Although this procedure understates the degree of intra-delegation agreement on this set of Democratic votes, it reveals more accurately the special influence of intra-delegation relationships by discounting the effect produced by a delegation's voting solidly with one of two cohesive wings of the party. For example, if the calculations for the 24-man New York delegation had been based on all 258 Democrats, the number of intra-delegation scores that might have been attributed to chance would have been two rather than four. Twenty-one members, rather than 19, would have had more intra-state

Table VI—Distribution of Intra-State Agreement Scores in Excess of Expected Incidence Within Ten Selected Republican State Delegations to the House of Representatives, 81st Congress

| | FIRST SESSION Intermediate Cohesion, 74 Roll Calls | | | SECOND SESSION | | | | | |
| | | | | Low Cohesion, 74 Roll Calls | | | High Cohesion, 66 Roll Calls | | |
STATE	Number in Delegation	Number with Excess Scores	Mean Excess Scores	Number in Delegation	Number with Excess Scores	Mean Excess Scores	Number in Delegation	Number with Excess Scores	Mean Excess Scores
California	13	8	1.75	12	9	2.4	12	4	1.0
Illinois	14	11	1.91	13	7	2.0	13	6	1.5
Iowa	8	5	1.2	8	8	2.25	8	0	0.0
Kansas	6	3	1.0	6	1	1.0	6	0	0.0
Massachusetts	8	6	1.5	8	6	2.0	8	0	0.0
Michigan	12	5	1.6	12	4	1.5	12	4	1.0
New York	20	4	1.75	20	14	2.64	20	5	1.2
Oregon	4	0	0.0	4	0	0.0	4	0	0.0
Pennsylvania	17	12	2.58	18	12	3.08	18	11	1.5
Wisconsin	8	3	1.0	8	5	1.2	8	1	1.0
10 States	110	57	1.79	109	66	2.32	109	31	1.32

scores than expected on a chance basis, and the mean of the excess scores would have been 4.85 rather than 2.89 (Table V).

In general the results of this analysis support the conclusions already tentatively stated, as the data in Table V and Table VI indicate. As expected, the pattern is not completely consistent from state to state in either party. Moreover, neither the per cent of delegation members with excess state scores nor the composite means of the number of excess scores correlate as closely with the median cohesion indexes as do the ratios in Table IV. And among the Democrats (Table V) the composite mean of the excess scores is a little lower for low-cohesion votes in the second session than for the intermediate set of the first session, contrary to expectation, largely owing to the remarkably high means of two good-sized delegations, Missouri and Texas, on the latter votes.

Nevertheless, the basic pattern identified in the previous analysis also appears here. The proportion in the Democratic delegations with a significant number of intra-state scores is inversely related to the average party cohesion of the sets. (The per cents are 50.7, 59.3, and 37.2 for the first-session votes and low- and high-cohesion sets of the second session, respectively.) For twelve of the thirteen Democratic delegations, North Carolina again being the exception, the proportion with a significant number of intra-state scores is highest in one of the two sets of roll calls on which party cohesion was relatively low. For five of the twelve—Alabama, Illinois, Minnesota, Missouri, and Texas—this proportion is highest on the 74 votes of the first session. Other partial exceptions to the expected pattern appear in New York and Pennsylvania, where the number with more than the expected quota of intra-state scores is larger in the high-cohesion set of the second session than in the first session votes, although the means of the numbers of excess scores among New Yorkers are of the anticipated relative magnitudes. (The high mean in the last column of Table V for the Ohio delegation can be ignored, since it represents the scores of only one man.)

The data on the Republican delegations (Table VI) are even more clearly consistent with the expected pattern. The proportion of Representatives in these ten delegations with a significant number of intra-state scores is inversely related to the average party cohesion on the three sets, the per cents being 51.8, 60.6, and 28.4 for the first-session votes and for the low-cohesion and high-cohesion sets of the second session, respectively. And the same proposition holds for the means of the numbers of excess scores. In nine of the ten delegations the highest proportion of

Representatives with a significant number of intra-state scores and the highest mean of the excess scores occur in one of the sets of votes with relatively low party cohesion, the only exception being Oregon, none of whose four-man delegation had a significant number of intra-state scores on any of the three sets of votes. In five of these nine delegations the highest proportion of significant intra-state scores occurs on the votes with the lowest average cohesion. The exceptions are Kansas, Michigan, Illinois, Massachusetts, and Pennsylvania, and in all but the first two of these the means of the numbers of excess scores are highest in the low-cohesion set of the second session even though the number with such scores is no higher than on the first-session votes. Michigan is the outstanding exception to the pattern in this group of delegations, since the number of its members with excess intra-state scores is the same for both the low- and the high-cohesion sets of the second session, although the mean is somewhat higher in the former. The New York delegation also deviates somewhat from the norm in that more of its members had excess scores on the high-cohesion votes of the second session than on the roll calls of the first, although again the mean of the number of excess scores is somewhat higher in the latter instance.

With proper allowance for the limits imposed by the case of a single Congress, it seems clear that in both legislative parties in the House of Representatives the issues that divide the party as a whole do not split the state delegations in similar fashion. Rather they tend significantly to increase delegation cohesion. In other words, agreement within the state delegations is not simply a reflection of high party cohesion. Nor, among the Democrats, is it merely a consequence of solid delegation adherence to one of two unified wings of the party. Rather the intra-delegation relationships seem to have an independent connection with the voting choices of Representatives, particularly on those issues that divide the party most sharply.

The fact of the significance of intra-delegation relationships and their apparent connection with levels of party cohesion is little more than a political curiosity, however, unless an explanation of the pattern can be adduced or demonstrated. What is there about the diminished cohesion of the party or the issues leading to such cleavage that should bring this result? What relevance has it for understanding the nature of the legislative party in the House?

Reflection suggests that the issues which most sharply divide a party are of two broad types. First, there are those which are difficult, highly controversial questions, the Representative's vote on which seems certain to produce important consequences both for the interests with which he identifies and for his own survival in public life. Although these are thus freighted with significant effects, the certainty of the latter may be much clearer than their precise nature. The Representative thus confronted with a situation both insistent and ambiguous is likely to look about him both for guidance and for reassurance. Consultation with the members of his own state delegation may serve those purposes, perhaps partly because there is defensive value in legislators from the same area and party presenting a solid front on issues of high controversy.[12] On such issues, moreover, the formal leadership may offer little guidance because it prudently avoids becoming identified with either faction on a hot and closely contested issue, because it cannot, in the intensity of the conflict, hope to carry more than a small majority of the party with it, or because the leaders themselves are not in agreement on the issues. Such issues are not necessarily, if this speculation is sound, "local" in their impact, in the sense that the effects of rivers and harbors legislation, a general tariff revision, or an inclusive agricultural bill are local. They may rather be "national" issues of either high or low intensity locally, as seems to be the case with many questions of foreign policy. Although the distinction here is probably more in degree than in kind, there does seem to be a difference between the locally concentrated access of national interests and the access of purely parochial interests, though legislative voting patterns on the two may be identical.

Second, the votes characterized by low party cohesion may be expected to include a number of issues of trifling importance, "free" votes on which the party leadership makes no position known because the outcome is a matter of complete indifference to them. The Representative who rushes over from his office or committee room in answer to the bell announcing a roll call on such an issue may be completely ignorant of its substance and import. He may get a quick and decisive briefing from the first acquaintance he meets on his way through the lobby, from a friend on the committee handling the measure, or from a familiar source within his state party delegation. On such votes, therefore, it is less accurate to say that the party is divided than to characterize it as not being united because the matter of party is irrelevant. But the influence of intra-state relationships may nevertheless be high.[13]

Correspondingly one would infer that the state delegation normally plays a diminished role on

votes of high party cohesion because there is no need for it to be influential. The issues in this type of situation are no longer controversial, are non-controversial—even if important in many instances—are trifling but unambiguous, or, if controversial, are by definition productive of cleavages between rather than within the parties. Some of the last would include those cases in which a unified leadership commits its reserves of influence, for whatever reason, in order to assure maximum support of a "party" position.

It is one thing to allege that votes of low and high party cohesion have these characteristics but another thing to demonstrate the point. Limitations of space prohibit the inclusion here of a list of all the roll calls, but examination of these six sets of votes indicates beyond much doubt that there are more issues of trifling importance among the low-cohesion votes of both parties than among the high-cohesion votes. For both parties roll calls such as those on authorizing daylight-saving time and changing the hours for the sale of liquor in the District of Columbia, on the omnibus rivers and harbors bill, on legislation for the benefit of limited groups of veterans, on efforts to rescind the curtailment of postal service, and on legislation authorizing library demonstrations in rural areas are much more characteristic of the low-cohesion sets than of either of the others. Minor issues, by any definition, are present in some measure on all the lists, but their distribution seems to accord with the expectation previously stated. "Important" issues of "national" consequence are also evident in all of the sets, but an assertion that they are more frequent on votes on which the party is unified can only be an inference from the more easily documented conclusion that minor matters are less common.

Since the six sets of roll calls by definition take into account intra-party controversy, there is need in characterizing the sets for some indicator of divergence within the House as a whole. Among several possibilities the simplest is the margin by which a motion is carried or lost as a per cent of the total number voting. This is not a completely satisfactory indicator, since "the House" is a constantly changing quantity. Thus a vote on a trivial matter settled by a close margin appears as a controversial item even though as few as 218 members bothered to vote on it at all. However, since failure to vote is often an act of avoidance as much as a reflection of indifference, refinement of the measure to take account of the number of non-voters does not seem readily practicable or entirely necessary.[14]

Table VII shows the distribution of the votes in the several sets according to these margins. In both parties the concentration of the low-cohesion and the intermediate-cohesion votes toward the lower end of the distribution indicates that these issues tend to be controversial within the House as well as within the parties. The U-shaped distribution of the two high-cohesion sets, on the other hand, reflects the fact that these votes tend to be either non-controversial or are straight party-votes—controversial only between the parties—and therefore are marked by a high degree of discipline on both sides.

It thus seems reasonably clear that the issues on which the state party delegations are most conspicuous and, presumably, most influential—the low-cohesion votes—are of two kinds. Either they are the tough, politically ambiguous questions on which the Representative finds himself genuinely uncertain and subject to mutually exclusive claims—"cross-pressured"—or they are matters of trivial or purely local importance. On both types the familiar associations within the state delegation provide guidance, reassurance, and the defensive advantages of solidarity or near solidarity among partisans exposed to the same or closely related publics.

The significance of the state delegation in the voting members of the House has been established, at least tentatively, and an explanation of these relationships has been offered and partially verified. But one further problem must be dealt with. Although the term "state delegation" has been employed throughout this paper, the data in Tables II through VI, above, indicate that there must be a good deal of variation within as well as between delegations. Specifically, is it not possible that what appears to be a "state" phenomenon is only an artifact of a classification that ignores locality and other factors which may constitute a more substantial basis of cohesion than associations within the state delegations?

Since none of the delegations in this study reaches or even approaches the theoretically possible—but highly improbable—perfect unity, some clustering of agreements within them is bound to exist. Examination of the scores within the delegations reveals, however, that such clustering is rarely to be accounted for primarily in locality terms.

Among the Democrats an outstanding exception is the Illinois delegation. Numbering eleven men in the second session, this group included nine men from Cook County (Chicago and its close suburbs), one from a district composed of seven "downstate" counties, including the city of Springfield, and one from a two-county district adjacent to the preceding and including the city of East St. Louis. As is evident from Figure 1, six of these men make up a cohesive and all but solid bloc on the low-cohesion roll calls of the second session. Among them these six account for all but three of the scores on which the per cent recorded in Table II is based, and all of them are from Cook County. Of the three Cook County members not part of this bloc, Yates was a freshman Representative from a district containing a number of high-income residential areas, and Dawson and Sabath were unrecorded on too many of these votes to have any scores of the minimum frequency. What has been described as "Illinois" solidarity, therefore, is in fact a closely knit portion of the Chicago delegation, a conclusion not entirely unexpected, since this group is reputed to be one of the few delegations in the House over which the county leadership can and does exercise continuous and effective discipline.

A very slight degree of the same sort of localization is evident in the New York Democratic delegation, twenty of whose twenty-four members in the second session were from New York City districts. Although the pattern is much less clear than in Illinois, there are signs of some clustering

Table VII—Distribution of Roll Calls by Levels of Cohesion and by Plurality Margins, House of Representatives, 81st Congress

HOUSE PLURALITY (%)	FIRST SESSION		SECOND SESSION			
	Intermediate Cohesion		Low Cohesion		High Cohesion	
	Republican	Democratic	Republican	Democratic	Republican	Democratic
0.1- 9.9	8	14	10	17	9	2
10 -19.9	12	19	15	14	11	12
20 -29.9	9	8	16	8	5	13
30 -39.9	13	14	13	8	2	7
40 -49.9	8	7	10	17	9	3
50 -59.9	2	2	4	5	3	2
60 -69.9	6	4	1	1	1	1
70 -79.9	5	2	3	4	4	3
80 -89.9	8	4	2	0	5	7
90 -99.9	3	0	0	0	17	12
Total	74	74	74	74	66	62

along borough lines, especially within the nine-man delegation from Brooklyn, a tendency that is not astonishing in view of the coalition character of the city's Democratic politics. While these signs appear, however, it is also clear that the pattern of agreements spreads over not only the whole city but all those parts of the state represented by Democrats. There is a solidarity within the delegation that is largely independent of locality solidarity.

In a few other Democratic delegations there are symptoms of intra-state localism, but they are not sharply defined. In the Alabama group, for example, there is some evidence that Representatives from the northern end of the state tend to agree with one another more frequently than with their colleagues from the southern end, and *vice versa*. This, however, may reflect no more than a tendency for pairs of legislators from adjoining districts to vote together with a high degree of frequency, a tendency apparent in many delegations in both parties.

Among the ten Republican delegations the only instance showing marked signs of intra-delegation localism is Wisconsin (Figure 2). It is not a highly cohesive group, as a comparison of the scores in Figure 1 and Figure 2 will indicate. Nevertheless, a division between the western districts (3, 9, and 10) and those in the eastern half of the state (1, 2, 7, and 8) is apparent, though it is not absolute. This cluster seems to reflect a fairly complex combination of ecological and strictly political or factional influences. The western districts include large portions of the cut-over forest land of the state and most of the poorer farm land, and in general are less prosperous than the sections nearer Lake Michigan. In the western section lies much of the area once given to strong support of the LaFollettes, and here are two of the three counties in the state carried by Stevenson in 1952. The cleavage between the two areas also corresponds roughly to the boundary between the western Protestant, Scandinavian dis-

Figure 1—Local Organization Control: Agreements Within the Illinois Democratic Delegation,† on 74 Low-Cohesion Roll Calls, House of Representatives, 81st Congress, 2d Session

Member and District	District Numbers											
	2	3	4	6	8	11	9	1	7	21	25	
O'Hara, 2d		61	59	61	61	58					58	
Linehan, 3d			63	62	63	63						
Buckley, 4th		63		60*	60*	61						
O'Brien, 6th	61	62	60		62	64						
Gordon, 8th	61	63	60	62								Cook County
Chesney, 11th		63	61	64								
Yates, 9th					56						58	
Dawson, 1st	(No scores of 38 or higher)											
Sabath, 7th	(No scores of 38 or higher)											
Mack, 21st	(None of first 10 scores from Illinois)											
Price, 25th	(None of first 10 scores from Illinois)											

† Counting only those intra-state scores included among the ten highest scores for each man. This figure should be read horizontally. Each row indicates those of the man's ten highest scores that are with others in the delegation.

* Only one of these scores counted in delegation total, as they were tied for 10th place on Buckley's list.

tricts and the Catholic, German sections in and around Milwaukee.

Evidences of factionalism not so clearly based on geography also appear among the Texas Democrats (Figure 3). The districts of the highly cohesive ten-man cluster in the lower part of Figure 3, those of the looser seven-man grouping in the upper corner, and those of the three less readily classified men in the middle all are pretty well scattered over the state. (Figure 3 is based on the roll calls of the first session, since they involved the largest number of state scores.) The cleavage, whose precise implications need not be examined here, can be characterized as that between the loosely cohesive cluster generally willing to accept the moderate leadership of Rayburn and the larger fraction of the delegation, often inclined to repudiate his initiative and to cast in with the more "typical" Southerners in the House.[15]

Aside from the sorts of exceptions mentioned above, the great majority of the state delegations examined show no internal clustering on a locality basis and none based on obvious factional lines. These findings, even in the case of some of the exceptions illustrated here, lend support to the proposition that there is political reality to the intra-delegation relationships in the House. And a reasonable inference from the evidence is that in many such groupings there is a conscious effort at concerted voting. Some equally plausible inferences, however, may operate in combination with this one or even in place of it, although the

last possibility seems improbable. An illustration is the California Democratic delegation, whose voting structure is built around four men, two from San Francisco (Havenner and Shelley), one from Los Angeles (King), and one from San Diego (McKinnon). It shows no locality cleavage, and it might reflect concerted action by the delegation. And yet there is a strong likelihood that the members of this nucleus were especially accessible to the legislative claims of organized labor. Supposing this to be the case, it might be argued that the statistical cohesiveness of the delegation is no more than a reflection of the accessibility of its individual members, as individuals, to the claims of the same national interest group. It is not necessary, that is, to conclude that intra-delegation consultation occurred at all, although the organizational functions of the state delegations in the legislative party and the political advantages of solidarity among neighboring legislators on issues of high controversy would support the view that both influences—interest-group demands and intra-delegation relationships—were operating simultaneously.

The California Democratic delegation also raises another question. Those top scores for each man which are not within the delegation typically are rather widely scattered, from New York to Washington. For example, the first ten scores of Representative Helen Gahagan Douglas on the low-cohesion votes of the second session included—in addition to four of her fellow Californians—Rep-

Figure 2—Geographic Factions: Agreements Within the Wisconsin Republican Delegation,† on 74 Low-Cohesion Roll Calls, House of Representatives, 81st Congress, 2d Session

Member and District	District Numbers								
	1	2	7	8	6	3	9	10	
Smith, 1st		51							} East
Davis, 2d	51			55					
Murray, 7th	44	48							
Byrnes, 8th		55							
Keefe, 6th	(No scores of 38 or higher)								
Withrow, 3d							53	53	} West
Hull, 9th							53	51	
O'Konski, 10th		43				53	51		

† Counting only those intra-state scores included among the seven highest scores for each man. This figure should be read horizontally. Each row indicates those of the man's seven highest scores that were with others in the delegation.

resentatives Price of Illinois, Karsten and Sullivan of Missouri, Jackson of Washington, O'Sullivan of Nebraska, and Feighan of Ohio. Much the same pattern occurs in Pennsylvania, Illinois, and other Northern delegations. Since the increases in intra-state scores are most apparent on the issues that divide the party between North and South, may it not be possible that what appears as increased delegation unity is no more than a tendency for the representatives from the larger urban areas to vote the same way on this kind of issue? This does not seem to be the case in California. Comparing the low- and high-cohesion sets of the second session, while the proportion of "big city" scores is higher on the former by 12.9 percentage points, the proportion of intra-state scores is greater by 16.9 points. Moreover, the incidence of intra-state scores is greater by 13.8 percentage points in the low-cohesion set of the second session than in the votes of the first session, while that of the "big city" scores is slightly smaller, by 3.5 percentage points. Comparable results were found for other delegations, further strengthening the conclusion that the increased unity of the state delegations is

Figure 3—Non-Geographic Factionalism: Agreements Within the Texas Democratic Delegation† on 74 Roll Calls of Intermediate Cohesion, House of Representatives, 81st Congress, 1st Session

Member and District	District Numbers																			
	1	2	3	9	10	14	15	18	19	8	16	5	6	7	11	12	13	20	17	21
Patman, 1st			59	54	57															
Combs, 2d	52		54																	
Beckworth, 3rd	59	54			58	54														
Thompson, 9th	54				58	58				55								52		
Thornberry, 10th	57		58	58			57													
Lyle, 14th	53		55	58	57				54											
Bentsen, 15th		51																		
Worley, 18th	43		44	45	47	45			46	43					48			41	43	41
Mahon, 19th			52	55	51	53					52				52	52		52	52	51
Thomas, 8th	(None of the first 19 scores with Texans)																			
Regan, 16th									46			53		49		52	50	48	49	49
Wilson, 5th											53			61	59	56	58	61	58	
Teague, 6th												50			52	53	48	51	55	
Pickett, 7th												61			60	55	53	58	57	
Poage, 11th			46*	50	52	48		48	52			47	47	46*		51	46*	49		47
Lucas, 12th												59		60			57	58	56	58
Gossett, 13th												56	53	55		57		54	56	58
Kilday, 20th												58		53	58	54			56	
Burleson, 17th												61		58	56	56	56			56
Fisher, 21st												58	55	57		58	58	52	56	

† Counting only those intra-state scores included among the nineteen highest scores for each man. This figure should be read horizontally. Each row indicates those of the man's nineteen highest scores that were with others in the delegation.

* Only one of these three scores was counted in the delegation total, as they were tied for nineteenth place on Poage's list.

not merely an artifact of the procedures employed in the analysis.[16]

Because the arguments and the evidence presented in this paper necessarily deal with tendencies and approximations in a legislative body of tremendous diversity and complexity, they should be summarized with a sharp eye on the dangers of overstatement. The basic position is that, unless one assumes that there is no pattern at all in the obviously rather fluid voting in the House, in the absence of institutionalized and fully operative cue-giving mechanisms within the legislative party proper, one would expect to find a variety of substitute devices performing this function. These would reflect associations within standing committees, friendships, and other structural features of the House. Among these the state party delegation, as a group within the legislative party, appears to have an important influence.[17] This statement is an inference from the evidence on intra-delegation agreements in voting. The delegation as a group of interacting legislators is strictly speaking an intervening variable in this interpretation; it is consistent with the evidence, but direct observation of its influence is normally not possible.[18]

The influence of the delegation is not completely consistent from state to state or from situation to situation. This was to be expected, since the delegation is not the only factor bearing upon the voting decision. At times the delegation's role is subordinate to or indistinguishable from centralized control by a strong local party organization, as in the case of the Illinois Democrats; from similarity of voting induced by similarities in the socio-economic composition of districts or by persistent factional cleavages within a state party, as among the Wisconsin Republicans and possibly the Texas Democrats; or from solidarity reflecting equal access to delegation members by the same national interest group, as the case of the California Democrats seems to suggest.

Such alternative influences as these are not inconsistent with a considerable measure of consultation and concerted action by the members of a delegation. Moreover, they do not seem fully to account for the persistent evidence of interaction and solidarity within most of the delegations. They do not adequately explain the occurrence of intra-delegation agreements in excess of what would be expected as a result of sharp regional cleavage within a party, such as the North-South split among the Democrats, or as a result of similarities in the constituencies of "big-city" Democrats.

A method of multiple correlation, if a suitable one could be devised, might not only assign weights to these varied influences but also might conceivably show that apart from these other factors—local party organizations, interest groups, similar constituencies, and the like—the relationships among the members of a delegation as a group were of no significance. In the absence of such a precise measure—and it is improbable that one can be developed—it is reasonable to infer that the face-to-face relationships within a delegation are an independent factor making for solidarity.[19] The evidence does not permit an estimate of the relative importance of the delegation as a group, and in some instances solidarity within a delegation can be accounted for on other grounds. But both the logic of the situation and the weight of the evidence seem to warrant assigning to the delegation as an interactive group an influence of its own upon the choices of its members.

Delegation influence is most apparent on the low-cohesion roll calls of both parties. Though the evidence is not completely satisfactory, these votes appear to contain a relatively large proportion of issues on which associations within a delegation—familiar through their use in connection with bids for committee assignments and a variety of other matters of legislative party organization—can be expected to function as a source of cues and of reassurance. These are the politically explosive but ambiguous issues of major importance, where solidarity at minimum offers defensive protection, and the genuinely trivial matters or those of largely local impact, where state colleagues, among others, are relied upon for advice. Presumably on both types of issues the leadership of the party as a whole does not or cannot supply guidance.

Though the functions of the delegation group are most apparent on the low-cohesion votes, this does not mean that the delegation is irrelevant even when the party is comparatively united. Intra-delegation agreements appear here in several cases more frequently than chance would explain. Reduced ambiguity and more effective operation of the party leadership on the high-cohesion votes would imply, however, a less prominent function for the state delegations on these matters.

Reflection on these findings point to a number of unanswered questions concerning the bearing of the general sociological literature about groups upon the legislative party in the Congress, and concerning the operation of the party group in the House and its role in the total political scheme. The legislative party is a system of mutually interdependent roles whose occupants share relevant attitudes and expectations, and thus satisfies the usual definition of a group. Yet it does not readily fit the specifications characteristic of the literature on groups. The character of the interdependencies and of the shared norms is not nearly so clear as in the case of the small groups from which most of the relevant sociological literature generalizes. Fluidity of internal structure, fractionation, and persistence all seem to be pertinent to a description of the legislative party. They are a paradoxical set of attributes because, given the first two, it is hard to account for the third.

This is not the place to attempt a thorough assault on this problem. It seems likely, however, that the incongruities emerge in part from two circumstances. First, the House and its parties are large, an elementary but fundamental fact that almost certainly has much to do with the peculiarities of structure in both. Second, and probably more important, they are an integral part of a more inclusive system in which variations and ambiguities in the distribution of risks and sanctions, from precinct to caucus to White House, have a bearing upon roles and upon the nature of structure and function. In the small, natural or contrived, "problem-solving" group of the experimental literature, in some larger associations such as militant labor unions, and presumably also in some highly disciplined state legislative bodies, the risks of the members and the sanctions to which they are subject are clear and integrated into the goals of the group. This is not the case with the legislative party in the House, but the persistent reality of party in the functioning of the chamber is unmistakable.

The generally accepted doctrines concerning leadership in formal groups assert that leaders display special attachment to the goals or norms of the group, and that their roles are functionally distinctive in that all members share a dependence on their performing in ways essential to the particular functions of the group. The application of these criteria to the legislative party as a system appears to extend little beyond the survival of the group as a scheduling device and as a means of allocating instrumental rewards such as committee assignments. Even these seem in many instances to be contingent upon the satisfaction of norms deriving from elsewhere in the political system, upon the reconciliation of the legislators' multiple group memberships. Yet the norms do seem at times to include more than procedural functions. When the competing demands of loyalties outside the legislative party are not dominant, the norms of the legislative party apparently can reach into areas of significant substantive policy. Apparently the leadership functions are then similarly extended, though perhaps permissively more often than as a positive role requirement, and they seem to retain a considerable element of contingency. Even under these circumstances there clearly are a number of significant substantive issues on which the leadership cannot or does not set a party line and on which relationships like those within the state delegations presumably tend to be determining.

More concretely, the present study raises a question of the extent, if any, to which leaders attempt to gear into the power that seems inherent in the intra-delegation relationships. These data can throw no light on this question, nor can they indicate whether the intra-delegation relationships reflect a power vacuum within the legislative party which a strong leadership might come to occupy, or merely an inevitable restriction upon the leadership role. To the extent that fractionation along delegation lines is a response to ambiguity in the House rather than to claims from the constituency—and some of the evidence here points in the former direction—further research may reveal a power vacuum. Further investigation may also indicate the conditions, such as the leverage provided by skilled and persistent policy initiatives from the White House, under which the role of the legislative party leader is broadened and the influence of relationships such as those within the state party delegations reduced. The broad theoretical questions and the more concrete descriptive ones raised by these observations may present a challenge worthy of further research effort.

Notes

1. Julius Turner, *Party and Constituency: Pressures on Congress* (Baltimore, 1951).

2. These statements are based on a number of interviews with Members of Congress from both parties, conducted during March, 1956. They do not reflect a systematic sampling. Confidence in them rests rather upon the consistency with which these views were reported.

3. The study of party leadership in the Congress, of which this report is part, was made possible by a grant to Columbia University from the Carnegie Corporation of New York. The author also gratefully acknowledges the help of a fellowship from the John Simon Guggenheim Memorial Foundation, which released him from his usual academic duties during 1955-56, the generosity of the Watson Scientific Computing Laboratory of Columbia University and its able staff, an indispensable resource for the study, and the creative assistance of Elinor G. Truman.

4. The number and size of the sets was dictated by the number of roll call votes with cohesion indexes of less than 100 in each of the sessions and by restrictions in the chosen procedure for IBM machine computation, which permitted analysis at one time of not more than and, for reasons of efficiency, not appreciably less than 74 votes. These procedures were adopted for the major purpose of a modified Rice-Beyle bloc analysis of the two party groups which would locate the formal party leadership in the voting structure and permit inferences concerning leadership roles. For the basic procedure see Stuart A. Rice, *Quantitative Methods in Politics* (New York, 1928), ch. 16, and Herman C. Beyle, *Identification and Analysis of Attribute-Cluster Blocs* (Chicago, 1931).

5. The largest state party delegation was chosen from each of eight regions if it amounted to at least three men,

and the second largest party delegation if it amounted to more than three. In addition, one extra Democratic delegation was selected from the South (Alabama) and one extra Republican delegation from the East North Central region (Wisconsin). The regions used were New England, Middle Atlantic, East North Central, West North Central, Border, South, Mountain, and Pacific. No Republican delegations qualified from the Border, South, and Mountain states. The states selected were, for the Republicans: Massachusetts, New York, Pennsylvania, Michigan, Illinois, Wisconsin, Iowa, Kansas, Oregon, and California; for the Democrats: Massachusetts, New York, Pennsylvania, Ohio, Illinois, Minnesota, Missouri, Oklahoma, North Carolina, Alabama, Texas, Colorado, and California.

6. "Agreements," as used here, include more than actual votes. Any declared position officially recorded in the permanent edition of the *Congressional Record* was included along with the "yeas and nays." Thus a Representative who voted "nay" on a roll call and one who was paired or announced against would be counted as in agreement on that vote. "Absences" thus cover all unrecorded preferences, including general pairs in which neither partner announces his position.

7. The formula for the number of possible pairs of items in a group of N size, $N(N-1)/2$, cannot be used in this case because of the wide discrepancies possible between the top scores of two men in a delegation. For example, in a delegation of ten one would be interested in the first nine scores of each man in the group. If, on 74 votes, the top score of man A is with man B of the same delegation and they vote the same way on 45 of the roll calls and if man B's ninth score is 55, A will not appear among B's intra-state agreements, although B's name will appear on A's list.

8. These figures are based on the sum of the actual agreement scores in the thirteen delegations divided by the sum of the theoretically possible scores.

9. In this connection it is important to bear in mind that the three sets of Democratic votes and the equivalent Republican ones are not identical, since the issues which divide the one party are not necessarily those which split the other. In the first-session set 50 roll calls appear among the 74 votes of both parties. In the low-cohesion sets of the second session the overlap is 43 out of 74 and in the high-cohesion set it is 29 out of 66 Republican and 62 Democratic votes. It is also true, of course, that, even if a vote appears in the equivalent set in both parties, it may occur at the upper end of the distribution in one and at the lower end in the other.

10. Speaker Rayburn was omitted from all calculations because he so rarely exercised his right to vote.

11. The delegations from the two Border states, Missouri and Oklahoma, were treated in this way after inspection indicated that on the whole both were somewhat more closely tied to the non-Southern legislators.

12. Among the many informal but continuing partisan and bi-partisan gatherings on Capitol Hill, many of which may be of far more consequence than their place in the literature would suggest, the ostensibly social but politically functional meetings of state and regional party delegations are common. (An interesting example is discussed in Tom Connally, *My Name is Tom Connally* [New York: Crowell, 1954], pp. 89-92. For a suggestive case of a somewhat different sort see Stephen K. Bailey and Howard D. Samuel, *Congress at Work* [New York: Henry Holt, 1952], pp. 125-26.) Both Senators and Representatives testify to the value, on controversial measures likely to cause difficulty in election campaigns, especially primary elections, of solidarity in state party delegations. Unless deep personal or political differences intervene, two Senators from the same state and party may work out a common position on a set of votes about to be taken in the chamber. Much the same thing takes place, apparently, within the House delegations. On occasion such arrangements may bridge the wide gulf between the two wings of the Capitol and, of course, they may cross party lines as well.

13. For an illustration of this see Bailey and Samuel, *op. cit.*, p. 132.

14. The plurality margin in the House is a more satisfactory indicator of controversy within the House, however, than the incidence of "party votes," on which a majority of Democrats oppose a majority of Republicans. As the cluster of votes at the upper end of the distributions in the last two columns of Table VII suggests, the high-cohesion votes of both parties contain a disproportionate number of non-party votes, which testifies to the non-controversial character of many of these roll calls. When one party or both are badly split, however, the incidence of party votes need not be high, though it may be, since controversy within the House does not necessarily follow party lines. For instance, in the Democratic low-cohesion set of the second session there were 31 votes of the 74 on which the corresponding Republican cohesion indexes were relatively high. When these roll calls involved a coalition between the Republicans and the northern wing of the Democrats, who constituted a majority of the Democratic representatives, a non-party vote typically resulted. However, when the votes reflected a coalition between the Republicans and the southern wing of the Democrats, a minority of the party, the result was a party vote. Thus, though party votes slightly outnumber non-party among all the low cohesion votes of both parties, the difference—six percentage points—is not great.

One might further assume that if a considerable proportion of the high-cohesion roll calls concerns issues no longer controversial, among them there would be a concentration of votes on final passage and on the acceptance of conference reports—ratifying roll calls taken after the hotly contested phases of the legislation have passed and the final outcome is clear. Conversely, the low-cohesion votes would include a disproportionate number of votes on modifying amendments, dilatory motions, and the like —votes reflecting the unsettled, controversial character of the issues. Votes on recommittal motions might lie between, since they often provide the only opportunity in the House to register opposition to a measure but also may be merely ratifying actions.

Analysis of the roll calls classified in this fashion raises some interesting questions about the roles of the two legislative parties but contributes little to determining the degrees of controversy within the House. The Democratic distribution fits the expected pattern, but the Republican reverses it. This suggests that the Democrats draw together on the ratifying type of motion because they are the responsible majority party, whereas the Republicans are more likely to be united on the preliminary skirmishes, splitting, when the ultimate result is clear, into a group opposed to the impending majority decision and one willing to go along with it. The latter choice is for them the "tough" one, on which colleagues in the state delegation may be influential, whereas the reverse tends to be true of the majority party. Whether this pattern is indeed a feature of the roles of the majority and minority parties or whether, as the material in Duncan MacRae's forthcoming monograph, "Dimensions of Congressional Voting," suggests, it is a reflection of persistent ideological tendencies in the two parties, only analysis of a Congress in which the majority and minority positions were reversed could determine.

15. Both these state studies and the inclusive bloc matrices underscore the lack of solidarity in the representation of the South, race issues apart, of which the Texas cleavage is illustrative.

16. Since almost all Northern Democrats come from "urban" districts, devising a test of this sort presents difficulties. "Big city" districts are here defined as ones which 1) are in or contain a Standard Metropolitan Area *and* 2) are in or contain a city of 100,000 or more or 3) contain a county of 100,000 or more. The per cents on which the statements in the text are based are not

identical with those in Table II, since all tie scores were included in this calculation, there being no defensible way of discriminating among out-of-state scores.

17. In his forthcoming study, "Dimensions of Congressional Voting," an application of scaling technique to roll calls in the House in the 81st Congress, Duncan MacRae, Jr., presents evidence to much the same effect, particularly in his chapter entitled "Scale Positions and Constituency Characteristics."

18. Occasional bits of direct evidence on delegation functions are encountered, in addition to those referred to earlier. For example, the twelve-man Missouri Democratic delegation in the 81st Congress, seven of whom were newcomers to the House in 1949, reportedly made a special effort at delegation solidarity as a way of sup-porting their fellow Missourian in the White House. This incidentally may account for some of the peculiarities in the Missouri data in Tables II and V.

19. The peculiarly personal character of these agreements is suggested not only by the clustering within the delegations but also by the fact that the number of agreements within the delegations is unrelated to two fairly obvious formal factors, seniority and primary or general election pluralities. The data could not be presented within the limits of this paper, but analysis of the intra-state scores in these terms shows that freshman Representatives are no more likely to tie to others in the delegation than are those who have served for several terms and that occupants of "safe" seats are no more likely to behave in this way than are legislators from "close" districts.

10. URBAN-RURAL CONFLICT: THE CASE IN ILLINOIS*

David R. Derge

FEW ASPECTS of state and local government have received more attention from political scientists than urban representation in state legislatures, and the political implications of urban under-representation. Murray Stedman states that "Rural minorities control many state legislatures and thereby penalize urban majorities. The virtual serf-dom of the urbanite to the rurally controlled state legislatures in many areas is a recurrent plaint in the writings of political scientists."[1] Commenting on the tendency of state legislators to form blocs reflecting individual localities, local and regional interests, Alfred De Grazia concludes that "every American state with any considerable urban population has undergone protracted conflict between rural and urban blocs, often regardless of party lines."[2] Textbooks on municipal government, and state and local government, universally condemn urban under-representation in state legislatures and state, or imply, that the result is consistent defeat or frustration of urban interests in the legislative arena.[3]

In general, the argument might be stated as follows: 1) there exist urban and rural interests which are incompatible; 2) urban legislators will forward urban interests, rural legislators rural interests; 3) since rural population is over-represented, rural interests will prevail over urban interests; 4) a redress of numerical representation to favor the urban areas will reverse the outcome of the conflict and urban interests will prevail.

Published for the first time in this volume.

* The research on which this study is based was made possible by a grant from the Committee on Political Behavior of the Social Science Research Council.

An illustration frequently selected to demonstrate the above argument is the urban behemoth, Chicago, in the state of Illinois.[4] In the 1949 through 1955 sessions of the Illinois General Assembly, Cook County, comprising most of the Chicago Urbanized Area, held only 37% of the Assembly seats while accounting for 52% of the Illinois population. Legislative reapportionment in 1955 gave Cook County 51% of the House seats, and continued control of the Senate in areas outside of Cook County.

This study examines the behavior of the Chicago area delegations in the Illinois General Assembly and response to this behavior by downstate legislators to determine the frequency and intensity of conflict between the two groups. The five legislative sessions chosen for analysis, 1949, 1951, 1953, 1955, and 1957, cover a ten-year legislative period in Illinois.

The recorded roll-call vote is used in this analysis to determine position-taking by legislators, and to uncover group conflict. The organization and conventions of the Illinois General Assembly operate to produce a large number of roll-calls each session, and to guarantee that a small minority of the membership can force floor action, and a roll-call vote, on any measure. Observation of the Assembly, and interviews with Assembly members, have led the writer to conclude that most substantial legislative conflict, such as that between urban and rural legislators, will be permanently recorded in the form of a roll-call at some stage of legislative action. Based on his observation of a session of the Illinois Assembly, W. J. Keefe comments that the roll-call is the proper criterion for measuring party attitudes on legislation and that most of the legislation deemed important to one of the parties will receive some sort of floor action.[5] Numerous other studies of legislative behavior in both national and state governments have relied heavily on roll-call analysis.[6]

All of the 14,052 House and Senate roll-calls which occurred during the five-session period were examined. Conflict on a majority of these roll-calls was slight or nonexistent, so for purposes of analysis a group of "contested roll-calls" was selected. To qualify as "contested" a roll-call must contain 15% of the membership on the losing side of the vote. This reduced to 1,605 the number of roll-calls to be subjected to the more elaborate analyses in which voting cohesions of party and geographical groups were determined for each roll-call. The use of punched cards and high-speed data-processing computer programs facilitated the analysis of the nearly 200,000 individual legislator votes.

In this study, tests of cohesion are based on the percentage of the elected membership of the delegation representing the majority position of the delegation on any given roll-call. Except for comparative data, this test of "absolute cohesion" is used throughout. For example, if 100 seats are held by Democrats and if 67 Democrats vote "yes," the Democrat cohesion on that vote would be 67% regardless of the number of Democrats who vote "no" or the number who were absent. This test retains the simplicity of a single, easily understood expression useful in identification of groups in conflict without adding the bi-dimensionality of intra-group cohesion which is not the main concern in most of the analyses and which is handled by certain manipulations of the "absolute cohesion" test when necessary.[7]

During the 1949, 1951, 1953, and 1955 sessions of the Illinois Assembly, 54 of the 57 Cook County seats were held by legislators whose districts were wholly or substantially within the city of Chicago. Consequently, the whole Cook County delegation is treated as the "urban" delegation in the analyses of those sessions. The 1955 legislative reapportionment produced districts either wholly within or wholly without Chicago, and this is reflected in the 1957 analyses by the use of the Chicago delegation as the "urban" delegation and by the exclusion of the greatly enlarged suburban Cook County delegation. The area wholly outside of Cook County, often referred to as "downstate," is treated as the "rural" delegation, although it includes both such substantial urban populations as Peoria (pop. 111,856) and legislative districts in which 80% or more of the population resides in places of less than 5,000 population. Statements about urban-rural conflict are usually couched in terms of the big city vs. the rest of the state, a dichotomy which obtains in popular beliefs about urban-rural conflict in Illinois.

1. *The urban delegation does not regularly vote with high cohesion.* Table 1 contains data on the voting cohesion of Chicago and Cook County delegations on contested roll-calls. During the ten-year period studied, the urban delegation voted with a cohesion of more than 90% on 32 of the contested roll-calls (2%), more than 80% on 163 roll-calls (10%), and more than 66% on 482 roll-calls (30%).[8] On 70% of all contested roll-calls the urban delegation voted with a cohesion of less than 67%.

The conclusion is that the urban delegation is not in the habit of voting solidly on issues which cause conflict in the legislature. Such an occurrence on a contested roll-call is the exception rather than the rule.

2. *The urban delegation almost always wins when it votes with a high cohesion.* In determining what would be considered an urban victory or defeat it was necessary to decide what degree of voting cohesion would be necessary to indicate "support" or "opposition" by the urban delegation. In this study, if the voting cohesion of the delegation was 67% or more on a given roll-call, the delegation is considered to have "supported" or "opposed" the measure involved. Although such a definition is necessarily arbitrary, certain considerations are apparent in the determination of delegation support or opposition. A vote on which

Table 1—Voting Cohesion of Cook County Delegation on Contested Roll-Calls: Sessions of 1949 Through 1957

| VOTING COHESION OF COOK COUNTY DELEGATION | NUMBER OF ROLL-CALLS | | | | | | | | | |
| | 1949 | | 1951 | | 1953 | | 1955 | | 1957* | |
	House	Senate	House	Senate	House	Senate	House	Senate	House	Senate
91-100	0	2	1	3	0	0	7	13	4	2
81-90	14	11	5	6	1	2	18	31	9	34
67-80	26	35	21	24	27	11	57	32	56	30
Less than 67	74	102	135	108	107	42	169	47	253	91
Total	114	150	162	141	135	55	251	123	322	157

* Chicago

less than half of the delegation was in agreement (possibly when some members of the delegation abstain from voting) would be eliminated on the basis that a minority expression does not represent a position imputable to the majority. On the other hand, to demand cohesion of 100% would eliminate all contested roll-calls from the analysis. Interviews with observers of the Assembly indicated that, if anything, this 67% level of significance tends to be too low.

Tables 2 and 3 contain data showing the wins and losses of the urban delegation when it voted with a cohesion of 67% or more. Out of 482 roll-calls on which the urban delegation voted with high cohesion, there were 384 wins (80%) and 98 losses (20%). Three-fourths of the losses were in the Senate, where the party division within the urban delegation confused high urban cohesion with high Democratic cohesion.

Because of the unique system of cumulative voting in the election of each House district's three-person delegation, House districts are certain to elect two members of the majority party in the district and one member of the minority party. Thus, although Chicago is a Democratic area, the House urban delegation contained a substantial percentage of Republicans during each of the five sessions. In no session did the Republicans have fewer than 36% of the House urban delegation seats. A roll-call reflecting a cohesion of 67% or more in the urban delegation necessarily included both Democrats and Republicans. This situation provides an opportunity to examine the success of the urban delegation when it not only voted with a high cohesion (67% or more) but also with substantial support from both parties within the delegation (at least 51% of each party group). Table 4 contains these data for House sessions.

On 168 of the 974 contested roll-calls the House urban delegation voted with high cohesion and with intra-delegation bipartisan support. The delegation was on the winning side of 153 of these roll-calls (91%) and on the losing side of 15 (9%). On 10 of the 15 losing roll-calls, the urban delegation lost by one vote at a time when 17 members of the delegation were voting against the delegation majority position.

The urban delegation in the Senate included enough Republicans in 1949, 1951, and 1953 to make feasible an analysis of roll-calls on which the test of cohesion (67% or more) also included at least 51% of each party group. The wins under this redefinition of urban cohesion in the Senate were 89 (95%) as compared to 71 (76%) when the requirement was simply a cohesion of 67% or more.

The total losses under the two definitions of high urban cohesion must be viewed in relationship to the 14,052 roll-calls of this ten-year period. The House and Senate urban delegations lost on 98 (seven-tenths of one per cent) when the test of cohesion was 67% or more of the delegation, and on 71 (five-tenths of one per cent) when the test was 67% or more of the delegation including at least 51% of each party group.

Table 2—Number of Contested Roll-Calls on Which the Cook County Delegation Won and Lost When It Voted with a Cohesion of 67% or More: House Sessions of 1949 Though 1957

VOTING COHESION OF COOK COUNTY DELEGATION	NUMBER OF ROLL-CALLS									
	1949		1951		1953		1955		1957*	
	Won	Lost	Won	Lost	Won	Lost	Won	Lost	Won	Lost
91-100	0	0	1	0	0	0	6	1	4	0
81-90	13	1	5	0	2	0	18	0	9	0
67-80	25	1	20	1	25	1	42	15	52	4
Total	38	2	26	1	27	1	66	16	65	4

* Chicago

Table 3—Number of Contested Roll-Calls on Which the Cook County Delegation Won and Lost When It Voted with a Cohesion of 67% or More: Senate Sessions of 1949 Through 1957

VOTING COHESION OF COOK COUNTY DELEGATION	NUMBER OR ROLL-CALLS									
	1949		1951		1953		1955		1957*	
	Won	Lost	Won	Lost	Won	Lost	Won	Lost	Won	Lost
91-100	0	2	3	0	0	0	13	0	2	0
81-90	11	0	5	1	2	0	14	17	29	5
67-80	22	13	20	4	8	3	12	20	21	9
Total	33	15	28	5	10	3	39	37	52	14

* Chicago

In summary, the urban delegation lost on a small fraction of the contested roll-calls when both parties in the delegation were in agreement. It is notable that the urban delegation lost on only three out of 14,052 roll-calls when it voted with a cohesion of more than 90%, indicating that as urban delegation solidarity approaches 100% it is virtually certain that the delegation will be on the winning side of the vote.

3. *The rural delegation seldom votes with high cohesion against the urban delegation.* Assumptions about urban-rural conflict imply that the two groups clash in the legislative arena and that the urban delegation loses. The preceding section suggests that the urban delegation seldom loses on roll-call votes. The assumptions further imply that high urban cohesion is met by heavy rural opposition.

Tables 5 and 6 contain data showing the degree of rural opposition to the urban delegation when the latter voted with a cohesion of 67% or more. It is striking that over the five-session period (including 7,186 roll-calls) there was no instance of a House urban-rural clash involving over 90% of the urban delegation in opposition to over 90% of the rural delegation. Only one case of conflict at the level of over-80% of each delegation in opposition is found. In the Senate two instances of conflict at the over-90% level are found. Fifteen instances of conflict at the over-80% level occurred in the Senate, but twelve of these took place in the 1955 session when 89% of the urban delegation was Democrat and 94% of the rural delegation was Republican.

If the 1955 Senate session is excluded, the other four Senate sessions and the five House sessions produced six instances of urban-rural conflict at the 80% level of significance.

If the test identifying urban-rural conflict is lowered to the 67% level of conflict between delegations, seven such cases are found in the House and 28 in the Senate. Twenty-four of the Senate roll-calls occurred in the 1955 and 1957 Senate sessions when over 80% of the Democrats

were urban and over 80% of the Republicans were rural.

It is notable that during the five House sessions which produced more than 7,000 roll-call votes, there were only three instances of urban-rural conflict in which a combination of more than 67% of both urban Democrats and urban Republicans were opposed by more than 67% of the rural delegation.

It is clear that urban and rural delegations do not vote solidly against each other in the Illinois Assembly. These findings do not support a belief that urban and rural legislators regularly slug it out in the state legislature.

When there is opposition to the urban delegation, from what quarter does it come? Using roll-call votes on which the urban delegation voted with a cohesion of 67% or more, a support-opposition score was obtained for each legislator by subtracting the number of times he voted against the urban delegation from the number of times he voted with it. In the quartile of highest opposition to the urban delegation practically all legislators are rural Republicans, with rural Democrats clustering in the two quartiles of lowest opposition. Support-opposition scores were obtained for the three-member House districts by summing the scores of the three members. Results of analyses of House and Senate districts using the Spearman rank-order correlations significant at the .01 level indicate a positive correlation between: 1) degree of opposition of Senators and of House members of the same party from the same area; 2) opposition to the urban delegation and degree of "Republicanism" of the district as measured by proclivity of the district to elect Republican legislators. Each downstate district sends at least one Democrat to the House, and in each case the Democrat had a score showing higher support of the urban delegation than did his Republican colleagues from the same district.

The support-opposition scores of legislators from downstate urbanized areas throw interesting light on the hypothesis that the common problems faced

Table 4—Number of Contested Roll-Calls on Which the Cook County Delegation Won and Lost When It Voted With a Cohesion of 67% or More, Including at Least 51% of Both Cook County Democrats and Cook County Republicans: House Sessions of 1949 Through 1957

VOTING COHESION OF COOK COUNTY DELEGATION	NUMBER OF ROLL-CALLS									
	1949		1951		1953		1955		1957*	
	Won	Lost	Won	Lost	Won	Lost	Won	Lost	Won	Lost
91-100	0	0	1	0	0	0	6	1	0	0
81-90	13	1	5	0	2	0	18	0	8	0
67-80	10	1	18	0	20	1	29	10†	23	1
Total	23	2	24	0	22	1	53	11	31	1

* Chicago
† Cook County lost on these ten roll-calls by one vote.

Table 5—Percentage of Downstate Delegation Opposing Cook County Delegation on Roll-Calls on Which the Cook County Delegation Voted with a Cohesion of 67% or More: House Sessions of 1949 Through 1957

| | NUMBER OF ROLL-CALLS | | | | | | | | | | | | | | |
| Percentage of Downstate Delegation Opposing Cook County Delegation | 1949 COOK COUNTY COHESION (%) | | | 1951 COOK COUNTY COHESION (%) | | | 1953 COOK COUNTY COHESION (%) | | | 1955 COOK COUNTY COHESION (%) | | | 1957 CHICAGO COHESION (%) | | |
	67-80	81-90	91-100	67-80	81-90	91-100	67-80	81-90	91-100	67-80	81-90	91-100	67-80	81-90	91-100
91-100	0	0	0	0	0	0	0	0	0	0	0	0	0	0	0
81-90	0	0	0	0	0	0	0	0	0	0	0	0	0	1	0
67-80	0	1	0	1	0	0	0	0	0	2	0	1	0	0	0
51-66	1	2	0	5	2	0	1	1	0	7	0	4	3	0	0
0-50	25	11	0	15	3	1	25	1	0	48	18	2	52	8	4
Total	26	14	0	21	5	1	26	2	0	57	18	7	56	9	4

Table 6—Percentage of Downstate Delegation Opposing Cook County Delegation on Roll-Calls on Which the Cook County Delegation Voted with a Cohesion of 67% or More: Senate Sessions of 1949 Through 1957

| | NUMBER OF ROLL-CALLS | | | | | | | | | | | | | | |
| Percentage of Downstate Delegation Opposing Cook County Delegation | 1949 COOK COUNTY COHESION (%) | | | 1951 COOK COUNTY COHESION (%) | | | 1953 COOK COUNTY COHESION (%) | | | 1955 COOK COUNTY COHESION (%) | | | 1957 CHICAGO COHESION (%) | | |
	67-80	81-90	91-100	67-80	81-90	91-100	67-80	81-90	91-100	67-80	81-90	91-100	67-80	81-90	91-100
91-100	0	0	0	0	0	0	0	0	0	0	2	0	0	0	0
81-90	0	0	2	0	1	0	0	0	0	8	2	0	0	0	0
67-80	0	0	0	0	0	0	1	0	0	2	1	1	6	2	0
51-66	12	0	0	2	0	0	3	0	0	6	9	4	3	0	0
0-50	23	11	0	22	5	3	7	2	0	16	17	8	21	32	2
Total	35	11	2	24	6	3	11	2	0	32	31	13	30	34	2

by cities throughout the state may lead legislators from these different cities to work together. Although there are wide variations in voting behavior of legislators from non-Chicago urbanized areas, those legislators are distinguished neither for support of, nor opposition to, the Chicago legislators. There are some Republican legislators from Chicago and Cook County in the quartile of highest opposition to the Chicago delegation.

4. *Party conflict is more prevalent than urban-rural conflict.* Party loyalty exerts a greater pull on the legislator's loyalty than does his geographical base.

Tables 7 and 8 present comparative data on frequency of party conflict and urban-rural conflict. Keefe's findings and tests of group cohesion are presented to indicate that tests of relative cohesion produce the same conclusions as tests of absolute cohesion.[9] With the exception of the 1955 and 1957 Senate sessions, party votes occurred in one to six per cent of all roll-calls, while

urban-rural votes occurred in less than 0.3% of all roll-calls.

In the data on the 1955 and 1957 Senate sessions, the party divisions again cloud analysis of urban-rural conflict, a fact that is partially illustrated by the footnotes to Table 8 which list the urban-rural votes meeting the test of party-conflict votes. In all other sessions and chambers party divisions within the urban delegations control the party variable to some degree. It is obvious that Democrat vs. Republican was much more the significant conflict. This is further evidence that when party groups within the urban delegation can come to an agreement on legislative policy the delegation stands an excellent chance not only to prevail but also to avoid rural opposition.

5. *Urban Democrats and urban Republicans are more often in disagreement than agreement.* To conform with assumptions about urban-rural conflict found in the literature of political science, urban legislators must act together to support or

Table 7—Percentage of All Roll-Calls of Party Votes and Urban-Rural Votes According to Derge[1] and Keefe[2] Definitions: House Sessions of 1949 Through 1957

TYPE OF ROLL-CALL	1949 N	1949 %	1951 N	1951 %	1953 N	1953 %	1955 N	1955 %	1957 N	1957 %
All roll-calls	1082	100.0	1417	100.0	1158	100.0	1669	100.0	1860	100.0
Party votes (Derge definition)	33	3.	24	1.7	19	1.6	30	1.8	90	4.8
Party votes (Keefe definition)	38	3.5	27	1.9	20	1.7	58	3.5	108	5.8
Urban-rural votes (Derge definition)	1	0.09	1	0.07	0	0.	3	0.18	2	0.11
Urban-rural votes (Keefe definition)	1	0.09	1	0.07	0	0.	2	0.12	3	0.16

1. Derge definition: 67% or more of elected membership of one group opposed to 67% or more of elected membership of other group.

2. Keefe definition: 80% or more of the voting members of one group opposed to 80% or more of voting members of other group.

Table 8—Percentage of All Roll-Calls of Party Votes and Urban-Rural Votes According to Derge[1] and Keefe[2] Definitions: Senate Sessions of 1949 Through 1957

TYPE OF ROLL-CALL	1949 N	1949 %	1951 N	1951 %	1953 N	1953 %	1955 N	1955 %	1957 N	1957 %
All roll-calls	1242	100.0	1376	100.0	1201	100.0	1483	100.0	1564	100.0
Party votes (Derge definition)	60	4.8	34	2.5	13	1.1	20	1.3	26	1.7
Party votes (Keefe definition)	54	4.4	43	3.1	16	1.3	35	2.4	55	3.5
Urban-rural votes (Derge definition)	2	0.16	1	0.07	1	0.08	16[3]	1.1	8[5]	0.51
Urban-rural votes (Keefe definition)	3	0.23	2	0.14	5	0.41	29[4]	2.	15[6]	1.

1. Derge definition: 67% or more of elected membership of one group opposed to 67% or more of elected membership of other group.

2. Keefe definition: 80% or more of the voting members of one group opposed to 80% or more of voting members of other group.

3. All of these votes met Derge definition of party vote.

4. Eighteen of these votes met Keefe definition of party vote.

5. Seven of these votes met Derge definition of party vote.

6. Fourteen of these votes met Keefe definition of party vote.

oppose legislation, and rural legislators must oppose these efforts. This overlooks the probability that in large urban areas there will be power struggles between Democrats and Republicans for control of the city government and political machinery and that urban legislators emerging from this struggle will divide in the legislature just as they divide in urban politics.

Table 9 contains data on the frequency of votes showing high bipartisan cohesion and partisan conflict within the House urban delegations of 1955 and 1957. Two significant findings are obvious. First, urban Democrats and Republicans are in conflict more often than all Democrats and all Republicans in the chamber. Second, urban Democrats and Republicans are more often in disagreement with each other than in agreement. It should be noted that on 42 of the 61 roll-calls showing such agreement less than 25% of the total membership of the chamber was on the losing side of the vote, a clear indication that most of the chamber was in agreement.

of the 32 bills. On 85% of these roll-calls Chicago Democrats and Republicans were in disagreement, with a high level of conflict on 60% of the votes. On two (5%) of the roll-calls both urban party groups took the same side, each with a cohesion of 67% or more.

The past five sessions of the Assembly have produced numerous bills introduced by Chicago and Cook County Republicans to embarrass or damage the Democrat-controlled Chicago administration. Conversely, Chicago Democrats introduced bills to consolidate their political advantages against Republican incursions. The downstate response to such measures tends to be partisan, producing chamber party votes rather than urban-rural votes. It should be noted, however, that in a number of cases the downstate legislators adopted a wait-and-see policy, refusing to take sides in an intra-city fight. Several downstate legislators have said in interviews that they are willing to support Chicago legislation on which both urban parties agree, but are themselves unwilling to settle intra-urban po-

Table 9—Number of Contested Roll-Calls on Which Party Groups Voted with a Cohesion of 67% or More, and Were in Agreement or Disagreement: House Sessions of 1955 and 1957

	1955		1957	
	N	% all contested roll-calls	N	% all contested roll-calls
Urban Democrats and Republicans in agreement	27	10.8	34	10.6
Urban Democrats and Republicans in disagreement	31	12.4	95	29.5
All Democrats and Republicans in disagreement	30	12.	90	27.9

The behavior of 1957 House Chicago Democrats and Republicans on 32 bills applicable only, or primarily, to the Chicago metropolitan area reveals that the urban delegation seldom acts with unity on municipal problems which give rise to conflict in the state legislature. Table 10 contains a summary of the agreement and disagreement pattern on 47 roll-calls taken during consideration

Table 10—Level of Agreement or Disagreement of the Chicago Democrats and Republicans on 47 Roll-Calls Involving Urban Legislation in the 1957 Illinois House

	N	%
67% or more Democrats opposed 67% or more Republicans	28	59.5
Democrats and Republicans in disagreement below 67% level	12	25.5
Democrats and Republicans in agreement above 67% level	2	4.5
Democrats and Republicans in agreement below 67% level	5	10.5
Total	47	100.0

litical disputes. It is a rare occasion when legislation supported solidly by both urban parties fails to pass.

S. B. 310 in the 1957 session provides a good illustration of intra-city conflict in the state legislature. This bill, introduced by three Chicago Republican Senators and one Cook County Republican Senator, simply restored a tax-rate limit for the City of Chicago after the 1955 session had failed to place limits on how much money the city administration could take from the taxpayers. To place such a tax limit would not only impose an important financial restraint on the Democratic city administration, but would also carry the implication that this administration could not be trusted to act in accordance with the interests of the people of Chicago.

The bill passed the Senate on a straight chamber party vote, the Chicago and Cook County Republicans lining up with downstate Republicans against Chicago Democrats. In House debate on this bill, Representative Pollack (R-Chicago), the House majority whip, accused Chicago Democrat legislators of political treachery in failing to keep 1955 promises to continue the tax-peg limit under which Chicago had been operating until that time. Two bills were introduced in 1955 by Chicago Democrats to continue this limit, but both bills were allowed by their sponsors to die on the calendar. In moving to overrule a Municipalities Committee "do not pass" report on S. B. 310, Pollack charged that without the tax limit "the taxpayers will be at the whim and caprice of the City of Chicago, and the taxpayers of Chicago deserve the protection of a limit." He further urged that "the people will be at the mercy of a city council controlled by the city administration" and that "the 'home rule' argument that Chicago should not be limited by the legislature is an attempt to take the lid off property tax, contrary to the historical practice in the state of Illinois."

Rep. De La Cour (D-Chicago), House minority leader, countered that "we (sic) of Chicago have treated our taxpayers fairly" and accused Pollack of unfair and dilatory action. The debate was wholly between Chicago Democrats and Chicago Republicans on the House floor. The vote which defeated Pollack's motion to overrule the "do not pass" report illustrates both the internecine urban party behavior and the tendency of downstaters to line up along party lines or to ignore the dispute. Chicago Democrats and Republicans lined up solidly against each other, the downstate Democrats voted with the Chicago Democrats and the downstate Republicans with the Chicago Republicans, and a small but decisive number of both downstate Democrats and Republicans abstained from voting. The absence of 21 downstaters killed Chicago Republican chances to restore the tax limit when the motion went down 71-69, 18 votes short of the required constitutional majority.

6. *Reapportionment may not guarantee a more favored position to big cities.* The previous sections of this paper have suggested that Chicago and Cook County, even though in the minority, were quite successful in being on the winning side of votes particularly when high cohesion tended toward bi-partisan unity. Downstate opposition to high urban cohesion seldom reached a significant level of conflict. It was also found that urban intra-delegation partisan conflicts exceeded bipartisan agreements.

With these points in mind the possible effects of the 1955 Reapportionment Act may be examined. Table 11 indicates that the net gain in House seats of the Chicago and Cook County Democrats in 1957 was 5.3% while the net Republican gain was 8.7%. The party division within the Chicago

delegation remained about the same as in 1955. Heaviest gains in seats was made by the suburban Cook County area, a Republican stronghold. The Chicago and Cook County Republican gains in the Senate are more spectacular. While Chicago Democrats suffered a 7% loss in seats in 1957, Chicago and Cook County Republicans enjoyed a 17% gain. Much of this is accounted for by the addition of five new Senate seats in Republican suburbia. Because reapportionment of the Senate requires a constitutional amendment, it is unlikely that Republican gains will be offset in the near future. Political habits of suburbia and the pattern of urban growth point toward a continued Republican domination of Cook County outside of Chicago, the area most likely to gain in seats as the House is reapportioned decenially. If it is true that the strongest opposition to Chicago comes from Chicago and Cook County Republicans rather than rural legislators, then in the 1957 Assembly Chicago was actually in a weaker position than before the reapportionment. Redress through fundamental changes in political loyalty in Republican suburban Cook County and downstate areas would seem remote.

It is interesting to speculate whether increased representation of the suburban Cook County area in the legislature may encourage enemies of the Chicago city administration to transfer much of the intra-city and county power struggle to the legislative arena. The Cook County and Chicago Republican gain in 1957 House seats was 8.7% as opposed to a downstate Republican loss of 6%, and the Senate gain was 17% compared to the downstate Republican loss of 9%. If Cook County and Chicago Republicans have enjoyed a corresponding increase in power in the Republican legislative parties, it is reasonable to conclude that they will be in an even better position than before to line up downstate Republican colleagues in the harassment of Cook County and Chicago Democrats who speak for Chicago city hall. This role of Chicago Democratic legislators is demonstrated by a statement in debate by Representative De La Cour (D-Chicago), 1957 House minority leader. De La Cour described the Democratic Mayor of Chicago as "Director of the Board, a captain of the ship, a commanding general."

It is not with shame that I say to you 'the Mayor of Chicago is the Democratic Central Committeeman and he is expressing what the people of Chicago want.' Orders have to be given, and I am happy as minority leader to get those orders, because it is in the interest of the wishes of the people of Chicago and of Illinois.

Needless to say, Chicago and Cook County Republicans do not perceive the Democratic Mayor as De La Cour describes him, either in city politics or in the state legislature.[10]

Political scientists propose "home rule" as one solution to the "stepchild lot" of the big cities in the state legislatures, although many of them feel that without "fair representation" the solution could never be forced. Paradoxically, in Illinois at least, the reapportionment which many counted on to make grants of power to Chicago more possible may indeed have created a political situation making such grants even more remote. The Republicans of Chicago, and their allies across the city limits in suburban Cook County, may develop into the strongest opponents of giving their political enemies more autonomy in the operation of Chicago city government. The more independent a Democrat-controlled Chicago becomes, the less secure will be Chicago Republicans and Republican suburbs fearful of big-city intrusions. With their increased legislative power resulting from reapportionment, they may effectively veto ambitions for home-rule powers.[11]

This analysis suggests that the traditional belief in bitter urban-rural conflict in state legislatures must be rejected for Illinois at least at the roll-call stage. Such conflict is rare in the Illinois General Assembly, perhaps because issues calling up such conflict are rare. When the big city comes to Springfield, backed by support from both urban Democrats and Republicans, it usually gets what it wants. Its legislators are not trampled on by rural legislators, even when the latter are in a numerical majority.

Rather, a different type of conflict emerges in which the big city finds its legislative friends in the urban legislators of the party which controls the city administration, and in rural legislators of that party. Its bitterest opponents in the state legislature are political enemies from within its own walls, and those camped in adjoining suburban areas. The balance of power is held by the rural colleagues of the city minority party. These rural legislators have demonstrated their willingness to cooperate in the solution of urban problems providing urban legislators of both parties can reach agreement on the solutions. They have demonstrated equally well that when the urban parties bring their squabbles to the state legislature, rural legislators will usually divide along party lines if they are attentive to the dispute at all. This situation places grave responsibilities on both urban parties to resolve differences on policy before putting their case before the legislature.

Intra-city party conflict may well be in the finest tradition of the doctrine of party responsibility, according to which party conflict is a healthy phenomenon and the majority party must be under the constant scrutiny and criticism of the minority party. If large cities are to have two-party systems, and if this doctrine, which has been forwarded by so many political scientists and has had the official blessing of the American Political Science Association, is to be pursued in large cities, it is only reasonable that urban parties should behave in this manner in the state legislature where many urban problems seek their solutions.

As long as partisanship has a role in governing big cities, and only a few political scientists now

Table 11—Seats Held in 1955 Session (Old Apportionment) and 1957 (New Apportionment) by Party Groups from Chicago and Cook County Outside of Chicago

HOUSE	1955		1957		
	N	% all seats	N	% all seats	% gain or loss in 1957
Chicago Democrats	34	22.	42	24.	+ 2.
Cook County Democrats	1	0.7	7	4.	+ 3.3
Total	35	22.7	49	28.	+ 5.3
Chicago Republicans	20	13.	27	15.	+ 2.
Cook County Republicans	2	1.3	14	8.	+ 6.7
Total	22	14.3	41	23.	+ 8.7

SENATE	1955		1957		
	N	% all seats	N	% all seats	% gain or loss in 1957
Chicago Democrats	17	33.	15	26.	− 7.
Cook County Democrats	0	0.	0	0.	0.
Total	17	33.	15	26.	− 7.
Chicago Republicans	1	2.	3	5.	+ 3.
Cook County Republicans	1	2.	6	16.	+ 14.
Total	2	4.	9	21.	+ 17.

believe that it does not, it is likely that the city's success in the state legislature will be determined by partisan considerations. To ask for more than this is to avoid the hard facts of political reality.

Notes

1. Murray S. Stedman, Jr., "American Political Parties as a Conservative Force" 10 *Western Political Quarterly* 395 (1957).

2. Alfred DeGrazia, "General Theory of Apportionment" 17 *Law and Contemporary Problems* 261 (1952).

3. For example, see: C. M. Kneier, *City Government in the United States*, Revised Edition (New York, 1947), Chapter VI; S. A. MacCorkle, *American Municipal Government and Administration* (Boston, 1949), pp. 52-54; C. F. Snider, *American State and Local Government* (New York, 1950), pp. 169-172.

4. See Kneier, *op. cit.*, Snider, *op. cit.*, Benjamin Baker, *Urban Government* (Princeton, 1957), pp. 325-328. Gordon E. Baker, *Rural versus Urban Political Power* (Garden City, 1955), pp. 15-19.

5. W. J. Keefe, *A Study of the Role of Political Parties in the Legislative Process, Illinois General Assembly* (Unpublished Ph.D. thesis, Northwestern University, 1951), pp. 73-74. See also Keefe's "Parties, Partisanship, and Public Policy in the Pennsylvania Legislature" 48 *American Political Science Review* 450 (1954), in which roll-call analyses are used.

6. M. Jewell, "Party Voting in American State Legislatures," 49 *American Political Science Review* 773 (1955); W. Lockard, "Legislative Politics in Connecticut," 48 *American Political Science Review* 166 (1954); A. L. Lowell, "The Influence of Party Upon Legislation," *Annual Report of the American Historical Association*, Vol. 1, 1901; D. MacRae, "Relation Between Roll Call Votes and Constituencies in the Massachusetts House of Representatives," 46 *American Political Science Review* 1046 (1952); Julius Turner, *Party and Constituency*, (Baltimore, 1951).

7. A number of quantitative tests of voting cohesion are available. Stuart A. Rice developed an index of cohesion which is useful when a single expression of unity within the delegation is needed, and intra-delegation conflict must be expressed. See *Quantitative Methods in Politics* (New York, 1928). Other writers have used a "relative cohesion" test which is based on the percentage of a delegation voting on a particular roll-call. The expression of cohesion is obtained in the same manner as in "absolute cohesion" tests, but is not related to the total membership of the group being studied.

The chi square test has been used to determine whether the distribution of votes cast by two or more groups on one roll-call can be attributed to random chance. See Murray C. Havens, *City versus Farm* (University, Alabama, 1957). This test yields a statement of statistical risk involved in rejecting hypotheses that distributions of elements are random. Havens established the level of significance at $P = .05$, the usual choice of social scientists using the X^2 statistic. At this level he accepts a relationship between variables involved in the roll-calls, in this case urban and rural groups. Thus, on those roll-calls where distribution of urban and rural votes yields $P = .05$ or less, Havens accepts the hypothesis that urban-rural conflict was present. There are several criticisms of this method. Assuming a hypothetical legislature in which urban and rural groups each hold 100 seats, a division of 57 urban "yes," 43 urban "no," and 43 rural "yes," 57 rural "no" would produce a X^2 value of 3.92, which is significant at the .05 level, and would lead to a conclusion of urban-rural conflict. This is substantially below the levels of significance used in this study and in roll-call analyses of party behavior cited in footnote 6. Further, no good comparison can be made between roll-call votes if no more than the X^2 and P values are available; that is, the X^2 test does not by itself provide a measure of the strength of correlation between variables (urban or rural constituency and position-taking on roll-calls), but only a statement of probability that randomness can account for distribution of votes. Unless this test is further refined by a coefficient of contingency, or similar statistic, no comparison can be made of association of variables on different roll-calls.

One merit of a fixed absolute percentage of delegation membership as a test for level of significant cohesion lies in being able to state that a delegation did vote with a given high cohesion, and that it was or was not opposed by another delegation voting with a given high cohesion. On the contrary, the X^2 test opens the door to conclusions of urban-rural conflict which may hardly be justified if "conflict" is to be endowed with its usual meaning. For example, Havens obtains a $P = .01$ for a roll-call on which the urban group divided 18 "yes," 15 "no," and the rural group 32 "yes," 0 "no." This meets his requirements for "urban vs. rural" although the urban delegation is almost evenly divided, and a majority of *both* urban and rural groups voted on the *same* side. (p. 54, *op. cit.*) Testing the distribution of votes within the urban delegation with a 50-50 hypothesis, one concludes that in this case the distribution must be attributed to random chance $(P = .30)$. Thus, one might conclude that this roll-call, and several others meeting Havens' test of "urban vs. rural" show a difference in behavior of urban and rural groups, but not a conflict between these groups.

Finally, Havens' application of the X^2 test to that portion of the total membership of a delegation which voted on a given roll-call resulted in the labelling of several roll-calls as "urban vs. rural" when less than half of either or both groups represented the majority position of the group on the roll-call.

8. The relatively higher incidence of voting cohesion from 67-91% in the 1955 and 1957 sessions of the Senate may be accounted for by the fact that Democrats comprised 83% of the Chicago delegation in 1957, and 89% in 1955. In all other House and Senate sessions, some Republican votes were needed to push delegation cohesion above 67%. The 1955 and 1957 Senate data reflect party conflict.

9. Keefe, *A Study of the Role of Political Parties in the Legislative Process, Illinois General Assembly*, pp. 232-233.

10. It is interesting that in the 1957 House, after reapportionment had placed all Cook County districts either completely inside or completely outside the city of Chicago, there were only four of the 322 contested roll-calls displaying a cohesion of more than 67% for the combined Chicago-Cook County group which had a numerical majority in the House. This should ease the fears of those downstaters who predicted that reapportionment would mean "control of the state by one county."

11. Edward C. Banfield has pointed out the inherent political difficulties of metropolitan area organization stemming from control of the central city and the suburbs by two different political parties. "The Politics of Metropolitan Area Organization," 1 *Midwest Journal of Political Science* 77 (1957). He states that "it seems likely that the central cities will become more and more Democratic" and that "the Republican suburban vote has in general suffered little from the increase in population." As a result "these facts suggest that for many years to come it will be difficult or impossible to integrate local governments where the two party system operates" because "in effect, advocates of consolidation schemes are asking the Democrats to give up their control of the central cities or, at least, to place it in jeopardy." It may be that Banfield's argument can be broadened so that the same forces which bring the central-city Republicans and the suburbs into collision with the Democrat central-city administration in metropolitan-area organization can be expected to appear in legislative consideration of expanded "home rule" powers for the central city.

11. A CASE STUDY OF THE LEGISLATIVE PROCESS IN MUNICIPAL GOVERNMENT

J. Leiper Freeman

THIS STUDY of the legislative process in municipal government focuses upon a city council's decisions involving the public works budget submitted by the mayor for the ensuing fiscal year. The data were collected through a series of intensive interviews with participants and an examination of the pertinent documents, several months after the action occurred. The study was exploratory, followed by a much larger project intent on illuminating community decision-making in "Bay City," a Massachusetts industrial center of nearly 50,000 persons.[1]

The basic objectives of the public works appropriations study were (a) to learn as much as possible about public decision processes and the kinds of influence impinging upon members of a public legislative body in a city, and (b) to determine the effectiveness of the technique of *ex post facto* interviews-in-depth with participants. The researchers were convinced that the technique can provide considerable evidence on the subject. At the same time, they felt that *ex post facto* interviews obviously furnish qualitatively different data from those provided by direct observation and on-the-spot interviews. The first type brings forth those more generalized events and relationships which are recalled as significant from the perspective of a later date. The second approach leads to more emphasis upon the idiosyncratic and momentary and is less likely to let minutiae slip through the net of recollection.[2] In the balance, despite limitations in the technique, the researchers felt that they had probed sufficiently to illustrate some significant elements in decision-making by municipal lawmakers. It was felt that willful deception, deliberate distortion, and the like were minimal. The biases of the findings were chiefly those inherent in the perceptions and recollections of the participants even after they had been stimulated to talk freely and to recall with thoroughness.

Basic Story of the Public Works Appropriations Process. Bay City in 1952 had a government which political scientists would classify somewhere between a "strong mayor" and a "weak mayor" type.

This paper was written especially for this volume.

Its mayor was elected for a two-year term and paid a salary of about $5,000 annually, for which he was supposed to spend most but not all of his time on the job. He had to share his executive powers in some cases with commissions or boards, but he usually named the members of these, subject to council confirmation, as vacancies occurred or terms ended. Department heads were for the most part under civil service and therefore generally immune to "spoils" reprisal either from the mayor or the council. Nevertheless, most department heads tended to feel that the mayor was the "boss" of the municipal enterprise within limits, and they generally did not like to be at cross purposes with him. Even those municipal administrators with separate boards or commissions to shield them were not insensitive to the mayor's status as the chief political officer of the city and to his budgetary controls. The mayor had the authority to determine the budget requests for each department, except the schools, and to submit them to the council. The council could either approve or lower the amounts requested, but could not raise them. The mayor also had considerable authority over the transfer of funds from one budget category to another. In the case of public works, he had special authority to alter the priority of expenditures for authorized projects of similar nature, thereby being able to push ahead the laying of a sidewalk in a favored neighborhood and to retard the laying of another in an unfavored area.

The council was composed of eleven members, also elected for two-year terms, five from the city at large and one each from the six wards of the municipality. They were paid nominal sums, and their councilmanic duties were not envisioned as consuming a major part of their time. They annually elected one of their number as president of the council and divided themselves into ten different standing committees on special subjects for the conduct of much of their work. The most important of these commitees, playing a vital part in the appropriations process, was the finance committee, which was always composed of the council president and two other members.

In the boiling pot of Bay City's municipal politics, the "Progressives" (local counterpart of the national Democratic party) held a nearly two-to-one majority, as long as they could hold together. At the time of this study, traditional local party lines were in a state of some fluidity, occasioned by the formation of a "Coalition" composed of most of the "Non-Partisans" (local counterpart of the Republican party) and significant elements of their traditional opponents. The Coalition was pictured in the press as the answer to a need for respectability, economy, and less partisanship in city hall. In the 1949 election it had defeated a staunch Progressive mayor whom some compared to Boston's James M. Curley, using a third candidate to help split the Progressive vote. That Progressive had won the mayoralty in 1947 by galvanizing his party into a crushing majority, and it had been in reaction to this event that the Coalition was formed. The Coalition in 1951 re-elected its mayor, again defeating the Progressive "boss" with the help of a third candidate. The Coalition also elected a majority of six members to the council. The local newspaper, the *Bugle,* which was bed-rock Republican in outlook and had taken a leading part in devising and promoting the Coalition, looked forward to another two-year regime in which their mayor would be able to pursue the policies advocated by the newspaper with the support of the legislative body.

Shortly after the election and long before the mayor's budget was to be submitted to the council for consideration, however, three of the Coalition members of the new council joined with three members from the anti-Coalition faction to form a new majority. They named one of their men council president and reserved for themselves the choicest council committee posts, including especially the finance committee. The other three Coalition members of the council and the two remaining members then became a loyal minority in support of the mayor. Managers of the Coalition and representatives of the *Bugle* tried in vain to stop the revolt of the insurgents and to hold a majority together which would follow their leadership. They even suggested that the leader of the revolt flip a coin with one of the loyal members of the Coalition on the council to determine the presidency. But the insurgents remained adamant and resorted to their majority power. Thereupon, the *Bugle* complained vigorously that the mayor had received a "double-cross" from the new majority leaders of the council.

Facing this hostile majority led by defectors from his cause, the mayor went about the business of preparing his budget in a pattern that differed somewhat from previous years. As usual, the budget requests for public works were initially set up by the commissioner, relying largely upon the previous year's figures. Then the mayor together with the auditor worked out a final form for presentation to the council, reducing nearly half the items in the commissioner's requests. In contrast with previous years, however, at this point the mayor did not work informally with the finance committee of the council, now composed of three of the majority who had turned against him. Instead, when he had finished his budget preparations, the mayor simply turned the document over to the council, or, as he put it, he "dumped it on their desks."

The finance committee therefore held its own hearings on the budget instead of working with the mayor, and finally in its executive sessions it cut the mayor's public works requests in 17 out of a total of 29 items. When the report of the finance committee came to the whole council for vote and adoption, 12 of the reductions in the mayor's requests were sustained by a vote of six to five, while five of the reductions made by the finance committee failed to be sustained, losing five to six. All other items, reported by the committee in the same amounts as requested by the mayor, were approved by a unanimous vote.

In the eyes of much of the community, this represented a substantial reversal for the mayor and a vigorous exercise of sheer power by the legislative majority. Many citizens of Bay City, like residents in other contemporary American communities, had become accustomed to executive leadership in budgetary matters. They had also been accustomed to collaboration and communication between the executive and legislative branches in working out many details of government. The separation of powers was usually moderated by the practice of informal consultation.

The *Bugle* coined a name for the council majority, the "Sasser Six," an epithet intended to connote that they followed the dictates of the council president, Robert Sasser. The newspaper depicted the Sasser Six as an obstructionist group concerned only with self-interest and playing "irresponsible politics" with the budget.

The Sasser group had no real opportunity to explain their position to the public through the newspaper, although they did have some opportunity to get their position across via the radio, since the council meetings were broadcasted. The majority members of the council tried to argue that the mayor had not been sufficiently economical in devising his budget. The *Bugle* and other Coalition spokesmen had to contend that the mayor, whom they had avowedly helped to get elected to establish more economy in city affairs, should be allowed to spend more money than the council was willing to permit. The Coalition's rationale for this somewhat anomalous position was that the mayor had formulated an efficient and economical budget, but that the insurgent council majority had made irresponsible cuts in order to make political capital.

The aftermath of the budget fight was that the *Bugle* continued to hound the Sasser Six on many issues, particularly in a drawn-out struggle by the mayor to secure the passage of a bond issue to expand the water supply of the city. Finally, in the latter part of the year, individual members of the Sasser Six one by one switched to vote with the mayor on the water bonds. Then in the autumn elections Sasser was badly defeated in a race for the state legislature. By the end of the year when the time had come to reorganize the council, the insurgents had lost their cohesion. But their actions prior to their dissolution provided valuable insights into the legislative process.

Legislative Decisions and Voting Alignments. In the decisions on the public works budget, three patterns of voting alignments occurred. First, there were *non-controversial* decisions which were represented by *unanimous* votes in the council. Second, there were *controversial* decisions settled by a vote of the *organized majority*, defeating the minority by six to five. Third, a different type of *controversial* decision entailed a *factional alliance* of the council minority and one member who defected from the organized majority. The *unanimous* decisions were the ones taken on budget items where the finance committee had recommended the same amounts as the mayor. The *organized majority* decisions were those in which the finance committee's reductions in the amounts requested by the mayor were adopted. The *factional alliance* decisions were those in which the finance committee's reductions in the amounts requested by the mayor were not adopted, allowing the mayor's requests to stand.

These three types of decisions are variations of three logical and empirical types which one might find in any American legislative body. There are first those decisions which are beyond controversy and are taken in an atmosphere of consensus attributable either to overwhelming agreement or indifference. Second, there are decisions taken in conformity with the pattern of majority vs. minority organization of the body. These are often called "party-line" votes where the organization of the legislature has been accomplished on the basis of party affiliation in a two-party political system. Finally, there are many types of combinations of minority factions which on given issues can form a voting majority, even though the members of the particular voting alliance have not stood and would not stand together to organize the legislative body.

Historically, in American legislative bodies, a vast proportion of actions taken are not controversial, but are accomplished by unanimous consent or without objection.[3] Most of the controversial decisions are normally taken by majorities composed of alliances of factions, even though "party affiliation appears to be the factor more closely associated with individual legislator's votes than any other."[4] In other words, relatively few decisions appear to be determined by straight, down-the-line votes between organized majorities and minorities in American legislatures. More often, while a predominant number of the organized majority may vote on one side and a predominant number of the minority organization may vote on the other side controversial decisions are made by an *ad hoc* alliance of factions, with those who cross organization lines tipping the scales.

Obviously, the proportions among the three types in the 29 decisions made by the Bay City council in this study are not representative of the historic proportions found in American legislative bodies generally. In the first place, the proportion of non-controversial decisions was much lower than might have been expected. In the second place, the proportion of organized majority decisions was much higher among the controversial decisions than might have been expected. The conditions contributing to these phenomena are of interest and will be explored.

Furthermore, the three types of decisions noted in the literature on legislative processes are sufficiently represented in this study to permit an attempt at explaining the factors which seem basic to each type. The factors to be considered are as follows: (a) the nature of the issue (i.e., relative values attached to the rational objective sought by the legislation); (b) the internal group structure of the legislature; (c) the norms of the system; (d) external relationships of the legislators, including those with constituency, party, pressure groups, the press, and the executive.

The Nature of the Issue as a Factor. The nature of the issue in most instances where the members of the council voted upon the 29 items of the public works budget was not perceived in terms of the relative values of the designated objectives but more often tended to be a question of human relations. The values of specific objectives in most cases were subsumed in questions about group relations within the council, about norms of council behavior, or about relations with the mayor, the newspaper, or other external factors.

For example, there was no discernible pattern of either controversial or non-controversial support for all "salary" items or all "expense" items, nor was there any consistent pattern of voting peculiar to most of the substantive objectives of the budget such as highways, bridges, sewers, snow removal, rubbish disposal, and the many other kinds of services performed by a public works department.

Certain exceptions should be noted. First, the mayor's requests for general administrative costs and engineering costs, both in personnel and expenses, were treated in a non-controversial manner. This set of facts proves nothing about the legislative process except that on these particular items, which the mayor had already cut to levels existing two years previously, the Bay City legislators were able to agree unanimously. The items may have been of such indifference to the legislators that they were treated without controversy. The values reflected in these objectives *per se* which made them non-controversial are difficult to find.

Second, all of the mayor's requests for purposes of sidewalks and for water supply were upheld in controversial decisions by factional alliances despite the recommendations of the finance committee that they be reduced. In each of these issues, one member of the Sasser Six defected from that group to join with the minority in support of the mayor, producing a factional alliance of six councilmen on that particular vote. Since the loyal minority of the council voted in every instance to support the mayor, they were not demonstrably swayed to do so in these cases by the nature of the objectives at issue. Each council member who defected from the Sasser Six, however, could be said to have done so because of the particular objective of the item concerned. On the other hand, it was not clear from the evidence that they, as individuals, attached more intrinsic value to sidewalks or to water supply than did any of the other councilmen as individuals. Instead, the more demonstrable fact was that the councilman placed sidewalks or water supply higher in his priority of values because of the constituency interests he represented. Each of the two councilmen who switched from the Sasser Six did so because he was "very interested in sidewalks" or "very interested in water supply," but further investigation supported the view that his special interest was a derivative of ecological needs widely recognized in his ward.[5]

The Internal Group Structure of the Council as a Factor. A key which unlocked the problem of understanding the division between the Sasser Six and the council minority, thereby serving to explain the organized majority votes and much other council behavior was to be found in the internal relationships of the council itself. Once elected to the council, the legislator became part of an organization in which members had different roles to play and different degrees of prestige, participation, and authority. Which roles he played and how much prestige, participation, and authority he enjoyed depended in considerable measure upon the committee posts assigned him. As in most other legislative bodies in the United States, the criterion of seniority was a traditional basis in the Bay City council for determining committee assignments.[6] Of course, the actual power to organize the council was in the hands of whatever majority was formed to exercise it, but usually the majority had recognized experience and seniority when organizing councils in the past.

In the formation of the Sasser Six, a group of junior members of the council, only two of whom had served a previous term, banded together and used the power of majority rule to prevent senior members from occupying the higher positions. This bargain struck at the outset of the legislative year constituted the foundation of the Sasser Six. Once founded, they held together in reaction to the criticism directed at them by the newspaper, the mayor, and the senior councilmen throughout the decisons on the budget and for over half the legislative year, until they finally disintegrated in the latter part of the year under the pressures previously noted.

The importance of the cohesion of the Sasser Six in terms of boosting their power in the structure of the council is demonstrated in the evidence which follows. First, a consensus ranking of the preference for and prestige of the ten committees of the council was obtained from the council members, showing the following results: (1) Finance; (2) Public Works; (3) Public Safety; (4) Legislative Affairs; (5) Claims; (6) City Property; (7) Printing; (8) Records; (9) Election Returns; (10) Hospital. By taking the committee memberships of each councilman and weighting them according to their rankings above, each legislator was assigned a score reflecting his position and rank in the structure of the council during 1952, the year that the Sasser Six dominated the organization. For comparative purposes, the same scores and rankings were made in a follow-up study of the council in 1953, the year after the Sasser Six had disintegrated. The relative scores and the relative rankings for the two years are presented in Table I.

It can readily be seen that the six members who grouped around Robert Sasser obtained for themselves positions of much greater importance within the council than the five minority members and much higher than they were able to obtain when their majority no longer held together. It is also evident that the junior members used their majority power to subordinate seniority as a criterion of leadership. Once committed to this internal structure, the organized majority resisted giving it up. They realized that if they did not stick together their political gamble and their revolt against the mayor, the newspaper, and tradition would probably come to naught. They seemed to hope that they would be able by their cohesive behavior to use council power to win public approval.

The organized majority decisions of the council in this situation were not "party-line" decisions in the ordinary meaning of a party which had won a majority at the polls. They were the product, instead, of an intra-legislative group formed after the election to seize council power, which operated in the pattern of party government without the external reinforcement that a majority party can usually command.

The Norms of the System as Factors. Surrounding the legislative process were expectations of both a legal and extra-legal nature which conditioned the action of the councilmen. For example, it was well recognized that by law some of the appropriations decisions to be taken by the council members lay within narrow ranges of alternative, if indeed there were alternatives. There were explicit legal requirements that prevented the council from curtailing the salaries of persons under civil service. Another law prohibited the council from increasing the amounts

of budget items above the mayor's requests. An additional law was very exact in fixing the time of decision. On the basis of these, one could explain why certain items were non-controversial, why no items were raised above the mayor's figures, and why the decisions of the council were made within a specified time. In studying the legislative process, it would be a mistake to overlook the formal, legal requirements because participants do many things simply because the laws say that they should be done.

Other norms were less explicit, but were widely acknowledged by councilmen as usually applying to budget legislation. They were informal and extra-legal adaptations that guided the process at several stages, under ordinary circumstances. These norms involved expectations of (a) executive limitations upon the ranges of choice available to councilmen; (b) cooperation and communication between the mayor and the council in working out the budget; and (c) a maximum of public harmony in the council in making budget decisions. Note that these informal norms set forth much more limited roles for councilmen in this process than even the somewhat limited roles allowed by law.

Despite the legal restrictions previously mentioned, councilmen *legally* and *formally* were in a position to deal independently and even harshly with the mayor's budget. *Informally*, however, they expected under ordinary circumstances to be limited by the calculations of the department head, the auditor, and the mayor who would present a budget strongly shaped by the figures of previous years. At the outset, then, they expected the budget to be tied to an inscrutable

Table I—Committee Position Scores and Ranking of Councilmen in Bay City: 1952 and 1953

	Councilman	Senior or Junior Mem.*	COMMITTEE POSITION SCORES:		RANK:	
			1952	1953	1952	1953
SASSER SIX	Sasser	Jr.	Pres.	15	1	9
	Mullins†	Jr.	43	30	2	4
	Martin	Jr.	40	14	3	10
	Kelly	Jr.	33	22	4	6.5
	Wrenn	Jr.	26	13	5	11
	Jauno	Jr.	25	15	6	8
	Lafevre	Jr.	17	29	7	5
	Blais	Sr.	13	22	8.5	6.5
	Arnett	Sr.	13	Pres.	8.5	1
	Galloway	Sr.	12	43	10	2
	Sideburns	Sr.	11	31	11	3

* Senior members are those with more than one prior term on the council.

† Mullins made a crucial switch during the latter part of 1952 which helped restore the power of the mayor's loyal group and appeared to prevent Mullins' slipping far in rank after the Sasser Six fell apart.

and somewhat authoritative past. Furthermore, the councilmen expected the budget presented to them to have been carefully examined by the auditor whom they regarded as a "watchdog" with twenty years of experience in the mysteries of budget laws and figures. Normally, he and the mayor were expected to make up much of what would turn out to be the final budget.

Legally, there were no requirements that the mayor and the finance committee confer. Yet an expectation had grown up that they would get together informally and work out most of the executive-legislative differences, so that the council's challenges of the mayor's requests would be largely delivered in a quiet and compromising atmosphere.

Legally, there were no requirements that the finance committee's and the mayor's recommendations be supported. But there was an informal expectation that, under ordinary circumstances, the most important actions in council would be taken in the finance committee, followed by closed meetings of the whole council at which the committee might present its recommendations and most of the remaining differences might be resolved. Thus, controversy in public meetings on most budget items was not ordinarily to be expected.

Generally speaking, the longer a person had been a member of the council, the more he accepted these informal norms. Especially, he seemed to view controversy on budget items between the executive and legislative branches or within the legislature itself as *exceptional* rather than as the *dominant mode* of making decisions. The disparity between the senior and junior members in their endorsement of these norms was dramatized by the respective answers of an extreme representative of each group to the question: "If the council has several informal meetings on the budget and then is ready to take formal action, should the debates on some items be opened up in a formal public meeting?"

SENIOR MEMBER: "After decisions have been agreed upon in the committee of the whole, then *differences should not be aired in public.* Give the committee of the whole four nights— then four more if necessary. Then come out and adopt the budget as a whole. This is a small city. You got to have harmony."

JUNIOR MEMBER: "The council meetings on the budget should be *open to the public* so that the real issues can be heard. And *never mind the friction* that the older members want to avoid. They and the mayor would like to have star chamber preliminary meetings called to avoid friction. This results in a cut-and-dried procedure."

Of course, not all of the senior members of the council felt as strongly as the oldtimer quoted above that budget decisions should be non-controversial and according to informal traditions, nor did all of the junior men feel as strongly in favor of open controversy as did the newcomer quoted. But the senior members, under ordinary circumstances regarded as the elder statesmen and custodians of the standards of the council, seemed to view the council as a body whose functions were to negotiate, to work things out cooperatively with the mayor and among themselves, and to avoid public divisions as much as possible. This conception stands in contrast to the formal notion of a legislature as an extremely independent body dedicated to crystallizing issues, focusing debate, and deciding by divided votes. The junior members seemed to have more of this formal but less sophisticated view of the council's functions, less appreciation of the informal norms, and a belief that the council should function with greater independence from the executive, with more public debate, and with public divisions in its votes.

In the decisions made by the council in this study, the informal norms had little effect, and therein lies one value of the inquiry. The fact that the informal norms were inoperative in this case does not demonstrate that they are ordinarily unimportant for an understanding of the legislative process. Rather, one should expect that in the majority of cases an understanding of the norms should lead to an understanding of the process. In fact, the follow-up study of the Bay City council on the budget process for the year subsequent to the one presently under analysis demonstrated that the informal norms were highly operative, once the senior members of the council had been restored to their "normal" positions of leadership. In this follow-up study, the actions of the council on the budget were explainable to an overwhelming extent on the basis of the same informal normative system that had been rejected under the leadership of the Sasser Six.

In the 1952 budget decisions, the operation of the informal norms was disrupted initially by the insurgence of the organized majority led by Sasser when they denied important posts to senior councilmen, thereby forestalling the leadership of those most clearly attached to and most familiar with the informal system. The insurgence in itself was regarded by the senior members and the mayor as a signal that informal procedures were not operative. Once started, it reduced the likelihood that most budget items would be decided in a non-controversial fashion.

The mayor reacted by violating the informal

custom of working with the finance committee. The committee in turn used this violation as a basis for contending that the mayor was the aggressor in destroying executive-legislative co-operation and asserted its power to cut the mayor's requests. The finance committee ignored the views of the council minority defending the mayor. The loyal minority in turn reacted to this rebuff by voting solidly against every recommendation of the finance commitee which differed with the mayor's requests.

In short, a chain reaction was set off by an unusual political maneuver in which the norms most firmly espoused by the elder statesmen of the council were violated not only by their antagonists but by themselves. As a consequence, the proportion of controversial decisions rose sharply. Non-controversial decisions became matters largely of coincidence or legal compulsion. Both sides in the controversy resorted to more formal and legalistic procedures. Finally, the feelings of the two groups about the way things ought to be run served to reinforce the conflict, as the senior members were constantly irate with the junior members for violating the traditions of harmony, while the junior members took refuge in the notion that they were fighting to open up a closed shop.

External Relationships as Factors. Three aspects of the external relationships of council members will be considered as they affected the appropriations decisions. They are, respectively, as follows: (a) constituency relationships; (b) relationships with the press; and (c) relationships with the executive. Party differences and pressure group contacts, ordinarily considered major factors in the decision-making process, were found to be of such negligible influence as not to merit detailed discussion in this case.

Constituency Relationships. There was no clear effect of constituency interests cutting across all patterns of decisions on the public works budget. Ruling out non-controversial, unanimous decisions, since they showed no divisions, consideration of the two types of controversial decisions indicates that constituency relationships were effective primarily in making individual members of the Sasser Six switch on particular issues to vote in factional alliances with the loyal minority.[7] Organized majority votes did not seem to have any clear relationship with constituency patterns. Two of the Sasser Six had been elected by the city at large, while three of the loyal minority had been elected at large, so that the majority-minority cleavage in the council was not based on an at-large vs. ward division.

In terms of the wards in which the councilmen *resided,* but which were not necessarily the only constituencies they represented, there was a pattern which coincided rather closely with the majority-minority cleavage, but it was not complete nor was it prominent in the calculations of the legislators. All of the members of the loyal minority lived in two of the six wards in the city, while all but one of the organized majority lived in the four other wards of the city. However, in view of the facts that the residential alignment was not complete and that ward alignments were not prominent in the calculations of the councilmen, the conclusion is that this residential phenomenon was secondary and incidental to other considerations in maintaining the Sasser Six in opposition to the council minority. Certainly, since residence was not coincidental with constituency for the at-large councilmen, the residential alignment could not be used to buttress the contention that the majority-minority cleavage was based on differences in constituency.

Relationships with the Press. General pressures by the press and mass communications media constitute another type of external relationship which might affect the legislative process. It might be regarded as basically of the same gender as pressure group relationships, yet a newspaper is sufficiently different from other community organizations so that it deserves separate treatment. Legislators are not "members" of newspapers in any ordinary sense.

As the only daily newspaper in Bay City, the *Bugle* performed a significant function in the legislative process, but it was difficult to determine the effect of the other media of mass communication, especially the radio station which broadcasted the council meetings. As nearly as one could ascertain, broadcasting the meetings served primarily to make the members of the Sasser Six more cohesive and more aggressive against the mayor. They viewed the broadcasts as unique opportunities to make appeals to the general public and to offset the *Bugle's* very unfavorable portrayals of their actions.

The newspaper accounts of the council meetings and the slanting of the news and issues by the *Bugle* in general were calculated to make the Sasser Six villains in a municipal drama. The effect of this constant barrage appears to have been as follows: (a) First, it reinforced the defensive cohesion of the Sasser Six, at least for several months. By giving them a name and making them more conscious of themselves as a majority caucus, the newspaper helped to encourage the Sasser Six to act as an organized majority during the budget decisions and for some time afterward. (b) Second, the effect of the *Bugle* upon the councilmen it attacked did not come from any mass antagonisms demonstrably stirred up by the publicity. Instead, the things the besieged councilmen read directly about themselves in the newspaper led to their feeling defensive and eventually dismayed and frustrated. For all they knew, a majority of the people were for them, but the main channel of publicity was against them, and this raised great anxieties as they read the *Bugle* and speculated about its influence. As one of the leaders of the Sasser Six stated, after he had finally switched to vote with the mayor late in the year on the water bond issue: "There wasn't no protests to the council. I didn't get a call, but the paper kept at it until I was saying 'water, water, water' in my sleep." (c) Finally, the newspaper attack seems to have played an important part in wearing down the members of the Sasser Six so that they fell apart several months after the budget was adopted. Even though their initial reaction was toward more cohesion, eventually the six majority councilmen began to feel isolated and demoralized as the newspaper attack continued month after month. Despite their righteous indignation against the *Bugle's* journalism and their cognizance of its biases, they appeared ultimately very dependent upon the paper for obtaining some sort of public images of themselves.

Relationships with the Executive. Of course, the mayor became in this action by the council a prominent symbol serving to stabilize the differences between the organized majority and its opponents. All of the six-to-five votes in which the Sasser Six held together were votes against the mayor. The loyal minority on the council never deviated from a position in which they voted to uphold the mayor's budget requests. But it would be inaccurate to conclude that the formation of the Sasser Six was primarily a product of legislative antagonism toward the executive. To be sure, the revolt of the three insurgent Coalition members leading to the formation of the Sasser Six necessitated a break with the mayor as long as the latter chose to stand by the three senior Coalition councilmen and the newspaper. However, their antagonism toward the executive was more a product of the formation of the Sasser Six, which was organized to satisfy the ambitions of the newer members of the council and to forestall the domination of municipal politics by senior politicians working in collaboration with the newspaper and the managers of the Coalition. Of course, once the insurgent majority

had been formed and the mayor chose to remain as the symbol of the Coalition, then the Sasser Six proceeded to play the role which their political situation seemed to dictate, and they opposed the mayor on many counts almost automatically.

Summary. The foregoing case illustrates three major types of legislative decisions and furnishes some insights as to the way several kinds of factors affected the legislative process. The three major types of decisions, as expressed in terms of alignments in the voting patterns of the councilmen, were (a) non-controversial, unanimous decisions; (b) controversial, organized majority decisions; (c) controversial, factional alliance decisions. They were similar to those that might be found in any legislative body, although they were not present in the same proportions in this case as one might expect in the "typical" American legislative body.

Considering the nature of the issue as a factor, the following propositions were supported by the analysis of this case: (a) The nature of the issue *per se* was not a strong factor in determining council voting alignments. (b) Although many issues may be matters of such indifference or such overwhelming acceptability to legislators that they produce non-controversial voting patterns, this study did not indicate that they were necessarily so. (c) The nature of the issue seemed most clearly a factor in producing legislative alignments of the factional alliance type. However, the particular issue did not seem to sway marginal legislators because of their personal values as much as because of the needs of their constituencies. Factional alliances appeared to be built *ad hoc* around issues according to constituency interests as perceived by legislators. This observation supported the argument for analyzing legislative behavior in terms of constituency characteristics rather than probing into individual motivation. (d) Otherwise, the nature of the issue in this case seemed to become enmeshed in the web of relationships—the internal structure, the formal and informal norms, and the external relations—of the legislative body.

In this study, the council's internal structure was shown to be one of the most important factors in the legislative process. (a) The organized majority, operating in a manner similar to a majority party caucus, was founded upon the agreement by which committee posts and legislative power and prestige were distributed after the members were elected. (b) This majority caucus cohered over a lengthy period of time, voting a "party-line" in most instances (except in several cases where some member defected on a particular issue af-

fecting his constituency to vote in a factional alliance) even though members of the caucus differed as to party affiliation and had been elected
on different tickets. (c) The desire for power and
prestige within the council was so strong that the
junior members were willing and able to use their
majority to overrule the normally accepted principle of seniority as a basis of assigning council positions. As long as they stuck together,
they preserved their positions within the council,
but once they lost their cohesion, they lost their
power.

Furthermore, certain general contentions were
supported about the effect of norms upon the legislative process. (a) Formal, legal requirements
furnished norms having a direct effect upon legislative behavior, and they had to be understood in
order to explain certain kinds of decisions. They
particularly explained, for example, why some decisions were non-controversial, since the councilmen felt that the law simply would not allow them
to alter the mayor's proposal. (b) Other informal
and extra-legal norms would have, under ordinary circumstances, explained a great deal about
the legislative process in the Bay City council.
Many of these informal norms, cultivated by senior
members of the council, were designed to minimize open controversy and to maximize non-
controversial decisions. Had the senior members
been in positions of leadership in the council,
these norms would have probably had more effect
than they did in this case. (c) The fact that the
informal norms were rendered inoperative by the
insurgence of the junior members of the council
produced two consequences. First, it increased the
proportion of controversial decisions. Second, it
forced the council to rely more upon legalistic
methods of operating and resolving conflicts.

A brief recapitulation of the effects of external
relationships upon the legislative process in this
study of the Bay City council shows the following:
(a) Constituency relationships were most important in the decisions of marginal legislators who
crossed organizational lines to vote in factional
alliances on particular issues. (b) At-large vs.
ward constituencies did not show any unusual
tendency to line up against each other. Other factors furnished more important, competing bases
of alignment. (c) Party differences were fragile
foundations for the maintenance of an organized
majority. This in part was due to the unstable
condition of party alignments in the community
where the Coalition had urged an attempt at bipartisanship. The weakening of traditional two-
party lines furnished an environment in which the
council could organize on the basis of the internal

distribution of council positions of power and prestige, ignoring partisan differences. (d) Pressure
group contacts appeared to be very highly over-
rated factors in legislative decisions. They seemed
to be neither as numerous nor as effective as some
conceptions of the legislative process might have
led one to believe. Nor did this case demonstrate
any great relevance of group memberships, either
organizational or categorical, for the kinds of
decisions made by the councilmen. (e) Of all the
external relationships considered, those with the
press and with the chief executive appeared to
have the greatest consequences, especially in maintaining a voting cleavage between the organized
majority and minority on the public works appropriations. The majority caucus, once it had organized and seized control of the council, was
committed to maintaining its position, and it reacted defensively to the public image portrayed
by the press and to the leadership symbolized by
the chief executive. (f) The influence of the press
appeared to be direct, i.e. the councilmen reacted
to what they had themselves read in the newspaper
rather than to any demonstrable pressures from
others whom the press had stirred up. (g) The effect of attacks in the press upon the council majority was at first to produce more cohesion, so that
in the appropriations decisions external attacks
helped to reinforce the organized majority decisions. Eventually, the effect of a prolonged attack
in the press was to frustrate and demoralize the
organized majority, since they lacked adequate
alternative ways of supporting themselves in the
community. (h) Hostility of the majority caucus
toward the mayor was not the cause of the formation of the caucus so much as it was an out-
growth of the organization of the caucus. Once
the alignment of the council had taken place, however, the executive became an important symbol
in the process of making decisions on the budget.
Wherever the leaders of the majority caucus differed with the mayor, a controversial decision
ensued. Wherever they did not differ, no controversy occurred.

Notes

1. The "Bay City" project was conducted under the
auspices of the Harvard Graduate School of Education
with funds from a grant by the W. K. Kellogg Foundation.
The author is particularly indebted to the other two principal researchers, Peter H. Rossi and James M. Shipton,
whose ideas and comments have been invaluable for preparation of this article. Others who took part in this phase
of the research in some fashion were Leo Barry, Alice
Bauer, Eugene Belisle, Jim Davis, Russell Davis, George
Flower, Carl Freudenreich, Tom Guilford, Andrew

Manges, Austin McCaffrey, Kermit Morrissey, Sam Morse, Cyril Sargent, and Claire Zimmerman.

2. Furthermore direct observation also produces data of a sort different from any kind of interview data.

3. Avery Leiserson, *Parties and Politics*, New York: Alfred A. Knopf, 1958, p. 339; V. O. Key, Jr., *Politics, Parties, and Pressure Groups*, New York: Crowell, 1952, p. 706.

4. Leiserson, *op. cit.*, p. 340.

5. This point will be further discussed under the topic of "Constituency Relationships."

6. This theme is strongly stressed in W. S. White, *Citadel*, New York: Harper, 1957. See also Roland Young, *The American Congress*, New York: Harper, 1958, ch. 3 and related references at pp. 289-94; Leiserson, *op. cit.*, pp. 333-39 and references cited.

7. See Julius Turner, *Party and Constituency: Pressures on Congress*, Baltimore: Johns Hopkins Press, 1952; Duncan McRae, "Roll Call Votes and Constituencies in the Massachusetts House of Representatives," *American Political Science Review*, Vol. 46, December, 1952, pp. 1046-55; Leiserson, *op. cit.*, pp. 344-46.

The Social and Psychological Bases of Legislative Behavior

INTRODUCTORY NOTE

UP TO THIS POINT legislators have been treated as a special class of persons, set apart from others by their holding legislative office. Despite their official distinction, however, legislators remain human beings, subject to whatever laws and principles apply to human beings as such. It seems obvious, therefore, that much of the legislator's behavior will be guided by his own qualities and characteristics as a person. In many instances these are qualities or characteristics he possesses before becoming a legislator, which shape his actions in his legislative role along with his actions in all his other social roles. In others, they are qualities and characteristics personal enough to him, but acquired as a result of his own particular legislative experiences. In any case, analysis of legislative behavior must reckon with behavioral characteristics which are variable from one legislator to another, according to their individual social background and psychological makeup.

The numerous tabulations of occupation, age, sex, income-level, and similar characteristics of members of various legislatures testify to the frequency with which it has been assumed that legislators' behavior is significantly influenced by their social background. The assumption behind all such descriptive accounts is that it makes a difference in the functioning of a legislature whether there are in it more farmers than workers, more old than young persons, more men than women, more lawyers than business men, and so on.

However, it is impossible to say what difference it makes unless one has some notion of how different personal backgrounds affect the persons concerned. An apparently common assumption is that social class fits a person with determinate ideological biases, so that legislators will carry into the legislature with them conceptions of goals and means appropriate for legislative action which they acquire from their social origins. A. W. Martin, in "The Legislative Assembly of New South Wales, 1856-1900," not only examines the connection between social origins and ideological beliefs and its consequences for legislative action, but also provides an excellent critique of the general problem of legislators' social origins.

However, it would be dangerous to accept a simple class theory equating social origins with legislative performance. The determinate effect of social class varies from one culture to another. What constitutes a "class" in one place may not do so in another. Are American farmers a "class," distinct from "businessmen" and "workers," or are farmers and businessmen together members of a class distinct from workers? Which is more important in shaping a person's behavior, the fact that he is "middle class" or the fact that he is a farmer? In many cases it is desirable to consider the problem not in terms of class but in terms of "interest."

Moreover, a person's occupation can affect his perceptions and behavior in many more ways than just giving him a particular ideological bent. Charles S. Hyneman, in "Who Makes Our Laws?" suggests, for example, that lawyers in the legislature may well act primarily not as spokesmen for the middle class or as spokesmen for some particular interest in society, but as lawyers representing the public as their clients—that lawyers, in other words, when they enter American legislatures, act as "professional representers" for the American public. While Hyneman makes his specific point with respect to lawyers, he also suggests the more general point that occupational and social background may be less significant in determining legislators' behavior than is commonly suggested.

Whether or not this is so, the evidence—as illustrated in Otto Kirchheimer's "The Composition of the German Bundestag, 1950," and Martin's article—shows that the proportion of legislators from different kinds of social or occupational backgrounds changes relatively slowly through time in any given legislative system. While one can not say with assurance what their results are for legislative behavior, it can at least be said that the social bases of legislative behavior are a fairly stable factor in a legislative system.

Background studies of legislators commonly tabulate not only class or occupational status of legislators but age and sex distributions as well. But they rarely say much about the differences in behavior, if any, resulting from these different characteristics. Perhaps, as often implied, increasing age makes a legislator more "conservative" both in his style of performance and in his policy-views, whereas youth inclines him toward radical and experimental views of legislative problems and a more precipitous style of action in the legislature. If this is so, available studies certainly offer no empirical evidence.

Somewhat more attention has been given to the distributional facts and the possible consequences of varying experience of legislators in non-occupational contexts. In particular, studies of tenure and turnover have revealed striking differences from one legislative system to the next in the amount of legislative and, in some cases, other political experience for legislators. Some of these, for example, Hyneman's, demonstrate that experienced legislators tend to occupy positions of greater power and influence within a legislature than do novices and less experienced legislators. In "Local Government Experience of Legislators," W. J. M. Mackenzie discusses the differences in experience with local government between members of various legislative systems. The assumption is that such experience will lead a legislator to see at least some problems before the legislature in a different light than do his fellow legislators not having that experience. But in all these cases, again, the actual connections between experience—whether in the legislature, in local government, or elsewhere—and legislative behavior are by no means clear.

In general it seems fair to say that legislative studies to date reveal statistically significant differences among legislatures with respect to the kinds of social background and experience of persons recruited into them. But they offer little firm knowledge about the relationship of those differences to either the functions and output of legislative systems or to the behavior of members as legislators.

Whatever his origins and background, entrance to the ranks of the legislature presents each legislator with his own personal problems of adapting himself to his situation. As was intimated in the first section of this book, and as Herman Finer's article, "The Tasks and Functions of the Legislator," makes more explicit, the functional tasks of the legislature require members to assume certain tasks and functions. The modern legislator—given the particular policy-making functions of modern legislatures—must to a considerable extent forbear to be a philosopher or a scholar, whatever his own personal inclinations in that direction, and become something of a broker, a politician, and a parliamentarian. He may find it advantageous to become a specialist in some subject-matter area or in some particular facet of the legislative operation.

Behavioral imperatives of this kind are closely related to the institutional context of the legislature as a law making body. It is well known, however, that any human group, in time, develops rules and norms of behavior for its members which are not so directly the result of the functional character of the group, but which seem in many cases to result from historical accident, chance repetition solidifying into habit, or some other seemingly irrelevant cause. Legislative bodies normally present their members with many such informal and unwritten norms of behavior. Ralph K. Huitt, in "The Operation of Norms in the U. S. Senate," describes how such informal rules affected the behavior of legislators in one particular case. Huitt also offers some cogent suggestions about the conditions under which such rules become more or less significant and about the way in which legislators relate them to their loyalty to party, personal friendship for fellow members, and other components of their legislative behavior.

Neither Finer nor Huitt discusses the problem, but it may be assumed that all legislators will not adjust in the same way to the functional requirements of their job or the rules of the legislature. Different persons will react quite differently to the often impossible burdens legislators are called upon to bear. How this task of adjustment to legislative tasks and legislative folkways looks to a legislator is forcibly described by Duane Lockard, a political scientist who has had personal experience as a member of the Connecticut legislature, in "The Tribulations of a State Senator." An important dimension of these differences in personal reaction is analyzed by Corinne Silverman in "The Legislator's View of the Legislative Process," which shows how some legislators are class-oriented, some party-leader-oriented, and some program-oriented in their approach to policy issues. Some of the consequences for legislative action are set forth, although the reasons why some legislators have one while others have another conception of their job as legislators are not. Because the legislator is dependent upon the whims of electoral choice to remain in office, personal concern about his prospects of continued incumbency can reasonably be expected to affect his approach to his duties as legislator. It may be that many of his votes and other legislative actions can be best understood as devices by which the legislator seeks to cope with electoral insecurity.

However influential the formal and informal requirements of office, a legislator's behavior continues to reflect intensely personal and unique properties of his own individual personality and character. It seems probable, in the first place, that some such factors are important in leading some people but not others to become legislators at all. No doubt legislators are, on the whole, more "politically inclined" than the average person in the general population. But what makes a person that way? What is there in the personality and life history of legislators differentiating them in this respect from laymen and, perhaps, from other classes of political actors? The article by Eulau and others on "The Political Socialization of State Legislators" describes some of the circumstances under which a number of American state legislators were "politically socialized."

A person's basic emotional and cognitive set toward the world around him, or what is popularly understood by the term, his psychological makeup, can be presumed to be a vital factor underlying his behavior as a legislator, just as it underlies all his other behavior. John B. McConaughy, in "Some Personality Factors of State Legislators in South Carolina," adds to the study of legislators' political socialization the finding that legislators, at least in this particular case, seem to be slightly more stable, more aggressive, and more sociable persons than members of the general population they represent.

Such findings as these may tell something about the motivational structure of the people who become legislators. But very little is known so far about the way in which their psychological makeup

might affect the way they act as legislators. One can, of course, make certain inferences about their legislative behavior, such as the inference that they will be more malleable, more compromising, and more tolerant of ambiguities in their legislative setting than would other persons. And one can make further inferences from here to the consequences for the legislative system, such as that legislatures are enabled to integrate and harmonize conflicting demands more readily by the presence of persons having a particular personality makeup. But in neither case is there research to support or to deny the validity of such inferences. This field of legislative study is still virgin territory.

Even if it cannot yet be related directly to the psychological or social bases of behavior, something is known about variations in legislators' individual behavior. One of the most significant contributions to this knowledge involves the recognition that different legislators entertain different conceptions of their role as legislators or their more specialized roles within the legislative system. Ralph Huitt's study, "The Roles of Congressional Committee Members," describes and interprets variations in behavior among individual legislators in terms of the roles they take. While Huitt's article is not concerned with relating the different roles to different psychological or social bases of behavior, the reader will undoubtedly be able to construct many hypotheses about such relationships.

The same might be said about the relationship of legislators' attitudes to social and psychological bases of behavior. Although James N. Rosenau's article, "Senate Attitudes toward a Secretary of State," seeks primarily to describe significant differences in the attitudes of United States Senators to a Secretary of State, without suggesting sociological or psychological explanations of them, numerous hypotheses about the relationship will undoubtedly suggest themselves. Rosenau's article, like Huitt's, it should be pointed out, is more concerned with exploring the consequences for legislative action of the differences described than with exploring their causes.

A suggestive discussion of the consequences for legislative behavior of the emotional attitudes of legislators and their underlying causes is found in Edward A. Shils's article, "Resentments and Hostilities of Legislators: Sources, Objects, Consequences." Shils outlines certain kinds of resentment and hostilities to which modern legislators are peculiarly prone, describes how these emotions may often govern legislative investigatory activities in particular, and shows how they stem not just from the innate psychological makeup of individual legislators, but from their emotional reaction toward the place of the legislature in modern government and public attitudes towards the legislature.

Studies of the kind presented in this section represent a comparatively recent development in political science. It cannot be said that they provide a clear and consistent theoretical viewpoint for the study of legislative behavior. It cannot be said that they explain more about legislative behavior than do studies of its political bases. They are cast in diverse conceptual frameworks and they are aimed at fragmentary and often unrelated aspects of the general problem.

But such studies do have the peculiar merit of focussing attention upon the central problem of legislative study—the behavior of legislators. Insofar as they seek to discover and to set forth in explicit terms significant uniformities in the behavior of human beings, they represent a step forward toward fuller understanding of legislative behavior. Once these uniformities are described, it becomes clear that the central task of legislative study includes both explanation of when and why the given uniformities occur and explanation of what difference their existence makes in the functioning of the legislature as a political institution. Because their central focus is on the behavior of human actors, they make it clear that legislative study, like any study of human behavior, requires a viable model of the human actors who make up legislatures.

A. The Recruitment and Composition of Legislatures

1. THE LEGISLATIVE ASSEMBLY OF NEW SOUTH WALES, 1856-1900

A. W. Martin

PROBABLY the most significant of current trends in the writing of English political history is that symbolised in the "great collective effort" of the *History of Parliament*. The immediate direction taken by this project is an effort to "record the names, and . . . the careers of the persons elected to serve in Parliament from the reign of Edward I to a date as far into the nineteenth century as circumstances may permit."[1] The ultimate end of the work is naturally more than merely biographical. As its inspirer, Sir Lewis Namier, has frequently intimated, it is to serve as a tool for attacking some crucial problems of English political history. He referred, for example, to one of these in his 1952 Romanes lecture:

> In 1761 not one parliamentary election was determined by party, and in 1951 not one constituency returned a non-party member. To trace how that change has come about will require a most thorough knowledge of constituencies and elections, of members and parliaments, and of constitutional ideas and realities throughout the formative period: to acquire that knowledge is one of the tasks of the *History of Parliament*.[2]

The type of analysis to which Namier refers here is exemplified in his well-known work on eighteenth century politics,[3] and it is not too much to speak of a "Namier technique" of investigation having already been established in this field. An important line of modern British historians, directly or indirectly influenced by Namier, has vindicated this technique by suggesting, through meticulous study of elections and of parliamentary personnel and groupings, some important modifications for received interpretations of various phases of English political history.[4]

The nature of formal political divisions and procedure is not, of course, the only aspect of parliamentary history which has been illuminated by

Reprinted from *Australian Journal of Politics and History*, Vol. 2 (1956), pp. 46-67, by permission of the author and the publisher.

biographical material. As long ago as 1913, C. A. Beard made the provocative suggestion that hidden facts emerge from statistical analysis of the membership of a whole legislature.[5] More recently we have had a spate of work in the same vein, ranging from the ambitious studies of Ross and Thomas,[6] to Guttsman's briefer surveys of the post-1885 British "political élite."[7] This approach to biography in political history may for convenience be broadly defined as the "statistical technique," and distinguished from the Namier tradition, though the two are closely connected, and often intermingled in practice. W. O. Aydelotte, a contemporary exponent of the "statistical technique," justifies it on the simple ground "that insight into the character of a representative body or any other body of men may be obtained from a biographical analysis of its individual members, and that the results of such a survey may be most readily grasped by counting them, by a quantitative method."[8] He suggests that the resources of the statistical method offer to historians an opportunity of drawing from the diffuse data of biographies the type of revealing correlations for which they are constantly in search, but which so often elude their grasp through the sheer multiplicity of the factors involved. Aydelotte is probably more acutely aware than many others of the limitations of such methods; he has provided the most thorough discussion yet published of the difficulties of applying them to historical data, together with a frank admission of his misgivings about his own work. He has to modify the charming dictum of Dr. Johnson on "the good of counting"—"that it brings everything to a certainty, which before floated in the mind indefinitely"— but for all his reservations, he still retains a faith in the capacity of statistical analysis to suggest new insights. After this stimulating preview, we await Aydelotte's final work with great interest.

Both branches of the biographical school of political history have been strongly criticised, on the one hand by those who distrust the contribution of the "measurers"[9] to historiography, and on the other by some who see in the work of men like Namier a crippling narrowness. The first objection is one aspect of a wider debate about the use of statistics in history, and as such is beyond the scope of the present discussion. It is to be noted, however, that the achievement of related disciplines, like sociology, in handling material by statistical methods, deserves the respectful attention of historians. And studies such as Guttsman's suggest how very narrow the borderline between sociology and history can be. Further, as Barraclough has pointed out, statistics may provide one solution for a dilemma agitating the minds of contemporary historians—that of reconciling the particular with the general in historical writing.[10]

The criticism of the Namierites' "narrowness" is of more moment. Probably the most cogent expression of this objection has been that recently made E. J. Hobsbawm. The "Namier method," he says, "falsifies history . . . by retelling the story of politics without the issues, the passions and movements which make up political history." Thus, for instance, he takes Gash to task because, thanks to his methodological limitations, he can write a book on *Politics in the Age of Peel* without adequately treating "the great bourgeois-radical reforms [or] the Chartists."[11] The reply to this is surely that Gash did not purport to write political history in the total sense that Hobsbawm demands. If his and Namier's methods seem to exclude some of the conventionally treated "ideals and passions," they take account of equally important matters whose omission can lead to the facile type of interpretation that—to take only one example—Namier's work on the eighteenth century has corrected. Hobsbawm's further argument, that the implication of the approach of Namier and his followers is "Conservative," because "it suggests that politics are and were always the same: struggles for power, for office, rivalries and bargaining, careerism and cheating," is unjust.[12] The whole point of Namier's work is to show that such struggles were *not* always the same: to demonstrate the fallacy of projecting back into the eighteenth century the political assumptions of the late nineteenth and twentieth centuries. The mechanisms of bargaining, the groups involved, the electoral system, accepted assumptions about the sources of executive power—these and other things are unique in particular times and places; Namier shows how the empirical examination of such problems is basic to a proper understanding of a political milieu in its own terms. Careerism, rivalries, and the rest are the common factors of political struggles in only the most general sense.

There is surely no dichotomy between the methods of the new school and those of historians who deal with "the ideals, passions, and movements" of political history; the work of the one complements and illuminates that of the other. Further, a persistent following-up of parliamentary analysis logically takes one deep into the social and intellectual foundations of a period. Namier demonstrated the workings of George III's Parliament, traced its connections with the electorate, and proved that political parties in the modern sense did not exist. But this only raised the further question: what social, economic and intellectual factors could produce such a parliamentary system? Even in the process of elaborating that system, he found himself considering such factors, while those who turn later to the task of rounding off his picture will be even more deeply concerned with them. Hobsbawm is probably correct in maintaining that Namier's techniques are particularly suited for investigating formless and corrupt politics, but his contention that they can be expected to "break down" when applied to other situations is difficult to accept. From Ostrogorski, Michels and Duverger, it has come to us as a commonplace that the organisations through which political movements operate mould as well as serve those movements, and therefore demand accurate and detailed investigation. Both Parliaments and parties provide modes of expression for the political needs of a community. To begin empirical study with either implies no disregard of the nature of the political movements at work therein. At the same time, such an approach can make possible the difficult task of assessing the interaction between such movements and the mechanisms through which they operate.

These reflections seem to me to have particular significance for those interested in nineteenth century politics in the Australian colonies.

*   *   *

In a sense, indeed, the history of Parliament in Australia could have a special significance: besides being a study in its own right, it might also be a tool for the investigation of a colonial society whose lines of social development in the last four decades of the nineteenth century are in many respects still a mystery to us. However remote and meaningless the parliamentary struggle before 1890 may have appeared to contemporaries and to the later propagandists—and even historians—of the Labor movement, it remains true that the colonial legislatures were linked directly through the electoral system, and indirectly through the contemporary "climate of opinion," to colonial

Table II—Legislative Assembly of New South Wales: Occupations of Members, 1856-1900 (Percentages)

| | YEAR OF ELECTION | 1856 | 1858 | 1859 | 1860 | 1865 | 1870 | 1872 | 1875 | 1877 | 1880 | 1882 | 1885 | 1887 | 1889 | 1891 | 1894 | 1895 | 1898 |
	Parliament	1	2	3	4	5	6	7	8	9	10	11	12	13	14	15	16	17	18
Pastoral	Pastoralist	42.6	40.7	37.5	26.4	25.0	25.0	23.6	23.6	19.4	20.4	19.8	14.0	14.3	14.1	7.7	7.2	8.8	10.4
Agricultural	Agriculturalist	1.9	–	–	1.4	1.4	2.8	2.8	2.8	–	0.9	0.9	–	–	1.5	–	1.6	2.4	0.8
Mining	Mine Owner or Manager	–	–	–	–	–	–	–	1.4	2.8	2.8	1.8	4.1	3.9	3.7	1.4	3.2	4.0	3.2
Commercial	Merchant (Import and Wholesale)	14.8	16.7	5.0	2.8	1.4	5.6	5.6	6.9	4.2	3.7	3.6	6.6	4.8	4.4	3.5	4.0	3.2	4.0
	Retail Trader	5.6	3.7	3.8	5.6	4.2	4.2	6.9	10.8	6.9	6.5	6.3	9.1	8.7	9.6	8.5	6.4	6.4	7.2
	Stock and Station Agent	–	–	–	–	–	–	1.4	1.4	2.8	2.8	4.5	0.8	3.2	2.2	2.8	1.6	1.6	0.8
	Land Agent	–	–	–	1.4	1.4	1.4	1.4	1.4	–	–	–	2.5	0.8	0.7	–	1.6	1.6	0.8
	Commission Agent	–	–	1.2	–	–	–	–	–	–	–	0.9	2.5	3.2	2.9	2.1	1.6	0.8	2.4
	Other Agent	–	1.9	2.5	1.4	–	–	–	–	–	2.8	0.9	–	1.6	2.2	1.4	0.8	–	0.8
	Auctioneer	–	–	–	–	2.8	1.4	2.8	1.4	4.2	2.8	2.7	2.5	1.6	2.9	2.1	1.6	2.4	1.6
	Country Entrepreneur	3.7	1.8	3.8	1.4	2.8	1.4	–	2.8	2.8	1.9	2.7	4.9	3.9	3.7	5.6	7.2	7.2	4.8
	Country Storekeeper	–	–	1.2	1.4	1.4	6.9	5.6	2.8	4.2	3.7	2.7	2.5	3.2	3.7	2.8	2.4	1.6	1.6
	Other Commercial	–	–	–	–	–	–	–	–	–	–	–	–	–	–	1.4	–	–	–
	Shipowner and Manager	–	–	1.3	–	2.8	1.4	2.8	1.4	2.8	0.9	1.8	0.8	2.4	2.2	2.8	2.4	1.6	1.6
Service	Publican	–	–	–	2.8	5.6	2.8	2.8	–	1.4	1.9	2.7	4.9	2.4	2.2	1.4	0.8	0.8	0.8
	Undertaker	–	–	–	1.4	–	–	–	–	–	0.9	0.9	0.8	0.8	0.7	0.7	–	–	–
Manufacturing and Processing	Manufacturer	1.9	1.9	1.2	4.2	4.2	2.8	5.6	6.9	4.2	6.5	6.3	5.8	6.3	5.9	4.9	4.0	4.0	4.0
Professional and Semi-Professional	Medico	–	3.7	1.3	1.4	1.4	1.4	1.4	–	1.4	2.8	1.8	3.8	3.2	0.7	1.4	2.4	2.4	1.6
	Barrister	11.1	9.3	12.5	6.9	10.0	10.0	5.6	6.9	6.9	7.4	6.3	4.9	3.9	3.7	4.9	2.4	2.4	3.2
	Solicitor	1.9	1.8	3.7	6.9	5.6	6.9	6.9	6.9	10.0	10.2	13.5	10.6	11.8	9.6	7.0	10.4	9.6	7.2
	Engineer	–	–	–	1.4	–	–	1.4	–	1.4	1.9	1.8	0.8	2.4	1.5	0.7	0.8	1.6	0.8
	Surveyor	–	1.9	–	–	–	–	–	–	1.4	1.9	1.8	0.8	0.8	0.7	0.7	1.6	1.6	1.6
	Accountant	–	–	–	–	–	–	–	–	–	–	–	–	–	0.7	0.7	2.4	2.4	2.4
	Journalist-Proprietor	–	–	–	–	–	–	–	–	–	0.9	0.9	–	3.2	4.4	4.9	6.4	4.8	7.2
	Journalist	1.9	3.7	2.5	2.8	2.8	2.8	2.8	2.8	2.8	2.8	2.7	4.1	3.2	4.4	5.6	4.8	4.8	4.8
	Schoolmaster	–	–	1.2	–	–	–	–	–	–	–	–	–	–	–	–	2.4	2.4	1.6
	Civil Servant	–	1.8	–	4.2	2.8	1.4	2.8	2.8	2.8	2.8	1.8	–	0.8	2.9	1.4	0.8	0.8	–
	Other	–	–	1.3	1.4	1.4	–	1.4	1.4	–	0.9	–	2.5	1.6	0.7	1.4	2.4	2.4	1.6
Artisan	Carpenter	–	–	–	–	–	–	–	–	1.4	0.9	0.9	–	0.8	–	0.7	1.6	0.8	0.8
	Compositor	–	–	–	–	–	–	–	–	–	–	–	–	–	–	2.8	1.6	1.6	1.6
	Miner	–	–	–	–	–	–	–	–	–	–	–	–	–	–	3.5	6.4	6.4	7.2
	Other	–	–	–	–	–	1.4	–	–	–	–	–	–	0.8	–	9.6	5.6	5.6	3.2
Private Means		7.3	1.8	5.0	4.2	5.6	4.2	5.6	4.2	5.6	3.7	2.7	4.1	3.2	2.2	1.4	1.6	0.8	1.6
Unidentified		7.3	9.3	15.0	20.6	17.4	16.2	10.8	10.0	7.8	5.3	7.3	6.6	3.2	5.9	4.2	–	3.2	8.8
TOTAL		100	100	100	100	100	100	100	100	100	100	100	100	100	100	100	100	100	100

society. If what has been said about the method of Namier and others is correct, it seems obvious that an understanding of Australian parliamentary history might enable us to discover new and stimulating questions to ask about Australian social history.

* * *

In the political history of New South Wales during the second half of the nineteenth century, a central question is the simple one, who were the politicians? It is my purpose now to suggest an answer, and in the light of this, to discuss certain neglected trends in the politics of the period. What follows might thus be viewed as an adaptation of some of the British techniques mentioned above, since it necessarily depends both upon biographical material and upon a familiarity with contemporary parliamentary and electoral events.

Table I* shows the occupations of members of the New South Wales Legislative Assembly for each Parliament (1 to 18) between 1856 and 1900. The same information is recorded in percentages, for comparative purposes, in Table II. Table III refers to the same politicians, giving in

Table III—Members of the N.S.W. Legislative Assembly, 1856-1900 Place of Residence, by Percentages

Date of Election	Parliament	Rural	Country Urban	Metropolitan	Unknown	Total
1856	1	44.4	5.6	44.4	5.6	100
1858	2	38.9	3.7	46.3	11.1	100
1859	3	35.0	7.5	41.2	16.3	100
1860	4	26.4	11.1	41.7	20.8	100
1865	5	25.0	12.5	45.8	16.7	100
1870	6	26.4	13.9	41.7	18.0	100
1872	7	23.6	20.8	41.7	13.9	100
1875	8	23.6	15.3	48.6	12.5	100
1877	9	15.3	20.8	50.0	13.9	100
1880	10	17.6	23.1	48.2	11.1	100
1882	11	17.1	18.9	52.3	11.7	100
1885	12	13.2	21.5	52.1	13.2	100
1887	13	13.5	27.0	53.2	6.3	100
1889	14	14.1	29.6	48.2	8.1	100
1891	15	7.0	37.3	47.2	8.5	100
1894	16	7.2	38.4	49.6	4.8	100
1895	17	8.8	36.8	46.4	8.0	100
1898	18	10.4	35.2	42.4	12.0	100

percentage form a digest of their places of residence. In order to make all figures comparable from Parliament to Parliament, only those members were included who gained their seats at a general election.[13] Variations in total numbers thus reflect changes in the electoral laws, and not the effect of by-elections to replace members who failed to serve their full terms.[14] Similarly, in the interest of consistency, the occupation recorded

* Editor's Note: Table I is omitted.

for each man was that being followed on the eve of his entry into the Assembly.

The Tables are founded upon biographical studies of almost 600 politicians.[15] But due to the unevenness of available data, the amount of detail in these "biographies" varies greatly. This partly explains why occupation has been selected for special attention, since it is the only information which can be traced about some of the more obscure members. At the same time, of all characteristics which could be observed when studying the composition of a group of men such as these, occupation is probably the most promising. It is, for instance, the most important single indicator of social status. Within limits, it suggests something of each individual's dominant economic interests. It is of special significance when considering some of the relationships between politicans and organised extra-parliamentary groups.

The occupational categories were determined empirically, as far as possible from the biographical studies, rather than according to some predetermined pattern. Because considerable compression was required to reduce the Tables to manageable proportions, some classifications encompass a wide variety of activities. "Retail Traders," for example, includes produce, fuel and timber merchants, wine merchants, grocers, druggists, booksellers, drapers, tailors, ironmongers, butchers. Those described as "Agents" were middlemen operating on a commission basis in various types of activity: stock and station, land, shipping and commission agents, woolbrokers, stockbrokers, auctioneers. Pottery, rope, soap, boot and woollen manufacturers are included in the "Manufacturing and Processing" group, together with millers, brewers, ironfounders, builders, a tanner and a woolscourer. In short, the type of business *function* seemed to be the most useful criterion in arranging these men in groups.

No attempt has been made to construct a separate Table to show employer-employee status. With minor exceptions, those in the pastoral, agricultural, commercial and manufacturing groups were working on their own account or were employers.[16] Economic independence of this kind was also characteristic of the majority of professionals. Of the few artisans in the Tables, most were undoubtedly employees.

A special explanation is perhaps necessary for the two unusual titles, "Country *entrepreneurs*" and "Journalist-Proprietors." The first was suggested by the recurrence of a type of capitalist who ran a variety of businesses simultaneously in rural areas.[17] The second refers to men who both owned and edited newspapers. The size of both groups increased markedly in the 'eighties, and this was of some political importance.

This is not the place to discuss the general difficulties that arise in collecting and arranging even the simplest of biographical data, or the humility one feels in presenting the results. The interested reader can best be referred to Aydelotte's definitive treatment of these matters in the article already cited, with the assurance that almost all the major problems and doubts to which he refers were experienced in constructing the Tables presented here.

Perhaps the most striking general impression conveyed by the Tables is that the Assembly was overwhelmingly "middle-class" in its composition before 1891. "Impression" is probably the best word to use here, since occupation is but one index of social class; however, economic independence —another middle-class characteristic in the nineteenth century—was common to all groups, except for a small minority of those engaged in the professions.

It is not surprising that men of independent means should have monopolised parliamentary representation in this period. Payment of members was not introduced in New South Wales until 1889, and this was undoubtedly the chief reason why artisans so rarely reached the legislature. In addition, the franchise was, until 1893, slightly weighted in favour of the well-to-do.[18] Nevertheless, it is doubtful whether the wage-earner's incentive to challenge the political hegemony of his superiors was very great before the 'eighties: the developing trade union movement absorbed incipient class animosity, and fairly consistent economic prosperity bred political apathy. We have had many elaborations of the theme that the middle class in Australia has rarely, if at all, acted independently, that its "characteristic role is that of a buffer between the contemporary group with oligarchical tendencies and the working class."[19] Yet it is now clear that it was the urban men of substance—not the "levelling" democrats hysterically conjured up by the imagination of Wentworth—who in the 'fifties prevented the pastoralists from working their oligarchical notions into the Constitution.[20] Within the new Parliaments, men of the same type were clearly responsible for the passage of the Land Acts, which provided the final demonstration of the pastoralists' inability to capture a dominant share of political power. From this time onward, there was little indication that the political philosophy of pastoralist members of the Assembly differed greatly from that of urban members. It is true that they were given to complaining that country areas received too little of the funds spent on public works, and that they could act as a tight pressure group in the scramble for concessions when land legislation amendments were under discussion. But after 1860 little remained of that "Conservatism" for which they have been credited in earlier Parliaments.[21] In any case, the direct political power of the pastoralists steadily waned after 1856, as is to be clearly seen in Table II. This trend was partly a measure of the development of urbanisation in the Colony, and partly a reflection of the inevitable tendency—where politicians were unpaid—for country elements hostile to squatters to find their champions among the men of provincial towns and the metropolis. The rapid overall shift of political power to the latter areas is even more markedly shown by the figures of Table III.

It is, then, reasonable in the light both of the position of the pastoralists, and of the structure of the Assembly, to see the middle classes as dominant in the politics of New South Wales between 1856 and 1890. On the practical import of that dominance there is perhaps room for argument: the politicians may at times have been muddle-headed, mediocre or even corrupt. But if one recalls only the solutions hammered out in these years for major problems like land settlement, education, immigration and public works development, the members of the Assembly appear not as mere "buffers" between some oligarchical group and the working class, but as effective political leaders.

This leadership seems to have been epitomised in the formulation of an *ethos* which set the tone for politics in New South Wales until the 'eighties. In reading the debates of the period, one constantly has the impression that at least outward acceptance of the few simple tenets of contemporary "Liberalism" was a condition of success both in Parliament and in the constituencies. This philosophy was in some ways merely the politicians' rationalisation—foisted upon a lethargic electorate —of the facts of their political practice. But undoubtedly it also represented to many an honourable and just approach to the problems of democratic government. For both these reasons, it was of singular importance in the political history of the Colony, while its apparent breakdown towards the end of the century was a significant political reflection of social change.

The name "Liberal," as used in the New South Wales Legislative Assembly until the mid-'eighties, did not denote a man committed to a closely defined set of political policies, or identifiable as a member of any single parliamentary group. Indeed, it was possible to think of a "Liberal Party" that transcended the normal faction divisions which underlay the struggle for office. In 1882, for instance, a politician of high repute expressed this idea, amid murmurs of general approval, from the floor of the House. He was speaking of the chief opponents of the time, Parkes and Robertson:

> The honourable gentlemen, though personally opposed, have voted for all the great measures which have been passed in this country. They have voted for a Lands Act, a Public Instruction Act, an Influx of Chinese Restriction Act, and all the great measures which have distinguished the Liberal Party. They have voted together, although they have sat on opposite sides of the House.[22]

This does not take us far in understanding what "Liberal measures" were, but it does suggest that membership of the "Liberal Party" was believed to be a matter of attitude of mind rather than of formal political alliance. The essence of this favoured attitude can best be seen by noting several connected instances in which it was imputed by contemporaries to politicians of whom they approved. In 1872, the member for Kiama, James Stewart, declared to his constituents:

> I do not wish to be captious, but I do think that the members of the present government do not represent so large a mixture of the Liberal element as I would desire. The Premier, Mr. Parkes, is a Liberal-minded statesman—a man devoted to doing good for the country. Mr. Farnell and Mr. Sutherland are Liberals, but Mr. Butler and Mr. Innes, men of ability, are Conservatives.[23]

Earlier, when the Government referred to here was being formed, Parkes had written to an old colleague to ask his opinion on the wisdom of including Butler in the Cabinet.[24] He had received the following reply:

> I do not know whether he is really bigoted or of the same practical Catholicism which now best goes down even in Ireland—and with which you need not scruple to join without prejudice to your true liberalism.[25]

Stewart's definition of a "Liberal-minded statesman" as "one devoted to doing good for the country" is vague indeed, but it is given point when considered in relation to De Salis' suggestion that Parkes' "true liberalism" is safe in alliance with a colleague who is not committed to advancing a sectional interest. The "Liberal," by implication, sought the welfare of the *whole* community, not that of a part of it. This was an idea repeated time and again at the hustings, where it had a special relevance. To take but one example, we may cite the words of a candidate in the Northumberland by-election of 1877, when, horrified by a suggestion that the local coalminers should return a representative to Parliament, he urged upon voters their duty not

to elect a man of some class interests or for some particular object. When a man was so elected to the Legislative Assembly, he was sent there as a mere delegate, and that was one of the most objectionable forms of representation. Any man going into that Assembly did not go there simply to represent a constituency, but to represent the Colony at large, and it was the bounden duty of every constituency to return a candidate who would represent the whole colony.[26]

Faith in the possibility of finding, for all political problems, solutions that were objectively beneficial to society as a whole was thus the core of the "Liberal's" creed. He did not attempt to elaborate precisely the lines that such solutions would take. He believed merely that men of sincerity who recognised their responsibility to the community could find them naturally, by untrammelled discussion and the interplay of opinion.[27]

An essential element of the creed was insistence upon the need for "independence," for it was argued that no man committed to party, or bound to obey post-election dictates from his constituents, could hope to consider any issue on its intrinsic merits. Debates in the House were sprinkled with ostentatious declarations of independence, and partisanship was one of the most serious charges one politician could level against another. Such a charge amounted to questioning integrity, and the person accused often went to extraordinary lengths to demonstrate his innocence.[28]

These ideals were taken to refer especially to the legislative activities of the politicians, but they also had important implications for administration; indeed "Good Government" was a phrase often equated with "Liberalism." No-one seriously questioned the correctness of that state paternalism to which the peculiar conditions of settlement in the Colony had led, but the politician did see himself as the guardian of integrity and efficiency in its administration. This was especially important while the railways and civil service remained under political control, and while the low density of population in rural areas held up the spread of local government. There were plenty of opportunities for logrolling and pork-barrel politics: to pose as the implacable enemy of group or personal gain at the expense of the general interest, the politician had to maintain a rigid front of independence.

Before the 'eighties, New South Wales had no formal political parties; the parliamentary groups which jockeyed for power could be compared to the eighteenth century English cabals. They were personal factions of an evanescent nature, which shrouded their methods—and often their membership—from the public gaze. Their strength, it seems, depended chiefly upon the skill of their leaders in the arts of intrigue and in the techniques of parliamentary manoeuvre. The demands they made upon the loyalty of their members were usually slight: the whole situation was put in a nutshell by a contemporary newspaper editor:

Ours is a system of government by majorities, but not a system of government by parties, in the sense of party being based on definite political principles. As party divisions do not represent, as they have done in England, distinctly marked differences of political principle and tendency, it is utterly impossible that honest and independent men can be expected to give to any government more than steady support which may, when the occasion requires it, be withdrawn without violation of party fidelity.[29]

To explain fully why political groupings were of this nature, one would require a much deeper understanding of the social and economic history of New South Wales than we at present possess. But it is clear that one factor of particular importance was the degree of social homogeneity among the politicians. This left room for great variety of opinion on minor matters, but seems to have diminished the possibility of disagreement on broader issues. Economic prosperity undoubtedly supported this tendency. Public finance, for instance, threw up no tricky problems like that of devising a taxation policy, since it was supported until the mid-'eighties by phenomenal land sales. Similarly, tariff policy was rarely an issue: there were few economic reasons for calling into question the traditional adherence to Free Trade. In short, given the composition of the Assembly in these years, it is hardly surprising that the politicians were not divided deeply enough on fundamental questions to produce political parties.

The peculiar *ethos* of the period was, however, more than a mere rationalisation of this political situation. Its similarities to mid-century English Liberalism suggest that it can also be viewed as an expression of faith natural to the classes from which the legislators came. The colonial "Liberal" was tolerant of state paternalism, but in other respects he saw eye to eye with his English namesake. The value he attached to independence, in the political sphere, represented one expression of his ideal of individual responsibility. And behind his recipe for wise lawgiving lay a Utilitarian vision of society as an agglomeration of individuals, whose wellbeing merely demanded legislators of "competence, inspired by a wise purpose."[30] That existing politicians were in fact drawn from a restricted social background made this view appear, in New South Wales as in England, a theoretical justification of a *status quo*

in which some groups were denied access to the forum of Parliament. But it is doubtful whether its adherents—or even those outside the charmed circle—saw it in this light. Group consciousness had yet to develop to the point where political "delegation" was respectable; meantime it found other modes of expression satisfactory. It may be, indeed, that the politicians, themselves in many cases self-made men, expressed in their Liberal ethic not merely a class philosophy, but a lingering wider faith in the reality of equal opportunity through the power of self-help in a fluid colonial society.

The first definite indication of the breakdown of the "Liberal" view of parliamentary representation came in the 'eighties, with the birth of the Protectionist party. Its appearance precipitated the formation of the first Australian "party of resistance," devoted to the cause of Free Trade. Both parties sprang from the work of organisations outside Parliament, and they represented the culmination of a tendency, first apparent in the 'seventies, for minority interest groups to combine with the idea of intervening directly in politics.

The exertion of *pressure* upon the legislature by organised opinion—through such means as delegations to members, and propaganda activities in elections—was already established practice, compatible with the theory of "total" representation. Temperance bodies, sectarian associations, the U.L.V.A. and a host of evanescent organisations devoted to reforming land, education and other legislation, normally pressed their views on candidates at general elections. Other institutions, like the Chamber of Commerce, and the developing trades unions, though rarely active in the constituencies, were consistently effective mouthpieces for the interests they represented. Sectional opinion had thus never been silent; what was new in the 'seventies was its attempt to secure direct representation in the House. In 1874 the Sydney Trades and Labour Council successfully sponsored the election of Angus Cameron, as an avowed working-class representative. A body known as the Workingmen's Defence Association tried in 1875 and 1877 to follow suit, but failed both in this object and in its efforts to unite with Selectors' Associations to sponsor joint candidates. These activities were transitory. Cameron soon showed himself unwilling to accept the dictates of the trade union movement, which, turning in upon itself, then eschewed the idea of seeking political representation for another decade.[31] The W.D.A. seems to have disappeared after 1877. Nevertheless, received notions of parliamentary representation had been seriously challenged.

Of greater importance was the growth of the Free Selectors' Associations. The first of these bodies was formed at Yass in the early 'seventies; others soon sprang up in the western and south-western districts, and at a general Conference of their representatives in Sydney in 1875, one member predicted that "the selectors would soon become a political power which would be able to put any party in or turn any party out."[32] Squatter-selector animosity was at its height at the time, and the movement, dedicated to land reform in the interest of the "small" man, took on a radical tone. Selectors' associations acted as distinct electoral organisations in 1877, usually choosing as their champions solicitors or journalists of "advanced" views, or country storekeepers and *entrepreneurs*. From this time onward a small knot of such men were usually distinguishable in the Assembly as the avowed champions of the "selector interest."[33]

A lull in the land controversy came in 1883, when Stuart's Act reorganised the whole basis of land settlement, granting many of the selectors' claims. The Associations now concentrated upon a secondary plank in their platform—the search for agricultural markets. Early agitation in this respect took the form of a demand for reduced railway rates, but, as this could not be granted, relief through Protection became an increasingly popular alternative. In the mid-'eighties, selectors' organisations formally merged with the Protectionist movement.[34]

This movement, established chiefly by intellectuals and manufacturers, sought the support of trades unions, and posed as a radical force hostile to the "dominant class of monopolists who have ruled our country too long . . . merchants, squatters and bankers."[35] The leaders of the small organisations which composed the movement[36] presented Protection as a panacea for the economic ills of classes other than those who "ruled the country,"[37] and as the chief tenet of a new "democratic" sentiment needed to revitalise politics. The difficulties of farmers, manufacturers and workingmen in the depression of 1883-5 lent some colour to these claims, and in 1886 existing Protectionist bodies united with the Free Selectors' Associations to form a Protection Union. A major function of this body was to be "to arrange, provide, and assist candidates for the various electorates," through its associated branches, and thus, as an external agency, to promote a Protectionist party in the Assembly.[38] Freetraders responded by forming similar associations, at first for propagandist work, and then for electoral intervention.

Meantime, the Land Act of 1884 had brought a drastic decline in land revenue, and, together with the business recession, this produced in 1885 a serious deficit in the public accounts. In the bitter debates that issued from a search for additional sources of revenue, the Free Trade-Protection controversy became a major issue within the legislature.[39] This stimulated the new electoral bodies to perfect their organisation, and linked their activities with a real parliamentary conflict. In the elections of 1887 and 1889 two distinct party machines faced each other,[40] and produced in the legislature a form of political division which seemed to make the traditional "Liberal" *ethos* an anachronism. For how were the old doctrines of "independence" and "total representation" to be maintained in the face of the existence of two political parties, one of which made its appeal frankly to the interests of a section of the electorate?

In general terms, it seems reasonable to interpret this challenge to accepted notions of representation as an expression of two facets of increasing social and economic diversification within the Colony. On the one hand, the sense of group solidarity among people with similar needs and ideals was becoming too strong to find adequate expression in the old safety valve of extra-political combination for limited ends. On the other, the groups themselves were increasing in number and diversity, to produce—even within the middle classes—a variegation bound to diminish faith in the idea of society's "oneness." This was strikingly demonstrated within the bosom of Parliament itself by the increasing diversity of occupations followed by members.[41] The appearance of political parties can thus, in the long view, be interpreted as a political readjustment to social reality.

The change was not at first greeted with equanimity on all sides, but its logic was inescapable. The reactions of the conservative *Sydney Morning Herald* reflect something of the revolution in local opinion on this issue during the critical days of the late 'eighties. This newspaper in 1877 had bitterly attacked the attempts of selectors to elect champions to Parliament, denouncing such men as mere "delegates" and not representatives,[42] and pointing out that "an eager, clamorous and organised minority will always overpower an inert and unorganised majority."[43] Yet ten years later it found little to complain of in the appearance of the new political parties. Though displaying some concern at the likenesses between local party machines and the English Liberal Caucus,[44] it lent its wholehearted support to the Free Trade cause, applauding the party's every move to augment its strength by refining both its organisation and its doctrine.[45] The *Herald's* reaction to the arrival of the Labor Party in 1891 made explicit a changed view of political representation foreshadowed in this acceptance of the party system of the 'eighties.

> The perplexing element of the [present] political situation is . . . the entrance of the Labor Party as a constituent factor into Parliament. In saying this we are not to be supposed to dispute the right, and we may add the duty of the electors if they consider any particular interest or class is not duly represented in Parliament, to take steps to secure its more effective representation. Parliaments are elected for no other purpose but to give effect to the will of the majority of the people, and when that is declared it is the duty of Parliament to adjust itself and its labours accordingly.[46]

To say that the political changes of the late 'eighties reflected in general some recognition of social divisions is not to claim that either the Free Trade or the Protectionist Party directly represented definable sectional interests. By 1889 each was trying to widen its appeal; while many of the old faction politicians—though forced by the electoral machines into a two-party mould—either refused or were unable to forget their former political methods and animosities, and so tended to blur further the content of the new alignments. And almost immediately after their appearance, the new parties were faced with unforeseen problems, like Federation, the great strikes and financial depression, which confused and split them. All these matters require detailed study before we can understand properly the nature of the somewhat battered parties that found themselves suddenly confronted in 1891 by the new political force of Labor. But at least one thing can be said with certainty: from 1887 onward the Free Trade Party rapidly outdistanced its rival in the elaboration of a political philosophy of widespread appeal, becoming the heir to the "Liberal" doctrine, and appearing as the party most devoted to the advancement of the "general" welfare.

There is naturally ample evidence to confirm the early Protectionists' claim that Free Trade was the policy of the mercantile classes.[47] But they erred in believing that the other hated group of "monopolists," the pastoralists, were Freetraders to a man.[48] Freetraders, in fact, had never addressed themselves openly to a section of the electorate. Indeed, they constantly drew attention to that part of Protectionist propaganda which appealed directly to the sectional interests of miners, farmers and manufacturers, and posed as the guardians of the general interest by interpreting Free Trade first as a symbol of individual liberty, and second as a doctrine which implied legislative action to ensure social justice for all.

A tentative approach to the first of these ideas appeared in the electoral campaign of 1887, when many Free Trade candidates insisted on using "the word 'freetrade' in its broadest and most comprehensive sense."[49] Thus one of them told the voters that

> a freetrade policy was more in sympathy with our institutions than any other they could imagine; it was more instinct with the ideas of a free people like ourselves—with liberal notions and liberal institutions, than any other policy.[50]

The ideas towards which these men were fumbling were properly formulated in the next two years. In 1889 a group of doctrinaires under McMillan reorganised the machinery of the Free Trade Party, renaming the local bodies upon which it was based "Free Trade and Liberal Associations," and officially adopting for the parliamentary party the name of "Liberal."[51] The propagandist A. B. Smith produced a body of doctrine for the reconstituted party in his pamphlet *Freetrade and Liberal Associations, Their True Province,* supported by B. R. Wise, in his *Position of the Liberal Party.* Smith gave in his pamphlet a historical survey of the "growth of liberal principles," particularly in England, designed to show that the name "Liberal" could more properly be assigned in New South Wales to Freetraders than to Protectionists. He examined the concept of liberty in terms reminiscent of J. S. Mill, and carefully defined a number of "fields" in which it ought to be preserved, adding that "in our own colony, at the present time, the portion of the Liberal citadel which is being threatened is that of our commercial freedom."[52] This argument against Protection was given a special slant, on the one hand to appeal to middle-class opinion, and on the other to suggest that another important matter, taxation, was also involved.

> The policy of Protection affords a striking example [of breach of liberty]. It is an infringement of the principle of security of property. It involves the infliction of a penalty on every citizen who chooses to purchase an article made outside his own country; and it is an inroad made upon that citizen's property, not as a contribution towards the fund for guarding the community from internal or external harm, which is a proper ground for taxation, but merely for the purpose of enabling certain fellow citizens to obtain for their manufactures a larger price than their quality would otherwise demand in competition with the outside world.[53]

Here the old colonial "Liberal's" notion of the injustice of seeking to advance the interest of a sectional group was restated, with an implicit suggestion that the sanctity of property was also involved.

But in accepting this formulation of its beliefs,

the party was saved from the crudities of an extreme *laissez-faire* position by the special significance of the taxation problem. The Free Trade-Protection controversy had originally flared up in Parliament when Jennings attempted to bolster declining state income with a revenue tariff. Protectionists had swung to his support, believing any tariff better than none. After 1887, the "Protectionist" party absorbed those who saw the customs house as an instrument of taxation, as well as those who would use it to block imports altogether. Protectionist division on this issue was never properly reconciled, and, against a background of growing difficulties in state finance, the Freetraders were able to depict their opponents as the party of indirect taxation. They, on the other hand, incorporated direct taxation as a central plank in the Liberal platform—the arm of Liberal policy calculated to confer some measure of social justice by distributing the burden of state upkeep in proportion to means.[54]

This approach to the taxation issue was not simply a matter of political expediency. Most Liberals—from the radical Wise to the conservative McMillan—genuinely believed direct taxation to be the one instrument of social reform consistent with Liberal principles.[55] Smith and the theorists of 1889 had explicitly rejected as illiberal the idea that the state could fix wages, control prices, limit working hours or by any such direct intervention seek to increase social welfare.[56] Many Liberals in the 'nineties came to reject this limited interpretation of their creed, and to concede justice to some of the demands of the Labor Party. But it was around the issue of direct taxation that the astute Reid was able to gather all shades of Liberal opinion, and to engineer a six-year Liberal-Labor coalition which produced some of the most progressive legislation ever placed on the Colony's statute book.[57]

It may reasonably be argued, then, that the appearance of political parties in New South Wales during the 'eighties did not destroy so much as modify the traditional "Liberal" *ethos*. The Freetraders took it over, and remoulded it to suit changing circumstances. In doing this, they found a way of reconciling the old individualist-based concern for "the general good" with a clear need for political action to improve the lot of particular *sections* of society. It is perhaps not too fanciful —given the composition of the Legislative Assembly in these years—to think that this achievement expressed the desire of at least a section of the middle classes to meet honestly the challenge of a new insight into social reality.

I have suggested that consideration of the structure of the New South Wales Legislative Assembly before 1900 raises the problem of understanding the political role of the middle classes of the period, and that for this the twin themes of "Liberalism" and of political organisation are important. But even within these limits, many unanswered questions remain. How far, for example, is it just to assume a large measure of agreement in political values before 1880? What precise conflicts occurred within the middle classes after that date, and how were they related to the participation of erstwhile "Liberals" in the early political Labor movement? What was the significance of the Free Trade-Liberal strength in urban areas? And, clearly related to this last question, to what extent was local "Liberalism" inspired by contemporary English political thought, especially during the last decade of the century, when there were significant parallels between colonial ideas and the "new Liberalism" produced in England by what J. A. Hobson called "a movement along the lines of the strongest human feeling"?

All these problems demand close study if we wish to gain a fully rounded picture of nineteenth century politics in New South Wales. For their proper elucidation, the political historian will certainly need—to adapt the words of Namier—"a most thorough knowledge of constituencies and elections, of members and parliaments, and of constitutional ideas and realities throughout [this] formative period." So large a task will require here—as in England—the interest and energy of many workers.

Notes

1. F. M. Stenton, "The History of Parliament," *Times Literary Supplement*, 6 Jan. 1956.

2. L. B. Namier, *Personalities and Powers*, London, 1955, p. 14.

3. L. B. Namier, *The Structure of Politics at the Accession of George III*, 2 vols., London, 1929.

4. J. E. Neale, *The Elizabethan House of Commons*, London, 1950; N. Gash, *Politics in the Age of Peel*, 1830-1850, London, 1953; R. Pares, *King George III and the Politicians*, Oxford, 1953.

5. C. A. Beard, *An Economic Interpretation of the Constitution of the United States*, New York, 1952.

6. J. F. S. Ross, *Parliamentary Representation*, London, 1948; J. A. Thomas, *The House of Commons, 1832-1901*, Cardiff, 1939.

7. W. L. Guttsman, "The Changing Social Structure of the British Political Elite, 1886-1935," *British Journal of Sociology* (*Br. J. Sociol.*), Vol. II, No. 2, June 1951; "Aristocracy and the Middle Class in the British Political Elite, 1886-1916," *Br. J. Sociol.*, Vol V, No. 1, March 1954.

8. W. O. Aydelotte, "A Statistical Analysis of the Parliament of 1841: Some Problems of Method," *Bulletin of the Institute of Historical Research*, Vol. XXVII, No. 76, Nov. 1954, p. 141.

9. This term was used by an Australian professor in a recent inaugural address, of which a principal theme

seemed to be a plea for reducing the use of statistics in historical research.

10. Barraclough commends Aydelotte's attempt "to establish criteria for the use of statistics in the modern history of Parliament" as an effort "to break through the limits of particularity" (G. Barraclough, "The Larger View of History," *Times Literary Supplement*, 6 Jan. 1956).

11. E. J. Hobsbawm, "Where are British Historians Going," *Marxist Quarterly*, Vol. 2, No. 1, Jan. 1955, p. 21.

12. *Ibid.*

13. As shown in the official *N.S.W. Parliamentary Record.*

14. The Constitution Act established an Assembly of 54, which was increased to eighty by the Electoral Act of 1858. When Queensland was separated from N.S.W., this number was reduced to 72. Redistribution of electorates in 1880 increased membership to 108, establishing a basic set of 72 constituencies, which could increase their representation in accordance with a sliding scale as population grew. By 1891 the Assembly thus had a membership of 141. Multiple constituencies were finally abolished by the Parliamentary Electorate and Elections Act of 1893, which set the boundaries of 125 new single-member electorates.

15. In the collection of this extensive material, I wish to acknowledge the assistance of my wife, and of Mrs. Wardle, of the History Department, Australian National University. I am also indebted to Mr. L. F. Fitzhardinge for innumerable references and suggestions.

16. The exceptions were those included in "Other Commercial"—a clerk, an insurance agent and a commercial traveller—and a few managers of mines and shipping companies.

17. For example, Morris Asher (Hume, 1859). General storekeeper at Wombat and Gundagai. Sold out and went to New Zealand, where he ran a general store and fitted up two whaling stations. Returning to Australia, Asher settled in the Albury district, subsequently owning a store, a boiling-down works, a flourmill and three hotels.

18. Besides the vote to which all males over 21 were entitled, through living in one place for six months, businessmen and landowners had a vote in each additional electorate in which they owned or leased property or premises of a clear value of over £100, or a rental of over £10 per annum. Also, as Labor leaders later urged, the "residence" clause undoubtedly disfranchised many migratory workers.

19. C. Hartley Grattan, *Australia*, Berkeley, 1947, p. 275. The most recent assertion of the supposed political impotence of the Australian middle class is a provocative article by A. Barcan who quotes Grattan with great approval: "The Australian Middle Class," *Past and Present*, No. 8, Nov. 1955.

20. See, *e.g.*, I. D. McNaughton's comments on this matter in G. Greenwood (ed.), *Australia, A Social and Political History*, Sydney, 1955, pp. 102-3. The same viewpoint is skilfully presented in an unpublished thesis by P. Loveday, *"Democracy" in New South Wales in the 1850's*, University of Sydney.

21. Whether pastoralists in fact led the Conservative movement in the earlier Assemblies is a question still uninvestigated. The reminiscences of some participants suggest that this was not altogether true: *e.g.*, W. Forster (*N.S.W. Parl. Debs.*, Series 1, Vol. IV, p. 1596), "We had a division of parties when responsible government first began. There was a sort of Conservative Party, which was associated with the old officialism of the colony."

22. Robert Wisdom, 24 Aug. 1882. *N.S.W. P.D.*, Series 1, Vol. VIII, p. 106.

23. *Sydney Morning Herald*, 1 Oct. 1872.

24. Edward Butler, prominent Sydney barrister, and a Roman Catholic.

25. L. F. De Salis to Parkes, 19 March 1872. (*Parkes Correspondence*, Vol. A881, p. 395a, Mitchell Library).

26. Speech of Wallace, Northumberland Nomination, *S.M.H.*, 20 July 1877.

27. There was a significant parallel here with the mid-century English tendency to define "a Liberal Government . . . not so much by its aim, as by the method employed to pursue it." See E. Halévy, *A History of the English People in the Nineteenth Century*, Vol. IV, London, 1951, p. 409.

28. See, *e.g.*, the *furore* caused in the Assembly by the case of H. H. Cooke, denounced as a "discredit to the House" for stating openly that on a Criminal Amendment Bill he would "vote whichever way the Government go." *N.S.W. P.D.*, Vol. VII, 26 Sept. 1882, pp. 549 *et seq.*

29. *S.M.H.*, 7 Dec. 1874.

30. John Bowle, in a discussion of "The Liberal Compromise," *Politics and Opinions in the Nineteenth Century*, London, 1954, p. 208.

31. For an excellent discussion of internal reasons for the trade union attitude to participation in politics in these years see N. B. Nairn, *Some Aspects of the Development of the N.S.W. Labor Movement*, 1870-1900, unpublished thesis, University of Sydney.

32. *S.M.H.*, 2 Dec. 1875.

33. Typical of such men were J. J. Wright, *entrepreneur*, of Queanbeyan; A. Affleck, storekeeper, of Gundaroo; L. F. Heydon, solicitor; E. W. O'Sullivan, journalist. Table I shows significant increases in the number of men of these types in the Assembly from the late 'seventies onward.

34. *Golden Fleece* (Special issue of *The Farmer and Settler*, 31 Aug. 1907), p. 77. Annual meetings of Free Selectors' Conferences were held from 1877 to 1883. In 1883 the Conference formed a Land Law Reformation League, designed to be a continuing organisation for promoting selector interests. But after the passage of Stuart's Land Act this body merged with existing Protectionist organisations (1884).

35. L. F. Heydon, President of the Land and Industrial Alliance, speech at a "Political Conference" of Protectionist organisations, July 1885. (*Daily Telegraph*, 31 July 1885).

36. The Democratic Alliance, the Land and Industrial Alliance, the Protection and Political Reform League.

37. Heydon, *op. cit.*

38. Constitution of Protection Union of N.S.W. (*S.M.H.*, 12 Nov. 1886).

39. The Jennings Government in 1886 proposed a three-point plan to restore state finances by imposing stamp duties, a land tax and a five per cent *ad valorem* tariff, with additional specific import duties. Protectionists hailed this as the "thin edge of the wedge," and Parkes declared that Free Trade *versus* Protection was now the real political issue of the day. (See, *e.g.*, his "challenge" to Protectionists on the eve of the 1887 election, *N.S.W. P.D.*, Vol. IV, p. 113).

40. See B. Mansfield, "Party Organisation in the N.S.W. Elections of February, 1889," *Royal Australian Historical Society, Journal and Proceedings*, Vol. 41, Part 2, Sept. 1955, for one examination of the extent of party activity in these elections.

41. Table I shows only ten occupational types in 1856, and 27 in 1889. These figures are actually an understatement of the contrast, since the Table represents a condensation of available data. If all sub-categories are included, the figures for 1856 and 1889 respectively are twelve and 42. (In 1889 there were, *e.g.*, ten types of retail traders to three in 1856, four types of manufacturers to two, etc.).

42. See, *e.g.*, *S.M.H.* editorial of 7 Nov. 1877.

43. *S.M.H.*, 13 Oct. 1877. See also editorial of 12 Oct. 1877, in which were criticised other organised minorities which a parliamentary candidate "must condescend to court."

44. See, *e.g.*, comment of 26 Jan. 1889 on the dangers of permitting electoral associations to act as "political conscience-keepers."

45. The *Herald* reported fully and with approval all details of Free Trade Association activity—propaganda, supplying candidates, and general liaison work between

local and central bodies—during the elections of 1887 and 1889. It was especially enthusiastic about the party's reorganization in 1889, and the attempt to extend its "range of action" by adopting a new name and platform (Editorial, 2 Ap. 1889).

46. *S.M.H.*, 30 June 1891.

47. For example, all six merchants elected to the Assembly in 1887 were Freetraders.

48. For example, ten pastoralists elected to the Assembly in 1887 were Freetraders, and seven Protectionists. In 1889 the numbers were seven and eleven respectively.

49. W. McMillan, manifesto, *S.M.H.*, 3 Feb. 1887.

50. S. Burdekin, *ibid*.

51. For accounts of these developments, see *S.M.H.*, 2 March 1889, 28 March 1889, 2 Ap. 1889, 8 Ap. 1889.

52. *Freetrade and Liberal Associations*, p. 42.

53. *Ibid.*, p. 28.

54. Party debate on new platform (*S.M.H.*, 2 Ap. 1889).

55. Wise was in the early 'nineties a founder of the "Free Trade and Land Reform" movement, which saw land taxation as a means of bringing "the poorer classes more nearly on a level with all the classes in the distribution of the comforts and necessities of life." (Speech, reported in *S.M.H.*, 16 Jan. 1894). McMillan was in favour of direct taxation because he believed "that the propertied classes of this country bear nothing whatever in the form of taxation in proportion to the privileges which they enjoy," and that " 'making the shoe pinch' will arouse [them] to a sense of their duty as citizens." (*N.S.W. P.D.*, Vol. XXV, p. 724).

56. *Free Trade and Liberal Associations*, pp. 28 *et seq.*

57. For a detailed discussion of Reid, the Free Trade Party, and direct taxation in the 'nineties, see A. W. Martin, "Free Trade and Protectionist Parties in New South Wales," *Historical Studies, Australia and New Zealand*, Vol. 6, No. 23, Nov. 1954.

2. WHO MAKES OUR LAWS?

Charles S. Hyneman

SOME POET, philosopher, or soothsayer of the past is supposed to have remarked that he cared not who made the laws of a nation if he but knew who wrote its songs. This article is based on the assumption that it is important to know who makes the laws of a people, no matter who produces the songs which they sing. It is concerned with the men who manufacture statutes—the legislators. It is limited to members of state legislatures only—Congressmen and members of city councils do not figure in the data and observations which follow; and it inquires only into the occupations and professions—ways of earning a living —of lawmakers.[1]

Facts about the men who enact statutes are, presumably, significant only if they bear some relation to legislative behavior—significant only if they affect the content or form of laws, or influence the procedure by which laws are enacted. Throughout the American literature of legislation one encounters the supposition that the ways in which legislators earn their living are worthy of careful analysis. The validity of the supposition is usually not argued; such rationalizations as have been offered seem to me not very convincing. But the widespread interest in occupations which the literature reveals seems to justify an extended analysis here, even though there be severe limitations on the reliability of data and sharp doubt that con-

clusions which may be drawn will be of social significance.[2]

Occupational Distribution of Legislators. Table 1 shows the numerical importance of different occupational groups in a composite of twenty-five legislative chambers (occupations of California senators are not available) and indicates the relative importance of the more numerous occupational groups in the several chambers. Lawyers are seen to be the most numerous single group; lawyers and farmers together constitute slightly less than one half of all legislators.[3]

Most significant are the statements of rank. Lawyers were the most numerous group in seventeen chambers; in the other eight chambers they were either second or third in importance. In those chambers where lawyers were not preëminent, farmers outnumbered them. In only two chambers were farmers less than third in importance. Merchants and business men not otherwise classified (henceforth referred to as merchants) were the third most important group. In three chambers, they were the second most numerous group; in twelve chambers, they were third in importance.[4]

The information which appears in Table 1 is shown separately for each of the twenty-five chambers in Table 2. In addition, Table 2 shows for each house the numerical importance of the five leading groups. It will be noted that in only one case did either lawyers or farmers (one of which group is first in each house) constitute one half

Reprinted from *Political Science Quarterly*, Vol. 55 (1940), pp. 556-581, by permission of the author and the publisher.

the six-session membership of a chamber. Farmers constituted 55.7 per cent of the 648 members who served in the Iowa House from 1925 to 1935. In only one other chamber (Iowa Senate) did farmers come within 10 per cent of a majority of all members. Lawyers amounted to more than 40 per cent of the six-session membership of eight different chambers. The best showing achieved by any occupational group other than lawyers and farmers was that of merchants who constituted 20.6 per cent of the Maine House.

But laws are not made by a composite of the members who serve in a series of legislative sessions; laws are enacted by the men who are present in a particular assembly. To what extent do lawyers or farmers control individual sessions of state legislatures?

It appears that in only one of the thirteen states, during the six-session period covered by this study, were farmers ever able to outvote all other groups. Farmers controlled five different sessions of the Iowa House of Representatives by majorities ranging between 54 per cent and 62 per cent of the entire membership; in 1925 they constituted 56 per cent of the Iowa Senate. The nearest approach of farmers to a clear majority in any other state seems to have been in the Mississippi Senate of 1925 when they constituted 42.9 per cent of the total membership of the chamber.

While lawyers were the most numerous single occupational group over a six-session period in seventeen of the twenty-five chambers studied, they seem to have enjoyed a clear majority in only six instances—twice in the Arkansas Senate (51.4 per cent and 60 per cent), twice in the New Jersey Senate (52.4 per cent and 55 per cent), and twice in the New York Senate (51 per cent and 54.9 per cent). In two sessions of the New Jersey House, lawyers, if correctly counted, represented exactly 50 per cent of the membership. In one session or another lawyers constituted more than 40 per cent of the membership of the lower houses of Arkansas, New Jersey and New York, and of the Senates of Arkansas, Illinois, Indiana, Louisiana, Minnesota, Mississippi, New Jersey and New York.

Occupations and Positions of Leadership. Any account of the importance of occupational groups in legislative bodies must take into consideration the distribution of offices of power and positions of influence. Examination of the allotment of committee chairmanships in twenty-five chambers during six regular sessions shows that the occupational groups which dominated the total membership also controlled most of the chairmanships, and, further, that chairmanships were divided among these occupational groups in approximately the same proportions as were all memberships. Lawyers were the most numerous single occupational group in seventeen of the twenty-five chambers; lawyers held more chairmanships than any other occupational group in twenty of the twenty-five chambers during the same period. Farmers were first or second in membership in nineteen chambers; they were first or second in number of chairmanships held in seventeen chambers. Merchants were second in importance in three chambers; they were first in point of chairmanships in one chamber, and second in two chambers.

Table 1—Distribution According to Occupation of All Members of Thirteen Lower Chambers and Twelve Senates During 1925-1935

	Number of Memberships	Per Cent of All Memberships	NUMBER OF CHAMBERS IN WHICH EACH OCCUPATIONAL GROUP OCCUPIED A GIVEN POSITION OF IMPORTANCE				
			First	Second	Third	Fourth	Fifth
Farmers	2722	21.5	8	11	2		2
Lawyers	3555	28.0	17	7	1		
Newspapermen	369	2.9			2	2	1
Other Professional Men	639	5.0		1	1	7	5
Bankers and Brokers	352	2.8		1		3	
Contractors	273	2.2			1		
Manufacturing and Industry	445	3.5		1	1	4	1
Insurance	484	3.8			2	3	1
Real Estate	385	3.0			2		1
Merchants and Other Business Men	1263	10.0		3	12	7	2
Engineers and Machinists	184	1.5					
Salesmen and Clerks	525	4.1		1		1	1
Laborers	205	1.6					
Not Otherwise Classified	704	5.5			2	1	10
Unknown	584	4.6					
Total	12,689	100					

Table 2—Showing the Five Most Important Occupational Groups in Thirteen Lower Chambers and Twelve Senates During 1925-35

OCCUPATIONAL GROUP AND PERCENTAGE OF TOTAL MEMBERSHIP

Chamber	All Members	First Occupations	%	Second Occupations	%	Third Occupations	%	Fourth Occupations	%	Fifth Occupations	%	Total Five Leading Occups.
Arkansas House	600	Lawyers	34.2	Farmers	26.7	Merchants	8.3	Prof. Men	7.3	Unclassified	6.2	82.7
Senate	210	Lawyers	49.1	Farmers	18.1	Merchants	8.6	Prof. Men	5.7	Unclassified	3.8	85.3
California House	480	Lawyers	34.3	Farmers	12.7	Merchants	8.5	Newspapermen	8.1	Real Estate	7.7	71.3
Illinois House	915	Lawyers	29.7	Farmers	12.6	Insurance	8.3	Merchants	7.9	Unclassified	7.7	66.2
Senate	306	Lawyers	32.7	Merchants	11.4	Farmers	9.2	Prof. Men	6.9	Insurance	4.2	64.4
Indiana House	600	Farmers	24.0	Lawyers	23.5	Merchants	12.7	Unclassified	6.0	Prof. Men	5.7	71.7
Senate	300	Lawyers	34.3	Farmers	14.7	Newspapermen	7.7	Merchants	7.0	Mfg. & Ind.	7.0	70.7
Iowa House	648	Farmers	55.7	Lawyers	11.6	Merchants	6.6	Bankers	4.8	Unclassified	4.2	82.9
Senate	300	Farmers	43.6	Lawyers	23.0	Merchants	7.0	Insurance	5.7	Prof. Men / Unclassified	4.0 / 4.0	87.3
Louisiana House	600	Lawyers	32.4	Farmers	19.3	Merchants	12.5	Prof. Men	9.7	Salesmen	9.5	83.4
Senate	232	Lawyers	46.5	Merchants	13.8	Farmers	12.1	Mfg. & Ind.	4.7	Salesmen	4.7	81.8
Maine House	906	Farmers	23.8	Merchants	20.6	Lawyers	8.9	Mfg. & Ind.	8.2	Unclassified	8.0	69.5
Senate	190	Lawyers	23.8	Farmers	18.9	Merchants	15.8	Mfg. & Ind.	7.4	Prof. Men / Unclassified	6.8 / 6.8	79.5
Minnesota House	786	Farmers	36.9	Lawyers	18.1	Merchants	9.8	Insurance	3.6	Prof. Men	3.4	71.8
Senate	402	Lawyers	40.3	Farmers	20.4	Contractors	6.2	Merchants	5.0	Newspapermen	4.5	76.4
Mississippi House	839	Farmers	38.7	Lawyers	30.9	Prof. Men	8.2	Merchants	5.8	Unclassified	4.3	87.9
Senate	294	Lawyers	45.9	Farmers	24.8	Merchants	7.8	Prof. Men	6.8	Unclassified	3.4	88.7
New Jersey House	360	Lawyers	42.0	Prof. Men	6.1	Unclassified	5.3	Merchants	4.4			62.2
Senate	124	Lawyers	45.9	Bankers	9.7	Newspapermen / Prof. Men	8.1 / 8.1	Insurance	8.1	Farmers	4.4	75.0
New York House	900	Lawyers	43.9	Farmers	12.1	Insurance	7.5	Merchants	7.1	Unclassified	6.9	77.5
Senate	306	Lawyers	46.1	Farmers	10.1	Mfg. & Ind.	9.5	Bankers	8.2	Merchants / Prof. Men	5.2 / 5.2	84.3
Pennsylvania House	1245	Lawyers	17.7	Salesmen	15.4	Unclassified	14.2	Merchants	11.6	Farmers	7.2	66.1
Senate	300	Lawyers	33.0	Mfg. & Ind.	14.0	Real Estate	9.3	Prof. Men	6.3	Merchants	6.0	68.6
Washington House	586	Farmers	27.5	Lawyers	15.4	Merchants	13.8	Newspapermen	5.5	Prof. Men	5.5	67.2
Senate	260	Farmers	20.8	Lawyers	18.4	Merchants	17.7	Bankers	7.3	Mfg. & Ind.	6.5	70.7

Table 3 shows that in six instances, one occupational group held as many chairmanships as all other groups combined. Farmers held, during the six-session period, 53.6 per cent of the chairmanships of the Iowa Senate. Lawyers held 51.5 per cent and 51.9 per cent of the Senate chairmanships in Louisiana and Minnesota, respectively, 57.9 per cent of the House chairmanships in Mississippi, and exactly 50 per cent of the chairmanships of the Arkansas and Mississippi Senates. In only four other chambers did lawyers hold more than 40 per cent of the chairmanships.

Assuming that continuity of experience in legislative service reflects itself in ability to influence legislative product, it will be of interest to observe the tendency of different occupational groups to survive for long periods of service. Table 3 affords opportunity to do this. It takes into account the 1363 house members and 1021 senators who, at any time during the six sessions studied, were serving their fifth or later session of service. A comparison of this table with Table 2 reveals that farmers constitute about the same proportion of veteran legislators as they do of all members. Farmers constituted 55.7 per cent of the six-session membership of the Iowa House; they constituted 58.7 per cent of the veterans of that chamber during the same period. Farmers were the most numerous occupational group in the six-session membership of eight chambers; the long-service farmers outnumbered the veterans of every other occupation in five chambers.[5] Farmers constituted more than 30 per cent of the six-session membership of four chambers; they comprised more than 30 per cent of the veterans of five chambers.

The advantage which lawyers have because of their number in the membership of the state legislature is heightened in some assemblies by their tendency to return for session after session of service. Whereas lawyers constituted a majority of the six-session membership of not one single chamber, they constituted a clear majority of the veterans in three chambers (Arkansas Senate, Mississippi House and New Jersey Senate). In eight chambers lawyers amounted to more than 40 per cent of the six-session membership; in exactly the same number they constituted more than 40 per cent of those who were serving their fifth or later session. If one checks Tables 1 and 2 by chambers, he will see that lawyers improved their position in fifteen chambers—i.e., in fifteen chambers lawyers constituted a greater proportion of the veterans than of all members. The gains in the fifteen chambers only slightly outweighed the losses in the other nine houses, however, the net averaging only a bit more than one-half of one per cent for the twenty-five houses.

At least four facts emerge conspicuously from the mass of data concerning occupations which has been compiled: (1) our bicameral system is not producing senates which differ from the lower houses, so far as means of livelihood of legislators is concerned; (2) the farmer is not, as commonly supposed, in possession of too many seats in legislative chambers; (3) the lawyer is representative for all population groups—our professional representor; and (4) that part of our population

Table 3—Prominence of Lawyers, Farmers and Other Occupational Groups as Measured by Possession of Committee Chairmanships and Tendency to Continue in Service

State and Chamber	PER CENT OF ALL CHAIRMANSHIPS WHICH WERE HELD BY			PER CENT OF ALL LEGISLATORS SERVING 5TH OR LATER SESSIONS WHO WERE		
	Lawyers	Farmers	All Other Occupations	Lawyers	Farmers	Other Occupations
Arkansas						
House	42.8	19.6	37.6	45.0	35.0	20.0
Senate	50.0	16.9	33.1	57.1	14.3	28.6
California						
House	35.7	12.8	51.5	37.0	12.3	50.7
Illinois						
House	36.8	15.1	48.1	36.8	10.6	52.6
Senate	36.0	8.1	55.9	24.2	15.6	60.2
Indiana						
House	22.4	19.1	58.5			
Senate	32.2	11.3	56.5	17.3	17.3	65.4
Iowa						
House	23.8	43.9	32.3	13.8	58.7	27.5
Senate	13.9	53.6	32.5	18.4	36.8	44.8
Louisiana						
House	30.0	19.1	18.5	23.0	18.7	58.3
Senate	51.5	8.2	40.3	43.6	18.2	38.2
Maine						
House	11.7	16.8	71.5	9.1	4.5	86.4
Senate	24.5	19.1	56.4	36.0	28.0	36.0
Minnesota						
House	25.4	29.4	45.2	20.6	27.6	51.8
Senate	51.9	8.2	39.9	48.5	15.2	36.3
Mississippi						
House	57.9	16.5	25.6	60.8	22.8	16.4
Senate	50.0	20.5	29.5	27.7	34.0	38.3
New Jersey						
House	39.6	2.7	57.7	42.8	2.4	54.8
Senate	46.7	7.8	45.5	52.0	3.8	44.2
New York						
House	35.7	23.9	40.4	42.5	15.2	42.3
Senate	49.6	13.2	37.2	44.8	12.7	42.5
Pennsylvania						
House	26.7	7.1	66.2	22.5	6.6	70.9
Senate	37.0	1.0	62.0	34.0	4.3	61.7
Washington						
House	14.3	33.3	52.4	14.4	43.9	43.1
Senate	20.9	18.5	60.6	32.5	24.2	43.3

which, under any definition, could be called the industrial proletariat enjoys very little membership.

Bicameralism and Occupations of Legislators. Table 2 alone is probably sufficient to convince the reader that the occupational character of the house and senate is essentially the same. This is most conspicuously so in the case of Arkansas where the five most important occupational groups of the House are also, and in the same order, the five most important occupational groups of the Senate. In Mississippi the same five occupations provide the five most important groups in each house, though the order of importance is not the same.

The widest difference in occupational character of the two chambers seems to exist in New Jersey. Even in that state, however, lawyers are of almost equal strength in the two chambers. Four fewer attorneys in the Senate or sixteen more in the House in the six-session period would have made them of almost identical importance. I do not know just what occupational groups are likely to be in alliance, if any such alliances exist in the legislature. None the less, it may be pointed out that a combination of bankers, merchants and manufacturers could control 10 per cent of the New Jersey House and 16.2 per cent of the Senate; and that such a bloc in combination with the lawyers could outvote all other occupational groups in either chamber.

Farmer strength, during the six-session period, was nearly twice as great in the New Jersey Senate as in the House, but this is a fact of little significance since farmers are so small a minority in either chamber (7.3 per cent of the six-session membership of the Senate, entirely missing from that chamber in 1931 and 1935). Any occupational group or groups which might, under the most inclusive classification, be identified as proletarian (laborers, salesmen and clerks, engineers and machinists) whether taken singly or in combinations are of nearly identical strength in the New Jersey House and Senate and taken in their entirety are of little importance numerically in either chamber—5.8 per cent of the six-session House membership; 5.6 per cent of the Senate.

The significance of the foregoing observations as to differences in the occupational content of the two chambers is greatly reduced, of course, by the fact that they describe a composite of six sessions. A view into the data for individual sessions of a sample of states, including New Jersey, shows, however, that the foregoing observations are essentially true for individual sessions.

The Farmer. It will be of interest to relate, as far as possible, the actual legislative membership of the various occupational groups to an ideal membership based upon the numerical importance of each group in the whole population of the state. This can be done with some satisfaction for farmers since the magnitude of the farm population reduces the likelihood of important error in the census figures. The other occupational groups differentiated in this study, however, constitute so small a proportion of the states' population that one can put very little confidence in the census figures. In spite of this limitation, however, such calculations have been made for lawyers—because of their numerical importance in legislative assemblies. It may be noted, furthermore, that newspapermen and publishers, bankers and brokers, insurance men, and real estate brokers doubtless hold far more seats in most legislative chambers than their numbers in the whole population would entitle them to.

The prominence of law-trained men and the scarcity of wage-earners in the state legislature will be discussed at length in the course of the next few pages. Attention should be called at this point to the fact that, contrary to the supposition of most writers, the farmer does not enjoy membership in the state legislature greatly out of proportion to his numerical importance in the whole population.[6] It appears that in ten of the twenty-five chambers farmers constituted a higher proportion of the six-session membership than their ratio to the whole population would have justified. In at least four of these instances, however, the advantage which the farmer held was so slight that it might well be discounted. In the Indiana House and the Senates of Iowa, New Jersey and Washington, farmers had, during the entire six sessions, from three to six more members than a system of proportional allotment would have given them.

On the other hand, in six chambers (the New York Senate and the lower chambers of Iowa, Maine, Minnesota, New York and Washington) the excess of actual farmer-membership over a membership ideally determined is substantial. Farmers held 290 seats in the Minnesota House during the period 1925 to 1935; on a basis of numerical importance in the whole population they were entitled to 272 seats. The excess, 18 seats, represents 6.6 per cent of the ideal; i. e., 18 is 6.6 per cent of 272. The comparable figure for over-membership of farmers in the remaining five of the six chambers just listed was: Maine House, 15.5; Iowa House, 32.2; Washington House, 51.4; New York Senate, 63.1; and New York House, 94.6.

In the other fifteen chambers the farmer held fewer seats than he would have been allotted under an apportionment based on numerical importance in the whole population. The difference between his actual representation and the ideal (i. e., the deficiency in representation), as measured by percentage of the ideal, ranged from a low of 3.1 per cent in the case of the Iowa Senate to a high of 69.1 per cent in the Arkansas Senate. In eleven of these fifteen chambers the under-representation of the farmer amounted to more than 25 per cent of his proper share on a numerical basis; in five chambers it amounted to more than 50 per cent.

The Lawyer's Prominence. According to the census figures attorneys at law constitute a very small part of the population of any state—ranging, among the states covered in this study, from a low of .24 per cent (24 one-hundredths of 1 per cent) of the gainfully employed population above the age of twenty in Mississippi, to a high of .69 per cent in New York. The median of the thirteen states studied was Indiana, where .39 per cent were lawyers. The small magnitude of the figures for lawyer-population and the certainty of error in ascribing occupations to legislators makes generalization as to the relative over-membership of law-trained men very hazardous. Subject to this limitation several observations may be of interest.

If representatives were distributed among the various occupations in strict accordance with their numerical importance in the total population, lawyers would have been entitled, for the entire six-session period, to less than one member in the Senates of Arkansas, Louisiana, Maine, Mississippi, New Jersey and Pennsylvania, and they would have been entitled to less than two members in the lower chambers of Arkansas, Louisiana and New Jersey. In only two bodies could the legal profession have laid claim, for a six-session total, to more than four representatives—the Illinois House of Representatives (4.5 members) and the New York House (6.3 members).

The excess of actual lawyer-membership over a true proportional membership for the legal profession may be presented in percentages. Allowing a lawyer for every fraction of an ideal proportional membership (i. e., allowing five lawyer-members instead of 4.5 as ideal membership in the Illinois House) the percentage relation of actual to ideal membership of lawyers ranges from a low of 2,400 per cent in the case of the Washington Senate to a high of 13,500 per cent in the case of the Mississippi Senate (ideal membership, 1; actual membership, 135). The median of the twenty-five chambers studied is the Pennsylvania House where the number of seats actually held by members of the legal profession was 5500 per cent of the maximum number of seats to which their importance in the state's population would have

entitled them (ideal membership, 4; actual membership, 220).

If one insists on viewing the excess strength which lawyers enjoy in the state legislature as a usurpation of the rightful membership of other occupational groups, certain other figures will be found of interest. The legal profession was, on a basis of numerical importance in the total population, entitled to a maximum of two seats in the Minnesota Senate; actually there were 162 lawyer-members. Lawyers thus had all the places they were entitled to in the upper house of that state and purloined 160 (40 per cent) of the 400 seats which rightfully belonged to other occupational groups. The figure arrived at in this manner—shall we call it the coefficient of thievery?—ranged from a low of 8.6 per cent in the case of the Maine House, to a high of 48.8 per cent in the Arkansas Senate. The median of the coefficients was 32.1 per cent—the Louisiana House.

It must be stated emphatically that this *over-membership* of lawyers in the legislature cannot be viewed as a matter of *over-representation* of the legal profession. The attorney is the accepted agent of all politically effective groups of the American people. As the lawyer is habitually the representative of the grasping and the abused in litigation, as he is increasingly the negotiator between business men with conflicting interests, as he is more and more the spokesman of individual and corporation in public relations—so is the lawyer today depended upon to represent citizens in the lawmaking body.

Reliance upon the lawyer as legislative representative is spread in surprising uniformity among all kinds of constituency. In a previous paragraph some percentages of over-membership of lawyers were presented; the range of excess membership was shown to be from 2,400 per cent in the Washington Senate to 13,500 per cent in the Mississippi Senate. Both Washington and Mississippi are, of course, basically agricultural and rural rather than industrial and urban, yet they represent the extremes in undue presence of lawyers. Of the thirteen states embraced in this study, three (Arkansas, Iowa and Mississippi) may be called strictly agricultural; in each, farmers constitute more than 40 per cent of the gainfully employed adult population. Three other states (New Jersey, New York and Pennsylvania) may be called strictly industrial; in each of them farmers amount to less than 10 per cent of the employed adult population. A study of the percentage of lawyer-excess in these twelve chambers shows that there is no correlation, direct or inverse, between the degree of over-membership of lawyers and the agricultural content of the population. The three chambers in which lawyers enjoy, relatively, the least advantage are, in order: Iowa House, Iowa Senate and New York Senate; the three chambers of greatest over-membership of lawyers are, in order: Mississippi Senate, Arkansas Senate and Arkansas House. The lawyer is thus shown to have made both his weakest and his strongest bid for power in states where the farmer is most strongly entrenched.

In order to probe further into the possibility that the lawyer-legislator may breed especially in a certain type of district, districts have been classified according to the urban-rural character of their populations. Four distinct district types were differentiated, which, for further discussion, may best be identified by number, as follows:

Type 1—80 per cent or more of the population of the district lies within a city of one million or more population.

Type 3—80 per cent or more of the population lies within a city or cities of 300,000 to 999,999 population.

Type 5—80 per cent or more of the population lies within a city or cities of 100,000 to 299,999 population.

Type 11—80 per cent or more of the population lies in places of less than five thousand population.[7]

Two or more of these district types were utilized in the selection of representatives to seventeen of the twenty-five chambers for which occupational data were available. These seventeen chambers are incorporated in Table 4 which shows for each of these district-types what percentage of their representatives in the legislature were members of the legal profession. The variance in the tendency to send lawyers ranges between the ultimate possible extremes—all of the members in the New York Senate from district-type 5 (dominated by such cities as Albany, Syracuse and Yonkers) were lawyers; none of the members in the New York House from district-type 11 (strictly rural) were lawyers.

It is hard to find in Table 4 any evidence of an established relationship between degree of urbanization and tendency to send lawyers to the legislature. In the case of thirteen chambers, the strictly rural districts (Type 11) included a smaller percentage of lawyers in their delegations than did districts of any other type. On the other hand, there were two chambers (Senates of Illinois and New Jersey) whose rural delegations contained a higher proportion of lawyers than did the delegations sent by the cities. If the forty-seven figures which are entered under the district-type headings (exclude the figures for "all districts") are arranged in order from the smallest to the

largest (i. e., from 0. to 100.), it will be found that seven of the ten smallest figures represent the strictly rural districts (district-type 11) and that only one of the ten largest figures represents the strictly rural, or district-type 11. Fourteen of the seventeen figures which represent district-type 11 fall below the median figure. On the other hand, four of the figures for the strictly metropolitan districts (district-type 1) fall below the median, as compared with three which appear above. Cities from 100,000 to 999,999 are definitely lawyer-inclined. Only three of the figures for these types of district (district-types 3 and 5) appear among the ten smallest figures; eight appear among the ten largest figures. Five of the twenty-three figures for districts of these types fall below the median; sixteen lie above the median; two are tied with a rural figure for the median position.

It is frequently suggested that the lawyer-legislator is not really a practitioner at law, or, if he is, not a very good one, and, therefore, that figures such as I have given greatly overstate the importance of the lawyer-mind in the legislative assembly. This conclusion seems not to be justified. The members of five senates and six lower houses who,

Table 4—Showing, by Chambers, Percentage Relation of Lawyer-Representatives to All Representatives Sent by Various Types of District, Classified on an Urban-Rural Basis

State and Chamber	URBAN-RURAL CHARACTER OF DISTRICT				
	Type 1	Type 3	Type 5	Type 11	All Districts
California					
House	22.2	51.8	59.1	32.4	34.3
Illinois					
House	31.2			23.9	29.7
Senate	24.2			46.7	32.7
Indiana					
House		36.5		19.7	23.5
Senate		52.8		19.2	34.3
Louisiana					
House		42.3		25.6	32.4
Senate		51.9		26.9	46.5
Minnesota					
House		47.7	33.3	7.1	18.1
Senate		62.5	60.0	29.7	40.3
New Jersey					
House			33.3	16.7	42.0
Senate			50.0	55.6	45.9
New York					
House	62.6	42.3	51.6	0.0	43.9
Senate	49.2	53.3	100.0	33.3	46.1
Pennsylvania					
House	23.9	16.1	14.3	12.6	17.7
Senate	47.8	12.5		18.8	33.0
Washington					
House		26.1	29.5	8.3	14.8
Senate		57.9	47.1	6.0	18.4

in the 1934 or 1935 session, identified themselves as lawyers or attorneys were checked against the listings in *The Martindale-Hubbell Law Directory,* 1936 edition.[8] Of 205 house members who called themselves lawyers, 149 (72.7 per cent) were listed in the legal directory as practicing lawyers; 65 of 78 senators (83.3 per cent) were listed; and 214 of the 283 (75.6 per cent) lawyer-members of the houses and senates combined were found in the *Directory.* Considering that the *Directory* presumably omits some bona fide lawyers and that many lawyer-legislators were difficult to locate in the volume because of uncertainty as to their business addresses, it seems fair to say that nearly all lawmakers who call themselves lawyers have adequate justification for doing so.

It also seems necessary to conclude that the lawyers who get elected to the legislatures are on the whole respectable members of the legal profession. Of ten Iowa senators, 1935 session, who identified themselves as attorneys, nine were listed in the *Law Directory*; of these nine, five were rated, "very high" as to legal ability; two others were rated "high," and the remaining two were rated "fair." No other chamber fared so well, though the Pennsylvania Senate approached this record.

Table 5 compares 149 house members and 65 senators (lawyer-members of six lower chambers and five senates in 1934 or 1935) with 200 practicing attorneys in Syracuse, New York, and 200 picked at random from Iowa cities of less than 15,000 population. This table seems to establish the lawyer in the legislature as a shade better than the members of this profession at large.

The Worker Class in the Legislature. The overabundance of law-trained men in the state legislature is intimately associated with another fact which, as pointed out above, emerges conspicuously from the quantitative data on which this study is based—namely, the absence from the legislature of any substantial number of persons who can be identified as belonging to the proletariat.[9]

By no stretch of the imagination can it be said that a propertyless worker-unemployed class is occupying seats in the legislature in keeping with its numerical importance in the whole population. If, giving that class a most inclusive definition, we assume that all legislators who declared themselves to be laborers, engineers, machinists, salesmen, or clerks belong to the worker class, we find a maximum of less than 1000 legislators, out of a total of nearly 13,000 members in the six sessions of the twenty-five chambers, who can be identified with the proletariat. At their greatest strength in the Pennsylvania House of 1935, they would have enjoyed 26.1 per cent of the voting power if they had stood together; in the chamber across the hall, however, their combined strength in that session would have equaled only 10 per cent of the total membership. In no other state could the proletariat, as above liberally defined, marshall anything like the strength which they enjoyed during the six-session period in Pennsylvania. In New Jersey, for instance, they constituted 5.8 per cent of the six-session membership of the House and 5.6 per cent of the Senate. In New York the comparable figures were 5.4 per cent for the House and 2 per cent for the Senate. This propertyless class was without so much as one member in the New York Senate of 1927 or 1929 or in either chamber of the New Jersey legislature of 1935. At no time during the six sessions did any member of the upper chambers of New Jersey or New York identify himself as any sort of manual laborer, other than what I have classified as "engineer or machinist."

Those interested in speculating on the likelihood that propertyless people will in the immediate future pave their way to power by conquests of state legislative positions will be interested to learn that the New Deal overturn seems to have worked no appreciable advantage to the propertyless worker-unemployed class, so far as possession of legislative seats is concerned. The personnel of seven lower chambers was checked in order to compare the occupational membership of the sessions of 1925, 1927 and 1929 (pre-landslide) with that of the sessions of 1933 and 1935 (post-landslide). Each major occupational group maintained or in-

Table 5—Comparison, as to Legal Ability, of 149 Representatives and 65 Senators Who Were Listed in the Law Directory with 200 Syracuse and 200 Iowa Attorneys

	No. of Lawyers	PERCENTAGE RATED Very High	High	Fair	Total Rated	Percentage Given No Rating
Members of six lower chambers	149	14.1	21.5	12.1	47.7	52.3
Members of five senates	65	40.0	16.9	12.3	69.2	30.8
Members of eleven chambers	214	22.0	20.1	12.1	54.2	45.8
Syracuse attorneys	200	14.5	7.0	10.5	32.0	68.0
Iowa attorneys	200	29.5	25.0	10.5	65.0	35.0
Syracuse and Iowa attorneys	400	22.0	16.0	10.5	48.5	51.5

creased its relative strength in one or more chambers, but suffered substantial losses in others. There is no basis for saying that, on the whole, one occupational group or class gained or lost in number of seats as a result of the landslide.

The Significance of the Occupational Distribution of Legislators. Throughout this discussion I have tried to avoid any suggestion that the *representation* which any class or part of society enjoys is measured by its *membership*—the number of seats—which it possesses in the legislature. Mr. A. N. Holcombe seems to me to fall into error on this point. He estimates the proportion of the American people which falls into each of the seven great economic classes which Bukharin identified: proletariat, capitalists, landlords, intermediate, transitional, mixed, unclassified. In answer to the question, "Which classes gain most from the normal operation of the American representative system?," Mr. Holcombe says: "It is possible to make a rough classification of the Federal Senators and Representatives upon the same basis as that adopted for the classification of the people at large. Such a classification should make it easier to answer the question, which classes are in a position to gain the most power under the American system of government?" Lawyers, together with "the whole intermediate class," he says, "are very greatly over-represented."[10]

Bukharin's classification of society may be valid for purposes of Marxist doctrine; it seems to me that it has only a very limited usefulness for contemporary analysis of legislative bodies. It may well be that when the social classes which Marx envisaged and Bukharin attempted to identify are forced into cleavage by the class struggle, spokesmanship for the different classes will be accurately measured by their numbers in the forum. But it should not be supposed that effective representation of the capitalist or the landowning class at the present time is in any sense measured by the relative numbers of capitalists and landowners in the legislature—which, I understand, is what Mr. Holcombe does suppose. Undoubtedly in the American political arena today the lawyer, the real estate broker, and the tenant farmer speak quite as confidently in the interest of a capitalist and a profit system as do those who, according to Marx, monopolize the advantages of that system. The *over-membership* of the "intermediate class," including lawyers, is our way of accomplishing the *over-representation* of the bourgeois classes, *grande* and *petite*.

The task of devising a representative system for legislative assemblies as practiced in the modern world is not simply one of assuring spokesmen, directly or indirectly, for all classes of people or

for all identities of interest. The task is, perhaps fully as much, one of making sure that the demands of certain groups will be submerged in the general public. I am not clear as to why the territorial or geographical constituency was originally established as our basic unit for representation. At least one of the reasons for our refusal to abandon territorial representation in favor of some form of economic or functional representation seems, on the other hand, to be pretty obvious— we are not willing to abandon our traditional symbol of equal representation for all; at the same time we are not willing to permit a propertyless worker-unemployed group to have places, proportionate to their numbers, in our policy-making bodies. The use of territorial constituencies has at least up to now permitted us to maintain capitalist-middle class control without avowedly violating the principle that, within the limits of enfranchisement, a man biologic is a man politic.

Discussion of alternatives to territorial constituencies seems to have centered upon one or the other of two possibilities: representatives might be allocated to people according to their economic status (landowners, industrial entrepreneurs, wage-earners), or representatives might be apportioned to people according to their societal function (bankers, farmers, coal miners).[11] If the first of these alternatives were adopted, if representatives were apportioned according to economic status, then surely little likelihood of retaining our symbol and at the same time maintaining our present class supremacy would exist. Mr. A. N. Holcombe, accepting Bukharin's classification, estimates that 51.7 per cent of our national adult population is of the proletariat. To allocate over 50 per cent, or even a much smaller proportion, of our congressional or state legislative seats to the propertyless worker-unemployed class is surely to invite that part of our population to take over not only our political system, but, through their control of political power, to take over the economic system as well.

It is not so clear what would be the effect on our present distribution of power between classes if representatives were allotted according to societal function (distinguished from economic status). Perhaps the aspirations of caretakers and charwomen who work in bank buildings could be smothered by declaring them to be bankers and thereby subordinating them to the greater voting power of the bond salesmen and customer's men who mistake themselves for captains of finance. On the other hand, if the janitor at the bank is thrown into a common constituency with all other caretakers, or cast into a more inclusive soviet of skilled or unskilled workers, he is in either event invited to send representatives to the legislature who are uncompromising in their spokesmanship and manuevering for the advantage of a worker class.

It is not to be supposed that the adjustment of the legislative constituency to either economic status or societal function will accomplish the immediate surrender of the class or classes which control the newspapers, write the public school curricula, and in other ways make attitudes what they are. Whether or not those who are now in power could, through some equivalent of gerrymandering and through the manufacture and manipulation of attitudes, maintain their position under an alternative system of representation, it is poor politics to give an inch to a man or to a group who will bend every effort to convert it into a mile.

The moral to this tale is that those who desire the perpetuation of bourgeois control in American legislative assemblies will do well to defend the use of geographic constituencies; and, no doubt, they will be well advised to resign themselves to farmers and lawyers as their representatives. Where, indeed, are the American capitalist and middle classes to find more effective spokesmen than in the individualistic, tradition-bound farmer and the fee-taking lawyer?

A great deal has been said about the "unfortunate consequences of farmer-dominated legislatures." Those who deplore the numerical importance of farmers in the legislature usually betray a confusion of *membership* with *representation*. Undoubtedly the city man has ample reason to bewail the existence of apportionments unduly limiting the number of representatives which urban centers may send to the legislature. But the over-representation of rural areas is not the same thing as "too many farmers." If apportionment were fairly handled—let us say, if one-member districts of equal population were laid out without conscious effort to discriminate for or against the city—farmers would dominate the voting in a very high percentage of districts and it is unlikely that the farmer contingent in the legislature would be materially reduced in more than a half dozen of our state legislatures.

The Lawyer as Lawmaker. It is popular also to decry the prominence of the lawyer in our lawmaking bodies. The lawyer, it is said, has his nose buried so deeply in the past that he cannot elevate his eyes sufficiently for a good look at the present. "It is almost an inevitable characteristic of the legal mind," says Harold Laski,

that it should tend to conservatism. It is largely engaged in the study of precedent. What it can do is most often set by the statutes of a preceding genera-

tion. Its chief exponents are, as a rule, men already well past middle age who come to positions of authority just when new wants they have not known are coming to be expressed. Lawyers, in fact, are more definitely the servants of tradition than any other class in the community; for the demonstration that novelty is desirable is, with them, more difficult, because more impalpable, than with any other aspect of social life.[12]

Mr. Laski does not say specifically that these thought and habit patterns beset the lawyer while he is acting in a lawmaking capacity, but the context in which the statement appears testifies to a belief that they do. Mr. Brooke Graves, now rising to prominence in the American literature of politics, says that just such a character as Mr. Laski ascribes to the legal mind is "significant because it constitutes a considerable part of the explanation of the fact that it is difficult to secure the passage, by our state legislatures, of liberal measures of a social or economic character."[13]

Nowhere in the literature of the subject do I find any *evidence* to support the supposition that law practitioners, when considering legislation, are bound up by a precedent-mongering habit. No doubt the attorney meets many of his problems of counseling clients in the state of mind which Mr. Laski ascribes to the lawyer in the above quotation. But to say that lawyers, when counseling clients, must constantly keep in mind the rules under which men's actions will be judged if they come to litigation surely constitutes no strong reason for saying that when they are in a position to change the rules lawyers can act only to confirm the existing understandings. If the lawyer transfers his client-advising and court-arguing ways to the legislative assembly, must it not be supposed that the same state of mind rules him when acting as a functionary in that other great policy-making institution, the family? Will it be said that when the lawyer is admonishing his children he shows especial tendency to harken back to ancestral ways—that lawyers above other people are prone to say, "Your grandfather would not permit me to shoot firecrackers in the living room; let the decision stand."

If lawyers reckon from existing understandings in advising clients, so also they advise clients as to possible interpretations of the law which will permit the action which the client wishes to take. Indeed it might be said that the more prosperous practitioners of law specialize in avoidance of understandings. Might we not say then that lawyers make our most progressive legislators because they are practiced in studying how old rules might yield to new for the benefit of present and future generations? It is said that lawyers rank next to engineers in their ability to win high executive positions in business corporations. Is this because lawyers demonstrate a tendency to paralyze action or is it possibly because business men have found that lawyers are facile in devising and executing programs of action?

If lawyers carry their professional thought and habit patterns into the legislative assembly, do other occupational groups do likewise? Are farmers, as legislators, inclined to plant small seeds and husband them into flowering social institutions? And if so, do they insist that the fruit be ready for harvest within a foreseeable time? Does the architect, in the legislature, demonstrate richness in capacity for planning social institutions? Does the taxi driver, when making laws, forge straight to his objective, looking neither to left nor to right? Are preachers useless above all men because their learning is in the ways of ancient Judea and Israel and their professional concern is for a life where statutes of limitation can have no effect?

The foregoing paragraphs may clear the lawyer-legislator of the charge of precedent-mongering, but still leave him indicted as a chief opponent of legislative change. Any individual lawmaker can be expected to defend his personal interests against legislative attack, and members of any occupational group can be expected to stand side by side in opposition to measures adverse to their common interests. Doctors furnish the principal resistance to socialization of medicine; insurance men are ever ready to protect the stake of widows and orphans in insurance policies. Quite naturally lawyer-members of the legislature are constantly on watch to protect the lawyers' interest in the law.

But the stake of the legal profession in the existing law is nearly all-embracing. Law is the material with which the lawyer works, as clay is the medium of the sculptor, and religion the stock-in-trade of the preacher. Every proposed enactment is a challenge to the attorney serving in the legislature. If it alters an important relationship, he may have to reassociate a great body of knowledge; if it alters an important procedure, his skill may be rendered obsolete.

Impelled by this catholicity of self-interest and fortified by numbers, the lawyer group in the legislature stands as a potential obstruction to every statutory innovation. The force of this resistance has never been objectively measured; my own observations suggest that the literature greatly overstates its importance.

The basic data of this article are descriptive of twelve state senates and thirteen lower chambers. It is improbable that the story would change greatly if it were extended to embrace all of the American state assemblies. But the account, even for the twenty-five chambers examined, is only a partial one. The fate of a very large proportion of proposed legislation is determined by the action of the reporting committee. Perhaps lawyers monopolize the committees on the judiciary and the criminal code, and thereby lay a withering hand on legislation which would alter the organization and procedure of courts, and the substantive and adjective law of crimes. Perhaps farmers, by holding all appointments to the committees on agriculture, really write the agricultural law of the forty-eight states. An extension of the investigative method used for this article would reveal the truth or fallacy of such suppositions.

Notes

1. This article is part of an extended study of thirteen representative state legislatures, during six sessions from 1924 to 1934 or 1925 to 1935. The thirteen states are: Arkansas, California, Illinois, Indiana, Iowa, Louisiana, Maine, Minnesota, Mississippi, New Jersey, New York, Pennsylvania and Washington. The six sessions chosen bridge the political landslide beginning in 1930 and represent periods of both Republican and Democratic dominance. In case of legislatures having annual sessions (New Jersey and New York) only figures for the odd year sessions are used. For explanation of the methods used in compiling data, see article by C. S. Hyneman and H. Lay, "Tenure and Turnover of the Indiana General Assembly," (1938) 32 *American Political Science Rev.*, pp. 55-57, notes 9 and 10; and M. Fletcher, "The Use of Mechanical Equipment in Legislative Research," (1938) 195 *Annals of American Academy of Political and Social Science*, pp. 172-175.
The study was made possible in part by grants of money from the Graduate Research Fund of the University of Illinois; in part by the resources of the Bureau of Government Research of Louisiana State University.

2. The principal limitations on the reliability of data are: (1) Only information given in printed biographical sketches and in tables printed in journals or other documents was available for twelve states; for Louisiana, data were collected by questionnaire or conversation. No doubt many of the data supplied in this fashion were inaccurate; perhaps many a man who called himself a contractor had better been classed as a workman. (2) Occupations were arbitrarily classified. Dorothy Schaffter found 152 different occupations and combinations of occupations in fifteen sessions of the Iowa legislature. All occupations are combined into fourteen occupational groups in this study. A "banker-lawyer," for instance, is called a banker, but a "lawyer-banker" is called a lawyer. (3) For many members, the occupation could not be learned. This makes all percentages inaccurate. Of 786 members who served in the Minnesota House of Representatives during 1925 to 1935, the occupations of 93 are unknown. This missing factor (11.8 per cent of the total membership) forces a large margin of error into any comparative figures which can be derived.

3. Figures in Table 1 relate to memberships and not to different individuals. Any man, for instance, who served in three sessions during the period embraced in this study was counted three times.

4. Table 1 indicates that ten different occupational groups were third in importance in twenty-six chambers, that eight different occupational groups were fourth in importance in twenty-eight chambers, and that nine dif-

ferent occupational groups were fifth in twenty-four chambers. Yet exactly twenty-five chambers were examined. This apparent error is due to the fact that when two occupations were equal in importance, they were accorded the same rank. Table 2 shows, for instance, that newspapermen and professional men were of equal importance in the New Jersey Senate. Both were listed as third in numerical importance in that body.

5. Table 3 shows that farmers and lawyers were evenly matched in number of veterans in the Indiana Senate. Contractors took first place with 23.2 per cent of all members.

6. In the following analysis references to the "whole population" are to the gainfully employed population above the age of twenty, and all computations relating to the importance of occupations in the general population are founded on the gainfully employed population above the age of twenty. This rules out any consideration of the unemployed, but that seems inevitable in an analysis of occupational groups, in view of the character of available census data. The unemployed receive attention later in this discussion.

7. The peculiar numbering (1, 3, 5, 11) is due to the fact that districts were grouped into twelve classes on an urban-rural basis, only four of which are believed to be significant for the present analysis. The numbers used here are consistent with those which will be used to refer to the urban-rural character of districts in forthcoming studies.

8. Published by Martindale-Hubbell, Inc., New York City. The six lower chambers selected are those of California, Illinois, Iowa, Louisiana, New York and Pennsylvania; the five senates are those of the same states, except-ing California for which senate occupations are unknown.

Only attorneys who have been in practice at least ten years can get a rating of "very high" in the *Directory,* and only those who have been in practice at least five years can get a rating of "high." An effort was made to check the members of certain 1925 sessions in the 1936 *Directory* to see how many lawyer-members subsequently achieved a "high" or "very high" rating, but this proved not feasible because of changes in address which made checking extremely difficult.

9. Efforts to obtain data as to income of legislators from federal and state income tax authorities failed. The statements of occupation by legislators supply the crudest sort of basis for estimating the numerical importance of workers in the legislature, yet that is the information relied on in this study.

10. A. N. Holcombe, *Government in a Planned Democracy* (New York, 1934), pp. 44 *et seq. Cf.* Holcombe, *The New Party Politics* (New York, 1933).

11. "The term functional representation is used in political science to describe the representation of specific economic groups, such as the workers or the employers in particular industries or both workers and employers together, the members of a profession and so forth. It must be distinguished from representation by class or rank or wealth, although in some cases the two groups may coincide." W. A. Robson, "Functional Representation," in *Encyclopaedia of the Social Sciences,* vol. 5, p. 518.

12. H. J. Laski, *A Grammar of Politics* (New Haven, 1925), p. 572.

13. W. B. Graves, *American State Government* (New York, 1936), p. 182.

3. THE COMPOSITION OF THE GERMAN BUNDESTAG, 1950*

Otto Kirchheimer

AFTER A SEVENTEEN-YEAR interval without parliamentary government, Western Germany elected a representative assembly on August 14, 1949. Though German enthusiasm over the election was not excessive, electoral participation (78 per cent of those eligible to vote) compared favorably with that under the Weimar Republic. Invalid ballots (3.1 per cent) were higher than under the Weimar regime (1 per cent) but not high enough to attest to any appreciable opposition to the convocation of the parliament. The election boycott called for by a few rightist organizations failed to materialize, despite the fact that the parliament was elected within the framework of a provisional constitution which, while drafted by a German Parliamentary Council, owed its existence to Allied sanction.

Reprinted from *Western Political Quarterly,* Vol. 3 (1950), pp. 590-601, by permission of the author and the publisher.

* The author gratefully acknowledges the collaboration of Mr. Wallace F. Doer, of the Department of State, in the compilation of the statistical material.

Moreover, the election law set a very low residence requirement—three months in the territory of the Republic[1]—thus enabling most of the refugees, with the probable exception of a few thousand who had just arrived from the Soviet Zone, to participate in the elections. The number of those excluded from voting through decisions of the denazification tribunals or of Allied authorities did not amount to more than 0.2 to 0.4 per cent of the total electorate.[2] For these reasons, the *Bundestag,* in spite of the assertions of East German propagandists, can justifiably be called a truly representative body.

What kind of representatives did the West German electorate send to the *Bundestag?* Did they emphasize the need for a clean break with the past, or did they endorse former Nazis or old-time politicians from the Weimar period? To what extent did their choices follow their economic interests? How did the refugees fare? These are questions which are answered by the data presented in this essay.

Age-Composition of Members. The present *Bundestag* is no gerontocracy, although 16.2 per cent of its members are over sixty years of age. The average age of members at the time of the election was fifty, as it was for the "Indian Summer" Reichstag of 1928. Almost as many members were in their fifties (34.3 per cent) as were in their forties (35.1 per cent). The generation born immediately before, during, and after World War I is distinctly underrepresented; although representing 36.3 per cent of the eligible voters, it accounts for only 14.4 per cent of the *Bundestag*. However, this is not a feature peculiar to the Weimar or Bonn assemblies, but is equally true of the Canadian (19.1 per cent), American (13.8 per cent), and British parliaments (17.8 per cent). Only the Crisis Reichstag of 1932, containing its heavy contingent of Nazi "legislators" with an average age of forty-four years, reached even a rough balance between voters and members in the lower age group.

The average age of the opposition Social Democratic Party (SPD) members is somewhat lower than that of the Christian Democratic Union (CDU) members. There is no discernible age pattern among the other parties. Members of the Communist Party of Germany (KPD) are in the middle ranges, and the few members of the rightist opposition are relatively young.

Status of Members Under the Third Reich. A detailed knowledge of the activities of members during the Third Reich would be valuable in determining their present political outlook; but there are fairly large gaps in the information available about them, even though the biographical accounts have been furnished by the members themselves. Of the 402 deputies, 15.6 per cent have omitted data on their background during this period, except to designate military service in World War II. Some, as chance investigations have brought out, have done so because of involvement in Nazi politics; others (probably a minority), because they apparently have not desired to reveal their earlier obscure positions in life.

The greatest number of deputies (45.7 per cent) are men who throughout the pre-World War II period were clerks, insurance agents, salesmen, farmers, etc. While few members served in professional government positions under the Third Reich, a relatively high number (12.2 per cent) held leading positions in business, agricultural organizations, or the academic world. At the other extreme, the smallest number of deputies (6.8 per cent) are refugees who returned to Germany after 1945. A fairly large number (8.7 per cent) were in concentration camps or prisons for an extended period before and during the war. A slightly smaller number (7.7 per cent) suffered minor persecutions accompanied by loss of rights during the Nazi period.

Table I—Age of Bundestag Members on August 1, 1949, Compared with 1928 and 1932[1]

Age Group[2]	CDU/CSU	SPD	FDP	BP	DP	KPD	WAV	Z	NR[3]	Total, 1949	Per Cent, 1949	Comparative Figures, 1928 in Per Cent of Total 1928 Membership	Comparative Figures, July 1932 in Per Cent of Total 1932 Membership
Less than 30	1	2	1	..	..	1	1	..	1	7	1.7	.8	5.6
30 to 39	13	13	6	6	..	3	3	3	4	51	12.7	16.1	34.0
40 to 49	43	55	16	5	9	6	4	2	1	141	35.1	35.9	28.5
50 to 59	54	47	22	3	4	4	2	2	..	138	34.3	34.9	24.3
60 to 69	28	12	7	3	4	1	2	2	1	60	14.9	10.2	6.9
70 to 79	2	1	..	..	..	..	..	1	1	5	1.3	1.9	.7
80 to 89	..	..	..	..	..	..	..	..	..	..	..	.2	..
Total	141	130	52	17	17	15	12	10	8	402[4]	100.0	100.0	100.0

1. The average age of the 1928 and 1949 members was 50 years and the average age of the 1932 members was 44 years.

2. The dates chosen for each age group are August 2 for the lower age, and August 1 for the higher age. For instance, men were placed in the 30 to 39 age group whose birthday fell between August 2, 1919 and August 1, 1909.

3. And Independents.

4. All figures in tables I to IV refer to the composition of the *Bundestag* as of July 1, 1950 without the members from Berlin.

SOURCE: *Die Volksvertretung—Handbuch des deutschen Bundestags*, ed. Fritz Saenger (Stuttgart: J. G. Cottasche Buchhandlung, 1949); *Reichstagshandbuch, IV. Wahlperiode, 1928; Reichstagshandbuch, VI. Wahlperiode, 1932* (Berlin, 1928 and 1932).

ABBREVIATIONS:
BP—Bavarian Party
CDU/CSU—Christian Democratic Union/Christian Social Union
DP—German Party
FDP—Free Democratic Party
KPD—Communist Party of Germany
NR—National Right
SPD—Social Democratic Party
WAV—Economic Reconstruction Party
Z—Center Party

From the standpoint of party affiliations, a definite pattern emerges. Figures for members who held positions of leadership during the Nazi period are highest among the right-wing German Party (DP) and the Free Democratic Party (FDP), lower among the CDU, and insignificant among the SPD. Politicians who fled from Nazi Germany and later returned are almost exclusively Social Democrats or Communists. Similarly, those who served long sentences in concentration camps or prisons are predominantly SPD or KPD members, with only a few belonging to the CDU and FPD. The remaining categories—those who suffered minor persecutions during the war, those who held jobs of small importance, and those with unspecified status—are fairly evenly distributed among all political groups. While records of active struggle against and persecution by the Third Reich are found mostly among the political left, those who held leading positions in that regime are generally among the political right. However, a great number of members in most of the parties survived the Nazi regime in small jobs, without having ever desired or obtained positions which closely identified them with the Nazis.

Refugee Representation. The representation of refugees was cut down somewhat by certain military government rules prevailing at the time of the election. In order to encourage the assimilation of refugees into German political life, military government refused to sanction refugee parties except on a local basis. Refugee candidates running for the election as representatives of refugee organizations were, therefore, excluded from sharing in the distribution of the 160 regional seats accruing to the parties admitted on a *Land*-wide basis according to their share in the regional vote.[3] They could, however, enter the contest in the 240 single-member constituencies where election was by simple majority of the votes cast. Though they did so in some cases, winning approximately one million votes on lists of their own, in only one constituency was a refugee candidate victorious. In the main, therefore, refugees had to utilize the channels of the established national or regional parties in order to gain representation. Such compromises between refugee groups and established parties were effected in many regions and by many parties. It is difficult, however, to determine the exact number of *Bundestag* members that may be called primarily refugee representatives. In this connection, the figure of 24.8 per cent of the members born outside the present boundaries of the Republic does not have much meaning because mobility among those with an urban background has been rather high. Even pre-1939 or pre-1945 domicile outside the present territory of the Republic would not be controlling because many members settled in Western Germany immediately after the war ended, becoming fully assimilated in Western German social and political life. If allowance is made for all these factors, the number of members who may be styled representatives of refugees would be somewhere in the thirties. With an approximate total of three million refugee votes,[4] this group is decidedly underrepresented in the parliament.[5] Judging from their success in some of the Diet elections held in 1950, the refugees' share of the representation is bound to increase to about sixty to seventy in future elections.

There are sharp differences in the regional pattern of representation among the various parties. The SPD, with its tradition of a strongly centralized national organization, has a comparatively high percentage of members who come from outside the present federal territory, including those who fled from the Eastern Zone, where the party

Table II—Background and Activities of Members During Pre-World War II Nazi Period, 1933-1939*

	CDU/CSU	SPD	FDP	BP	DP	KPD	WAV	Z	NR†	In Per Cent of Total Membership
Government Officials, Exclusive of Teachers and Minor Officials	3	..	4	1	..	..	1	..	1	2.3
Financial, Industrial, Agricultural and Academic Leaders	20	3	17	3	6	..	..	..	..	12.2
Armed Forces Career	1	..	1	..	..	..	2	..	..	1.0
Major Persecutees	4	20	..	..	..	11	..	..	..	8.7
Other Persecutees	11	12	3	2	..	..	..	..	3	7.7
Refugees Abroad	..	22	..	..	..	4	1	..	..	6.8
Minor Positions	85	55	16	7	9	..	4	6	2	45.7
Unspecified	17	18	11	4	2	..	4	4	2	15.6
										100.0

* Statistical data prepared from *Die Volksvertretung—Handbuch des Deutschen Bundestags*, ed. Fritz Saenger (Stuttgart: J. G. Cottasche Buchhandlung, 1949).

† And Independents.

was forced to merge with the Communist Party. At the other extreme, the CDU, representing more an agglomeration of independent regional organizations than a national party, and drawing a considerable amount of its strength from the indigenous rural and small town population, has relatively few members who come from outside the federal territory. Some other parties, particularly the FDP and the WAV have usually built their election strategy on alliances with refugee groups, as reflected in the relatively high percentage of refugee representatives among them.

Occupational Status of Members. The Parliaments of the Weimar Republic were elected according to strict proportional representation in large election districts, from lists prepared by regional party conventions and central party offices. Parliaments were made up of public and party officials and party journalists, intermingled with representatives of special interest groups, with members of the professions representing only a minor share of the composition. As to their social and educational background, members of the 1928 parliament coming from the working and white collar groups (42.8 per cent) did have a slight edge over members with a university education or a teacher's certificate (36.8 per cent).

The following analysis will try to show that neither political and social upheaval nor change in the electoral system (with 240 of the 402 representatives elected in single-member constituencies, and the remainder taken from lists prepared by *Land* party conventions) has brought about any substantial change in the occupational pattern of the representatives. The analysis will also try to separate social and educational background from present professional status.

To start with the social and educational background: In keeping with German tradition, 41.1 per cent of the *Bundestag* members hold university degrees or teacher's certificates; these furnish the strongest contingent. Approximately 50 per cent of the middle-class and rightist representatives have university training, while members with business backgrounds without previous academic training amount to only 6.7 per cent. The second largest group comprises those who have come up from the rank of the white-collar professions (22.1 per cent); these are most heavily represented in the SPD. Of the members of the Bonn Assembly, 16.7 per cent began as manual workers, the proportionally highest number of them belonging to SPD and CDU. If their percentage has been on the decline since the Weimar assemblies, this is largely due to a steep decrease of KPD representation in the present *Bundestag*.

Educational and social background has no direct bearing on present professional status, however; nor is this professional status always expressed by official membership in a specific professional group. Many a member calls himself a worker or employee, although he may have been ordained as a clergyman or inscribed in the lawyer's register. Furthermore, although their profession may have served such members as jumping off points for their political careers, once in parliament they may represent certain groups which have no connection, or only a slight one, with their professional listings. Table III, therefore, lists the members according to the major interest they represent and according to the role they actually play in public and political life, irrespective of their formal professional classification.

Group Listings. The presence of a considerable number of public officials seems to be a permanent feature of German political assemblies. Their representation in the *Bundestag* (22.1 per cent) is even higher than that in the 1928 *Reichstag*.

Table III—The Professional and Educational Background of Members*

	KPD	SPD	Z	CDU/CSU	FDP	DP	BP	WAV	NR†	Total	In Per Cent of Total Membership	Comparative Figures 1928 in Per Cent of Total 1928 Membership
Manual Worker	10	41	1	11	2	..	..	1	..	66	16.7	27.5
White Collar	4	46	4	19	2	4	1	5	4	89	22.1	15.3
University and Teachers, Officer Training	..	40	4	68	31	6	10	3	4	166	41.1	36.8
Business	..	1	..	9	10	3	2	2	..	27	6.7	4.1
Small Business	..	1	1	12	1	3	1	..	..	19	4.7	5.1
Agricultural	..	..	..	18	6	1	3	1	..	29	7.2	10.6
Housewife	1	1	..	4	..	..	..	..	..	6	1.5	0.6
Total	15	130	10	141	52	17	17	12	8	402	100.0	100.0

* Statistical data prepared from *Die Volksvertretung—Handbuch des Deutschen Bundestags*, ed. Fritz Saenger (Stuttgart: J. G. Cottasche Buchhandlung, 1949); also from *Reichstags-Handbuch, IV. Wahlperiode 1928* (Berlin, 1928).

† And Independents.

However, closer scrutiny shows that today, as under the Weimar Republic, the overwhelming number of public officials elected to parliament (20.9 per cent) hold their jobs on an elective and temporary basis as representatives of political parties.[6] This applies—in addition to the federal ministers—to the *Land* ministers, the mayors, and the *Landräte*. They are the middlemen between the professional civil service and the legislative assembly, and they also act as special pressure groups for their regional interests and the public bodies which they represent. Whether all of them should simultaneously hold two responsible public jobs—where one is more than enough—is debatable. It is especially so in the case of the *Land* ministers, as the federal constitution has made provision to enable them to make their influence felt in the *Bundesrat*. Consequently, the Rhineland-Westphalia constitution of June 1950 (Article 64 [4]) establishes incompatibility be-

*Table IV—Present Professional Status of Members**

	KPD	SPD	Z	CDU/CSU	FDP	DP	BP	WAV	NR†	Total	In Per Cent of Total Membership	Comparative Figures 1928 in Per Cent of Total 1928 Membership
Officials with Political Background	..	30	1	40	7	2	3	..	1	84	20.9	15.3
Career Officials	..	1	1	1	..	1	1	..	..	5	1.2	3.6
Party and Related Functionaries	8	30	2	8	2	1	3	3	4	61	15.2	20.0
Journalists, Writers Publishers	4	19	..	5	5	..	..	..	..	33	8.2	12.0
Refugee and War Damaged Leaders	..	10	1	6	6	1	..	6	3	33	8.2	...
Proprietors and Managers of Financial and Industrial Enterprises	..	4	..	13	13	3	2	..	..	35	8.7	5.7
Officers of Industrial Associations	..	..	..	3	..	2	..	..	..	5	1.2	2.5
Proprietors of Agricultural Enterprises and Officers of Agricultural Organizations	..	2	1	20	7	2	3	2	..	37	9.2	13.7
Artisans and Proprietors of Other Retail Enterprises and Officers of Retail and Artisan Organizations	..	1	..	11	2	2	1	1	..	18	4.5	6.5
Trade Union, Consumer, Cooperatives and Sickness Insurance Officials, and Works Council Officers	2	20	1	8	1	2	..	..	..	34	8.5	10.6
Workers	..	..	..	1	1	..	..	..	..	2	0.5	0.2
White Collar Employees	..	1	..	..	..	..	..	..	..	1	0.3	...
Professions												
Lawyers	..	4	2	11	5	1	3	..	..	26	6.3	3.3
Teachers	..	4	1	7	2	..	..	..	..	14	3.7	3.5
Clergymen	..	1	..	3	..	..	..	..	..	4	1.0	0.4
Doctors	..	2	..	1	1	..	..	..	..	4	1.0	0.3
Architects	..	..	..	1	..	..	1	..	..	2	0.5	...
Housewives	1	1	..	2	..	..	..	..	..	4	1.0	0.4
Total	15	130	10	141	52	17	17	12	8	402	100.0	100.0

* Compilation of statistical data was made with reference to *Die Volksvertretung—Handbuch des Deutschen Bundestags*, ed. Fritz Saenger (Stuttgart: J. G. Cottasche Buchhandlung, 1949); also to *Reichstags-Handbuch, IV. Wahlperiode* (Berlin, 1928). However, see above for method of interpretation.

† And Independents.

tween holding the office of *Land* minister and membership in the *Bundestag*.[7]

This prohibition against dual political office on the federal level and *Land* level, deriving both from the need for greater efficiency and for a clearer delineation of federal and *Land* functions, has little relation to the traditional fear of subservience of the legislative members to the executive branch of the government, which has lost its meaning in the modern, party-directed democratic state. So has the need for protecting the officials' political neutrality, at least so far as political officials themselves are concerned.[8] However, the old concept of incompatibility, though it has less applicability today, is upheld both in American-inspired military government legislation and, in a diluted form, in the *Bundestag* election law,[9] though it is honored more in the breach than in the observance. Yet, the survival of the old style incompatibility concept may be one of the reasons why the number of career officials, never very high in the German political assemblies of this century, has dropped to insignificance in the present *Bundestag* and is now much lower than the corresponding number of public officials in the total population whose interest they ostensibly represent. Moreover, among the appointed officials who have been elected to the *Bundestag*, there are not only old-style career officials but also administrators, such as directors of labor exchanges or deputy *Landräte*, who hold their jobs on account of their trade union or political background. In contrast to the Weimar Reichstag, there is no member of the judiciary in the *Bundestag*.

The triads of political officials, party functionaries, and the closely related group of journalists comprise well over one-third of the total membership. The new grouping of refugee leaders (8.2 per cent) forms the transition from the established professional political personnel to the representatives of special interest groups. In the representation of special interest groups, business stands out with 9.9 per cent. The fact that an increase in numbers of proprietors and managers has been accompanied by a decrease of full-time officers of industrial associations may probably be traced exclusively to the late start in the reorganization of such associations. The representation of agriculture has declined greatly since Weimar days, from 13.7 per cent to 9.2 per cent, because the most important agricultural regions of Germany are now outside the federal boundaries.

Next in importance are the trade unionists, and related professions whose percentage (8.5 per cent) seems rather low, if only for the reason that solely those members are counted who are directly employed by the trade unions, excluding those members who have risen from the union ranks and are now holding political or party office. Representation of artisans and retail enterprises has declined only moderately (4.5 per cent as against 6.5 per cent), in spite of the fact that the present *Bundestag*, unlike the old *Reichstag*, does not have a specific party for the representation of the interests of what in Germany would be regarded as small business. The deputies from professions, medicine, law, teaching, architecture, and the clergy with a total of 12.5 per cent, are somewhat more numerous than in 1928 (7.5 per cent). Among them the independent lawyers (as distinct from those retained by specific interest groups) though on the increase (6.3 per cent as against 3.3 per cent), do not amount to more than about half of the professional group.[10]

The same traditional patterns may be observed in the occupational distribution among the various parties. Though the majority of SPD members of the *Bundestag* originally came from the working or white-collar classes, they are now party officials, in government positions or journalists. Moreover, in spite of the official political neutrality of the German Trade Union Federation, twenty of its own or of closely related functionaries hold seats as SPD *Bundestag* members. In contrast, the CDU accounts for only eight of the trade union functionaries. Being a major government party in both the *Bundestag* and most *Länder*, its leaders are frequently found among political officials. Officials and representatives of agricultural and business interests together make up half of the total representation of the CDU in the *Bundestag*. The FDP as well as the DP (the latter a smaller, more regionalized party), both closely resembling the German People's Party and the German Nationalist Party of the Weimar Republic, show the strongest concentration of business interests, amounting to one-fourth of their members; although in absolute numbers of business representatives, they both have fewer than the CDU.[11]

The Return to Traditional Patterns. Thus, the change of the election system and the ensuing greater possibility and pressure for picking personalities, rather than machine politicians and special interest representatives, have not left any decisive imprint on the composition of the *Bundestag*. The picture which has emerged, as in so many other fields, is clearly one of restoration and return to old institutional patterns. Additional evidence of this is the fact that about 65 per cent had been active in pre-Hitler politics in some capacity although only eighteen members belonged to the Weimar Reichstag.

What are the reasons for this *Wiederkehr des Gleichen?* Is there a conspiracy of old-timers, of party hacks, and of business groups to bar new elements from entering the parliament? Such a theory, however conveniently it may serve as a propaganda device for those who oppose the new regime, has little foundation in fact. With somewhat more justice, as the age composition shows, one might point to the failure of the younger generation to get adequate representation. Yet this is neither a postwar nor a specific German phenomenon. There are always difficulties for younger people in finding recognition, and especially in the Germany of 1949, where, unlike other countries, a record of war heroism was no special recommendation. Moreover, many whose education and background might point to a political career, have been avoiding any association with present-day German politics. They feel the same deep-seated scepticism toward parliamentarianism that was so widespread in the Germany of the 1920's. Others simply fear to compromise their future careers by participation in politics under the occupation regime. Many may also have reservations about exposing their records during the Third Reich to public scrutiny, and may be waiting until denazification has been completely shelved. Whatever the reasons, there were many explanations which strongly favored the return of the traditional parliamentary pattern. On the political left, there was a fairly compact and loyal clientele of the former trade unions and of the Social Democratic and Communist parties. They considered it as natural, as the first stage of reidentifying themselves with the nation, to renew allegiance to their old leaders, who had emerged from concentration camps, from exile, or oblivion, and had started to rebuild their former organizations. Many of them—almost half of those now in the *Bundestag*—were now fifty and sixty years old, or older; but they recruited some of the younger party and union functionaries, together with a number of intellectuals who would carry on the cause.

To a lesser extent, the same pattern may be found among the middle-class groups. Men who had suffered for loyalty to their church or political organization, and had been forced out of office, were ferreted out by military government and put back into active politics. Their numbers, however, were quite small. In the first years after 1945, there was often a lack of suitable middle-class political personnel able and willing to serve under the conditions of the pre-currency stabilization society, with the pickings slim and the constant threat of having to cope with military government and denazification procedures. The Economic Council, instituted in 1947 as a preparatory step toward a full-fledged West German parliament, together with the 1948 currency reform, changed this situation. With the quickening pace in shifts of authority from Allied to German personnel, political jobs became more important as the making of legislative and administrative decisions reverted to German hands. The parties, though still very much in the formative stage, now served as more than mouthpieces for German claims and schools of democracy, where generous platforms for future reference could be elaborated. Yet these middle-class parties were desperately short both in politically acceptable leaders and, especially after currency reform, in funds. Thus, quite naturally, the politicians who during the high tide of denazification had helped to reestablish the businessman, now welcomed the financial and political support of the business interests.[12] Election platforms were trimmed accordingly, though the scramble for the refugee vote necessitated many concessions in verbiage, as well as the acceptance of some refugee candidates on the election lists in order to attract the votes of these new and politically untested groups.

Conclusion. The present *Bundestag*, therefore, is characterized—as were the Weimar assemblies —by two elements: (1) the representation of well-defined interest groups, the size of whose membership corresponds more to their economic power than to their numerical strength in the country; and (2) a considerable body of professional politicians. The small part played by the independent lawyer, as distinct from the legally-trained, interest-group representative or government official, is explained both by the prevalence of these well-organized groups and by the continuing, fairly-rigid party patterns. While primary groups, industrial and agricultural producers, unions and others thus continue to strive for direct group representation,[13] the necessary interparty arrangements continue to be effected by the political and party officials rather than by the free-wheeling parliamentary lawyer. In some contrast to its Weimar predecessors, the *Bundestag* is a hard-working, though very pedestrian assembly, it discourages political oratory of its small bunch of irregulars and radicals and is content with taking its political lights and directions from its two antagonistic leaders, the Chancellor and the leader of the Social Democratic Party.

Notes

1. Election law for the first *Bundestag* and the first *Bundesversammlung* of the Federal Republic of Germany of June 15, 1949; BGBL, p. 25, par. 1 (3).

2. *Ibid.*, par. 2 (3) and (4). In the U.S. Zone, where denazification was more severe than in the other Western Zones, 100,000 people had been temporarily deprived and 25,000 permanently deprived of their civil rights, including

the right to vote. However, by August, 1949 many, if not the majority, of the 100,000 had regained their status as full-fledged citizens, e.g., in Hesse, only 13,000 from a total of 2,901,000 eligible voters have remained disqualified as of August, 1949.

3. This share was to be calculated after the D'Hondt maximum figure system (*Federal Election Law*, quoted *supra*, par. 10).

4. For a more detailed study of the vote, see Otto Kirchheimer and Arnold Price, "Analysis and Effects of the Election in Western Germany," Department of State *Bulletin*, Vol. XXI (Oct. 17, 1949), pp. 563-73.

5. Their proportional share would have been fifty to sixty members.

6. As to the necessity to differentiate between political and career officials, see Max Weber, *Wirtschaft und Gesellschaft*, Vol. I, Part III, chap. VI.

7. For the more recent literature see: K. J. Partsch and W. E. Genzer, "Inkompatibilität der Mitgliedschaft in Bundestag und Bundesrat," *76 Archiv des Oeffentlichen Rechts* (1950), 187-204, and the discussion in the *Bundestag* of October 18, 1950, 92 Sitzung, pp. 3416-19. The problem of incompatibility cannot be discussed in full in this article, as it would need a total reappraisal of the relationship between parliament, government, and civil service. See however, Hildegard Krueger, "Gibt es eine Inkompatibilität für die Mitglieder der Gesetzgebungsorgane nach dem Grundgesetz?" in *106 Zeitschrift für die gesamte Staatswissenschaft* (1950), pp. 700-718.

8. The best survey of the whole problem of parliamentary incompatibility is still Werner Weber, "Parlamentarische Unvereinbarkeiten," *19 Archiv des Oeffentlichen Rechts* (1930), 161-254; see also Otto Kirchheimer, *The Historical and Comparative Background of the Hatch Law in Public Policy* (Cambridge: Graduate School of Public Administration, 1941), Vol. II, pp. 341-73.

9. See Military Government Law No. 20, concerning the election of certain public servants to the first *Bundestag;* the *Oeffentlicher Anzeiger für die Vereinigten Wirtschaftsgebiete*. 1949, No. 46, Art. I; and *Federal* Election Law quoted *supra*, par. 5, c(2). See also the *Landessatzung* for Schleswig-Holstein of January 12, 1950 (G. V. Bl., p. 3) par. 10, I and II.

10. A comparison between the present professional status of *Bundestag* members and the members of the 1947 elected Swiss *Nationalrat* shows significant similarities.

Switzerland's Lower House: Officials with political background, 21.2 per cent; journalists, 6.2 per cent; career officials, 4.6 per cent; functionaries of economic organizations (no distinction is made between trade union officials and officials of industrial organizations), 13.9 per cent; lawyers, 13.9 per cent; professions (teachers, engineers, doctors), 12.4 per cent; farmers, 11.4 per cent; industrialists, merchants, retailers, managers of corresponding enterprises, 13.9 per cent; unaffiliated workers or employees, 1.5 per cent; pensioners, 1.0 per cent. (Source: *Nationalratswahlen 1947, Beiträge zur Schweizerischen Statistik* [Bern, 1949], Vol. 22, p. 180.)

11. Since the completion of the present paper an article by Dolf Sternberger "Berufspolitiker und Politikerberufe" (*Die Gegenwart*, Vol. V [November 15, 1950], pp. 9-11), has come to the attention of this writer. Sternberger agrees with this writer on what both of us call the professional politicians, and the functionaries of social and economic interest groups, notwithstanding inevitable differences of evaluation. However, Sternberger does not give separate figures for the important postwar phenomenon, the refugee politician. Our opinions vary, however, on the usefulness of Sternberger's third and most important category, formed after Max Weber's "Honorationenpolitiker," the 38 per cent "amateurs" in politics. On the possibility of their survival Sternberger ostensibly pins whatever hopes he has for German politics. But the only common denominator between the lawyer, the industrialist, the farmer, and the professor and career civil servant, seems to lie in their formal independence from party pressure. This has not much to do with their independence of judgment. The paid party secretary and organizer may have as little or as much independent judgment as the chairman of the leather industrialists or of the regional farmers association even though the latter keeps their parties alive through their subsidies whereas the party functionnaire owes his job to the political organization.

12. The return to traditional middle class party financing by business, even to the extent of channelling subsidies through the same middleman used for such purposes before 1933, has been revealed in the hearings before the special committee of inquiry set up in the *Bundestag* session of October 5, 1950, 89. Sitzung, pp. 3288 ff.

13. See the discussion in H. F. Gosnell, *Democracy, the Threshold of Freedom* (New York: The Ronald Press Company, 1948), p. 231, and Kirchheimer, *op. cit.*, p. 350.

4. LOCAL GOVERNMENT EXPERIENCE OF LEGISLATORS

W. J. M. Mackenzie

IN AN ARTICLE PUBLISHED in *Public Administration* in Winter, 1951, I made some points about the representation of local government in the House of Commons, and illustrated them by statistics based on the biographies of M.P.s in *The Times* guide to the General Election of 1950. The statistics given were far from comprehensive, but seemed to me to show that "the House of

Reprinted from *Public Administration*, Vol. 32 (1954), pp. 409-423, where it appeared under the title, "Local Government in Parliament," by permission of the author and the publisher.

Commons is not really strong in experience of local government outside London."[1]

In preparing his book about the General Election of 1951, Mr. D. E. Butler collected from a variety of sources much fuller information about all candidates successful and unsuccessful, and he published a brief analysis referring to "Local Government in Parliament" in *Public Administration* in Spring, 1953.[2] His table, based on fuller information than mine, showed a rather higher proportion of M.P.s with experience in local government. His conclusion was that "when at least

36 per cent of M.P.s have served in Local Government, Local Authorities cannot seriously claim that they lack representation."

This is the sort of disagreement which arises when conclusions are drawn incidentally from data collected for other purposes, and there can be no real solution without a specially designed inquiry. In particular, we have been using in a rather loose way phrases like "experience in local government," and "representation of local government," which would have to be defined much more clearly in a proper inquiry. There are, however, two preliminary questions on which one can get some further light from material already available:

(*a*) Does information about candidates in Great Britain suggest any points of interest for further analysis, for instance about variations in practice between different parties, different areas, different types of local authorities, different types of M.P.s?

(*b*) There is no "absolute" standard of "adequacy" in these matters: can any "relative" standard be established by comparison between British practice and that of other countries?

The figures given here are given under considerable reserves as to their accuracy and comparability, and they do not justify elaborate statistical analysis. But they suggest some points which may be worth following further.

LOCAL GOVERNMENT AND THE HOUSE
OF COMMONS

I am greatly obliged to Mr. Butler for giving access to his card index of candidates in the election of 1951 and to Mr. G. M. Higgins for analysing Mr. Butler's data from the point of view of local government.

The information comes mainly from the candidates themselves. On general grounds one would expect its accuracy to be fairly high. The following are the most important points of definition:

(*a*) So far as possible, Mr. Higgins has followed the same practice in the definition of "Conservative" and "Labour" candidates as was adopted by Mr. Butler in his book about the election of 1951.

(*b*) The figures given cover all constituencies in England, Scotland and Wales, but exclude Northern Ireland.

(*c*) "Local Government experience" has been defined as past or present membership of any local authority in this area except a parish council. It may be wise to remind readers that this is a "conventional" definition, and says nothing about the length or quality of the experience; and that

it does not distinguish between present membership and membership in the past, recent or remote.

(*d*) I have continued to write rather loosely about the "representation" of local government in Parliament and in central assemblies in other countries. This is convenient, but "representation" is a word with various complex implications, and in a more formal study it might be wise to use a more colorless word such as "integration" to describe inter-locking membership of elected bodies at different levels.

Table I—Successful and Unsuccessful Candidates

CANDIDATES	CONSERVATIVE			LABOUR		
	Succ.	Unsucc.	Totals	Succ.	Unsucc.	Totals
Totals	312	293	605	295	318	613
With Local Government Experience	68*	102	170	155*	136	291
Percentages	22%	35%	28%	53%	43%	47%

* Mr. Higgins has found two more M.P.s with local government experience than has Mr. Butler.

Table 1 confirms for candidates what is already known about M.P.s: Labor candidates as a whole have more experience in local government than Conservative candidates. The difference is narrower for unsuccessful candidates than for M.P.s: that is to say, safe seats go more readily to local government men in the Labour Party than in the Conservative Party.

If the figures are analysed by type of constituency (as in Table II) it can be seen that the discrepancy between the Parties is largest in County Boroughs in England and Wales, and that Labour practice seems to vary less than Conservative practice between constituencies of different types. But too much weight should not be placed on these figures. The official classification of Parliamentary constituencies is from the political and social point of view rather arbitrary; and in any case national averages conceal wide local variations. For instance, it looks at first sight as if there were striking differences between Conservative practice in English County Boroughs and in Scottish Burghs; on a percentage basis Conservative candidates with local government experience seem to do four times better in Scotland than in England. But when the figures are looked at in detail it can be seen that the Scottish figures are based only on Edinburgh and Glasgow, and that there are wide variations between different English cities.

This is illustrated by Table III, which points to the danger of generalisation about local and national politics. In the last resort the political system is unified by party discipline in the House of Commons, and figures for the whole country bring out important facts about the House of Commons. But they also conceal wide local variations which are still of great importance in British politics.

If Labour on the whole gives more seats to men and women with local government experience than do the Conservatives, this suggests that it may be worth correlating the Labour figures with those for Trade Union M.P.s who hold a high proportion of safe Labour seats. The figures are familiar:[3] in the election of 1951, out of 137 Labour candidates backed by Trade Unions 104 were successful, out of 476 other Labour candidates 191 were successful. Out of 37 Labour M.P.s with majorities of over 20,000, 29 are T.U. M.P.s. Mr. Higgins has taken the seven Unions which are most active in parliamentary representation, and also all other Trade Union candidates, and the result is shown in Table IV.

These figures are interesting and may be unexpected. They can be re-expressed in two ways. The proportion of Trade Union Members with local government experience was far higher than that of any other class of M.P. (between 70 and 75 per cent) in both these Parliaments. Trade Union members are about one-sixth of the House of Commons, they supply about one-third of its experience of local government. It is hard to say what this means for the representation of local government: but the figures suggest that we should look again at some of the commonplaces about the place of the Trade Union M.P.s in British politics. Many of these men are local leaders as well as being Trade Union officials, and there are some areas in which this is very important both for Trade Unionism and for local government.[4]

But the matter can only be taken further by detailed study of particular areas and Unions.

Mr. Higgins has correlated local government experience with size of majority, and (as could be expected) a rather high percentage of Labour M.P.s with big majorities have had local government experience. This is largely a reflection of the position about Trade Union M.P.s, and it is unnecessary to reproduce his table here.

One point raised by Mr. Butler and myself was that of experience in local government "outside London." The definition of "London" is notoriously difficult: I took a wide definition of the Metropolitan area, Mr. Butler took a narrower one. To my mind, "political London" lies somewhere between the two: but there is no convenient statistical area that corresponds to it exactly, and it is certainly safer to use Mr. Butler's definition than mine, since there is no doubt that the whole of his area is metropolitan in character.

Mr. Butler found that out of 258 authorities mentioned by M.P.s a third (83) were in the Metropolitan area; 32 out of 67 Conservative M.P.s with local government experience had obtained it in that area, 41 out of 154 Labour members. Mr. Higgins has prepared an analysis by "regions" which puts the matter in a rather different light. Table V gives his figures in so far as they suggest points of interest.

The Metropolitan area in the narrower sense is outstanding in both parties for its ability to call on candidates with experience in local government; and the South-East, which (besides the East Anglian countryside) includes the outer suburbs of London, is also pretty high in its percentage of local government candidates. These

Table II—Successful and Unsuccessful Candidates by Type of Constituency

CONSTITUENCY	CANDIDATES	CONSERVATIVE			LABOUR		
		Succ.	Unsucc.	Totals	Succ.	Unsucc.	Totals
County Borough Constituencies (E. and W.)	Totals	69	106	175	106	71	177
	Local Government Experience	13	41	54	55	26	81
	Percentages	19%	39%	31%	52%	37%	46%
Other Parliamentary Boroughs (E. and W.)	Totals	56	72	128	73	56	129
	Local Government Experience	17	23	40	44	28	72
	Percentages	30%	32%	31%	60%	50%	56%
Scottish Burghs	Totals	12	19	31	20	12	32
	Local Government Experience	6	5	11	11	4	15
	Percentages	50%	26%	35%	55%	33%	47%
County Constituencies (Great Britain)	Totals	175	96	271	96	179	275
	Local Government Experience	32	33	65	45	78	123
	Percentages	18%	34%	24%	47%	44%	45%

areas together return 196 out of 613 M.P.s for Great Britain, so that their position in the House of Commons is extremely important and they contribute a large share of the *total* candidates with local government experience.[5] But the *percentage* of candidates from local government is not greatly above that in other areas, with the possible exceptions of the Midlands and the South-West, which include a high proportion of constituencies of a relatively old-fashioned rural type.

It should be noted that Table V relates to candidates with local government experience anywhere in Great Britain; the figures do not therefore match Mr. Butler's figures of 32 Conservative M.P.s and 41 Labour M.P.s with experience of "local government in or around London." This point is better illustrated by another set of figures

Table III—Successful and Unsuccessful Candidates: Some Large Cities

CITY	CANDIDATES	CONSERVATIVES			LABOUR			TOTALS (both Parties)
		Successful	Un-successful	Totals	Successful	Un-successful	Totals	
Birmingham	Total	4	9	13	9	4	13	26
	Local Government Experience	0	5	5	5	3	8	13
Edinburgh	Total	4	3	7	3	4	7	14
	Local Government Experience	2	1	3	0	0	0	3
Glasgow	Total	7	8	15	8	7	15	30
	Local Government Experience	4	1	5	8	4	12	17
Leeds	Total	2	5	7	5	2	7	14
	Local Government Experience	1	2	3	3	2	5	8
Liverpool	Total	5	4	9	4	5	9	18
	Local Government Experience	3	1	4	3	1	4	8
L.C.C. area	Total	14	28	42	29	14	43	85
	Local Government Experience	6	12	18	20	7	27	45
Manchester	Total	4	5	9	5	4	9	18
	Local Government Experience	1	3	4	3	1	4	8
Sheffield	Total	2	5	7	5	2	7	14
	Local Government Experience	0	1	1	1	0	1	2

Table IV—Trade Union Sponsored Candidates

UNION	CANDIDATES	1950 ELECTION			1951 ELECTION		
		Successful	Unsuccessful	Totals	Successful	Unsuccessful	Totals
N.U.M.	Total	37	0	37	36	1	37
	Local Government Experience	26	0	26	26	1	27
T.G.W.U.	Total	16	3	19	14	3	17
	Local Government Experience	12	0	12	11	1	12
N.U.R.	Total	10	2	12	9	2	11
	Local Government Experience	8	1	9	7	1	8
U.S.D.A.W.	Total	8	1	9	8	2	10
	Local Government Experience	3	1	4	2	1	3
R.C.A. (T.S.S.A.)	Total	8	4	12	7	4	11
	Local Government Experience	6	2	8	6	2	8
A.E.U.	Total	8	2	10	7	6	13
	Local Government Experience	7	0	7	5	4	9
N.U.G.M.W.	Total	6	4	10	4	1	5
	Local Government Experience	5	2	7	3	1	4
Other Unions	Total	18	14	32	19	14	33
	Local Government Experience	15	6	21	13	10	23
All Unions	Total	111	30	141	104	33	137
	Local Government Experience	82	12	94	73	21	94

NOTE: The Labour Party Annual Conference Reports have been taken as the authority for T.U. sponsorship: the details for 1951 are from Mr. Butler's card-index; those for 1950 are taken from other sources, chiefly *The Times* guide, and are thus less complete, particularly for unsuccessful candidates.

Table V—Successful and Unsuccessful Candidates by Regions

REGIONS	CANDIDATES	CONSERVATIVE			LABOUR			TOTALS (both Parties)
		Successful	Un-successful	Totals	Successful	Un-successful	Totals	
England:	Total	46	49	95	50	46	96	191
Metropolitan	With Local Government Experience	17	17	34	32	21	53	87
	Percentage	37%	35%	36%	64%	46%	55%	46%
*N.W.	Total	43	40	83	40	44	84	167
	With Local Government Experience	8	19	27	25	20	45	72
	Percentage	19%	47%	33%	62%	45%	53%	43%
Rest of England	Total	182	142	324	143	183	326	650
	With Local Government Experience	34	50	84	70	77	147	231
	Percentage	19%	35%	26%	49%	42%	45%	36%
Scotland	Total	35	35	70	35	36	71	141
	With Local Government Experience	8	8	16	16	14	30	46
	Percentage	23%	23%	23%	46%	39%	42%	33%
Wales	Total	6	27	33	27	9	36	69
	With Local Government Experience	1	8	9	12	4	16	25
	Percentage	17%	30%	27%	44%	44%	44%	36%

* Cumberland, Westmorland, Lancashire, and Cheshire.

Table VI—Candidates with Local Government Experience in Their Own Constituency

REGIONS	CANDIDATES	CONSERVATIVE			LABOUR			TOTALS (both Parties)
		Successful	Un-successful	Totals	Successful	Un-successful	Totals	
England:	Total with L.G.E.	17	17	34	32	21	53	87
Metropolitan	L.G.E. in own constituency	8	3	11	19	7	26	37
	Percentage	47%	18%	32%	59%	33%	49%	43%
North-West	Total with L.G.E.	8	19	27	25	20	45	72
	L.G.E. in own constituency	5	10	15	9	7	16	31
	Percentage	62%	53%	56%	36%	35%	36%	43%
Rest of England	Total with L.G.E.	34	50	84	70	77	147	231
	L.G.E. in own constituency	13	17	30	22	21	43	73
	Percentage	38%	34%	36%	31%	27%	29%	32%
Scotland	Total with L.G.E.	8	8	16	16	14	30	46
	L.G.E. in own constituency	6	7	13	14	6	20	33
	Percentage	75%	87%	81%	87%	43%	67%	72%
Wales	Total with L.G.E.	1	8	9	12	4	16	25
	L.G.E. in own constituency	1	2	3	9	3	12	15
	Percentage	100%	25%	33%	75%	75%	75%	60%
Totals	With L.G.E.	68	102	170	155	136	291	461
	L.G.E. in own constituency	33	39	72	73	44	117	189
	Percentage	49%	38%	42%	47%	32%	40%	41%

(Table VI), which relates to candidates with local government experience in the area for which they stood as candidates. The definition of "area" here is a little arbitrary, and there are minor discrepancies between the figures reached by Mr. Butler (who found 113 M.P.s with local government experience in their own constituency) and Mr. Higgins (who found only 106). This does not affect the general picture; once more the Metropolitan area and the North-West stand rather apart from the other regions of England, and it becomes obvious that Scotland and Wales have a pattern of their own which is unlike the English pattern.

Table VII (*a*) and (*b*) illustrates the special position of London more forcibly. There seems

Table VII—(a) Candidates with L.G.E. in Metropolitan Area

CANDIDATES	CONSERVATIVE			LABOUR		
	Succ.	Unsucc.	Totals	Succ.	Unsucc.	Totals
Total with L.G.E.	17	17	34	32	21	53
L.G.E. in Metropolitan Area	16	13	29	30	17	47
Percentages	94%	76%	85%	94%	81%	89%

Table VII—(b) Candidates with L.G.E. in L.C.C. Area

CANDIDATES	CONSERVATIVE			LABOUR		
	Succ.	Unsucc.	Totals	Succ.	Unsucc.	Totals
Total	14	28	42	29	14	43
Total with L.G.E.	6	12	18	20	7	27
L.G.E. in own M.B.	4	3	7	13	3	16
L.G.E. in Metropolitan Area	6	10	16	19	5	24

to be here a pretty strong indication of an established "ladder" from local to national politics, such as is familiar in some other countries. Nothing like this exists generally over a wide area elsewhere in Britain: but there are some marked local exceptions. For instance, 12 out of 15 M.P.s for Glasgow have had experience in local government: all 12 have served on Glasgow City Council.

OTHER COUNTRIES

When I suggested originally that local government is "under-represented" in the House of Commons, I was implying a rough comparison with the position in a number of other countries. It is a commonplace that in Britain the "carpet-bagger" has been a great figure in politics from the time of Queen Elizabeth I:[6] and that in many other countries there is (by con-

trast with this) a political "career" which leads from a local assembly to a regional assembly, and from there to the national assembly. We have all been told about the importance of the "locality rule" in American politics, as a means of bringing the parish pump to the Capitol. Where a ladder of this sort exists it may be much more important than the legal structure of local government. French local government is legally subject to strong central control; but many *Députés* are also members of local authorities, party discipline is not strict except in the Communist Party (which is now purely an opposition party), and the result is that political localism is often a good deal stronger than legal centralism. At the other extreme is Russia, where a relatively loose legal structure is made to work with rigid centralism by strict discipline within the governing party, which transmits orders down the party "ladder" to the aspiring party men in the local authorities. My original hypothesis, not very clearly framed, was that the forms of British law give local government a status of exceptional freedom, but that legal autonomy was over-ridden in practice by party discipline and the prevalence of the "carpet-bagger." I had hoped, after reading Mr. Butler's note, that it might be possible to put this in more exact form by statistical comparison with other countries: but on the whole I have to report failure. The trouble is that it is impossible to get adequate statistics on a fully comparable basis for any two independent parliamentary systems. I am, however, very much indebted to those who have helped in collecting figures, and I think it is worth presenting some of their material.[7] The figures seem to me to illustrate my point, but it is clear that they do not prove it; perhaps all that statistics can do in this field is to suggest problems for investigation in more direct ways.

WESTERN EUROPE

France. In the National Assembly elected in 1946, 219 *Députés* out of 544 had been or still were elected members of local authorities.[8] By the time of the 1951 elections matters had settled down somewhat, party discipline had weakened, and the focus of politics had moved from left centre to right centre. Probably the representation of local government had increased: out of 627 *Députés*, 185 were at that time elected members of Departmental Councils (including 26 who were chairmen of such councils) and 157 were *Maires* of fairly important Communes.[9] These figures partly overlap; on the other hand, they disregard past experience, membership of

Communal councils, and the smaller communes.

The second chamber (the *Conseil de la République*) is for the most part elected indirectly by members of local authorities, and the representation of local government is correspondingly high. Out of 200 members elected in France in 1946, 130 had local government experience. In 1953 among 320 members there were 138 serving Departmental Councillors (19 of them chairmen), 200 serving Communal Councillors (132 of them *Maires*). There are, of course, overlaps: but the 1953 figures relate only to present membership of local authorities.

This indicates that local representation in the first chamber is somewhat stronger than in Britain, and that in the second chamber it is very much stronger.

Its strength can be illustrated in another way. There are 90 Departmental Councils in France, and in 1953 the chairmen of 45 of them were members of one of the Houses. From the elections of June, 1951, up to November, 1953, 70 *Députés* had become Ministers; 30 of them were members of local bodies in 1951, six of them as Chairmen of Departmental Councils, ten as *Maires*.

Italy, Belgium and the Netherlands. These follow a similar pattern which can be illustrated briefly.

Table VIII—Experience in Local Councils of Members of the Italian Parliament in 1953

MEMBERS	TOTAL GIVING INFORMATION	LOCAL GOVERNMENT EXPERIENCE		
		Regional	Provincial	Communal
Deputies	434	9	41	208
Senators	243	3	41	121

These figures include some overlaps.

In Belgium, the important terms are *Bourgmestres* (Mayors with large executive powers), *Echevins* (members of the "steering committee" of a local authority) and Communal Councillors.

The corresponding terms for Holland are Burgomaster, member of a College, and local councillors: to these should be added membership of a Provincial Council and of a Provincial Executive, bodies intermediate between local and central government.

Table IX—Participation in Local Government of Members of the Belgian Parliament in 1950

Members	Total Membership	Bourg-mestres	Echevins	Councillors
Representatives	212	45	36	130
Senators	175	33	17	29

These figures do not overlap, and do not reckon past experience.

Sweden. This country is difficult to bring into the reckoning, because a good deal of administration at the local level is done by *ad hoc* bodies appointed by the elected local councils not necessarily from their own number; the position is that in 1950 out of 230 members of the Lower House, at least 177 had experience in a local council or *ad hoc* committee; out of 150 members of the Upper House, at least 109 had such experience.

These figures, rough though they are, illustrate the normal pattern in the democracies of Western Europe. There is a considerable range, of which one extreme is the Belgian Lower House, composed almost entirely of serving members of local authorities, and the other is Holland, where the percentage of experience in local government is about 40. This Dutch percentage is not much higher than the British percentage: but this is an extreme case, and on the whole the integration of local and national politics is much closer than in Britain.

SETTLED DOMINIONS

It is generally believed that local government is politically weak in the settled Dominions, with the possible exception of New Zealand. Unfortunately, I have no figures for New Zealand, Australia or South Africa; such figures as are available[10] for Canada suggest a situation more British than European or American. It is said that of the new members elected to the Canadian House of Commons for the first time in 1945, 32 per cent had experience of local government in municipalities or counties only, a further 9 per cent (some of whom may also have had "local" experience) had been members of provincial legislatures. The proportion of members recruited "from below" in this way had been declining at previous general elections: in 1945 the percentage of all members who had local experience was presumably still above the level of 32 per cent and 9 per cent.

Table X—Experience in Local Government of Members of the Dutch Parliament in 1953

House	Total Membership	Provincial Exec.	Provincial Council	Burgomaster	Member of a College	Member of a Local Council
Lower House	98	3	8	8	6	18
Upper House	49	2	2	6	6	3

These figures do not overlap, but do allow for past experience.

UNITED STATES OF AMERICA

The phrase "carpet-bagger" is American and spread at the time of the irruption of Northern candidates into the Southern States immediately after the Civil War, seeking to be returned by the new negro vote; there is an unwritten law that every member of the Federal House of Representatives must reside in his constituency, and it is generally regarded as improper to establish residence simply for political purposes. There is, therefore, no "squad" of national politicians detached from connections with local politics, as there is in Britain; this has important effects on the conduct of American government in general, and on the position of local and state government in particular. Table XI gives the figures for the 83rd Congress as it was in March, 1953; it includes some overlapping.

Table XI—State and Local Government in Congress

House	Total	State Governors	Members of State Legislatures	Locally Elected Officers
House of Represen- tatives	432	1	174	297
Senate	96	29	39	76

Source: biographies in the Congressional Directory.

Table XII—U.S. Legislatures: Experience in Locally Elected Bodies

State	House	Total Membership (not including vacancies)	Service on Some Locally Elected Body
Wisconsin (1949)	Assembly	100	72
	Senate	33	23
South Carolina (1951)	House	123	12
	Senate	45	1
West Virginia (1951)	House	94	13
	Senate	32	6
Nebraska (1951)	Single Chamber	45	15

Sources: Wisconsin figures from a survey made by the State Legislative Service of Wisconsin. The other figures from biographies in the State Reference Handbooks.

Congress has no direct responsibility for local government (except in so far as it refuses to concede it to the District of Columbia), and one ought, therefore, to follow the question into the State legislatures. But this raises great difficulties of comparability, as well as of the extent of the materials. The figures in Table XII illustrate the position in four very different States.

This shows a range from over 70 per cent in Wisconsin to 8 per cent in South Carolina. The variation may be partly due to variations in information given by members in their official biographies, some of which are extremely sketchy; but there is no doubt that conditions vary greatly and there is no basis for any generalisation below the Federal level.

EASTERN EUROPE

It would be interesting to follow this into Eastern Europe, if it were possible. The question of the integration of local and central authorities arises even in a dictatorship, and the original Soviet formula was that of "election up" through a pyramid of local authorities, so that all members of the Supreme Soviet were associated with some local Soviet. The 1936 Constitution replaced this system by one of direct election; no complete statistics are available, but what information there is suggests that the practice bears traces of the old system and that it is quite common for members of the Supreme Soviet to be also members of a local Soviet.

This is certainly the position in Yugoslavia, which has deviated from Stalinism without any fundamental change in constitutional structure. There are fairly reliable figures for the position in the Assembly of the Federal Republic of Croatia in 1953: out of 250 members, 97 were then members, and another 86 had previously been members, of local elected bodies. I have no figures for the central parliament of the Federation: the figures for the other Federal Republics are unsatisfactory because they include under this heading only members not otherwise classified. The total figures must, therefore, considerably exceed those shown in Table XIII.

Table XIII—Members of Federal Assemblies in Yugoslavia in 1953 Classified as Members of Local Authorities

Assembly	Total Membership	Membership of Local Authorities
Serbia	338	134
Slovenia	283	47
Bosnia-Herzegovina	270	123
Macedonia	245	81
Montenegro	160	62

CONCLUSION

This reference to Eastern Europe may serve to illustrate again my main point. In different countries there are varying degrees of integration between local government and central government on two different scales, a legal scale and a political scale. The legal situation may not correspond closely to the political situation, and the latter may be difficult to assess, because close and loose integration may both work in two ways. Close integration may mean that the localities move the centre or that the centre moves the localities: a looser relationship may mean that the local authorities are free—or simply that they are disregarded. The matter is one of political structure, and is too delicate to be measured by the very crude statistics available. Perhaps the statistics do something to confirm what one would expect on other grounds, that there are four main patterns of relationship: that of Britain and the settled Dominions, in which local government has much freedom in law, but is apt to be disregarded in practice; that of the democracies of Western Europe, in which local authorities are more limited in law, but have greater political influence (this is obviously related to differences in cabinet systems and party systems, as well as in the tradition of administrative law); that of the U.S.A., where peculiar conditions are created by great diversity of local forms and by the separation of powers, which enables Congress to remain obstinately local without doing serious damage to the national interest; and that of Eastern Europe, where Party overrides State, and the important matters are those decided in the inner councils of the Party.

Notes

1. *Public Administration*, Winter, 1951, p. 355.
2. *Public Administration*, Spring, 1953, p. 46.
3. These given here are taken from the Labour Party Annual Conference Report for 1951; it is known that they are in some respects inaccurate.
4. Co-operative M.P.s conform more closely to the ordinary Labour pattern; out of 17 elected in 1951, 7 had local government experience.
5. 96 out of 223 M.P.s, 168 out of 461 candidates.
6. Compare, for instance, the work of Professor Neale, Mr. Pennington and Mr. Brunt, Professor Namier and Professor Gash.
7. My thanks are due to Mr. P. W. Campbell (France), Dr. Brian Chapman (Italy), Mr. John Grundy (Holland and Belgium), Mr. N. C. M. Elder (Sweden), Mr. J. W. Grove and Mr. A. M. Potter (U.S.A.), Mr. D. J. R. Scott (Yugoslavia); some of these gentlemen obtained private information from officials, to whom we are much indebted. Published sources have been specified where used.
8. *Le Monde*, "Elections et Referendums," Vol. 1.
9. *Notices et Portraits* of the National Assembly.
10. N. Ward, *The Canadian House of Commons: Representation* (University of Toronto Press, 1950), p. 122.

B. Conceptions of the Legislator's Office and Role

5. THE TASKS AND FUNCTIONS OF THE LEGISLATOR

Herman Finer

WHETHER the mandate comes from the constituency or from an association or the party, its exercise requires the member to think, discuss, and determine—the last being expressed by his vote. In modern legislatures everywhere, the large majority of members does little more than vote; only a few discuss; and a very small minority thinks effectively. The composition of these functions varies a little from country to country, but generally the emphasis is upon will or power—that is, upon the vote. This is a direct corollary of the majority principle; and it seems a parlous condition until we reflect that, after all, the real thought has already been accomplished outside the legislature and will yet be accomplished, completed, and applied to all points of practical detail by the opposing groups of leaders and the permanent officials. Fundamentally, a legislature is a forum where men may measure the strength of each other's will as expressed in their numbers and in other demonstrations of strength of feeling and purpose, and may either enter into agreements by mutual concessions or vote each other down.

Legislators as Policy Makers. Broadly, policies are made or adopted by political parties. This does not always or chiefly mean that the members of a party or its leaders are inventive, that they conceive and elaborate schemes of reform or conservation. They are certainly disposed to do this by character and the stimulus of their experience. Some, indeed, do discover the answer to problems and the means of fulfillment. Upon reflection, however, it will be seen that not many such inventions are due to party and legislative persons. The politician is a broker rather than an inventor. And not infrequently he must be prompted vigorously before he satisfies his clients.

Those who discover issues, and explore and plan the means of their settlement, are the thoughtful and sensitive among the population, though they may be, and in our own day usually are, voluntarily attached to some specific party. Consider the immense industrial and commercial associations, the social groups of all sorts with which every country now teems, the municipalities and their associations; consider the reformers and thinkers like Bentham and Chadwick, Tom Paine, Judge Lindsey, Henry George, Bernard Shaw, the Webbs, Lassalle, Mazzini, Raffeisen, Plimsoll, the Prohibitionists, the Bimetallists, Adam Smith, Rignano, Tolstoy, Marx, Marie Stopes, Veblen, Jane Addams, Octavia Hill, Florence Nightingale, Bellamy, Jevons, Keynes, Havelock Ellis, and others who first pursued lonely paths and were later joined by disciples who surged forward to harass, press, and sometimes to convince political parties. All these geniuses of sensitiveness and intellectual comprehension, these masters of history and moral value, are the true manufacturers of the politicians' stock-in-trade. This is quite natural, for to govern well has always required the rarest degree of knowledge and wisdom.

* * *

The world of special groups, philosophy, and social speculation, then, furnishes the politician with his material. Nor must we forget that in that world the politician has his own salaried professional philosophers and contrivers—the civil service, which not only thinks and plans but also explores and formulates what the rest of the world is thinking and planning. It is a professional machine to acquire, to assimilate, to cut and dry the world's intellectual and emotional produce and put it up in the form which politicians may understand and employ. Of major importance is it also that, in our own time, international secretariats of the specialized agencies—first in the League of Nations and now in the United Nations Organizations—have grown up to add to their carefully formulated thoughts and ideals.[1]

Politicians not Philosophers. The politician is not always chosen for his knowledge, nor always for his character. He is chosen because he represents the views of a certain party, and because he

Reprinted from *The Theory and Practice of Modern Government* (New York: Henry Holt and Company, revised edition, 1949), pp. 379-384, by permission of the author and the publisher.

can win the seat (and this implies, quite naturally, that talented men without campaigning qualifications—kinetic, pachydermatic, confidence-winning—are rarely chosen as candidates).

* * *

The member is a vehicle of the party, and the party is chosen because, fundamentally, it embodies the material and spiritual interests of the people who choose, and it is chosen to dominate the state, as far as it can, in the sense of its avowed and explained policy. As far as it can! In that phrase resides the virtue of legislatures and politicians! For in spite of the extralegislative activities of the parties—their researches, their considered formulations of policy, their crosscountry debates, and the incessant war in the press—the policy of each party is not complete and cannot be complete until the other side is heard. When members enter the legislature, were they conscious of anything but their electoral victories and the messianic programs of their "side" and the chances of reform and distinction, they would solemnly admit (1) that much in their program was tactical, included to "catch votes"; (2) that a good deal in heaven and earth had not been thought about at all; and (3) that they must expect the unexpected: events, contingencies, calling for quick thought and the improvisation of a policy. They would realize, upon a little reflection, that even when the policy was not tactical, but had been considered in all its facets with care and with a calculation of their opponents' strength, not all could be foreseen, not every detail sifted, not every force truly evaluated until it had been discussed with hostile elements possessing the parliamentary power to enforce some at least of the drive of their opposition. Not until there is a personal confrontation in a small assembly, with systematic procedure, can the detailed expression of policy, which means everything, be considered, or the full spiritual force of majority and minority be measured and applied. Further, the good in dialectic is not only that it causes one person or party to triumph over another, but that it sometimes causes some truth to triumph over both by provoking the explanation of self to self.

Therefore legislatures and politicians still have their invaluable place in the modern state, and deliberations and debate still occupy a central place in their functions.

* * *

The Politician as a Broker. The politician is, therefore, as near as any single term can signify him, a broker. His business is to apply the power resident in his constituency to convert desires into statutes and administrative actions by alloying them with the possible. He attempts to get as near

the desirable as he can, and what is possible he will learn, whether he is in the government or in the opposition. The ways are many and devious. But let us attempt to paint a portrait in broad outline of the best type of member. The portrait will do for all legislatures. And we sketch, not the art of succeeding to high place or of obtaining favors —that will appear as we proceed—but simply the equipment of the member to convert his mandate (poor, poor word!) into governmental realities.

The Legislator as Scholar. He need not be a scholar, and indeed, this would entangle and embarrass rather than help him, for his function is to act, to fight, and to seize advantages, not to meditate upon them. Were he a scholar, an expert, he would be encumbered by doubts and details, and it is notable that scholars who have entered legislatures have either been silent or silenced (think of Acton, J. S. Mill or de Tocqueville); and Francis Bacon, a member of Parliament, and Lord Chancellor some 250 years before explained why this must be in his *Advancement of Learning* on the mentality of scholars. Or they have had to jettison their scholarship and become men of affairs, carrying the least baggage and allowing passion to vanquish their scruples. The legislator has no need to be a scholar, for he can get all the information he needs for debate in a desiccated preparation from the party pamphlets and newspapers (or, in the United States, from the Legislative Reference Division of the Library of Congress). Further, if he has to a sufficient degree the energy of reform, or the desire to shine in the legislature and the constituencies, the government printing offices turn out a spate of reports by official experts and investigating committees. Only the few more serious members make any pretense of trying to master these, for again the party and the press offer short versions (though it has been recounted by a witty member of the French parliament that a member has been known to sleep on the reports in a literal sense, owing to poverty so great that he could not afford a bed!).

Truth compels me to say that very many members are unable to master the meaning of a lengthy and complicated report by their own efforts, owing to insufficient native ability and education. A few, however, are able to understand the complex and technical information. Some, realizing the impossibility of being masters of all trades, wisely specialize. The specializers and others who are less fortunate may have friends who are experts; and then successful intervention in debate may be assured by persistent and acute interrogation, so that the most abstruse points are cleared up. Indeed, this is a very important part of the work of an able member—to discover the experts and philosophers and get himself coached by them. He may easily do this if he is a little energetic, for such people are usually good-natured and easily succumb to the flattery that they and their knowledge are of practical importance, and the belief that in this way they become the real sources of government, that "philosophers are kings." Nor are the hopes of these expert friends altogether vain, but they are imperfectly realized owing to practical exigencies—or, in other words, the confounded obstinacy of other people, and the fact that the advice of rival experts and philosophers has been taken by the other side.[2] But what the legislator cannot learn from print he may learn from verbal exchange.

The Legislator as "Politician." The member who has gone so far has gone very far, and it now behooves him to keep friendly with other members. Popularity on personal grounds is exceedingly important, for it takes the edge off sharp truths and opens a way for their acceptance. It is even more important to be popular with opponents than with friends, for they will grant concessions on that account, believing that such "a jolly fellow" could hardly be ill-willed or stupid: or at least the concession is granted before they come upon these truths, by which time they have lost the battle.[3] Hence the lobbies, the social life of the legislature, *la buvette,* and the political clubs play a large part in the evolution of the member and of policies. The full list of ingredients for success in this direction, universally valid, cannot be given—each person is born with his own way to the hearts of other people. The need to do social favors involves an incessant vigilance for friends who have social graces and power. Their value must be justly estimated— that is, their value in the political exchange—and they must be held in corresponding regard and offered corresponding respect and political favors. Friends must be made and dropped in accordance with this rule. If you wish to waste time on useless people you may do it, of course, but it should be recognized as waste. Here, in the activity of the man in politics, as everywhere in life, the function has its specific nature, and its commands are peremptory. On the political exchange, men and things are valued in terms of the desirable power which can be purchased with them: quite properly, for victory must not be jeopardized by giving way to a desire to gaze at the stars.

The Legislator as Parliamentarian. To the qualities already described, another is indispensable. It is a knowledge of the rules of legislative procedure. There the member will find all the permissions and prohibitions affecting his right to intervene in discussion. He will discover weapons

to defeat his rivals and opportunities to advance his own cause, obstacles to his progress, and roads which will require a process of sapping. By adroit use of these rules he may exact concessions by threatening to obstruct his opponents' path with amendments; and in modern parliaments so much has to be done at the insistent call of the constituencies that men are willing to concede in order to proceed. He will also be able to obtain concessions by the intrinsic merits of his argument, his rhetoric. These together will stem the tide of his opponents' policy by exhibiting to them its results, as the simple technical consequences they have not had sufficient imagination to foresee, and as the extent of human opposition which will be aroused and has been underestimated. Further, a speculative portrayal of results in terms of votes at the next election will help.

The Legislator as Party Member. Where the party is in opposition, the member's activity is favored by the leaders and it may bring him reputation and power (Senators Vandenberg and Taft in the first two sessions of the 79th Congress were outstanding examples). For then any stick is a good weapon; and the government must be unmercifully harassed. But when the party is in office, then the private member is sworn to cheer and vote, to cooperate and not to oppose. Even a trifle is a waste of time and may wreck the strategy resolved upon by the leaders. The party has many means of enforcing this unwritten rule, the principal method being to set officers to watch the conduct of the member, or to meet together and discuss and determine their course, and to threaten the refractory with expulsion or the withdrawal of aid at the next election.[4] The discipline is effective, for without the party there is no nomination, and no opportunity to play an effective part in the legislature, and the expenses of election are so great that most members must rely upon party help.

Thus it is an illusion, and a quite unnecessary one, to believe that members of the legislature are creators of policy. They are parts of an embattled national host whose objective and strategy have long since been prepared, and they are needed for the purposes of minor tactics, which are not, however, without importance. Or, to change the metaphor, they are merchants buying votes in the cheapest market, the constituencies, and selling in the dearest, to the forces opposed to them, which is always the official opposition, and often to their own colleagues and leaders. It is not derogatory to the function and dignity of legislatures to say this; for we merely say that not in the members do the initiative and the need for thought reside, but in the party leaders.

The work of the assembly is important, but the ordinary member cannot, does not, and need not, contribute much to its execution. To say that the average member was ever in a much (if any) better position, in a parliamentary "Golden Age," is to repeat legend, not history. Where, indeed, as in France, the private member has much independence and the parties are of small authority, *no* business is done, and the work of the legislature dissolves into an interminable series of oratorical skirmishes, with guerilla tactics and destructive ambuscades.

This is far from meaning that the quality of a legislature's work is independent of the ability and work of its members. But we are concerned to say that almost everything depends upon the leaders, and that is due to electioneering methods in large populations with universal suffrage, to the complex technical nature of modern civilization, and to the large amount of business which legislatures must get through. However, the better the followers the better (though the more embarrassed) the leaders. Above all, for the day-by-day supervision of executive policy in action, the work of the departments of government, the multifarious acts of administration by hundreds of thousands of career officials, and the diverse outlook and critical attentions of the popular representatives are of the greatest value.

On the whole, then, in a country with well-organized and purposive parties, the constituencies do not cause much damage in returning mediocrities, but so far as such qualities are lacking—as in France and the United States (especially in the South)—their choice may be very damaging not only to their civilization but to the very notion of parliamentary government. Even this evil is partially overcome by that disbelief in the logical extreme of democracy which shows itself in the establishment of permanent, professional, career administrative officers.

Notes

1. Cf. Herman Finer, *The Economic and Social Council of the United Nations* (Boston, 1945).
2. Cf. T. V. Smith, *The Legislative Way of Life* (Chicago, 1940).
3. Cf. D. Kirkwood, *My Life of Revolt* (London, 1935), pp. 202-307.
4. The British Labour party's Standing Orders, *q.v.* reproduced in each Report of the Party's Annual Conference, are particularly severe. Practice is far more lenient, though it is not possible to refrain altogether from disciplinary measures, as indiscipline spreads. In May, 1948, for example, two Labour members were expelled from the party: one for publicly denouncing the Labour government's intention to nationalize the iron and steel industry, and another for contumaciously leading a group of members against the government's policy of fighting against the Left-wing Socialists of Italy who were in company with the Italian Communist party during the crucial election of April, 1948. The expulsion took place after a long process of persuasion and a hearing at party headquarters.

6. A CASE STUDY IN SENATE NORMS[1]

Ralph K. Huitt

THE SENATE of the United States, like other institutionalized groups, operates in accordance with a complex of norms for members' behavior which are understood by few outsiders and perhaps not completely by all senators. Formal written rules governing the behavior of members take into account the division of functions between the two major parties and the operation of the Senate's institutionalized sub-groups, the committees. These are supplemented by unwritten rules that are often more consequential. Members have generally-accepted notions of the way the Senate as a body ought to perform its public business and regulate

Reprinted from *American Political Science Review*, Vol. 51 (1957), pp. 313-329, where it appeared under the title, "The Morse Committee Assignment Controversy: A Study in Senate Norms," by permission of the author and the publisher.

its internal affairs, and the way members ought to behave toward the Senate and toward each other.[2]

Senatorial behavior would be difficult enough to study if this were all, but it is not. For one thing, the norms are by no means undifferentiated for the entire membership. Within the Senate a number of identifiable official and unofficial "statuses" (or "positions") besides that of United States Senator can be distinguished, each carrying with it a "role" in the form of behavior expected by the Senate and the public of the person occupying that status. The leadership positions in the two parties and the committee chairmanships come immediately to mind as examples of official statuses. The status of "elder statesman" occupied at one time by, say, Senators Walter George and Alben Barkley may be suggested as an example of the unofficial kind. Furthermore, even senators who occupy no specialized statuses must accommodate themselves to the demands of many groups. Some of these are sub-groups of the Senate itself: the senatorial party, with its formal and informal structure; the committees; friendship groups; and groups of sectional, ideological, and interest allies. Many are outside the Senate: the national party, with its need to make a record and capture the presidency; the constituency, sometimes conceived broadly as all the people in a state and sometimes more narrowly as the groups that supported the senator; interest groups broader than a state, perhaps sectional or national in their scope. The demands these groups make on a particular member often conflict, and they must moreover be reconciled with the ambitions, philosophy, and personality of the member himself. The "reference group" for the substance of the specific behavior may then be exclusively the one in which the senator is physically participating, the Senate, or it may be one which is psychologically important to him, even though he may not be a formal member of the group. The Senate itself will be the reference group for the style of the behavior and the form in which he interacts with other senators and the symbols and agencies of the Senate.[3]

These are commonplace observations; the existence and power of norms for behavior are apparent to anyone who reads about the Senate in the daily newspaper. When the "liberal" senators mass their forces in a vain effort to change the closure rule it is plain that the written rules, including the one that makes a change so difficult, have crucial importance, as does the unwritten convention that the Senate is a "continuing" body. There is even some general awareness of the more subtle working of the norms regulating the conduct of members toward each other; this is implied in the fairly common reference to the Senate as an "exclusive club." The generally more subterranean operation of norms of this kind comes to the surface when a sanction is applied—when virtual ostracism was imposed on Huey Long, or when a public rebuff is administered to an overly aggressive junior member. The sanction may be covert, as in the Senate's displeasure with Senator Case of South Dakota in 1956 for embarrassing his colleagues by revealing publicly the offer of a campaign contribution by a lobbyist interested in natural gas legislation. This apparently exceeded their annoyance with the lobbyist who embarrassed Senator Case. Much less frequently it is overt, as in the official censure of Senator McCarthy, who, more than one competent observer has suggested, was disciplined finally for continued flouting of the "club rules" rather than for his aggressions on persons outside the Senate which were considered by many of his critics to be more grievous departures from proper conduct.[4]

Incidents of this kind do not carry us far; they substantiate the existence of the norms without telling us much about their content. Learning more about them is not easy. The written rules and official interpretations of them, when they are observed, present no great problem. The norms that are not explicit, the "oughts" that are shared by Senators because they are members of the "club," are another matter; perhaps only those members who are in the process of acquiring them understand them at the self-conscious level. They offer quite difficult problems to the non-member student. The kind of participant observation that has revealed the norms of some other groups is neither entirely adequate for, nor permitted by, a group as complex and secretive as the Senate. Perhaps a good beginning for a study of norms would be a series of political autobiographies such as no retired senator so far has seemed willing or able to write. At the present, political scientists and journalists are left to make inferences about these "oughts" from observations of how senators, as a group, "normally" behave with respect to each other, and, more clearly, from critical instances in which the Senate formally or informally applies sanctions against proscribed behavior, or is in an obvious conflict-of-norm situation among its members.

Political scientists have made some studies of the relative effectiveness of competing claims on political representatives over time, in regard to categories of issues.[5] But the fact that a senator votes more frequently with his party than with a sectional group does not necessarily mean that he puts party allegiance first; it may only mean that the sectional group makes fewer demands on him. Again, it tells us nothing about the kind of situation in which the senator will put the claim of one ahead of the other.

This study rests on two assumptions. The first is that particular conflict situations may furnish clues about the norms that affect behavior and their relative strength among different members of the group. The situation chosen for analysis here is the controversy in the Senate over the assignment of Senator Wayne Morse of Oregon to standing committees after he had bolted the Republican party in the presidential election of 1952. The bare facts of the controversy will be stated, followed by analysis of the relative strength of behavioral norms involved in the contest. The second assumption is that it should be possible to make valid, if crude, inferences about norms for behavior from the printed record which is available to everyone. After all, much of Senate behavior that counts is *public* behavior; whatever their private motives, senators must live with their public records. Accordingly, the study was made, and tentative conclusions reached, wholly from the printed record. After that, persons were interviewed in Washington who had first-hand participant knowledge of the controversy. If the second assumption were correct, no basic alterations should then have been necessary; and that proved to be the case. Some refinements were made, but the conclusions (which are wholly the author's own) did not have to be altered as a result of the interviews.

I. What Happened to Morse. Wayne Morse was an early supporter of Eisenhower, but a progressive estrangement from the candidate and his campaign declarations was climaxed by Morse's announcing for Stevenson in the middle of October and resigning from the Republican party a few days later.[6] The break was complete: Morse campaigned for Stevenson and later declined the invitation of the Republican Senate conference to attend its first session. He asked not to be assigned committee seats by the Republicans, now the majority party in the Senate, saying that he would seek his posts as an Independent from the Senate itself. The Republicans accordingly filled their list with party members; the two vacant seats not filled by either party when committee appointments were considered by the Senate on January 13, 1953, were on the District of Columbia and Public Works committees. (By law, a Senator must be given a seat on at least two standing committees.) Morse wanted to retain his old assignments to the Armed Services and Labor and Public Welfare committees. A suggestion that unanimous consent be given for Morse and an additional Republican member to be added to each of these committees met the objection of the minority leader. Morse then nominated himself for the Armed Services committee. A written ballot was taken and Morse lost, 81-7. Morse next introduced a resolution which would add himself and one majority member to each of the committees to which he had belonged, for the duration of the 83rd Congress, and asked and received permission from the Senate to postpone his appointment to committees until the resolution could be acted upon by the appropriate committee and the Senate.[7]

The wait was a long one. The Committee on Rules and Administration unanimously reported the resolution adversely in mid-April, but the Senate did not debate it until May 25. The resolution was defeated 56-19, whereupon the Senate elected Morse to the vacancies on the Public Works and the District of Columbia committees.[8]

The third vote on Morse's committee assignments came in January, 1954, a full year after the beginning of the 83rd Congress. A resolution changing the committee structure gave Morse's friends an opportunity to offer an amendment which would return Morse to the committees he had served on during the 82nd for the remainder of the 83rd Congress, enlarging them by one member each and reducing by the same number the committees he would leave. Thus it would not be necessary, as it would have been a year earlier when the ballot was taken, to strike anyone from a committee list; but (on the assumption Morse would vote with the Democrats) four committees thereafter would not be controlled by either party. On this proposal Morse mustered his largest vote, but nevertheless lost 59-26.[9]

The bare summary of events gives no indication of the vigor with which Morse fought for his old committee seats. He charged the Republicans with engaging in "terrorism" to enforce conformity, and demanded rights in regard to committee assignments based on eight years seniority in the Senate. The Senate had ample opportunity to become familiar with the argument supporting his case; Morse repeated it frequently in 1953 from January until the end of May in his reports of the "committee of the whole of the Independent party" on Friday afternoons. Morse's argument rested upon the Constitution of the United States and the formal and informal rules of the Senate. Article V of the Constitution states, among other things, that "no State, without its consent, shall be deprived of its equal suffrage in the Senate." To Morse, this meant that "to deny any fraction of the normal rights of a Senator, not in his own capacity but as a representative of a State, is to compromise . . . [that] basic guaranty." And what are the "normal rights of a Senator"?—under the Legislative Reorganization Act, to seats on two standing committees, and under a long-standing rule of the Senate, to be appointed to them by ballot by the Senate itself. Furthermore, not just any two committees would do; as Haynes put it: "Once placed upon a congenial committee, a Senator is likely to retain that assignment as long as he remains in the Senate, or until he requests to be excused from further service thereon."[10] Not since 1871, said Morse, had the Senate departed from this practice. If the Senate were in fact a continuing body (and Morse agreed with the majority that it was) its committees likewise had an unbroken life; the parent body need only fill vacancies and assign new members. It was true that Republicans who bolted the presidential candidate in 1924 had lost intra-committee *rank* in the next session of Congress, but Morse was not concerned about that. He believed that committee rank properly should be determined by party seniority, and as the freshman Independent he was prepared to go to the bottom of the list. But committee *assignments,* he argued, depended upon seniority in the Senate, and his colleagues could not deny him his rightful place on his old committees without placing in jeopardy their own rights under the seniority system. Morse therefore declined to request appointment by the conference of either party, insisting that the whole Senate should elect him to committees in accordance with his rights as a Senator.

The Republican leadership denied any wish to discipline Morse. What they wanted was to control the Senate. As Taft pointed out, the Republican margin was paper-thin; with Morse an Independent the Senate division stood at 48-47-1. There were fifteen standing committees. The Legislative Reorganization Act allowed 11 majority members and no minority members to serve on three committees. The Republicans had sought to amend the rule to allow 18 majority and three minority members to hold three seats each. The Democrats had scaled down the ratio to 14-3, leaving the majority's margin the same as before. Thus the Republicans could control only 13 committees; Morse and the Democrats would control the other two. The majority therefore had chosen to lose control of the two least important committees. Case explained that the Republicans had taken Morse at his word and had not assigned Republican seats to him; they had filled Republican requests for committee assignments until only two were left, on Public Works and District of Columbia (Morse contemptuously dismissed this as the "garbage can disposal principle" in committee assignments). If the Democrats had consented to the 15 member margin, it was implied, Morse could have had his old seats.

Lyndon Johnson, the minority leader, thought that Morse was not the responsibility of the minority. In the division of committee assignments between the parties, the Republicans had been given two seats each for 49 members, including Morse. Johnson had expressed the hope that Morse could retain the seats he wanted, but he would not interfere with the majority's assignments. He made clear his intention to vote for the Republican and the Democratic nominees; to break the party lists would invite the majority to meddle with the minority and elect all the committees.

Johnson's determination to respect the other party's committee list was reciprocated by the Republicans. When the resolution adding Morse and a Republican to two committees was debated in May, Johnson opposed it, saying that he was "willing to share the junior Senator from Oregon 50-50 with the majority party, but I am not willing to have the Senate say it will add 4 seats to 2 committees and completely disregard the 47 members who make up the minority party." Knowland, acting for the majority leader, agreed that the minority did not have to accept a change in ratio disadvantageous to them, and the Republicans voted almost solidly against the resolution.

The rebuttal of Morse's arguments was shared by both sides. It was contended that no more was guaranteed the States by the equal suffrage provision in the Constitution than that each should have two Senators. Morse's distinction between the Senate and the majority conference was deemed to be formal only; actually a majority had the right to appoint all committees, and in practice this meant the majority party. Members tended to follow the party leadership simply because that was a practicable way to organize the Senate. The Legislative Reorganization Act, they said, really was designed to reduce the committee load of the Senators, not to guarantee anything new to them. As for that, Morse could have had two committee seats in January, and by election of the Senate, if he had not asked for a postponement. His opponents would agree that he had a right to two seats; what they denied was that he had a right to say which two. There was no mention of seniority in the Constitution nor in the Legislative Reorganization Act; consideration of seniority was a convention of the Senate. Moreover, as Senator George (himself the ranking member of the Senate in seniority) put it, "prior seniority is purely a political matter . . . essentially a matter of party determination, regulation and control." It was party seniority therefore which determined not only rank on committees, but assignment to committees as well.

II. The Appeal to Precedent. The one respect in which little effort was made to rebut Morse on the floor was in his oft-repeated contention that removing him from committees against his will violated the precedents of the Senate. This is curious behavior on the part of a body which ascribes so much importance to precedents. It is useful to an institutionalized group like the Senate to preserve at least the illusion of consistent behavior; it is impressive to the layman, and it makes possible the settling of many problems through appeal to the authority of usage. Precedents that are generally followed are useful to the student of senatorial behavior: they help to identify the working rules of the group, and behavior which violates them is worth investigation.

According to Morse, only one Senator had ever been removed from a committee without regard to his seniority. That was Sumner, chairman of the Foreign Relations Committee, who lost his seat in 1871 because of his opposition to Grant's determination to occupy Santo Domingo. In the only modern instance of such party discipline, the Republicans placed Ladd (who had been chairman of Public Lands), Brookhart, and Frazier at the bottom of their committees in 1925, to punish them for campaigning for LaFollette. But they were not removed from their committees, Morse asserted; that was the point he wanted to make. And against this example of discipline he could and did cite numerous instances when bolting went unpunished. Moreover, when two Farmer-Laborites were elected from Minnesota in 1923 several committees had been enlarged to avoid reducing the ratios of the major parties, as Morse now suggested be done in his case. Thus it seemed to him that the action against him followed an isolated and unhappy precedent, and ignored established practices of the Senate.

We shall not be concerned with the 19th century here. But 1925 is another matter; one member of the Senate today was sitting then, and the party strife which the Republicans sought by Draconian measures to end is by no means ancient history. First we shall look briefly at what happened in 1925; then we shall seek out the party bolters in subsequent presidential campaigns to see what happened to their committee positions. It must be recognized, of course, that there are many degrees of party defection and numerous ingenious modes of effecting it. Morse himself distinguished between "bolting"—campaigning for the other party's candidate, which he thought properly should be preceded by resignation from one's old party —and "taking a walk," a matter of campaigning for neither but voting for the opposition's candidate, which he thought does not call for resignation. There are other ways, of course. The politician may "go fishing" (not vote), vote but remain noncommital, avow party loyalty while studiously ignoring the candidate, damn with faint praise, or stage a "sitdown" (announce for the candidate but not help him). The infinite variations on this single theme are worth a study of their own, but we shall be concerned here only with outright bolting—the overt act which cannot be recalled nor misunderstood.

The objects of party discipline in 1925 were bolters. George W. Norris and Hiram Johnson left little doubt that they were for LaFollette, but they did not openly support him; in the formal sense, they remained within the party fold. Ladd, Brookhart, and Frazier, on the other hand, were bolters, whose break with their party's candidate was overt.[11] The Republican conference voted therefore not to invite the three rebels or La Follette to the party conference, nor to place them on committees to fill Republican vacancies. Moreover, each of the four was placed at the bottom of the committees on which he served, below the lowest-ranking Democrat. In a word, the Republican conference treated them like independents. But these bolters, unlike Morse, were not willing to consider themselves independents. Brookhart stated flatly: . . . "I did not leave the Republican party. I am a better Republican than is the Senator from Indiana [Watson, chairman of the Committee on Committees] today." They were stoutly supported by Norris and Borah, who raised the old, troubling question: what is a Republican? The Democrats did not know, but they thought it was a problem for the Republicans. Pat Harrison requested and received permission for Senators to vote "present" ("I do not want to enter into the family row over there . . .") on the motion to return Ladd to his chairmanship, and 26 Senators did so vote. Ladd was replaced by Stanfield, a "regular" Republican from Oregon;[12] LaFollette was dropped from the chairmanship of the Interstate Commerce Committee and Watson took his place. But the action of the Committee on Committees went further than demoting the bolters. In a move that today would scarcely seem like chastisement, but obviously ran counter to his preference, Frazier was transferred from Indian Affairs, whose business he understood, to Banking and Currency, whose business he did not. The reason given was forthright. With LaFollette also on the committee, the progressives and the Democrats together would control it; and since LaFollette ranked him, Frazier had to go. The Democrats had been unwilling to increase the committee size to let them both stay. So Morse was mistaken: the action of 1925 provided a precedent for just what was done to him in 1953. But what of the intervening years?

III. Others Who Bolted. No Presidential campaign in this period has lacked bolters. The disciplinary action of 1925 did not prevent bolting even in 1928. Trouble for the Republicans came once more from midwestern progressives. Norris left his irksome position on the sidelines and actively supported Smith, as did John J. Blaine of Wisconsin.[13] Both sides wooed Robert LaFollette, Jr., his Democratic opponent obligingly dropping out of the senatorial race and Curtis, Hoover's running mate, speaking out for LaFollette in Wisconsin. But LaFollette contented himself with denouncing the Republican platform as "reactionary," praising some of Smith's views, and calling for the election of progressives to Congress.[14] The Democratic rebels were both southerners, but there the resemblance ended. Tom Heflin of Alabama was always a problem to the party, and his campaign against Smith was characteristic of him; he abused Catholics and attacked Tammany Hall in meetings patrolled by his "rangers" (klansmen).[15] Simmons of North Carolina, who called his party's campaign "two-faced and hypocritical," was the senior Democrat on the Finance Committee and had been a regular party leader in his state for a quarter of a century. His single act of rebellion was provoked by Smith's opposition to Prohibition.[16]

The Democratic ranks held in 1932, but not so the Republican. Hiram Johnson declared he would not "taint" his record by supporting Hoover, and campaigned for Roosevelt in California.[17] LaFollette still thought progressive congressmen were the country's best hope, but supported the Democratic candidate because Hoover was "wrong on every issue" and had "a 100% reactionary record."[18] Norris's response to Roosevelt was more positive. Declaring that "what this country needs is another Roosevelt in the White House," he served as chairman of a non-partisan National Progressive League for Roosevelt and stumped for him around the country.[19] Bronson Cutting, a progressive Republican from New Mexico, acknowledged his mistake in ever supporting Hoover and called for universal support for the President's opponent.[20]

By 1936 LaFollette, like Norris, was for Roosevelt as well as against his opponent. In addition to speaking for Roosevelt, LaFollette helped arrange the withdrawal of Minnesota Democratic nominees for governor, senator, and one congressional seat, in favor of the Farmer-Labor candidates, thus effecting a coalition of the two parties.[21] Subsequently, Henrik Shipstead (Farmer-Labor senator from Minnesota) announced for Roosevelt, the first presidential candidate he had supported in twelve years.[22] Norris made a clean break with his party, not only campaigning for the New Deal incumbent in the White House, but also winning his Senate seat as an Independent over nominees of both major parties.[23] Gerald P. Nye said he would stay out of the presidential campaign as a courtesy to Lemke, the North Dakota congressman running as a minor party nominee, but Nye did make two speeches for Norris.[24] The other North Dakota senator, Frazier (who had been disciplined for bolting in 1924), supported Lemke.[25] Two other Republican senators, Couzens of Michigan and Norbeck of South Dakota, bolted their party's nominee, but both were dead before the next Congress convened. No Democratic senator openly left the party fold. Even Rush Holt of West Virginia, who keynoted the first convention of Father Coughlin's National Union for Social Justice, and who also had lunch with Landon, in the end was silent as to whom he would support.[26]

Despite the third term issue in 1940, outright bolting was rare. Burke of Nebraska endorsed Willkie and later joined the Republican party, while Holt sponsored an anti-third term resolution in the Senate; but both had lost in the Democratic primaries in their states. On the other hand, Norris and LaFollette continued their championship of Roosevelt. The Wisconsin senator, in the face of a fight for reelection, announced his position on the eve of the platform conventions of his state's three parties.[27] Norris again headed a non-partisan group for Roosevelt and campaigned actively for him in Nebraska and the West.[28]

Each party suffered the defection of one senator in 1944. Joseph Ball of Minnesota, after hearing Roosevelt's speech to the Foreign Policy Association, announced that he would support the President for a fourth term.[29] The Democratic bolter was O'Daniel of Texas, who was a frequent supporter of Republican policy in the Senate.[30]

What is striking about the election of 1948, in which Truman won despite rebellion from both wings of the Democratic party, is the lack of widespread overt disloyalty in the Senate. Glenn Taylor of Idaho was Wallace's running mate, and at least two southerners—Ellender of Louisiana and Eastland of Mississippi—seem to have campaigned for the States' Rights ticket;[31] but what confronted Truman in the South apparently was the kind of hostility of which senators are masters, which makes itself plain without committing the irrevocable act.

Party defection in 1952 came in a variety of shades. Morse's was the most complete, ending, as it did, in resignation from his party. Price Daniel of Texas was as forthright in supporting the opposition's candidate, but felt no compulsion, apparently, to leave the Democratic party.[32] Two other Democrats performed equivocal but effective maneuvers within their own states. Harry Byrd, without endorsing the Republican slate, announced that he would not endorse Stevenson, in a speech which doubtless was understood in Virginia.[33] Pat McCarran exchanged mutually uncomplimentary remarks with Stevenson without bothering to oppose him, but in Nevada his organization supported the Republican Malone for reelection to the Senate against the young Democrat who had dared to beat McCarran's man in the primary.[34]

IV. What Happened to the Bolters. In the record of the twenty year period from 1929 through

1949, which covers assignments to committees of the 71st through the 81st Congresses, there is nothing that remotely resembles punishment of senatorial bolters through loss of seats or rank on committees.

Bolters were treated like other senators when their parties—whether in the majority or not—assigned them to committees. Norris retained his chairmanship of the Judiciary Committee in the 71st and 72nd Congresses, after supporting Smith in 1928. Heflin and Simmons kept their places after opposing him. Bronson Cutting was dropped from the Foreign Relations Committee in 1933, but that was because the Republican quota was reduced from 13 to eight. All those who retained their seats ranked Cutting. Bolters seem to have received normal promotions to better committees. For instance, Robert LaFollette, Jr., went from Post Office and Post Roads to Foreign Relations in 1929. Bolters were regularly advanced in rank on their committees. Not even leaving the party (as Morse did in 1952) hurt them. The 77th Congress in 1941 furnishes an example with two rebels, Norris the Independent and LaFollette the Progressive, listed as the ranking minority members of every committee that either of them served on except one (LaFollette on Foreign Relations). Between them they held the ranking minority position on seven of the Senate's 33 committees.

Except in the case of Morse, the committee assignments in the 83rd Congress reveal no hint of punitive intent. Daniel of Texas was appointed to the Interior Committee, a choice spot for a solon from an oil-producing state. It need hardly be added that no inconvenience was suffered by Byrd or McCarran.

The contemporary record seems clearly to support the proposition that the Senate norm is that a senator who bolts his party's presidential nominee shall not be punished by loss of what is perhaps his most important senatorial perquisite, his regular place in the committee structure. Any departure from that norm must be regarded as unusual behavior of genuine significance. Why were party bolters punished in 1925 and 1953, and not in the years between?

V. Why Some Bolters Are Punished. Some of the variables which might be supposed to have affected the behavior of the Senate appear to have had no influence. Among them are:

(1) *Degree of defection.* Brookhart was demoted on all his committees for little more than criticizing the Republican vice-presidential candidate, an action that usually is overlooked. Morse campaigned actively for the opposing party's candidate, but so did several bolters who were not punished. Robert LaFollette, Sr., took the field himself against his party's candidate and was punished; his running-mate on the Progressive ticket, Senator Wheeler, was not.

(2) *Degree of estrangement* (formality, conclusiveness of break). The 1924 rebels stayed in the party and were disciplined; Norris and the young LaFollette, like Morse, left the party but were not penalized.

(3) *Frequency of defections.* The 1924 bolters were old troublemakers, but so were Norris, LaFollette, and Heflin. Morse, on the other hand, left the party fold only once.

(4) *Strength and importance of the bolters.* The four senators who were disciplined in 1925 represented a stubborn and not inconsequential wing of the party, with a long tradition. Morse did not. Among the senators not disciplined, Norris and the junior LaFollette were formidable individuals. Ball and O'Daniel, to mention only two, were not.

The variable which does prove out is the *ideological division* of the committee to which the bolter belonged. Thus where such a committee is not divided along lines of interest group ideology, or where it is divided but the majority group has a workable margin, it is not necessary to penalize an insurgent member. On the other hand, where the dissident element holds the balance of power, the defection furnishes a pretext for securing effective control of the committee for the majority.

That is what happened in 1925. The Republican party was split between east and west; the east had the White House but the west had the seniority in Congress. With the party ratio in the Senate 55-40-1 the Republican margin looked better than it was. Five Republicans (LaFollette, Brookhart, Ladd, Frazier, and Norris) and the Farmer-Labor member (Shipstead) would vote with the progressive Democrats and at least five other Republicans (Borah, Johnson, McMasters, Howell, and Schall) were generally undependable.[35] A year earlier a coalition of Democrats and insurgent Republicans had made Smith, a Democrat from South Carolina, the chairman of the Interstate Commerce Committee. In this political climate, the Republican leaders in the Senate were determined not to lose control of any committee, however unimportant, if they could help it. The bolt of 1924 gave the leadership an opportunity to gain ground. LaFollette and Ladd were relieved of their chairmanships of otherwise manageable committees. Frazier was shifted from Indian Affairs, where he and LaFollette could team up with progressive Democrats to control it, to Banking and Currency, where his vote was not needed. The party leaders' strategy was explained bluntly by Reed of Pennsylvania, who said that an effort had been made to effect a similar change on Manufactures (which he thought had "gone to the devil" the last two years) where LaFollette and Brookhart held the balance, but it had failed.[36] The bolters were allowed to keep their other committee assignments, with loss of rank, because they did not endanger conservative Republican control of those committees.

In 1953, one of Morse's assignments as a Republican presented no problem of control. Though not free from group conflict, the Armed Services Committee was not divided into two camps either by partisanship or by interest group ideology. Control of the committee did not turn on any one member's vote. This was freely admitted in the debate. Morse pointed out that the Armed Services watchdog subcommittee chaired by Lyndon Johnson (successor to the Truman-Mead subcommittee) had submitted 41 reports, all of them unanimous.[37] There was a rumor at one stage that Morse would be reassigned to the Armed Services Committee, but not to the Labor and Public Welfare Committee; but Morse, by declining the invitation to the Republican conference and announcing that he would seek his seats from the Senate, made it easy to drop him from both committees without precipitating a fight along lines of interest group ideology or raising an intraparty punishment issue. The question put was the "rights" of a senator *qua* senator.

The Labor and Public Welfare Committee presented a quite different case. At the beginning of the 84th Congress it was the most sharply divided committee, along both party and interest group lines, in the Senate. The split extended even to the professional staff, who did not work for the whole committee but were divided between the majority and the minority.[38]

The character of the Committee split could be demonstrated by ranging all Senators at the beginning of the 83rd Congress along a "liberal-conservative" continuum to find where the Committee members would fall. For the purposes of this study that was done by preparing a table which ranked members of the Senate according to the percentage of times each cast a "liberal" (or "progressive") vote over a six-year period on a series of issues selected by *The CIO News*. Eighty senators were ranked; the other sixteen were new and so had no voting record for this period. Similar computations were made for votes selected by two other organs of "liberal" opinion, the AFL's Labor's League for Political Education,

and *The New Republic*. Correlations with the percentages based on the votes selected by *The CIO News* were so high, however, that only the latter were used in the table. In addition to correlating closely with the other two, the selection made by *The CIO News* covers more roll-call votes spread more evenly over the six years.[39] A senator who voted "liberal" at least half the time on the issues so chosen will be referred to here as "liberal." It is not argued that a ranking of senators according to this criterion measures the "liberalism" of senators in a philosophical sense. What *is* assumed is that it gives a fair approximation of the relative acceptability of senators to the urban-labor interests who were loyal to the New Deal-Fair Deal and who would be extremely concerned about the work of the Labor and Public Welfare Committee. Presently, data from the table will be used to mark the people who eventually supported Morse in his fight to regain his committee seats, and to raise the question why they did not vote for him at first. At this point it may be used to show the split on the Labor and Public Welfare Committee.

As the 83rd Congress convened, the four Republican holdover members on the 13-member committee ranged from the moderate liberalism of Tobey and Ives through the moderate conservatism of Smith (of New Jersey) to the strong conservatism of Taft. The five Democrats (Lehman, Douglas, Neely, Murray, and Hill), on the other hand, were all of a piece; they could be counted on to support the "liberal" side 90 per cent or more of the time. And the new Democratic appointee, John Kennedy, was their kind; in his six-year tenure as a member of the House of Representatives, Kennedy's voting record was substantially like theirs.[40] The new Republican appointees (Goldwater, Purtell and Griswold) could be counted on to strengthen the conservatives, but *two* of them would not be enough. With the Democrats voting as a bloc, the best they could get was a tie. Morse, with his voting record like the Democrats', would decide the outcome. When it is remembered that the Republicans in 1953 controlled both White House and Congress for the first time in twenty years, and that both parties had promised to revise the Taft-Hartley act, it is clear why the Republicans were reluctant to allow Morse to occupy the "swing position" that Ives accused him of wanting.[41] As it turned out, the partisan division on the committee, even with a dependable Republican margin of one vote, was so sharp that the committee accomplished little in the 83rd Congress.

VI. The Conflict of Loyalties. Morse's support, first and last, came from the liberal Democrats.

The CIO selection of roll calls shows 33 senators who cast "liberal" votes at least half the time. Twenty-seven of these were Democrats, one (Morse) an Independent, and two (Langer and Tobey) relatively independent Republicans. Three (Aiken, Ives, Smith) were more regular Republicans—and none of them ever voted for Morse. In January of 1953 Morse got his own vote, five liberal Democrats, and Tobey. In May he was supported by 19 of the 27 liberal Democrats. Among the eight who did not support him were Lyndon Johnson, the leader; Clements, the whip; Kerr and Hennings, members of the Policy Committee; and Smathers, close to the leadership group though not formally a member of it. Others who supported him were Tobey, Langer (paired for), and Cordon, his Oregon colleague. A year later he added the votes of Hennings, in the leadership group, and two other liberal Democrats, plus a handful of others not easily explained.[42]

It is evident that the Republicans generally, and the conservative Democrats, suffered no very strong cross-pressures in casting their votes. It was the liberal Democrats who were torn between the line adopted by the party leaders and their loyalty to a friend and ally. This may be inferred from their voting behavior, and it is supported by persons who shared their experience. This was especially true in the case of a group of about a score of them who met regularly in a bi-weekly informal meeting (their administrative assistants meeting on alternate weeks) for program planning. They were Morse's friends, and they received support from the same kinds of groups that helped him. It was because Morse shared their convictions that he left the Republican party. It was their aid that Morse could and did expect. It was they who failed him the first time, in Morse's view, but who eventually rallied to him handsomely. What explains this contradictory behavior?

It is not the last two votes that need explaining, but the first; there is no reason to believe that Morse's friends were not sympathetic with him in January, as they were later. But Morse could hardly have posed the issue that first time in a less palatable way—a way which was only partially of his own choosing. He did not himself know very early what the Republicans planned to do about his committee assignments. Then after announcing that he would seek appointment directly from the Senate, Morse stood aloof from his friends, neither asking nor receiving their counsel or support. Through a tactical error Morse failed to give the Senate the customary notice at least one day in advance of his resolution to increase the size of two committees to include himself and an additional Republican, so that the resolution had to go to committee. As a consequence he had to nominate himself, request a written ballot (a maneuver that took his friends by surprise), and ask that his supporters strike from the ballot a party-nominated member, Republican or Democrat.

This is what most of Morse's friends declined to do—to interfere with the committee selections of the other party. The position of the Democratic party leadership never changed; it opposed Morse every time. Nevertheless three members of the Policy Committee voted for Morse the second time, despite a Policy Committee decision to make it a party issue, and four the third. But to vote for him in January 1953 involved more than going counter to the leadership of their party.[43] It would also violate a *Senate* norm of long standing and general acceptance. The principle had been stated by Henry Cabot Lodge in 1919 when the Democrats had tried to reduce the Republican margin on four committees. Said Lodge: "We feel that the makeup of your committees is your business and your responsibility, and that the makeup of our committees is our business and our responsibility. That is the ordinary rule of courtesy and good manners which I have never before seen violated in the Senate."[44] The Democrats accepted his statement of the rule and voted for his list intact. This was the rule which prevented the majority party from making all the committee selections, as it had the power to do; and this rule proved stronger than the ties of friendship and interest group ideology which bound liberal Democrats to Morse in 1953.

Heavy pressures bore upon the liberal Democrats between January and May of 1953, and not the least of them from Morse himself. It is hard to convey a sense of the bitterness with which Morse attacked the liberal Democrats and their party leader.[45] His heavy defeat had placed him in an untenable position; "even the liberal Democrats have deserted him" taunted the Oregon newspapers, and Morse's harsh cry of pain filled the chamber. His position improved in the spring of 1953; labor rallied to his support, and his filibuster against the Tidelands bill won prestige for him with many liberal groups. Yet no better reason for the behavior of his friends comes to mind than the one they insistently gave themselves: a vote for Morse in January 1953 required that a committee member chosen by the opposing party be struck; four months and again a year later, it did not.

VII. Conclusions. From this study some tentative conclusions regarding norms for behavior in the Senate may be suggested as hypotheses for further testing:

(1) Bolting the party ticket in a presidential election is not usually punished in the Senate by loss of rank or membership on committees. Senators who bolt are most likely to be deprived of committee rank or membership when the deprivation will affect a close ideological division on one or more committees in a way that is favorable to the majority. Paradoxically, discipline is most likely to be applied when it is least likely to be effective—i.e., when a close division of power gives the disciplined member maximum leverage. Thus the two examples of punishment did not seriously hurt the victims. The bolters disciplined in 1925 regained their committee rank in the next congress. Wayne Morse received better committee assignments from the Democrats in 1955, just before he joined their party, than he had lost two years earlier. Discipline has not seriously inhibited bolting; the 1924 bolters repeated their offense and there have been party defections in every presidential election since 1924.

(2) The response of senators under cross-pressures of claims of friendship or ideological allegiance, on the one hand, and loyalty to the party leadership on the other, will depend on the structuring of the situation:

(a) The requirements of party regularity are generally binding on questions pertaining to the organization of the Senate, which include the working arrangement that each party will accept without question the committee list of the other. This norm is generally stronger than the claims of friendship or ideological allegiance. Senators who supported the proposal to add Morse and a Republican to two committees apparently believed they had not violated this norm when their vote would not deprive any senator of his regular committee assignment nor the majority party of its control of a committee, even though their vote was opposed by their party leaders.

(b) Unless other interests can be exploited to reenforce an appeal to party loyalty, it will probably prove weaker than strongly pressed claims of friendship or ideological allegiance. This may be true even with members of formal party leadership groups. The apparent weakness of the appeal to party loyalty may be deceptive, however; when the outcome is not in doubt it may not be strongly pressed.

Notes

1. This study was made possible by funds granted by The Fund for the Advancement of Education. That Corporation is not, of course, responsible for any of the statements made or views expressed here.

2. "A possible objection to the word *norm* itself is that we may easily confuse two different things: norm A, a statement of what people ought to do in a particular situation, and norm B, a statistical, or quasi-statistical, average of what they actually do in that situation. Sometimes the two coincide, but more often they do not." George Homans, *The Human Group* (New York, 1950), p. 124. The term is used here, as Professor Homans uses it, in the first sense, as the behavior expected of members of a group by the members themselves, a departure from which in practice is followed by some punishment, such as a decline in the member's social standing in the group.

3. See Eugene L. and Ruth E. Hartley, *Fundamentals of Social Psychology* (New York, 1952), pp. 456-81.

4. See William S. White, "The 'Club' that is the U. S. Senate," *New York Times Magazine*, November 7, 1954, and *Citadel: The Story of the U. S. Senate* (New York, 1957); and Richard Rovere, *Affairs of State: The Eisenhower Years* (New York, 1956), pp. 217-29.

5. See, e.g., George L. Grassmuck, *Sectional Biases in Congress on Foreign Policy* (Baltimore, 1950), and Julius Turner, *Party and Constituency: Pressures on Congress* (Baltimore, 1951). See also David B. Truman, "The State Delegations and the Structure of Party Voting in the United States House of Representatives," *American Political Science Review*, Vol. 50, pp. 1023-45 (December 1956).

6. *The New York Times*, October 19, 1952, p. 1, col. 7; October 25, 1952, p. 1, col. 4. For Morse's account of his break with the party, see *Congressional Record*, Vol. 99, pp. 3752-60 (April 24, 1953); and *U. S. News & World Report*, Nov. 19, 1954.

7. *Congressional Record*, Vol. 99, pp. 327-52 (January 13, 1953). The vote is at pp. 346-49. All page references herein are to the bound volumes, not the daily edition.

8. *Ibid.*, p. 3053 (April 14, 1953); p. 5224 (May 20, 1953); pp. 5421-44 (May 25, 1953). The vote is at p. 5444. See also Sen. Repts. No. 142 and No. 304, 83rd Cong., 1st Sess.

9. Deaths in the Senate had changed the party ratio to 48-47-1 in favor of the Democrats, but the votes of Morse and the Vice President kept the Republicans in organizational control. The resolution was S. Res. 180, sponsored by the leadership of both parties and reported favorably by the Rules Committee. It provided for the enlargement of two committees (Post Office and Civil Service, and Public Works) from 11 to 13 members. It also established a sliding-scale ratio of majority members who were to be allowed assignment to three (instead of two) committee seats, to minority members accorded the same privilege, a move designed to preserve a one-member margin for the majority party on each committee. The Morse amendment, introduced by Anderson, was sponsored by 12 Democrats and Langer. *Congressional Record*, Vol. 100, pp. 97, 120-21 (January 11, 1954); pp. 218-28 (January 13, 1954). The vote is at p. 228.

10. Quoted from George H. Haynes, *The Senate of the United States*, 2 vols. (Boston, 1938), Vol. 1, p. 294.

11. Kenneth C. MacKay, *The Progressive Movement of 1924* (New York, 1947), p. 195; Alfred Lief, *Democracy's Norris: The Biography of a Lonely Crusade* (New York, 1939), pp. 268-70; George W. Norris, *Fighting Liberal* (New York, 1945), pp. 286-87.

12. The debate is found in *Congressional Record*, Vol. 67, pp. 15-16, 41-67 (March 9, 1925). The vote is at p. 63. Harrison missed a nice point: if the Republican conference was correct, the bolters were *not* Republicans and the question of their chairmanships and committee assignments was not a "family row" but the business of the Senate—as Morse made it in 1953 by staying out of the party and away from the conference.

13. *The New York Times*, October 25, 1928, p. 1, col. 7 (Norris); October 16, 1928, p. 15, col. 1; and October 21, 1928, p. 21, col. 3 (Blaine).

14. *Ibid.*, October 9, 1928, p. 2, col. 3; October 10, 1928,

p. 2, col. 4; July 8, 1928, p. 2, col. 5; October 27, 1928, p. 9, col. 1.

15. *Ibid.,* July 5, 1928, p. 21, col. 4; July 3, 1928, p. 6, col. 2.

16. *Ibid.,* October 13, 1928, p. 5, col. 3; October 22, 1928, p. 1, col. 4; October 26, 1928, p. 2, col. 2.

17. *Ibid.,* October 15, 1932, p. 9, col. 1; October 29, 1932, p. 1, col. 7.

18. *Ibid.,* October 20, 1932, p. 15, col. 2.

19. *Ibid.,* September 26, 1932, p. 1, col. 7; September 29, 1932, p. 1, col. 6.

20. *Ibid.,* October 27, 1932, p. 12, col. 5.

21. *Ibid.,* September 29, 1936, p. 23, col. 3; October 4, 1936, p. 1, col. 6.

22. *Ibid.,* October 19, 1936, p. 2, col. 4.

23. *Ibid.,* September 18, 1936, p. 9, col. 1.

24. *Ibid.,* October 2, 1936, p. 9, col. 6.

25. *Ibid.,* October 4, 1936, p. 1, col. 6.

26. *Ibid.,* August 11, 1936, p. 8, col. 2; August 15, 1936, p. 1, col. 4; September 17, 1936, p. 9, col. 1.

27. *Ibid.,* October 1, 1940, p. 15, cols. 7-8.

28. *Ibid.,* October 21, 1940, p. 8, col. 5.

29. *Ibid.,* October 23, 1944, p. 1, col. 1; October 24, 1944, p. 15, col. 1.

30. *Ibid.,* October 22, 1944, p. 38, col. 3; November 3, 1944, p. 18, col. 8.

31. *Ibid.,* November 19, 1948, p. 21, col. 1; November 25, 1948, p. 30, col. 5.

32. *Ibid.,* October 16, 1952, p. 14, col. 3.

33. *Ibid.,* October 18, 1952, p. 1, col. 5.

34. *Ibid.,* October 25, 1952, p. 11, col. 4; October 28, 1952, p. 1, col. 8; October 29, 1952, p. 33, col. 5.

35. "Purging the Republican Ranks," *Literary Digest,* Vol. 84, pp. 7-8 (March 21, 1925). See also George Creel, "What Do These Senators Want?", *Collier's,* Vol. 71, pp. 9-10 (March 10, 1923), and "Non-existent Republican Majority," *Outlook,* Vol. 142, p. 350 (March 10, 1926).

36. *Congressional Record,* Vol. 67, p. 67 (March 9, 1925).

37. *Ibid.,* Vol. 99, pp. 342-43 (January 13, 1953).

38. George B. Galloway, *Congressional Reorganization Revisited* (College Park, Md., 1956), p. 6. Morse, Douglas, and Humphrey, in arguing for Morse's resolution in May, all admitted there was a "philosophical division" on the committee, which would not be affected if a conservative Republican were added along with Morse.

39. Sixty-nine votes selected by *The CIO News* are found in the issues of August 11, 1947; July 19, 1948; January 2, 1950; August 14, 1950; December 17, 1951; and August 18, 1952. Duplications were eliminated. Thirty votes selected by Labor's League for Political Education may be found in their booklet, *Voting Records of Sen-*

ators and Representatives, 1947 Through 1952. Sixty votes selected by *The New Republic* are shown in the issues of September 27, 1948, pp. 28-30; November 14, 1949, pp. 24-25; October 9, 1950, pp. 14-15; and September 22, 1952, pp. 16-17.

40. In a similar selection of votes in the House of Representatives, Kennedy voted "right" 93 per cent of the time on 30 votes in *The CIO News,* and 100 per cent "right" on 20 votes in the AFL's tabulation and 12 votes in *The New Republic.*

41. *Congressional Record,* Vol. 99, pp. 343-44 (January 13, 1953). A note of caution, however, should be added. The Committee on Rules and Administration recommended in January of 1953 (S. Res. 1) that nine committees, including Labor and Public Welfare, be increased by two members, and six others be reduced by two; as amended and passed (S. Res. 18), Labor and Public Welfare remained the same size. (*Congressional Record,* Vol. 99, p. 233, 279-81, January 7 and 9, 1953). In May 1954 two lesser committees were increased by two members each (see n. 9, above), but the motion to enlarge Labor and Public Welfare again was defeated. Failure to increase the committee's size, which would have strengthened Morse's claim to a seat, strongly supports the argument that there was indeed an element of punishment in the majority's attitude.

42. Jackson (D. Wash.) also voted for Morse in May 1953 and January 1954; he was a freshman senator. A similar selection of votes cast in the House of Representatives showed that in his six years in the House Jackson's percentage on a total of 61 votes selected by *The CIO News* was 92, on a total of 26 votes selected by the AFL's LLPE was 100, and on a total of 59 selected by *The New Republic* was 97.

43. The authority of the leadership in January 1953 was strengthened by two other actions in regard to committees. First, Lyndon Johnson went against ancient usage in the Senate by insisting that each freshman Democratic senator be given one good committee place. It is significant that Jackson was the only freshman Democrat ever to vote for Morse and that he did not do so the first time. Second, the enlargement of the more important committees made possible some attractive transfers. Eight Democrats who did not vote for Morse in January 1953 but ultimately did so, were beneficiaries of transfers to better committees.

44. Quoted in Haynes, *op. cit.,* Vol. 1, p. 290.

45. See, e.g., the colloquy on March 6, 1953, *Congressional Record,* Vol. 99, pp. 1679-86. Morse said he had refused the apologies of the liberal Democrats and he threatened to campaign against them in 1954.

7. THE TRIBULATIONS OF A STATE SENATOR

Duane Lockard

HAVING GONE THROUGH the process of trying to attract the attention of the voters in a campaign for the Connecticut senate, I am certain that most people are unaware of their state legislators. I campaigned in a district of some fifty-five thousand people in the eastern part of my state, and although the area is small it was impossible to

Reprinted from *The Reporter,* May 17, 1956, pp. 24-28, by permission of the author and the publisher.

meet and talk with more than a small fraction of the voters.

My qualifications for the job—that I had studied and taught and written on state government—were never very widely known, in spite of newspaper advertising, speeches, posters, and even one costly TV appearance. My political mentors, incidentally, were rather concerned over the fact that I am a professor. They were careful to emphasize that I had once been a coal miner.

Early in the campaign my party's candidate for governor spoke at a dinner meeting and I followed him on the rostrum. One man in the rear of the room said to the ladies at his table, who included, as it happened, my wife: "Who's this guy? Nobody ever heard of him; they sure were stupid to nominate him." My wife, without identifying herself, argued my merits but left him unimpressed. "You gotta be well-known to win that job," he asserted with assurance.

How wrong he was! I won as an unknown, and largely, I am forced to admit, because the Democratic Party was doing well, for most of my votes were certainly cast by people who had hardly even heard of me. Campaigning and publicity helped me, no doubt, but the margin of victory must have come from those who knew next to nothing about me. Even now most of my constituents do not know me. On one occasion when I was introduced to someone as a senator, he asked me how things were in Washington.

* * *

Roughly half of the six thousand legislators elected in 1956 were probably entering the legislatures for the first time. Most legislators cannot afford to serve more than one term. In Connecticut we are paid a handsome $300 a year for the months of work we put in at Hartford. You have to be rich, retired, or crooked not to suffer financially in most state legislatures.

The game of musical chairs at the state capital cuts the efficiency of the legislature. It is a rare first-termer who can contribute much. A handful of veteran legislators and in many, if not most, states a few party leaders make the important decisions. Even the conscientious newcomer can be misled into playing the game of the crafty few. I once voted unknowingly for a bill containing a rider exempting legislators from highway tolls while increasing them for other motorists. It was weeks after the close of the session before most of us realized that the rider had been stuck in by the chairman of the house's finance committee. Although the bill has since been repealed, few actions of the Connecticut General Assembly have done more to lower its prestige, and it illustrates the power the well-placed few can exercise.

Not even committee chairmen in Connecticut wield more power than the party leaders, however, and by party leaders I do not mean the majority and minority leaders but persons outside the legislature. State party chairmen and important city and county leaders are often the ones who decide a bill's fate. Caucuses are held frequently —in the senate daily and in the house once or twice a week—and there the party position is decided. Once the decision is made it is unusual for a legislator to vote independently.

At times I refused to go along with my Democratic colleagues, but in general I did not find it impossible to agree with the group decisions.

One advantage of the caucus, whatever its drawbacks, is that the party in the legislature takes a stand as a unit so that the public may judge the party's policy. To have every man go his own way often is tantamount to elimination of responsibility, for, if my argument about the relative anonymity of state legislators is correct, the records of individuals are simply not scrutinized. The record of a party as a whole cannot easily be hidden.

In Connecticut the caucus combines with strong party leadership to provide a tightly controlled system. State party chairmen traditionally are strong in Connecticut. J. Henry Roraback typified the old-time state party boss; John Bailey is a perfect example of the more modern type.

* * *

During legislative sessions, so the story goes, Roraback had delivered to him after every day's session a black box containing all the following day's bills. After examining the bills, he cleared, rejected, or suggested revision of them as he personally saw fit.

The day is probably gone when any one man can exert that kind of power from outside state legislatures (at least, one hopes so), but lesser approximations of Roraback remain in vogue in more than one state. Connecticut's contemporary parallel is John Bailey, Democratic state chairman. If you want to get a bill through the senate when it is Democratically controlled, you would be well advised to consult with Bailey. A Harvard Law School contemporary of former Governor John Lodge, a Republican, Bailey is independently wealthy, intelligent, and incomparably well versed in the political and legislative history of Connecticut. He sits in on and influences Democratic caucuses, even though his power to discipline is virtually nonexistent, at least when compared with Roraback's. Although he refers to himself as "nothing more than a messenger boy for the governor," his actual authority in many policy matters is great.

Right now, Connecticut Republicans have no leader comparable to Bailey. Since Lodge's defeat for re-election in 1954, the Republicans have been unusually disorganized. His defeat was the signal for the beginning of an all-out fight for control of the party. The lobbyist therefore has to deal with at least three Republican leaders nowadays: the state chairman and the G.O.P. leaders of Fairfield and Hartford Counties.

Although divided, the Republican Party leadership still has considerable power in the legislature. For example, during the 1955 session the House (Republican) and the Senate (Democratic) took opposite positions on two education bills, and it appeared that both might fail, although there was some sentiment for a swap—each chamber agreeing to pass the other's bill in return for safe passage of its own. In discussing this problem with Bailey, I was advised to talk to a Republican house member who would in turn get in touch with Meade Alcorn, Hartford County G.O.P. leader, who would arrange the swap. Bailey told me: "If Alcorn agrees to go for this, there won't be any trouble. His word is good." Bailey was right. I made the suggestion to the House Republican, who talked to Alcorn. In short order both bills were passed without further difficulty.

It would be wrong, however, to assume that these political leaders are omnipotent. They are utterly unable to get some bills through and they cannot stop others. The primary-election law is a good example. Nearly every party leader around Hartford in 1955 was opposed to the idea of a primary. Why should they want one? As things stood, Connecticut was the only state without a primary in any form, which simply meant that it was easier for the bosses to choose their candidates in a convention without outside interference. Yet by luck, maneuvering, and the misfiring of one of the time-tested methods for killing a bill, the primary bill did become law.

Some Republicans were won over to the primary when they realized it might be a weapon to use against Bill Brennan, the G.O.P. boss of Fairfield County, who, they feared, might win party control in a convention. Probably the law would never have passed, however, had it not been for the misfiring of the "improve-it-to-death" weapon. This technique involves the amendment of a bill in one chamber so as to "improve" it (by making its restrictions more rigorous or its terms more inclusive), always in the hope that the other chamber will not accept the changes. Then you can piously point to your "record" of having passed the "best" bill, which the other chamber defeated. The primary bill made five trips between the two houses in this manner before both passed it.

In the final stages there was no place to hide; further amendment would have made it obvious to everyone that the leaders were trying to kill the bill. Thanks to the identification of the party with its legislative record—not that of scattered individuals—the political leaders' fears of the primary were overcome by their greater fear of retribution at the polls.

*   *   *

To be efficient, a legislative body must have adequate time for the lawmakers to give some consideration to the questions they must decide. In Connecticut, legislators feel lucky when they know what's going on.

Before you conclude that we are a bunch of dolts to get into such a position, look first at the demands placed upon a member's time. He is a part-time legislator to begin with. At $300 a year how can he be anything else? Time that he might spend studying bills has to be spent making a living. Nearly all the legislators commute to and from Hartford while the session is in progress. I spent more than two hours a day driving fifty miles each way from home to legislative hall. There are, in addition to strictly legislative chores, hundreds of minor errands to be run for constituents. I do not object to the task of acting as liaison man between the citizen and the bureaucracy—over unemployment compensation or eligibility for old-age relief and the like—but such chores take up time.

In the 1955 session of the Connecticut General Assembly we considered no fewer than 3,600 bills. I undertook to read every one of them as they came from the printers but soon had to give up. Later I tried to read the bills with favorable committee reports. Finally, in the end-of-session rush, not even that was always possible. All this work has to be done within five months. Constitutionally, the session must end when five months have elapsed.

Nor does the state legislator have a staff to assist him in research on bills or in handling constituents' problems. These jobs are his alone. One constituent, writing in to request a minor but time-consuming chore of me, said he knew I was busy and he did not want to waste my time, but could my office do it for him? My office! I had no office staff and indeed no office except for a corner in my hallway at home, where unsorted and unfiled letters, brochures, notes, and thousands of bills constantly threatened to bury my children under a paper cascade. It is the same way with most other state legislators. We are on our own, and you get worse laws as a result.

Patronage questions also eat away at one's time. In one sense this may be the most useless use of legislative hours, but by the mores of American politics it appears unavoidable. The staffs of Connecticut's local courts are politically appointed, and with each change of administration there is a turnover of court personnel. When I had originally been asked to run for the senate, I had warned my backers that I would insist on a veto on court personnel recommended to the governor.

I did not want to control the process or to appoint my own slate, but I did insist on a veto.

Making this veto stick for one of the towns in my district was a touchy job. Those whom I did not deem fit to be judges were outraged when I objected to their nomination. Meeting after meeting, often lasting until two or three o'clock in the morning, was called to iron out the matter. The rejectees pleaded with me in hurt tones: "Haven't we served the party well for years? Why kick us in the face like this?" My argument that professional competence as well as party service was a relevant consideration for appointment made little impression. I finally got my way, but malcontents told me to my face that I would be denied renomination and that "some old jerk without your smart-aleck ideas" would be nominated.

The number of utterly insignificant bills is downright incredible. These trivia are of three kinds: local bills for specific municipalities, insignificant administrative matters, and minor economic-interest conflicts.

In Connecticut a high proportion of the proposals we consider are strictly local. We deliberate bills to decide whether clerks can be transferred from one municipal office to another in a given town. We approve the number of dogcatchers a small town should have. I spent considerable time getting a bill passed to permit a change in the title of the chief of police in New London.

To these local bills must be added a great number of proposals that are of no general importance. Why should the Connecticut legislature have to decide, for example, whether cuspidors should be permitted in barbershops? To let such trivia be decided by administrative agencies makes far more sense than to ask legislatures to decide them. And where the local bills are concerned, it is foolish, not to say destructive of local government initiative, to turn over such questions to the state legislature.

State laws regulate many professions and most businesses in considerable detail, and it is not uncommon for a business or professional group to try to rig the law so as to trim down or eliminate competition. Insurance agents try to deprive automobile dealers of the sale of auto insurance. Civil-engineering firms fight individually licensed engineers. Large garages try to keep gas stations out of the repair business. Liquor distributors oppose liquor distillers; one type of oysterman is against another; dentists argue with dental laboratorists over rights to dispense false teeth. And endless array of economic interests combat each other, all fighting in the name of free enterprise, public health and safety, or fair trade.

These conflicts come to the legislator. Often he doesn't know anything about the particular interest involved and would prefer to ignore the matter, but he can't. A drumfire of propaganda and pleading is his lot on each of these questions. I was deluged with material on the matter of the sale of insurance by auto dealers. Dozens of letters and telegrams poured in. Local dealers telephoned to plead with me—this in response to urging by their paid lobbyists to get after their local legislators. (I certainly got more than my money's worth out of the telephone company during that period. At times we had to take the phone off the hook to eat dinner without interruption.)

This sort of legislation brings out the least noble traits of legislators. The lawyer, insurance man, druggist, real-estate dealer, or automobile dealer who is a part-time legislator is not always scrupulously careful to separate his two roles.

One question often put me about my legislative experience is: Did you find that state legislators were crooked? Speaking of Connecticut, I must say that they are not crooked. Bribery is almost unheard of in my state. A few years ago a legislator was convicted of bribery in connection with a fireworks-regulation bill, but he was an exception. On the whole, there is probably less unethical behavior among legislators than among businessmen. Indeed, some more or less accepted business practices would be a ticket to political defeat or prosecution if legislators tried them. Whatever the reason—and I am inclined to think it is partly because of the absence of horse racing in the state—Connecticut legislators have a pretty clean record.

Another question I am frequently asked is: "With all the pulling, hauling, deceit, and backstage maneuvering that goes on in the legislature, weren't you disgusted and disillusioned?" I answer that I was not particularly disillusioned because I had watched the Connecticut legislature enough from the outside to see how the game was played, and therefore I had no illusions to be shattered. I admit that at times I was disgusted with the way in which my fellow legislators—and even I, for that matter—behaved. I sometimes made blindfold decisions and went along with propositions that I doubted, and I knew others were doing the same.

However, I have no feeling of revulsion about politics or about my membership in the legislature. Since the interests behind some proposals involved the pursuit of thousands or even millions of dollars, I did not expect the legislature to be a Sunday-school picnic. The stakes are high not only for those who seek monetary gain but also for those interested in court reform, mental health, or indeed the improvement of legislative practices. In the process of working for goals compromises are inevitable, even though it is often distasteful to have to make some of the compromises demanded.

Far from shrinking from political participation, though, I hope to continue it and I highly recommend it to my friends. Some fourteen thousand places are open on the ballots for state legislatures this fall. Are there any takers?

8. THE LEGISLATORS' VIEW OF THE LEGISLATIVE PROCESS*

Corinne Silverman

MANY FINGERS attempt to reach into the pie of the legislative process. There are the political parties, more or less organized, with a hierarchy of formal leadership and a framework of policies and sanctions. There are lines running to and from the executive. The administrative departments, in some respects adjuncts to the power and policy role of the executive, can also have their own parts to play, and can serve as leverage points for configurations of clientele groups. Each legislator faces a somewhat unique situation in his relationship with his constituency, and his constituency is one of infinitely varied patterns of needs, interests, social and economic compositions and political preferences. Criss-crossing these elements of the legislative process are the activities and aims of organized interest groups with their own hierarchy of formal leadership and framework of policies and sanctions. Not only do each of these seek participation in the legislative process. The views of the legislators themselves about the place of each factor in the process to some extent define the nature and role of these various elements.

Based on interviews with twenty-six members of the 1952 session of the Massachusetts General Court, this study reports the legislators' concepts of the legislative process and tentatively proposes what appear to be meaningful categories among these concepts. It will first describe the different views of the role of party, for party was the first concern of the legislative respondents. The concept of party was related with the different views of the role organized group activity played and should play in the legislative process. Views of party were also related with the amount of organized interest

Reprinted from *Public Opinion Quarterly*, Vol. 18 (1954), pp. 180-190, by permission of the author and the publisher.

* The research was carried out and this report prepared under the direction of Oliver Garceau as part of a project financed by a grant from the Rockefeller Foundation to Bennington College.

group activity visible to the legislator, and with the different criteria used by the legislator in identifying the interest or activity of such groups. It is also possible to report something of the legislator's perception of other factors in legislative decision-making, and of his broad concepts of representation.

The Political Setting. Massachusetts is a densely populated, highly urbanized and industrialized state. The two-party margins in both the presidential and gubernatorial elections have been close for the last twenty-five years; but the gerrymandered state legislature does not accurately reflect this closeness of the balance between the parties. Although seven Democratic governors have been elected since 1928, the year Massachusetts moved from the "sure" Republican column to that of a "close" state, the Democratic party has not had a majority in the state senate once in the 20th century. In 1948 the Democrats for the first time gained control of the lower house, by a one-seat margin. In the 1950 election, the Democratic governor, Paul Dever, was re-elected, and again the lower house was controlled by the Democratic party, this time by a majority of eight seats (52.3 per cent of the 240 seats). The Republicans maintained control of the senate, and increased their majority from the 20-20 division in the 1949-1950 legislative sessions to a 22-18 margin in the 1951-52 sessions. Thus, 1952, the year of this study, was the last session of a legislature in which, for the second time, a Democratic governor and a lower house with a slim majority of Democrats faced a Republican senate. The Massachusetts legislature, elected for two years, and meeting annually for increasingly long sessions, is composed of members with, for the most part, substantial legislative experience as compared with some highly amateur bodies. In 1952, the members of the lower house had, on the average, four years of service, while the state senators averaged four years in the house and six years in the senate.

The issues and episodes chosen for investigation concerned the major business associations and involved their active participation. The background for events in the legislative arena was examined by interviews with lobbyists, journalists and members of the relevant legislative committees during the sitting of the 1952 session, and by study of the minutes of meetings of several interest groups. The interviews with the legislators were begun immediately after the session adjourned. The business groups directly active were not the trade associations, but organizations purporting to represent broader business interests. The Associated Industries of Massachusetts is composed primarily of manufacturers, though many sizes and shapes are represented. The Boston Chamber of Commerce is a more heterogeneous group. A third group, the Massachusetts Federation of Taxpayers' Associations, is, as its title implies, a federation of local associations which include among their members real estate, commercial, manufacturing and financial interests and a considerable number and variety of individual citizens. The Boston Retail Trade Board also participated in the events under scrutiny. Both the AIM and the Taxpayers Association have members in all parts of the state. Although the Boston Chamber and the Boston Retail Trade Board are, by name, Boston organizations, the local counterparts of these groups are affiliated with, and to a degree followers of, the metropolitan units.

The staff executives of these business groups agreed upon two 1952 issues as the most important for their membership. One issue was a proposed amendment to the Massachusetts State Constitution to permit a graduated income tax. This proposal had already been passed once, and required a second legislative endorsement before being submitted to popular referendum. The four major business groups claimed that not only had they considered the defeat of the amendment a major item on their agenda, but that many of the trade associations had also been concerned and active. The proposed amendment was supported by Governor Dever and by the major labor groups in the state.

The other issue involved a group of bills dealing with the Massachusetts Employment Security Law, the state unemployment compensation law. This issue had come to a boil in the previous session when a major revision of the Employment Security Law had been undertaken. At that time, Ray Long, a staff executive of the Massachusetts Federation of Taxpayers' Associations, started a movement for business group cooperation on the

issue. This is not a tactic often used formally by organized groups, although ad hoc and informal intercommunication is frequent. Groups, so the story goes, are built on voluntary memberships and contributions. What group leaders can raise depends pretty largely, they feel, on their ability to point to a record of accomplishment over the past legislative session. Accordingly, groups are reluctant to get together on a formal basis, since they would have to share the credit, and possibly the contributions, or, conversely, share the blame for the errors of others. In this case, however, the threat to business was thought to be so serious as to warrant the step, especially since the business groups were dealing with a Democratic governor and Democratic lower house. The unemployment compensation rate was felt to be high to the point of competitive disadvantage. Due to the drain imposed on the fund by the 1949 depression in Massachusetts, it was not impossible that the rates would rise even further. Many business interests wanted an overhaul of the administrative machinery and of the substantive objectives and provisions of the law.

Ray Long contacted Roy Williams, the executive vice-president of the Associated Industries, who agreed to a cooperative approach. Ed Connelly, AIM legislative counsel, was included in the leadership of what became an ad hoc holding company of business groups. The overall scheme was to gather together representatives of many business groups and interests to plan concerted policy and action on the proposed revision. Accordingly, Long, Williams and Connelly met several times in the spring of 1950 to draw up a preliminary program. The Employment Security Council was formally launched in June at a meeting of some twenty-five businessmen representing major business firms in the state, widely diversified by type of enterprise. By the end of 1951, the Employment Security Council could correctly claim to represent, directly or indirectly, almost every business organization and interest in the state. And by the end of 1951 the revision of the Employment Security Law had been accomplished. The legislature adopted the Council's proposals on experience ratings, taxation rates, the solvency account and its scale of rates, additional disqualifications from benefits, and a new system of reporting to employers and the public by the Employment Security Division of the Massachusetts Department of Labor and Industries. The Council did not succeed in changing the benefit rates, nor was the administrative machinery of the Employment Security Division tightened in accordance with its recommendations. The tally of victories was high and was immensely satisfactory to the executives of the Council.

The bulk of the legislative activity had been carried on by Long and Connelly, though Clifford Fahlstrom, also on the staff of the Associated Industries, was nominally the head of the Council. The former two were in all probability those who would have been most active in any event as representatives of the organizations most interested in the issues. But by using the form of a "new organization," and by using Fahlstrom who was not so well known to the legislators, they were able to present their case as one supported by the businessmen of the entire state acting in spontaneous concert. To some extent, they could hope to avoid such old antagonisms as might exist. The Council was successful in arousing the interest and response of many individual businessmen over the state. Particularly noteworthy was the large attendance of businessmen at the legislative hearings.

By 1952, the purpose of the major business groups was merely to hold the line against attempts by labor organizations to re-revise certain provisions of the bill. During the session, a series of conferences on unemployment compensation proposals were held in the Governor's office between representatives of the AIM, the Taxpayers, and the A.F. of L., with the director of the Division of Employment Security taking an active part. The Employment Security Council remained in existence as far as appearances were concerned, but Connelly, Long, and Fahlstrom carried the load, as representatives of the Taxpayers and AIM. The legislature took no action during the session to disturb the statute.

The Legislators' Picture of the Session. In the summer of 1952, immediately after the close of the session, a sample of the legislature was interviewed.[1] Although all the legislators interviewed agreed that party was the most visible factor in the legislative process, they did not agree on how the two relatively well organized parties in fact influenced decision-making. These differences of opinion were evident throughout the interviews, but they appeared most clearly in response to a specific question about identifying a party issue. Each legislator was asked, "What makes an issue 'a party issue'?" There were, in general, three types

of answers. The three answers were based on three views of the nature and operation of party, and the views of party were associated with differences in the weights the legislators assigned to other aspects of the legislative process.

One group of legislators held the firm conviction that there was a distinct difference between the two parties, a difference self-evident to all the legislators. Usually they spoke in terms of a polarized party system, founded on a class interest base. "An issue supported by labor is a Democratic party issue, and an issue supported by management is a Republican party issue." Some expressed this in more generalized terms, saying that there was a traditional, philosophical difference between the two parties, elaborating in some cases to say that this difference was based on a "liberal-conservative split," a "labor-management split," a feeling that "a man should help himself versus the government should help him," or often in the generalization, "Republicans think differently from Democrats." There was no reference to the organized structure of party leadership or to the specific content of the party programs. To simplify later discussions, these legislators will be called the "class party oriented."

A second group of legislators, while they often expressed similar feelings about the difference between the two parties, used as their criterion for defining a party issue the activity of the party leadership. These legislators said that the "tip-off" on a party issue came when their floor leader stood up on a standing vote, or called for a roll call vote. In the absence of overt action by the Democratic leaders, a few respondents assumed that the report of the committee could be taken as the Democratic party's position on a bill, since the Democratic majority had organized the house. A vote by a party caucus was seldom mentioned by Republicans or Democrats, and was never cited as the sole criterion. All of these legislators defined a party issue in terms of party leadership, and will be considered in later discussions to be the "party leader oriented."

The third group of legislators, who might be described as the "program oriented," discussed the nature of a party issue by combining the perspectives of the first and the second groups.

An issue is made a party issue in two ways: first by virtue of the fact that legislators will follow the

Table 1—Viewpoints on Party as a Factor in Defining Issues

VIEWPOINT	DEMOCRATS		REPUBLICANS		TOTAL	
	No.	Per Cent	No.	Per Cent	No.	Per Cent
Class party oriented	5	41.7	6	42.9	11	42.3
Party leader oriented	6	50.0	6	42.9	12	46.2
Program oriented	1	8.3	2	14.2	3	11.5
Total	12	100.0	14	100.0	26	100.0

opinions of the leadership . . . and second, party issues become such because certain issues carry with them an historical backlog of opinion—perennial issues which are associated with one party or the other.

Since the Democrats had control of the lower house and the Governor was a seasoned party leader, the Democratic party might be presumed to have had more opportunity to exercise party sanctions and enforce party regularity. It is interesting, therefore, that the Democratic legislators interviewed were neither more nor less likely to respond in any of these three ways than were the Republican legislators interviewed. There was almost exactly the same distribution of viewpoints on the nature of a party issue among members of both parties.[2]

An early section of the interview centered on the graduated income tax amendment and the employment security bills. The legislators were asked to name those business organizations which they recalled as having been interested or active. There was no substantial difference between the Republicans and Democrats in their ability to recall such activity or interest. Indeed, unless specifically noted, it can be assumed that no differences appeared along party lines. However, a relationship appeared between the various views on the role of party in the legislative process and the observation of business group activity associated with these two issues. The legislator who saw the parties as polarized along essentially class lines, and who defined for himself the relationship of each issue to this character of the parties, was least able to recall which organized groups had been involved in the issues. The party leadership oriented legislator was able to recall more group activity and the legislator with the complex definition of party—involving the action of party leaders, the content of the party program, and the traditional value preferences of the party—was able to describe the greatest variety of organized group participation.

The same correlation was found with the ability of the legislators to identify correctly the lobbyists for the major organized business groups.[3]

The legislators interviewed mentioned a number of criteria for identifying organized group activity on an issue. These criteria included communications from individual constituents believed to have been stimulated by an interest group, information and opinion flyers sent by the groups to the legislators, legislative contacts made by local affiliates of the organized groups, lobbying activity by group representatives, appearances at relevant legislative committee hearings, gossip in the legislative halls, and newspaper advertisements by the groups. As might be expected, the range of criteria referred to by any one legislator varied with his viewpoint on the role of party in defining issues. The "class party oriented" used the fewest number of criteria, averaging 1.8. The "party leader oriented" legislators averaged 2.8, and the "program oriented" legislators used an average of 3.3 criteria.

Summarizing, then, all the legislators were concerned in the first instance with the importance of party in the legislative process, but they held different views on how to identify a party issue and on how party policy was implemented. These differences were associated with differing capacity to recall detail about business group activity, to identify lobbyists associated with these groups, and to see evidences of organized group interest and activity. These findings are suggestively comparable with the results of a survey made of Vermont legislators in 1951. Four perspectives on the legislative process were identified in the Vermont study, three of which are similar to the viewpoints on the role of party held by the Massachusetts legislators.[4] Although Vermont is a strongly Republican state, there were in 1951 two loosely organized Republican factions developed within the legislature, and the Vermont legislators responded to these factions much as the Massa-

Table 2—Relationship between Viewpoints on Role of Party, and Awareness of Elements in the Legislative Process

Aware of Elements in Legislative Process	Class Party Oriented (N = 11)	Party Leader Oriented (N = 12)	Program Oriented (N = 3)	Total (N = 26)
Organized group activity				
Percent able to identify more than average number of state business groups active on two major issues (Average was 3.6)	36.4%	58.3%	66.7%	50.0%
Average number of business group lobbyists correctly identified	1.7	2.5	3.0	2.2
Average number of criteria used to identify organized group interest or activity	1.8	2.8	3.3	2.4
Per cent of legislators able to cite instances of political activity by state administrative departments	18.2	33.3	66.7	30.8
Per cent of legislators able to cite instances of constituent response to group stimuli	63.6	75.0	100.0	73.1

chusetts legislators responded to the nature of the parties. There also appeared to be the same relationship in Vermont between attitudes toward factional leadership and program on the one hand, and awareness of organized group activity. Those legislators who discounted the importance of factional leadership and program in resolving the important issues of the session were those who were least able to recognize the organized groups in the state, to cite instances of organized group interest in legislative issues, or to identify the lobbyists representing the groups. The "faction oriented" legislators, corresponding roughly to the "party leader oriented" in Massachusetts, were more aware of organized group activity, and the "program oriented" were those most aware of organized group activity.

Whether this relationship between viewpoints toward the role of faction and the participation of organized groups would extend to a legislator's ability to handle detail about other aspects of the legislative process was a question toward which much of the Massachusetts survey was directed. Two further elements in the legislative process were explored: the legislator's awareness of political activity on the part of the various administrative departments and the legislator's awareness of constituent response to group stimuli. In the first case it was hoped to determine whether the legislators had been aware of situations where an administrative department had taken an active role in the development of an issue, through mobilization of a clientele group, through specific activity by the department head himself, or through other means.[5] Of the members of the sample, 30.8 per cent were able to relate instances ⟨ᵉ such activity by administrative departments in one or another of these forms. The relationship between the viewpoint on party and the awareness of political activity by administrative departments was comparable to the relationship between viewpoints on party and awareness of organized group activity. Such policy involvement by adminstrative departments was reported by 18.2 per cent

of the "class party oriented," by 33.3 per cent of the "party leader oriented" legislators, and by 66.7 per cent of the "program oriented" legislators. It is true that with a small sample and the time frame of a single session, there could well be a large element of chance in data such as these, but the fact that the same relationship turns up between concept of process and reports of administrative involvement as between the other items studied must be interesting if not conclusive.

The relationship was the same on the questions relating to constituent response to group stimuli. Instances of hearing from their constituents in a way indicative of interest group action were reported by 63.6 per cent of the "class party oriented," 75 per cent of the "party leader oriented" legislators, and 100 per cent of the "program oriented" legislators.

The Role of the Representative. What a legislator looks for as evidence of group activity may provide a clue to how he defines the norms of democratic government and the role of the representative. Table 2 shows that the legislator who was program or party leader oriented would look for more kinds of evidence of interest group activity. But interesting variations in the individual types of evidence are shown in Table 3. More of the "class party oriented" mentioned "response from individual constituents" than might have been expected, and in the case of the "group appearances before legislative committee hearings" there is a scaling in reverse.

These relationships, considered together with the other responses of the legislators, may suggest the different ways in which the legislators define the role of the representative in the decision-making process. The selections of evidence of group activity, with the class party oriented scoring high on constituent activity and committee hearings, may be explained by the legislator's definition of representation. The definition of the class party oriented legislator requires that he heed closely the call of the represented, and that he follow the rule book of legislative procedure

Table 3—Legislators' Criteria of Interest Group Activity

	PER CENT OF LEGISLATORS WHO CITED EACH CRITERION			
Criteria	Class Party Oriented (N = 11)	Party Leader Oriented (N = 12)	Program Oriented* (N = 3)	Total (N = 26)
Constituent response to group stimuli	81.8%	66.7%	100.0%	71.4%
Group flyers	36.4	66.7	66.7	50.0
Local group activity	18.2	66.7	66.7	42.9
Lobbying at state level	18.2	50.0	66.7	35.7
Committee hearings appearances	18.2	16.7	00.0	14.3

* The two out of three who turn up in these scores of the program oriented are not consistently the same two respondents.

in order that the democratic process be inviolate. These legislators were the ones who excluded from their verbal responses the role of party leadership and of party program. They stressed their personal ability, or perhaps their duty, to judge each issue on such grounds as they deemed important.[6] These were also the legislators who were least likely to report in any detail the entrance into the legislative process of organized groups, and who were least able to discuss the state administrative departments as active in legislative decision-making. Some findings in the Vermont survey lend support to this analysis, for the legislators in Vermont who had the narrowest view of the legislative process were those who referred to the legislative committee for the resolution of issues. The committee member was thought most capable of reaching a correct decision and the legislature was expected to accept the committee report. Further, these respondents believed that this was indeed the fact.

Party affiliation per se is not significant in these findings. There seems, however, to be a relationship between the legislator's view of process and the social character of their constituencies, broadly defined. The "class party oriented," with their simplistic perceptions of process, were either Democrats elected from metropolitan Boston or Republicans from non-metropolitan, non-suburban districts. The "party leader oriented" legislators tended to come from metropolitan centers outside of Boston. All the "program oriented" come from suburban districts.[7]

There is no definitive explanation for this. Speculations cannot claim to be informed. Clearly the political forces operative in the dominant metropolitan area of the state differ from those operative in cities outside of Boston and from those in the suburbs. Granting this, it should follow that different motivations, political skills, and viewpoints are more likely to be successful in producing electoral victories for political aspirants in each of these situations. The electoral margins of the various legislators are not at all related to any of the material presented. With more cases one might find that among legislators representing suburban districts, for example, those with a close electoral margin were more likely to be "party leader oriented" than "program oriented," although as a group, the suburban legislators tend to be "program oriented" to a greater extent than legislators from metropolitan centers. But it may be the political climate of metropolis, suburb, small city, and township in Massachusetts provides its own stereotype of representation as well as its own type of representative.

The emphasis throughout this presentation has been on the different ways the legislators view elements of the legislative or decision-making process, rather than on the decisions themselves —the roll call votes. Although the "yeas" and "nays" are in a real sense a pay off in the legislative process, one "yea" is likely to reflect a different degree of acceptance than another and a different evaluation of consequences. The dichotomized choice finally available to the legislator is only a crude verbal summary of what has actually been accomplished or what the participants believe should be accomplished. The bill voted upon has a content determined by the forces operating in the process of formulating, discussing, and deciding. To a large degree, the ways in which these forces enter the legislative process are dependent upon the extent to which they are considered useful, proper, or desirable by the legislators themselves.

Notes

1. A non-structured interview of the focused type was used. The sample was drawn purposively to represent the lower house members in distribution of both parties by geographical location, previous legislative experience, present committee membership and committee chairmanship. The total sample was 30 members, and the analyses below are based on completed interviews with 26 members.

2. The lack of difference between the Republicans and the Democrats in this respect may well be a function of the small size of the sample, as may be the analyses to follow. In a sample of 26 cases, findings can only be regarded as suggestive, not conclusive.

3. To get comparability of the results, each legislator was given the opportunity to name whatever groups he wished, but before the interview ended he was asked specifically about the major business groups mentioned in the introduction of this study: the AIM, the Taxpayers, the Chamber of Commerce, the Retail Trade Board, and, in the case of the employment security bills, the Employment Security Council. In scoring the results of the interviews, therefore, each legislator was given credit for each of these groups plus any one additional business group he discussed. A total of five business groups could have been credited to any legislator on the graduated income tax issue, and a total of six on the employment security bills.

Similarly, though there were three or four lobbyists from each major business group, the legislator was scored on his ability to name correctly one lobbyist associated with a group. A "perfect score" would have been six, one each from the AIM, Taxpayers Federation, Chamber of Commerce, Retail Trade Board, Employment Security Council, and one from another group such as insurance, public utilities, hotels, etc.

4. The fourth perspective in Vermont was not found in Massachusetts and may be appropriate to a one-party state with a loose factional structure. There were a few legislators in Vermont who, although aware of the factional split in the party and the importance of the program differences between them, were more concerned with gaining positions of leadership for themselves on particular issues only peripherally of interest to the factional leaders.

Leadership, independent of the party system, did not in Massachusetts seem to have developed, and certainly did not turn up among the members of the sample.

5. Since almost 100 per cent of the sample mentioned as an example of such activity the patronage power of the Commissioner of Public Works, the results described in the text refer to all citations other than this.

6. This is not at all to say that these legislators were more likely to bolt the party on roll call votes. They were not more or less likely to jump party lines.

7. In the Vermont survey, the degree of education and amount of previous legislative experience was correlated with perspectives on the legislative process. This would seem to be true in the Massachusetts sample, but the smaller size of the group imposes caution in attempting to draw conclusions from the somewhat ambiguous data.

C. Personal and Interpersonal Orientations of Legislators

9. THE POLITICAL SOCIALIZATION OF AMERICAN STATE LEGISLATORS*

Heinz Eulau, William Buchanan,

LeRoy C. Ferguson, John C. Wahlke

AS LONG AGO as 1925, Charles E. Merriam, viewing the promises of political research, proposed that "the examination of the rise and development of the political ideation and the political behavior of the child has in store for us much of value in the scientific understanding of the adult idea and conduct."[1] Yet, over thirty years later, we know next to nothing about "political socialization"—the process by which people selectively acquire the values, attitudes, interests or knowledge that fit them for particular political roles and make them take these roles in characteristic ways. Studies of voting behavior suggest that, under certain conditions, family tradition can be an important factor in a person's orientation towards politics, influencing the degree, kind and direction of his political involvement. We also know that religious, ethnic, and class perceptions and attitudes are formed rather early and, through time, become integrated into a system of values which tends to shape a person's social outlook and changes only slowly when it comes into conflict with opposed social values.[2] But these studies shed little light on the developmental pattern of a person's political socialization.

If little is known about the initiation to politics of the population at large, not much more is known about the initiation of those for whom

politics is a matter of central concern—politicians. Biographies, of course, tell us a great deal about the political socialization of particular, usually distinguished, public figures, but they represent unique cases which cannot be generalized. On the other hand, what systematic analyses have been made of political elites, are limited to data about the social bases of political recruitment and changes in the composition of elites.[3] These studies do not include systematic information on questions such as these: When do politicians become interested in politics? How do they become oriented to politics? Who are the agents of political socialization? What political or social events seem to arouse attention to politics? What kind of predispositions seem to accompany the initial interest in politics? Are political or other social beliefs involved in the process of political socialization?

This study presents some data on the political socialization of a particular type of politician—the American state legislator. In soliciting recollections about these legislators' earliest interest in politics, we did not consider it appropriate to think in motivational terms. Motivational analysis would have required more intensive interviewing than our research design permitted.[4] Hence, even though some of our respondents might use motivational language in trying to explain "why" politics interested or attracted them, we are not prepared to take such comments at face value. It seems doubtful that even those with some sense of self-awareness could accurately tell the reasons or motives that directed them to politics. We are therefore not concerned with "why" state legislators became interested in politics, but rather with "how" they perceive what happened in the

Reprinted from *The Midwest Journal of Political Science*, Vol. 3 (May, 1959), by permission of the publisher.

* This study was made possible by grants from the Political Behavior Committee of the Social Science Research Council. Neither the Committee nor the Council is responsible for the study. The data reported in the study come from interviews with 474 state legislators in California, New Jersey, Ohio and Tennessee, conducted by the authors and research assistants during the 1957 sessions of the four legislatures. The samples are 91% in Tennessee, 94% in California and Ohio, and 100% in New Jersey.

course of their political socialization. Recollections of this kind, it seems to us, have a functional reality of their own in constituting a part of the situation in which state legislators define their political roles.[5]

Time of Political Socialization. In a recent review of voting behavior studies, Lipset and his associates reported that "it is difficult, if not impossible, to make any reliable estimate, on the basis of empirical evidence, of the age at which politics becomes meaningful to children or youth." After examining the skimpy research evidence, they inclined to focus on the period of adolescence —"the period in the life cycle where the individual first encounters strong influences ^utside of his family and must proceed to define his adult role."[6] Assuming Lipset's conclusion to be correct, our data (summarized in Table 1) suggest that politicians see themselves as exposed to the political environment at an earlier stage of their

Table 1—Time of State Legislators' Earliest Recollections of Political Interest

Time of Recollection	Cal. N = 113	N.J. N = 79	Ohio N = 162	Tenn. N = 120
Childhood/grammar school	39%	23%	35%	32%
Adolescence/high school	16	10	15	11
College/equivalent period	8	10	13	7
After college	17	14	11	18
Time of entry into politics	18	15	23	13
Time not specified/codable	2	28	3	19
Total	100%	100%	100%	100%

personal development than the average citizen. With the exception of New Jersey,[7] about a third of state legislators recalled their childhood or the grammar school period as the time when they first became interested in or aware of politics. But only ten to sixteen per cent mentioned a period roughly coinciding with adolescence and high school. Altogether, almost one half had recollections locating their first political interest in the pre-college or equivalent age period. The childhood-grammar school period is perceptually more salient for state legislators than the time of adolescence or any single later period.

Nevertheless, as Table 1 shows, a sizeable proportion of state legislators reported first paying attention to politics either after college and its equivalent period or at the very time of entry into active politics. As one legislator put it:

Well, this might come as a surprise to you, but I was never interested in politics. I first became interested in politics after I was elected.

The data suggest that the process of political socialization, even for those who are most active in politics, is not necessarily restricted to the early years of the life cycle. As Talcott Parsons has argued, socialization may occur at almost any phase of a person's development and is part of a continuous process of growth.[8]

If we look at the inter-state differences with regard to the time of political socialization, no particular pattern emerges. The fluctuations from state to state in each time period are small. Apparently, the process of political socialization in the four states follows a relatively similar time scale.

What accounts for the fact that legislators are initiated into politics in different periods of the life cycle? The evidence suggests that differences in the time of political socialization would seem to be a function of different influences which come into play in different periods of an individual's personal development.

Primary Group Influence in Political Socialization. An interest in politics is probably related to the opportunity to hear about it or directly experience it. The opportunity to become acquainted with political life is given when significant persons in an individual's most immediate social environment are themselves in close and continuing contact with politics. Having parents, relatives or close friends in politics is likely to facilitate an individual's own awareness of and familiarity with public affairs. The strong influence exerted by primary groups on voting behavior, for instance, is a reasonably well-documented finding of recent social research.[9] Earlier research on non-political social participation has also shown that family members tend to be either all participants or all non-participants.[10] While precise data concerning the general population are lacking, it is plain that state legislators tend to come from families which are much more involved in politics than the average American family. As Table 2 indicates, from 41%, in the case of New Jersey legislators, to 59%, in the case of Ohio and Tennessee legislators, reported that one or more of their family had been or were in politics, although in a few cases they went back several generations to find them.

Table 2—Relatives of State Legislators in Politics

Relatives in Politics	Cal. N = 113	N.J. N = 79	Ohio N = 162	Tenn. N = 120
One or more	43%	41%	59%	59%
None	57	59	41	41
Total	100%	100%	100%	100%

State legislators, in recalling their earliest interest in politics, indicated that they are sensitive to primary group influence and attributed their political awareness to parents, relatives or friends and associates. Between 34 per cent, in the case of the California respondents, and 47%, in the case of the New Jersey respondents, spontaneously mentioned members in their immediate circle as agents of their political socialization. But if we look in more detail at those who attributed their political interest to persons with whom they were in direct and sustained relationship, we find that many more mentioned family members than friends and associates as having been instrumental in this respect (Table 3). Moreover, in the case of two states, New Jersey and Ohio, substantial

Table 3—The Influence of Primary Groups on State Legislators' Interest in Politics

Primary Group	Cal. N = 113	N.J. N = 79	Ohio N = 162	Tenn. N = 120
Family members/ relatives active in politics	18%	32%	31%	19%
Family members/ relatives interested in politics	12%	2%	8%	16%
Friends/associates active or interested in politics	7%	13%	4%	8%

pluralities of those who mentioned primary group influence as the source of their political consciousness—32% and 31%, respectively—recalled that their family had been more than occasionally active and attributed their own political awakening to this fact, and in New Jersey friends and associates were named more frequently than elsewhere. Whether the differences between Ohio and New Jersey, on the one hand, and California and Tennessee, on the other, are meaningful reflections of possibly differing functions of the nuclear family in the political socialization of youth in these states can only be a matter of conjecture.

Political interest is seen as a matter of family tradition or inheritance: "I was born into a political family. . . . I grew up in politics"; or, "I guess it's pretty much a combination of environment and heredity. . . . We are all sort of involved in politics," were typical comments. Others were more explicit. Familiarity with political campaigning by his father going hand in hand with earliest awareness is illustrated in this comment:

My first recollection of politics was when I was four years old and my father was a member of the House of Representatives. I played here in this room when I was a little boy. . . . Then, too, I experienced

a brief congressional campaign when my father was a candidate. He was defeated, but the whole thing left a deep impression on me. I met lots of people in politics through my father.

The family as a source of the politician's early identification with a political party and awareness of a political issue is described as follows:

My father was a member of the city council. He ran for Congress on the Republican ticket and was defeated. I went to political meetings with him, I was always interested in politics. I therefore always felt a close identification with the Republican Party. On my mother's side the family was Democratic. . . . And my mother's mother was a suffragette. There was much discussion about the woman franchise.

The vividness of these and many other accounts testifies to the important role played by family members in shaping the politician's orientations. Ties with a political party, consciousness of public issues, knowledge of both the serious and pleasurable aspects of political behavior, or sense of public responsibility, appear as products of political socialization in the most intimate form of primary group life.

What strikes one in reading some of the comments is the casualness of the socialization process when the agents are friends or associates. As one respondent put it, "some of the boys I was going around with were interested in politics, so I just went along." Another put it this way:

I would say that I was catapulted into politics without any approach. My law partner had been city councilman and had held other political jobs. So I went naturally to work in his behalf in these campaigns. This I did for a number of years. So from there I was asked to run for the legislature. I didn't seek the job, I was asked.

In the first case, political interest seemed to be a by-product of one's need to be socially acceptable; in the second case, it derived from activity on behalf of a politically involved professional associate. In both cases apparent political apathy is transformed into political awareness and participation as a result of primary group contact.

Political Interest as Result of Participation. Political socialization does not necessarily precede some form of political activity. A person may participate in political action of one kind or another without any previously crystallized political affect. For instance, he may find himself involved in "school politics" because his political potentialities are sensed by his peers; he may become active in political campaigns because of other social ties with other campaign workers; or he may even participate in low-level political party work, as an errand-boy or leaflet distributor, without really understanding the meaning of his activity. As Table 4 indicates, these types of participation are reported as stimulants of political

Table 4—*Political Interest as Result of Political and Non-Political Participation*

Type of Participation	Cal. N = 113	N.J. N = 79	Ohio N = 162	Tenn. N = 120
Activity in school politics	12%	4%	4%	*%
Study of politics	20%	9%	14%	8%
Political work: general (campaigns, meetings)	20%	6%	10%	13%
Party work	12%	32%	10%	7%
Civic/community work	11%	8%	6%	8%
Activity in occupational/professional groups	8%	4%	6%	*%
Activity in ethnic/religious groups	*%	3%	—	—
Legislative lobbying	3%	1%	—	2%
Politically-related job (teaching civics; journalism; law; etc.)	8%	4%	3%	7%

* Less than one per cent.

interest. California respondents, in particular, mentioned these directly political forms of activity as sources of their political involvement, though New Jersey legislators exceed the Californians in the "party work" category.

Secondly, a person may become exposed to politics by experiences which are themselves non-political in character, but which are close enough to politics to serve as agencies of political socialization. For instance, school learning, or even self-education, may stimulate political awareness; so may participation in civic or community affairs, as well as activity in occupational, professional, or minority groups. Finally, a person may come to be politically conscious by performing professional tasks which are relatively close to politics, like lobbying, newspaper work, law practice, teaching of civics, or public employment. As Table 4 shows, some of these forms of non-political participation were recalled by state legislators as avenues of their political socialization. Again, these forms of activity seem to play a somewhat more important role in California than in the other states, though inter-state differences are consistently small.

Two aspects of the distributions in Table 4 deserve special mention. First, the study of civics, politics or related subjects in school does not seem to serve as a potent lubricant of political consciousness or interest. With the exception of

California, where a fifth of the legislators pointed to their formal schooling as having had relevance to their political interest, a surprisingly small percentage gave responses such as: "I guess it started with my getting interested in the study of civics in grade school and high school. I suppose this study of civics was my first inspiration."

Secondly, it seems that, for a number of the politicians who populate the four state legislatures, political or party work itself was the source of their political initiation. This seems to be particularly the case in New Jersey, and might be due, in part, to the highly politicized atmosphere characteristic of that state's metropolitan areas. In other words, party politics operates as its own socializing agent. Getting involved in political work, either occasionally in connection with a campaign, or by doing regular party work, seems for some of these politicians to have been a first stimulus of a more permanent dedication to public life. Running errands, handing out leaflets, or door-to-door canvassing work was given by some as their earliest recollection of interest in politics, usually among those whose family had been active or interested in politics before them. For others, being recruited by a party to run for party or public office seems to have been the source of a political orientation. As one legislator put it, "I got politically interested in 1938 when I became involved in county and state politics. I then became the chairman of the county committee."

Among non-political forms of participation mentioned by legislators as decisive in their political socialization, activity in civic affairs or community work ranks first in all four states. That such activity served as a direct incentive to political interest might be expressed as follows:

This is actually an extension of my activities in the school and community. I was interested in service clubs, civic progress and community problem-solving. It was getting so I was going to meetings ten nights a week. It's only a short step from this to public office.

Activity in occupational and professional groups, or contact with politics as a result of actually non-political but politically-connected jobs, was recalled by a few legislators as influencing their interest in politics. A newspaperman would say that, of course, he became interested because of his profession. Another "became interested in political intrigue as a young cub reporter, and was hired to write publicity for a state senator." A former union leader recalled that his interest was aroused when politicians catered to him to win the support of his membership. A lawyer recalled his work for a property owners association before government bodies, or a teacher of civics suggested that his political interest was stimulated when he took his classes to visit the state capital. Finally, contacts with politicians in service jobs were reported by some as having been instrumental in developing their political interest. A number of legislators mentioned having served as pages in the state legislature while in college. As one of them recalled, "I attribute my early interest in politics to my employment in the legislature." Public employment, in administrative departments of the state government or in the elected office of county trustee, was reported by some as a source of their first political interest.

The impression one gets from these recollections is one of the great variety of agents and activities which can operate as influential stimuli of political socialization. One is struck by the great heterogeneity of the sources which stimulate a political focus of attention. Most of those who mentioned these stimuli became interested in politics, at least in their own definition of what it means to be "politically interested," rather late in their personal development—in support of the notion that political socialization is not restricted to the earliest years of the life cycle, but that it is a process which takes place at later phases as well. While it is likely, of course, that the foundations of political interest were laid earlier, it is the later phases which apparently stand out in these legislators' perceptions of their political socialization.

Political Interest as Result of Public Events. Great public events, either of a periodic character, like election campaigns, or of more singular though far-reaching nature, like wars or economic depressions, may have a politically mobilizing impact on persons not previously concerned with public affairs. Similarly, relatively unimportant local or state problems become public issues which may involve people who before their occurrence had paid no attention to politics. Forty-two per cent of California, 25% of New Jersey, 21% of Ohio, and 18% of Tennessee legislators recalled particular events or conditions as stimuli of their first political interest. While the percentages in particular categories are small (Table 5), except in the case of California, in connection with political campaigns, and in New Jersey, in connection with local conditions or issues, the tenor of these recollections suggests that political socialization occasioned by public events may be accompanied by a special intensity of feeling not generally experienced under other circumstances.

The Presidential campaign, in particular, seems to have a latent socializing function in the American political system. It serves not only to activate voters, but the excitement, the turbulence, the color, the intrusion of the Presidential campaign into the routine existence of a relatively little politicized society seem to make a profound impression, so that many years later a particular election or administration may be recalled with a good deal of relish as a source of political interest—as if the election had been held only yesterday:

In the Hughes campaign of 1916 my grandfather said to me: "My boy, I'll meet my maker. There's only one thing I regret, that I voted in the re-election campaign for Cleveland's second term." People streamed through the house to find out from the old man how to vote.

During the Bryan-McKinley campaign I hanged a picture of McKinley on my bedroom wall. My father took it off and I hanged it up again. He took it off and took me to the woodshed. I've been a Republican ever since.

Remarks made about gubernatorial, senatorial or other election campaigns were less colorful than recollections of Presidential contests. War, on the other hand, was recalled in more intensely personal terms by the few who ascribed their political interest to this experience. "Many of us, when we came back, had a new awakening, a new interest in civic affairs," or, "In prison camp I decided that we should do everything that we could on a local level instead of joining big organizations to influence grand policy."

Some California and Ohio legislators mentioned the depression as the origin of their political awakening. One respondent reported, for instance, that in the thirties, while he was employed in county agricultural work, "the plight of the farmers brought my interest." Another said that "during the depression everybody was politically conscious, and that interest stayed with me." For some of those who claimed to have become politically aware in the depression, politics seems to have meant a job. As one of them put it, "Well, during the depression, we weren't selling any automobiles. The situation was favorable for me to get on the ticket for county auditor." In this case, for in-

Table 5—Political Interest as Result of Particular Events or Conditions

Events or Conditions	Cal. N = 113	N.J. N = 79	Ohio N = 162	Tenn. N = 120
Presidential campaigns or administrations	14%	4%	11%	8%
Other political campaigns	19%	5%	2%	3%
War	2%	3%	2%	3%
Depression	5%	—	2%	—
Local conditions/issues	5%	15%	2%	4%
State conditions/issues	5%	—	1%	—

stance, a first interest in politics seems to have coincided with the respondent's active entry into politics. Finally, state or local conditions were reported by a few legislators as having been instrumental in their political socialization.

Personal Predispositions and Political Socialization. As we mentioned earlier, our research orientation was to find out "how" state legislators became interested in politics, not "why" they became interested. Nevertheless, it is noteworthy that half of the California, New Jersey and Ohio legislators, and a third of the Tennesseans, seized our question of "how" they had become interested as an opportunity to reflect on certain personal predispositions which, they apparently felt, preceded or accompanied their political awakening. It is possible, of course, that these recollections are nothing more than current rationalizations. Yet, even if we are not prepared to interpret these responses as anything else, they are probably quite genuine perceptions and, as such, constitute significant elements in legislators' self-definitions as politicians.

Table 6—Personal Predispositions and Political Socialization

Predispositions	Cal. N = 113	N.J. N = 79	Ohio N = 162	Tenn. N = 120
Political power	3%	6%	2%	3%
Admiration for politicians	19%	3%	5%	2%
Indignation	9%	8%	5%	2%
Sense of obligation: general	15%	5%	8%	*%
Sense of obligation: to special groups	3%	6%	*%	*%
Desire for sociability	2%	5%	1%	2%
Physical handicaps displaced	*%	—	*%	*%
Long interest: unspecified	14%	24%	33%	23%

* Less than one per cent

Of those who expressed themselves in predispositional terms, a good many simply said that they had always been interested in politics, and left it at that. But perhaps the most interesting finding revealed in Table 6 is that only very few of these politicians spontaneously mentioned political power, influence or authority as the kind of stimuli which predisposed them towards a political orientation. While it is, of course, impossible to say whether such power motives were really present or absent among those who admitted to them and those who did not, there is no reason to suppose that in a democratic society, where a large part of the community participates in the selection of public officials, politicians are neces-

sarily and only recruited from power-motivated persons. Even if politicians differ from average citizens in the degree of their political involvement, values other than power are likely to bring would-be leaders to public attention.[11] The fact that only few of these legislators indicated power as a predispositional correlate of their political socialization is, therefore, quite understandable. Only a few were as explicit as the legislator who said that it was hard for him to explain what first interested him in politics, but continued:

> I would say that I'm the sort of person interested in doing things. I feel I should contribute from the policy point of view. I'm not a good joiner. I feel the same sort of thing carries over into government and politics. I have always some desire not to be in the crowd. I'm never content to go to meetings and just listen and go home. I like to get my oar in.

Admiration for politicians—as ego-ideals—was suggested by others as having had some influence on their developing political interest. That favorable impressions of other politicians formed at an early age have an impact on political awareness seems plausible, as the following example illustrates:

> I do remember that one summer I was staying with my uncle. I guess I was about 13. I attended an old-fashioned town meeting with him. My uncle was quite active at the meeting, and it made quite an impression on me.

While some legislators recalled having become politically interested as a result of admiring certain politicians, others reported having become interested for just the opposite reason—because they were dissatisfied with politicians or political situations:

> This is a somewhat long story. I was an officer of a club, and in this capacity I had to call upon a city councilman to speak with him about getting the use of (some facility). He promised me to look into it and have my request heard before the commission, but he never did. He just ignored me.

Sense of obligation appears, not surprisingly, as a relatively frequent category of predispositional responses. This kind of answer is, of course, part and parcel of a politician's armor of rationalizations and can hardly be taken at face value:

> Well, it came about twelve or fourteen years ago when I decided I had spent all my life tending to our business and had done nothing for the community. I looked around to see how I could help out and decided to run for the legislature. I thought my business experience would be useful in the legislature.

Yet, there is an element of genuine commitment in this response that is in sharp contrast to mere political rhetoric. In other words, a distinction must be made between the politician for whom "public service" is a convenient device of deception, of himself, his audience, or both, and the politician who really feels a sense of obligation.

A few legislators suggested that their interest in politics was stimulated by the "social" possibilities which politics seemed to offer, as, for instance, the former school superintendent who upon retirement missed the chance to meet people which his occupation had given him and who, for this reason, claimed to have become interested in politics. Finally, three legislators attributed their initial interest in politics to the existence of a physical handicap and implied that politics offered them a compensatory opportunity. As one of these pointed out, "As a kid I had a bad leg, couldn't participate in sports and developed an interest in politics. I thought a legal background qualified a fellow for anything in public life."

It requires re-emphasis that our data do not tell us "why" these legislators were "moved" to seek a political career, while others in the general population, with similar ostensible experiences were not so moved. In other words, the perceptual data on legislators' pre-political activities, or the events surrounding their earliest political interest, or even what they described as predispositional factors, cannot be interpreted in a motivational sense. If there is a personality syndrome of which one may think as "political man," the data do not and cannot reveal its existence among these state legislators.

Ideology and Political Socialization. Not unexpectedly in a society like the American where politics is pragmatic rather than ideological, political beliefs seem to play a minor part in the process of political socialization. As Table 7 shows, only very small minorities in all four states linked our question of how they had become interested in politics with a discussion of political beliefs. This is all the more significant because the open-ended character of the question represented a perfect opportunity for ideological discourse if the respondent wished it. One can only guess, of

Table 7—Socio-Economic Beliefs in Political Socialization

Beliefs	Cal. N = 113	N.J. N = 79	Ohio N = 162	Tenn. N = 120
Liberal	7%	1%	2%	—
Conservative	4%	1%	1%	2%
Pro-business	—	—	*%	—
Pro-labor	3%	3%	*%	—
Pro-farmer	*%	1%	1%	—
Pro-religious/ethnic groups	—	3%	*%	—

* Less than one per cent

course, that in a European country where ideology constitutes a more important item of political culture, a legislator would probably have seized this opportunity to express political opinions or beliefs. And those who did mention beliefs gave them only most cursory attention.

Summary: Major Sources of Political Interest. If we look at a summary of the major sources of political interest as spontaneously reported by legislators themselves, some state-to-state patterns emerge. We cannot say absolutely that these patterns are not due purely to chance, but the very fact that patterns do occur suggests that interstate differences may be genuine expressions of political socialization processes among the four states. Table 8 summarizes the responses in our major categories. The most obvious difference to be noted is between California and the other states

Table 8—Summary: Major Sources of Political Interest

Major Sources	Cal. N = 113	N.J. N = 79	Ohio N = 162	Tenn. N = 120
Primary groups	34%	47%	43%	42%
Participation	70%	60%	49%	43%
Events/conditions	42%	25%	21%	18%
Predispositions	52%	53%	52%	33%
Beliefs	16%	10%	6%	3%

in regard to the influence of primary groups. One possible explanation of the relatively low percentage in the California column is that primary groups are less effective as political socializing agents in California because primary group influence is predicated on a reasonably stable population structure. But California is distinguished from the other three states by the fact that it is an immigrant state, and it may be that the population movement into the state has not permitted the formation of stable primary groups which can act as effective agents of political socialization. On the other hand, New Jersey, the oldest of the states in terms of admission to the Union, shows the greatest percentage in the primary group category, with Ohio and Tennessee in close middle positions.

What California may lack by way of primary group influence, it seems to make up in the categories of participation and events or conditions as stimulants of political interest. With regard to participation, it may be suggested that social and political activity is seized upon by an immigrant population to make itself feel at home in a new environment. In newly created communities, fewer legislators are "born into" politics, more become politically active in the process of community life. Similarly, political beliefs seem to play a slightly more important role in a state where stable political party patterns have had less of a chance to crystallize than in states characterized by very definite, if different, party-system structures. In both the participation and event categories, as in the category of political beliefs, the pattern of responses ranks California first, New Jersey second, Ohio third, and Tennessee last. Moreover, Tennessee legislators were less likely to mention personal predispositions than the legislators from the other three states. Just why this should be the case we cannot say.

What do our data tell us about the political socialization of state legislators? In general, it seems that a great many sources are operative in initiating political interest. Perhaps the most significant finding is tentative support for the hypothesis that political socialization—the process by which political interest is acquired—may occur at almost any phase of the life cycle, even among men and women whose concern with public affairs is presumably more intense and permanent than that of the average citizen. But it seems to take place more often at a relatively early age. Whether the differences we found from state to state, either with regard to the agency or time of socialization, are significant as evidence of differing political sub-cultures would require more detailed and systematic inquiry than we were able to execute here.

Notes

1. Charles E. Merriam, *New Aspects of Politics* (Chicago: University of Chicago Press, 1925), p. 85.

2. See Herbert Hyman, *Political Socialization* (Glencoe: The Free Press, 1959).

3. See Morris Janowitz, "The Systematic Analysis of Political Biography," *World Politics*, VI (1954), 405-12, for a review of such studies.

4. The interview question read: "How did you become interested in politics? What is your earliest recollection of being interested in it?" It should be pointed out that the problem of legislators' political socialization was only peripheral to our main research interest—the analysis of state legislatures as political role systems. We did not intend to collect as full a set of data as might be desirable—the story of politicians' socialization could be the subject of a full-scale research project in its own right. This study therefore aspires to nothing more than a descriptive presentation of state legislators' perceptions of their political socialization, and the analysis has not been guided by specific hypotheses.

5. It should also be pointed out that the open-ended character of the question makes it mandatory to consider the results of this study as suggestive rather than definitive. While open-ended questions have the advantage of making for spontaneity and a wide range of response, and of allowing the respondent himself to formulate or "structure" the topic under investigation, there are certain drawbacks which limit their usefulness in statistical analysis. Heterogeneous answers make statistical controls difficult, if not impossible, and they make statistical inference of doubtful validity. For instance, some respondents mentioned primary groups they considered instrumental in stimulating their first political interest; others referred to some form of activity, political or otherwise, as a source of their first interest; others described events or conditions with which they associated their political concerns; still others referred to personal predispositions accompanying their initiation to politics; and a few mentioned political beliefs. Moreover, many respondents gave more than one "reason" for their political socialization. This makes it difficult to single out any one factor as more important than any other.

Secondly, the respondents differed a great deal in a number of personal characteristics which are significant in answering open-ended questions. A few were suspicious of the interview and gave minimum, if not evasive, answers, while others, more favorably inclined, were more candid. Some were genuinely pressed for time and failed to elaborate as fully as those who were willing to devote a great deal of time to the interview. Still others—especially those with relatively little education—were unable to articulate answers to a question about which they evidently had thought little prior to the interview. Fluctuations in mood, in attitude towards the interview, in verbal facility or in self-consciousness made undoubtedly for considerable variability in answer patterns.

These differences are inherent in the open-ended type of interview question and in the interview situation. They do not allow us, therefore, to make categorical statements about the actual distribution of perceptions of factors in political socialization which we might have found if we had asked direct, closed questions about the particular factors which we were able to code. For instance, the fact that a certain percentage of our respondents mentioned some form of primary group influence does not mean that others, who did not mention this, were not possibly affected by family or friends in the process of their political socialization. In other words, the percentages of responses occurring in any particular category are, at most, suggestive indices of the extent to which legislators recalled certain socializing influences.

6. Seymour M. Lipset, Paul F. Lazarsfeld, Allen H. Barton, Juan Linz, "The Psychology of Voting: An Analysis of Political Behavior," in Gardner Lindzey, ed., *The Handbook of Social Psychology* (Cambridge: Addison-Wesley, 1954), II, 1145.

7. There is reason to believe that the low percentage figure for New Jersey legislators having political recollections from childhood is not too accurate. For, as we shall see, New Jersey legislators, more than those from at least two other states, mentioned family influence as an important factor in their political socialization. As Table 1 shows, the low percentage of New Jersey legislators recalling the childhood period must be accounted for by the fact that, compared with the other states, an inordinately large percentage could not be coded on the time dimension. In other words, it is unlikely that New Jersey represents a special case.

8. "The term socialization in its current usage in the literature refers primarily to the process of child development. This is in fact a crucially important case of the operation of what are here called the mechanisms of socialization, but it should be made clear that the term is here used in a broader sense than the current one to designate the learning of *any* orientations of functional significance to the operation of a system of complementary role-expectations. In this sense, socialization, like learning, goes on throughout life. The case of the development of the child is only the most dramatic because he has so far to go." Talcott Parsons, *The Social System* (Glencoe: The Free Press, 1951), pp. 207-8.

9. See Paul F. Lazarsfeld, Bernard Berelson, and Hazel Gaudet, *The People's Choice* (New York: Columbia University Press, 1948), pp. 140-5; Angus Campbell, Gerald Gurin, and Warren E. Miller, *The Voter Decides* (Evanston: Row, Peterson and Company, 1954), pp. 199-206;

Bernard R. Berelson, Paul F. Lazarsfeld, and William N. McPhee, *Voting* (Chicago: University of Chicago Press, 1954), pp. 88-109.

10. W. A. Anderson, "The Family and Individual Social Participation," *American Sociological Review*, VIII (1943), 420-4.

11. See Harold D. Lasswell, "The Selective Effect of Personality in Political Participation," in Richard Christie and Marie Jahoda, eds., *Studies in the Scope and Method of "The Authoritarian Personality"* (Glencoe: The Free Press, 1954), p. 221, for a discussion of political personality in democratic settings.

10. SOME PERSONALITY FACTORS OF STATE LEGISLATORS IN SOUTH CAROLINA

John B. McConaughy

SOME TWENTY YEARS AGO Harold D. Lasswell, in his *Psychopathology and Politics*,[1] attempted to show by case histories some of the motivations and personality characteristics of certain political types. This book was a pioneer in its field because it applied the psychoanalytic "free fantasy" technique to the field of political science. The case histories were chosen from those in selected hospitals and from the official files of certain psychiatrists. From these case histories, Lasswell was able to obtain information which threw new light on the actions of such political types as the agitator and the administrator. He then developed the formula $p\}d\}r = P$; where p equals private motives, d equals displacement onto public objects, r equals rationalization in terms of public interest, $\}$ means "transformed into," and P signifies the political man.[2]

Lasswell's techniques are invaluable for the study of political personalities and motives. It is unfortunate that others have not utilized them more fully and thereby added to the store of knowledge concerning the personalities of politicians; but a partial explanation lies in the fact that the techniques themselves present obstacles to their ready use by political scientists. In the first place, the case histories are usually confidential and difficult to obtain. In the second place, in order to evaluate them validly the political scientist needs training as a psychiatrist as well as a political scientist. Finally, most of the case histories deal with either neurotic or psychotic individuals who came to the hospital or the psychiatrist only because they were somewhat abnormal. Although the study of the abnormal helps one to understand the normal, it would be a contradiction of terms to consider the abnormal typical of the

normal. And while it is true that abnormality is a matter of degree rather than *non sui generis*, still the degree of difference can be so great as to be the difference between the reactions of politicians in a democratic United States and a nazi Germany or a communist Russia. There is no question about the validity of Lasswell's analysis concerning the individuals whom he studied; but because of the nature of his data and their selection, it is difficult for others to corroborate his findings and to determine whether or not his individuals are typical or representative of the average politician.

The Political Science Department at the University of South Carolina, in cooperation with the Psychology Department,[3] has been interested in developing new techniques which could be applied more widely to politicians at present active in politics. These techniques have the advantage of studying the normal rather than the abnormal; they are more objective than subjective, and are capable of being checked by other political scientists with a minimum amount of training in psychology, rather than in psychiatry. The principal disadvantage of these techniques is that they are extensive rather than intensive. A political scientist using Lasswell's methods could probe deeper into individual cases than the researcher using the new techniques.

The procedure followed consisted of giving a battery of personality and opinion tests to eighteen legislators, state senators and representatives of South Carolina. The majority of the tests were administered at the State House during the regular session of the General Assembly; a few, however, were given to the men in their home offices. The legislators were promised absolute anonymity in order to encourage truthful answers. One control group for two of the tests, the Unlabelled Fascist Attitude Test and the Lentz C-R Opinionaire, was composed of a South Carolina service club of 28 members. A second control group for

Reprinted from *American Political Science Review*, Vol. 44 (1950), pp. 897-903, where it appeared under the title, "Certain Personality Factors of State Legislators in South Carolina," by permission of the author and the publisher.

the C-R Opinionaire was composed of 21 adult men who had finished four years of college work and had received their A.B. degrees. A graduate student, with training in both political science and psychology[4] administered the tests and did the statistical research.

In general the legislators were quite cooperative in taking the tests, once they were assured that their identity would not be disclosed. The principal difficulty in administering the tests to them was the fact that they were extremely busy most of the time while the legislature was in session; consequently, each individual had to be given one test at a time. This operation required a high degree of patience. On the other hand, the fact that the legislators were meeting in Columbia, where the University is located, offered some compensating advantages.

Some explanation should be made of the statistical methods used in this research, since political scientists may not be as familiar with them as are psychologists.[5] Whenever equivalents were available, the raw scores of the tests given were converted into percentiles before comparisons were made, so that as many as possible of the scores would be given in the same unit of measurement. There were eleven factors tested by this particular battery of tests, and for each factor the following seven statistical values were found:

1. The frequency distribution, . . .
2. The average, . . .
3. The median, . . .
4. The standard deviation, . . .
5. The correlation of scores of the legislators with their ages by the rank-difference method. . . .
6. A comparison of the averages of the scores of the older men with those of the younger. . . .
7. Scattergrams. . . .

The tests given in this survey were the Bernreuter Personality Inventory, the Guilford-Martin Inventory of Factors G-A-M-I-N, the Edwards Unlabeled Fascist Attitude Test and the Lentz C-R Opinionaire. All have the advantage that the traits being measured are not discernible by the person taking the test, thereby increasing the validity of the test.

The outstanding feature of the Bernreuter and the Guilford-Martin tests is that they measure several different factors of personality at one time, saving much time in administration. The following traits are measured by the Bernreuter Personality Inventory:

(1) B1-N. A measure of neurotic tendency. Persons scoring high on this scale tend to be emotionally unstable. . . . Those scoring low tend to be well-balanced emotionally.

(2) B2-S. A measure of self-sufficiency. Persons scoring high on this scale prefer to be alone, rarely ask for sympathy and encouragement, and tend to ignore the advice of others. Those scoring low dislike solitude and often seek advice and encouragement.

(3) B3-I. A measure of introversion-extroversion. Persons scoring high on this scale tend to be introverted; that is, they are imaginative and tend to live with themselves. . . . Those scoring low are extroverted; that is, they rarely worry, seldom suffer emotional upsets, and rarely substitute day-dreaming for action.

(4) B4-D. A measure of dominance-submission. Persons scoring high on this scale tend to dominate others in face-to-face situations. Those scoring low tend to be submissive.[6]

Norms have been compiled for male and female high school students, college students and adults, with which the scores of examinees may be compared. The Bernreuter Test has been criticized because of the fact that it shows a positive correlation between introversion and neurosis, which may be an artifact due to the use of some identical items in the two scales B1-N and B3-I. A test which could have been used in place of the Bernreuter would have been the Guilford-Martin S-T-R-D-C test, but the Bernreuter test was adopted because it is the most widely used test and therefore affords the best basis for comparison.

In interpreting the above table, the average adult male would score 50 per cent. The table indicates that the South Carolina political leaders are far less neurotic than the average male adult, far less introverted, more self-sufficient, and slightly more dominant. Indeed, the political leaders seem to be better adjusted to life and more stable than the average male voter. The results would seem to throw serious doubt on the theory sometimes advanced by psychoanalysts that politicians go into politics because of feelings of insufficiency or an inferiority complex. The politician is no dreamer; apparently he is a realist who enjoys meeting people and going on parties.

Table I—Bernreuter Personality Inventory

	Average P.R.	Median P.R.	S.D.	Rho-Correlation with Age
B1-N	32.83%	28.33%	24.19	− .04
B2-S	65.89%	72.50%	21.99	− .08
B3-I	28.78%	26.00%	20.93	− .02
B4-D	58.33%	62.50%	22.26	− .02

Table II—Guilford-Martin Inventory of Factors G-A-M-I-N

	Average P.R.	Median P.R.	S.D.	Rho-Coefficient with Age
G	54%	59%	25.68	— .30
A	67.17%	72%	21.61	— .30
M	69.72%	67%	19.09	.35
I	76.83%	83%	23.15	.06
N	60.19%	61.67%	26.50	.41

The traits measured by the Guilford-Martin Inventory of Factors G-A-M-I-N are:

(1) G. General pressure for overt activity.
(2) A. Ascendency in social situations as opposed to submissiveness.
(3) M. Masculinity of attitudes and interests as opposed to femininity.
(4) I. Lack of inferiority feelings; self-confidence.
(5) N. Lack of nervous tenseness and irritability.[7]

As Table II shows, the politicians tested were only slightly more energetic than the average male population, but they were much higher than average in respect to ascendancy in social situations, masculinity and lack of nervous tenseness and irritability. The political leaders were highest in lack of inferiority feelings. Only 23.17 per cent of the total adult male population ranks higher in lack of inferiority feelings than the average South Carolina political leader tested. The findings on lack of inferiority feelings also agree with B2-S on the Bernreuter Personality Inventory.

The Edwards Unlabelled Fascist Attitudes Test is based on a similar test, composed by Stagner, which arrived at the conclusion that while subjects may reject any statements labelled "fascist," they may accept the same statements if they are not so labelled.[8] Stagner's pioneer work in the field measures such phases of fascism as militarism, nationalism, anti-radicalism, contempt for the lower classes and opposition to labor unions.[9] Edwards' purpose was to include attitudes toward birth control, education, status of women, status toward religion, etc., for these phases can be a more delicate and less recognizable test of a fascist tendency.[10]

The lowest possible score obtainable on the Edwards Test is 20; the highest possible score is 100. In order to be sure of the meaning of the Edwards Test in South Carolina a control group composed of 28 adult members of a service club in South Carolina was used to provide a comparison with the legislators. This control group consisted of persons of varying ages.

It can be seen from Table III that the South Carolina political leaders averaged below the control group in fascist tendencies. (The political leaders also averaged from 1.3 points to 6.6 points, according to age, below the average made by the students who took the tests under Edwards.) In addition, this table shows that fascist tendencies increase with age but are inversely proportional to county sales, high school education and urban percentage of the voters who elect the South Carolina political leaders.

The Lentz C-R Opinionaire, which tests conservatism-radicalism, is based on the assumption that the conservatism-radicalism difference among persons is dependent upon the degree of their opposition or favor toward change.[11]

Although the South Carolina political leaders are among the top 36.22 per cent of the most conservative male adults in the United States, they average only slightly more conservative than the two South Carolina control groups. As indicated in the table, conservatism increases heavily with age and decreases quickly when legislators are from counties with high retail sales, which is an index of prosperity. The effects of education and urbanity of the electorate upon the political ideas of their representatives are too small to be statistically significant.

In conclusion, the Bernreuter Inventory given to eighteen of 170 South Carolina legislators indi-

Table III—Edwards Unlabelled Fascist Attitudes Test

	Midpoint	Average	Median	S.D.	Rho-Age and Score
Legislators	60	58.72	55.33	11.96	.38
Control Group	60	59.33	57.00	10.98	

	Rho County Sales and Score	Rho H. S. Graduates and Score	Rho Urban Percentage and Score
Legislators	— .31	— .42	— .38

Table IV—Lentz C-R Opinionaire

CONSERVATISM

	Av. P.R.	Median P.R.	S.D.	Rho with Age
S.C. Legislators	64.78%	67.50%	26.58	.41
Control Group No. 1	60.00%	68.50%	21.74	
Control Group No. 2	54.26%	59.50%	20.37	

	Rho with Sales	Rho Education	Rho Urbanity
S.C. Legislators	— .45	— .03	— .13

cated that the political leaders were decidedly less neurotic than the general male population; that they were more self-sufficient; that they were decidedly more extroverted; but that they were only slightly more dominant. The Guilford-Martin Inventory of Factors G-A-M-I-N indicated that South Carolina political leaders have, to an insignificant degree, more general pressure for overt activity than the average person; that they are decidedly more masculine than the general male population; that they are, to a large degree, more self-confident than the average person and have fewer feelings of inferiority; and that they are less irritable and tense than the average person. The South Carolina leaders, according to the Edwards Unlabelled Fascist Attitude Test, are less fascist than those treated by Edwards. The acceptance of fascist ideas by the leaders decreases with the prosperity, education and urbanity of the county which they represent. The C-R Opinionaire indicates that South Carolina political leaders are, to a significant degree, more conservative than the general college population, but not much more conservative than the samples of South Carolina population used as control groups. The counties in South Carolina with the largest · retail sales send more liberal political leaders to the state capitol than counties with low retail sales.

In conclusion, it must be stressed that the results reported are highly tentative and should be used with extreme caution. The sample of eighteen political leaders is too small to be conclusive for the country as a whole. The eighteen leaders came from only one state, and personality traits might differ in other areas. It is to be hoped, consequently, that political scientists using similar techniques in other parts of the country may be able to add information which either corroborates or refutes the results obtained in South Carolina.

Notes

1. (Chicago, 1930).
2. *Ibid.*, pp. 261-262.
3. Especially with Dr. M. Kershaw Walsh, Head of the Psychology Department.
4. Marie Joyce Hayes, whose unpublished M.A. thesis, "The Personality Factors of Contemporary Political Leaders of South Carolina" (University of South Carolina, 1948), deals with some of the findings of the tests.
5. For a fuller discussion of the statistical procedures involved, see Henry E. Garrett, *Statistics in Psychology and Education* (New York, 1926).
6. Robert G. Bernreuter, *Manual for the Personality Inventory* (Stanford University, 1935), p. 1.
7. *Manual of Directions and Norms for the Guilford-Martin Inventory of Factors G-A-M-I-N*, p. 1.
8. Allen L. Edwards, "Unlabelled Fascist Attitudes," *Journal of Abnormal and Social Psychology*, Vol. 36, p. 572 (1941). The Edwards Test was standardized on only 91 college students at the University of Akron in 1940, and may be a little hyper-sensitive. Its reliability has sometimes been questioned.
9. *Ibid.*, p. 575.
10. *Ibid.*, p. 576.
11. Theodore F. Lentz and Colleagues, *Manual for C. R. Opinionaire* (St. Louis, 1935), p. 1.

11. THE ROLES OF CONGRESSIONAL COMMITTEE MEMBERS*

Ralph K. Huitt

EACH HOUSE of Congress is a human group, with leadership, a hierarchy of influence, and a set of norms which control, more or less, the behavior of its members. The man who goes to Congress joins a going concern. He accepts and shares a group life.[1] One factor in any decision he makes is the influence on him of his house as an institutionalized group. But the group life of the congressman is exceedingly complex. Like other men he is a member of many groups, with any one of which he might identify in a particular situation; but unlike most other men he is a *representative*, under obligation consciously and deliberately to take into account the wishes of the groups which support him. As we have said, he is part of the status pattern in his legislative house, in which both formal and informal leadership patterns impose obligations and afford access to power. His success as a professional legislator depends to a large extent upon his conforming with the group norms of his colleagues. But congressmen, too, follow the election returns; prestige and influence in the internal system of the legislature are responsive to success in meeting external demands upon the member. In these respects, to be sure, the group life of a legislative body is not different in kind from that of those small groups which have been studied with impressive results.[2] But it certainly is more complex and its members are more sophisticated. Consequently, it presents more formidable problems than do simpler groups.

A study of the group life of Congress might well begin with the standing committee. It *is* a small group, susceptible in most of its operations to close observation. Because its membership is relatively stable, its leaders men of long committee tenure, it has a continuous group life of its own. One factor in that group life, of course, is the pressure from the house whose creature it is, but the committee is worth studying as a human group

in its own right. Furthermore, there is the attractive possibility that techniques so developed will be useful in the more difficult undertaking with the larger group of which it is a part. And it is relatively accessible to research: most of its hearings are open to the public and an adequate record is kept. The public hearing is only a part of the activity of a committee, but it is an important and often revealing part.

The standing committee then is a promising group with which to begin a study of the behavior of congressmen in the legislative struggle for at least four reasons. One is the greater *frequency of interaction* of individual congressmen in committees than on the floor of their house. On the floor a congressman may speak seldom, and on a particular issue may confine himself to a single prepared speech. But in a committee in which he is active he talks many times and with less formality. A second reason is that in the committee hearings a group of congressmen are subject to *common stimuli*. They hear the same witnesses and react to the same comments. The third is that the committee is a group of *manageable size* for intensive study. It is possible to observe it closely, and its members are few enough that roles can be kept straight and relationships plotted. A fourth is that it has, within limits, a *continuous life*. Its membership changes, but members are encouraged by the seniority principle to stay on a committee. And the change of membership is never complete and seldom drastic at one time; group norms can easily be transmitted to new members. Thus the committee is a subgroup of its house which is itself a going concern.

Some Hypotheses About the Committee. We are not without generalizations about the roles that committees — and inferentially committee members — play in the legislative process. The general literature on legislation and the political process furnishes several which might serve as hypotheses for further testing. One of the most tenacious of the basic concepts has the committee discovering, protecting, and advancing the general interest out of the welter of special interests contending for support. As Professor Chamberlain puts it: "The committee itself must be the

Reprinted from *American Political Science Review*, Vol. 48 (1954), pp. 340-365, where it appeared under the title, "The Congressional Committee: A Case Study," by permission of the author and the publisher.

* The research on which this article is based was made possible by a grant from The Research Committee of the Graduate School, University of Wisconsin.

guardian of the general public interest, too large and too vague to be organized. What is in the general interest is for the committee to determine, after hearing advocates of the special interests who appear before it."[3] After giving a number of examples of committee actions, he asserts that "the committee played principally the part of a *legislative court,* listening to the evidence of fact and law brought before it by interested parties, considering their suggestions . . . ," then deciding what should be done.[4]

This notion of the committee's function perhaps is accepted implicitly in the recent emphasis on the committee's role as a *fact-finding agency.* Political scientists, and some congressmen, have insisted that committees need professional staff with secure tenure, capable of serving either party with equal competence.[5] To insure the non-partisan and objective character of their service, some have urged a legislative career service, perhaps with staff members to be drawn from a pool, with a professional personnel director in charge of recruitment. The argument is that the professional staff could get objective facts for the committee, thus ending the committee's dependence upon the selected facts of lobbyists and the not disinterested experts borrowed from the bureaus.

A second function, not unlike the first, is that of providing, through its public hearings, an open *public forum.*[6] The special interests still vie with each other, the general interest still must emerge from their clamor, but the stage is highlighted, and a larger audience participates in the decision.

A somewhat different set of generalizations— or hypotheses—rests upon the conception of the legislative process as simply one phase of the political struggle, in which contending groups seek access to governmental power at a number of points, the legislative committee being one.[7] The committee members are not judges, discovering the general interest; they are themselves participants in the political struggle, as indeed are all other governmental officials. No one knows what the "general interest" is; there is none in which everyone shares. Public policy emerges from the pull and haul of groups, and the whole thing is kept from flying to pieces because overlapping memberships in groups prevent the perfect mobilization of any interest. In this frame of reference Professor Truman sees the committee using its public hearing for three purposes.[8] The first, and probably least important, is that of *"transmitting information,* both technical and political, from various actual and potential interest groups to the committee." The second use is as "a *propaganda channel* through which a public may be extended

and its segments partially consolidated or reinforced." Thus the public forum is provided but the committee is not neutral; what is presented is not so much a fair debate as a set piece. The third use is to provide a *catharsis* for frustrations and grievances, "a quasi-ritualistic means of adjusting group conflicts and relieving disturbances through a safety-valve."

This is not, of course, an all-inclusive list of the general propositions about the roles of congressional committees, nor is it suggested that these propositions are mutually exclusive. But they are useful hypotheses for empirical research. The purpose of this study is to see how well these generalizations explain what took place in a series of public hearings before a particular committee on a given issue. The hearings chosen for a case study are those held before the Senate Committee on Banking and Currency in the Spring of 1946 on the question whether the price control and stabilization program of 1942 should be continued, and if so, whether and what changes should be made in it.[9] No claim is made that these are "typical hearings," from which valid generalizations about all committee hearings can be made. No doubt there are numerous "types." But there are several reasons why these hearings are selected for the purposes of this study. (1) The problem is intensely political, i.e., many powerful groups have a stake in the issue and are prepared to make strong efforts to influence the outcome. (2) It is a problem which involves the "general interest"; everybody in the country will be affected in some degree by the outcome. (3) Facts would seem to have some relevance in arriving at the policy decision. There are huge quantities of data available and there are substantial bodies of politico-economic theory to which they can be related. (4) This is not a new problem. It has a history in the three years of administration of public policy in a war economy and nearly a year in a peacetime economy. It is the kind of problem, therefore, which should bring into play all the elements necessary to test the generalizations about committee behavior which we have stated.

The limitations of this kind of study are obvious. It is limited to the public hearings, although much that is important, and perhaps what is decisive, takes place elsewhere. Moreover, it is limited to the printed record of those hearings, where only what is said can be found, and that subject to editing. Inferences therefore must be made from behavior which is recorded incompletely, and perhaps inaccurately. The principal defense of a study thus restricted lies in the fact that it is made with materials which are available in profusion to the kind of people who will make most of the studies of legislative behavior. Few academic persons have data-gathering organizations at their disposal, or freedom for continuous participant-observer research. But the printed record is within the reach of the most modest seminar, making possible endless repetition and refinement. Furthermore, hypotheses which are formulated in crude studies may be used to guide studies which can employ more precise procedures.

Roles of Committee Members. From even a casual reading of the record it would seem that these generalizations may be extended and refined by focusing on the behavior of individual members of the committee. A multiplicity of roles are played by various members, and sometimes by a single member. The status *committee chairman,* for example, can be described by formal and informal powers attributed to that status. But the human chairman is a man in space and time, interacting with other men. More than that, the human chairman occupies more than one status. He is a committee chairman, but he is also a representative of a district, and a member of a complex of groups which make claims upon him and with which he identifies from time to time. And not even the status chairman can be simply defined: at one moment the status is that of the fair presiding officer, under a moral obligation to treat all interested groups fairly; at another moment it may be that of the party leader with a commitment to a program; and again it may be that of a champion of the clientele his committee serves. The role the human chairman will play, his behavior itself, will depend upon many things: upon the constituency, sectional, and party interests in the issue; upon the size of his majority and his hold over it; upon the power and popularity and party of the man in the White House.

The concepts *status* and *role* which we are using here are neither novel nor very complicated. They are used in the sense that Professor Linton uses them in his *The Cultural Background of Personality.*[10] Every culture, no matter how simple, is organized into a number of systems which relate the individual to his culture, among the most important being those of age-sex, family, occupation, and association groups. In a complex society with a high degree of division of labor such as our own, these systems are multifold and overlapping. "The place in a particular system which a certain individual occupies at a particular time" is referred to by Linton as "his *status* with respect to that system." The term *role* he uses "to designate the sum total of the culture patterns associated with a particular status. It thus includes the attitudes, values, and behavior ascribed by the society to any and all persons occupying this status. It can even

be extended to include the legitimate expectations of such persons with respect to the behavior toward them of persons in other statuses within the same system. . . . In so far as it represents overt behavior, a role is the dynamic aspect of a status: what the individual has to do in order to validate his occupation of the status." A role thus is defined by what other people expect of the person filling it. Behavior consists of what the person actually does in filling the role. An individual congressman may occupy a number of statuses: he is a middle-aged man, a father, a congressman, a Democrat, a member of the Ways and Means Committee third in seniority, and so on. In each of these statuses he has learned to play certain roles, and to expect other people to play certain roles. He cannot play all these roles simultaneously, of course; "although he occupies statuses and knows roles at all times, he operates sometimes in terms of one status and its role, sometimes in those of another." The congressional role probably is most usefully conceived not as a single role but as a multiplicity of roles, defined for the congressman by the varying expectations of the groups which he represents or with which he identifies. These roles may be and frequently are conflicting, requiring the individual congressman temporarily to abdicate one or another of his roles, or to find some way to conciliate them, or perhaps to withdraw from the conflict which he cannot resolve.

The price control controversy in the Spring of 1946 subjected congressmen to just such conflicting demands, and by the time the issue reached the Senate Committee they were well-defined. The extensive hearings before the House Committee on Banking and Currency, which culminated in a series of proposed amendments to the existing law, made certain of that. It is easy, as a consequence, to identify a representative sample of congressional roles from the behavior of the members of the Senate Committee.[11]

The only person to play clearly the role of a national party leader was Senator Robert A. Taft, and he seemed to play it consistently. To him the price control contest was simply one round in a continuing battle with the Administration. Officials of the Administration he regarded not as individuals but as representatives of a generalized program which he was attacking on all fronts. Taft made this explicit when Chester Bowles protested that Taft was criticizing him for opinions which he (Bowles) did not hold: "Mr. Bowles, may I say this: I don't distinguish you from the administration. The administration has one policy; you are the Director of Economic Stabilization. What your particular views are make no difference to me. You are carrying on the policies of the administration. When I say 'You' I should be more explicit. I mean the administration. I am not attacking you personally on it, or anything of the sort. I am criticizing your analysis of the situation which is only affected by administration policy; not by what you personally think. That makes no difference to me."[12] The loan to Britain was a special target of Taft's frequent attacks on aspects of the Administration program not within the Committee's jurisdiction. But in his role of national leader, Taft did not hesitate to tell representatives of specific industries that he did not believe they should be decontrolled.[13] His role apparently was appreciated by the spectators; when he excused himself from the session with Bowles, Senator Millikin noted that Taft's departure cost the Committee half its audience.[14]

There was no Democratic counterpart of Taft. The chief burden for the Administration was carried not by the aging and ailing chairman, Senator Wagner, but by Hugh Mitchell. It was Mitchell who apparently was forewarned of the nature of impending testimony against OPA, and so was ready to confront a hotel association's witness with the statement of a firm specializing in hotel accounting that "the hotel industry of this country is at its peak"; a meat institute's spokesman with a retail grocers' attack on the institute's market survey; the automobile dealers' representative with a court decision upholding the OPA cost absorption policy complained of; and a retail dry goods association's director with a Small Business Committee report claiming that prevailing prices were not hindering production by established firms.[15] Mitchell's favorite tactics were to call for figures and more figures, and then discredit or interpret the figures if possible. But he was content to undertake no more than his role on the Committee required, leaving a general defense of the Administration to another time and place.

Another familiar legislative role, that of representative of a sectional interest, was played with almost classic purity in these hearings by Senator Bankhead. His concern was the Southern cotton farmer and the textile industry which buys his product; like a sensitive seismograph picking up vibrations in far corners of the globe, Bankhead reacted to testimony which remotely affected his chief interest. A lumber manufacturer was asked about timber on land owned by farmers, and the price of southern pine compared with western pine. A general discussion of how OPA figured profits was turned into a specific discussion of how it was done on cotton textiles. No suggestion that the industry was doing better than during an OPA base period was acceptable.[16] A general discussion of industry advisory committees led him

to point out that the 15-member committee on women's blouses had not a single member from the South, and get a promise of OPA action.[17] Pankhead's interventions were devoted almost exclusively to his one interest, and when witnesses equipped to talk about that were on the stand his usual taciturnity vanished. On one morning the Committee heard seven witnesses, three of whom represented the cotton textile industry.[18] With these three witnesses Bankhead accounted for more than one-third of all the interruptions (questions and comments). Of the other four (representing apartment owners and hotels) he asked no questions at all. Bankhead presided over the hearings on two occasions; on one, the principal witnesses represented the American Farm Bureau Federation, the National Grange, and the National Cooperative Milk Producers Federation; on the other, the witness was the Secretary of Agriculture.[19]

The Committee members seemed most impressive when they were acting as representatives of specific constituency interests in their states. Here they seemed to speak as experts in their own right. The cliches fell away, the fuzziness and amateurishness disappeared; here the facts were clear and the grasp sure. As a consequence, when the senators talked details of the products and industries of their states with each other they could get together on what they meant, the frustrations of contradictory figures and shifting frames of reference relieved for the moment. Mitchell on the dairy industry in Washington, Murdock and Millikin on dairy cattle in Utah and Colorado, Hickenlooper on land prices in Iowa, Fulbright on strawberries and poultry in Arkansas[20]—these are but a few examples of members speaking easily and with authority on the interests of their states.

This role occupied Senator McFarland to the virtual exclusion of any other. He took very little part in the hearings. His interest was in the subsidies paid to the lead, copper, and zinc industries, which were important in Arizona. Early in 1942 the OPA froze the prices of these metals, and then sought to increase production by awarding subsidies for increments over base-period output on a mine-to-mine and month-to-month basis. McFarland proposed an amendment, supported by the industries, which would shift 60 per cent of the subsidies into the prices of the metals and put the remainder on a noncancelable basis. McFarland came late for Bowles' presentation and made sure the matter had not come up. In the meeting devoted to it, McFarland carefully guided the testimony of the industry representatives and answered many of the senators' questions himself. He displayed no interest in the subsidy question in regard to anything else. He took little part in the remainder of the hearings until the last day, when the OPA administrator of meat prices was called by the Committee in reference to several telegrams from Arizona meat dealers received by McFarland.[21]

There is a difference, of course, in seeking to amend a law, which is the legislative function in its primary form, and interceding with an administrative agency in behalf of a constituent. The latter is the "errand-boy" role, and by the accounts of legislators themselves a large part of their time is spent playing it.[22] There is eloquent testimony in the hearings to the importance of the role to both legislator and administrator: in the senators' complaints that OPA handled congressional mail slowly, and in Paul Porter's reply that the agency got 1500 congressional letters a week and had a rule, not always carried out, that they must be answered in three days.[23] The errand-boy role was not dropped at the committee room door. Capehart brought up three wires from merchants in Indiana complaining about the trouser problem ("Do you have a trouser expert here, Mr. Porter?"); Taylor the case of a packer in Idaho; Mitchell that of a packing company in Tacoma, Washington; Buck that of a factory in Johnstown, Pennsylvania, about which he had a letter; and Bankhead that of a Mr. Flagg of Florence, Alabama.[24] Names were called and action solicited. Hickenlooper, for example, instructed Porter to "make available to me all of the records of Mr. Slotkin and his meat operations for the last 4 years and whatever investigations you have made and alleged infractions and shortcomings; all the meat quotas and his record of ceiling purchases. . . . I would like to see the file and know why something has not been done about it."[25] Tobey raised the case of a New Hampshire veteran who thought OPA was stopping him from fabricating lumber he had logged himself. The OPA man present could not answer the question, but it was later handled to Tobey's satisfaction, although, curiously enough, not to that of Millikin of Colorado.[26] Senatorial interventions in the administrative process, of which these are samples, were made frankly and the administrators commended for prompt service. Hickenlooper spoke appreciatively of Porter's alacrity in the one case the Senator asked him personally to handle, and Capehart stated: "I personally have been over to OPA on any number of occasions, and I must say that I think my batting average has been about 99 per cent in the matter of getting adjustments."[27]

Still another role is involved when an industry brings its problems before the Committee and, in effect, gets a review of the policy and rulings of the administrative agency. This happened several times during the hearings. Typically, the industry in question was not one in which any individual senator was particularly interested; it simply was one which was not satisfied with the results it had gotten in its dealings with OPA. The senators allowed themselves to become entangled in the technical details of the industry's problems, frequently accepted the industry's version, and then called on OPA for action. A good example occurred early in the hearings, when representatives of the underwear industry appeared and complained in detail of OPA procedures and policies. It soon became obvious that their problems had a long history and that the Committee was not competent to legislate in detail for the underwear industry. An OPA man was sent for, and there followed a confrontation scene between him and the underwear maker he allegedly was driving out of business.[28]

The usual effect of the Committee's interest in a particular industry or business was that the OPA then tackled the complainant's applications with speed, giving him real service. The Committee thus constituted itself a kind of superadministrative agency, intervening capriciously and depending upon business to initiate the process. Capehart got an assurance that a price increase would be granted the cheese industry, and Taft a promise of immediate action on evaporated milk.[29] In some cases the outcome was ambiguous, as with Capehart's efforts in regard to the price of butter and oil, and Millikin's attempt to "get an airtight promise out of OPA to decontrol poultry."[30] In one instance a glovemaker under suit for alleged violation of the law brought his case to the Committee, and strong pressures were placed on the OPA enforcement chief by Committee members, apparently in an effort to persuade him to drop the case.[31]

One way to intercept the shifting roles of the Committee members is to observe the variations in their behavior when different witnesses appear before them—representatives of the Administration, of interest groups, businesses, etc. The Administration point of view, in support of extension of price control "without crippling amendments," was well represented on the Committee. Wagner, Mitchell, Barkley, Taylor, Radcliffe, Murdock, Fulbright, and Tobey (a Republican), were usually dependable, and sometimes aggressive, supporters of OPA. But it would have been hard to tell it during the testimony of Bowles or Porter, the first two witnesses before the Committee. Despite Bowles' hopeful introductory comment that he would like to read his statement through and then answer questions on it, Taft, Capehart, and Millikin promptly took charge. In his first appearance there is no page of uninterrupted testimony, in his second only three.[32] So intensive was the barrage that at one point the roles were reversed, with Bowles cross-examining Taft on the Senator's statements.[33] In all of Bowles' testimony, there are no more than four interventions by Administration senators to ask leading questions in support of the witness. In the two early appearances of Porter, who on the whole was treated more gently than Bowles, there are only three.[34] It is hard to escape the conclusion that the senators were content to let the bureaucrats take care of themselves as best they could. The role of the legislator versus the bureaucrat is an old one, rooted in an institutional jealousy never hard to arouse. Anti-OPA witnesses were well aware of it: statements that "Congress treated us fairly but OPA interpretation stripped away relief" and charges of "OPA usurpation" were staples of their testimony. And the target was well-chosen; even the gentle Barkley, staunch friend of OPA, remarked once ". . . I won in the Senate, but I lost in OPA."[35] Administration witnesses were not all treated the same, needless to say; Fred Vinson was the only important witness who was allowed to read his statement through without interruption.[36] Among his many services to his country, the Secretary of the Treasury could count six terms in the House of Representatives.[37]

The lethargy of the Administration senators, which hung on through the appearances of several spokesmen of particular industries, disappeared instantly with the appearance of Robert R. Wason, president of the National Association of Manufacturers.[38] Before Wason had read two hundred words of his statement, his right to speak for the public, for industry, or even for the NAM, had been challenged. From that point on the fight seems pretty even, as it was later when James B. Carey, secretary-treasurer of the Congress of Industrial Organizations, appeared.[39] NAM and CIO were the principal ideological protagonists in the fight over the extension of price control, and this was clearly reflected in the interest group split on the Committee when their representatives appeared.[40] Neither man was allowed a page of uninterrupted testimony. The role here was that of legislator pro-or-con interest groups. The senators clearly were identifying with private interest groups in a struggle which cut across the separate branches of the government.

Other group identifications can be perceived in the hearings. For instance, the special position of farm groups in American politics was underlined. In the welter of name-calling and exaggerated charges, there is not one criticism of farmers. Everyone agreed they deserved well of the re-public. On one occasion Taylor came dangerously close to a critical remark; in defending the government's paying a premium price for grain, he said: "The farmers knew that they [starving people] had to have it, but unfortunately they have held on to the wheat and corn. I don't think it is to the credit of the American farmers themselves. . . ." But Capehart forthwith restated the official congressional position: ". . . I don't agree with the Senator that the American farmer is unpatriotic. I think they are among the most patriotic people this Nation has and I want the record to so state. I don't agree with that statement at all."[41] Ed O'Neal, president of the American Farm Bureau Federation, reflected the magnificent immunity of the farmers when he blamed the inflation, with fine impartiality and without challenge, on the Congress, both parties, the Treasury, the Federal Reserve, and the whole Administration, as well as OPA.[42] Again, it was reflected in the lack of any interrogation of James G. Patton, president of the National Farmers Union, whose record as a political actionist might have been expected to invite cross-examination.[43]

One identification any congressman is likely to make is that with his former, or other, occupation. This is borne out in the lawyer-like conduct of the legislative hearing itself, with its cross-examinations and its concern for "the record." As Ernest Griffith has remarked, "The majority of congressmen were (and still are) lawyers, and, to a lawyer, truth emerges from a battle of protagonists."[44] But other occupations also are represented, and the label "lawyer" frequently covers a variety of activities. It is a virtue of the legislature that it is made up of "general" men, and it is natural that legislators should test what they hear against the commonsense of their own experience. The senators on this committee did so; Murdock, for example, talked to a livestock man about his own grass-fed steers, and Millikin remarked: "I am speaking somewhat categorically on this because I have had considerable experience in the oil business."[45] But this is not the same thing, quite, as identifying with an occupational group and perceiving facts in their frame of reference. That is what Capehart seemed to do. A farmer and manufacturer, Capehart had been in the Senate less than two years. He made reference to both of his other occupations, but it was clear that Capehart saw price control in his role as businessman. Over a quarter of a century of experience had conditioned him to trust a businessman's judgment and resent the bureaucrat's interference in the economy. As he put it himself (objecting to questions asked of a businessman): "My observation is that anyone that comes in here from an industry knows his business. They are the people who are trying to make things and do business under all the difficulties that confront them, and trying to be honest and sincere and conscientious, and in the hope that they will be permitted to remain in business. I think that to question their integrity and honesty . . ." To which Barkley replied, in part: "We had a witness here yesterday who questioned the sincerity and honesty and integrity of everybody in the Government and you didn't complain about that."[46] But Barkley, who first went to Congress in 1913, *had* complained the day before, as he did on every occasion when government officials were attacked indiscriminately.

That Senator Capehart continued to regard price control as a businessman would, so long as he remained a minority member of the Committee, is suggested by his writing in 1951 what President Truman called "the terrible Capehart amendment," which Truman said made price control impossible. But in 1953 Capehart assumed the new status of Chairman of the Banking and Currency Committee, and with it a new role requiring him to accept primary responsibility for the legislation reported by the Committee. In his new role he advocated stand-by controls for prices, wages, and rent. He found it hard to understand the intransigence of groups which were "unalterably opposed" to any concession to the principle of controls, and understandably shocked to hear himself accused by a business lobbyist of espousing a philosophy of the "left." It would be hard to find a more striking example of the effect of a change of status.[47]

Senator Tobey appeared briefly from time to time in his peculiarly personal role of moral prophet. He was inclined to indict the whole people for lacking the moral fiber to resist the tainted opportunities afforded by the black market. In the tones of Jeremiah, later to become familiar to the television audience of Kefauver's crime investigation, he called upon the people "to rise up and say 'Unclean, unclean.' "[48]

Some of the roles which might have been anticipated were not played by anybody. That of the dictatorial chairman, sure of his power, was one. That of the subject-matter expert, whose prestige in a given field is widely accepted (e.g., O'Mahoney on economic questions[49]), was another. The hectoring-inquisitor role was not played consistently by anybody.

The limitations upon what can be done in a study of behavior from the printed record alone have already been acknowledged. The pattern of interactions among the members can be studied fully only from first-hand observation. What does it mean in the climate of the hearing for a par-

ticular member to be present? Or absent? It can be seen from the record that questions, and sometimes tempers, tended to get shorter when Senator Taft was on hand. That is tantalizingly suggestive, but not enough. Who supports, who opposes, whom? Who retreats into silence from whom? Such questions can be answered only by the observer. The item in the record which might reveal significant interactions may be the very one which is subsequently edited from it.

It is hard to evaluate the role of leadership with any method, and especially so when reliance must be placed on the printed record. On the surface, it would appear that Senator Wagner had little control over his Committee in the price control controversy. The power of the committee chairman is justly celebrated in political journalism, but it may be that like so many other concentrations of power in the Congress, it can be used most effectively against a majority only in a negative way. The chairman can prevent committee consideration, prevent a report, prevent floor consideration, much more easily than he can command a balky majority to do something positive. When Congress passes legislation requiring periodic reenactment, as it does so often now, it must counteract to some extent the power of the few to control the many. Wagner was not able to get his way with this Committee. He refused to sign the report. Barkley signed it only to get it on the floor, making clear his opposition to it. What went on in the executive sessions, where the bill was amended heavily over the opposition of the chairman, obviously is not to be learned from the record, and perhaps not in any other way.

Some elaborate studies based on role theory have been made of complex organizations,[50] and the congressional committee would seem to be an inviting subject for such research. That much, at least, seems clear from the foregoing analysis; no generalizations about the committee are valid which do not take into account the varied and complex statuses which congressmen hold, and the shifting roles which they play in filling first one and then another of them. A congressional committee is an agency for the implementation of the purposes of congressmen. Functionally, it gives to bills the detailed consideration which the full house cannot, but in other ways it is simply another point of focus of the political process, as its parent house is also. It is a part of "the legislative struggle," to use Bertram Gross's term, but, as he indicates, the struggle is a confused one in which the participants fight for different and changing purposes and represent many and sometimes opposing causes. National and parochial ends are inextricably entwined in the Congress, and so they are in the committee. Taft, holding no elective party office in the Senate and sharing eighth rank in seniority with three others, nevertheless chooses the role of national leader for himself and effectively shapes the expectations of others to that role. The committee hearing is no more than a shift of scene for him. McFarland, soon to lead the Democrats in the Senate, chooses for reasons of his own to use this time and place to plead narrowly for the industries of his state. Therein lies the value of the committee hearing for the student of political behavior: within a more manageable compass, the congressmen behave like congressmen.

The Committee as a Fact-Finding Agency. The Committee's performance as a fact-finding agency is worth special consideration. Quantitatively, at least, an impressive job was done. Nineteen days were consumed in public hearings, during which 12 public officials, 38 spokesmen of business and business groups, five representatives of organized labor, eight farm group leaders, and nine persons representing other groups—72 witnesses in all—testified before the Committee. The printed record ran to 2212 pages, including 541 exhibits, charts, statements, letters, and telegrams. Thousands of questions were asked and answered. Out of this welter of facts and opinions, what did the Committee learn about the problems of economic stabilization? What kinds of questions did its members ask? What picture of the factual situation emerged from the answers they got? In the light of the Committee's performance, what might be done to make legislative committees generally more effective as fact-finders?

These questions would be easier to answer if the Committee had ever formulated a set of questions to which the hearings should supply answers. That the Committee did not do. Nevertheless there were questions which, because of their pertinence, were raised again and again, by the witnesses and by the senators themselves. For the purposes of this study, several of these recurring questions were traced carefully through the hearings, to see whether any or all of them could be answered, unambiguously, from the record. Careful attention was paid to the leading questions and gratuitous statements of the senators, to see what facts they accepted, and whether their conceptions of the "facts" ever changed. From this procedure there emerged, not one picture of the factual situation, but two. The senators who supported OPA accepted one, those who opposed OPA the other. Some sharpening of details in each picture doubtless occurred, but there was no indication of a change in the general picture for

either group. Each group seemed to come into the hearings with a ready-made frame of reference. Facts which were compatible were fitted into it; facts which were not compatible, even when elaborately documented, were discounted, not perceived, or ignored. This is not so hard as it sounds. A disagreeable fact is not an isolated fact, but one of a constellation of facts. Which is the relevant one? And when statistics seem accurate beyond dispute, there is the question of selecting the relevant variable or the proper base period, or perhaps of whether there is not a serious contrary trend which began too late to be reflected in the figures. Thus contradictions need not be resolved, and in these hearings they were not resolved. The hearings could be said not to have progressed. At the end the same questions were being asked as at the beginning, and were receiving the same sets of answers.

There was not necessarily agreement within either group over what should be done about price controls. The *pro forma* claim that "I don't know how I'm going to vote on this matter" was made frequently, and most of the senators would say that price controls ultimately would be extended —with modifications. What divided them was that one group would accept statements of fact which put the OPA in a good light, and receive sympathetically the claims of groups which supported the OPA and the Administration. The other group would not. The first group was made up loosely of the Democrats Wagner, Mitchell, Barkley, Taylor, Fulbright, Murdock, and Radcliffe, and the Republican Tobey. The opposing group was composed of the Republicans Capehart, Millikin, Taft, Hickenlooper, Buck, and Butler, and the Democrat Bankhead. Other members of the Committee did not participate frequently enough to be placed with any confidence. The first group's conception of the facts was shared roughly with Administration spokesmen, labor representatives, the president of the National Farmers Union, and several other group representatives purporting to speak for the "liberal" or the consumer point of view. The second group listened most receptively to business spokesmen and the representatives of the other farm groups. These classifications are rough, of course, and should be taken that way. They are not meant to indicate anything approaching complete uniformity.

Some of these questions, and the ways in which the two groups answered them, may now be considered.

What Was the "Lesson" of World War I? The Administration clearly thought that the experience of World War I supported the extension of price controls. Every Administration witness mentioned it, and charts were brought in to support their story.[51] Starting back in 1914, it ran, prices rose precipitously until some voluntary controls were partially successful in checking the rise in 1917-18. After a brief post-Armistice recession, with controls off, prices rose sharply again in 1919-20, causing a snowballing of demand and a hoarding of inventories, in anticipation of even higher prices. Ultimately a buyers' strike caused collapse; deflation and depression were the result of the unchecked spiral of prices. To these witnesses and their supporters the moral seemed clear: weakening the price control program in 1946 would bring the same disastrous results.

To the other side it was not clear at all. They doubted the relevance of the earlier experience to the problem at hand. Or they were impressed with the shortness of the periods of inflation and deflation in World War I. Taking the post-Armistice figures alone (which they frequently did), neither the climb nor the subsequent drop looked so bad. They pointed out that a "flood of goods" had eventually forced prices down, forgetting that prices had gone up three times as much as industrial production, and that the "flood of goods" had been released—not produced—by deflationary dumping. Even recollections of the period fell conveniently into place; Glen Taylor remembered it as a dreadful experience, Capehart as not bad at all.[52] Millikin was perhaps the most intransigent. He could see on the government's charts only one fact, that prices had gone down. The buyers' strike had prevented an "explosive inflation"—by which he meant not the 150 per cent increase the World War I charts showed, but the kind of runaway inflation the Germans had.[53]

What causes inflation? This question caused difficulty, because whenever it was discussed seriously it took the Committee quickly outside its jurisdictional field. Farm policy, fiscal policy, the wages of labor, and many other things not the Committee's business were involved in the stabilization program. But the question had to be raised. The Administration group saw the principal inflationary threats in the economic forces OPA sought to control. The pent-up demands from the war period, supported by 225 billions in purchasing power, exceeded the total current supply of goods. Production was at a record high level, despite labor shortages and the problems of reconversion, but it would take time to "fill the pipelines" from producer to consumer and meet the demand. In this interim period, price controls were imperative to prevent a disastrous spiral. These were the bed-rock economic facts, but this group suspected more. They believed that businessmen were hoarding inventories, thus aggravating the shortages, in order to make huge profits if price controls were removed. They also believed that speculation—"betting on inflation"—made the control job harder.

The charge of inventory-hoarding is a good example of the influence of group ideology on the perception of facts. It was made repeatedly by pro-OPA witnesses, and apparently believed implicitly. Yet when the opposing senators demanded proof, it was sometimes promised but never furnished. Paul Porter could report an incident he knew about, and surmise that the situation, whatever it was, would get worse as the date for the expiration of controls drew near.[54] A member of a CIO local told about finding a back room full of oil at a place where he had been told there was no oil.[55] That was the extent of the proof of inventory-hoarding, but the charge would not down; it was an essential element of the version of the facts held by OPA supporters. Their opponents, curiously enough, accepted inventory-hoarding as a fact sometimes, justifying it on the grounds that the hoarders could not make a profit under OPA, or that they hoped OPA would see "the light" and treat them fairly.

Anti-OPA witnesses and senators found the chief causes of inflation in the policies of OPA itself. OPA kept prices unrealistically low, forcing producers to concentrate on high price lines or inferior substitutes. By refusing to recognize rising costs of production, OPA impeded production. OPA propaganda and "scare talk" created an inflation psychology, leading to panic buying and hoarding. Other Administration policies, including the unbalanced budget and the loan to Britain, compounded the pressures on prices. So did the wage increases which the Administration permitted. To this group, wage increase always started an inflationary spiral, just as a price increase did for the pro-OPA group. Similarly, Taft would not agree with Bowles that repeal of the excess profits tax was inflationary, but he was sure the loan to Britain was.[56]

What has been the overall effect of price controls on the economy? OPA and its friends were sure that OPA had stabilized the economy and prevented inflation. Their charts showed it; the cost-of-living index had risen only about 30 per cent since 1939.[57] They claimed that the cost-of-living had risen only about 3½ per cent since price controls became effective in 1943, and had gone up only .7 per cent since V-J day. In this time, controls had prevented neither production nor profits. Everyone knew that production had been enormous, and the charts showed that it had risen at its wartime peak nearly 140 per cent over the 1939 level. Their opponents would contest it, but OPA was prepared to support the claim that business profits had been high, too. OPA believed that it had preserved economic stability and made planning possible.

Its opponents believed that the overall effect of OPA on the economy had been bad. Some were willing to accept it as a wartime necessity, and to make a grudging admission that it had done an acceptable, even a good job, if only its powers could be terminated soon. But others would not concede that it had done a good job. The kindest view was that it was not OPA's fault: the economy was too complex for controls, and besides, price controls could only treat effects, not causes. Some argued that inflation had been serious in spite of OPA (amounting to 32 per cent over 1941)[58] but generally the figures did not seem to matter much; they did not settle the question, as they might have been expected to do. Millikin said again and again that OPA never had held a line when there was real pressure on it, that the goods simply flowed into the black market and the price line became a "fiction." OPA had made it impossible for farmers, dry goods wholesalers, retail meat dealers (and others, explicitly and by inference) to operate legally. The government's figures actually demonstrated a chief vice of OPA: the agency concentrated on controlling the cost-of-living *index*, rather than encouraging production through incentive prices where needed. The bill of particulars against OPA was a long one; in addition to hampering production, penalizing the efficient producer, and diverting goods to the black market, OPA had used its consumer subsidy program to increase the demand for the limited supply of goods. The overall effect of OPA, they believed, had been to aggravate inflationary pressures.

What is the administrative record of OPA? The administrative performance of OPA was under continuous attack; the agency and its friends never got off the defensive. OPA was charged with handling appeals slowly, with issuing orders that were hard to understand, with tying up business with red tape. It was not improving, or if it were, it still was not good enough. OPA was inflexible; it handled individual firms with industry-wide orders, and refused to modify those orders. These criticisms were to be expected, but there were worse. The agency had "continuously and directly violated the Price Control Act,"[59] Taft said, and Goss, master of the Grange, was even more sweeping when he said: "For four years the OPA has thumbed its nose at Congress, has violated the basic law under which it was created, and has pursued an illegal but politically expedient course which has fed the fires of inflation

and then tried to control the fire by stopping up the chimney."[60] Its "vicious propaganda" had created a "scare psychology" among buyers. OPA was accused especially of refusing to grant relief in hardship cases, as provided for by law, and of holding up production by maintaining inadequate ceiling prices which they had the power to raise. This line of criticism fell into a syllogism: every increase requested is necessary to production; any delay in granting it holds up production; therefore, OPA is responsible for critical shortages (e.g., in housing for veterans).[61] Since there was no question of the righteousness of every request for an increase, if OPA held one up a year it was only because of administrative ineptitude; the fact that it was granted ultimately proved it was right all the time, without regard to any change in circumstances which might have occurred.

Under this drum-fire of criticism, OPA was pushed into defending itself by citing the number of adjustments it had made and price increases it had allowed.[62] The agency officers contended they had a "realistic" approach to price control (i.e., one which allowed prices to go up). The ambivalence in their position was resolved by claiming that, while they had held the line against general inflation, they had granted adjustments to get production or relieve hardship. The Administration group was willing to admit mistakes, but insisted that OPA's procedures had been improved and made more than reasonably efficient. A detailed account of procedures employed to reduce delay in handling individual adjustment cases was placed in the record, with statistics demonstrating their effectiveness.[63] Breakdowns in production were traced to shortages in labor and materials, not to administrative delay. But the criticisms, needless to say, were not affected in the least.

The influence of group ideology on fact perception was clearly reflected in the image of OPA as a human organization which each group held. The opponents of OPA saw the agency people as theorists, inexperienced in business, telling experienced businessmen what to do. The complaint that "OPA does not understand the underwear industry" (or the construction industry, or any other) was frequently heard, and doubtless it was true. As one OPA official put it, it was impossible to have an expert in every line. To a businessman involved in the unique particulars of his own business, the edicts of an agency which of necessity sought to generalize its rules were bound to seem amateurish and arbitrary. Thus the professor, whom the Congress had tried to legislate out of OPA, proved as a stereotype to be ineradicable.

Consequently, the anti-OPA senators were prepared to accept assertions of industry representatives that inexperienced men were dictating terms to their particular industries. Detailed statements of the experience of men in those branches of OPA were of no avail.[64] The automobile dealers complained that there were no persons remaining in OPA who had experience in the retail automobile business; Porter listed four in the Automotive Branch, and the dealers carried the debate into the appendix of the record.[65] In answer to the lumbermen's charge, Porter listed 17 employees with a total experience in the lumber business of 400 years.[66] But Taft was sure that no retail lumberman knew anything about pricing for the industry. And so it went. That there was more involved than the legislator's stereotype of the bureaucrat is clear from the persistence with which the Administration senators defended the competence and experience of OPA administrators, whom they believed to be able and patriotic men who frequently were hired away from OPA by business.

What Are the Motives of OPA? The contrary images of OPA extended to the motives imputed to the administrators themselves. Their opponents saw them as enemies of capitalism, who hated profits, liked controls for their own sake, and wanted to perpetuate their own jobs. "Last year, this year, next year, the year after" was heard again and again, summing up the anti-OPA belief that OPA would always ask for extension of its regulatory powers. The statements were bitter. Bowles was compared to Hitler and Mussolini, without rebuke from anti-OPA senators. OPA officials belonged to that "school of thought that believes that the wholesaler, jobber, and distributor are excrescences on the body politic." Again, ". . . the fundamental philosophy of OPA is the abolition of profits, the regulation of profits, and the stifling of private enterprise." The kindest construction put on their motives was that they were "a group of very sincere, honest young people that want to reshape the world nearer to their heart's desire . . . but they seem to disregard the effect of these regulations on legitimate established business.[67] Given this image of OPA, it was easy to believe in specific acts of duplicity and abuses of power. When a price increase was granted an industry the day before its spokesman appeared before the Committee, Capehart was sure the timing was deliberate. The OPA contention that at least two months were required to clear a price order did not move him (although usually he would accept the argument that OPA could do nothing in a hurry).[68] OPA was charged with allowing a rental 50 per cent above ceilings on some new

apartment buildings in New York, just to prevent apartment owners from claiming there was no new building under OPA.[69]

OPA's own statements of its policies and practices obviously would not be acceptable to senators who saw them in this light. Porter stated the decontrol policy of OPA this way: ". . . if we can find that there is a reasonable prospect that there will not be inflationary increases to the extent that would jeopardize the general policy of stabilization, we can take [price control] off." But Millikin was sure that if OPA should take "a long look through the future and if you see some little dislocation ahead that might interfere with prices, you are not going to decontrol."[70] Some of the senators favored writing a rigid decontrol formula into the law, on the ground that OPA could not be trusted to decontrol otherwise. Perhaps the blackest picture of OPA was painted by Millikin in grilling the OPA deputy administrator for enforcement. Millikin insisted that OPA set quotas for its enforcement officers, smeared innocent business men and set traps for them with sweeping injunctions, and forced federal judges to render judgments they knew to be unjust. Murdock finally was moved to protest that OPA did not write the law, nor confirm the federal judges, and "that if you go to the length that Senator Millikin wants you to, we must assume that we have a fool on the bench as well as a rather vicious fool in the OPA Enforcement Section."[71]

The Administration group could see no justification for impugning the motives of OPA officials. As they saw it, "they are all down here on loan from business enterprises and at a financial sacrifice, most of them, and they are anxious to get back.[72] OPA administrators were selfless, patriotic men, who believed in the profit system and allowed for profits in their pricing, and who were motivated by a desire to save the business system from the evil effects of an inflationary spiral.

How Has Labor Fared in the Postwar Economy? If one question were wanted, of all those asked in the hearings, to provide an index to the whole constellation of facts accepted as true and relevant by the person answering, this one probably would serve as well as any other. The result would turn on whether the answer mentioned hourly wage rates, which generally were up, or take-home pay, which generally was down.[73] This is another way of saying that the two groups divided sharply on their attitudes toward organized labor. The pro-OPA group, senators and witnesses (including the consumer groups and the Farmers Union), was sympathetic toward it; the other was not. One brief exchange perhaps will serve to illustrate. Ed O'Neal, president of the American Farm Bureau

Federation, presented a series of elaborate tables designed to show, generally, that the earnings of labor had advanced much faster than the cost-of-living, and that conversely the cost of food had advanced relatively very little.[74] Senator Mitchell pointed out that the NAM compilation showed the cost of food and the price of farm products as having gone up more than the AFBF figures did. Replied O'Neal: ". . . We farmers are getting awfully tired of the *workingmen in America* and a lot of *propagandists in the administration* blaming the farmer. We are all pretty mad about it." To which Mitchell countered: "How about the National Association of Manufacturers? Their compilation shows that the farmer is getting more out of the increase, a greater increase, than anybody else." But Mitchell could not make O'Neal criticize the NAM.[75]

Obviously, hourly wages and take-home pay are two aspects of the same thing, and both were relevant to the Committee's problem. Hourly wages are part of the cost of production and affect the price at which a producer can sell. Take-home pay is what the worker relates to the cost-of-living; together they determine whether he makes ends meet. But both groups were reluctant in the extreme to consider both factors. Taft, for instance, wanted the AFL to put in the record "a figure on the increase in *straight-time hourly earnings* since before the war." Green did not have those figures, but "I have a few figures here," he said—all showing declining earnings *since VE-day*. Taft did not want postwar figures; he wanted a simple comparison of the increase of the cost-of-living and of straight-time hourly earnings since January 1, 1940, which he believed would show that labor had done very well. Needless to say, when the figures were submitted he got a great deal more than that, but never precisely that, and the showing did not come out his way at all.[76]

The cleavage on facts related to labor never was closed. Earlier in the year a wage increase had been granted to steel-workers, followed by an increase in the price of steel. These related facts were neatly divided in the testimony; neither side willingly talked about both. To one, the wage increase meant that the government had abandoned wage controls; to the other, the "$250,000,000 bribe to the steel industry" was a hard blow at stabilization. Goss and O'Neal, like the businessmen, stressed the wage increase; Patton and Carolyn Ware (speaking for the consumer) said that their organizations had protested the price increase. One group saw labor's preferred position relative to other groups continuously being improved by a sympathetic Administration which allowed wages to rise unchecked and forced businesses to absorb increased costs without price relief. The other saw disadvantaged labor striving to meet increased costs of living with diminished take-home pay, and forced to bargain with businesses which could recoup strike losses from tax returns.

Other Questions. Many other questions showed the same division as to what the facts were; a few, briefly treated, will have to suffice.

One of the cliches accepted by everybody was that production was the only thing that would solve the problem of inflation. What, then, was the level of production at the time of the hearings? The Administration group offered figures many times to show that production was at the highest level in our history, that only the pent-up demand of a population loaded with purchasing power made it insufficient.[77] This made the problem simply one of what to do about prices until the excess of demand could be satisfied. Higher prices, they were sure, would not increase production, when the real bottlenecks were shortages of labor and materials. There was no indication that the figures ever convinced anybody. "How do you get production?," remained the crucial question for the opponents of OPA. Even the everyday experiences of the protagonists seemed to be affected by what they thought to be true. Senator Taylor found the evidences of production in the stores; he had found tools he wanted with no trouble. A representative of the National Retail Associations, on the other hand, could not buy a little hatchet, search as he would.[78]

A related question concerned the profits of business. In an economy of hundreds of thousands of businesses, it may be doubted whether aggregates or averages could mean much; but the profits of business were part of the picture and a try had to be made. Some elaborate statistics were presented, but the Committee never really got beyond the question of how profits should be computed. Profits before, or after, taxes? Figured as a percentage of net worth, or net sales? Bowles' figures were based on net worth; Taft countered with tables showing the percentage of national income paid out to various types of recipients between 1929 and 1945, and corporate profits before and after taxes as a percentage of national income for the same period.[79] Similar difficulty was had with a question of business practice. One of the House amendments would require OPA to set a ceiling price for every product which would allow the cost of the product plus a reasonable profit for both producer and distributor. OPA argued that most industries make a variety of products, some of which make high, others low profits and still others no profit at all. What mattered to the industry was its overall profit. OPA supporters could and did buttress, with personal experience, their contention that no businessman expected to make a profit on every item. But their opponents had had contrary experience in business; they were equally sure no businessman ever willingly lost money on anything.[80]

A question with which the public was concerned in 1946 was what had happened to meat, and what should be done to get more of it. The question was extensively discussed in the hearings, by the persons best qualified to give the answers. The several levels of the meat industry all wanted price ceilings removed. They quoted Department of Agriculture figures to show a great supply of cattle, enough to meet demand, and needing to be reduced. They argued that legitimate packers had trouble getting steers because they had been diverted to small black-market operators, who wasted valuable by-products as well as overcharging the public. They estimated that the removal of controls would send prices up 15-20 per cent (again based on Agriculture figures), which was about what they thought people were currently paying in the black market. With decontrol, the industry people believed, meat would flow into legitimate channels, probably forcing prices down. If meat were not decontrolled now there never would be a better time.

The experts in OPA, and their friends on the Committee, thought the black market in meat and the wastage of by-products had been greatly exaggerated. They recognized that there had been diversion of meat into the black market, but they pointed out that a new control order put into effect on May 1 had within a week increased the volume of inspected slaughter cattle by 12 per cent to a figure only one per cent below the volume for the same time in 1945. They believed, therefore, that the problem was being solved. Some of them questioned the Agriculture Department's figures; they did not believe there was enough meat. But Patton and the CIO packinghouse workers both thought the "shortage" was deliberately engineered by the large packers.[81] They were sure that the removal of ceilings would send prices up at least 50 per cent, wreck other food controls, and end stabilization. It would be better to decontrol later, when a larger supply of durables and consumer goods would drain off purchasing power and relieve the pressure on foods.

The disagreement extended even to small and ascertainable facts. What is the most efficient use of grain? Fulbright asserted that "a pound of wheat, used in bread, will produce about 2,400,-000 calories, and if it is fed to a beef cow it will produce only a little over 200,000 calories." To which Hickenlooper replied: ". . . I am quite cer-

tain that the statistics show in every study that has ever been made of ultimate food values that human beings get more definite, substantial value out of grain fed through meat animals than they do from the grain itself. That is they get more proteins and more vitamins. . . ."[82] Like the large contradictions, this small one remained unresolved.

Many facts, of course, have handles on both ends. Wason, of NAM, for instance, produced newspaper advertisements to show that grocery prices had gone up more than Bowles claimed. This might seem to prove that Bowles had lied and that OPA had failed to control grocery prices, or it could show that the grocers had no reason to complain of OPA.[83] When a CIO member recited high prices he had to pay, it might demonstrate, as he thought, the laborer's need for continued protection; but perhaps it was unwitting testimony to OPA's ineffectiveness.[84] Or take the question of the level of production of any commodity. If it were conceded to be low, and not equal to demand, it could be said to prove that price control was needed until production could meet the demand, or, contrarily, that control should be abolished in order to get production. If it were conceded to be high, it might prove that production and profits could be gotten under price control, or that control could now be abolished with safety.

Influence of Group Ideology on Fact Perception. What has been argued in the preceding section is that the Committee and its witnesses were made up of two loose groups of people who disagreed, not so much in their opinions upon what should be done about a known or ascertainable fact situation, as upon what the underlying facts themselves were. As advocates, neither side could afford to accept the other's conception of the facts, for that would be to concede the battle; policy is rooted in the assessment of the situation. But if common experience can be trusted, the people on both sides believed in good faith that they were stating *the* facts, and from this flowed the sincerity and even passion with which they seemed to talk. As Walter Lippmann put it, "a public opinion is a moralized and codified version of the facts."[85] The interest group orientation furnished the pattern of preconceptions through which the facts were screened. It was easy for one side to see an entrenched bureaucracy meddling with a free economy, for the other to see a democratic government protecting the helpless from exploitation. After that it was just a matter of filling in the details.

There is, to be sure, nothing new in this conception. It is at least as old as Plato, who expressed it with moving beauty in his allegory of the cave.[86] But it has a relevance for a theory of the group process in politics that has not been sufficiently appreciated. In the price control controversy (and surely in others like it) the senators were not sitting as arbiters of the group struggle, but as participants; it flowed through them. But it was not perceived so clearly and simply as that by those in the struggle. It is generally accepted that there are many opinions, but not that there are many versions of the facts—or at least, not that there is no single *true* one. This is the crucial problem of communication between social groups, as it is, to a greater degree, of intercultural communication. Given its own version of the facts, and believing it to be the only true one, each side could fight for the general interest and impute bad motives to its opponents in all sincerity. In this sense the Committee *was* concerned with promoting the general interest, but so were most of the spokesmen of special interests who appeared before it. Social conflict over group interests, clearly perceived and rightly identified, should be easy to mediate; a rough appraisal of the balance of power and frank bargaining should be enough. It is the quantum of concern for the general interest in every calculation that makes the trouble.

It should be emphasized that the price control question was highly political, with a long history. The kinds of information committee members would want, the kinds of facts they would be able to perceive, their willingness to accept relatively objective data, surely would vary with the kind of question under consideration. Nevertheless, the conception of the social nature of fact perception should be useful to political science. In regard to policy, it suggests one of the limits to the usefulness of uncommitted social intelligence to the politician. In regard to research, perception of the fact situation surely is one of the crucial variables, both in the group struggle which is the political process, and in the behavior of the individual actors in it.[87] Conversely, the perception of the fact situation by public officials might provide a useful index to their group orientations.

Conclusion. This study began with two sets of generalizations, one of which suggested that committee members sit as judges representing the general interest presiding over the public debate of the special interests; the other suggested that committee members themselves are participants in the struggle of contending groups, one phase of which is the public hearing. The analysis of the hearings conducted in 1946 by the Senate Committee on Banking and Currency on the question of extending price control would seem to support the latter. The members of this Committee did not sit as

legislative judges to discover an abstract general interest, nor did they seem concerned with presenting a balanced debate for public consideration. On the contrary, most of them did take sides. The Committee hearings clearly were used as a public platform for opposing groups with which the senators identified. A great deal of information was received from interested groups, which the senators accepted or rejected in accordance with their preconceived notions of the facts. What was made perfectly clear was that the groups opposing price control were more numerous and more militant than the groups supporting it. This was, of course, crucial information. The remark of Kefauver and Levin (in urging professional staff for committees), that "Congress cannot function today without lobbyists,"[88] will always be true, for only the lobbyists can tell what their groups will fight for and how hard they will fight. It is reasonable to suppose that some social catharsis was provided by the institutionalized conflict, as Professor Truman suggested, but there was no way to tell in this study.

But this is not to be taken to mean that Professor Chamberlain's generalizations are wrong. What is suggested rather is that members of the Committee behaved in a variety of ways, depending upon the roles they chose to play. It seems indeed unlikely that we have exhausted the repertory of committee roles; quite the contrary. In hearings on a different issue, under other circumstances, some or all of the members surely might choose the judicial role, some or all of the time. The number and range of roles permitted by the norms of a given committee, the variations in what is acceptable which may exist between committees, are matters for further research.

Other questions should be asked. Why does a legislator choose a particular role, and not another? What is the effect of the subject matter of the hearing upon role selection? Upon the perception of facts, and the willingness of committee members to accept relatively objective data? The records of hearings of congressional committees, readily accessible in embarrassing abundance, can be used extensively to formulate hypotheses based on these and other questions, which might then be tested in more intensive research. State legislatures, which seldom keep verbatim records of committee hearings, nevertheless multiply the opportunities for studies involving close observation, interviews, and other techniques in the arsenal of behavior research. It should not be too much to hope that ultimately some general propositions might be fashioned which would contribute to a viable theory of politics.

Notes

1. See David B. Truman, *The Governmental Process* (New York, 1951), pp. 343-46.

2. See especially George C. Homans, *The Human Group* (New York, 1950), in which five distinguished studies in social behavior are examined in detail to develop both an organic theory of the human group and a system of analysis for further study of the group.

3. Joseph P. Chamberlain, *Legislative Processes: National and State* (New York, 1936), p. 79.

4. *Ibid.*, pp. 72-73. Emphasis added.

5. *The Reorganization of Congress*, A Report of the Committee on Congress of the American Political Science Association (Washington, D.C., 1945), p. 79; Galloway, *Congress at the Crossroads*, pp. 158-61; Ernest S. Griffith, *Congress: Its Contemporary Role* (New York, 1951) pp. 70-75; Estes Kefauver and Jack Levin, *A Twentieth Century Congress* (New York, 1947), pp. 167-68; *Organization of the Congress*, Report of the Joint Committee on the Organization of Congress, pursuant to H. Con. Res. 18, H. Rep. No. 1675, 79th Cong., 2d sess., pp. 9-11; and Report from the Special Committee on the Organization of Congress, Sen. Rep. No. 1400, 79th Cong., 2d sess., pp. 21-24. See also the frequent recommendations of this nature in *Organization of Congress*, Hearings before the Joint Committee on the Organization of Congress, pursuant to H. Con. Res. 18, 79th Cong., 2d sess.; *Legislative Reorganization Act of 1946*, Hearings before the Committee on Expenditures in the Executive Departments, U.S. Senate, 80th Cong., 2d sess.; *Organization and Operation of Congress*, Hearings before the Committee on Expenditures in the Executive Departments, U.S. Senate, 82d Cong., 1st sess.

6. Chamberlain, p. 64.

7. See especially Arthur F. Bentley, *The Process of Government* (Bloomington, Ind., 1949), first published in 1908; Truman, *The Governmental Process* (cited in note 3); and Bertram M. Gross, *The Legislative Struggle* (New York, 1953). The latter devotes three chapters (14-16) to a realistic description of the operations of congressional committees.

8. *The Governmental Process*, pp. 372-77. Emphasis added.

9. *1946 Extension of the Emergency Price Control and Stabilization Acts of 1942, As Amended*, Hearings before the Committee on Banking and Currency, U.S. Senate, 79th Cong., 2d sess., on S. 2028. Cited hereafter as *Hearings*.

10. Ralph Linton, *The Cultural Background of Personality* (New York, 1945), pp. 76-77.

11. The Democratic members of the Committee were Robert F. Wagner, New York, Chairman; Carter Glass, Virginia; Alben W. Barkley, Kentucky; John H. Bankhead 2d, Alabama; George L. Radcliffe, Maryland; Sheridan Downey, California; Abe Murdock, Utah; Ernest W. McFarland, Arizona; Glen H. Taylor, Idaho; J. William Fulbright, Arkansas; Hugh B. Mitchell, Washington; and E. P. Carville, Nevada. The Republican members were Charles W. Tobey, New Hampshire; Robert A. Taft, Ohio; Hugh A. Butler, Nebraska; Arthur Capper, Kansas; C. Douglass Buck, Delaware; Eugene D. Millikin, Colorado; Bourke B. Hickenlooper, Iowa; and Homer E. Capehart, Indiana.

12. *Hearings*, p. 43.

13. *Hearings*, pp. 965, 1265.

14. *Hearings*, p. 29.

15. *Hearings*, pp. 986-87, 1094, 1295-96, 1311.

16. *Hearings*, pp. 704-6, 1730-31.

17. *Hearings*, p. 325. There followed this colloquy:

Senator Tobey: That is not Senator Claghorn speaking. That is Senator Bankhead.
Senator Bankhead: What was that?
Senator Tobey: That was a joke, Senator. I said it was not Senator Claghorn, it was my friend Senator Bankhead speaking about the South.
Senator Bankhead: I am always trying to get justice for them. That is a hard task very often, I will say to my New England Senator friend.

18. *Hearings*, pp. 931-1041.

19. *Hearings*, pp. 637-777, 1043-88.

20. *Hearings*, pp. 176, 687-88, 1046-49, 1721-23.

21. *Hearings*, pp. 74-75, 436-95, 1733, 1791-93.

22. See the statements in Galloway, *Congress at the Crossroads*, pp. 57-63.

23. *Hearings*, pp. 1725-26. Tobey suggested that a review board be established to handle congressional cases faster.

24. *Hearings*, pp. 175-76, 181, 182, 130-32, 110.

25. *Hearings*, p. 1743.

26. *Hearings*, pp. 1667, 1693.

27. *Hearings*, pp. 132, 111.

28. *Hearings*, pp. 229-73.

29. *Hearings*, pp. 845-46, 1725.

30. *Hearings*, pp. 853-58, 1087, 1724.

31. *Hearings*, pp. 1516-38.

32. *Hearings*, pp. 6-75.

33. *Hearings*, pp. 25-26.

34. *Hearings*, pp. 77-208.

35. *Hearings*, p. 956.

36. *Hearings*, pp. 1551-78.

37. In the 68th to 75th Congresses, except for the 71st.

38. *Hearings*, pp. 392-428.

39. *Hearings*, pp. 573-603.

40. Consider this fine exchange:
Mr. Carey: There are no such things as "natural economic laws."
Senator Millikin: Who repealed those?
Mr. Carey: They never existed.
Senator Millikin: My God! That is astounding information.
Mr. Carey: In the first place, economic laws are a prostitution of the *aims of nature, whose first purpose* is to fill the needs of man . . . (*Hearings*, p. 576. Emphasis added).

41. *Hearings*, p. 800.

42. *Hearings*, pp. 668-69.

43. *Hearings*, pp. 691-99.

44. *Congress: Its Contemporary Role* (cited in note 7), p. 63.

45. *Hearings*, pp. 1205, 1718. Millikin is an example of the lawyer in Congress: his biography in the *Congressional Directory* includes law, the army, and politics, but not the oil business.

46. *Hearings*, p. 1316.

47. See Robert Bendiner in "The Apostasy of Homer Capehart," *The Reporter*, May 12, 1953, pp. 30-32, for an interesting description of the Senator's discomfiting experience.

48. *Hearings*, p. 1673.

49. See Earl Latham, *The Group Basis of Politics* (Ithaca, N. Y., 1952).

50. See Eugene Jacobson, W. W. Charters, Jr., and Seymour Lieberman, "The Use of the Role Concept in the Study of Complex Organizations," *The Journal of Social Issues*, Vol. 7, pp. 18-27 (No. 3, 1951), and the publications of the Survey Research Center, University of Michigan, which are listed there.

51. The statements used in this section were all selected because they were made many times. Therefore, no attempt will be made to document them except where a particular quotation is used by way of illustration. For a representative Administration statement of the World War

I experience, see the testimony of John D. Small, head of the Civilian Production Administration, at pp. 1449-50.

52. *Hearings*, p. 206-7.
53. *Hearings*, pp. 1585-86.
54. *Hearings*, p. 198.
55. *Hearings*, p. 608.
56. *Hearings*, p. 39.
57. *Hearings*, p. 1450.
58. *Hearings*, p. 866.
59. *Hearings*, p. 1243.
60. *Hearings*, p. 674.
61. *Hearings*, pp. 301-4.
62. *Hearings*. See, for example, pp. 82, 155-56, 159-62, 783-84, 1580, 1727.
63. *Hearings*, pp. 138-45.
64. See the list of OPA personnel connected with pricing of textile industries, *Hearings*, pp. 118-25.
65. *Hearings*, pp. 1272, 1760, 1874-76.
66. *Hearings*, p. 1713.
67. *Hearings*, pp. 1185-86, 1356, 971, 1356. See p. 971 particularly for the contrast in the images of OPA held by the president of the National Apartment Owners' Association and by Senator Glen Taylor.
68. *Hearings*, pp. 1311, 1319.
69. *Hearings*, p. 1492.
70. *Hearings*, p. 1718.
71. *Hearings*, p. 1691. This remarkable cross-examination is worth a complete reading. See pp. 1663-1705.
72. *Hearings*, p. 971.
73. See the colloquy of Taft and Bowles, *Hearings*, p. 58.
74. *Hearings*, pp. 654-65. Significantly, the only group chosen for comparative purposes is labor.
75. *Hearings*, p. 667. Emphasis added. Contrast the at-

tack on NAM by James Patton, president of the Farmers Union, pp. 694-98.
76. *Hearings*, pp. 787-93. Emphasis added.
77. *Hearings*, pp. 870-71, 1449-51, 1461-62, 1708-9.
78. *Hearings*, p. 867.
79. *Hearings*, p. 42. Perhaps the most remarkable piece of statistical gymnastics was performed by James Carey, CIO, who put corporate profits during the war years at 52 billion dollars (before or after taxes?). Although he stated that 25.9 billions had been paid to stockholders, he then said: "For every dollar of these unused reserves [sic] it means one hour of unemployment for some American worker. In other words, $52,000,000,000 means 52,000,000,000 man-hours of unemployment" (p. 585).
80. For representative examples of these exchanges, see *Hearings*, pp. 47-48, 286, 807, 987, 1589-90, 1623-25.
81. Resolution of United Packinghouse Workers of America, CIO, *Hearings*, pp. 641-44; testimony of James Patton, pp. 698-99.
82. *Hearings*, pp. 1209-10.
83. *Hearings*, pp. 395-402.
84. *Hearings*, pp. 604-9.
85. *Public Opinion* (New York, 1922), p. 125.
86. This was the central idea of Lippmann's *Public Opinion*. See especially Karl Mannheim, *Ideology and Utopia* (New York, 1951), and Ralph K. Merton's essay, "The Sociology of Knowledge," in *Twentieth Century Sociology*, eds. G. Gurvitch and W. E. Moore (New York, 1945).
87. See the distinction between process and behavior made by David Easton in *The Political System* (New York, 1953), pp. 203-6.
88. *A Twentieth Century Congress* (cited in note 7), p. 156.

12. SENATE ATTITUDES TOWARD A SECRETARY OF STATE

James N. Rosenau

EXTENSIVE CONCERN about the office of the Secretary of State has accompanied the postwar expansion of American commitments abroad. From the abundant literature now available,[1] a standardized picture has developed of the various roles which the Secretary must perform and of the problems inherent in his office. He is portrayed as necessarily faced with the task of achieving a delicate balance between a variety of incompatible roles: he must simultaneously maintain an alliance system, advise the President, placate the Congress, administer the State Department, inform the public, consult with interest groups, interact with the Defense Department, and relate to some fifty-eight other executive agencies that participate in the formulation of foreign policy. The Secretary's job, in short, is a tough one, perhaps even an impossible one.

Of all the potential conflicts built into the Secretary's multiple roles, his relationship to Congress

is seen as especially difficult. In fact, it has become commonplace to assert that he is inevitably destined to incur the wrath of Senators and Representatives, and that this Congressional hostility seriously undermines the formulation and conduct of foreign policy. The Secretary is said to be vulnerable to legislative criticism because, unlike the heads of the Agriculture and Labor Departments, he lacks a domestic constituency which commands the respect of large blocs in Congress. Even worse, he always appears to be asking Congress to assist people abroad, so that resentments are heightened by the conviction that his clients are "furriners" rather than Americans. Furthermore, as the official largely responsible for steering the ship of state through angry and uncertain waters, the Secretary emerges as an ideal scapegoat for Congressmen who have to make difficult but unavoidable choices with respect to complex situations that they can neither comprehend nor tolerate. Forced to recognize that

Published for the first time in this volume.

the international environment is precarious and threatening, legislators gravitate to the Secretary as the most logical and convenient target upon whom can be projected the frustrations to which all the evil in the world gives rise. These considerations are supposed to foster an attitude whereby Congressmen assume that they will never lose votes if they attack the Secretary and that they might even add to their political fortunes by compiling a record of opposition and antagonism. Lastly, such an attitude is said to be bulwarked by a long-standing antipathy, particularly on the part of Midwesterners, to the eastern, "Ivy League" character of the foreign service, with the result that the Secretary inherits socio-economic as well as political liabilities when he dons striped pants and enters his office.

Compelling as this analysis may be, it breaks down in a number of ways when subjected to empirical verification. More precisely, a systematic investigation of Senatorial attitudes toward Dean Acheson indicates the need for considerable modification of the notion that all or most legislators are antagonistic to the Secretary. Even more precisely, such a simplified and all-encompassing conception of the direction, nature, and sources of Senatorial behavior does not correspond with the findings, reported here in summarized form,[2] derived from a content analysis of the more than thirty thousand pages which constitute the formal deliberations of the Senate during the 1949-52 period.[3]

Perhaps the most significant finding yielded by the inquiry concerns the extent to which Senators participated in the debate about Acheson. Of the one hundred twenty-one persons who served in the Senate during the four-year period, eighty-seven referred so infrequently to Acheson that an attitude could not reasonably be inferred from their behavior.[4] Regardless of whether the passivity of this Passive Majority was due to the absence of an attitude or to an attitude of purposeful silence, the fact is that more than two-thirds of the Senate stood on the sidelines while thirty-four members (the Active Minority) engaged in controversy over Acheson.

The extent of this passivity is plainly revealed by the quantitative data. From the convening of Congress on January 3, 1949, to its adjournment on July 7, 1952, a total of 3,502 references[5] to Acheson were recorded on the Senate floor. Although this amounts to an average of about 29 references per Senator, the median figure of 6 references more accurately suggests the inactivity of most Senators. Indeed, twenty-nine made no references whatsoever, while the most registered by any one Senator was 346. Table I presents a general view of the distribution within this range. Here it can be seen that a small proportion of the Senate recorded a preponderance of the references. Or, to put this datum even more strikingly, while the Passive Majority accounted for 71.9 per cent of the Senate membership, they tallied only 10.7 per cent of the total references.

Table I—Distribution of Senators by Total Number of References

Number of References	Number of Senators
0	29
1-5	29
6-10	19
11-15	5
16-20	7
21-40	4
41-60	12
61-80	4
81-100	4
101-150	4
151-200	—
201-300	2
301-346	2
Total 3,502	121

Conceivably, of course, the ranks of the Passive Majority may have been swollen by considerations entirely unrelated to attitudes toward Acheson. Frequency of reference may also have been a measure of how Senators varied in their conception of the Senatorial role, in seniority, in attendance, and in such idiosyncratic factors as taciturnity and talkativeness. The possible presence of these extraneous variables can, however, be easily exaggerated. There is no evidence that any of them correlated highly with the distinction between the Passive Majority and the Active Minority, thereby indicating that the procedures employed did subject attitudes toward Acheson to measurement. The Passive Majority was not, for example, comprised largely of Senators who acquired their seats subsequent to January, 1949, and whose reference frequency may thus have been inhibited by the seniority tradition. On the contrary, not only did fifty-one members of the Passive Majority serve in the Senate for the full four-year period, but fifty entered upon their duties in 1947, and thirty-nine were present when Acheson was confirmed as Under Secretary of State in August, 1945. Similarly, it seems unlikely that varying attendance rates produced the distinction between Active and Passive Senators, as is demonstrated by the fact that Vandenberg, Kefauver, and Taft were members of the Active Minority even though illness, crime investigation, and presidential aspirations respectively took them

; way from the Senate and Washington for long stretches of time.

Nor did brevity of tenure during the 1949-52 period swell the ranks of the Passive Majority. This factor was circumvented by basing the activity-passivity delineation on the number of references recorded per month of 1949-52 Senate tenure rather than on the total number of references registered. Senators who made a reference rate in excess of 0.7 were regarded as having engaged in behavior sufficiently patterned to warrant the assumption of a structured attitude, whereas those whose rate was less than the cutoff point were judged as too passive to entitle the researcher to posit the existence of an attitude. Accordingly, Senators whose tenure was shortened by late entry or early exit were not excluded from the Active Minority because they had fewer chances to compile a high number of total references.[6]

In short, while extraneous variables relating to the organization, procedures, and traditions of the Senate were undoubtedly operative, the absence of clear-cut evidence in this respect suggests that the substantial size of the Passive Majority stemmed in part, probably in large part, from a lack of attitudes toward Acheson or from purposefully passive attitudes. Positive as well as negative findings also point to such a conclusion. In particular, it is noteworthy that on the few occasions when Passive Senators did refer to Acheson, they engaged in behavior which, in other attitudinal studies,[7] has been repeatedly attributed to the relative lack of an attitude. Just as one study found that enlisted men who neither liked nor disliked their officers placed low on a scale of attitude intensity,[8] so does it emerge that Senators who had most of their references coded as neutral[9] also registered low reference rates. Taken as a whole, 60.1 per cent of the 378 references tallied by the Passive Majority were coded as neutral.[10] In contrast, the Active Minority had only 26.1 per cent of their 3,124 references so designated. This close linkage between frequency of reference and judgmental direction on the one hand, and between infrequency of reference and neutral content on the other, clearly points to the presence of attitudinal factors as determinants of passivity: whereas it is possible to conceive of many irrelevant reasons why Senators might not have participated in debate, it is difficult to imagine any extraneous variables that might have also inclined them toward neutrality on the few instances when they did refer to Acheson.

If some Senators were intentionally silent and neutral, presumably this was due to an ambivalence toward Acheson that they found most easily resolvable by studiously avoiding reference to him. In terms of the definition of an attitude used here, silence was their "way" of responding to him. Traces of such an attitude can be most clearly discerned in the behavior of Passive Democrats, some of whom appear to have experienced a conflict between severe criticism of some of Acheson's policies and unconditional support of his actions in other areas. Such a conflict is suggested by one of Eastland's few references:

I want to say this for Mr. Acheson, that while I do not agree with his Asiatic policy and I think it is inadequate, yet I think Mr. Acheson is a fine gentleman who is doing the very best he can. In the light of history, however, I think he is wrong. I think his policies are totally inadequate to stop communism, but I say that our forei:n policy to restore world trade is sound and that, after all, the great bulwark to prevent Communist expansion is to make friends with people by doing business with them. I think that Mr. Acheson in that respect has shown both courage and intelligence, and I endorse that policy 1,000 per cent.[11]

Other Passive Democrats were apparently torn between doubts about Acheson's policies and a reluctance to criticize a key official of their party. This type of ambivalence is to be seen in Chavez's inability to contain his silence after Communist China entered the Korean war:

I do not say this in any criticism of the Secretary of State, and this is not a question of personalities; but situations come and go. The flag means more to me, the Constitution means more to me, the Declaration of Independence means more to me, and the American system means more to me, than any personality. . . . I do not know what the Secretary of State had in mind six months ago. I shall take it for granted, until I know differently, that he was acting in good faith. But the point is not whether he was right or wrong. The point I am trying to make is that action should be taken now. . . . What I am saying is not said with the idea of criticism of the motives of the Secretary of State, his sincerity of purpose, or his integrity. I may be mistaken, but I think that his trouble is that he is trying to make up his mind from the thinking of the central part of the North Atlantic states, and it does not involve the thinking of Bolivar or Clinton Corners, N. Y., Eaton, Ky., or Sullivan Hollow, Miss., or Los Chavez in New Mexico, or Fort Scott, Nebraska. . . .[12]

The silence of some Republicans may have also stemmed from ambivalence, or at least hints of it can be detected in the behavior of the fourteen (out of seventeen) Northeastern[13] Republicans who were members of the Passive Majority. It seems likely that among these Senators there was a distaste for the extremism of some of their Republican colleagues which conflicted with an uneasiness about the adequacy of Acheson's policies. Being unwilling to align themselves with Acheson's most outspoken critics, and being unwilling or unable to rise to the defense of a Democratic official, such Senators thus refrained from entering the controversy, maintaining instead a studied passivity with respect to it. Indeed, the muteness of these fourteen Senators could hardly have been more conspicuous: while they served a combined total of 406 legislative months during Acheson's Secretaryship, they made only 71 references to him. One of these, made by Flanders, succinctly reflects the conflict which may have underlain the silence of some Northeastern Republicans:

The papers carry the story that the Republicans are trying to get rid of Mr. Acheson as Secretary of State. I wish to disassociate myself from this undertaking, but I do wish to join with those who are seeking to assist him toward a more constructive line of policy than that which has been followed for some time past.[14]

But it would be overtaxing the data to conclude that every Passive Senator possessed an attitude of purposeful passivity. Conceivably some did not have an attitude toward Acheson and therefore were not ready to respond to him in any "way." Specialization and the division of Senatorial labor presumably led some Senators to concentrate upon domestic policy issues and to pay relatively little attention to foreign policy, with the result that they had no occasion to respond to Acheson and develop an attitude toward him. Like the commander of the western front who is so preoccupied with his own difficulties that he is only remotely concerned about the course of battle on the distant eastern front, probably such Senators operated with the assumption that their interests in the foreign policy area were being advanced by particular members of the Active Minority.

In any event, regardless of the sources of passivity, it is a major conclusion of this inquiry that, in terms of their behavior on the Senate floor, most Senators were indifferent to Acheson. The notion that all or most legislators become preoccupied with the Secretary of State still stands in need of empirical demonstration.

The conception of widespread antagonism to the Secretary breaks down further in the light of the finding that Acheson did have friends in the Senate. Thirteen of the thirty-four Active Senators recorded more favorable than unfavorable references. Indeed, this Cordial Minority accounted for 77.0 per cent of the 537 favorable references tallied during the 1949-52 period. To-

gether the thirteen Cordial Senators[15] had 54.5 per cent of their 759 references coded as favorable, 40.2 per cent as neutral, and 5.3 per cent as unfavorable—behavior which certainly indicates that Acheson was not without defenders in the Senate. In fact, the Cordial Minority were capable of vigorously expressing their approbation. Theirs was not necessarily the perfunctory and routinized praise so habitual to Senators. Rather they described him as "a brilliant man,"[16] as "reliable, helpful, cooperative, and trustworthy,"[17] as possessing "a sense of calm and poise that comes from his great intellectual capacity and moral courage,"[18] as "a public servant of vision, profound intelligence, courage, resourcefulness, and high patriotism—qualities without which we would have no hope of winning in the great struggle for peace."[19] With equal vigor did the Cordial Minority deny that Acheson was disrespectful of Congress; he was portrayed as

a man of great ability who has many qualities and intellectual attainments that are very helpful to the [Foreign Relations] committee and its members. He is always thoroughly cooperative with the committee, and in addition, he is always willing to confer with individual members. I am sure that he does not withhold any information which would be helpful to us in our deliberations. . . . I do not recall any time when the Secretary refused to appear or refused to discuss any foreign policy question raised by committee members.[20]

Nor did Cordial Senators concede that Acheson was "soft" on communism. On the contrary, they knew of "no man who has held more stalwartly to his course that we could not rely upon the Russian word,"[21] with the consequence that "'the present Secretary of State is an able, conscientious, patriotic, devoted public servant, who has dedicated a lifetime of service in the struggle for freedom, and has dedicated his physical energy, his emotional and mental capacities in the struggle against communism."[22] Indeed, not only was the United States "most fortunate to have at this time a man of his vast experience and wisdom at the post of Secretary of State,"[23] but one Cordial Senator even ventured "to suggest that no group of free nations in the history of mankind, faced with such an overwhelming threat to their security, ever owed so much to a foreign minister as the free nations of the world owe today to Dean Acheson."[24]

The Cordial Minority was also capable of berating the Hostile Minority for "the excess of vituperation which has splattered the composite image of Mr. Acheson."[25] Perhaps the most forceful expression of this capacity occurred when a Hostile Senator denied that he had launched "an attack on the Secretary himself," a remark to which Connally replied in no uncertain terms:

No, it was no attack at all—it was merely kicking him in the ribs, punching him in the nose, and pummeling him. It was no attack at all. Of course it was an attack; not such an attack as a witness might make under oath in court. It was not an attack like that of a witness who must produce facts. But it is an attack by way of insinuation.[26]

While the foregoing demonstrates that Acheson was championed by friends in the Senate, it must be noted that Cordial Senators were most aggressive in praising his personal qualities[27] and deploring the attacks upon him,[28] but that their capacity for vigorous support was less than extensive with respect to his performances.[29] Such a distinction is perhaps most noticeable in the behavior of the four Cordial Senators who made 38 of the 40 unfavorable references tallied by the Cordial Minority. These four Senators had 80.0 per cent of their 35 references to his personal qualities coded as favorable, whereas only 12.5 per cent of their 104 references to his performances were so designated, a contrast which clearly indicates that their cordiality was limited in the latter respect. In fact, their lesser enthusiasm for his actions gave way to outright criticism when Acheson violated strong convictions which they held about particular policy questions: 35 of their 38 unfavorable references were classified in the performance category, and these focussed exclusively on Acheson's posture toward European unity (Fulbright), Atlantic Union (Kefauver), troops-to-Europe (Hickenlooper), and the Far East (Smith of N. J.).[30] For two of these Senators, Fulbright and Kefauver, this conflict between a favorable image of his person and an unhappiness over certain policy matters had the consequence of invigorating their readiness to defend Acheson when their special preoccupations were not involved. Indeed, they posited themselves as especially competent to deplore unwarranted attacks upon him, frequently citing their own criticism as entitling them to denounce the behavior of Hostile Senators.[31]

Although the other nine Cordial Senators made no unfavorable references, traces of lesser enthusiasm for Acheson's policies can also be discerned in their behavior. Notwithstanding their capacity for unreserved praise, the cordiality potential[32] of these nine Senators did not approach one hundred per cent. Rather they modified their approval to the extent of registering a neutrality potential of 37.3 per cent. Even more suggestive, these nine Senators consistently responded cordially to Acheson's personal qualities, but their responses to his performances were cast as much in unevaluative as in favorable terms: only 10.7 per cent of their 140 references to his person were given a neutral designation, whereas the equivalent figure for their 280 references to his performances was 48.2 per cent. This sensitivity to Acheson's policies is also apparent in the content of their references to his performances. While they praised his leadership in general, and while they insisted that he did cooperate with the Congress, they did not rebut the main charges made by the Hostile Minority. For the most part they avoided reference to his role in the Korean conflict, just as they were virtually silent about the contention that he permitted the Communist conquest of China, that he caused the removal of General MacArthur, and that he tolerated subversion in the State Department. Nor did they counter such criticism by effusive praise of those performances which Hostile Senators ignored and which were widely regarded as being outstanding accomplishments: only a very few of their favorable references, for example, were devoted to Acheson's performances with respect to the developing strength of N.A.T.O. or the "Uniting for Peace" resolution adopted by the United Nations. In short, Acheson's friends applauded his personal qualities and they deplored the attacks upon him, but their counteroffensive did not include a vigorous and exacting defense of his performances in substantive policy situations.

It is interesting to note that the Japanese Peace Treaty conference of September, 1951, constituted the one concrete policy situation in which Acheson's role was elaborately and unrestrainedly acclaimed by the Cordial Minority. They extolled "the brilliance with which he presided at San Francisco,"[33] describing it as "a grand job"[34] which necessitated

a special tribute to the Secretary of State, Mr. Acheson, for the commendable and brilliant way in which he handled the conference. The Russians and their satellites . . . were defeated because of Mr. Acheson's skill in handling the entire meeting. . . .[35]

Why did the Cordial Minority refer so wholeheartedly to this particular performance and so cursorily, if at all, to most of his actions? Perhaps the main difference lay in the fact that the proceedings of the conference were nationally televised, thereby permitting Cordial Senators to assert perceptions that were also readily available to the public. Whatever reasons they may have had for limiting their approval of his actions and policies, these were probably nullified by this unique situation in which the spectacle of Acheson thwarting the Russians was witnessed by a nationwide audience. Indeed, they were quite explicit about the relevance of this consideration:

By means of the television broadcast of the recent peace conference, many persons for the first time saw the Secretary of State as he really is. They learned to appreciate the fine man that he is and the fine character that is his. The American people have found, as they have come to know him better, the Secretary of State to be one who is skilled, trained, experienced, and informed.[36]

Despite their response to the Japanese Peace Treaty, it is difficult to estimate why Cordial Senators were so selective in their defense of Acheson. The data do not indicate whether their silent posture toward his performances stemmed from doubts which they were unwilling to concede to the Hostile Minority, or whether it was fostered by a fear of the political liabilities that may have attended a defense of his more controversial actions. Probably both considerations were operative to a certain extent. Such a conclusion, however, must be placed in a proper perspective. It pertains to what Acheson's friends did not say. No less significant is the fact that they did engage in cordial behavior, that they did surmount their doubts and fears rather than lapse into passivity, and that not infrequently they did so in a vigorous and combative fashion. Plainly it would be erroneous to dismiss their cordiality simply because it did not offset the hostility of his critics. Indeed, given the temper of American society during the 1949-52 period, it is perhaps more relevant to inquire about the sources of such support than about the limits within which it flourished.

A few hints as to some of the factors underlying cordial attitudes are implicit in the composition of the Cordial Minority. Of its thirteen members, nine were Democrats and four were Republicans. No Cordial Senator hailed from the Pacific Coast or from the Mountain states; rather, five came from the Midwest and four each from the South and the Northeast. Three of the Republicans came from the Midwest, a finding which demonstrates the fallacy of assuming that Midwestern Republicanism necessarily produces hostile attitudes toward the Secretary. Even more suggestive is an apparent correlation between cordiality and proximity to the foreign policy-making process: eight of the Cordial Senators were members of the Foreign Relations Committee and this included all four of the Republicans. Since the ranks of the Cordial Minority did not include every member of the Foreign Relations Committee, however, and since it did include five Senators who never held such an assignment, it is only safe to conclude that affiliation with either the Democratic party or the Foreign Relations Committee seems to have been a minimum prerequisite to the development of a cordial attitude.

But there need be no caution with respect to the finding that some Senators did develop cordial attitudes. Whatever the sources of their behavior, and although they may have possessed certain criticisms and reservations about his actions, thirteen Senators did speak on Acheson's behalf. The notion that the Secretary of State is so vulnerable to Congressional hostility that no legislator is likely to befriend him also fails to withstand the test of empirical investigation.

Acheson's supporters were no match for the twenty-one Active Senators who made more unfavorable than favorable references. Together this Hostile Minority accounted for 67.5 per cent of the 3,502 references registered during the 1949-52 period and for 94.1 per cent of the 1,921 unfavorable references. The predominance of Hostile Senators is further indicated by a directional and chronological breakdown of the total references (Table II). Here it can be seen that not only

Table II—Directional Distribution of References by Years

Percentage of Total References Recorded as	1949	1950	1951	1952	All Four Years
Favorable	24	15	12	10	15
Unfavorable	35	56	63	63	55
Neutral	41	29	25	27	30

was their criticism considerably greater than the praise of Acheson's friends, but also that, proportionately, it continued to mount during the first three years and held steady in the fourth year.

Although Hostile Senators dominated the Acheson debate, not all of them evidenced an inclination to treat him as a scapegoat for the insecurities of a troubled world. A significant distinction can be made between those who tended to confine their criticism to Acheson's performances and those whose hostility tended to be more indiscriminate and embraced him in all his capacities. These tendencies have been operationalized by attributing a discriminately hostile attitude to those Senators who recorded less than 10.3 per cent of their hostility potential in the personal qualities and symbol-collectivity[37] categories, and by ascribing an indiscriminately hostile attitude to those who registered more than 10.3 per cent of their unfavorable references in these two categories.[38] On this basis the Hostile Minority breaks down into clusters of eight Discriminates[39] and thirteen Indiscriminates.[40]

That the Discriminates were primarily ready to respond to Acheson as a performing official is illustrated by the median of 83.4 per cent of their unfavorable references which they recorded in the performance category. That they were not ready to respond critically to his personal qualities, and that they were essentially unconcerned about him as a symbol-collectivity, can be seen in the small proportion of their unfavorable references which they tallied in these two categories: the median figure of 3.65 per cent reflects the very limited extent to which their hostility was comprised of personalization and symbolization. Clearly their generalized potential of hostile responses was not very general. It was confined to and circumscribed by certain situations in the foreign policy environment. In a figurative sense it might be said that theirs was hardly a hostility toward Acheson, that rather it was a readiness to respond hostilely to the Secretary of State. One Discriminate Senator, Cain, made this distinction quite explicit when he interpolated into a critical speech the comment that "I make no possible reference to him as a person, but I refer to him as one of the most powerful officials on the face of the earth."[41] On another occasion Cain observed that his remarks were "without prejudice to the Secretary of State, whose personal name I have not used."[42]

The tendency of the Indiscriminates, on the other hand, to respond to Acheson as a complex of personal qualities and as a symbol-collectivity can be seen in the median proportion of their hostility potential, 20.3 per cent, coded in these two categories. The Indiscriminates were also concerned about Acheson's performance. A median of 61.3 per cent of their unfavorable references was so classified, and their perceptions of him as a performing official were not so confined to selective policy areas as those of the Discriminates, encompassing instead a much broader range of situations in the foreign policy environment. Theirs was indeed a generalized potential of hostile responses. For the Indiscriminates, Acheson was a generalized evil: they had a hostile attitude toward what he was and what he did and what he symbolized.

Given their more generalized hostility, it is not surprising that the Indiscriminates criticized Acheson more consistently than did the Discriminates: the median hostility potential compiled by the latter was 46.3 per cent, whereas the equivalent figure for the former was 83.5 per cent. As a result of this hostility which verged upon 100 per cent, the Indiscriminates were hardly ready to refer to Acheson in an unevaluative fashion and under no circumstances were they prepared to register approval of him: their median neutrality ₁otential was 16.5 per cent, while their unwillingness to express praise is amply demonstrated by their median cordiality potential of 0.0 per cent.

On the other hand, being less disposed to criticize Acheson at all times, the Discriminates were capable of frequently recording neutral references to him: their median neutrality potential was 48.65 per cent. Moreover, being highly selective in their hostility, the Discriminates even had a limited capacity for responding favorably on occasion, a tendency which is reflected in their median cordiality potential of 4.2 per cent and which was perhaps most pronouncedly expressed when Knowland, "without any mental reservation whatever," asserted "that the job which Secretary Acheson did in presiding over the [Japanese Peace Treaty] conference was outstanding. . . . I think he handled himself in a superb manner."[43]

The Discriminates not only confined their criticism to Acheson's actions, but they did so in a highly selective fashion. Rather than contesting everything Acheson did, they tended to specialize in such matters as the Far East (Knowland), the normalization of relations with Spain (Brewster), the immigration laws (McCarran), the procedures employed for issuing passports (Morse), and the constitutionality of various treaty arrangements (Donnell and Watkins). Aside from these particular preoccupations, the Discriminates were apparently prepared to accept Acheson's actions as reasonable and legitimate—or at least they did not make substantial reference to him with respect to other issues. Knowland, for example, had 77.7 per cent of his 130 references classified in the Far Eastern category, whereas only 3.8 per cent were coded in the West European category. Indeed, Knowland specialized so thoroughly in Far Eastern matters that, unlike his Hostile colleagues, he did not wait until disaster occurred in the region before blaming Acheson for the course of events: he made 38.6 per cent of the 44 references to the Far East recorded by the entire Senate in 1949, and, even more significantly, he was the only Senator to criticize Acheson for omitting Korea from the American defense perimeter *before* the Korean conflict broke out in June, 1950.[44]

A few clues as to the sources of hostility, as well as to the factors which inclined the Discriminates to be so much more selective in their criticism than the Indiscriminates, can be derived from the party, regional, and committee affiliations of the Hostile Minority. Except for McCarran, all twenty-one Hostile Senators were Republicans. All thirteen Indiscriminates were Republicans, and ten of these represented Midwestern states (with two of the remainder hailing from Mountain states and the other from the Northeast). Only two of the eight Discriminates, on the other hand, came from the Midwest, while three came from the Pacific coast, two from the Mountain states, and one from the Northeast. None of the Hostile Senators served on the Foreign Relations Committee until April, 1951, when Brewster, a Discriminate, replaced the deceased Vandenberg. Since these party and committee ties of the Hostile Minority were exactly contrary to those of their Cordial colleagues, it seems safe to conclude that, excepting McCarran, membership in the Republican party and nonmembership in the Foreign Relations Committee were necessary to the development of hostile attitudes. Likewise, since the two Hostile Minorities differed greatly in their regional composition, it would appear that indiscriminate hostility received its strongest nourishment in the soil of Midwestern Republicanism.

This is not to say that such affiliations were sufficient to foster one or the other form of hostility. On the contrary, they were only minimum prerequisites to the formation of such attitudes, as is indicated by the fact that the Hostile Minority did not embrace all the Republicans and that the ranks of the Indiscriminates did not include every Midwestern Republican. However, while the data again do not permit precise inferences as to attitudinal sources, they do plainly indicate that at least two distinct types of hostility were operative. This finding is especially noteworthy. Too often it is assumed that legislative hostility has only one dimension in the foreign policy field, that Senatorial critics can only strike wildly and blindly at administrative officials. The Indiscriminates did just that (below), possibly reaching unparalleled heights of vituperation and intemperance. But it is equally remarkable, given the hectic tenor of the 1949-52 period, that while the Discriminates were no less critical, they were much less frenzied. Their behavior clearly demonstrates that it was possible to engage in lengthy and frequent criticism of Acheson's performances without necessarily resorting to personalization and symbolization. This should hearten those who see no alternative between excessive partisanship in foreign affairs and bipartisanship which bridges the separation of powers gap at the loss of responsible criticism. It should also give pause to policymakers who never vary their response to legislative hostility because of an assumption that all their critics operate at the same level of irreconcilability. In this sense, the ability of a Knowland to restrain his distaste for Far Eastern policy is highly significant, perhaps even more so than the bitter extremism of a Jenner or a McCarthy.

Although stress has been placed upon the finding that most Senators were passive toward Acheson, that some were cordial, and that a few were selective and restrained in their criticism, the foregoing is not intended to obscure the central role played by the thirteen Senators who were highly antagonistic. Their predominance is readily discernible in the quantitative aspects of the data: the Indiscriminates, comprising 10.7 per cent of the total membership, made 48.3 per cent of all the references recorded by the entire Senate and 76.1 per cent of all the unfavorable references. Indeed, the 1,691 references tallied by the thirteen Indiscriminates constituted more than four times as many as the 378 registered by the eighty-seven Passive Senators, nearly three times the 674 recorded by the eight Discriminates, and more than twice the 759 tallied by the thirteen Cordial Senators. Moreover, their 1,691 references amounted to more than twice the 837 recorded by all sixty-seven Democrats and to more than three-fifths of the 2,665 compiled by the fifty-four Republicans.

But the quantitative data do not fully portray the extent to which the Indiscriminates dominated the Acheson controversy. In addition to its sheer volume, the inconsistency, ambiguity, and malevolence of their criticism also shaped the tone and terms of the debate. From their references to his performances, for example, a composite picture emerges of an actor who had a prior history of undesirable performances and who, as Secretary of State, acted deceptively, straightforwardly, meekly, and authoritatively to complicate horrendous situations that he caused to exist in the first place. The Indiscriminates were the only Senators to attribute consequences to his performances, describing him as causative of everything from the Communist conquest of China to "the awful [potato] marketing year of 1950."[45] Indeed, so consequential were his performances that "every passing hour produces additional proof of how Secretary Acheson is continuing to double talk us even deeper into Communist booby traps all over the world.[46] With respect to China, the Indiscriminates were inclined to posit Acheson as a mortician: he was accused of having "driven the final nail in the coffin of Nationalist China"[47] with such force that he was prepared "to not only bury the Republic of China, but to heap refuse on its grave."[48] Nor were their assertions of his responsibility for the Korean war any less picturesque: "The blood of our boys today is on his shoulders, and not on the shoulders of anyone else."[49] And how did Acheson's actions produce the Korean conflict? Aside from attributing causation to his defense perimeter speech, the Indiscriminates did not analyze the chain of events in very precise terms: "Mr. Acheson zigged, and he zagged, until he zigzagged us into war."[50]

As the foregoing suggests, Acheson could do nothing that would have satisfied or placated the

Indiscriminates. Under no circumstances, for instance, were they ready to perceive him as having cooperated with the Congress. He was seen as either failing to consult or as consulting deceitfully, as either withholding information or as pressing for legislation by providing information, as either ignoring the Congress or as thwarting it. Nor did they modify their conviction that Acheson ignored or bullied the Congress when confronted with the fact that he did consult with the appropriate committees and that some of their colleagues regarded him as cooperative. Such evidence was dismissed on the grounds that the Congress was "spineless," composed of "dummies" who "nod their heads" when "Mr. Acheson pulls the strings."[51] Indeed, such Senators were "used as pawns by the master architect of our over-all foreign policy, Mr. Acheson. . . . They have been lied to, double-talked to, and completely duped by the master-mind of our State Department."[52]

That the Indiscriminates were intent upon finding fault with whatever he did can also be seen in their references to Acheson's actions relative to the Soviet Union. If he condemned the Russians in strong language, then his action was described as a "supposed anti-Communist outburst,"[53] as an effort "to blame Stalin for his own criminal blunders."[54] Or, if it was conceded that he was capable of taking an anti-Communist position, then he was criticized for "trying to contain communism with his left hand while he coddles communism with his right."[55]

By positing him as possessing extraordinary power and influence, the Indiscriminates supplemented their perceptions of the damage wrought by Acheson's performances. Often they indirectly traced causation back to him by insisting that he wielded an evil and undue control over a wide variety of officials, agencies, and situations. Even the President was perceived as subject to his domination: notwithstanding their distaste for Truman, the Indiscriminates occasionally exonerated him by noting that "the Acheson hand [is] quicker than the Truman brain,"[56] and that "he is blind to the devious paths down which Acheson has advised him."[57] This excessive influence was also cited as the reason why Truman did not remove Acheson from the Secretaryship: "In the relationship of master and man, did you ever hear of man firing master?"[58] The Indiscriminates devoted equal energy to explicating how military personnel and policies fell under Acheson's jurisdiction. Among other things, they contended that "the army has become an implement of foreign policy, subject to the orders and commands of the Secretary of State,"[59] and that

The State Department has its obedient, political generals, its stooges in battle dress, whom it has moved into top positions. They impose total silence on the professional military men, while Acheson makes our military plans. . . .[60]

Nor were specific officials and agencies the only objects which the Indiscriminates posited as submissive to Acheson. At a higher level of generalization they perceived that "the Secretary of State is managing our Armed Forces, our political life, our private press,"[61] that "Mr. Acheson today is not only writing our foreign policy but he more than any other man in the United States is dictating our domestic economy."[62] All of this authority was perceived as amounting to a process which put "Mr. Acheson in full charge of the throttle,"[63] so much so that it was "turning . . . the Government of ours into a military dictatorship, run by the Communist-appeasing, Communist-protecting betrayer of America, Secretary of State Dean Acheson."[64] In short, as far as the Indiscriminates were concerned, "Dean Acheson has muscled in on so many of the vitally important policy-making commissions and boards of our Government that he is not only Secretary of State, but has become Mr. Government itself."[65]

Despite the pervasive and deep-seated nature of their hostility, it seems doubtful that the Indiscriminates derived their antagonism simply from a negative reaction to Acheson as a human being. Their tendency to exaggerate his influence suggests that the word "Acheson" meant more to them than merely the name of an individual official. This is further indicated by the content of their 279 references to his personal qualities. Together these add up to an image of his person that, whatever its accuracy, was so lopsided and ambiguous that it is by no means certain what it was about Acheson that the Indiscriminates found so distasteful. Their references to his personality and abilities were conspicuously vague and unsubstantial, hardly amounting to impressive evidence in support of the oft-asserted observation that Acheson's manner and talents were a major source of Congressional antipathy to him. Evasiveness and disloyalty, for example, were the only traits attributed to his character; but these attributions were so extreme that they appear to have served other purposes for the Indiscriminates than that of describing their conception of his person. Surely a variety of considerations may have underlain this fairly typical evaluation of his loyalties:

I have studied Acheson's public utterances sidewise, slantwise, hindwise, and frontwise; I have watched the demeanor of this glib, supercilious, and guilty man on the witness stand; I have reflected upon his career, and I came to only one conclusion: his primary loyalty in international affairs runs to the British labor government, his secondary allegiance is to the Kremlin, with none left over for the country of his birth. The only trouble Acheson ever encounters is when Socialist-British and Russian-Communist policy diverge. . . . Then he reluctantly follows the lead from Socialist-London.[66]

The widespread notion that Senators were irritated by Acheson's "Ivy League" origins and his appearance also seems dubious in the light of the data. The Indiscriminates made no reference whatsoever to his social and educational background. And only 10 references, made by three Indiscriminates, were coded in a subcategory embracing perceptions of his physical appearance and dress. These described him as a "handsome and polished gentleman,"[67] as "well-groomed,"[68] as "the great Red Dean of fashion"[69] and the "diplomatic dean of fashion,"[70] and as "the elegant and alien Acheson—Russian as to heart, British as to manner."[71] Given the heavy emphasis that has been placed on Acheson's appearance as a stimulant of legislative antagonism, it is surprising that the Indiscriminates did not make more references along these lines.

But, it might be argued, perhaps they indirectly expressed reactions to Acheson's person in their perceptions of his performances. A special performance subcategory designed to yield evidence of this bootlegging process, however, had only a minimum of references coded therein, and these were no more substantial than the personal qualities which the Indiscriminates perceived directly. To be sure, his person may have been irritating to them without becoming the subject of extended verbalization. It is conceivable that his manner and talents nourished their hostility in the first place and that they then emphasized other issues because such were viewed as more comprehensible and reprehensible to the public. Yet no inkling of this syphoning process can be found in the data and the fact is that they did not refer either frequently or precisely to the varied qualities which are supposed to have been so vexing to them.

The tendency of the Indiscriminates to use Acheson's name as a symbol of some ambiguous phenomenon, or as a label for some unspecified collectivity, constitutes additional evidence that their attitudes were more than a direct response to who he was or what he did. They recorded 91.8 per cent of all the references coded in the symbol-collectivity category. In so doing they most frequently referred to the "Acheson crowd" or the "Acheson group," but they also linked Acheson's name with a wide variety of hyphenated collectivities, including "the Truman-Acheson clique,"[72] "the Hiss-Acheson combine,"[73] "the Acheson-Jessup crowd,"[74] "the Acheson-Hiss-

Yalta crowd,"[75] "the Acheson-Lattimore-Jessup group,"[76] "the Hiss-Lattimore-Acheson clique,"[77] and "the Truman-Acheson-Marshall trio"[78] (sometimes called "the Unholy Three"[79]). Nor were the collectivities limited to three: there was also "the Hiss-Acheson-Lattimore-Marshall group"[80] and "the Hiss-Acheson-Lattimore-Jessup crowd."[81]

In addition to positing the operation of hyphenated collectivities as explanatory of all that was undesirable, the Indiscriminates perceived that hidden groups and mysterious forces were causing untold damage. As if they could neither tolerate nor comprehend a world consisting of concrete officials and concrete socio-political processes, they often referred to a world composed of surreptitious figures and ominous tendencies. And, in the world, Acheson was viewed as "the very heart of the octopus,"[82] as the expression of "a sinister, ruthless undertow,"[83] as the product of "the inner circle . . . with its hidden rooms and hidden corridors."[84] For the Indiscriminates, in short, the course of events was determined by "a rather sinister monster of many heads and many tentacles, a monster conceived in the Kremlin, and then given birth to by Acheson, with Attlee and Morrison as the midwives, and then nurtured into Frankenstein proportions by the Hiss crowd, who still run the State Department."[85]

Certainly this "sinister monster" approach points to the conclusion that Acheson signified more than an identifiable human being to the Indiscriminates. Plainly they used his name as symbolic of activities and processes far more comprehensive in scope and consequence than any single individual. Whatever the reasons for their vituperative hostility and symbolic thinking, it would appear to have been derived from sources far more profound than irritation with what they conceived him to be. Indeed,

Acheson is not important in himself. He is a vastly over-rated figure. He is important because of the power which is now gathered in the Department and managed by our hidden government, while he serves as the well-groomed front.[86]

If Acheson's qualities and actions had little relevance to the development of indiscriminate hostility, what factors did foster the growth of such attitudes? Undoubtedly partisan considerations were operative. The Indiscriminates made quite explicit their calculation that political capital was to be derived from their hostility:

Dean Acheson, the man who by his record elected me to the United States Senate, is riding in the saddle today. If it had not been for his philosophy of Americanism and his handling of the far eastern question, this young country lawyer would not have been elected to the Senate. I crusaded in my State, telling of the planning, the errors, the blundering of his State Department. Yes, the people of my State understood Dean Acheson as long ago as November 7, 1950.[87]

On the other hand, other Republicans engaged in partisan activity without resort to symbolization and extreme vituperation. Surely it would be a gross oversimplification to explain the "sinister monster" approach as simply a means of gaining political advantage. Presumably the socio-psychological underpinnings of Midwestern Republicanism were equally important sources of their behavior, as, in all probability, were developments abroad during the 1949-52 period. In fact, the chronological and substantive pattern of their references suggest that the Indiscriminates would not have been especially preoccupied with Acheson if events in the Far East had unfolded in a less tumultuous fashion. Neither the volume nor the venomous quality of their references reached overwhelming proportions until the status quo in that part of the world began to alter. While the party battle and regional influences may have predisposed them to engage in extensive criticism, all the evidence points to the conclusion that their attitudes were mobilized and intensified by events in China and Korea. This is not to say that the extremism of their language originated with the Far Eastern crises. Presumably the tendency to describe the world in these terms stemmed from other, more idiosyncratic sources. However, since their calls for Acheson's resignation, as well as their tendency to posit him as a symbol-collectivity, did not attain climactic proportions until the latter part of 1950, it seems clear that as events in the Far East became increasingly uncontrollable so did the criticism of the Indiscriminates.

For these most Hostile Senators, then, Acheson apparently served as a scapegoat for the frustrations and insecurities of a situation which they were either unable or unwilling to fathom, much less accept. In this sense it seems doubtful whether their criticism stemmed, as some Cordial Senators contended, from a desire to undermine the direction and objectives of American foreign policy. Their attacks on Acheson correlated too closely with upheavals abroad to be viewed as an effort to reverse or restrain the pattern of commitments which had evolved subsequent to 1945. Had such been the intention of the Indiscriminates, presumably they would have condemned him for the Atlantic Pact and its implementation rather than virtually ignoring this aspect of his performances. While they may have been discontent with the status quo that existed prior to the Korean war, such an irritation was not fully

projected upon Acheson until after the uneasy peace in the Far East was shattered. For example, it was not until then, some six months later, that they became concerned about his refusal to "turn my back" on Alger Hiss, his speech in which Korea was omitted from the American defense perimeter in the Far East, and his responsibility for the Communist conquest of China. Moreover, the superficiality of many of their perceptions further indicates that concern about the bases of a sound policy did not underlie the attention which the Indiscriminates paid to Acheson. For them he was less a policy-maker and more a chaos-maker.

It is, of course, difficult to isolate a particular event in the Far East which precipitated an increased readiness to respond to Acheson. Presumably successive events had a cumulative effect, beginning with the collapse of Nationalist China in late 1949, heightened thereafter by the outbreak of war in Korea, sustained by the unexpected duration of the conflict, and culminating in Red China's entry into the war in November of 1950. Of all these developments, perhaps the most important was the entrance of Red China into the Korean war. Conceivably, had this not happened, Senatorial preoccupation with Acheson would have subsided with a quick termination of the Korean conflict and a return to the status quo. But China's entry raised the specter of an enlarged conflagration of indeterminate duration and possibly of disastrous consequences. Thus it might be argued that in November of 1950 attitudes toward Acheson became an irreversible commitment, an argument which is further substantiated by the fact that the Republicans in both houses of Congress adopted a resolution calling for his removal after, not before, the 1950 elections, on December 15th, less than three weeks subsequent to China's entry into the war.

To concentrate on this one event as *the* determinant of Senatorial behavior, however, would be to grossly distort the dynamics of attitude formation. It is safer to attribute causation to the whole series of interrelated developments which marked the Far Eastern scene, while emphasizing at the same time that it seems doubtful whether Acheson would have been a center of Senatorial controversy if these events had not occurred. To be sure, Senators with special grievances would have railed against him even if the world scene had remained calm. Yet, if the foregoing analysis is accurate, the Acheson controversy would have been little more than a mild and cursory dispute if the course of events had not unfolded as tempestuously as they did. Under less hectic circumstances the extremists would have been silenced or nullified by his defenders, just as they were forced to deny on several occasions early in 1949 that they had attacked him.

If it took a major change in the status quo to arouse the Indiscriminates, then it might well be said that all Senators, like citizens, lack an active orientation to the Secretary of State so long as developments abroad do not impinge upon their other pursuits. They are, it is true, constantly alert to Soviet maneuvers and to the requirements of a policy capable of preventing an alteration of the status quo. Nevertheless, until such an alteration occurs their concern for the Secretary would seem to operate within narrow, specialized limits. The party battle has much upon which to thrive without requiring nourishment from the insecurity of world politics. Indeed, since it flourishes upon that which is local and personal and close to the daily life of the community, an ordered and secure, and therefore remote, international situation is unsuited to, if not incompatible with, the party battle. Thus, except for those who had a specialized interest in a limited aspect of the external world, it would appear that Senators were content to ignore Acheson to the extent that international developments did not intrude upon their domestic concerns. That he became a focal point of debate is a measure of the upheavals which occurred during his tenure as Secretary.[88]

This is not to say that the rapidly changing world scene was the only attitudinal source or even the most important one. If such was the case, if Senatorial behavior was simply a response to external developments, then all Senators would have behaved in the same way. That they did not indicates that party, regional, and committee affiliations combined to produce varying frameworks through which foreign affairs were interpreted. In short, each of the components of this affiliative framework, as well as alteration of the status quo, was necessary to the formation of attitudes toward Acheson, but none was sufficient in itself. Only in the sense that the course of events was the chief mobilizer of Senatorial attitudes can it be cited as a more important factor than any other.

In any event, whatever the sources of their attitudes, clearly the Indiscriminates dominated the Senatorial scene in so far as Acheson was concerned. Given the virulence of their attacks, it is little wonder that most observers have assumed the existence of widespread hostility toward him. Even if the extent and depth of the antagonism has been exaggerated, certainly the predominance of the Indiscriminates gave the impression of widespread hostility. And, to the extent that other officials or citizens acted in terms of this impression, then to such an extent this was tantamount to a situation of widespread hostility.

There is a strong temptation, not entirely without merit, to be skeptical of empirical findings that fail to conform to existing conceptions of how behavior occurs. Often, however, such skepticism stems less from scientific caution and more from an inclination to reaffirm the prevailing theoretical model by way of avoiding the difficult task of revising it. And reaffirmation is easily accomplished: by challenging and denying the premises and procedures whereby the empirical findings were uncovered, the original notions can be preserved in all their logic, untarnished by the efforts of systematic inquiry.

Since only thirteen Senators were found to behave in such a way as to approximate the prevailing conception of legislative attitudes presented at the outset, this inquiry is perhaps especially vulnerable to challenge on methodological grounds. A number of arguments might be mustered to reaffirm the notion that all or most Senators are antagonistic toward the Secretary in order to gain votes or to relieve themselves of frustration. The behavior of Passive and Cordial Senators can be dismissed by contending that Senators do not publicly express what they really think, by arguing that the silence of the former and the praise of the latter was intended to obscure the existence of indiscriminate hostility. Reflecting as it does a widespread tendency to posit legislators as steeped in hypocrisy, as capable of divorcing their personal convictions from their public actions, this is a very compelling argument. It is also largely unanswerable, since data can always be rejected on the grounds that they fail to describe what is "really" the case. Yet, even if it could be demonstrated that Senators are able to exclude, neatly and thoroughly, their private thoughts and values from their public expressions whenever they find it convenient to do so, the fact remains that it is the verbal behavior of Senators, and not what they "really" think, that has consequences for the conduct and formulation of foreign policy. Although it is conceivable that a Senator, in the privacy of his own home, spoke critically of Acheson to his wife while at the same time making speeches which portrayed Acheson in a very favorable light, only the latter action is of significance to the policy-making process. The student of foreign policy is concerned with Senators as Senators and not as husbands, with actors in foreign policy situations and not with whole persons.

To be sure, Senators may have privately expressed views as Senators which they either contradicted or did not articulate in public (e.g., their colleagues or reporters, or even the Secretary himself, might have been the recipients of confidential opinions), and which thus may have been relevant to the policy-making process. Such data, however, have always been elusive to the researcher,[89] and all he can do is to restrict his interpretation to the available evidence. In a strict sense, then, the foregoing pages describe Senatorial attitudes toward Acheson as they were publicly expressed. Yet, this is hardly a major qualification of the findings, since the compilation of a public record constitutes the essence of the Senatorial role and since it is by no means certain that private values and attitudes can be thoroughly excluded from the public record, especially when the latter is examined over a full four-year period.

The adequacy of the *Congressional Record* provides another set of arguments by which the findings might be discounted. Reasoning along this line would grant that the public record contains reliable data about Senatorial attitudes, but would insist that serious distortion occurs in the limitation of the public record to the words expressed on the floor of the Senate. Such an argument would assert that, given the rules of procedure and tradition which govern formal debate, Senators regard speaking on the Senate floor as a special situation which does not obtain elsewhere, so that what they say in the Senate chamber is unrepresentative of what they say in committee deliberations, in press, radio, and television interviews, and in speaking tours of their constituencies. While this contention cannot be refuted by empirical evidence derived from systematic inquiry, neither can it be substantiated. Thus it is probably no more valid to assume that the *Congressional Record* is unrepresentative of the public record than to assume that it is an adequate sample. Here the latter assumption was made, partly because it greatly facilitated quantitative analysis[90] and partly because a wide group of competent observers were found to agree that Senators speak with the same tongue whether they are on or off the Senate floor, that they are addressing the same audiences regardless of the particular forum in which they exercise their vocal chords.[91]

Even if it is conceded that floor debate is typical of Senatorial behavior, there remains the contention that a variety of extraneous variables serve to distort the data and to render measurement difficult, if not impossible. Certainly a number of problems do arise from the fact that although Senators have an equal opportunity to address their colleagues in formal debate, some avail themselves of it considerably more than others, with the result that, as previously noted, the quantitative aspects of the data are a measure of such factors as seniority, attendance, role definition,

and personality as well as of attitudes toward Acheson. Inability to isolate a particular variable, however, does not mean that its operation has not been subjected to measurement. Rather it emphasizes the necessity of proceeding with caution and of accompanying attitudinal inferences with other possible interpretations of the data.

While these arguments, taken separately or together, facilitate reaffirmation of the notion that the Secretary must inevitably confront a hostile legislature, it should be noted that they cannot presently be supported by empirical evidence and that they are therefore founded on a chain of assumptions no less arbitrary than those which have led to contrary findings. Furthermore, even if it is granted that Senators do not say what they "really" think, that they speak differently on the Senate floor than off it, and that attendance and other extraneous factors largely determine their contribution to formal deliberations, the fact remains that, in so far as their four-year behavior in the Senate chamber was concerned, most Senators were silent in regard to Acheson, a few were friendly, and only a small minority were extensively and irreconcilably hostile.

Notes

1. See, for example, the following: Dean Acheson, "Responsibility for Decision in Foreign Policy," *Yale Review*, Vol. 44 (September, 1954), pp. 1-12; Dean Acheson, "What a Secretary of State Really Does," *Harper's Magazine*, Vol. 209 (December, 1954), p. 48; John Robinson Beal, *John Foster Dulles: A Biography* (New York, 1957), Chaps. 13-16; Daniel S. Cheever and H. Field Haviland, Jr., *American Foreign Policy and the Separation of Powers* (Cambridge, 1952), pp. 24-32, 200-24; Robert A. Dahl, *Congress and Foreign Policy* (New York, 1950), *passim;* Douglas Southall Freeman, "Introduction," in McGeorge Bundy (ed.), *The Pattern of Responsibility* (Boston, 1952), pp. xvii-xxi; Arthur Krock, "In The Nation," *New York Times* (January 22 and 29, February 7, 1957); James L. McCamy, *The Administration of American Foreign Affairs* (New York, 1950), *passim;* Paul H. Nitze, " 'Impossible' Job of Secretary of State," *New York Times Magazine* (February 24, 1957); James Reston, "Secretary Acheson—A First-Year Audit," *New York Times Magazine* (January 22, 1950); Richard C. Snyder and Edgar S. Furniss, Jr., *American Foreign Policy* (New York, 1954), pp. 238-243, 275-306; Henry M. Wriston, "The Secretary of State Abroad," *Foreign Affairs*, Vol. 34 (July 1956), pp. 523-540.

2. For the complete study, see James N. Rosenau, *The Senate and Dean Acheson: A Case Study in Legislative Attitudes*, unpublished Ph.D. thesis, Princeton University (Princeton, 1957). It should be stressed at the outset that this is not a study of the consequences of Senatorial behavior. While it would surely be a worthwhile enterprise to trace the impact of what Senators said about Acheson upon the course and conduct of foreign policy during the 1949-52 period, such is not within the scope of this inquiry. Here the concern is with the sources of legislative behavior and not with its consequences. The hope is that greater understanding of the former will lead to a more sophisticated comprehension of the latter.

3. For an extended presentation of the nature and use of the analytic categories employed in the content analysis, see *ibid.*, Chaps. 1-2 and Appendix I. So as to facilitate comprehension and evaluation of the material presented here, brief explanations of the major categories and procedures are provided in footnote form where appropriate.

4. Like other mortals, Senators do not behave in a random or arbitrary fashion; rather, their behavior stems from a readiness to respond to situations or events or persons in certain ways. This "readiness to respond in certain ways" is the definition of an attitude used here. "Ways" in this concept does not mean a set of specific courses of action, but rather it refers to a generalized potential of responses that might, in any given situation, be expressed in a variety of forms of action. Based on a readiness to respond in a certain way, Senators then "sized up" Acheson in order to give concrete form to their verbal behavior (i.e., to engage in a specific course of action). This "sizing up" is the definition of a perception used hereinafter. Of course, the observer never sees attitudes and perceptions; he only observes behavior, from which the attitudes and perceptions must be inferred. As operationalized, then, attitudes consist of inferences derived from the verbal behavior of Senators which was repeated and consistent, thereby indicative of a generalized "readiness," while perceptions have been inferred from behavior which was descriptive and momentary, thereby indicating a selection process or a "sizing up." This conceptualization has been drawn from the following sources: Richard C. Snyder, H. W. Bruck, and Burton Sapin, *Decision-Making as an Approach to the Study of International Politics* (Princeton, 1954), pp. 92-109; Theodore M. Newcomb, *Social Psychology* (New York, 1950), Part II; Wilbur Schramm (ed.), *The Process and Effects of Mass Communication* (Urbana, 1954), pp. 209-250.

5. A "reference" constitutes the basic unit of measurement. The limits of a reference were determined by the limits of five mutually exclusive categories corresponding to the ways in which Senators identified Acheson as an object in their environment. That is, a reference is not equatable to every time Acheson's name was mentioned by a Senator. Rather *one* reference was defined as existing whenever a Senator mentioned *one* personal quality, or *one* performance, or *one* authority of Acheson's, or *one* symbol-collectivity performance or quality, or *one* of the three complexes subsumed under a residual category (the nature of these identification categories is noted below). Thus a reference may have been a word, a phrase, a sentence, a paragraph, or several paragraphs in length (by procedural definition, however, it could not be longer than one column of the *Congressional Record*).

6. An exception was made, however, in the case of four Senators, three of whom (Baldwin, Barkley, and Dulles) were not included in the Active Minority because their service in the 81st Congress was so exceptionally brief that their few references, while contributing to a reference rate in excess of 0.7, were insufficient in number to permit the derivation of an attitude. The fourth Senator, Tydings, was assigned to the Passive Majority because such a high proportion (78.9 per cent) of his 19 references was classified as neutral that a positive attitude could not be inferred from his behavior.

7. See, for example, the following: Hadley Cantril, "The Intensity of an Attitude," *Journal of Abnormal and Social Psychology*, Vol. 41 (April, 1946), pp. 129-135; H. J. Eysenck and S. Crown, "National Stereotypes: An Experimental and Methodological Study," *International Journal of Opinion and Attitude Research*, Vol. 2 (Spring, 1948), pp. 26-39; Daniel Katz, "The Measurement of Intensity," in Hadley Cantril (ed.), *Gauging Public Opinion* (Princeton, 1944), pp. 51-65; Samuel Stouffer, *et al.*, *Measurement and Prediction* (Princeton, 1950), *passim*.

8. See Edward A. Suchman, "The Intensity Component in Attitude and Opinion Research," in Samuel Stouffer, *et al.*, *op. cit.*, pp. 222-233.

9. In addition to being coded in substantive categories, each reference was also categorized in terms of whether the quality, performance, authority, etc., appeared to be cited by the Senator in favorable, unfavorable, or neutral (i.e., as unevaluative description) terms.

10. Of their remaining references, 20.6 per cent were classified as favorable and 19.3 per cent as unfavorable.

11. *Congressional Record* (hereinafter abbreviated as C.R.), Vol. 96, Part 5, p. 5760: April 26, 1950.

12. C.R., Vol. 96, Part 12, p. 16047: December 4, 1950.

13. Since the process of subdividing the United States into political regions becomes arbitrary at a certain point, especially with respect to the "border states," the basis of assigning states to regions was that of facilitating comparisons between this study and other recent analyses of Congressional behavior in the foreign policy field. Accordingly, the regions used here correspond to those employed by H. Bradford Westerfield, *Foreign Policy and Party Politics* (New Haven, 1955), pp. 28-29.

14. C.R., Vol. 96, Part 3, p. 3920: March 23, 1950.

15. Benton (D-Conn.), Connally (D-Tex.), Fulbright (D-Ark.), Hickenlooper (R-Ia.), Humphrey (D-Minn.), Kefauver (D-Tenn.), Lehman (D-N.Y.), Lucas (D-Ill.), McMahon (D-Conn.), Pepper (D-Fla.), Smith (R-N.J.), Vandenberg (R-Mich.), Wiley (R-Wis.).

16. C.R., Vol. 95, Part 1, p. 466: January 18, 1949 (Hickenlooper).

17. C.R., Vol. 95, Part 1, p. 460: January 18, 1949 (Vandenberg).

18. C.R., Vol. 97, Part 9, p. 11371: September 14, 1951 (Humphrey).

19. C.R., Vol. 96, Part 3, p. 3769: March 22, 1950 (Lehman).

20. C.R., Vol. 96, Part 4, p. 5420: April 20, 1950 (Connally).

21. C.R., Vol. 96, Part 12, p. 17002: December 22, 1950 (Pepper).

22. C.R., Vol. 97, Part 1, p. 1221: February 12, 1951 (Humphrey).

23. C.R., Vol. 97, Part 9, p. 11371: September 14, 1951 (Humphrey).

24. C.R., Vol. 97, Part 9, p. 11366: September 14, 1951 (Benton).

25. C.R., Vol. 97, Part 9, p. 11367: September 14, 1951 (Benton).

26. C.R., Vol. 95, Part 1, p. 710: January 31, 1949.

27. Acheson's personal qualities constituted one of the five identification categories in which the data were coded. References were classified here whenever Senators identified Acheson in terms of what he *was, is,* or *should be* irrespective of what he *did, does,* or *should do.* Any aspect of Acheson which was seen as existing independent of any given performance (or of the phenomena subsumed by the other identification subcategories) was defined as a quality. The distinction between a complex of personal qualities and a complex of performances has been adapted from Talcott Parsons and Edward A. Shils (eds.), *Toward a General Theory of Action* (Cambridge, 1952), p. 57.

28. References in which Acheson was identified as a subject of attack were separately coded under a subcategory of the residual identification category.

29. Acheson's performances comprised another of the five identification categories, embracing references in which he was identified in terms of what he *did, does, will* or *should do* irrespective of what he *was, is,* or *should be.* A performance was defined as *an* expenditure of energy by Acheson toward one or more of the other objects in the environment (the object categories are explained in the next footnote).

30. Data pertaining to the matters upon which Senators focused were obtained by coding all references among a wide range of categories and subcategories corresponding to the other objects in the environment to which Senators saw Acheson, however identified, as relating. That is, after being classified in one of the five mutually exclusive identification categories, each reference was

then coded in terms of the objects other than Acheson mentioned therein. The categorization of objects included both persons and collectivities, with the latter being defined as "systems of action composed of a plurality of individual actors in determinate relations to one another" (Parsons and Shils, *op. cit.*, p. 57). Thus categories were established for references citing such objects as a government agency (the Defense Department), a country (Germany, the Germans), a continent (Asia, Asians), and special systems of action involving either an aspect of American life (immigration) or an implementation of American foreign policy (troops-to-Europe).

31. See, for example, C.R., Vol. 96, Part 3, p. 4121: March 27, 1950 (Kefauver); Part 12, p. 16694: December 18, 1950 (Fulbright).

32. So as to account for varying degrees of cordiality, hostility, and neutrality, as well as for descriptive purposes, the percentage of a Senator's (or a group's) total references coded as favorable, unfavorable, and neutral is hereinafter cited as either his (or their) cordiality, hostility, or neutrality potential.

33. C.R., Vol. 97, Part 9, p. 11366: September 14, 1951 (Benton).

34. C.R., Vol. 98, Part 2, p. 2340: March 14, 1952 (Wiley).

35. C.R., Vol. 97, Part 8, p. 11121: September 11, 1951 (Smith of N.J.).

36. C.R., Vol. 97, Part 9, p. 11371: September 14, 1951 (Humphrey).

37. The symbol-collectivity category was established to account for references in which Acheson was identified neither as an individual possessing certain qualities nor as an official performing certain acts, but as a symbol of an ambiguous phenomenon ("the Truman-Acheson policy") or as a member of an indeterminate collectivity ("the Acheson crowd").

38. It must be emphasized that this subdivision of the Hostile Minority is not founded on the imputation of a magical quality to the quantity of 10.3 per cent. Such a percentage is an arbitrary demarcation which was employed by way of permitting a more concrete analysis of what were regarded as significant, albeit relative, differences within the Hostile Minority. It was employed because it happened to fall at the midway point in the widest gap in the center of the distribution, and thus it more neatly separated the two Hostile Minorities than would have any other percentage.

39. Brewster (R-Me.), Cain (R-Wash.), Donnell (R-Mo.), Ferguson (R-Mich.), Knowland (R-Cal.), Morse (R-Ore.), McCarran (D-Nev.), Watkins (R-Utah).

40. Bricker (R-Ohio), Bridges (R-N.H.), Capehart (R-Ind.), Dirksen (R-Ill.), Jenner (R-Ind.), Kem (R-Mo.), Langer (R-N.D.), Malone (R-Nev.), McCarthy (R-Wis.), Mundt (R-S.D.), Taft (R-Ohio), Welker (R-Idaho), Wherry (R-Neb.).

41. C.R., Vol. 97, Part 10, p. 12538: October 3, 1951.

42. C.R., Vol. 98, Part 4, p. 4994: May 9, 1952. That Cain was consistent in the appelation he used can be seen in the fact that he spoke of Acheson as "the Secretary of State" 137 times during the 1949-52 period, as "Secretary Acheson" 11 times, as "Mr. Acheson" 12 times, and as "Acheson" 6 times. Indeed, this separate word count of how Acheson was designated provides considerable evidence that Cain was not alone in distinguishing between the man and the office, that the appelative behavior of all Senators was derived from their attitudes rather than from mere habit (see the discussion of "The Nomenclature of Identification," in my unpublished thesis, *op. cit.*, pp. 98-102). The difference between the two Hostile Minorities is especially noteworthy in this respect: while the Discriminates spoke of "the Secretary of State" in 69.0 per cent of their total designations and of "Acheson" in 4.4 per cent, the equivalent figures for the Indiscriminates were 29.9 per cent and 29.7 per cent.

43. C.R., Vol. 97, Part 8, p. 11081: September 10, 1951.

44. C.R., Vol. 96, Part 2, pp. 1558, 2645: February 7 and March 2, 1950; Part 4, p. 4985: April 10, 1950.

45. C.R., Vol. 97, Part 4, p. 5676: May 23, 1951 (Welker).

46. C.R., Vol. 96, Part 4, p. 5086: April 12, 1950 (Jenner).

47. C.R., Vol. 98, Part 2, p. 2585: March 20, 1952 (Malone).

48. C.R., Vol. 97, Part 5, p. 6603: June 14, 1951 (McCarthy).

49. C.R., Vol. 96, Part 9, p. 12591: August 16, 1950 (Wherry).

50. C.R., Vol. 96, Part 12, p. 16057: December 4, 1950 (Kem).

51. C.R., Vol. 97, Part 8, p. 10811: August 30, 1951 (Malone).

52. C.R., Vol. 96, Part 4, p. 5088: April 12, 1950 (Jenner).

53. C.R., Vol. 96, Part 4, p. 4648: April 4, 1950 (Jenner).

54. C.R., Vol. 96, Part 4, p. 4461: March 31, 1950 (Langer).

55. C.R., Vol. 98, Part 1, p. 226: January 16, 1952 (Kem).

56. C.R., Vol. 96, Part 12, p. 16178: December 6, 1950 (McCarthy).

57. C.R., Vol. 96, Part 9, p. 12744: August 17, 1950 (Wherry).

58. C.R., Vol. 97, Part 5, p. 6602: June 14, 1951 (McCarthy).

59. C.R., Vol. 97, Part 2, p. 2870: March 22, 1951 (Bricker).

60. C.R., Vol. 97, Part 2, p. 2596: March 19, 1951 (Jenner).

61. C.R., Vol. 98, Part 4, p. 4888: May 7, 1952 (Jenner).

62. C.R., Vol. 96, Part 2, p. 2555: March 1, 1950 (Wherry).

63. C.R., Vol. 96, Part 11, p. 14923: September 15, 1950 (Malone).

64. C.R., Vol. 96, Part 11, p. 14916: September 15, 1950 (Jenner).

65. C.R., Vol. 96, Part 11, p. 14917: September 15, 1950 (Jenner).

66. C.R., Vol. 97, Part 5, p. 6592: June 14, 1951 (McCarthy).

67. C.R., Vol. 96, Part 3, p. 4119: March 27, 1950 (Bridges).

68. C.R., Vol. 97, Part 4, p. 5718: May 23, 1951 (Jenner).

69. C.R., Vol. 97, Part 2, p. 2390: March 14, 1951 (McCarthy).

70. C.R., Vol. 96, Part 3, p. 4119: March 27, 1950 (Bridges).

71. C.R., Vol. 97, Part 5, 6557: June 14, 1951 (McCarthy).

72. C.R., Vol. 97, Part 3, p. 3719: April 12, 1951 (Bridges).

73. C.R., Vol. 96, Part 1, P. 755: January 23, 1950 (Capehart).

74. C.R., Vol. 97, Part 8, p. 10329: August 20, 1951 (McCarthy).

75. C.R., Vol. 97, Part 5, p. 6559: June 14, 1951 (McCarthy).

76. C.R., Vol. 96, Part 7, p. 9718: July 6, 1950 (McCarthy).

77. C.R., Vol. 96, Part 12, p. 16068: December 4, 1950 (Malone).

78. C.R., Vol. 97, Part 3, p. 4069: April 18, 1951 (Malone).

79. C.R., Vol. 97, Part 2, p. 2788: March 21, 1951 (Malone).

80. C.R., Vol. 97, Part 5, p. 6573: June 14, 1951 (McCarthy).

81. C.R., Vol. 97, Part 4, p. 5772: May 24, 1951 (McCarthy).

82. C.R., Vol. 97, Part 4, p. 5774: May 24, 1951 (McCarthy).

83. C.R., Vol. 97, Part 3, p. 4069: April 18, 1951 (Malone).

84. C.R., Vol. 97, Part 4, p. 5718: May 23, 1951 (Jenner).

85. C.R., Vol. 97, Part 3, p. 4261: April 24, 1951 (McCarthy).

86. C.R., Vol. 97, Part 4, p. 5718: May 23, 1951 (Jenner).

87. C.R., Vol. 97, Part 3, p. 3724: April 12, 1951 (Welker).

88. This analysis also helps to explain the supposed discrepancy between Senatorial attitudes toward Acheson during his 1945-7 tour of duty as Under Secretary and his later tenure as Secretary. That is, while the cold war gained considerable momentum in the earlier period, the prevailing status quo, though tenuous, was not radically altered, so that presumably Senators had less of a need to focus attention upon the Secretary of State, much less the Under Secretary.

89. At best they can only be partially ascertained through the technique of interviews and questionnaires, a technique which was not employed for several reasons, not the least of which is the fact that Senators cannot make sufficient time available to the researcher who confronts them with an elaborate interview schedule. Furthermore, since Senators would have had to recapture feelings and thoughts which possibly no longer existed or had since been altered, data derived from interviews might have been somewhat distorted. In limiting research to the public record, there need be no concern that the data used have been revised in the light of subsequent events.

90. Because Senators have an equal opportunity to speak in the Senate chamber, whereas material pertaining to their verbal behavior elsewhere is not equally available for all Senators. Quantitative analysis would hardly be possible if it was based upon data which included the press releases or radio transcripts of some Senators, the comments made in committee hearings by others, and only the Senate speeches of still others. What might be gained in breadth by the inclusion of such sources would certainly be dissipated by the almost unsurmountable problems of weighting to which they would give rise.

91. George B. Galloway, *The Legislative Process in Congress* (New York, 1953), p. 558; Bertram M. Gross, *The Legislative Struggle* (New York, 1953), pp. 365-6; James Reston, "The Decline of Eloquence in Congress," *New York Times* (January 31, 1954).

13. RESENTMENTS AND HOSTILITIES OF LEGISLATORS: SOURCES, OBJECTS, CONSEQUENCES

Edward A. Shils

CONGRESSIONAL investigating committees have brought about valuable reforms in American life. They have performed services which no other branch of the government and no private body could have accomplished. They have also—like any useful institution—been guilty of abuses. Like many institutional abuses, these have been products of the accentuation of certain features which have frequently contributed to the effectiveness of the investigative committee. In the following essay, we shall not concern ourselves with the description of these abuses, nor with the ways in which certain valuable practices, when pushed to an extreme, have become abuses. These abuses have included intrusions in spheres beyond the committees' terms of reference, excessive clamor for publicity, intemperate disrespect for the rights of witnesses, indiscriminate pursuit of evidence, sponsorship of injudicious and light-hearted accusations, disregard for the requirements of decorum in governmental institutions, and the use of incompetent and unscrupulous field investigators. Here we shall take as our task the exploration of factors which may assist in understanding some of these peculiarities and excesses of congressional investigations.

In the view here taken these excesses arise out of the conditions of life of the American legislator: the American constitutional system itself, the vicissitudes of the political career in America, the status of the politician, the American social structure and a variety of other factors. This analysis does not claim to be a complete picture of the social pattern of the American legislator; it is not intended to be an exhaustive analysis. It seeks only to point out those factors which have produced certain features of the investigative process—especially the tone of acrimony, of hostility toward witnesses and of disregard for the standards of propriety and respect which are even more necessary in political democracies than in other systems of government.

We shall accordingly begin with an exposition of some of the sources of strain on the legislator. Then we shall go further into the manner in which these strains become intensified in the relations between politicians on the one hand and administrators, intellectuals, and, occasionally, business men on the other.

In the United States as in any other large demo-

Reprinted from *University of Chicago Law Review*, Vol. 18 (1950-51), pp. 571-584, where it appeared under the title, "The Legislator and His Environment," by permission of the author and the publisher.

cratic government, the burden on the legislator is great. The volume of legislation is vast and its complexity beyond the judgment of laymen. Even an expert could not hope to understand and master fully all the bills which are produced. This is particularly true in the United States where many bills are produced on the same subject and where individual legislators often have their own legislative ambitions, in addition to the program of their party leaders. The legislator is overwhelmed by his legislative work alone, the amount aggravating the difficulty. He frequently votes on measures on which he has not formed his own judgment and on which he has not had his judgment authoritatively and reassuringly formed for him by his party organization. The fact that he leaves so much uncovered has a disquieting effect on him; it causes him to feel that matters are slipping beyond his control.

The structure of the American party system and its manifestation in Congress accentuate the strains on the American legislator. He is very much on his own. The national party does not arrange his candidacy; it has little control over the machine on which the congressman depends for his re-election; and its financial aid for the conduct of his campaign is much less than adequate. He must keep his machine going. Like an ambassador who is uneasy that his enemies at home are undoing his work and undermining his position while he is away, the legislator must always keep his eye on the machine at home—fearing that it might break out of his control during his absence in Washington.

American constituents, at least a sector of them, are often very outspoken in their demands. The American legislator is moreover hypersensitive to the faintest whisper of a constituent's voice. Unable to depend on the national party for re-election, he must cultivate and nurture his constituency more than legislators in other democratic countries where constituents are less clamorous and parties are stronger at the center.

To satisfy the demands of some of his constituents the American legislator wastes his time and energy running errands for them in Washington and receiving them when they visit the capital for business or for sight-seeing purposes. He himself is often quite pleased to have this opportunity for personal contact with his constituents even though it distracts him from his job in Washington.

In addition to trying to please those whom he sees, he is constantly harried in his mind's eye by those whom he does not see or from whom he does not hear. His remoteness from them does not make him less sensitive to their sentiments or

fearful of their displeasure. The distance from the voter and his anonymity make the sensitivity even greater and more delicate. The nature of the recruitment process favors the man with a delicate ear for the voters' sentiments, and an eagerness to gain their approbation; American politics favors the person who can present himself as a man of the people, who is proud that he deviates from them in no significant way and who fears that any known deviations would be interpreted as snobbery or stand-offishness.

This eagerness to gratify an unseen constituency and to rank high in their favor helps us to understand why it is that legislators who have no strong convictions on a given topic might sometimes be among its most fervent investigators. They do so simply because they believe it will appeal to their constituents and because they cannot allow any rival for the affection and votes of their constituents to pre-empt this theme.

Far from his home base and insecure about his tenure and support, he is hard put to find a procedure for keeping in touch with his constituents and fixing himself in their minds. The congressional investigation is often just the instrument which the legislator needs in order to remind his constituents of his existence. That is the reason why investigations often involve such unseemly uses of the organs of publicity. Publicity is the next best thing to the personal contact which the legislator must forego. It is his substitute offering by which he tries to counteract the personal contact which his rivals at home have with the constituents.

The frequent recourse to personal intervention on behalf of individual constituents has greater consequences than the maintenance of a sensitive attachment of the legislator to his audible constituency and the wasteful expenditure of his time. It fosters in him a particular attitude of personal expectancy toward the bureaucracy and towards the individual administrator.

The American legislator, whose professional traditions date back to a social order in which government intervention played no great part and in which patronage was the main method of recruitment, tends to look on the administrator's tasks as something which is properly his own responsibility—as something which is only transitorily delegated to the administrator. He draws no fine line between legislation and administration and he likes to co-operate in and assist in administration as well as to specify the administrator's tasks and powers. The modern separation of powers is indeed often felt as an implicit rebuff.

To these particular strains in the vocational life of an American legislator should be added the more general strains. For one thing the career of the professional politician is full of hazards. In all democracies the legislator is recurrently in danger of not being re-elected. In the event of being unsuccessful he must go back to a career which he has neglected. In the United States very few of our professional politicians are recruited from the classes which live from inherited wealth. If he is in the professions or in business he will have to make up the distance which his contemporaries have gained on him. Although he might have improved certain "connections," some of his skill other than political skill might well have deteriorated. Whatever the effect on his skill he faces the humiliation of return as a political failure, and the need to begin at a lower level than those who were his equals a few years before. Moreover, since our politicians do not come from classes which have as part of their tradition a normal expectation of entering a political career, they tend to a greater extent to be selected from among persons who enjoy the game of politics, to whom it has a special psychological appeal. For such persons, the threat of exclusion from politics through failure is especially menacing. Thus the situation of the political career in the United States makes legislators faced with the possibility of failure take eager refuge in devices which will recommend them to their constituents. Well publicized activity as a member of an investigative committee is one of these devices.

Even when successful, however, the professional politician in the United States cannot always have the pleasure and comfort of feeling that he is participating in a highly honored profession. The fact that he is so often made into an errand boy or handmaiden to his constituents is indicative of their attitude towards him and of his attitude towards himself. Government in the United States, where established institutions are not usually objects of deep reverence, is far from the most esteemed of institutions. Living off the public treasury, from the taxpayers' money, whether as legislator or administrator, has until recently been looked down upon by the hard-working taxpayer and his newspaper spokesmen. This view is still at work in American public opinion. The image of the politician in the organs of mass communication is not a laudatory one. Pomposity, vanity, an unbalanced sense of importance and occasionally sheer dishonesty are part of the traditional American conception of the professional politician —although the reality has been far different. Even though this popular image has been changing in the past decades, the term "politician" still has a derogatory overtone. The occasional outbursts of an excessive desire to please on the one hand

and of vindictive aggressiveness on the other are both products of this perception by the professional politician of his ambiguous status. The legislator's suspicion of the administrator as one who lives wastefully on the taxpayer's money is also an expression of his discomfiture concerning his own ambiguous status.

Congressional investigations often provide favorable occasions for the manifestation of this deeplying distrust. It is not only the social status of politics that influences the legislator's mood. The geographical location of the center of national political life also has its effect. The almost exclusive position of politics as the chief employment of Washington has an influence on the life of the legislator. It means that he is forced to live almost entirely in an atmosphere of politics. It is true of course that many enjoy this type of life with its incessant stress on influence, rivalry, ambition and frustration—it sharpens political wits and has a brilliance of its own. It does however strengthen and even overdevelop the political orientation of men who have already entered voluntarily upon such a career. By political orientation is meant that exclusive preoccupation with political events to the point where every human activity becomes evaluated not in terms of its intrinsic value but in terms of its political significance. In Washington legislators must associate in their leisure hours almost entirely with other legislators or with journalists, administrators, and business men whose presence in Washington is almost always evidence of their own predominantly political interests. In such a society where the talk is invariably centered about who is getting what from whom, both the sensitivity and the insecurity of the legislator are increased. It strengthens his tendency to interpret everything in political terms and to look on the world as engaged at every moment in arranging political combinations, intended to advance some individual or group and to ruin another. This type of social life offers no respite from the tensions and anxieties of the individual legislator's own political career—it provides a stimulant rather than a soothing calm. The gossip and rumors agitate him and cause him to worry more about his own political fortunes. Hearing so much of what others are doing or are having done for them to secure their political fortunes, he feels he must exert himself more to establish and advance his own prestige. Whoever blocks him is his enemy. Whoever has a deficiency, real or imputable, which can be attacked in the name of a major political value, becomes a fair target in the competition to keep oneself politically afloat.

As a result of these factors—not all of which

operate equally for all our legislators—the life of the American politician holding a seat in the Senate or in the House of Representatives is far from an easy one. He is always confronted with more demands on him than he can satisfy; he is always in danger of displeasing someone and he is never sure of just what it will take to please them or how he can do it when he knows what it is; he is always dependent on someone else's judgment for his equanimity and for his security. The result is a state of stress and disquiet, often flaring up into rage and sometimes into vindictiveness.

The emotional moods and the deeper attitudes to which they become fixed enter very intimately into the conduct of congressional investigations. The chief victims of congressional investigation are administrative officials and political dissenters, with big business men occasionally emerging as targets. We shall now deal with them in that order.

The traditions of the American Congress and the outlook of our congressmen are the products of a free society in which it was neither necessary nor desirable that large powers be assigned to the executive branch of the government. The inevitability of the delegation of power is often intellectually acknowledged by our legislators but there is also resentment against this necessity and a deep unwillingness to accept it. As we have already indicated, the bureaucrat or the administrator is regarded as the usurping rival of the legislator. General laws, when implemented in detail by administrators, often work hardships on particular constituents. The legislator is often unable to persuade the administrator to remove that hardship. In many cases the derogation of his power and status which this implies is bitterly felt by the legislator and animosity against particular administrators and against the executive branch and bureaucracy in general is fostered.

This attitude is also affected by the gradual diminution of the patronage system in the recruitment of the federal civil service. A civil servant appointed by patronage is the creature of the legislature. The prevailing atmosphere of the American political system, despite the establishment of the merit system in the federal civil service, is still that of patronage. The important role in the national parties of local and state "machines," subsisting on patronage, is responsible for this. A legislator who has passed through the lower levels of the party on his way upward still tends to expect civil servants to respond to him as though they are personally beholden to him. The fact that this is not so is well appreciated by the ordinary administrator and manifested in his behavior.

The contact between legislators and admini-

strators who appear before the various standing committees and subcommittees is often frustrating to the legislator. There is seldom the element of direct challenge to the personal status of the legislator but the authoritative and self-assured way in which the administrator disposes of his own knowledge and the legislator's questions can also become a source of uneasiness. The administrator deals self-confidently with a matter which the legislator does not always grasp with the same measure of self-confidence. When the subject matter of the hearings is one about which the legislator already has some grievances, the result is apt to be a further rankling of his sentiments. The resulting "soreness" occasionally reveals itself in the support and conduct of investigations directed against the particular administrator and against bureaucrats in general.

This particular friction is, in part, one of the by-products of the merit system. The civil servant, particularly the civil servant of the level called before congressional committees, tends to be considerably more educated and probably of a higher social and economic status as regards his origin, than the legislator who is requesting a service of him or interrogating him. He is as we have indicated not only more expert in the matter at hand but he usually, either wittingly or unwittingly, is also more the master of the situation than the legislator. Resentment against those whose fortunate accidents of birth gave them educational opportunities which were not available to the legislator is heightened—it certainly was heightened during the Roosevelt administration—by an attitude of personal, social and intellectual superiority on the part of the administrator. This sense of superiority very often does not exist at all but is nonetheless often assumed to exist and is as bitterly resented.

The concurrent elevation of the educational level of the civil service and the delegation of vast legislative powers to a resourceful and ingenious executive only reinforced a difficulty which is endemic in the American constitutional system—namely, the sharp, personal separation of the legislative and executive branches. The fact that the leaders of the executive branch—the President to some extent, and even more, his cabinet members (except generally the relatively insignificant Postmaster General)—cannot usually be regarded as "one of the boys" deepens the breach between the legislators and the executive branch. It increases the likelihood of misunderstandings which accumulate and which cannot easily be cleared up by informal personal interchange, or prevented by the existence of close personal relations or friendship.

Some of these frictions are in the nature of our constitutional situation. If legislators are intended to watch over the execution of the laws they pass and to scrutinize the laws recommended to them by the executive branch, some friction will necessarily exist. It is however exaggerated by the adventitious element of the legislator's representation of the private interests of particular constituents. It is also driven further by the fact that except for personal intercessions and questioning in committees, the American legislator has no control over what he regards as injustices or inefficiencies in the working of the administrative system. He must intervene personally, often at the cost of much time and energy, or he must attempt to hold up the appropriation of an entire section of the administration. If he fails in the first and the second alternative is not available to him, he has only the investigative committee left to him. It is certainly not always easy to start such a committee and a long accumulation of hurts and grievances will usually have been felt before the committee can be created and got under way. He must wait until enough other legislators think the issue is a good one or until, for some other reason, enough other legislators are willing to allow him to go ahead. The long period of waiting and the gradual fusion of resentments from a great variety of sources make it more likely that the investigation will be rough. Even if he is not on the committee himself, he will often support it because it is a vicarious way of soothing the many hurts he has experienced. There is little opportunity for the release of pressure by moderate means, such as the question period in the House of Commons, which provides a regular opportunity for the airing of small injustices and prevents an accumulation first of personal animosity and then of animosity in general. The possibility of having a particular wrong corrected imposes a sense of responsibility on the person who is trying to bring about the correction. If the situation has been allowed to go so far that accusations are generalized and no immediate corrections expected—when the legislator feels that he is shouting into the wind—then his accusations will become louder and angrier and his wrath will be less easily and efficiently appeased. Yet this is the atmosphere in which investigations are too often launched.

The strains which arise from our constitutional system and our cultural background are aggravated during periods of strong executive leadership and expansion of the executive. Strong executive leadership appears, while it is in operation, to cure the ailments, but under our present conditions it nonetheless leads inevitably to aggravation. The dry fruit of this aggravation is harvested in the period of weakest leadership. And jealous though they are of their powers and prerogatives, legislators normally renounce some of them during periods of national crisis. This was what happened under the administration of Franklin Roosevelt. His brilliant personality and self-confidence in confronting the domestic crisis of the thirties and the succeeding international crisis encouraged as great a delegation of power as any American Congress has ever participated in. Legislative regret and resentment over this delegation was already gathering force in the late 1930's. Pressure accumulated because of the insolence and brilliance of the exceptional group of energetic administrators and advisors whom the President gathered round him. The demand for a redress of the balance—for revenge against the disrespectful usurpers—grew through the thirties and was scarcely held in check by the continuation of the crisis and the exceptional personal and political capacities of the late President. His replacement by Mr. Truman and the renaissance of demands for normality after the war released the flood of resentment which had been storing up against the chief executive and against the bureaucrats.

The animus of the legislator against the bureaucrat is fed further by another cleavage in American life. We refer here to the tension between intellectuals and politicians. Although this country, more than any other, owes its origins as a state to intellectuals, ever since the Jacksonian revolution there has been a distrust of intellectuals in politics and a distrust of politics among intellectuals. For nearly one hundred years the intellectuals of this country were identified with the genteel tradition— a tradition which stood in conflict with the rough-handed politics of the big city machines, and particularly with the urban, predominantly immigrant working classes of the big cities and the dour, commercially minded farmers of the Middle West. They stood apart too from the energetic capitalistic enterprisers of the great periods of economic expansion which followed the Civil and First World Wars. Academic intellectuals inspired by Germany and Great Britain had contributed greatly to the establishment of the merit system in the federal civil service. In many other contexts their estrangement from the prevailing modes of activity of the "hail fellow well met" politician was evident. Those who lived in the light of the genteel tradition identified themselves with a cultural pattern which was waning. In doing so a large section of the American intellectual classes found themselves in opposition to most of the prospering tendencies in American life; they felt a stronger kinship with European cultural standards and practices and with sections of the population of the Eastern seaboard—the Eastern "aristocracy"—which felt an inner sympathy with the British pattern of life.

This attitude was by no means universal among the intellectuals. There was already much intellectual hostility towards the genteel tradition before the First World War, and afterward the flood engulfed it. Nonetheless the intellectual liberalism which drew its inspiration from Veblen, Dewey and Mencken and which opposed the genteel tradition was at least as antagonistic towards politics and politicians as the intellectuals whom they criticized. Although with the exception of Mencken and a few of the literary men, these critics of American politics were not admirers of European institutions, their critical attitude towards America and their sympathy with the socialistic aspects of the Russian Revolution made it easy for those who regarded themselves as the chief incorporation of American values to label the critics as un-American. This latter view was common among many politicians long before the Roosevelt administration.

The 1930's saw the entry of the "intellectuals" into the government on an unprecedentedly large scale, and at an unprecedentedly rapid rate. The shock to the legislator of the loss of his power to the bureaucracy was certainly not rendered easier to bear by the fact that it was being surrendered to the intelligentsia. It was as if two enemies combined to become a single enemy; the hostility previously directed against the separate enemies now fused on the single object. This has been another element in the acerbity of congressional investigations.

Still other strands in this thread of legislative hostility have been a pervasive and peculiar form of xenophobia and the fear of the consequences of disloyalty. We shall deal first with the former. Although the proportion of foreign-born persons in the United States has dwindled greatly in the past quarter-century, concern over imperfect assimilation is still strong on both sides of the line. It is strong both among the more assimilated and less assimilated. Both proclaim the successful achievement of their Americanization, and the deficiencies of those who are less Americanized. It is natural for human beings who are uncertain of their own conformity with a given standard to abuse others for inadequate conformity with it. The United States is a country which has undergone rapid changes; it is loose in its attachment to most traditions except those of individual freedom and reverence for the Constitution. Americans are relatively unbound by professional and occupational ties and by local loyalties. When we are

uncertain about the genuineness of our loyalties, we tend to suspect others of not being genuine in their loyalties. When our loyalties are loosely anchored to particular places and institutions, we sometimes feel the need to be loyal more urgently than do those persons and societies which are more firmly established in traditional loyalties. The very looseness of our loyalties, which on the one hand is a condition of our freedom, makes us on the other hand more sensitive about our loyalties. Periods of crisis make men feel the need for protection; they also make them need to feel loyal to some powerful protective institution such as a mighty national state. The less they are bound by professional and local loyalties, the more will they feel the need for the more inclusive loyalty, and the more suspicious will they be of the genuineness and sufficiency of the loyalty of others. The weakness of the former type of loyalty will strengthen the disposition to think in terms of crisis, to interpret situations as if they were crises. Mobile, traditionless people will be quicker to see and proclaim a crisis than those whose professional and local loyalties hold them fast.

In the United States politicians have an unusually high degree of social mobility. Politicians, more than any other profession, represent the realization of the idea of the poor boy who takes advantage of the opportunities of an open society and rises to the top. Even more than business men and intellectuals, American politicians have moved from the society of their birth and youth. They have moved from their earlier residences to Washington where they live away from their old friends and associates. They have given up their earlier occupation and as we have already said, they live in a world full of pitfalls and threats to their professional success. Many of them are, in the old term, "hyphenates" of fairly recent generations, and would like to live it down. The one firm foundation of their faith is therefore America and all which threatens them is interpreted as a threat to America. There is in consequence a general suspicion among legislators of disloyalty to American standards, of un-Americanism, on the part of those who deviate from them in other respects. Those who challenge them and make them uneasy—bureaucrats and intellectuals—are therewith cast outside the circle of the saved, at least until they have been cleared. The vague and troubling nature of the animosities makes it difficult to formulate them precisely and to check them justly. They overflow the bounds of reason: all sorts of ancient enemies, individuals and groups become the targets of these animosities. Once an investigative committee is started to satisfy these passions, it brings with it so many other advantages such as publicity, advancement, and approbation from more vocal constituents, that it keeps going on its own steam.

The second factor, the fear of disloyalty which might culminate in subversion, is a relatively new one on the scene. It points however in the same direction and gives a certain form to the vague animosities towards the bureaucratic usurpation of legislative power. Whereas earlier fears of revolution were focussed on dissidents outside the government—outcasts of society who would attack the seats of governmental power from the outside— the experience of recent years has given rise to fears and phantasies of the revolutionary seizure of power by persons within the government. The Communist method of subversion, which was illustrated by their interest in the ministries of interior and defense, had its efficacy demonstrated in the Czech *coup d'état* in 1948. The shock caused by events in Prague combined with the anti-bureaucratic disposition and the exaggerated sensitivity to disloyalty to add heat and fury to investigations into the workings of the administrative branch of the American government. The discovery of some genuine cases of espionage and intended subversion has given such subjective plausibility to these fears that they have now come to seem, to those who shared the more general apprehensions, to justify any accusation.

It must not be thought that the strong emotions of uneasy legislators are reserved only for bureaucrats, intellectuals, and agents of foreign subversion, etc. Congressmen conducting investigations are not always the friends of the existing economic system or of the "vested interests" of big business. In the main, congressional investigations, even when they are hostile to great economic organizations, usually treat individual business men politely. It is also probably true that in this most recent period where the various categories of the legislator's internal and foreign enemies have preoccupied them, "big business" has been treated rather respectfully. It is not always so however. Congress in its sentiments is disposed to sympathize with the small business man and to look with suspicion on the great organizations. Legislators in the United States are disproportionately of small town origin and their values too are those of the small town society. Big business represents a negation of these values. Moreover in addition to these fundamental sentiments and principles which favor small business, many of the legislator's errands on behalf of constituents are conducted for small businessmen. Not all the grievance which flows from injustice or rebuff is directed toward the bureaucrat. Some of it goes towards big business.

On the other hand big business represents the successful culmination of the aspirations of the small business man; he who sympathizes with the latter cannot withhold some admiration from the former. Many of the great American industrial achievements which make legislators proud of their American nationality are the achievements of "big business men." Their attitude towards big business is therefore ambivalent. Big business is vast, impersonal and often creates hardships for their small business constituents. Moreover it very often works through sophisticated lobbyists whose personal charm and favor do not always eradicate the guilty feeling of having allowed oneself to be seduced by the "vested interests," and do in fact generate guilt for having yielded to their blandishments. As a result of this ambivalence in loyalties to the different strata of the business community, legislative attitudes towards big business are more fluctuating than they are towards bureaucrats, intellectuals and subversives. When the tide turns against the big business man, as it did for instance in the 1930's, and they become the objects of investigation, the violence of tone and the acrimonious method of conducting an inquiry can reach the extremes which the investigations of other targets have reached since the Second World War.

In the tense atmosphere of the legislative investigation, where accumulated passions are released against potential or imagined enemies, each accusingly worded question or hostilely intended general statement sets the stage for more bitter accusations and more violent denunciation. The pattern of discourse already too prevalent in American political life—that a point cannot be made unless it is overstressed and reiterated in the strongest possible terms—has been further developed by congressional investigations and made into the standard currency of American legislative and political argument. Legislators who feel relatively little animosity against their opponents use this language because it has become a convention of their profession or because to be heard in the clamor of sensational words, they too must speak sensationally. It is not only that injustices are done to administrators and private individuals and that the processes of administration, even on the highest levels, are impeded by the way in which congressional investigations are sometimes carried on. The main defect does not lie in the fact that the conduct of the investigative committees, which are most unscrupulous in their desire for publicity, discredits investigative committees in general and causes their valuable achievements and outstanding merits to be overlooked. The deeper damage consists in what it is doing to the tone and etiquette of American political life. The tolerance and calm which are necessary for rational discussion of the extremely complicated and difficult alternatives confronting us are greatly diminished by the standards of political discourse which the most vociferous of congressional investigative bodies are establishing. This is a time when it is most desirable and necessary that the older crudities of mind and sentiment should be replaced by dispassionate reflection and carefully measured statement. The tact and self-restraint which are essential to the political life of a democracy are stunted in this atmosphere.

By their disrespect for the proprieties, without which an efficient democratic government cannot function, the reputation of the political profession is further besmirched and the quality of its performance is reduced. The injury which the low prestige of the political career has done to our country has fortunately been neutralized by the sound sense of the mass of the population, and the exceptional devotion to the public good of a small number of morally and intellectually eminent men in each generation. The nature of the tasks facing politicians today however is so taxing to every moral and intellectual resource that the questionable luxury of political savagery can no longer be afforded. Yet the situation is not easily curable. The misbehavior of a significant minority of legislators lowers the esteem in which the professional politician is held. This low esteem is in its turn one of the factors which accounts for the excesses in the conduct of the legislators in investigation and other activities. In a situation which seems much like a vicious circle at least part of the remedy must be sought in greater tactfulness and restraint. It is not too much to hope that if legislators, politicians and citizens can be made more aware of the delicate balance on which the free society rests, some of them will change their behavior and others will no longer support or tolerate practices which are harmful to the democratic system.

SECTION IV
Research Orientations and Techniques

INTRODUCTORY NOTE

NO HARD and fast line can be drawn between the studies in this section on research orientations and techniques, and the theoretical and empirical studies of the preceding sections. Many of the previous articles could have been included here as examples of particular research approaches, just as some of the papers presented in this section could have been fitted into the substantive parts of the volume. If, nevertheless, a separate methodological section seems to be called for, it is because the articles included here are more explicit in conceptualizing legislative behavior research or pay primary attention to research techniques.

Research on legislative behavior has been more sensitive to problems of technique than to problems of conceptual clarification. Yet, the most sophisticated technical developments, to be fruitful from the point of view of advancing knowledge about legislatures and legislative behavior, are meaningless unless research findings are presented in a theoretically, or at least conceptually, viable framework which will give more than *ad hoc* significance to the great variety of factors that constitute the legislative process. As one or two studies included in this section will show, brute empiricism, no matter how elegant or rigorous in design, if it is unenlightened by theory, adds little to our understanding of legislative behavior and the legislative process. Future advances in research depend on the continued interpenetration of theoretical, empirical and methodological developments.

The dominant mode of approach has been what one may call "limited-factor" analysis. Either "internal" attributes—the legislator's socioeconomic background or social-psychological characteristics —or "outside" factors—such as party, pressure group or constituency—are singled out, often quite arbitrarily, as particularly significant in "influencing" legislative behavior. The studies presented in sections II and III of this volume are, in large part, illustrative of the most widely practiced research strategies.

There is, of course, nothing intrinsically "wrong" with this approach. Undoubtedly, the variables involved in legislative behavior are so numerous that few can be treated simultaneously, and dealing with one or a few may be the better part of research wisdom. But the limits imposed by research strategy must not conceal the fact that no factor operates in isolation. It is for this reason that the theoretical criteria used in the selection of variables are crucial. Yet, only a few studies make the criteria explicit. At most, there seems to be the assumption that, under certain conditions, one variable will "yield" to the other, or at least neutralize it. Often the model implicit in these studies —regardless of how many factors are seen as influencing legislative behavior—is essentially mechanistic. The legislative process is conceptualized as subject to the play of "forces" over which the legislator has relatively little control. The model is made explicit by Stephen K. Bailey in his case study of the Full Employment Act of 1946, *Congress Makes a Law* (1950), characterized as "an attempt to make a vector analysis of legislative policy-making." Following E. Pendleton Herring, Bailey defined the policy-making process as "the interaction of ideas, institutions, interests, and individuals." Just how these four I's differ from one another, and how they "interact," if it is permissible to speak of interaction at all, is left to the imagination.

A more appropriately social model is suggested by Earl Latham in *The Group Basis of Politics* (1952). A legislature is more than the sum of its members who are subject to conflicting pressures. Legislatures "are groups also and show a sense of identity and consciousness of kind that unofficial groups must regard if they are to represent their members effectively." Once it is realized that legislators are not billiard balls responding mechanically to the pulls and pushes of outside forces, but approach decisions with sets of attitudes and identifications directly relevant to their legislative behavior, the conceptual schema underlying research has as its center the legislator himself and the roles he takes in his interactions with significant others in the legislative system.

A viable conceptual model of legislative behavior which is both theory-oriented and empirically relevant might make two assumptions: first, that the legislature, as an institution, is a sub-system of action in the larger political system; and, second, that it is linked with other political sub-systems—such as the party system, the system of pressure groups, or the system of constituencies—by the roles which legislators take in various sub-systems, including the legislature itself. The center of investigation, then, is the roles which legislators take in the sub-systems. Roles are the premises in terms of which legislators behave and make decisions. The model differs from both the mechanistic and the interactional models in that it sees the legislator involved in a continuing network of social relationships which constitutes a system. The whole system is maintained by legislators' taking appropriate roles in the various sub-systems. The approach implicit in the model is specifically structural-functional.

Mathematical models have been used only rarely to conceptualize or solve the problems with which political scientists are concerned. This has probably been due, in part, to the ambiguity and instability of the concepts used in political science, but, in part, it has been also due to the fact that the mathematical constructs did not seem particularly relevant. In recent years, however, the theory of games has come to the attention of political scientists because many of its assumptions also seem to be the assumptions of political science. Game theory, like political science, is concerned with conflict and coalition, with decision-making behavior and the prediction of consequences following alternative choices, with strategies and probabilities. The models of game theory are, of course, models of rational action, and to what extent they are useful in the explanation of political behavior is yet to be seen. Nevertheless, the two articles included here as examples of the application of game theory to legislative behavior—"A Method for Evaluating the Distribution of Power in a Committee System," by Shapley and Shubik,

and "A Game Theoretic Analysis of Congressional Power Distributions for a Stable Two-Party System," by Luce and Rogow—are pioneer studies in the field and suggestive of the kinds of model building which the theory of games might fertilize and guide.

Legislative research has availed itself of a great many research techniques. The use of documentary and statistical sources has been most frequent, but participant observation or direct observation have also been employed. Nothing needs to be said here about documentary and statistical analysis which is familiar enough. Participant observation, though giving insight into unique situations, is unsystematic. On the other hand, systematic direct observation of interaction patterns has proved so laborious that it has rarely been attempted. Interactional models have come to rely, therefore, on the interview as the most economical and reliable research technique. Yet, the interview has been used much less widely than one should expect, and only in recent years.

By far the most frequent and cheapest source of data for the study of legislative behavior has been legislative roll-calls. Roll-call analysis, in turn, has proved susceptible to a great variety of statistical and scaling techniques. As early as 1901, A. Lawrence Lowell used roll-call analysis to study the place of parties in the legislative process. More recently, Julius Turner, William J. Keefe and others have employed different indices of party voting for similar purposes. Stuart A. Rice's "index of cohesion," formulated in "Measuring Cohesion in Legislative Groups" included in this section, has proved useful in other than research on parties, though it requires theoretical specification of the groups to be studied. Finally, roll-call votes have been used to demonstrate that legislators are consistent in their legislative behavior through time. One of the techniques used is illustrated in Dean R. Brimhall's and Arthur S. Otis' "A Study of Consistency in Congressional Voting."

More recently, factor analysis and scale analysis have been applied to roll-call votes. Unfortunately, these analyses have often been distinguished by a crass empiricism. There is little indication that factor analysis has been employed to test particular hypotheses of interest to political scientists. Factorial analysis, as also the method used by Brimhall and Otis, employs rather arbitrary criteria in the selection of the roll-calls which are subjected to analysis. The value of these studies lies, therefore, in their technical execution rather than in their findings which confirmed what was generally known. On the other hand, as William Riker shows in "A Method for Measuring the

Significance of Roll Call Votes," determination of significance can be both theoretically meaningful and methodologically systematic.

Of all the techniques available for roll-call analysis, the construction of cumulative scales, invented by Louis Guttman, is likely to be the most profitable from the point of view of legislative behavior analysis. For, as a technique, it is predicated on some theory of legislative behavior without which meaningful selection of particular roll-calls to be scaled is impossible. George M. Belknap, in "Scaling Legislative Behavior," not only describes the technique, but suggests its utility from the point of view of a political scientist. And Charles D. Farris, in "A Scale Analysis of Ideological Factors in Congressional Voting," presents an illuminating application of the technique to one of the most elusive problems of American politics—the problem of political beliefs. For a fuller treatment of both theoretical and practical aspects of roll-call scaling, the reader should consult a recent publication by Duncan MacRae, Jr., *Dimensions of Congressional Voting* (Berkeley: University of California Press, 1958).

1. A METHOD FOR EVALUATING THE DISTRIBUTION OF POWER IN A COMMITTEE SYSTEM

L. S. Shapley and Martin Shubik

IN THE FOLLOWING PAPER we offer a method for the *a priori* evaluation of the division of power among the various bodies and members of a legislature or committee system. The method is based on a technique of the mathematical theory of games, applied to what are known there as "simple games" and "weighted majority games."[1] We apply it here to a number of illustrative cases, including the United States Congress, and discuss some of its formal properties.

The designing of the size and type of a legislative body is a process that may continue for many years, with frequent revisions and modifications aimed at reflecting changes in the social structure of the country; we may cite the role of the House of Lords in England as an example. The effect of a revision usually cannot be gauged in advance except in the roughest terms; it can easily happen that the mathematical structure of a voting system conceals a bias in power distribution unsuspected and unintended by the authors of the revision. How, for example, is one to predict the degree of protection which a proposed system affords to minority interests? Can a consistent criterion for "fair representation" be found?[2] It is difficult even to *describe* the net effect of a double representation system such as is found in the U. S. Congress (i.e., by states and by population), without attempting to deduce it *a priori*. The method of measuring "power" which we present in this paper is intended as a first step in the attack on these problems.

Our definition of the power of an individual member depends on the chance he has of being critical to the success of a winning coalition. It is easy to see, for example, that the chairman of a board consisting of an even number of members (including himself) has no power if he is allowed to vote only to break ties. Of course he may have prestige and moral influence and will even probably get to vote when someone is not present. However, in the narrow and abstract model of the board he is without power. If the board consists of an odd number of members, then he has exactly as much power as any ordinary member because his vote is "pivotal"—i.e., turns a possible defeat into a success—as often as the vote of any other member. Admittedly he may not cast his vote as often as the others, but much of the voting done by them is not necessary to ensure victory (though perhaps useful for publicity or other purposes). If a coalition has a majority, then extra votes do not change the outcome. For any vote, only a minimal winning coalition is necessary.

Put in crude economic terms, the above implies that if votes of senators were for sale, it might be worthwhile buying forty-nine of them, but the market value of the fiftieth (to the same customer) would be zero. It is possible to buy votes in most corporations by purchasing common stock. If their policies are entirely controlled by simple majority votes, then there is no more power to be gained after one share more than 50% has been acquired.[3]

Let us consider the following scheme: There is a group of individuals all willing to vote for some bill. They vote in order. As soon as a majority[4] has voted for it, it is declared passed, and the member who voted last is given credit for having passed it. Let us choose the voting order of the members randomly. Then we may compute the frequency with which an individual belongs to the group whose votes are used and, of more importance, we may compute how often he is *pivotal*. This latter number serves to give us our index. It measures the number of times that the action of the individual actually changes the state of affairs. A simple consequence of this formal scheme is that where all voters have the same number of votes, they will each be credited with $1/n$th of the power, there being n participants. If they have different numbers of votes (as in the case of stockholders of a corporation), the result is more complicated; more votes mean more power, as measured by our index, but not in direct proportion (see below).

Of course, the actual balloting procedure used will in all probability be quite different from the above. The "voting" of the formal scheme might better be thought of as declarations of support for the bill, and the randomly chosen order of voting

Reprinted from *American Political Science Review*, Vol. 48 (1954), pp. 787-92, by permission of the authors and the publisher.

as an indication of the relative degrees of support by the different members, with the most enthusiastic members "voting" first, etc. The *pivot* is then the last member whose support is needed in order for passage of the bill to be assured.

Analyzing a committee chairman's tie-breaking function in this light, we see that in an *odd* committee he is pivotal as often as an ordinary member, but in an *even* committee he is never pivotal. However, when the number of members is large, it may sometimes be better to modify the strict interpretation of the formal system, and say that the number of members in attendance is about as likely to be even as odd. The chairman's index would then be just half that of an ordinary member. Thus, in the U. S. Senate the power index of the presiding officer is—strictly—equal to 1/97. Under the modified scheme it is 1/193. (But it is zero under either interpretation when we are considering decisions requiring a two-thirds majority, since ties cannot occur on such votes.) Recent history shows that the "strict" model may sometimes be the more realistic: in the present Senate (1953-54) the tie-breaking power of the Vice President, stemming from the fact that 96 is an even number, has been a very significant factor. However, in the passage of ordinary legislation, where perfect attendance is unlikely even for important issues, the modified scheme is probably more appropriate.

For Congress as a whole we have to consider three separate bodies which influence the fate of legislation. It takes majorities of Senate and House, with the President, or two-thirds majorities of Senate and House without the President, to enact a bill. We take all the members of the three bodies and consider them voting[5] for the bill in every possible order. In each order we observe the relative positions of the straight-majority pivotal men in the House and Senate, the President, and also the 2/3-majority pivotal men in House and Senate. One of these five individuals will be the pivot for the whole vote, depending on the order in which they appear. For example, if the President comes after the two straight-majority pivots, but before one or both of the 2/3-majority pivots, then he gets the credit for the passage of the bill. The frequency of this case, if we consider all possible orders (of the 533 individuals involved), turns out to be very nearly 1/6. This is the President's power index. (The calculation of this value and the following is quite complicated, and we shall not give it here.) The values for the House as a whole and for the Senate as a whole are both equal to 5/12, approximately. The individual members of each chamber share these amounts equally, with the exception of the presiding officers.

Under our "modified" scheme they each get about 30% of the power of an ordinary member; under the "strict" scheme, about 60%. In brief, then, the power indices for the three bodies are in the proportion 5:5:2. The indices for a *single* congressman, a *single* senator, and the President are in the proportion 2:9:350.

In a multicameral system such as we have just investigated, it is obviously easier to defeat a measure than to pass it.[6] A coalition of senators, sufficiently numerous, can block passage of any bill. But they cannot push through a bill of their own without help from the other chamber. This suggests that our analysis so far has been incomplete—that we need an index of "blocking power" to supplement the index already defined. To this end, we could set up a formal scheme similar to the previous one, namely: arrange the individuals in all possible orders and imagine them casting *negative* votes. In each arrangement, determine the person whose vote finally defeats the measure and give him credit for the block. Then the "blocking power" index for each person would be the relative number of times that he was the "blocker."

Now it is a remarkable fact that the new index is exactly equal to the index of our original definition. We can even make a stronger assertion: *any scheme for imputing power among the members of a committee system either yields the power index defined above or leads to a logical inconsistency.* A proof, or even a precise formulation, of this assertion would involve us too deeply in mathematical symbolism for the purposes of the present paper.[7] But we can conclude that the scheme we have been using (arranging the individuals in all possible orders, etc.) is just a convenient conceptual device; the indices which emerge are not peculiar to that device but represent a basic element of the committee system itself.

We now summarize some of the general properties of the power index. In pure *bi*cameral systems using simple majority votes, each chamber gets 50% of the power (as it turns out), regardless of the relative sizes. With more than two chambers, power varies inversely with size: the smallest body is most powerful, etc. But no chamber is completely powerless, and no chamber holds more than 50% of the power. To illustrate, take Congress without the provision for overriding the President's veto by means of two-thirds majorities. This is now a pure tricameral system with chamber sizes of 1, 97, and 435. The values come out to be slightly under 50% for the President, and approximately 25% each for the Senate and House, with the House slightly less than the Senate. The exact calculation of this case is quite difficult because of the large numbers involved. An easier example is obtained by taking the chamber sizes as 1, 3, and 5. Then the division of power is in the proportions 32:27:25. The calculation is reproduced at the end of this paper.

The power division in a multicameral system also depends on the type of majority required to pass a bill. Raising the majority in *one* chamber (say from one-half to two-thirds) increases the relative power of that chamber.[8] Raising the required majority in all chambers simultaneously weakens the smaller house or houses at the expense of the larger. In the extreme case, where unanimity is required in every house, each individual in the whole legislature has what amounts to a veto, and is just as powerful as any other individual. The power index of each chamber is therefore directly proportional to its size.

We may examine this effect further by considering a system consisting of a governor and a council. Both the governor and some specified fraction of the council have to approve a bill before it can pass. Suppose first that council approval has to be unanimous. Then (as we saw above) the governor has no more power than the typical councilman. The bicameral power division is in the ratio 1:N, if we take N to be the number of councilmen. If a simple majority rule is adopted, then the ratio becomes 1:1 between governor and council. That is, the governor has N times the power of a councilman. Now suppose that the approval of only one member of the council is required. This means that an individual councilman has very little chance of being pivotal. In fact the power division turns out to be N:1 in favor of the governor.[9] If votes were for sale, we might now expect the governor's price to be N^2 times as high as the average councilman's.

Several other examples of power distribution may be given. The indices reveal the decisive nature of the veto power in the United Nations Security Council. The Council consists of eleven members, five of whom have vetoes. For a substantive resolution to pass, there must be seven affirmative votes and no vetoes. Our power evaluation gives 76/77 or 98.7% to the "Big Five" and 1/77 or 1.3% to the remaining six members. Individually, the members of the "Big Five" enjoy a better than 90 to 1 advantage over the others.

It is well known that usually only a small fraction of the stock is required to keep control of a corporation. The group in power is usually able to muster enough proxies to maintain its position. Even if this were not so, the power of stockholders is not directly proportional to their holding, but is usually biased in favor of a large interest. Consider one man holding 40% of a stock while the remaining 60% is scattered among 600 small shareholders, with 0.1% each. The power index of the large holder is 66.6%, whereas for the small holders it is less than 0.06% apiece. The 400:1 ratio in holdings produces a power advantage of better than 1000:1[10]

The preceding was an example of a "weighted majority game." Another example is provided by a board with five members, one of whom casts two extra votes. If a simple majority (four out of seven votes) carries the day, then power is distributed 60% to the multivote member, 10% to each of the others. To see this, observe that there are five possible positions for the strong man, if we arrange the members in order at random. In three of these positions he is pivotal. Hence his index is equal to 3/5. (Similarly, in the preceding example, we may compute that the strong man is pivotal 400 times out of 601.)

* * *

The values in the examples given above do not take into account any of the sociological or political superstructure that almost invariably exists in a legislature or policy board. They were not intended to be a representation of present day "reality." It would be foolish to expect to be able to catch all the subtle shades and nuances of custom and procedure that are to be found in most real decision-making bodies. Nevertheless, the power index computations may be useful in the setting up of norms or standards, the departure from which will serve as a measure of, for example, political solidarity, or regional or sociological factionalism, in an assembly. To do this we need an empirical power index, to compare with the theoretical. One possibility is as follows: The voting record of an individual is taken. He is given no credit for being on the losing side of a vote. If he is on the winning side, when n others voted with him, then he is awarded the probability of his having been the pivot (or blocker, in the case of a defeated motion), which is $1/n+1$. His probabilities are then averaged over all votes. It can be shown that this measure gives more weight than the norm does to uncommitted members who hold the "balance of power" between extreme factions. For example, in a nine-man committee which contains two four-man factions which always oppose each other, the lone uncommitted member will always be on the winning side, and will have an observed index of 1/5, compared to the theoretical value of 1/9.

A difficulty in the application of the above measure is the problem of finding the correct weights to attach to the different issues. Obviously it would not be proper to take a uniform average over all votes, since there is bound to be a wide disparity in the importance of issues brought to a vote. Again, in a multicameral legislature (or in any more complicated system), many important issues may be decided without every member having had an opportunity to go on record with his stand. There are many other practical difficulties in the way of direct applications of the type mentioned. Yet the power index appears to offer useful information concerning the basic design of legislative assemblies and policy-making boards.

Appendix

The evaluation of the power distribution for a tricameral legislature with houses of 1, 3, and 5 members is given below:

There are 504 arrangements of five X's, three O's, and one ϕ, all equally likely if the nine items are ordered at random. In the following tabulation, the numbers indicate the number of permutations of predecessors ( ) and successors [ ] of the final pivot, marked with an asterisk. The dots indicate the pivots of the three separate houses. Power indices for the houses are 192/504, 162/504, and 150/504, and hence are in the proportion 32:27:25, with the smallest house the strongest. Powers of the individual members are as 32:9:9:9:5:5:5:5:5.

Notes

1. See J. von Neumann and O. Morgenstern, *Theory of Games and Economic Behavior* (Princeton, 1944, 1947, 1953), pp. 420 ff.

2. See K. J. Arrow, *Social Choice and Individual Values* (New York, 1951), p. 7.

3. For a brief discussion of some of the factors in stock voting see H. G. Gothman and H. E. Dougall, *Corporate Financial Policy* (New York, 1948), pp. 56-61.

4. More generally, a minimal winning coalition.

5. In the formal sense described above.

6. This statement can be put into numerical form without difficulty, to give a quantitative description of the "efficiency" of a legislature.

7. The mathematical formulation and proof are given in L. S. Shapley, "A Value for N-Person Games," *Annals of Mathematics Study No. 28* (Princeton, 1953), pp. 307-17. Briefly stated, any alternative imputation scheme

would conflict with either *symmetry* (equal power indices for members in equal positions under the rules) or *additivity* (power distribution in a committee system composed of two strictly independent parts the same as the power distributions obtained by evaluating the parts separately).

8. As a general rule, if one component of a committee system (in which approval of all components is required) is made less "efficient"—i.e., more susceptible to blocking maneuvers—then its share of the total power will increase.

9. In the general case the proportion is $N - M + 1:M$, where M stands for the number of councilmen required for passage.

10. If there are two or more large interests, the power distribution depends in a fairly complicated way on the sizes of the large interests. Generally speaking, however, the small holders are better off than in the previous case. If there are two big interests, equal in size, then the small holders actually have an advantage over the large holders, on a power per share basis. This suggests that such a situation is highly unstable.

2. A GAME THEORETIC ANALYSIS OF CONGRESSIONAL
POWER DISTRIBUTIONS FOR A STABLE TWO-PARTY SYSTEM[1]

R. Duncan Luce and Arnold A. Rogow

THE THEORY OF GAMES (11) is a mathematical model for conflict of interest among intelligent and motivated agents; it is, therefore, not surprising that attempts are being made to apply it to some political science problems. So far, there are two such published efforts. The first consists of readings in game theory, assembled by Shubik (9), which serve to introduce some of the basic ideas and criticisms of the theory. The second, a paper by Shapley and Shubik (8), is the first actual application of a portion of game theory to a political science problem. The present paper outlines another application, which is in a sense a natural successor to the Shapley-Shubik work.

We must emphasize that this is an outline, for we do not view the content as a serious attempt to study Congress as such; rather it is a purposely oversimplified illustration of how a part of game theory may be applied to such studies.

To this end, we have taken pains to point out the nature of the assumptions made, the extent to which they are inherent in the model, and the extent to which they are simply matters of convenient exposition. We hold that a much more serious attempt must be made to abstract the central features of a legislature than we have undertaken before one can decide whether the particular model recommended is useful or not. In apparent contrast to our doubts that the formulation will sustain careful scrutiny by students of Congress, we have formulated a group of generalizations that summarize some of our detailed results and we have discussed these in the light of prevailing generalizations and some data. This should not be misinterpreted; it is only intended to demonstrate how it is possible to go from the mass of detail generated by the model to the types of generalization more familiar to a political scientist. We hope that our discussion will stimulate others to use these mathematical tools in deeper analyses of legislative bodies—studies in which data are related more closely to theory than we have done.

A legislature, as a voting body, can be viewed as having two inherently different aspects: a formal body of rules, called the legislative scheme, which establish the conditions under which a bill is passed, and the various peculiarities and limitations characteristic of a particular legislature working within the given scheme. Included in these limitations are such realities as the party structure, party discipline, the effects of pressure groups, etc. Following Shapley and Shubik, it appears that the scheme is usefully identified with one of the central notions in *n*-person game theory: the characteristic function. It is suggested that many of the "realities" of a legislature can be identified with another notion central to one of the several equilibrium theories. This theory is concerned with those couplings of a "power distribution" to a division of the participants into coalitions such that no changes occur. Since it is striking that the two-party system—a division of the participants into two disjoint coalitions—has remained stable for a long time, we shall assume that it *is* stable and inquire as to the theoretically necessary location of power in Congress and the presidency for such stability. We shall not attempt to discuss the much more profound question as to why the two-party system has evolved and why it is stable, but only what conditions are theoretically necessary on the power distributions in order that the system be stable. As will be seen, the theory is simply a formalization of the usual verbal discussions about the location of power—a formalization that can be readily extended to more complicated models of Congress where many of us would find it difficult or impossible to extend a nonsymbolic analysis.

Our work relates to the Shapley-Shubik paper

Reprinted from *Behavioral Science*, Vol. 1 (1956), pp. 83-95, by permission of the authors and the publisher.

1. This work was undertaken when the authors were Fellows (1954-55) at the Center for Advanced Study in the Behavioral Sciences, Stanford, California. The final revision was supported in part through funds extended to the Behavioral Models Project, Bureau of Applied Social Research, Columbia University by the Office of Naval Research. The paper may be identified as publication A198 of the Bureau of Applied Social Research. Reproduction in whole or in part is permitted for any purpose of the United States Government.

in the following way: They ignored any information one might have about specific legislatures and confined their attention to legislative schemes. Given such a scheme, they inquired into the possibility of a priori statements about the power distributions implied by the scheme. If one is willing to accept certain conditions as to the nature of such an a priori distribution, they establish that it is uniquely determined by the voting scheme. For the study of existing legislatures this is obviously insufficient and one must take into account some of the known realities and attempt to deduce from them other—known or unknown—assertions and to investigate the empirical truth of these consequences. Our purpose is to begin to deal with this problem.

Before turning to the details of the model, let us freely admit that to many—particularly to those with mathematical training—the following discussion will seem tedious and the content slight in relation to the length. It is true that the content could be contained in half a dozen or eight pages, but only at the expense of using more mathematics and thereby excluding as readers many of those we most want to address: political scientists concerned with the study of legislatures. One price of inter-disciplinary communication seems to be length.

1. A Mathematical Representation of a Legislative Scheme. For the purposes of this paper, we shall suppose that the only function of a legislative body is to vote on bills which are presented to it; of course, this is not actually the case, but it may prove to be a suitable first approximation to a legislature and, at the least, it should be of interest to see what consequences can be drawn from it. For the moment, we shall not consider how a legislature may be divided into chambers nor how it may be partitioned into parties; rather, we will simply think of it as a body of undifferentiated men who vote. Let us denote this set (the terms "class" or "collection" are also used) of men by the symbol L (which stands for "legislators"). Consider any subset S of the set L (for example, if L denotes the set of men in the United States Congress on January 1, 1955, then the Southern Democratic Senators form a well-defined subset of L). The rules of the legislative scheme under consideration must determine whether or not this set S is able as a voting coalition to pass a bill. Indeed, one way to prescribe the voting rules of the body is to list for each possible subset S whether or not it can pass a bill. Let us call those coalitions which can pass a bill *winning* and those which cannot *losing*.

The legislative scheme with which we shall be concerned is that of the United States. It involves two sets of men: Congress, which we shall denote by the symbol C, and the President, whom we shall denote by P. For our purpose, it will not prove necessary to take into account that Congress is divided into two houses, for we shall not be concerned here with the origination of bills, with committee activities, or with treaties, and we shall always assume similar majorities in both houses. A coalition in this scheme is winning if and only if either

1. it consists of a majority (in both houses) of Congress and the President, or
2. it consists of a two-thirds majority (in both houses) of Congress.

All other possible coalitions are losing. It should be noted that by ignoring the possibility of ties, we have made a minor idealization: this is not essential to the model and it can be eliminated at the cost of more *routine* labor later on.

Returning to the general case, we may assume that as a result of passing or defeating a bill, there are certain rewards accruing to those involved. These may range from outright money payments to individuals, through various forms of indirect compensation, to changes in relative prestige. Each of the individuals in the legislature is assumed to have a pattern of preferences among these outcomes. While it is very difficult to ascertain these preferences in practice, they may still be postulated. If they are defined over all risky outcomes, i.e., outcomes consisting of chance distributions over the basic outcomes, and if they satisfy certain axioms, then the theory of utility establishes how the preferences may be represented by numbers (11, pp. 15-30). Since there is an extensive literature on this subject, brevity dictates that we cannot delve into it deeply. Nonetheless, it must be emphasized that the theory is controversial and that many authors do not feel that people can be expected to exhibit the consistency demanded by the axioms. On the other hand, the axioms do have a certain compelling plausibility. One important difficulty in the theory, as it is now developed, is that the numbers representing preferences are not uniquely determined —the choice of both the zero and the scale unit is arbitrary. The important ambiguity is that of the unit, for it is impossible to say what changes in the underlying outcomes result in the same utility change for two different people. This is the famed problem of interpersonal comparisons of utility.

Assuming the existence of such utility functions and a solution to the problem of interpersonal comparisons, the theory of games shows how it is possible to derive a number for each logically possible coalition which represents, in utility units, the amount of the rewards that the coalition as a whole may insure for itself (11, pp. 238-243). The fact that interpersonal comparisons cannot now be made would seem to render this construction empty; however, it is not completely empty if one supposes there exists a solution to this problem and, in some contexts, it is possible to determine these summary numbers without actually obtaining the individual utilities (see below). In a sense, such a number associated with a coalition represents its power with respect to the single bill under consideration. When we use the word "power" in the rest of this paper, it shall mean only the numerical representation of rewards accruing to coalitions as evaluated by the members of these coalitions. It is important that no other meanings of this word be read into our results.

The power, in the sense of the numbers just described, of a coalition depends not only on the ability of the coalition to pass a bill, but also on the individual evaluation of the outcomes; thus, we cannot anticipate in general that these numbers will meet very strong restrictions. In fact, in the theory of games they are shown to satisfy only two very reasonable requirements; these are discussed in the Appendix. Since our work is primarily illustrative of a mathematical method, we shall not attempt to deal with the completely general case, but rather we shall suppose that the individual evaluations of the rewards resulting from passing the bill under consideration are such that each of the winning coalitions has identical power and each of the losing coalitions has identical power. This, very clearly, is an idealization, but one which may be approximately true in some cases. It is not, however, essential to the methods we are illustrating, as is pointed out in the Appendix, so long as one can devise empirical methods for estimating the relative power of the various coalitions. As we shall see, it will not prove necessary to have these estimates for all possible coalitions, but only for a relatively few relevant ones.

With the assumption of the power equality of all winning coalitions and of all losing ones, there is no loss of generality in setting the power of a winning coalition equal to 1 and that of a losing one equal to 0; this we shall do. If S is any subset of L, we denote by $v(S)$ the power of S acting as a coalition, i.e., $v(S) = 1$ if S is winning and $= 0$ if S is losing.

Of course, it is a theoretical fiction to speak of the power of a coalition. True, the power results from the collection of men acting as a coalition, and so in that sense it is associated with the coalition, but the rewards it represents must actually be rewards to individuals in the legislature. We cannot even say "rewards to just the members of the coalition which passes the bill," for the coalition may find it expedient to turn over some of the rewards to men not in the coalition. At least this is an a priori possibility and though it will not actually occur under the assumption of equality of power for winning and for losing coalitions, with more general assumptions it can. We, therefore, suppose that the distribution of total power to the different legislators can be represented by a collection of n numbers x_i, where i is an index running over the n legislators. For example, if we number the legislators from 1 to n, then x_{10} denotes the power accruing to the legislator numbered 10. We shall stipulate that *all* the power is distributed to the legislators, i.e.,

$$x_1 + x_2 + \cdots + x_n = 1,$$

and that the smallest amount of power is 0, i.e.,

$$x_i \geqq 0 \qquad \text{for } i = 1, 2, \cdots n.$$

(In the vocabulary of the theory of games, such a distribution is called an imputation.)

We shall suppose, subject to some limitations to be given later, that during the pre-vote haggling and threatening each of the legislators is attempting to achieve as large a portion of this distribution of power as he can. The purpose of our analysis, among other things, will be to establish which, if any, of the distributions of power are in equilibrium in the sense that further haggling will not result in a modification of the distribution.

At this point, it is convenient to interrupt our pursuits to indicate what Shapley and Shubik have done in the paper mentioned earlier (8). Given a legislative *scheme*, as described by the winning and losing coalitions, they inquired what, if any, a priori statements could be made about power distributions. They quite consciously ignored all the specific information one might have or might obtain about a specific legislature, such as Congress at a certain date, and they concentrated entirely on the information given by the legislative scheme. We shall not attempt to reconstruct their argument, but we may mention the nature of the important and surprising theorem of Shapley's upon which their work rests. He has shown (7) that if an a priori distribution of power is required to meet some (apparently) weak and possibly acceptable conditions, then there is a unique answer to the problem which can be expressed by a simple formula involving the numbers $v(S)$. The formula amounts to calculating for each legislator the chance that, if a coalition were built up successively by random selections from among the legislators, he would be the individual who converted it from a losing one to a winning one.

They presented several calculations of a priori power distributions for well-known voting schemes. For example, for the congressional-presidential scheme, the ratio of power of a single representative to the presidency is 2 to 350 and between a senator and the presidency the ratio is 9 to 350. If we take the House of Representatives and the Senate as single units, then they have equal a priori power and the presidency is two-fifths as powerful. If the congressional scheme were modified so that the presidential veto could not be overridden, then the House would have slightly less power than the Senate and the presidency would be about twice as powerful as either of them. As they point out, such a theory gives one a tool to examine the effect of revising legislative procedure, for ". . . it can easily happen that the mathematical structure of a voting system conceals a bias in power distribution unsuspected and unintended by the authors of the revision" (8).

Our purpose is to go beyond the Shapley-Shubik analysis of a legislative scheme to an analysis of a legislature. This will, of course, necessitate a model of what we mean by a legislature. In the next section, we shall present a model for Congress, which is illustrative of a class of models for legislatures. (The general class is discussed in the Appendix.) These models must attempt to capture some of the realities of specific legislatures —realities which are not part of the voting scheme. In the case of Congress, we mean by realities such facts as the party structure, the committee roles, the liberal-conservative dichotomy, the individual loyalties to party, personal animosities, etc. We shall not, by any means, attempt to deal with all of these in this illustrative example, but only with the party structure and an approximation to party loyalty. This will permit a plausible first approximation which is sufficiently simple to render the analysis fairly transparent. The effect of introducing other factors is only to increase the details of analysis without modifying the basic procedure.

2. A Model of Congress. We shall start with the fact that every legislator is identified with one or two non-overlapping political parties. We shall assume for simplicity, and with little practical loss of generality, that whichever party has a majority in one chamber of Congress has a majority in the other. Let us label the majority party as number 1 and the minority party as number 2, and let us denote by C_1 the set of congressmen in the majority party and by C_2 the set in the minority party.

An arresting fact about Congress is the stability of the two-party system, i.e., the simple fact that it has not split into more than two parties or reduced to one. One of the major questions to

which we shall address ourselves is whether there exist distributions of power for our model of Congress which permit a stable two-party system. Thus, if the President is a member of the majority party, we shall be interested in the stability (in a sense yet to be defined) of the partition of the voting body (which includes the President) into C_2 on the one hand and C_1 plus P on the other. Let the set consisting of C_1 and P be denoted by $C_1 \cup P$. Let τ_1 denote this partition, $(C_1 \cup P, C_2)$. Similarly, if the President is in the minority party, we shall be interested in the partition

$$\tau_2 = (C_1, C_2 \cup P).$$

While the two-party structure is known to be stable, it is equally clear that some, if not most, bills are passed by coalitions different from the party coalition. The conservatives of the two parties may join as a temporary coalition to pass a single bill without causing the disruption of the party structure. However, given a particular bill and a particular Congress, there are certain coalitions which could not conceivably form. If we restrict our attention to the partitioning of Congress by parties, these limitations on the formation of coalitions (to pass a bill) are, therefore, limitations on defections from the parties. Such limitations are produced by a number of factors such as pressure from constituents, party discipline, pressure from lobbies, the particular issue at stake, etc. However they may be generated, they can be described in terms of the set of Congressmen who can be induced to defect to the other party. Here we make two simplifying assumptions: first, that there are no abstentions from voting and, second, that the only defections are from one party to the other. Actually, the second of these omits the important possibility of defectors from both parties joining to form a winning coalition. Again, as will be seen, there is no inherent reason for making this assumption: it only reduces the amount of routine calculation and the amount of space needed to present the results.

Because of the nature of the legislative scheme, there are only two groups of defections which are of interest: a defection which swells the ranks of the other party to a two-thirds majority in each house, in which case a presidential veto can be overridden, and a defection which fails to achieve a two-thirds majority in at least one house but does result in a simple majority in each, in which case a coalition of the majority and the President can pass the bill. In either case, the party in question theoretically will only be interested in defections which just produce the desired majority—all other votes are technically superfluous. Now, at the time of any given vote, it does not seem too implausible to suppose that in principle the potential defectors in each party can be graded from the most to least willing to defect from their party. If so, and if the defectors are added to a coalition in order of decreasing willingness to defect, then there is a unique set of defectors which will just create a simple majority, if that is possible, and a unique set which will just create a two-thirds majority, if that is possible. So, when we speak of a set of defectors which create a certain majority, we shall mean that minimal set of congressmen, drawn from among those most willing to defect, which is just necessary to form the majority.

With this assumption, then, we may divide the congressmen of parties 1 and 2 into two non-overlapping sets: C'_1 and C'_2 will denote the sets of *potential defectors* from parties 1 and 2 respectively and C''_1 and C''_2 the remaining members of each party, who will be called the *diehards*.

There are a number of different cases which can occur in this idealized Congress. Since there is no a priori reason to exclude any of these we shall examine each of them separately, and on the basis of this exhaustive examination, we shall draw some general qualitative conclusions from the model (section 5).

First, there are four basically different partitions of Congress into the two-party system: either party 1 (which by assumption has a majority) fails to have a two-thirds majority in at least one chamber, or it has a two-thirds majority in both, and either the President is a member of party 1 or of party 2.

Second, there are twelve different possible limitations on coalition changes from the two-party partition. These twelve arise from a selection of one of the alternatives in each of the following three classes of alternatives:

1. either the President is (or feels) free to defect from his party, or he is not;
2. party 1 plus the defectors from party 2 either form only a simple majority, or they form a two-thirds majority in both houses; and
3. party 2 plus the defectors from party 1 either fail to form a simple majority in at least one house, or they form a simple majority in both houses but not a two-thirds majority in at least one, or they form a two-thirds majority in both houses.

We observe that not all these limitations are compatible with all the coalition partitions, e.g., it is not possible for the majority party to have a two-thirds majority in both houses and for the addition of defectors from the other party to reduce this to a simple majority. If such cases are excluded, then there are a total of 36 cases to be examined.

3. Equilibrium Power Distributions in a Special Case.

To introduce the equilibrium notion we shall use and to illustrate the typical calculations involved, we shall choose one of the 36 cases; it matters little which one we take. Let us suppose the President is in party 1 and that party 1 has only a simple majority in Congress. Thus, we shall be concerned with the partition $\tau_1 = (C_1 \cup P, C_2)$, where C_1 does not form a two-thirds majority. As the system of limitations on changes from τ_1, let us choose the case where

1. The President is free to defect;
2. party 1 plus the defectors from party 2 form only a simple majority; and
3. party 2 plus the defectors from party 1 form only a simple majority.

Now, from these assumptions, we see that a two-thirds majority does not exist among the possible changes; thus any winning coalition that can form must include the President. It is easy to see that there are only three such coalitions:

$$C_1 \cup P, \quad C_1 \cup C'_2 \cup P, \quad \text{and} \quad C_2 \cup C'_1 \cup P,$$

where, as before, if A and B are sets, $A \cup B$ is the set whose elements consist of those in A and those in B. One of these three will have to form to pass the bill; we shall not concern ourselves with which (there are certainly not enough assumptions even to begin to answer that question), but rather with the location of power in such a Congress under the assumption that the two-party system is stable.

Consider a power distribution x_i, $i = 1, 2 \cdots n$, which is offered as being compatible in this Congress with the two-party partitioning of Congress. If any legislator i not in $C_1 \cup P$ has $x_i > 0$, then we know that the sum of the x_j for j in $C_1 \cup P$, must be less than 1. But since $C_1 \cup P$ is winning it can command power of 1, and so it can form and each of its members can receive more than they did in the arrangement x_i, $i = 1, 2, \cdots n$. Since we are assuming each legislator is out to better his gains of power, we must conclude that if anyone outside $C_1 \cup P$ has power, then the combination of the two-party partition and the given power distribution cannot be in equilibrium. A similar argument applies to $C_1 \cup C'_2 \cup P$ and to $C_2 \cup C'_1 \cup P$, but not to any other set of legislators for either they are losing, and so can offer no power gains, or they are not among the admissible changes. Thus a power distribution x_i, $i = 1, 2, \cdots n$, is in equilibrium with τ_1 only if $x_i = 0$ for any legislator i not in *each* of the three coalitions. Thus, the power must be distributed over those who are in *all* three of the winning coalitions, i.e., over $C'_1 \cup P$. In other words, in this situation the power is distributed over the defectors from party 1 and the President. Exactly how it is distributed over these men is not determined in this simple model: it presumably depends upon factors which we have not taken into account. If we were to extend the model to include such things as the actions of committees, the origins of the bill, and so on, we could then expect a much more detailed determination of the power distributions.

4. The Equilibrium Power Distributions for the Two-Party System. In order that there shall be no ambiguity in our definition of equilibrium, we shall be somewhat more formal than we have been up to now. Let $v(S)$ denote the number representing the power accruing to the set S if it forms a voting coalition. Let X stand for the distribution of power x_i, $i = 1, 2, \cdots n$. Let τ denote a partitioning of the legislature into coalitions (while we have assumed partitions into only two coalitions, this assumption is by no means necessary). Let the symbol $\psi(\tau)$ stand for the class of coalitions which can form, if there is any reason to do

so, when the legislature is partitioned according to τ. Then, we shall say that the pair (X, τ) is ψ-stable (which is simply the name assigned to this particular definition of equilibrium) if for each set S in $\psi(\tau)$,

$$v(S) \leqq \sum_{i \text{ in } S} x_i.$$

(The last symbol, $\Sigma_{i \text{ in } S} x_i$, simply means the sum of the values x_i for each legislator i in the coalition S.)

A re-examination of the analysis of the special case discussed above shows that it is just a special case of this definition.

Actually, the definition we have given here is slightly different from that presented in the mathematical literature (3, 4). There it was stipulated that if a legislator receives no power at all, i.e., if $x_i = 0$, then he shall not be involved in a coalition with any other legislators. The argument for imposing this condition arises simply from asking why he should cooperate with others if this coop-

Table 1—The Power Distributions for a Stable Two-Party System Under the Given Conditions

No.	Presidential Defection	Party of President	Size of Party 1 Majority	Size of Party 1 plus Party 2 Defectors	Size of Party 2 plus Party 1 Defectors	Locations of Power
1.a.i	Possible	Either	simple	simple	less than majority	Party 1, President
ii					simple	Party 1 defectors, President
iii					two-thirds	Party 1 defectors
1.b.i				two-thirds	less than majority	Party 1
ii					simple	Party 1 defectors
iii					two-thirds	Party 1 defectors
2.a			two-thirds	two-thirds	less than majority	Party 1
b					simple	Party 1 defectors
c					two-thirds	Party 1 defectors
3.a.i		1	simple	simple	less than majority	Party 1, President
ii					simple	Party 1, President
iii					two-thirds	Party 1 defectors
3.b.i				two-thirds	less than majority	Party 1
ii					simple	Party 1
iii					two-thirds	Party 1 defectors
4.a.i	Not Possible	2	simple	simple	less than majority	Impass—no winning coalitions
ii					simple	Party 2, Party 1 defectors, President
iii					two-thirds	Party 2, Party 1 defectors
4.b.i				two-thirds	less than majority	Party 1 defectors, Party 2 defectors
ii					simple	Party 1 defectors, Party 2 defectors
iii					two-thirds	Party 1 defectors, Party 2 defectors
5.a		1	two-thirds	two-thirds	less than majority	Party 1
b					simple	Party 1
c					two-thirds	Party 1 defectors
6.a		2	two-thirds	two-thirds	less than majority	Party 1
b					simple	Party 1 defectors
c					two-thirds	Party 1 defectors

eration does not result in any gain for him. This is a powerful argument in situations which occur only once, but it seems less convincing in a legislature where one bill is but part of an on-going process.

Now, while we have in fact been ignoring the on-going process (see the Appendix), we shall at least take it into account to the extent of waiving the second condition. It may also be worth noting that from the mathematical point of view this does not constitute a very serious change in the definition for the second condition has not played an important role in most of the theorems proved.

We may now give (Table 1) the power distributions which coupled with the party partitioning of Congress are stable in each of the 36 cases described in Section 2. The conclusion in each case arises by an argument like that given in Section 3 (that case is number 1.a.ii in Table 1).

5. Conclusions. By examining the summary of results in Table 1, certain generalizations implied by the model are clear. We may list six which seem interesting:

1. In all cases the arrangement of Congress into two opposed party coalitions is stable provided the power is distributed as indicated. In very many cases, however, it is necessary to form coalitions other than along party lines in order to produce a winning coalition, i.e., to pass a bill. In only one case (4.a.i) are the limitations so stringent that no working majority can form: this is when the President is of the minority party and will not defect to the majority, the majority party has only a simple majority even with the defectors from the minority, and the minority does not have a simple majority even with the defectors from the majority. What is interesting is that in only one case of the 36 can such an impasse result.

2. In all circumstances, the President is weak when the majority party—whether he is a member of it or not—has a two-thirds majority. If this model has any relation to reality, we must conclude that a President should fear a real Congressional landslide for *either* party.

3. The President possesses power (from voting considerations) only when neither party can muster more than a simple majority even with the help of the defectors from the other party.

4. The only circumstances when the minority party is the holder of any power is when the President is in the minority party and he is unwilling to defect to the majority.

5. Under all conditions, if the defectors from party 1 added to party 2 fail to form a majority, then the diehards of party 1 possess power. The only other case in which they possess power is when the President is a member of party 1, he

is unwilling to defect, and party 2 plus the defectors from party 1 form only a simple majority (cases 3.a.ii, 3.b.ii, and 5.b).

6. The only case when the party 2 diehards possess any power is when the President is a member of their party, he is unwilling to defect, party 1 has only a simple majority, and party 2 plus the defectors from party 1 form either a majority or a two-thirds majority (cases 4.a.ii and iii).

In connection with these last two statements, we note that there are a large number of situations where the diehards are not in a position to command power in a stable two-party system, and those situations in which they do have power appear to be ones not likely to occur often in practice. Recall that when we introduced the concept of a ψ-stable pair (section 4) we noted that in the original mathematical definition it was stipulated that a nontrivial coalition would not exist if its members did not benefit from their participation in the coalition. While we waived this condition for our work in this paper, there is still some force to the argument if we think of the long-term existence of a legislature. Thus, if voting coalitions tend to stabilize in time and if consideration is not given to the diehards by the other party members, it should not be too surprising to find a sudden change in their behavior. Of course, it must be understood that this is not a conclusion from the model but an extrapolation, for the model (as a special case of game theory) is inherently static and does not attempt to deal with such changes in time.

Despite the various limitations of the model, which we have already noted, the generalizations we have drawn from it do not appear to be seriously inconsistent with a number of political science "findings" concerning Congress, and in several cases they appear to emphasize aspects of congressional power which may not have been given adequate attention. The sorts of statements with which the model is not in serious contradiction are:

The President, as a legislator, is weak when either

1. his party is in the minority;
2. his party is in the majority but is not committed to his program; or
3. either party can muster sufficient strength to overturn a veto:

and the President, as a legislator, is strong when either

4. his party is in the majority and is committed to his program;
5. his party is in the majority, whether or not it is committed to his program, provided that it

cannot muster sufficient strength to overturn a veto;

6. supporters from his own party and defectors from the opposition party constitute a pro-administration majority coalition.

Such statements as these are not in all cases fully acceptable generalizations from the model, e.g., the first one must be qualified by the condition that one or another congressional coalition has a two-thirds majority, for if not the President possibly does possess power (see cases 1.a.i, 1.a.ii, 3.a.i, 3.a.ii, and 4.a.ii). A careful examination of our results will show that several others of these statements need some qualification before one can say that they coincide with the results of the model, but the spirit of them is much the same. It would be of some interest to know how stable these generalizations are under slight changes in the assumed limitations on coalition changes (as given by $\psi(\tau)$): for example, one might examine the effect of including as possible coalitions those made up from the defectors of the two parties. This would result in many more cases to examine, but none would be any more difficult to deal with than those above.

Let us emphasize once again that both these statements and the generalizations arrived at using game theory refer only to one aspect of Executive-Legislative relations. They do not deal with the crucial power position of committees and party leaders, the special position of the Rules Committee in the House, the filibuster power in the Senate, or a number of other important factors. Consequently, no claim can be made that our generalizations would not be substantially modified were the model refined.

On the other hand, they do emphasize several factors which are sometimes neglected or which are occasionally minimized in political science literature. One of these is concerned with the power position of diehards vis-à-vis defectors. As V. O. Key, Jr.[2] and James M. Burns, (1, see also 2) among others, have noted, party defectors often constitute either the effective working majority or the effective opposition, irrespective of whether or not they are members of the nominal majority party. The model suggests that in only a relatively few (and relatively unlikely) cases do the party diehards possess effective power.

In the majority of the 36 cases, party defectors hold the balance of power.

This observation suggests that more attention needs to be paid to the analysis of Congress not in terms of nominal party majorities or minorities but in terms of cross-party groupings which might be tentatively classified as we have done. Thus far, empirical research does not provide a clear answer to the question of the extent of party cohesion,[3] let alone answers to such questions as: who are the diehards and defectors, from what areas of the country do they come, why do they operate as such, and is the theoretically greater power of the defectors reflected in the legislation which finally gets to a vote, in committee assignments, or in other kinds of prestige and influence?

Our game theory generalizations also point up a number of inherent features of Executive-Legislative relations. It is clear from the model that the President, under the prevailing system of loose party discipline, does not necessarily gain when his party is returned to Congress with an overwhelming majority. Although most students of legislative behavior are of the view that the party of the President should have the main responsibility for the organization of Congress, our analysis suggests that the President is not much advantaged when his party elects two-thirds or more of the Senators and Representatives. Other things being equal, the President's power as a legislator appears to be great when his own party controls between 51% and 66% of Congressional seats, and when no cross-party combination of diehards and defectors can total more than two-thirds of the membership. Tactically, this means that his party should have only about 55% of the seats.[4]

Rather paradoxically, the President's power can also be great even when his own party is in

2. "In the American Congress the weak ties of the majority encourage the minority to wean away followers from the majority party and to determine the outcome of at least some and at times many legislative issues. It is not uncommon for the working 'majority' to be composed of a substantial part of the minority plus a sector of the nominal majority . . . the genuinely effective 'opposition' often consists, not of the minority, but of recalcitrant members of the majority who hold a balance of power within the House or Senate" (6, p. 706).

3. The failure is reflected in the differing views held of the matter. Thus, Burns' view that "Party cohesion is still slight today," (1, 40) confirming A. Lawrence Lowell's analysis of fifty-four years ago, is similar to that advanced in the American Political Science Association's report "Toward a More Responsible Two-Party System." But a diametrically opposite position has been taken by a number of other political scientists. See for example, (10).

4. These generalizations are not contradicted by the record of Presidential vetoes cast during the Roosevelt Administration. As the following table shows, 69% of the vetoes cast by Roosevelt were cast during the three Congresses in which one or both houses were controlled by a two-thirds or better Democratic majority.

President	Year	Congress	House		Senate		Vetoes
			D	R	D	R	
Hoover	1931-33	72nd	220	214	47	48	18
Roosevelt	33-34	73rd	310	117	60	35	73
Roosevelt	35-36	74th	319	103	69	25	148
Roosevelt	37-38	75th	331	89	76	16	117
Roosevelt	39-40	76th	261	164	69	23	167
Roosevelt	41-42	77th	268	162	66	28	79
Roosevelt	43-44	78th	218	208	58	37	45
Roosevelt	45-46	79th	242	190	56	38	76

the minority, provided that he is still in control of a bloc of his party possessing at least 35% of the Congressional votes. For in such cases, and so long as the 35% is loyal to the party chief, the majority (and opposition) party can initiate legislation, but it cannot subdue the veto power. The President, therefore, holds effective power as either party diehard or defector; in the former role, he can bring about a legislative stalemate, and in the latter role, he can transform an opposition which is impotent, so far as positive power is concerned, into a governmental party.

In closing, we must once again return to the limitations of the present version of the model. Whether or not this game theoretic analysis can provide us with any illumination of the Congressional power structure depends very largely on its potentialities of refinement to include factors which are known to be of importance. Thus, the question reduces to our ability to determine the power of coalitions, $v(S)$, and the limitations on coalition change, $\psi(\tau)$, for more complex real situations. More sophisticated models may very well necessitate the collection of empirical data in an attempt to determine these quantities. Presumably, the limitations on coalition defections, etc., can be assessed from obtainable data, in which case there seems to be no reason to assume, a priori, that the model must remain in its present elementary state. Equally, there seems no reason to suppose, if the generalizations deduced from the present model are at all interesting, that future refinements will not produce results of similar but more subtle interest.

Appendix

The purpose of this appendix is to indicate a little more explicitly the general form of a game model which we have illustrated by a special case in the main body of the paper. As we have indicated in several places, we believe that the methods discussed here are applicable to more refined models of legislatures; however, such applications surely will be more tedious in labor and will, in all probability, require the collection of empirical data.

As we said, game theory begins with a situation consisting of possible choices by individuals and individual outcomes associated to the choices. The individuals are assumed to have patterns of preferences among the outcomes which meet the axioms of utility theory, and so their preferences can be represented numerically. From this structure, the theory of games establishes that to each

subset S of the individuals there is assigned a number $v(S)$, which is calculated from the individual preferences. While in the model we examined $v(S)$ was either 0 or 1, in general this is not the case. If, for example, different rewards or different evaluations of the rewards occur for passing a bill, then the power of different coalitions which could pass the bill will be different. Or if we do not focus our attention on one bill, but on a series of bills, then since it is unreasonable to suppose that they will all result in the same rewards, we must suppose that the values $v(S)$ will depend upon more than the ability of the coalition S to pass a bill. The task of estimating $v(S)$ is clearly an empirical problem of some magnitude; there can be no doubt that it is a major stumbling block to the successful application of these methods. In particular, the theoretical construction of passing from individual preferences to $v(S)$ cannot be used, except in very special circumstances, to calculate $v(S)$; the practical difficulties are too great. More direct procedures are needed. One which may be useful is educated guesses made by well-informed observers. Another is a proposed, but untried, technique closely related to the methods of utility theory but applied directly to the coalitions and not to the individual outcome; this is discussed by Luce and Adams (5).

The collection of numbers $v(S)$, for all subsets S of the given set L (of legislators), form what in mathematics is called a real-valued set function v. This construct of game theory is called the *characteristic function* of the game. It might appear that since there is wide latitude in the individual evaluations of outcomes which lead to the characteristic function v, there can be no constraints on v in general. While this is almost true, it can be shown that it must meet two conditions, but in general no others can be established. Let us suppose that R and S are two subsets of L which have no legislators in common, and let $R \cup S$ be the subset consisting of the legislators in R plus those in S. Then it can be shown that

$$v(R \cup S) \geqq v(R) + v(S).$$

In words, this simply means that the coalition $R \cup S$ can do everything R and S can do as separate coalitions, and possibly more. The whole is at least as great as the sum of its parts. The second condition, while mathematically significant, certainly appears trivial when one thinks of a legislature. It says the set ϕ which has no members —the empty set—has no power:

$$v(\phi) = 0$$

The interesting one is the former. In the case of the model we were discussing, it is particularly easy to see that it holds. If R and S are both losing $v(R) = 0$ and $v(S) = 0$. But $R \cup S$ may be either winning or losing, so the inequality holds. If R is winning and S is losing (or equally, R losing and S winning), then since $R \cup S$ is a set which includes the winning set R, it too must be winning. Thus, $v(R) = 1$, $v(S) = 0$ and $v(R \cup S) = 1$, and so equality exists. Finally, consider the case where both R and S are winning. Recall that we said R and S have no legislators in common, so we have the situation that if R passes a bill A which the coalition S does not like, then S can bring the negative of A before the legislature. Since S is winning it can pass not-A. Thus, the legislature would reach the deadlock where it could pass both A and not-A; clearly, no acceptable legislative scheme would have this property, so the assumption that both R and S are winning is not meaningful. Hence, we conclude that the inequality must be met.

As in the special model, the equilibrium states of the legislature, no matter what characteristic function is involved, are given in terms of a pair (X, τ), where X is a distribution of power to the individuals and τ is a partition of the legislature into coalitions. The distribution of power, or imputation as it is called, X must satisfy two conditions. It is a partitioning of the total power available:

$$x_1 + x_2 + \cdots + x_n = v(L).$$

and no individual receives less power than he can be certain of getting:

$$x_i \geqq v(i) \quad \text{for} \quad i = 1, 2, \cdots n.$$

Finally, the model supposes that the realities of the situation, insofar as they produce limitations on shifts from one partitioning of the legislature to another, can be given in the following way. For each partition τ one is interested in, there is given a list of admissible coalition changes, which we denote by $\psi(\tau)$. It will be recalled that where τ was taken to be the partition into parties, $\psi(\tau)$ involved coalitions formed through defections from one party to the other. Again, it is an empirical problem to estimate these limitations. This problem will become particularly grave when an attempt is made to refine the model to take into account committees and other relevant features of Congress. Yet students of Congress have discussed such limitations and it may not be impossible to employ careful statistical studies to gain the necessary detailed data.

The application of the model is straightforward if the two empirical problems can be overcome. First we choose a partitioning τ of the legislature which we wish to investigate (possibly along party lines, but not necessarily). Second we determine $\psi(\tau)$. Third for each subset S in $\psi(\tau)$, we determine $v(S)$. Observe that so long as we deal with only one τ, it is not necessary to determine the whole of the characteristic function, but only the values for the admissible coalitions as given by $\psi(\tau)$. Fourth, we determine those distributions X which with τ are ψ-stable using the definition given in section 4. The fewer coalitions that are admissible, the less precisely defined is X, the more that are admissible, the more precisely defined is X. In many games, if too many coalitions are admissible, there is no X which meets all the conditions of the definition of ψ-stability, in which case one is forced to conclude that the partition τ is not stable. The effect of the limitations given by ψ is to increase the stability of a legislature, or in general, of a game.

Notes

1. Burns, J. M. *Congress on trial*. New York: Harper, 1949.
2. Carr, R. K., Bernstein, M. H., Morrison, D. H., Snyder, R. C., & McLean, J. E. *American democracy in theory and practice*. (Rev. ed.) New York: Rinehart, 1955.
3. Luce, R. D. A definition of stability for *n*-person games. *Ann. Math.*, 1954, 59, 357-366.
4. Luce, R. D. *k*-Stability of symmetric and of quota games. *Ann. Math.*, 1955, 62, 517-527.
5. Luce, R. D., & Adams, E. W. The determination of subjective characteristic functions in games with misperceived payoff functions, *Econometrica*, 1956, pp. 24, 158-171.
6. Key, V. O., Jr., *Politics, parties and pressure groups*. (3rd Ed.) New York: Crowell, 1952.
7. Shapley, L. S. A value for *n*-person games. Contributions to the theory of games. II. *Annals of Mathematics Studies*, No. 28. Princeton, N. J.: Princeton University Press, 1953. Pp. 307-317.
8. Shapley, L. S., & Shubik, M. A method for evaluating the distribution of power in a committee system. *Amer. pol. sci. Rev.*, 1954, 48, 787-792.
9. Shubik, M. *Readings in game theory and political behavior*. New York: Doubleday, 1954.
10. Turner, J. Responsible parties: A dissent from the floor. *Amer. pol. sci. Rev.*, 1951, 45, 143-152.
11. von Neumann, J., & Morgenstern, O. *Theory of games and economic behavior*. Princeton, N. J.: Princeton University Press, 1947.

3. MEASURING COHESION IN LEGISLATIVE GROUPS

Stuart A. Rice

THE MOST TANGIBLE and measurable units of political behavior are *votes*. They are tangible because simple and precise. They are measurable, for although each is really a *gross measure* of opinion, the value of which may differ widely in different individuals, they are nevertheless assumed to have equal value and are counted and recorded officially.[1] The determination of popular attitudes by an analysis of popular votes upon a variety of issues would be the preferred method if the data were available. A few such analyses of referendum votes have been made.[2] Unfortunately for this purpose the number of issues that have been acted upon by referendum is still small. Moreover, an essential requisite is lacking in any popular vote conducted over a wide area, namely, identification of the individual votes with the individual voters.

Election returns in the aggregate—the only form in which they are usually available—must be dissected if they are to be of value in estimating the forces of opinion at work in the electorate. Just as biological science made no progress in discovering the laws of heredity until it dealt with unit characters, political statistics will be meaningless as refined tools or products of measurement until they enable the investigator to distinguish the votes of rural, urban and small-town dweller; Protestant, Catholic and Hebrew; farmer, laborer and capitalist; native and foreign-born in their numerous varieties. Intersecting groups such as these mould the *mores* of individuals attached to them. They determine those characteristic, habitual and largely unconscious individual attitudes that have their resultant in "public opinion" and the "popular verdict at the polls." Hence to understand the result of an election one must understand the groups in the electorate and the part played by each as a causal factor in the result. But as already pointed out, the data from which this part might be measured are largely unavailable.

A similar difficulty is not encountered in dealing with representative bodies. Roll-call votes in Congress and American legislatures are cast openly

and recorded officially. But may the votes of legislators be regarded as representative of the opinions of those who select them? The correlation would obviously be imperfect, and might not even be high. Yet with full cognizance of the numerous influences tending to deflect the legislator from a normal expression of his personal attitudes, the writer contends that he is representative of the groups in the electorate to which he belongs—at least to a degree. He is representative, first, because voters tend to select men of their own "kind" to office, even though the similarity in kind may be based in the voter's "identification" of himself with the social, economic or intellectual attributes of the office-holder. The legislator is representative in a second sense, based upon the first, because he responds to legislative issues on the whole in about the same manner as would his fellow group members in the constituency. However amenable to "influence" he may be, there is a constant "strain" in the legislator's behavior toward consistency with the *mores* of his various groups. In a sufficiently large number of cases, this strain toward consistency with his social heritage is certain to affect any numerical indices of the legislator's behavior that may be devised. Measurements of group behavior in legislative bodies, therefore, are regarded by the writer as indicative of the attitudes of corresponding groups in the electorate. Objective tests of these *a priori* assumptions are possible and should be undertaken. Regardless of their validity, however, measurements of legislative behavior have a value in themselves, not only to the theorist but to the practical politician as well. This will be apparent in the pages that follow.

The present paper, then, has two general aims: first, to present a method for the measurement and comparison of the voting behavior of groups in legislative bodies; second, to illustrate the method by presenting the results of analysis of the cohesion and comparative resemblance of certain parties and blocs in the New York State Assembly of 1921 and in the United States Senate of the Sixty-eighth Congress. As a subordinate aim the writer hopes to add precision to a number of terms in common use in political discussion,

Reprinted from *Political Science Quarterly*, Vol. 40 (1925), pp. 60-72, where it appeared under the title, "The Behavior of Legislative Groups," by permission of the author and the publisher.

such as "cohesion," "swing" and party "wing."

The first test that any legislative group must meet concerns its *cohesion*. Are the members of Group A in their voting behavior more like each other than are the members generally of the more inclusive Group B which includes not only A but non-A individuals as well? For example are the Republican members in a state senate more alike in their votes than are the members of the senate generally? If so, it may be inferred that they are more like-minded and the Republican group may be called more *cohesive* than the senate as a whole. Similarly it may be asked whether the Republican senators are more or less cohesive than are the Democratic senators. Or take a question still more definite: Was the tri-partisan "progressive" or LaFollette bloc in the Senate of the Sixty-eighth Congress more or less cohesive than were the various senatorial groups included under each of the formal party designations?

The writer has been able to obtain precision in answering such questions by the aid of what he has called an *index of cohesion*. This index is based upon the theory of probability.

If roll-call votes were cast according to pure chance, the most probable result in the case of any roll call would be a division in which fifty per cent of the members voted affirmatively and fifty per cent voted negatively. It is evident that the cohesion within the entire body in such a case would be *nil*. Hence a measure of cohesion will be obtained if we determine the degree of departure from the most probable chance distribution of votes, toward complete uniformity of action, i. e., a roll call in which all members vote alike. Referring only to the percentage of affirmative votes for the sake of convenience, it is apparent that zero cohesion (0.0) will be indicated by a roll call in which fifty per cent of the members vote affirmatively. Absolute cohesion (100.0) will be indicated whenever the group is unanimously either for or against a measure; i. e., when it votes either 100 per cent or 0 per cent in the affirmative. Further, an index of cohesion intermediate between 0.0 and 100.0 will be determined by the degree to which the percentage of affirmative votes departs from 50.0 in either direction toward 0.0 or 100.0. For example, when the votes of the group on a given measure are 30 per cent in the affirmative or 70 per cent in the affirmative, the index of cohesion will in both cases be 40.0, for in both there is a 20/50 or 40 per cent departure from 0.0 cohesion toward 100.0 cohesion. When the index of cohesion upon a series of roll calls is to be found, the writer has employed the arithmetic mean of the indices derived for the various individual roll calls in the series.

Allied to the problem of group cohesion, and likewise requiring measurement, are questions of the extent to which various groups are alike or unlike in their voting responses to political issues. It is useful not alone to the political scientist but to many laymen to know whether farmers and workingmen, when thrown together in a state legislature, tend to be in mutual opposition or in mutual support. If they tend to be in mutual opposition with respect to prohibition and its enforcement (as they do) are they likewise in opposition with regard to labor legislation or political reform? Or, to use the former illustration, was the LaFollette bloc in the Sixty-eighth Congress in closer affiliation with the regular Republican party or with the regular Democratic party? In either case, how much closer? Answers to such questions based on a "hunch" are unsatisfactory. Measurements are needed.

To place beside his index of cohesion within groups, therefore, the writer has derived an *index of likeness between groups*. The possible range of this index is likewise from 0.0 to 100.0. If, for example, all Republicans in a legislative session vote affirmatively on a given roll call while all Democrats vote negatively, it is obvious that the behavior of the two groups, so far as it can be expressed by votes, is absolutely dissimilar. One is 100 per cent affirmative, the other 0 per cent affirmative. The arithmetic difference between the percentages of affirmative votes in the two cases is 100.0. This figure thus gives an index of absolute difference in voting behavior between the two groups. If, on the other hand, Republicans and Democrats *both* divide, at the same time, 50-50, or 70-30, or 85-15, the responses of the two groups, as groups, will in each case be the same. It is to be inferred in such cases that the distribution of groups is determined by factors unassociated with party divisions, and Republicans and Democrats may be said to vote *alike* on the issue at hand. The arithmetic difference between the respective percentages of affirmative votes in each such case will be 0.0, and the complement of this figure, 100.0, will be the index of likeness. Thus the complement of the arithmetic difference between the percentages voting in the affirmative in each of two groups gives an index of likeness between them, so far as their voting behavior is concerned. The index of likeness upon a series of roll calls may again be regarded as the arithmetic mean of the indices derived for the separate roll calls in the series.

The use of the two indices will now be illustrated, first, by an analysis of roll-call votes in the New York State Assembly of 1921. This was the year of "normalcy" at its height. A number of "Lusk" bills, together with the disqualification of a Socialist member, were carried with ease by an overwhelming Republican majority in the New York Legislature.

The Assembly was composed at the outset of 150 members. Eight groups were selected for analysis and comparison as a result of preliminary study of the roll calls recorded in the Assemby *Journal*. These were: The Assembly as a whole, the Republicans as a whole, the New York City Republicans, the "Up-State" Republicans, the Democrats, the Socialists, the Farmers and the Labor members. It so happened that all of the members classified as Farmers or Laborites were also Republicans. Those placed in these categories were members who met certain objective documentary tests concerning occupation and residence. All of the Democrats but two were from New York City. We may classify the members as indicated in the two following tables in order to show the relationships existing between the several groups:

Table I—Composition of the New York Assembly, 1921, by Parties and Two Selected Occupations

Republicans	119
Farmers	27
Laborites	5
Unclassified	87
Democrats	28
Socialists	3
Assembly as a whole	150

Of 1296 roll calls taken during the session, all but 255 were unanimous. Out of an estimated total of 175,000 votes cast, only 7,595 or 4.3 per cent were cast in the negative. The study has been confined, therefore, to roll calls in which there were six or more opposing votes cast against the majority action.[3] The results of the study are presented in Tables III and IV, which follow.

The number of groups of assemblymen whose votes were analyzed might have been extended to

include categories based on religious or other lines. Similarly, the roll calls included in the study, 169 in number, might have been classified into an indefinite number of subordinate categories. Three sub-classes of measures only are shown in Table III. "State issues" include all measures other than those of purely local character. Among 76 roll calls affecting single municipalities or counties, 59 were selected which bore upon the affairs of New York City alone. Thus roll calls upon "state issues" and "New York City issues" are referred to in columns 4 and 5, respectively. In column 6 are shown the indices of cohesion for 8 roll calls affecting the issue of prohibition and its enforcement. The same classification of measures is employed in Table IV.

A number of conclusions might be drawn from Tables III and IV. Still others might be disclosed if a larger number of the possible comparisons of group likeness were carried through in Table IV. A few of the more significant points indicated in the tables will serve to illustrate the utility of the method:

1. The New York City Republicans, in effect, formed an intermediate party group or bloc between the Up-State Republicans and the Democrats. When all measures are taken together, this bloc of New York City Republicans was more like its Up-State party associates (74.4) than it was like the Democrats (53.0). Yet on such an issue as prohibition, its likeness with the Up-Staters was represented by the index 20.6 as compared with

Table II—Composition of the New York Assembly, 1921, by Parties and Localities

Up-State Members		88
Republicans	86	
Democrats	2	
New York City Members		62
Republicans	33	
Democrats	26	
Socialists	3	
Assembly as a whole		150

Table III—Indices of Cohesion Within Various Groups in the New York Assembly, 1921

1	2	3	4	5	6
Group	Number in Group	169 Roll Calls with 6 or more Opposing Votes	94 Roll Calls on "State Issues"	59 Roll Calls on New York City Issues	8 Roll Calls on Prohibition
Assembly as a whole	150	51.4	44.9	..	15.6
Republicans	119	74.8	66.0	..	44.9
Up-State Republicans	86	87.9	80.7	96.5	89.9
New York City Republicans	33	65.5	63.9	62.1	68.7
Democrats	28	77.4	73.0	79.6	100.0
Socialists	3	94.0	94.1	..	71.3
Farmers	27	91.2	85.6	..	100.0
Laborites	5	68.0	59.9	..	12.5

an index of 84.5 between itself and the Democrats. In cohesion, the New York City Republicans were low—65.5 as compared with 87.9 for the Up-State Republicans and 77.4 for the Democrats. This f_ct is suggestive of a conflict between party loyalty on the one hand, tending toward association with the Up-State Republicans, and sectional loyalty upon the other, tending toward association with the Democrats, all but two of whom represented New York City districts.

2. The Republican farmers formed a highly cohesive group (91.2) within the relatively cohesive group of Up-State Republicans (87.9). It is apparent that the common occupation is a cohesive influence. The cohesion of farmers was exceeded only by that of Socialists (94.0) who were represented a portion of the time by only two members.

3. The laborites showed relatively low cohesion (68.0) although this was probably the result of their division between the Up-State and New York City wings of the Republican party. The Republican laborites showed considerably more likeness to the Socialists (52.9) than did the Republican farmers (36.5).

4. The several groups are arranged in the same order with respect to their cohesion whether all roll calls entering the study or only those concerning "state issues" are considered. In each case, however, the cohesion of the group is less in the case of "state issues." We may infer that local issues, particularly those affecting the city of New York, promote a more uniform response within each group than do issues of more general state-wide significance. It is probable that the long-standing quarrel between the city and the

Up-State districts tends to produce a more habitual response in each group whenever the issue is presented, whereas "state issues" are more likely to be considered upon their merits and hence produce a more varied response in each group.

5. Up-State Republicans show almost perfect cohesion (96.5) on the 59 roll calls specifically affecting New York City. They are considerably more united upon these matters than upon any other type of measures segregated, and considerably more united than are the Democrats (79.6). Hence it may be said that common attitudes regarding the affairs of New York City constitute the outstanding characteristic of the voting behavior of the Up-State Republicans. The New York City Republicans, on the contrary, occupy with regard to city issues the same intermediate position as a separate but not very cohesive group that they occupy upon questions generally.

6. The Assembly was more sharply divided on the issue of prohibition than on legislative issues as a whole. There were eight roll calls taken in which this issue was mainly involved. In each case Farmers (who were all Republicans) and Democrats were completely in agreement among themselves, but in *opposite directions*. That is, the index of likeness between Farmers and Democrats on this type of issue was 0.0.

Without further inferences from Tables III and IV, the writer hastens to a second illustration of the use of the two indices that have been described. This is found in an analysis of the votes of the so-called "progressive" or LaFollette bloc on the first fifty-four senatorial roll calls in the Sixty-eighth Congress.

The formal party affiliations of United States

Table IV—Indices of Likeness Between Various Groups in the New York Assembly, 1921

	1	2	3	4	6
Groups Compared		169 Roll Calls with 6 or More Opposing Votes	94 Roll Calls on "State Issues"	59 Roll Calls on New York City Issues	8 Roll Calls on Probition
Whole Assembly and Farmers		78.8	76.9	..	58.1
Whole Assembly and Laborites		86.6	85.4	..	95.1
Whole Assembly and Republicans		87.3	88.1	..	85.3
Whole Assembly and Democrats		49.5	53.0	..	41.9
Whole Assembly and Socialists		48.9	..	..	54.6
Republicans and Farmers		90.4	88.5	..	72.5
Republicans and Laborites		88.3	86.4	..	83.8
Farmers and Laborites		84.8	79.9	..	60.2
Socialists and Laborites		52.9	..	..	56.1
New York City Republicans and Up-State Republicans		74.4	70.8	75.5	20.6
New York City Republicans and Democrats		53.0	60.6	50.9	84.5
Farmers and Democrats		..	..	..	0.0
Farmers and Socialists		36.5	..	..	12.4
Republicans and Democrats		37.1	..	..	28.0

senators are of record. Their affiliations or sympathies with conservative, progressive or other blocs are not. On the basis of a variety of criteria, such as attendance at conferences of "progressives," the writer has segregated the following list of thirteen senators in the Sixty-eighth Congress, composed of six Republicans, five Democrats and two Farmer-Laborites: LaFollette, Frazier, Brookhart, Norris, Ladd and Borah, Republicans; Wheeler, Dill, Sheppard, Walsh of Massachusetts and Ashurst, Democrats; Shipstead and Johnson of Minnesota, Farmer-Laborites. For convenience this group of thirteen senators may be called "radical." Similarly, a larger list of twenty-two senators who may be termed "progressive" has been formed by the addition to the first thirteen of nine others with a reputation for progressive leanings, who failed, however, to meet the first criteria of selection. The "progressive" group thus includes the "radical." The various indices of cohesion that have been derived are shown in the following table:

Table V—Cohesion of Various Senatorial Groups in the Sixty-eighth Congress

Group	First 54 Roll Calls Taken in the Sixty-eighth Congress	47 Roll Calls Derived by Omitting 7 of Comparative Unimportance
The Senate as a whole	44.2	46.5
Democrats (all so listed)	63.6	63.1
Republicans (all so listed)	70.0	66.3
"Radical" group of 13	66.6	71.0
"Progressive" group of 22	62.7	67.2

It is apparent from Table V that when all fifty-four roll calls were considered, the "radical" and "progressive" blocs were slightly less cohesive than the Republicans, including under the latter term all who gave this as their party designation in the Congressional Directory. The "radical" bloc, however, was more cohesive than the Democrats. Among fifty-one non-unanimous roll calls, the "radical" bloc was more cohesive than either Republicans or Democrats in the case of eighteen, and more cohesive than (or equally cohesive as) at least one of these parties in the case of twenty roll calls additional, leaving thirteen or 25.5 per cent in which both parties exceeded the "radical" bloc in cohesion.

But among the fifty-four roll calls, some were of greater importance than others. In the last column of Table V will be found the indices of cohesion when seven roll calls upon such matters as the award of individual war pensions and the election of a doorkeeper to the senate were eliminated. In this column it will be discovered that

if the more important roll calls alone be considered, both "radical" and "progressive" blocs were more cohesive than either of the parties. It should be remembered that the insurgent tendencies of the progressive and radical senators tend to diminish the cohesion of the formal party organizations. It is probable, though it has not been determined, that the radicals were not so cohesive as the "regulars" in either of the old parties when taken by themselves. Nor has the writer employed the index of likeness to determine whether the radicals and progressives were more closely aligned to the Republican or the Democratic group, for it is hardly to be questioned that their affiliations were with the latter.

The illustrations that have preceded have been comparatively simple because they did not involve as variables the factors of party affiliations themselves. But suppose it is desired to compare the cohesion of two groups cutting unequally across party lines: for example, the cohesion of farmers and laborites when all farmers are Republicans while laborites are found in both parties. A higher index of cohesion among farmers in such a case would not be significant, for the major vote-determining influences are associated with party affiliation. At least one practicable means of eliminating the party variable when it is thought to invalidate the result is by the method of classification. Republican farmers may be compared with Republican laborites or with Democratic laborites, but not with a bi-partisan labor group. The indices of cohesion and of likeness gain significance (when the party variable is held constant in this manner) by comparison with the indices that would be *probable* on the basis of party affiliations alone. Thus it would be "expected" that the index of likeness between Republican farmers and Democratic laborites would equal the index of likeness between all Republicans and all Democrats if farmers and laborites constituted *random samples* of their respective parties. If in fact the former index is the smaller it is clear that farmers and laborites have a tendency to differ in their votes *relative to their party affiliations,* i. e., more than their party affiliations would call for. Similarly, the cohesion of Group A in Party X relative to the cohesion of X, when compared with the cohesion of Group B in Party Y relative to the cohesion of Y, will indicate whether A or B is the more cohesive relative to party affiliations.

When subordinate groups A and B are both wholly affiliated with Party X, a comparison of their respective indices of cohesion may be made directly. But it is not so simple to ascertain whether they are tending toward like or unlike voting behavior. At this point precision must be sought for the concept of "swing." Do A and B tend to "swing" in the same or in opposing directions within the common Party X? Are they, that is, in opposing wings or in the same wing of that party? If the number within the party be large as compared with the numbers in the subordinate groups, the "swing" may be safely determined by comparing the percentage of affirmative votes in the party group as a whole with the respective percentages of affirmative votes in the two subordinate groups. For example, in one roll call on the question of prohibition enforcement in the Pennsylvania House of Representatives of 1919 the Republican group with 175 members voting was 51.4 per cent in the affirmative on a particular presentation of the issue. Of seven Republican farmers, one, or 14.3 per cent was in the affirmative, while of eight Republican laborites, all or 100.0 per cent were in the affirmative. It will be clear that farmers and labor members, as occupational groups, "swung" to opposing wings of the common Republican party on this particular issue.

Similarly, it is found that the farmer and labor groups in the New York Assembly session analyzed above tended to swing to opposite wings of the common Republican party group in the larger number of roll calls taken. For reasons which need not be related here, exact measurement of the amount of swing is difficult, but a mere summation of the number of cases in which the swing is in the same direction as compared with the number in which it takes place in opposing directions, will usually suffice for the inquiry in hand.

Close adherence to the technique of comparing an actual index of cohesion or likeness with the index that would be expected on the basis of party affiliations alone, will provide the student with answers at once logical and quantitative to many common problems of group action in politics—problems now being approached by intuition and impression; in other words, on the basis of "hunch."[4]

Notes

1. *Cf.* the writer's note, "The Political Vote as a Frequency Distribution of Opinion," *Journal of the American Statistical Association*, March, 1924.
2. *Cf.* for example, "The Political Thought of Social Classes," by William F. Ogburn and Delvin Peterson, *Political Science Quarterly*, Vol. XXXI, pp. 300-317; "The Referendum in Washington," by Stuart A. Rice, *Proceedings of the National Conference of Social Work*, 1923, pp. 508-510.
3. The high degree of like-mindedness indicated by the large proportion of unanimous roll calls is illusory owing (a) to constitutional specification of the occasions on which roll calls must be taken in the passage of a measure, (b) to the legislative device for evading the constitution in this respect known as the "short roll call." A short roll call is almost invariably indicated when the recorded number of votes in opposition to the majority action is ten or less. To be recorded in opposition on a short roll call, the member must rise in his seat and so request after the presumptive roll has been taken. For a precedent for disregarding unanimous and near-unanimous roll calls, *cf.* A. Lawrence Lowell, "The Influence of Party upon Legislation in England and America" *Annual Report of the American Historical Association*, Vol. 1, 1901, pp. 321-542.
4. For a more thorough examination of the principles and limitations of the method he has sketched, as well as for further illustrative material, the writer must refer to chapter vi and the appendices of his study, *Farmers and Workers in American Politics*, Columbia Studies in History, Economics and Public Law (New York, Longmans, Green & Co., Agents, 1924).

4. A METHOD FOR DETERMINING THE SIGNIFICANCE OF ROLL CALLS IN VOTING BODIES

William H. Riker

IN THE NUMEROUS recent studies of voting behavior in legislatures, the question of deciding upon the relative significance of roll calls remains a persistent and unsolved methodological problem. Whether the analyst studies the cohesion of groups in the legislature, arranges legislators along a scale of opinion, or correlates legislative behavior with

Published for the first time in this volume.

external events, if roll calls are his basic data, he must choose some roll calls from among many for his study, deciding which are trivial and which are important.

The difficulty of making this choice has often been mentioned. Matthews, in a recent paper summarizing studies of voting behavior in Congress, remarks:[1]

The use of these techniques [i.e., to measure party unity, etc.] is far less automatic and objective than at first it seems. First there is the question of *weighting* the roll calls. [Emphasis in the original.] Oftentimes, numerous roll calls will be held on the same measure —the Congressmen and Senators dividing up much the same way each time. Other roll calls are held on insignificant matters. The kind of blocs found, the cohesion [or] likeness of parties or other groups, will depend to some extent on whether all roll calls or just the "important" ones are included in the computation.

Again, Shapley and Shubik, writing of the difficulty of computing an empirical power index to compare with the ingenious *a priori* index which they invented, remark:[2]

A difficulty in the application of the above measure [a suggested empirical index] is the problem of finding the correct weights to attach to the different issues. Obviously it would not be proper to take a uniform average over all votes, since there is bound to be a wide disparity in the importance of issues brought to a vote.

Until some means is found to distinguish objectively between trivial and non-trivial roll calls, all studies of legislative voting behavior are bound to be suspect. I offer here, therefore, a technique of weighting roll-calls according to a quasi-objective scale of significance. With appropriate modifications, this technique is, I believe, feasible for roll calls in all voting bodies. Although it would doubtless be preferable to present this technique in connection with a report on some empirical study, it is offered here and in isolation because the problem it purports to solve is a pressing one for many scholars.

There are two preliminary difficulties in weighting roll calls: (1) variations in judgment arising out of personal bias—the scholar weighting them by his own subjective judgment cannot be certain that his judgment will agree with anyone else's; and, (2) variations in judgment arising out of differences in the temporal location of the observer —he cannot even be certain that his own judgments at different times will agree with each other.

Concerning the second difficulty, it is apparent that judgments about roll calls vary over time. Some of the most controversial roll calls of, for example, the 1930's now seem quite unimportant, and, conversely, some of the least controversial now seem to have enduring importance. Thus, the roll calls by which riders were attached to WPA appropriations were among the most controversial of the era. But the WPA did not become a permanent feature of our politics and the issues arising out of it have faded in our complacent memories. To us now the enduring features of the New Deal

are such things as the Wagner Act and TVA —but when these went through Congress they were hardly controversial at all. It seems wise, therefore, to draw a distinction between the *significance* of a roll call, a judgment made at the time a roll call occurs, and the *importance* of a roll call, a judgment made at some time after it occurs. Because discussion of the importance of a roll call, involving an indefinite locus in time, is necessarily inexact and probably futile, the analysis which follows is limited to discussing the significance of roll calls.

But the first difficulty, variations in judgment arising out of personal bias, still remains. In order to minimize this distortion, one needs a measure of significance that does not depend entirely upon the judgment of any single person. One might arrive at such a measure by arranging for a group of informed observers to weight a series of roll calls. But, since for most legislatures there exist no informed observers except the members themselves, it is doubtful that a panel of experts could be brought together. And, since the observers cannot be expected to use identical standards of judgment, it is doubtful that an average of their weightings would mean anything at all.

It thus appears that the judgment both of the individual scholar and of any conceivable panel of outside experts is suspect. The only remaining persons available to evaluate the significance of roll calls are the members of the legislature themselves. Legislators perform as a matter of routine all that one might expect from a panel of experts: by reason of their membership they are forced to evaluate every—or nearly every—roll call. The judgments they render are, of course, as subjective as any that might be rendered by other persons; and so it might superficially appear that a measure of significance based on their judgment is valueless also because it also is distorted by bias. But it is both impossible and foolish to attempt to eliminate bias from judgments of significance. Significance involves meaning; and meaning must have reference to some persons. The problem is not to eliminate subjective judgment, but to select the persons whose subjective judgment will be used to weight roll calls. It seems intuitively justifiable that the persons whose judgments are so used ought to be those who, by their actions, make the significance, that is, the members of the legislature themselves.

It is, of course, ordinarily impossible to secure from *all* members of any legislature the kind of self-conscious rating of significance a panel of experts might provide. Nevertheless, legislators do make judgments of the significance of every roll call and they record these judgments in their actions. As Turner has pointed out,[3] by their very decision to hold a roll call vote, Congressmen differentiate between (1) motions deserving a roll call and (2) motions not deserving a roll call vote. For the purposes of Turner's study, this crude differentiation was sufficient and so he weighted all roll calls equally, remarking that for him, "Congress has solved the weighting problem."

Turner's method is not universally applicable, however. Although it avoids the subjectivity of the scholar, it fails to differentiate among the roll calls in the first category (those measures deserving a roll call vote), which are the very roll calls most recent work has been concentrated on and which most research workers wish to differentiate among. The problem, then, is to find some way of extracting from the record of legislators' behavior their own judgments concerning the relative significance of measures which deserved a roll call vote.

Two features about every roll call reflect the combined judgment of significance passed by members of the legislature: (1) the degree to which the members participate in a roll call, and, (2) the degree to which they contest its outcome.

Therefore, I suggest the following definitions: The *most significant* roll call possible is one in which (1) all members vote, and (2) the difference between the majority and minority is the minimum possible under the voting rules. Conversely, the *least significant* roll call is one in which (1) a bare quorum votes, and (2) the outcome is unanimous. Thus, in the House of Representatives on motions requiring at least 218 members voting to pass, the most significant roll call is one resulting in a count of 218-217, while the least significant is one resulting in a count of 218-0. All other possible roll call results may be ordered (by standards similar to those just set forth) on a scale between these two extremes. Such an ordering represents legislators' collective judgment, indexed by behavior rather than talk, of the relative significance of all roll calls.

In making this ordering, the scales for attendance and for uncertainty must be combined in such a way as to give a unique value for each possible outcome. A general formula for one such combination is set forth in Appendix I, and an example of this combination is set forth in Figure 1. In the latter, all possible outcomes when all members participate are entered in Row 1, all possible outcomes when all members except one participate, in Row 2, and so on. In each row, the most significant outcome of the row (in terms of degrees to which issue is contested) is entered in Column 1, while the least significant for that row is entered in Column 5. The last row is of course

that which contains outcomes in which only a bare quorum participated.

Each outcome in the matrix can be given a value consisting of the sum of the number of the row and the number of the column in which it appears. For example, in Figure 1, the outcome 7-1 (Row 2, Column 3) is given a value of $2 + 3 = 5$. The value thus given is unique along each row and down each column, but along the negative diagonals the values are identical. For example, in Figure 1, the outcomes 8-1, 7-1, 5-2, 4-2, all have the same value.

Figure 1—Example of the Matrix of Outcomes in a Simple Legislature

ROW NUMBER	COLUMN NUMBER				
	1	2	3	4	5
1	5-4	6-3	7-2	8-1	9-0
2	5-3	6-2	7-1	8-0	
3	4-3	5-2	6-1	7-0	
4	4-2	5-1	6-0		
5	3-2	4-1	5-0		

n = number of members = 9
t = a quorum = 5
r_i = number voting on a roll call
m = minimum necessary for victory = $[1/2 \ r_i] + 1$
$5 \leq r_i \leq 9$

In order to distinguish among these it is necessary to add an additional weighting factor based on attendance, a procedure which, while arbitrary, seems intuitively justifiable. This extra weight is the ratio of the row number to the number of rows plus one. Thus, in Figure 1, the value of the outcome 7-1 is $2 + 3 + 2/6 = 5 \ 1/3$. In Appendix I, it is proved that this procedure yields a unique value for each possible outcome in any legislature. In as much as an array of the sort in Figure 1 is not feasible for a large legislature, it is also proved in Appendix I that a unique value for each possible outcome is obtained from the formula,

$$v(a_{ij}) = n - q_{ij} - m + 2 + \frac{n - r_i + 1}{n - t + 2}$$

where "a_{ij}" is any possible outcome,
　"$v(a_{ij})$" is the value of a_{ij},
　"n" is the number of members of the legislature,
　"r_i" is the number voting on a roll call in which the outcome is a_{ij},
　"q_{ij}" is the number on the losing side of a_{ij},
　"m" is the minimum necessary for victory when r_i participate,
and "t" is a quorum.

From this formula for the value of a roll call

it is easy to define a relation of significance among roll calls. Using "S" to symbolize the relation of "more significant than," S may be defined thus:

$$\text{If } v(a_{ij}) < v(a_{ef}), \text{ then } a_{ij} \, S \, a_{ef}.$$

In graphic terms, if $a_{ij} \, S \, a_{ef}$, then either (1) a_{ij} is closer than a_{ef} to the upper left hand corner of the matrix of outcomes, or (2) a_{ij} and a_{ef} are equidistant from this corner but $i < e$.

This definition of significance can be used to advantage in any discussion of roll calls, even highly literary discussions of them. The definition of S is, however, applicable only to comparisons between roll calls in legislatures of exactly the same size. A measure for comparing roll calls in legislatures of different sizes may be defined as follows:

$$s = 1 - \frac{v(a_{ij}) - v(a_{11})}{v(a_{dg}) - v(a_{11})}; \quad O \leq s \leq 1;$$

where s is a coefficient of significance and $v(a_{dg})$ is the value of the least significant roll call possible in the matrix of outcomes. Note that, if $t = 1$, then $v(a_{dg}) = n + 1 + \frac{n}{n+1}$, which approaches $n + 2$.

There is substantial intuitive justification for using the foregoing definitions to arrive at the legislators' collective judgment of significance. The degree of attendance indicates their judgment on whether or not it is worthwhile to express an opinion on a motion—and this judgment, in turn, reflects pressures from party, constituency and other sources. The size of the margin between the majority and minority indicates the degree to which the outcome is uncertain—and presumably the greater the uncertainty, the greater also is the tension and enthusiasm surrounding a roll call.

There are, it is true, instances in which these measures are not wholly accurate. Attendance may be high for accidental reasons or deliberate abstentions may render the degree of participation lower than actual interest justifies. But in almost all such instances, the distortion introduced by artificially high or low attendance is balanced by a compensatory distortion in the measure of uncertainty.

When attendance is accidentally high (e.g., when just after a highly significant roll call, many members remain to vote on a second roll call simply because they happen to be on the floor), then the measure of participation makes a roll call seem more significant than it actually is in the opinion of the participants. Yet in such instances the outcome is not seriously contested. (If it were, the participants in the second roll call would be there out of interest in the outcome rather than out of the accident of previous attendance.) Hence, a distortion in one direction is balanced by a reverse distortion in the other; while the measure of significance is increased by attendance, it is decreased by roughly the same amount by the fact that the margin between majority and minority is larger than it might otherwise have been.[4]

If attendance is artificially low by reason of deliberate abstention (such as occurs when legislators subject to intense cross pressures evade voting or when a group of legislators abstain in order to express, not indifference, but discontent), the following situations may occur:

(1) The abstainers are those who, if they had voted, would have voted on the winning side, so their abstention did not affect the outcome of the vote. In this circumstance, while the measure of the significance of the roll call declines by reason of lessened attendance, the measure of significance increases by reason of the narrowing of the margin between the majority and minority. Hence abstention does not affect the reliability of the measure.

(2) The abstainers are those who, if they had voted, would have voted on the losing side, but their abstention did not affect the outcome of the vote. In this circumstance, the measure of significance declines because of both lessened attendance and widened margins between majority and minority, there is no compensatory effect in the measure of significance, and the proposed measure appears to fail to reflect adequately the judgment of legislators. This failure is, perhaps, more apparent than real. One finds in many instances that a dissident faction of a minority takes the liberty of expressing its discontent only on those measures the outcome of which it knows it is unable to affect. On measures where there is a chance of the minority growing into a majority, the dissidents of the minority are probably not so prone to express their discontent in action. It may well be, therefore, that roll calls containing abstentions of this sort are properly measured by the coefficient of significance. If they were more significant in the opinion of legislators, the dissidents of the minority would not abstain.

(3) The abstainers are those who, if they had voted, would have voted with the losing side; and, if they had so voted, the losing side would have become the winning side. Here there at first appears little doubt that the measure of significance fails to reflect adequately the opinion of legislators. Imagine a nine-member legislature in which the members are divided four to three, with two abstainers who, if they had voted, would have voted with the minority. In such circumstances, the effect of abstention is to lower the coefficient

of significance from 1 to .65. Note, however, that the abstainers sacrifice their desired outcome on the roll call for their desired influence of their colleagues of the minority (or colleagues of the might-have-been majority). The only reasonable way to explain such behavior is to say that the abstainers value the effect of their abstention more than the effect of their vote. And this is another way of saying that they do not value their vote on this issue as highly as the effects of abstention. One cannot evade the conclusion, therefore, that the vote in itself is not of the highest significance, and may be properly described by a coefficient of significance of .65. Once again, therefore, the appearance of a distortion in the measure of significance is largely illusory.

Some intuitive indication of the accuracy of this measure of significance may be obtained from Figure 2, where the coefficient of significance, s, has been calculated for all presidential elections from 1888 to 1956, thus treating elections as roll calls of the whole nation. In these calculations it was assumed that t (a quorum) $= 1$, that n consisted of the adult citizens (prior to 1920, the adult male citizens) minus varying adjustments for adult negroes residing in the eleven states of the old confederacy, and that $m = \frac{r_i}{2} + 1$, except in the three-party elections of 1892, 1912, and 1924, when $m = \frac{r_i}{3} + 1$. By reason of the vast change in n in 1920 and by reason of the fact that women have only gradually come to exercise their right of suffrage, the coefficients before and after 1920 are incomparable. Within these two time periods, however, it is fairly clear that the relative values of s agree with the intuitive judgments of most historians. It is especially interesting that the election of 1896 is the most significant in the period 1888 to 1916 and the election of 1940 is the most significant in the period 1920 to 1956. Speaking as a historian rather than a statistician, the election of 1896 with its rejection of the agrarian radicalism of the South and West has always seemed to me to be the definitive triumph of the Republican Party in the post civil war era, while the election of 1940 with its issues of third term and war has always seemed to me the definitive vindication of the New Deal. The fact that the literary and statistical judgments bear each other out lends validity to each of them.

The calculations of Figure 2 are presented because most readers are equipped to consider intuitively the accuracy of s in relation to presidential elections. Nevertheless, s was not devised for this measurement and it is only with some distortion that it can be so used. Rather, s was designed to compare roll calls in an assembly. Even though fewer readers are equipped to make intuitive judgments about the relative significance of legislative roll calls, Figure 3 presents the coefficient of significance for the most significant roll calls in the Senate in the second session of the 83rd Congress (1954). While some may wish to argue about the ratings of some of these roll calls, it is again, I believe, fairly clear that these coefficients agree in the main with the intuitive judgments of experienced observers of Congress.

The absence from Figure 3 of any roll call concerned with the censure of Senator McCarthy may occasion some surprise, although reflection will convince most of the surprised ones that censure had ceased to be "important" by the time it came to vote. Most of the subjects actually included in Figure 3—income tax relief, the Bricker Amendment, and agricultural price supports—were the most controversial subjects of debate in the whole session. Only one item, the proposed amendment of the Taft-Hartley Act, seems out of place. I suspect its significance is high simply because anything connected with that exceptionally controversial statute is politically important in this era. Possibly the most interesting feature of this list is the fact that, of the four roll calls arising out of the Bricker Amendment, the one that stands highest concerns a motion for adjournment. Traditionally, motions for adjournments, when not offered by the majority leader for the purpose of adjourning, lead to some of the most "important" roll calls. Once again, literary and statistical judgments bear each other out.

In the application of the coefficient of significance to roll calls in particular legislatures, numerous institutional problems will inevitably arise. While the solution of them properly rests with those scholars who actually use this technique to study legislative behavior, still some comments on institutional problems seems in order—if only as an indication of the way this technique of measurement can be put to use.

Figure 2—Coefficient of Significance for Presidential Elections, 1888-1956

Year	Coefficient of Significance	Year	Coefficient of Significance
1888	.830	1920	.410
1892	.698	1924	.379
1896	.845	1928	.536
1900	.786	1932	.554
1904	.657	1936	.580
1908	.696	1940	.634
1912	.645	1944	.583
1916	.757	1948	.560
		1952	.621
		1956	.587

(1) In legislatures where party discipline is almost always strict and consequently legislators do not cross party lines in voting, the ratio between the majority and minority is usually about the same during one session. Hence variations in the coefficient of significance consist largely of variations in attendance. And since in such legislatures attendance is usually well enforced by party whips, the variation in the coefficient of significance from roll call to roll call is not very large. This means that, in legislatures with a well disciplined two party system, small variations in the measure must be accorded greater respect than in legislatures with more than two parties or with poorly disciplined parties. Yet small variations in the measure may occur by reason of irrelevant influences such as the time of day at which roll calls occur or the existence of an influenza epidemic. Owing to this possible distortion, the measure of significance requires much more literary interpretation in legislatures with two (and only two) well disciplined parties than in other legislatures. Yet even in legislatures with two well disciplined

parties, the measure of significance is exceptionally useful to highlight those roll calls in which a break in party discipline either increases or decreases the closeness of the margin.

(2) In many legislatures on some roll calls, the behavior of some legislators does not indicate their judgment of significance, but rather indicates the presence of entirely irrelevant considerations. For example, there was in the Tennessee legislature recently a wily old hand who repeatedly changed his vote on roll calls where there was a fairly wide margin between the majority and the minority. On investigation, this curious behavior turned out to be a test by the changeling of whether or not a pair of young and new legislators from neighboring counties were obeying the instructions of their county party leaders to follow the voting pattern of the old hand. Reports of students of American state legislatures suggest that similarly irrelevant considerations affect the outcome of roll calls in all parts of the country. Manifestly, if irrelevancies influence voting in a considerable degree, as I am convinced they do in some legislatures, then the coefficient of significance, which assumes rational behavior, is hardly a reliable measure of significance. When studying such legislatures, the scholar who uses this measure must, of course, take irrelevancies into consideration.

(3) In some legislatures there exist what appear to be institutional features that can be used to differentiate among roll calls. For example, when the executive is permitted to label some roll calls as votes of confidence, then those so labelled may be regarded as the most significant roll calls in a session. The existence of labelling seems an easier and superficially more realistic test of significance than the coefficient. The very act of labelling may, however, have direct consequences on the outcome. Probably in most instances, the labelling increases attendance. In some instances it may increase the margin between the majority and minority over what the margin would have been had the label not been attached. In other instances it may decrease the margin from what it might have been. In short, the labelling process may turn what promises to be an insignificant roll call into a significant one or what promises to be a highly significant roll call into an insignificant one. Thus, the labelling may have consequences which themselves deserve to be measured and the coefficient of significance is designed for just such a purpose. For example, it may be used to discover the relative significance of two or more votes of confidence.

*   *   *

It should be apparent that the coefficient of significance cannot be used in a wholly mechanistic

Figure 3[5]—Roll Calls with Coefficients of Significance Greater than .9 in U. S. Senate, 83rd Congress, 2nd Session

Coefficient of Significance	Subject of Roll Call	Page of Journal
.9719	Revision of Internal Revenue Code—motion to amend to raise personal exemption to $700 and for those over 65 to $1400	425
.9719	Revision of Internal Revenue Code—motion to amend to raise personal exemption to $700	424
.9436	Consideration of Bricker Amendment—motion to adjourn	152
.9297	Consideration of Bricker Amendment—vote on final passage	154
.9294	Consideration of Agriculture Appropriation Act—motion to support price of milk at 90% of parity	618
.9284	Consideration of Agriculture Appropriation Act—motion to raise support from 80% to 82.5% of parity in certain instances	617
.9283	Consideration of Agriculture Appropriation Act—motion to raise support from 82.5% to 90% of parity for cooperators	617
.9155	Consideration of Agriculture Appropriation Act—motion to support price of milk at 90% of parity	618
.9027	Consideration of Bricker Amendment—motion to amend	144
.9016	Consideration of Bricker Amendment—motion to amend	154
.9016	Motion to recommit bill to amend Taft-Hartley Act of 1947	289
.9007	Consideration of Agriculture Appropriation Act—motion to limit power of Secretary of Agriculture over county committees	627

manner. It was developed with the situation in the United States Congress in mind and, on account of its origin, probably measures Congressional behavior better than behavior in other legislatures. Nevertheless, with some adjustment and interpretation, it can be used in the study of any legislature. And while it is not completely automatic, it still can eliminate many doubts that have arisen around all previous roll call studies.

Appendix[6]

Define:

1. A set, N: $\{1, 2, \cdots, n\}$, (a legislature)
2. An integer, t, such that $1 < t < n$, and such that, if c is a constant (where $0 \le c \le 1$), then, if cn is an integer, $t = cn$, and if cn is not an integer, $t = [cn] + 1$ (t is a quorum).
3. A set, N': $\{r_i\}$, where $i = 1, 2, \cdots$, d, and where $r_i = n$, $r_2 = n - 1, \cdots, r_d = n - t + 1$ (r_i is the number voting on a roll call).
4. For each r_i, a set, A_i: $\{a_{i1}, a_{i2}, \cdots, a_{ig}\}$, where a_{ij} is an ordered pair of integers, (p_{ij}, q_{ij}), such that $p_{ij} + q_{ij} = r_i$, and such that, by the rules of the set N, p_{ij} is defined as the size of the winning coalition and q_{ij} is defined as the size of losing coalition; and where $p_{i1} = m$, $p_{i2} = m + 1, \cdots, p_{ig} = r_i$, where m satisfies the conditions of (5) below.
5. An integer, m such that m is determined by a constant, k (where $0 \le k \le 1$), and either r_i or n. (In cases (1)-(4) below, m is the size of the winning coalition. In cases (5)-(7), m is the size of minimum blocking coalition.) If m is determined by r_i,
   (1) if $k > 1/2$ and if kr_i is an integer, $m = kr_i$
   (2) if $k > 1/2$ and if kr_i is not an integer, $m = [kr_i] + 1$
   (3) if $k = 1/2$ and if r_i is odd, $m = [kr_i] + 1$
   (4) if $k = 1/2$, if r_i is even and if the rules of N provide for a casting vote, $m = kr_i + 1$

   (5) if $k = 1/2$, and if kr_i is even, and if the rules of N do not provide for a casting vote, $m = kr_i$
   (6) if $k < 1/2$, and if kr_i is an integer, $m' = kr_i$ and $m = r_i - m' + 1$
   (7) if $k < 1/2$, and if kr_i is not an integer, $m' = kr_i + 1$ and $m = r_i - m' + 1$.

N.B.: A note on the calculation of m for real legislatures:

   (a) if $k > 1/2$ and the nays win, use 5(6) or 5(7) and substitute k' (where $k' = 1 - k$) for k.
   (b) if $k > 1/2$ and the yeas win, use 5(1) or 5(2).
   (c) if $k = 1/2$ and the yeas win, use 5(3) or 5(4).
   (d) if $k = 1/2$ and the nays win, use 5(3) or 5(4); except, when N lacks rules for breaking ties, use 5(5).
   (e) if, as in the UN Security Council, the rules of N require that some $p \epsilon N$ vote yea for a measure to pass, and if it passes, use 5(1) or 5(5). If it does not pass, use 5(6), with $k = 1/n$ and r_i replaced by n.

If m is determined by n, the foregoing definitions stand with "n" substituted for "r_i."

6. A value, $v(a_{ij})$, for each a_{ij}:

$$v(a_{ij}) = n - q_{ij} - m + 2 + \frac{n - r_i + 1}{n - t + 2}$$

Theorem: $v(a_{ij})$ is unique.
Proof: Order all a_{ij} in an array, thus:

1. For each a_{ij}, i is the row number: $i = n - r_i + 1$
2. For each a_{ij}, j is the column number: $j = p_{ij} - m + 1$
3. The sum, $i + j$, yields a unique value for each $a_{ij} \epsilon A_i$ and for each a_{ij} in column j. For each pair, $(a_{ij}, a_{i+1, j-1})$, however, $i + j = (i + 1) + (j - 1)$.

	Col. 1 $p_{i1} = m$	Col. 2 $p_{i2} = m + 1$	Col. j $p_{ij} = m + j - 1$	Cols. $g, g', \cdots, g''$ $p_{ig} = r_i$
Row 1 $r_1 = n$	a_{11}	a_{12} $\cdots$	a_{1j}	$\cdots\cdots$ $a_{1g'''}$
Row 2 $r_2 = n - 1$	a_{21}	a_{22} $\cdots$	a_{2j}	$\cdots\cdots$ $a_{2g''}$
Row i $r_i = i$	a_{i1}	a_{i2} $\cdots$	a_{ij}	$\cdots$ $a_{ig'}$
Row d $r_d = n - t + 1$	a_{d1}	a_{d2} $\cdots$	a_{dj}	$\cdots$ a_{dg}

4. For each A_i, the fraction, h_i, where $h_i = \dfrac{n - r_i + 1}{n - t + 2}$, is unique, in as much as the numerator is the row number and the denominator is the number of rows plus one.

5. The sum, $i + j + h$, yields a unique value for each a_{ij} even in the case of the pair $(a_{ij}, \ a_{i+1, \ j-1})$, for $i + j + h_i \neq (i + 1) + (j - 1) + h_{i+1}$.

6. $i + j + h_i = (n - r_i + 1) + (p_{ij} - m + 1) + \dfrac{n - r_i + 1}{n - t + 2}$

$= n - p_{ij} - q_{ij} + 1 + p_{ij} - m + 1 + \dfrac{n - r_i + 1}{n - t + 2}$

$= n - q_{ij} - m + 2 + \dfrac{n - r_i + 1}{n - t + 2}$

$= v(a_{ij})$

Q.E.D.

Notes

1. Donald R. Matthews, *The Dynamics of Voting Behavior in National Legislatures: The American Congress* (mimeo, 1957, presented at the American Political Science Association Annual Meeting, New York City), pp. 3-4. Other participants in the panel at which Matthews' paper was read also emphasized the difficulty of distinguishing among trivial and important roll calls, not only in the United States Congress but also in the French National Assembly, the British House of Commons, and American state legislatures.

2. L. S. Shapley and Martin Shubik, "A Method of Evaluating the Distribution of Power in a Committee System," *American Political Science Review*, Vol. 48 (1954), pp. 787-792.

3. Julius Turner, "Party and Constituency: Pressures on Congress," *Johns Hopkins Studies in Historical and Political Science*, Vol. 49 (1951), pp. 1-190, at p. 20.

4. Note that this compensation is rather more likely to occur in legislatures, such as those in the United States, where the parties are not well disciplined, than in legislatures, such as those in England, where the parties display a very high index of cohesion in roll calls.

5. I am indebted to my former student, Mr. Peter Dohr, for the calculations in Figure 3.

6. I am indebted to my colleague, Professor Andrew Berry for suggestions about the form of the statements in this appendix.

5. A STUDY OF CONSISTENCY IN CONGRESSIONAL VOTING

Dean R. Brimhall and

Arthur S. Otis

CAN WE PREDICT from the past record of a congressman how he will vote in the future? The answer is yes—to a very marked degree.

This answer is based on a careful study of the votes cast by 512 congressmen on important propositions during the past five years.

Let us say that a congressman's position on a scale from *liberal* to *conservative* is represented by assigning him a scale value from 1 to 7, the value 1 representing the most liberal position and 7 the most conservative position, as shown in Figure 1. Then we may say, briefly, that if each congressman is given a scale value each year to represent his position on the scale for that year, there are 46 chances in 100 that his scale value will not change from one year to the next; there are 83 chances in 100 that his scale value will not

Reprinted from *Journal of Applied Psychology*, Vol. 32 (1948), pp. 1-7, 14, where it appeared under the title, "Consistency of Voting by Our Congressmen," by permission of the authors and the publisher.

change more than 1 unit from one year to the next; and there are 95 chances in 100 that his scale value will not change more than 2 units. The maximum change possible would be 6 units.

Source of the Data. The data upon which the study was based were reported in the *New Republic*. In various past issues the vote of each congressman is given for each of a number of important propositions on which a roll call was had.

Figure 1—Showing Seven Positions Along a Scale from Liberal to Conservative

In the case of each proposition the vote of each congressman was recorded as follows:

+ = a "progressive" vote, according to the

opinion of the editors of the *New Republic;*

— = an "anti-progressive" vote;

0 = absence or "paired."

For example the votes of the Arkansas senators on the 10 propositions reported on August 4, 1947, were recorded as shown in Table 1.

Table 1—Manner of Reporting Votes

Proposition	1	2	3	4	5	6	7	8	9	10
Arkansas										
Fulbright	+	—	+	+	+	0	+	+	—	+
McClellan	—	—	+	—	+	—	+	+	—	+

The table shows that in the opinion of the editors, Senator Fulbright voted "progressively" on Proposition 1, voted "anti-progressively" on Proposition 2, voted "progressively" on Propositions 3, 4, and 5, was absent or paired on Proposition 6, etc.

For convenience the data were grouped and designated as shown in Table 2.

Table 2—Source of Data

PERIOD	DATES OF REPORTS	NUMBER OF PROPOSITIONS Senate	NUMBER OF PROPOSITIONS House	DESIGNATION ADOPTED
I	May 8, 1944	18	18	"1944"
II	Feb. 4, 1945	5	6	"1945"
	Feb. 11, 1946	10	10	
III	Sept. 23, 1946	14	15	"1946"
IV	Aug. 4, 1947	10	10	"1947"
	Total	57	59	

Since the propositions reported upon were not the same for the House and Senate, a separate study was made for each legislative body. The study of the voting of senators is described first.

"Progressiveness" Expressed as a Per Cent. First, a percentage rating was obtained for each senator for each period by finding the number of votes cast by a senator during that period and then finding what percentage of these were "progressive" votes.

For example, if, during Period I, a senator voted on 15 of the 18 propositions and voted "progressively" on 12 of these 15, his percentage ratings for that period was 12/15, or 80%.

Assigned Scale Values. The percentage rating of each senator for each of the four periods was then converted into a scale value according to Table 3.

To assign these scale values it was necessary to find the distribution of percentage ratings and so arrange them in order.

Table 3—Scale Values

Highest seventh of the percentages	1
Next highest seventh percentages	2
Next highest seventh percentages	3
Next highest seventh percentages	4
Next highest seventh percentages	5
Next highest seventh percentages	6
Lowest seventh of the percentages	7

For purposes of assigning these scale values, use was made of the percentage ratings of only those senators who were present in all four periods. There were 57 such senators, as may be determined from Table 4.

The highest seventh of the 57 percentage ratings in Period I were, respectively, 100%, 100%, 94%, 94%, 94%, 94%, 93%, and 92%. These were therefore assigned the scale value 1. The percentages constituting the next highest seventh were 85%, 81%, 76%, 76%, 76%, 75%, 71%, and 63%. These were assigned the scale value 2. Those constituting the next seventh were assigned the scale value 3, and so on.

Table 4—Scale Values of Senators

	I 1944	II 1945	III 1946	IV 1947	Avg.
Alabama					
Hill	3	2	2	1	2
Arizona					
Hayden	2	2	2	2	2
McFarland	2	2	3	3	3
Arkansas					
Fulbright			3	2	2
McClellan	6	4	4	3	4
California					
Downey	1	1	1	2	1
*Knowland			3	4	4
Colorado					
Johnson	3	3	2	3	3
*Millikin	7	7	7	5	6
Connecticut					
McMahon			1	2	2
Delaware					
*Buck	7	7	6	7	7
Tunnell	1	2	1		
Florida					
Andrews	3	5	5		
Pepper	1	1	1	1	1
Georgia					
George	5	4	5	4	4
Russell	4	2	4	3	3
Idaho					
Taylor		1	1		1
Illinois					
*Brooks	6	6	6	7	6
Lucas	2	2	2	2	2

Table 4 (continued)

	I 1944	II 1945	III 1946	IV 1947	Avg.
Indiana					
*Capehart			5	7	6
*Willis	7	5	5		
Iowa					
*Hickenlooper			5	6	6
*Wilson	6	6	4	5	5
Kansas					
*Capper	4	4	6	6	6
*Reed	6	6	6	6	6
Kentucky					
Barkley	1	1	2	1	1
Louisiana					
Ellender	2	3	3	4	3
Overton	6	3	4	4	4
Maine					
*Brewster	4	6	5	7	6
*White	5	7	7	7	7
Maryland					
Radcliffe	2	4	4		
Tydings	5	4	5	3	4
Massachusetts					
*Saltonstall			3	5	4
Walsh	4	2	2		
Michigan					
*Ferguson	5	5	3	5	5
*Vandenberg	3	5	4	5	4
Minnesota					
*Ball	2	4	4	4	4
*Shipstead	4	4	4		
Mississippi					
Bilbo	4	4	5	7	5
Eastland	5	4	5	3	4
Missouri					
*Donnell			3	5	4
Montana					
Murray	1	1	1	1	1
Wheeler	5	4	3		
Nebraska					
*Butler	5	6	6	6	6
*Wherry	7	5	6	6	6
Nevada					
McCarran	3	4	3	4	4
New Hampshire					
*Bridges	5	6	7	6	6
*Tobey	4	3	3	3	3
New Jersey					
*Hawkes	7	7	7	6	7
*Smith		4	4	5	4
New Mexico					
Chavez	4	2	1	2	2
Hatch	2	2	2	3	2
New York					
Mead	1	1	1		
Wagner	1	1	1	1	1
North Carolina					
Bailey	5	6	5		
Hoey			4	4	4

Table 4 (continued)

	I 1944	II 1945	III 1946	IV 1947	Avg.
North Dakota					
*Langer	2	3	3	2	2
*Young			6	5	5
Ohio					
*Taft	5	5	4	7	5
Oklahoma					
*Moore	7	7	7	6	7
Thomas	3	4	4	2	3
Oregon					
*Cordon		5	4	7	6
*Morse		2	2		2
Pennsylvania					
Guffey	1	1	1		
Myers		1	2		2
Rhode Island					
Gerry	6	5	6		
Green	1	1	1	1	1
South Carolina					
Johnston			4	2	3
Maybank	3	3	4	3	3
South Dakota					
*Bushfield	7	7	7	6	7
*Gurney	4	6	7	5	5
Tennessee					
McKellar	5	4	3	5	4
Stewart	3	4	4	5	4
Texas					
Connally	5	5	6	4	5
O'Daniel	6	7	6	6	6
Utah					
Murdock	1	1	2		
Thomas	1	2	1	1	1
Vermont					
*Aiken	3	2	2	3	3
*Austin	3	5	4		
Virginia					
Byrd	6	6	4	5	5
Washington					
Magnuson		2	1	2	2
Mitchell		1	1		
West Virginia					
Kilgore	1	1	1	1	1
*Revercomb	7	6	4	6	6
Wisconsin					
LaFollette	2	2	1		
*Wiley	4	5	6	7	6
Wyoming					
O'Mahoney	2	3	3	2	2
*Robertson	7	7	7	6	7

The scale values for the four periods for the various senators are shown in Table 4. This table contains the names of only those senators who were present during at least two of the four periods. The starred senators are Republicans.

In order to present a single comprehensive

scale value for each such senator, Table 4 shows also the *average* scale value for each senator who was present in Period IV.

Consistency in Voting. A glance at Table 4 will show that there is a marked degree of consistency in the scale values. Note for example how Hayden of Arizona got 2, 2, 2, 2, for the four periods.

To obtain a measure of consistency of voting, each scale value was compared with the one preceding, to see whether it was the same or whether it differed by one unit or two units or three units.

Thus, Hill of Alabama shifted first from 3 to 2 (one unit of change), then repeated the 2 (zero units of change) and then shifted from 2 to 1 (one unit). In this way the 218 shifts were noted. They are shown in Table 5.

Table 5 is read as follows. There were 90 instances in which the shift was zero units; that is, in which the scale value remained the same as it was the year before. These 90 cases were 41% of the 218 shifts. There were 91 instances (42% of the 218) in which the shift in scale value was only one unit. The 41% and 42% together made 83% of cases in which the shift was not over one

Table 5—*Shifts in Scale Values of Senators from One Period to the Next*

Amount of Shift	No. of Cases	Per Cent	Sub-total
0 units	90	41	41
1 unit	91	42	83
2 units	34	16	99
3 units	3	1	100
Total	218	100	

unit. There were 34 instances (16% of the 218) in which the shift was two units, making 99% of cases in which the shift was not over 2 units. In only 3 cases (about 1%) were the shifts as much as 3 units, as from 4 to 1.

The following are the three senators who shifted 3 units: Overton of Louisiana, 6 to 3; Taft of Ohio, 4 to 7; and Cordon of Oregon, 4 to 7.

The following senators maintained the same scale value throughout the four periods:

Hayden, Arizona	2	2	2	2
Pepper, Florida	1	1	1	1
Lucas, Illinois	2	2	2	2
Reed, Kansas	6	6	6	6
Murray, Montana	1	1	1	1
Wagner, New York	1	1	1	1
Green, Rhode Island	1	1	1	1
Kilgore, W. Va.	1	1	1	1

The Representatives. A comparable study was made of the consistency of voting of the representatives. The degree of consistency of voting by representatives is shown in Table 6 which is comparable to Table 5.

Table 6 is read as follows: Of the 1076 shifts made by the representatives (in most cases 3 shifts by each), 504, or 47%, were zero units—no shift at all; 391, or 36%, were shifts of one unit, making 83% of cases in which the shift was not over one unit; 127, or 12%, were shifts of two units, etc.

Table 6—*Shifts of Scale Values of Representatives from One Period to the Next*

Amount of Shift	No. of Cases	Per Cent	Sub-total
0 units	504	47	47
1 unit	391	36	83
2 units	127	12	95
3 units	46	4.2	99.2
4 units	7	0.7	99.9
5 units	1	0.1	100.0
Total	1076	100.0	

The representative who made a shift of 5 units was Winstead of Mississippi, who shifted from 7 in "1946" to 2 in "1947."

Table 7 shows the data of Tables 5 and 6 combined; that is, for congressmen of both houses together.

Table 7—*Shifts in Scale Values of Senators and Representatives Together*

Amount of Shift	No. of Cases	Per Cent	Sub-total
0 units	594	46	46
1 unit	482	37	83
2 units	161	12	95
3 units	49	4	99
4 units	7	0.5	
5 units	1	0.1	

Table 7 shows that, as stated at the outset, there are 46 chances in 100 that a congressman's scale value will not change at all from any given year to the next; there are 83 chances in 100 that his scale value will not change more than one unit; and there are 95 chances in 100 that his scale value will not change more than 2 units.

The chances are less than 1 in 100 that a congressman's scale value will change more than three units out of a possible 6 units of change; and there is less than 1 chance in 1000 that a congressman's scale value will change 5 units.

6. SCALING LEGISLATIVE BEHAVIOR

George M. Belknap

ATTEMPTS TO SECURE reliable scientific laws about political behavior involve certain persistent problems regardless of what specific behavior is under examination. One of the problems is the development and refinement of concepts which will guide our observations and our analyses of data. Another involves the development of research methods which will enable us to relate our concepts to empirical observations. Conceptual and methodological inquiry go hand in hand. Talcott Parsons emphasizes this point in saying:

"The ideal is to have theoretical categories of such a character that the empirical values of the variables concerned are the immediate products of our observational procedures. In relatively few fields of social science is any close approach to this yet possible, but with further development both on the theoretical side and in the invention of new observational and experimental procedures great progress in this direction is to be expected."[1]

This paper deals with some methodological and conceptual problems in political science research. The two major objectives are to clarify certain key concepts in the study of political behavior and to establish a measurement scheme which will relate the concepts to ordered empirical observations. Legislative behavior was chosen for the first attack on these problems.

The legislative body is posited as an important area of behavior affecting what Easton calls "the authoritative allocation of values for a society."[2] The behaviors of legislators are clearly consequential in the determination of such value allocations as tax relief, social services, and security from foreign threat. The legislative body is seen also as a social system involving structured sets of behavior. The posited structure implies that uniformities can be traced in the legislative sub-set of all the behaviors which determine our value allocations. Having focused our inquiry on the part of the political process called the legislative process (and leaving for separate consideration the relations of the legislative process to other areas of

the political process), we can restate our objectives in terms of the legislative analysis.

(1) How can we isolate regularities in legislative behavior by the use of available or procurable data?

(2) How can we analyze these data in order to provide information on groups as well as on the individuals forming them?

(3) How can we communicate findings on individual and group legislative behavior through an unambiguous notation system? In other words, how can we symbolize through words or mathematical symbols the behavioral uniformities observed?

(4) How can we use our empirical orderings to clarify various concepts in legislative research?

A related objective achieved through viewing legislative behavior in the context of the total political process is the relation of the dependent variables of legislative behavior to such "outside" variables as constituency and group.

Approaches to the Study of Legislative Behavior. Before tackling these problems in legislative analysis, let us look at various approaches to the study of this part of the political process. One is the detailed, intensive examination of a legislative body as it performs certain characteristic functions. This approach, exemplified by Bailey's study of Congress,[3] resembles that of the anthropologist whose highly empirical research amasses large amounts of detailed information about a tribe, a clan, or a culture. Another approach is the study of key legislative positions, their development, and their functions in legislative life. Another involves the analysis of sub-groups of legislatures, especially committees. Still another approach, the most extensive of the three, is the study of general trends in the behavior of entire legislative bodies.

Each of these approaches calls for different research methods. The highly detailed empirical examination of the legislative body as a "society" requires the collection of large quantities of information about the functions of the society. It attempts to give a "full picture" of the actions within it, if only for a short period of time. Highly intensive studies of key offices or positions use institutional analysis of the offices and psycho-

Reprinted from *Midwest Journal of Political Science,* II (1958), 377-402, where it appeared under the title, "A Method for Analyzing Legislative Behavior," by permission of the author and the publisher.

logical analysis of the office holders. The legislative committee (a face-to-face group within the legislature) seems ideally suited for small-group analysis and sociometric delineation of the behaviors of group members. Ralph Huitt[4] and others seem to be working in this direction.

The method described here is suitable for *extensive* legislative analysis. It isolates regularities in the behavior of individual legislators, expresses the regularities within a group context, and provides a notation scheme for communicating the empirical regularities. Another function of the method is the isolation of behaviors which are deviant relative to the general trends which are observed.

The advantages of a mathematical approach to behavior analysis as presented here are numerous. As Stuart Rice has pointed out, "the quantitative expression of a social fact is to be preferred for scientific purposes whenever it can be used. It reduces individual bias to a minimum, permits verification by other investigators, reduces and at the same time makes evident the margin of error, and replaces the less exact meaning of descriptive words with the precision of mathematical notation."[5] Especially important in legislative analysis is the fact that the uses of mathematical approaches to behavioral analyses *are not* limited to quantification. Kurt Lewin states: "Mathematics handles quantity *and* quality . . . qualitative differences themselves can and should be approached mathematically."[6]

Some General Measurement Problems in Legislative Analysis. Most measurements of legislative behavior have involved the assigning of class scores on series of legislative roll calls. The word "class" is used here since we are referring to such formal aggregates as members of a particular political party, people coming from the same region, etc. We can thus reserve the term "group" for those persons who exhibit one or more common characteristics on the behavioral variables of central interest.

Classes are measured by indices such as those proposed by Stuart Rice,[7] Key,[8] Turner[9] and Grassmuck.[10] The classes for which these measures are computed are sub-sets of legislative bodies. So long as our interests are in descriptions of important classes within a legislature, (common party, common section, etc.) in terms of gross characteristics, then class scores are adequate. As Turner and others have shown, these measures help answer many significant questions about our national political parties and about other important factors affecting legislative behavior.

There are, however, some problems in extensive legislative analysis which call for measurements of the behavior of *individual* legislators. An example of an individual measure is the "liberalism-conservatism" score which is usually determined subjectively.[11] Another method of deriving individual scores is with reference to class tendencies. The most common example of the latter is a party-loyalty index. Our procedure here will be to establish individual and group measures simultaneously.

One advantage of using individual rather than class scores is analogous to the advantage of using statistics on people (as in a sample survey) over demographic statistics (as in a census tract). No matter how small the class or demographic unit, the people composing it will not be homogeneous enough to allow us to control statistically variables other than the ones under examination, and, since our generalizations are implicitly about people, the analysis unit of the person gets us more directly and less inferentially to him. Equally important is the fact that an individual score when expressed with relation to group tendencies allows us to study the individual and the group jointly.

Many of the individual measures which are needed for legislative analysis are readily assigned. Biographical data are available on party affiliation, length of time in the legisltive body, holding of important positions, etc. And since a legislator under our system represents a geographical unit, measures of that unit are assignable to a legislator in many studies.[12] If one specifies as his universe of analysis, the membership of a legislative body, statements about the voting behavior of the population are likely to be expressed as the *dependent* variables of the study. Measurements on the independent variables (personality, socio-economic constituency characteristics, etc.) are not our concern here. It is the dependent variables which pose the major measurement problem in legislative analysis. Subjective scores on "liberal-conservative" or "isolationist-interventionist" based on one's own judgment of which legislative votes are "liberal," "isolationist," etc., are not likely to be generally accepted by other investigators. And if we deal only with specific pieces of legislation, our results will have no general applicability. Our central problem is to establish generally acceptable yardsticks of legislative behavior which will cover significant areas of legislative action.

Scale analysis in psychology and sociology has helped solve analogous problems in those fields. It is possible to view a legislative vote as similar to a single response to a single question on a questionnaire. Then we find that the development of attitude scales covering various areas of attitude content suggests a solution to the problem of establishing standards for measuring legislative behavior. As early as 1924, Stuart Rice demonstrated the use of the legislative vote as an opinion index.[13] Using a series of legislative votes to form a behavioral scale analogous to the attitude scale which one forms from a series of attitude questions is only an extension of Rice's idea.

The Concept of Unidimensionality. The attitude scale which I have found most suitable for legislative analysis using individual behavioral scores is known as the Guttman scale.[14] It is widely used in social psychology and has undergone many improvements over the past few years. Guttman scaling not only provides individual scores but it also allows us to examine *patterns of individual behavior* within a group context. This, in turn, helps us clarify the variables upon which the measurements are made. "Scales may be used to measure, as well as to clarify, certain sociological variables. These variables are conceived as complex in two respects: they involve patterns of action on one hand, and structuring of individuals on the other."[15]

The central concept of Guttman scaling is *unidimensionality*. The Guttman scale is designed to measure one attribute at a time and to avoid the confusion experienced when arriving at common scores by different routes. Although much of our language describing legislative behavior implies unidimensionality, it is seldom examined from this standpoint. We speak of one legislator being more "liberal" than another and implicitly compare the two on legislative voting generally. When it becomes apparent that some legislators are "liberal" in domestic affairs and "conservative" in foreign affairs, we become aware of the descriptive inadequacies of the terms. Similarly, terms like "isolationist" and "interventionist" are highly time-bound and become more inadequate as the period of their origin recedes into the past. The problem of unidimensionality in measurement is basically a problem of designating behavioral uniformities along one or more "yardsticks." The problem of terminology is a related one in that verbal comparisons and descriptions are implicitly measurements (if only of an ordinary nature) along some dimension.

Unidimensionality, the central concept in scale analysis, is an analytical convenience. It would be very unlikely that any area of human behavior or attitudes could be expressed in terms of a single dimension or variable. When, however, there is high consistency or common content in an area of behavior, scale analysis traces the existence of the consistency by organizing the behavioral data on the population under examination. "The mathe-matical model is needed to allow the use of multiple indices, yet *provide an inherent check on the unitary character of the concept under investigation.*"[16]

The Value of Scale Analysis in Legislative Studies. The areas of behavior (it could be of attitudes, abilities, and various other things as far as the use of the method is concerned), when tested and found unidimensional, offer several things necessary for the objectives of legislative behavior analysis. They are: (1) Continua for the measurement and rating of legislators, (2) information on legislative groups within which individual activities take place, (3) clarification of the variables under examination for accurate, objective, descriptive terminology. Existing rating and measurement schemes as well as much of the language used to describe political behavior assume unidimensionality. This method provides an objective test of dimensionality in areas which are of importance to political science.

Because the theory of scales involves the analysis of *patterns* of behavior, an important concept is the attribute or qualitative variable. Such a qualitative variable could be a series of attitudes or behaviors toward some object or question, and members of a group of people might have various combinations of them. Values of this qualitative variable would present the various positions taken on the question at hand.

The Construction of a Scale. *A Scale Variable.* Scaling attempts to translate such attributes into a *quantitative* variable. By this we mean that the qualitative categories will be given definite sets of values. Using the concept of simple function, Guttman transforms positions on a qualitative variable into values on a quantitative variable. When a set of positions on several qualitative variables are simultaneously translated into a value on a quantitative variable, we have what Guttman calls a *scale variable.*

Take the attribute "attitude toward the abolition of the closed shop" with its three positions: favoring, opposing, and indifference; and represent them this way: Y is the attribute with the values Y_1, Y_2, Y_3, (Y_1 being "favoring the abolition of the closed shop," Y_2 "opposing the abolition of the closed shop," etc.).[17] Then take a population of legislators possessing the attribute Y, and suppose there are ten members of the population (ten values of X). The distribution of the attribute on the population might look like this:

X	0	1	2	3	4	5	6	7	8	9
Y	Y_1	Y_1	Y_1	Y_3	Y_3	Y_2	Y_2	Y_2	Y_2	Y_2

or like this:

In both of these cases for each value of X there is one and only one value of Y. For any value of X (any member of the population) we can reproduce the value of Y which is that person's value on the attribute.

In assigning the values of *several* attributes to members of a single population, we come to another important concept in scaling, what Guttman calls the *universe of attributes*. We spoke of the attribute, "attitude toward the closed shop," and how its values could be plotted for a population. Now it may be asked, "Is this attribute part of a cluster of attributes?" Are attitudes toward the closed shop part of general attitudes toward organized labor? Similarly, is a legislative vote on the closed shop issue part of a pattern of labor voting?

Universe of Attributes. The universe of attributes can be thought of as all of the attributes that are applied in the concept. The universe of attributes, "attitudes toward organized labor," consists of attitudes toward such things as the closed shop, industry-wide bargaining, union-pension programs, etc.

Another way of describing the universe is to say that it consists of all the attributes of interest to the investigation which have a common content, so that they are classified under a single heading which indicates that content . . . the investigator indicates the content of interest by the title he chooses for the universe, and all the attributes with that content belong in the universe.[18]

Such grouping of attitudes, behaviors, etc., is done every day. We make generalizations about "pro-labor attitudes," "isolationist attitudes," and "liberal attitudes." One could list the various things which *he* means to include when he uses the more general term. The question which is raised here is whether such a generalization is valid and whether or not its validity can be tested.

Scale analysis offers such a test. It allows us to take an area of attitudes which one believes to have a common content (and hence can be brought under a general term), and test it for its common content. If such a common content exists, the various attitudes, expressed as variables or attributes, will form a scale for the population holding them.

Selection of a Population. Having selected a universe of attributes which are believed to have a common content we proceed to plot their value for the population chosen for the study. Continuing with the example of labor attitudes, our problem is to test the relationship between such things as "attitude toward the closed shop," "attitude toward compulsory arbitration," etc. Perhaps they are independent; perhaps they form a general "attitude toward labor."

Having selected such items for our universe of attributes, the next step is to select a population for whom the selected attributes have a common content. Not all populations are expected to have structured attitudes on this problem, as such attitudes are the products of continued experience. Turning to farmers, for example, a group of farmers may never have thought about "labor problems" in a general way and may have unrelated attitudes toward, say, the closed shop and the secondary boycott. A position on one may be based on a single experience (the reading of the electrotyped newspapers during a printers strike, for example), while a position on the other might be based on experience involving a boycott of agricultural products.

We might choose, therefore, a population of legislators whose duties have required them to talk about and work with "labor problems" over long periods. Because of this experience it would be expected that their attitudes toward labor would be well structured. Now we can explore the kind of structure that exists.

Some way must be devised to record the characteristics of the population which are of interest to the investigation, to obtain data on the people being studied. It can be done through questionnaires, observations, or other data-gathering techniques. In the example as well as the findings reported, the legislative vote will be our basic datum.

Each member of the population must be assigned a numerical value (number the legislators 1, 2, . . . n). Then against each legislator, we plot values on the quantitative variables. For a small legislative body it is possible to use the actual names of the legislators if the analysis is done clerically. However, assigning a number to each member of the population is necessary whenever IBM equipment is used. By knowing the value of a member of a legislative population, we can reproduce all his votes on the attributes (issues) used to form the scale.

Chart Representation of Scale Analysis. To show how a set of attributes combine to form a universe and to form a particular arrangement of the population possessing them, let us go back to the example of the legislator and the "labor" attributes. The following questions might be asked of them in the form of roll-calls:

A. Do you favor the outlawing of the secondary boycott?

B. Do you favor the legalizing of the injunction as a means of stopping strikes?

C. Do you favor outlawing collective bargaining?

These questions might be chosen to tap the general "attitude toward labor."

Assuming that no members abstain or are absent, there are eight possible combinations of answers (2·2·2). Actually we would expect to find fewer combinations occurring in a population. Some people would be expected to vote "nay" to all three. Others might vote "yea" to all three. Another combination which would probably come up would be YYN; another YNN. If any general "attitude toward labor" exists, we would not expect to get such patterns as NNY or NYY where a person favors an extreme anti-labor move and opposes a moderate one.

Let us assume that this is what actually occurs when we record the votes, and that all members give one of the four patterns, NNN, YNN, YYN, and YYY. We can then assign values to the population on the basis of the pattern given—1-NNN, 2-YNN, 3-YYN, 4-YYY. This value would be the person's score. From the person's score we would know precisely what votes he cast on *all* the issues involved. A score of "2," for example, does not mean simply that the person cast one "yea" and two "nay" votes, but that he cast a "yea" vote on issue number one and "nay" votes on issues number two and three. A person's voting record is perfectly reproducible from his score. Each vote is a simple function of the score. *This will only be the case, however, when the series of issues form a scale for the population*; that is, where certain patterns of response occur and others do not.

A procedure for finding out whether the chosen issues form a scale for the population chosen is as follows: plot the values of the attributes (the votes) opposite the members of the population.

The parallelogram pattern of X's on the chart shows the relationship between the four patterns of votes. If someone had voted $Y_1N_2N_3$, the X's

Chart 1

	Y_1	Y_2	Y_3	N_1	N_2	N_3
1	X	X	X			
2		X	X	X		
3			X	X	X	
4				X	X	X

for these votes would not have fallen within the parallelogram pattern.

The relationship between patterns of variable values (in this example, votes) can also be shown by the use of bar charts. Suppose now we have a larger population casting votes on the same labor issues. Suppose on issue number one 80 per cent of the population voted "yea" and 20 per cent voted "nay." Suppose that the division on the second issue was 60 per cent "yea" and 40 per cent "nay"; on the third issue 10 per cent "yea," and 90 per cent "nay." These divisions could be represented simultaneously as shown in Chart 2:

Now by using vertical dotted lines to extend two of the "division" lines and scoring the marginal frequencies, we can divide the population on the basis of votes on *all three* issues.

These percentages, given inside Chart 3, indicate the way the population divides on the individual issues considered separately. The percentages shown at the bottom of the chart indicate the ways in which the population divides on all three issues considered simultaneously. These marginal frequencies of the Chart give us this information; 10 per cent of the population voted YYY, 50 per cent voted YYN, 20 per cent voted YNN, and 20 per cent voted NNN. *Because the three issues form a scale for the population, the above percentages can be shown simultaneously.*

This is possible (and a perfect scale exists) only if the 20 per cent voting "nay" on issue No. 1 (in the above example) are included in the 40 per cent voting "nay" on issue No. 2, and the 90 per cent voting "nay" on issue No. 3. The same thing must be true of the "yea" votes: The 10 per cent voting "yea" on issue No. 3 must be included in the 60 per cent voting "yea" on issue No. 2 and in the 80 per cent voting "yea" on issue No. 1. An essential fact here is not that the percentages are progressively larger as we go from one issue to another, but that *particular* percentages (people) are included in the larger percentages. If no scale existed, the 10 per cent of

Chart 2

Issue	Yea		Nay
No. 1	80%		20%
No. 2	60%	40%	
No. 3	10%	90%	

those who voted "yea" on issue No. 3 might be distributed in any way on the other issues—all could be on either side of the division, for example. If a scale exists, however, all must be on *one* side of each of the other issues.

Detection of Deviant Cases. Why does a universe of items form a scale while items selected at random do not? Why should only those particular patterns of votes described in the above example, i.e., those patterns which together form a parallelogram, be found and not the other possible ones? There is no necessary logical reason why a person could not be in favor of an extreme anti-labor measure and be opposed to a milder one. The reason for a scale emerging in such a context is largely cultural. Labor questions have been discussed and argued in relation to each other and general attitudes are developed in such a context is largely cultural. Labor questions have be expected that well-structured attitudes would come out of the political platforms, legislative programs, and the polarizing effect of party conflict.

If a person from a totally different culture were to become part of the population being examined for scalable attitudes, he might have quite unrealistic (from the point of view of American political practice) attitudes toward the individual items if he understood them at all. If there were enough such "foreigners" in our population, there would not be enough regularity in answers to form a scale.

The fact that a person having different values will give responses different from any pattern making up a scale shows a secondary function of scale analysis. Not only does scaling give us a rank ordering of the population for whom the scale exists, but it singles out those persons for further study whose behavior or attitudes cannot be expressed as a function of the scale scores. If there are many such deviants, of course, no scale exists for the population. The allowable number of deviant (non-scale) responses must be fixed in advance. Ten per cent is the figure which has generally been used. This is a problem which can be handled better in the context of particular scales.

Relating Scale Scores to Outside Variables. It has been emphasized how scale analysis tests for unidimensionality and gives a rank-order of the population along a dimension. Even more impor-

tant it also allows us to relate these characteristics to other outside variables. As Edwards and Kilpatrick put it:

Another important characteristic of scales is that a zero-order correlation between an outside variable and the rank-order score on a scale will be equivalent to the multiple correlation between the individual items forming the scale universe and the outside variable. This means that efficiency in prediction from a set of items is maximized.[19]

Scaling, multiple correlation, and factor analysis have this in common: they provide efficient means for combining data, and means which are objective in that they depend on data orderings rather than arbitrary classifications. Scaling is particularly appropriate for ordering legislative data in that it gives a rank-ordering of the population (the "rating" objective of this study) and at the same time demonstrates the data ordering on which the ratings are based. Scores derived from such a rank ordering are of the same predictive value as a series of scores based on the individual item forming the scale. Thus, instead of doing separate analyses of the relationship between attitudes toward the closed shop and an outside variable (per cent urban population in constituency, for example), attitudes toward industry-wide collective bargaining and the same outside variable, and so forth, we can do a single analysis to relate scale scores on all the labor questions to our outside variable.

An Exercise in Scale Analysis of Legislative Voting. In order to demonstrate the utility of scale analysis in legislative behavior measurement, Senate voting on the Taft-Hartley Bill was analyzed. (See Chart 4.) The writer has found that other areas of national legislation (taxation, European aid) can be scaled as successfully as trade-union legislation, but the results of the other analyses will not be reported in this article.

The Taft-Hartley debates covered numerous proposals and motions; some were carried, some defeated. Men involved in these were not divided into simple pro-labor or anti-labor ranks. The numerous proposals and amendments offered opportunities to each legislator to take one of several positions running from an extreme anti-labor position to an extreme pro-labor one. Relatively few men voted either for all the anti-labor proposals or against all of them.

Chart 3

Issue	Yea				Nay
No. 1			80%		20%
No. 2		60%		40%	
No. 3	10%			90%	
	10%	50%		20%	20%

Chart 4—Senatorial Voting on Taft-Hartley Issues

Senator	Score	PRO-LABOR							ANTI-LABOR						
		1	2	3	4	5	6	7	1A	2A	3A	4A	5A	6A	7A
Chavez	(0)	X	X	X	X	X	X	X	.	.	.	.	.	.	.
Downey	(0)	X	X	X	X	X	X	X	.	.	.	.	.	.	.
Green	(0)	X	X	X	X	X	X	X	.	.	.	.	.	.	.
Hayden	(0)	X	X	X	X	X	X	X	.	.	.	.	.	.	.
Johnson	(0)	X	X	X	X	X	X	X	.	.	.	.	.	.	.
Johnston	(0)	X	X	X	X	X	X	X	.	.	.	.	.	.	.
Kilgore	(0)	X	X	X	X	X	X	X	.	.	.	.	.	.	.
Lucas	(0)	X	X	X	X	X	X	X	.	.	.	.	.	.	.
McFarland	(0)	X	X	X	X	X	X	X	.	.	.	.	.	.	.
McGrath	(0)	X	X	X	X	X	X	X	.	.	.	.	.	.	.
Magnuson	(0)	X	X	X	X	X	X	X	.	.	.	.	.	.	.
Maybank	(0)	X	X	X	X	X	X	X	.	.	.	.	.	.	.
Murray	(0)	X	X	X	X	X	X	X	.	.	.	.	.	.	.
Myers	(0)	X	X	X	X	X	X	X	.	.	.	.	.	.	.
O'Mahoney	(0)	X	X	X	X	X	X	X	.	.	.	.	.	.	.
Pepper	(0)	X	X	X	X	X	X	X	.	.	.	.	.	.	.
Sparkman	(0)	X	X	X	X	X	X	X	.	.	.	.	.	.	.
Taylor	(0)	X	X	X	X	X	X	X	.	.	.	.	.	.	.
Thomas (Okla.)	(0)	X	X	X	X	X	X	X	.	.	.	.	.	.	.
Thomas (Utah)	(0)	X	X	X	X	X	X	X	.	.	.	.	.	.	.
Barkley	(1)	.	X	X	X	X	X	X	X	.	.	.	.	.	.
Hill	(1)	.	X	X	X	X	X	X	X	.	.	.	.	.	.
Langer	(1)	.	X	X	X	X	X	X	X	.	.	.	.	.	.
McCarran	(1)	.	X	X	X	X	X	X	X	.	.	.	.	.	.
McMahon	(1)	.	X	X	X	X	X	X	X	.	.	.	.	.	.
Morse	(1)	.	X	X	X	X	X	X	X	.	.	.	.	.	.
Wagner	(1)	.	X	X	X	X	X	X	X	.	.	.	.	.	.
Aiken	(2)	.	.	X	0	X	X	X	X	X	.	.	.	.	.
Connally	(2)	.	.	X	.	X	X	X	X	X	.	X	.	.	.
Ellender	(2)	.	.	X	.	X	X	X	X	X	.	X	.	.	.
Hatch	(2)	.	.	X	X	X	X	X	X	X	.	.	.	.	.
Fulbright	(5)	.	.	.	X	.	.	X	X	X	X	.	X	X	.
Holland	(5)	.	.	.	X	.	.	X	X	X	X	.	X	X	.
O'Connor	(4)	.	.	.	X	.	X	X	X	X	X	.	X	.	.
Russell	(5)	.	.	.	X	.	.	X	X	X	X	.	X	X	.
Stewart	(6)	.	.	.	X	.	.	.	X	X	X	.	X	X	X
Tydings	(4)	.	.	.	X	.	X	.	X	X	X	.	X	.	X
Umstead	(4)	.	.	.	X	.	X	X	X	X	X	.	X	.	.
Cooper	(3)	.	.	.	.	X	X	X	X	X	X	X	.	.	.
Ecton	(3)	.	.	.	.	X	X	X	X	X	X	X	.	.	.
Flanders	(3)	.	.	.	.	X	X	X	X	X	X	X	.	.	.
Ives	(3)	.	.	.	.	X	X	X	X	X	X	X	.	.	.
Knowland	(3)	.	.	.	.	X	X	X	X	X	X	X	.	.	.
Lodge	(3)	.	.	.	.	X	X	X	X	X	X	X	.	.	.
Malone	(3)	.	X	.	.	X	X	X	X	.	X	X	.	.	.
Revercomb	(3)	.	.	.	.	X	.	X	X	X	X	X	.	X	.
Saltonstall	(3)	.	.	.	.	X	X	X	X	X	X	X	.	.	.
Tobey	(3)	.	.	.	.	X	X	0	0	0	X	X	.	.	.
Wilson	(3)	.	.	.	.	X	X	X	X	X	X	X	.	.	.
Young	(3)	.	.	.	.	X	X	X	X	X	X	X	.	.	.
Baldwin	(4)	.	.	.	.	0	X	X	X	X	X	X	0	.	.
Cordon	(4)	.	.	.	.	.	X	.	X	X	X	X	X	.	X
Thye	(4)	.	.	.	.	X	X	X	X	X	X	X	.	.	.

Chart 4—(continued)

Senator	Score	PRO-LABOR							ANTI-LABOR						
		1	2	3	4	5	6	7	1A	2A	3A	4A	5A	6A	7A
Brewster	(5)	.	.	.	.	.	.	X	X	X	X	X	X	X	.
Bridges	(5)	.	.	.	.	.	.	X	X	X	X	X	X	X	.
Brooks	(5)	.	.	.	.	.	.	X	X	X	X	X	X	X	.
Butler	(5)	.	.	.	.	.	.	X	X	X	X	X	0	.	.
Cain	(5)	.	.	.	.	.	.	X	X	X	X	X	X	X	.
Capehart	(5)	.	.	.	.	.	.	X	X	X	X	X	0	.	.
Dworshak	(5)	.	.	.	.	.	.	X	X	X	X	X	X	X	.
Ferguson	(5)	.	.	.	.	.	.	X	X	X	X	X	X	X	.
Hoey	(5)	.	.	.	.	.	.	X	X	X	X	X	X	X	.
Jenner	(5)	.	.	.	.	.	.	X	X	X	X	X	X	X	.
McCarthy	(5)	.	.	.	.	.	.	X	X	X	X	X	X	X	.
Millikin	(5)	.	.	.	.	.	.	X	X	X	X	X	X	X	.
Overton	(5)	.	.	.	.	.	.	X	X	X	X	X	X	X	.
Smith	(5)	.	.	.	.	.	.	X	X	X	X	X	X	X	.
Taft	(5)	.	.	.	.	.	.	X	X	X	X	X	X	X	.
Vandenberg	(5)	.	.	.	.	.	.	X	X	X	X	X	X	X	.
Watkins	(5)	.	.	.	.	.	.	X	X	X	X	X	X	X	.
Ball	(6)	.	.	.	.	.	.	.	X	X	X	X	X	X	X
Bricker	(6)	.	.	.	.	.	.	.	X	X	X	X	X	X	X
Buck	(6)	.	.	.	.	.	.	.	X	X	X	X	X	X	X
Bushfield	(6)	.	.	.	.	.	.	.	X	X	X	X	X	X	X
Byrd	(6)	.	.	.	.	.	.	.	X	X	X	X	X	X	X
Capper	(6)	.	.	.	.	.	.	.	X	X	X	X	X	X	X
Donnell	(6)	.	.	.	.	.	.	.	X	X	X	X	X	X	X
Eastland	(6)	.	.	.	.	.	.	.	X	X	X	X	X	X	X
George	(6)	.	.	.	.	.	.	.	X	X	X	X	X	X	X
Gurney	(6)	.	.	.	.	.	.	.	X	X	X	X	X	X	X
Hawkes	(6)	.	.	.	.	.	.	.	X	X	X	X	X	X	X
Hickenlooper	(6)	.	.	.	.	.	.	.	X	X	X	X	X	X	X
Kem	(6)	.	.	.	.	.	.	.	X	X	X	X	X	X	X
McClellan	(6)	.	.	.	.	.	.	.	X	X	X	X	X	X	X
McKellar	(6)	.	.	.	.	.	.	.	X	X	X	X	X	X	X
Martin	(6)	.	.	.	.	.	.	.	X	X	X	X	X	X	X
Moore	(6)	.	.	.	.	.	.	.	X	X	X	X	X	X	X
O'Daniel	(6)	.	.	.	.	.	.	.	X	X	X	X	X	X	X
Reed	(6)	.	.	.	.	.	.	.	X	X	X	X	X	X	X
Robertson (Va.)	(6)	.	.	.	.	.	.	.	X	X	X	X	X	X	X
Robertson (Wyo.)	(6)	.	.	.	.	.	.	.	X	X	X	X	X	X	X
Wherry	(6)	.	.	.	.	.	.	.	X	X	X	X	X	X	X
White	(6)	.	.	.	.	.	.	.	X	X	X	X	X	X	X
Wiley	(6)	.	.	.	.	.	.	.	X	X	X	X	X	X	X
Williams	(6)	.	.	.	.	.	.	.	X	X	X	X	X	X	X
Wilson	(6)	.	.	.	.	.	.	.	X	X	X	X	X	X	X

NOTE: Bilbo was absent during all votes.

Explanations of Items on Table.

1. "Yea" on a pro-labor substitute bill.
2. "Nay" on overriding veto of the Taft-Hartley Act.
3. "Nay" on an amendment to outlaw unfair labor practices by unions.
4. "Yea" on a motion to have separate labor bills rather than a single general one.
5. "Nay" on a motion to provide for government control of union welfare funds.
6. "Nay" on a motion to outlaw industry-wide collective bargaining.
7. "Nay" on a motion to legalize the use of the injunction against labor unions.

Seven roll-calls were used to construct the scale for trade union legislation.[20] Roll-call number one marks off the most extreme pro-labor group composed of twenty Democrats and no Republicans. These twenty men who were alone in voting for roll-call number one held their ranks perfectly in voting for the other six issues. Roll-call number one was a substitute labor bill offered by Senator Murray. This was a move to have a less "anti-labor" bill, and its supporters were "strongly" pro-labor.

The second roll-call in the scale was the vote on overriding Truman's veto of the Taft-Hartley Bill. The group already mentioned (the twenty men voting for Murray's substitute bill) all voted "nay" on this roll-call and were joined by eight other men. These eight men formed a second group in the analysis;[21] they were pro-labor enough to vote "nay" on Taft-Hartley, but not as pro-labor as the twenty voting for Murray's substitute bill.

The next roll-call (No. 3) was a motion by Ball to make illegal "union coercion of employers." The pro-labor people voting "nay" to this were the above groups plus four additional Senators. These four form a new group being pro-labor enough to vote against Ball's amendment, but not pro-labor enough to vote for upholding the veto of Taft-Hartley or for Murray's substitute bill.

Roll-call number four was on a motion by Senator Morse to have separate labor bills rather than a single omnibus labor bill. In this move he was supported by all the members, except three, of the groups already listed as well as seven "new" men, six of them Southern Democrats. This is the group beginning with Senator Fulbright and continuing through Senator Umstead.

The next roll-call (No. 5) having to do with the control of worker welfare funds, found eleven men joining the pro-labor ranks. These are the "liberal" Republicans—Flanders, Ives, Knowland, Lodge, Saltonstall, Tobey, etc. In the more pro-labor groups the only Republicans were Morse, Langer, and Aiken.

Notice that none of the southern Democrats added to the pro-labor list by item No. 4 voted "nay" on item No. 5 (a vote which would have followed if item No. 4 had fixed their position and determined their pattern on the other items). Item No. 4 was evidently an all-out party effort which drew the more anti-labor Democrats into line. After this roll-call they resume their position far "down" on the scale.

The next roll-call (No. 6) was a move to limit industry-wide collective bargaining. Of the groups already listed, all but seven voted "pro-labor" on

this item, and a new group of Baldwin, Gordon, and Thye was formed.

The last roll-call used (No. 7) was a move to legalize the injunction in labor cases involving the secondary boycott and jurisdictional strikes. Some very "conservative" Senators would not go this far and voted with the groups which already had shown some degree of pro-labor feeling.

The remaining people, of course, are the most anti-labor of all. They voted for this last motion as well as anti-labor on all the others.

Seven roll-calls, then, form eight groups which are separated according to the degree of "labor" feeling which their voting expresses. If each member of each group had voted exactly as every other member of the group did, we would have a perfect scale. Actually, this was not the case.

With ninety-four Senators and seven roll-calls, 658 votes were recorded. Fifteen votes were "non-scale" votes. This gives an index of reproducibility of 97.7 per cent. A non-scale vote is detected after each person has been assigned to the group whose voting pattern most closely resembles his. Starting at the top of the list of Senators on the Chart, all of the first group (Chavez through Thomas) have identical voting records on the seven issues. These men will be scored "zero."

The next seven men (Barkley through Wagner) also have identical voting patterns. They will be scored (1).

The next group (Aiken through Hatch) will be scored (2). The scoring of people in the following group (Fulbright through Umstead) brings up a problem in the use of non-perfect scales. If this group had a common voting pattern they would all be scored (3). Actually, the item which brings these people into the list at the point at which they are shown on the Chart does not serve the purpose for which it was used and the men in this group will not be scored until the other items have been considered. Instead, the group Cooper through Young will be scored (3). The group Baldwin through Thye will be scored (4). The group Brewster through Watkins will be scored (5), and the group Ball through White will be scored (6).

All of the men casting non-scale votes can now be scored. The general rule here is that such people are scored with the group with whom they can be placed with a minimum number of alterations in their voting patterns. If the same number of alterations can place a man in either of two positions, he is placed nearest the mean score of the entire population.[22]

On the Chart, Malone cast a pro-labor vote on item No. 2. If he had gone on to vote pro-labor on items Nos. 3, 4, 5, 6, and 7, he would have been scored a (1). Actually he did not vote pro-labor again until item No. 5, and from then on his voting is consistent. By ignoring his one non-scale vote on item No. 2, Malone becomes a (3) along with Cooper, Ecton, Flanders, etc.

The next men casting non-scale votes are Connally and Ellender, who deviate from the voting pattern of the other members of their group by their votes on item No. 4. By filling in this one vote, each becomes a (2) (along with Aiken and Hatch).

All of the people (Fulbright through Umstead) have to be scored by this system. By altering the minimum number of votes (by changing the necessary "yea" votes to "nay" votes and vice versa to get a perfect vote pattern of a person) Fulbright, Holland, and Russell become (5) (along with Brewster through Watkins); O'Connor and Umstead become (4), and Stewart becomes (6). Tydings is a case of an unsymmetrical voting pattern turned up by scale analysis.

If item No. 4 were omitted, no changes would occur in the scoring of any of the members. No alterations would have been necessary to make Connally and Ellender become (2). Fulbright through Umstead would not have been listed until the issues were entered which eventually determined their positions.

Item No. 4 was entered even though it contributed nothing to the construction of the scale or the scoring of the population. It was entered to show the existence of a factor different from the main one underlying the series of items and hence the scale. The consistency of voting on six of the seven issues indicates a general attitude for each Senator on trade union issues. The "second factor" (besides trade union attitudes) is probably a party "loyalty" factor.

The complete scale on trade union issues shows both an ordering of the roll-calls and an ordering of the population of Senators. There are six distinct groups of Senators ranging from an extreme pro-labor position at one end to an extreme anti-labor position on the other.

The items in this scale tell us something about the attribute which describes the consistencies of voting by the population. The items were all in the area of government control of trade union activities. The general attribute should be defined accordingly: "behavior (or attitudes) toward government control of union activities." The voting on these issues was done in the context of a legislative policy. This policy was an attempt to write a new national labor bill providing for a more rigid government control over unions than the law then in effect. A Senator's score on this attribute should be interpreted as his position on this general policy question. If a new policy is initiated in a future session of Congress, the ordering of the population would be expected to differ to the degree that the new policy differed in content (dealing, say, with government control over wage issues rather than over union activities) from the one on which the scaled voting was based.

Scale Values and Correlations. One of the objectives mentioned at the beginning of this study was the clarification of concepts in legislative research. The concept of the unidimensional scale with a specific empirical content ("trade-union issue position") is the major one which has been examined. This delineation of an area of behavioral uniformity is offered as a more exact concept than the more common ones such as "liberal," "conservative," or "isolationist."

If it is agreed that scaling provides a reliable method for ordering legislative behavior, we can then proceed to use these orderings for further analysis. The next analytical step would be to relate the values on our dependent (behavioral) variables to those factors which we hypothesize as their determinants. Such correlations require the assigning of values for the same population on whatever independent variables are suggested as determinants of legislative behavior. Reliability means that other investigators would assign identical values to members of the population.

The independent variable which is most often set forth as a major determinant of legislative behavior is political party membership. Although our legislative system is not characterized by as strong political party control as is the English parliament, party membership would appear to be a major factor in American legislative life.

The variable "political party membership" can be considered a two-valued variable in national legislative analysis despite the "Independent" status of Senator Morse at the time of these roll-calls. However, the variable was set up as a combined region-party variable because of the well-known political uniqueness of the South. The following charts show how a single independent variable can be related to the variable: "trade-union issue position."

The fact that a much higher percentage of Democrats than Republicans fall within the pro-labor group would have been predicted by most political analysts. The fact that Southern Democrats fall somewhere between non-Southern Democrats and Republicans is also well known. The obviousness of the findings, however, should not obscure the importance of correlational analyses using legislative behavior scores. Not only are many simple relationships (between two variables) not so obvious, but there are the intriguing problems involving the joint effects of several factors on the voting behavior of legislators. Techniques such as analysis of variance would be particularly well suited for this.

Conclusions. Scale analysis can successfully be applied to legislative voting. Patterns of legislative votes can be isolated and quantified. Voting of individual members of a legislature can be examined in the context of group or bloc positions. Groups can be examined in the context of the entire legislative body.

The variables necessary for correlational studies of legislative behavior can be clarified conceptually by scale analysis. The clarified behavioral variable provides a stable basis for quantitative treatments of a legislative population. Such a variable serves also as a basis for unambiguous descriptive nota-

RELATIONSHIP BETWEEN PARTY MEMBERSHIP AND VOTING POSITIONS ON TRADE UNION ISSUES

Chart 5—Attitude Toward Labor as Independent Variable

	Pro-Labor*	Moderate†	Anti-Labor‡
Non-Southern Democrats	74%	15%	—
Southern Democrats	19%	15%	25%
Republicans	7%	70%	75%
	100%	100%	100%
Number of Members	27	20	48

Chart 6—Party Affiliation as Independent Variable

	Non-Southern Democrats	Southern Democrats	Republicans
Pro-Labor	87%	26%	4%
Moderate	13%	16%	27%
Anti-Labor	—	58%	69%
	100%	100%	100%
Number of Members	23	20	52

* Scores 0 and 1, Chart 5
† Scores 2, 3, and 4, Chart 5
‡ Scores 5 and 6, Chart 5

tion (replacing vague descriptive terms such as "liberal," "isolationist," etc.).

And "area" of legislation such as the "labor-union-government" issues treated in this paper seems best suited for unidimensional conceptualization. When attempts were made to scale all votes of a legislative session, the general standards of scalability were not met. Completely general terms such as "liberal" and "conservative" imply more order than has been found by this investiga-

tion. Especially striking is the lack of consistency between domestic and foreign-affairs voting.

Positive steps to operationalize political science concepts and clarify the variables related to them can and should be taken. Concepts referring to administrative behavior, group action, political leadership will be much more fruitful when they have clearly been linked to empirical orderings. Discussion can be clarified and the testing of propositions can proceed. Along with conceptual clarification (in terms of empirical referents) we need a simple, unambiguous notation system for the handling of political data. Finally, the related objective of establishing a measurement system upon our clarified variables needs to be emphasized. Conceptual clarification, empirical ordering, notation refinement, and measurement are elements of a general methodology. They are the steps which will help us move ahead in the development and testing of theories of political behavior.

Other parts of the political process (group analysis, for example) will probably be more difficult to treat in terms of the above objectives than legislative analysis. The legislative vote is a particularly neat and available datum. However, we have no choice except to attack the general problems and find out how difficult it is to do scientific research in each area of political behavior.

Notes

1. Talcott Parsons, *Essays in Sociological Theory Pure and Applied* (Glencoe, Illinois, 1949), p. 5.
2. David Easton, *The Political System* (New York, 1953), p. 129.
3. Stephen K. Bailey, *Congress Makes a Law* (New York, 1950).
4. Ralph Huitt, "The Congressional Committee: A Case Study," *The American Political Science Review*, Vol. 48 (June, 1954), pp. 340-365.
5. Stuart Rice, *Quantitative Methods in Politics* (New York, 1928), p. 3.
6. Kurt Lewin, "Concepts in Field Theory," *Field Theory in Social Science* [ed. Darwin Cartwright], (New York, 1951), pp. 30-31.
7. See index of cohesion and index of likeness, Rice, *op. cit.*, p. 3.
8. V. O. Key, Jr., *Southern Politics in State and Nation* (New York, 1949).
9. Julius Turner, *Party and Constituency: Pressures on Congress* (Baltimore, 1951).
10. George L. Grassmuck, *Sectional Biases in Congress on Foreign Policy* (Baltimore, 1951).
11. Somehow the methods of using judges and a consensus of their judgments for establishing criteria for measurement has never caught on in political science. See L. L. Thurstone, "Attitudes Can Be Measured," *American Journal of Sociology*, Vol. 33 (1928), pp. 529-554.
12. The difficulty here is that political and census boundaries do not usually coincide. Demographers seem to

be moving toward more "natural" units rather than political ones.

13. Stuart Rice, "The Political Vote as a Frequency Distribution of Opinion," *Journal of the American Statistical Association*, Vol. 19 (March, 1924), pp. 70-75.

14. Louis Guttman, "The Basis for Scalogram Analysis," from *Measurement and Prediction*, Samuel A. Stouffer, et al (Princeton, New Jersey, 1950).

15. Matilda White Riley, John W. Riley, Jr., and Jackson Tobey, *Sociological Studies in Scale Analysis* (New Brunswick, 1954), p. 21.

16. Riley, Riley, and Tobey, *ibid.*, p. 14.

17. The following discussion is taken almost literally from Guttman's own exposition of his scaling theory. This paper is in no way a contribution to scale theory but is rather an application of it to legislative behavior analysis. For a thorough discussion of Guttman scaling, see Louis Guttman, *op. cit.*, pp. 60-90.

18. Louis Guttman, *op. cit.*, pp. 80, 83-84.

19. Allen L. Edwards and Franklin P. Kilpatrick, "Scale Analysis and the Measurement of Social Attitudes," *Psychometrika*, XIII, No. 2 (June, 1948), p. 108.

20. Although the computations here were made clerically, IBM machinery should be used whenever possible in scale analysis. In legislative analysis, large legislative bodies can be treated as easily as small ones if we enter our data on Hollerith cards. Large populations make it possible for us to do analysis which cannot be done with small numbers (controlling on two variables and still having large enough cell entries, for example). See Riley, Riley, and Tobey, *op. cit.*, pp. 273-305.

21. Malone's later votes show his vote to be a non-scale response.

22. For a discussion of the scoring of non-scale patterns see Andrew F. Henry, "A Method of Classifying Non-Scale Response Patterns in a Guttman Scale," *The Public Opinion Quarterly*, Vol. 16 (Spring, 1952), pp. 94-95.

7. A SCALE ANALYSIS OF IDEOLOGICAL FACTORS IN CONGRESSIONAL VOTING

Charles D. Farris

THE PURPOSE of this essay is to propose a method of determining ideological groupings in an American legislative body, to illustrate the method by reference to the House of Representatives of the 79th Congress, and to suggest questions which this method might answer.[1] The argument supports the following hypotheses:

1. Some (but not necessarily all) of a legislator's roll call votes during a session (or term of office) define his "public ideology" for that session (or term).

2. Legislators may (in the present context, Representatives of the 79th Congress did) maintain enough consistency in their voting on related aspects of the same "major issue" so that their yeas and nays are "scalable" according to Guttman's ordinal scaling technique.

3. As a method of roll call analysis, Guttman scaling has certain advantages over other methods of roll call analysis.

4. Some scales based on roll call votes are more "ideological" in content than others.

5. Using the varying positions of legislators on a number of scales for selected "major issues," one can classify legislators into a relatively small number of "ideological groupings."

6. Further research can isolate and specify the

Reprinted from *The Journal of Politics*, Vol. 20 (1958), pp. 308-38, where it appeared under the title, "A Method of Determining Ideological Groupings in the Congress," by permission of the author and the publisher.

politically or theoretically relevant variables that differentiate (in a statistically significant sense) the members of one ideological grouping from those of another.

It is neither necessary nor appropriate to use all the roll call votes during a particular session or term in order to define the public ideological positions of legislators. Either because of their form or because of their content, it is appropriate to exclude certain roll calls from consideration. The analysis in this section justifies the exclusion of certain roll-calls on formal grounds. Substantive grounds for exclusion of other roll calls are treated in a later section.

During the 79th Congress (1945-1946), the House of Representatives took the yeas and nays 231 times. Of these roll calls, 94 may be excluded for "formal" reasons:

1. One of the 94 yielded *no quorum.*

2. On 61 of the 94, the Representatives who voted were substantially *unanimous,* 90 per cent or more of them voting on the prevailing side of the question.

3. On the remaining 32 roll calls, the House showed rather sharp *partisanship:* of the members who voted, 90 per cent or more of the nominal Democrats voted on one side of the question, and 90 per cent or more of the nominal Republicans voted on the opposite side.

Such exclusions as these are justifiable by common sense, by the logic of the present study, and by the previous practice of other roll call analysts. No-quorum roll calls, to be more specific, either commit a legislative body to nothing, or the votes that they "fail" to record—as in the case of the "disappearing quorum" in the national House of the last century, for example[2]—may be, politically, as significant as the votes that they record.

Earlier roll call analysts have frequently excluded unanimous or near-unanimous roll calls from their analyses. Of the justifications that they give,[3] none seems relevant to the analysis of roll call voting in the U. S. House of the 79th Congress. For present purposes, the best justification for excluding unanimous or near-unanimous roll calls is that they make merely gross, instead of comparatively fine, discriminations in public legislative sentiment. If 90 per cent or more of the Representatives who vote on a particular roll call vote on the prevailing side of the question, then the "reproducibility" of such a roll call, if it appears as an "item" in a putative Guttman scale, can not be less than .90. To include a unanimous roll call in such a scale, therefore, would "spuriously" inflate the reproducibility of the scale.

The best reason for excluding "partisan" roll calls from consideration is simply that, when the parties disagree sharply on a question, they are, after all, acting in a way that parties, by definition, are "supposed" to act. If the major parties are regarded as fundamental political institutions, then the finding that they sharply differ from one another is ordinarily enough to set at rest further inquiry into the reason for their disagreement. Inquiry is likely to cease, moreover, whether the inter-party disagreement is a matter of "principle" (ideology) or mere "power" (patronage, spoils, pelf).

The only moderately controversial question about the exclusion of "partisan" roll calls is the definition of "partisan." Lowell, in his early study, "arbitrarily defined" as a "party vote" any vote where nine tenths or more of each party (in a two-party system) were voting against each other,[4] and Turner has used the same definition.[5] Other roll call analysts—for example, Westerfield[6] and the editors of the *Congressional Quarterly Almanac*—define a "party-line vote" as one on which over half the voting members of one party stand against more than half the voting members of the other. There is a practical reason for using Lowell's 90 per cent criterion, rather than Westerfield's majority criterion: the latter would eliminate from consideration a very large number of roll calls and would confine analysis to a rather small collection of "bi-partisan" votes.

The elimination of 94 out of 231 roll calls by the foregoing criteria leaves a set of 137 roll calls with the following formal characteristics:
1. All of them produced at least a quorum, and most of them drew a participation much larger than that of a mere quorum.
2. In none of them did the House exhibit extreme partisanship, although in some of them, more than half (but less than nine tenths) of the voting Democrats opposed more than half (but less than nine tenths) of the voting Republicans.
3. Some of the roll calls in the 137 were "bi-partisan": more than half the voting Democrats and more than half the voting Republicans voted on the same side, rather than on different sides, of the question.

In subsequent sections of this article, the analysis classifies these 137 roll calls into a number of Guttman scales, and proposes a rationale for selecting certain scales as being more "ideological" in substance (content) than others.

If one assumes that each of the 137 roll calls presented at least one separate and distinct ideological issue, then it follows that, in order uniquely to describe the individual public ideology of a particular Representative, it would be necessary to specify how he voted on each of the 137 roll calls.

Fortunately, such a massive task of description is not necessary. Many of the roll calls dealt with different aspects of the legislative progress of a particular bill through the House, and the way a Representative voted on a particular one of these roll calls was, usually, not unrelated to the ways in which he voted on other roll calls dealing with different aspects (amendments, procedural motions, *etc.*) of the same bill.

Furthermore, many of the roll calls on questions about different bills were on questions that lay in the same broad policy area. For example, a series of amendments to the 1945 bill extending the Reciprocal Trade Agreements Act lay in the area of foreign policy as did a roll call on adopting a special rule for the British loan bill in 1946.

Because every roll call is not entirely *sui generis*, there is a possibility of grouping different roll calls on apparently related questions. There is the further possibility of using a set of related roll calls to construct a scale, in terms of which the Representatives can be ranked (within specifiable limits of error) according to the variable degree of favorableness or unfavorableness that they exhibit toward the common subject matter.

A scaling technique devised during World War II by a sociologist, Louis Guttman, makes it possible to scale sets of roll calls.[7] Belknap, Gage and Shimberg[8] have shown that Guttman scaling is applicable to the roll call votes of U. S. Senators, and others have demonstrated the applicability of the technique to the U. S. House.[9]

When a researcher is "successful"[10] in scaling a set of roll calls that share at least some common content (or relate to different aspects of some common issue), the end product of the scaling process is a Guttman scale. An example of such a scale appears in Table 1, which is based on five roll calls taken in the House during 1945. The issue which appears to be common to the five roll calls is the public worth of price control and OPA.

In terms of scale theory, a set of roll calls dealing with a common issue is said to "scale" if a Representative whose attitude toward the issue is more favorable than a second Representative's is, on each roll call in the scale, as favorable as, or more favorable than, the second Representative. In terms of this definition, the five OPA roll calls in Table 1 form a scale, with scale types ranging from 1 (least favorable to OPA) to 6 (most favorable). Any Representative in, say, scale type 5 is, thus, more favorable to OPA than any Representative in, say, scale 3. A type 5 Representative is *as favorable* to OPA as a type 3 Representative on three roll calls (121, 119, and 135) and is *more favorable* on two roll calls (122 and 123). Corresponding comparisons are possible for all other pairings of scale types in the scale.

Since perfect scales do not usually occur in reality, users of scale analysis have developed a number of criteria for evaluating the approximations to perfect scales that do actually occur.[11] In terms of all but one of these criteria, the scales used in this article are satisfactory scales. I have disregarded the criterion that a scale with dichotomous items (*i.e.*, roll calls) should always contain at least 10 items, simply because the House did not always supply as many as 10 roll calls in a particular subject matter category.

The application of Guttman scaling technique to the roll calls of the House for 1945 and 1946 yielded the 27 scales which are enumerated and classified in Table 2. Evidently, Representatives

Table 1—An Example of a Scale

ROLL CALL NO.	SUBJECT	DISTRIBUTION OF VOTES			+ Vote	Percentage +
		Yes	No	Total		
119	Amendment, HJ Res 101 (79 Cong, 1st sess), to extend price control for one year—put food pricing under Secretary of Agriculture	187	207	394	No	52.5
121	Amendment — require prices for meat products to include profit on each category of product	256	130	386	No	33.7
122	Amendment — require Secretary of Agriculture to approve all food prices set by OPA	223	167	390	No	42.8
123	Amendment—provide for court review of OPA actions	213	177	390	No	45.4
135	Adopt conference report	256	95	351	Yes	72.9

Selected Voting Patterns with Re-Ordered Roll Calls

"Perfect" Voting Patterns | | | | | | | **"Error" Voting Patterns***

Scale Type	Roll Call No.					Freq.
	121	122	123	119	135	
6	+	+	+	+	+	131
5	—	+	+	+	+	44
4	—	—	+	+	+	14
3	—	—	—	+	+	16
2	—	—	—	—	+	76
1	—	—	—	—	—	114
						384

Scale Type	Roll Call No.					Error
	121	122	123	119	135	
6	+	+	=	+	+	1
2	±	—	—	—	+	1
2	—	±	—	—	+	1
3	±	—	—	+	+	1
4	—	—	+	+	=	1
6	+	+	+	=	=	2

* Errors underlined.

Analysis of Actually Occurring Errors

Roll Call No.	121	122	123	119	135
No. of Errors	6	5	23	10	13
%age of Error	1.6	1.3	6.0	2.6	3.4

Coefficient of reproducibility (Rep) $= (1 - \dfrac{57}{1920}) = .970.$

maintain enough consistency of voting behavior —for this Congress, at least—so that practically all their roll call votes can be classified as part of one scale or another.

The 13 roll calls (from the 137 previously selected) that do not appear in the Table 2 total of 124 are of two kinds: some were the only roll calls taken on the subject to which they pertained; others essentially duplicated roll calls that are included in one of the 27 scales. As a standard to be used later in selecting certain scales for defining ideological groupings, Table 2 also shows the extent to which each scale, when dichotomized, correlates with nominal major party affiliation.

Although Guttman scaling obviously introduces elements of formal precision into roll call analysis, the question remains: what makes scaling a better method of roll call analysis than the techniques that earlier analysts have used? Why scale, especially since scaling is such a laborious operation?

An answer to these questions presupposes, for convenience, an elementary methodological analysis of the techniques of earlier roll call analysts.

A survey of earlier roll call research reveals that abstraction, classification, and counting are the operations that are common to much of the research. The operations yield particular facts which the researcher then predicates to one or another of these "things":

1. Roll calls.
2. Individual legislators.
3. Aggregates (or classes)[12] of legislators.
4. Relations between pairs of legislators or aggregates of legislators, or pairs of roll calls.

The researcher then typically compares the same set of "things" in respect of the co-variation, if any, between (or among) two or more sets of facts (including roll call data) predicated of those things.

Examples of each type of predication are not hard to find. Lowell, for instance, predicated "party vote" or "not a party vote" of each of the *roll calls* that he examined. He then determined, in both British and American jurisdictions, the varying incidence, in successive time periods, of "party votes" among all roll calls during each period. Turner, using similar procedures, has brought some of Lowell's series up into the twentieth century.[13]

An obviously elementary way to characterize an *individual legislator* is to specify whether he voted "yea" or "nay," "pro" or "anti," "majority" or "minority," "liberal" or "conservative," "administration" or "opposition" on a particular roll call. The legislator may, perhaps, be more reliably

Table 2—Classification of Scales, House, 79th Congress

Major Issues and Scales	No. of Roll Calls	Party Corr.
I. Foreign Policy		
1945 scale	4	.89
1946 scale	4	.86
	8	
II. Defense		
Atomic energy scale	2	.63
Civilian manpower draft scale, 1945	5	.56
Selective service scale, 1946	4	.23
	11	
III. "Socio-economic Distributionism"		
"Tidelands" oil scale	2	.83
OPA extension scale, 1945	5	.82
Welfare scale	12*	.70
Tax readjustment scale	2	.68
TVA steam plant scale	2	.62
OPA extension scale, 1946	12*	.58
Labor scale, 1945	12*†	.49
Labor scale, 1946	12*†	.43
	56‡	
IV. UnAmerican Activities		
"Scale No. 1"	4	.49
"Scale No. 2"	4	.47
	8	
V. Negroes: scale	11*	—.44
VI. Immigration and Naturalization scale	3	.14
VII. Government Administration and Operations		
Government organization scale	3	.53
Postal rates scale	2	.52
Non-legislative salaries scale	2	.51
D. C. appropriations scale	3	.39
Civil service retirement annuities scale	3	.30
Congressional compensation scale	3	.22
	16	
VIII. Miscellaneous		
"Pork" scale	4	.72
Airport construction scale	2	.69
Forestry scale	2	.30
Railroad bankruptcy amendments scale	3	.14
	11	
Total	124‡	

* Condensed to 4 "contrived" items. Cf. Samuel A. Stouffer et al., "A Technique for Improving Cumulative Scales," *Public Opinion Quarterly*, XVI (1952), 273-91.
† Includes 3 roll calls duplicated in the other labor scale.
‡ Excludes the duplication of 3 roll calls in one of the labor scales.

characterized by "summing" his votes on a number of presumably related roll calls.[14]

Aggregates of legislators have received a variety of characterizations from roll call analysts.

1. Using all roll calls cast during a particular time span on a particular subject or issue, Grassmuck has "summed" the "pro" and "anti" votes of the members of each party (during the time span) from each geographical section of the country. In the end, he was able to compare the percentage of, say, "pro-Navy" votes cast by, say, Northeastern Democrats with the percentages of "pro-Navy" votes cast by any other regional-partisan aggregates.[15]

2. Westerfield, having classified each roll call he studied as involving a "party-line" vote, a "two-party majority" vote, and "administration support" (or opposition), then computed, for each member of either House, the percentage of roll calls in each of these categories on which the member either supported his party's majority or supported the administration. Using this percentage as a predicate for each legislator, Westerfield made frequency distributions of the percentages among regional-partisan aggregates in both Houses, and then compared the several frequency distributions.[16]

3. Rice's "index of cohesion" is another example of a type of predicate that is designed to characterize the behavior of an aggregate of legislators. In its simplest form, the index applies only to the behavior of an aggregate on a single roll call, although typically, the researcher sums and averages the varying indexes of cohesion of the "same" aggregate on a number of roll calls and thus produces a mean index of cohesion of the aggregate. Different aggregates are then compared in respect of their mean indexes of cohesion.[17]

The remaining category of "particular facts" or predicates that earlier roll call analysis has used is the category of facts about *relations*—relations between (or among) legislators, aggregates of legislators, or roll calls. The end product of research which uses any of the first three categories of predicates already summarized is, to be sure, a comparison between (or among) two or more "things," and comparison, of course, implies the possibility of relation. But the fourth category of predicates differs from the first three in that, for the fourth, the research operations on the roll call data yield, "directly," a particular type of predicate (statistic, index) which is, itself, a statement of relation.

In the literature of roll call analysis, there appear a rather wide variety of kinds of relational predicates.

1. Rice's technique for the detection of blocs is the simplest—and most laborious—of the relational techniques. Using all roll calls in which every possible duo of legislators take part, the method yields the number (or percentage) of roll calls in which both members of each possible duo voted the same way—in which they agreed.[18] Although Rice's method is quite simple in principle, not many researchers have used it, because of the large number of possible comparisons between all different duos of members in a "large" (say, 30 or more members) legislative body. Beyle's study of the Minnesota Senate, although adversely criticized for its neglect of probability theory, is apparently the largest operation to have used the Rice technique.[19] Truman has made a somewhat limited use of the method, with regard to agreements among members of state delegations in the national House.[20] And Pritchett's studies of Supreme Court "voting" behavior involve, essentially, an application of Rice's technique to a nine-member "legislative" body, each of whose non-unanimous decisions Pritchett has treated, in effect, as "roll calls."[21]

2. Rice's "index of likeness" is one of the earliest techniques used to yield a "direct" index comparing two aggregates of legislators. Typically, the researcher calculates an index of likeness for the two aggregates on each of a number of roll calls, and then averages the several indexes of likeness.[22] As a relational index of the degree of closeness of party voting on roll calls, Turner has used not only the Rice index of likeness, but the statistic X^2 as well.[23]

3. There have also been two published studies whose authors have either correlated or compared votes on one roll call or on "summed" sets of roll calls with votes on either roll calls or sets. The relational index used in the correlation study was the tetrachoric correlation coefficient. It was in this study, also, that a factor analysis of roll call voting appeared.[24] In the comparison or consistency study, Brimhall and Otis, having computed "progressivism" scores for all Senators and Representatives in four successive sessions of Congress, tabulated the "magnitude" of the inter-session changes in the members' scores and arrived at an estimate of the members' consistency as "progressives."[25]

With the completion of this methodological summary, the question recurs: why scale? If scaling is a "better" technique than other techniques of roll call analysis, its superiority ought to be specifiable in terms of the ways in which it, in comparison with other techniques, copes with certain recurring problems common to all, or almost all, roll call analysis. The most important of these problems appear to be:

1. The problem of what roll calls should be selected for analysis.
2. The problem of absent or undeclared members.
3. The problem of reliability.
4. The problem of "adding" or "summing" a number of roll calls so as to yield an ordinal "metric."
5. The problem of flexibility.

The selection problem comes up in the literature in more than one way. The researchers or their critics worry about a system of "weights" that, if known, would lead to the selection of the "most important" roll calls for analysis.[26] Or the analyst—frequently a "lib-lab" publicist—will select certain roll calls during a session as "key" roll calls, without specifying what makes a roll call "key."[27]

Actually, the selection problem is not one problem, but two.[28] The first problem is for the researcher to identify the distinguishable issues—to determine the dimensionality—of the entire aggregate of non-unanimous roll calls taken during a session (or term of office) of a legislative body. The second problem is that of selecting a roll call on an issue that will dichotomize the members into two groups, one "pro" and one "con" on the issue.

So far as the literature is concerned, the roll call analyst has met both these problems by the exercise of "judgment" or "common sense" or by drawing on his personal stock of "lore." The difficulty with this way of meeting problems is that it is not consistently repeatable by different persons: the method lacks "publicness," or inter-subjective validity.

Scaling, by contrast, is of great assistance in identifying and defining the number of distinguishably different issues—major *or* minor, apparent or *not* to "common sense" and "judgment"—that lie implicit in all the non-unanimous roll calls of a particular session or term.

If a collection of roll calls "scales," the roll calls involve: (a) only one dimension or issue; or (b) two or more highly correlated issues; or (c) coalition behavior among legislators.[29] When a researcher, using his "judgment" and the criteria of scalability, has included the largest possible number of roll calls within the smallest possible number of scales, he is left with a collection—large or small—of roll calls that do not "belong" (in terms of the criteria of scalability) with any of the scales he has prepared. These "non-belonging" roll calls fall into two categories. One contains roll calls each of which presents an issue that is *sui generis* for the particular session or term. The other category contains roll calls each of which presents two or more issues and is multi-dimensional.[30] In

principle, the dimensionality of each roll call of the second sort can be demonstrated by cross tabulation with two or more of the uni-dimensional scales.

It follows, therefore, that the minimum dimensionality of a heterogeneous aggregate of roll calls—the minimum number of distinct issues inherent in them—is the sum of the minimum possible number of scales that can be prepared plus the number of *sui generis* roll calls.

Various roll call analysts have coped—whether consciously or not—with the dimensionality problem in different ways. Rice, for example, seems hardly to have been aware of it. Grassmuck and Westerfield, by restricting their concern to foreign affairs, by sub-categorizing roll calls in that policy area, and by making separate analyses within each sub-category, have probably avoided, in large measure, the dimensionality problem. Their "method" is not however, readily generalizable to the dimensional problems inherent in a more heterogeneous collection of roll calls. Correlational or factor analysis (the Harris technique) can yield dimensionality information—can identify most, if not all, of the distinguishably different issues—but such analysis is at least as laborious as scaling. A factor analysis, moreover, will not always leave the roll call data it has processed in a form that is usable for further research purposes, in other research contexts. Scaling avoids this disadvantage of factor analysis.

The dichotomy problem may be most clearly presented in an illustration. Given, for example, five roll calls on, say, labor issues, all of which "scale," where should the analyst dichotomize the scale—how should he dichotomize the members of the legislative body—if he wishes, for particular research purposes, to categorize members as either "pro-labor" or "anti-labor"? For the "judgment" researcher, the problem is, by "common sense," to pick one roll call which, somehow, "best represents" the entire collection of labor-issue roll calls. For the scale analyst, his scale will strongly indicate not only whether it is "appropriate" to dichotomize, but also, where the dichotomy should be made.

Consider the two examples in Table 3. Each set of roll calls, assumed to be all the labor roll calls taken in two different Congresses, shows a range of pro-labor percentages that runs from 20 to 80 per cent. In the absence of a scale, "judgment" can hardly yield a very certain cutting point—pick a representative roll call—for dichotomizing the members of either Congress. Scaling the two sets of roll calls, however, will yield distributions of members into scale types that closely approximate the expected distributions shown in the table. Clearly, the labor issue does not divide the members in Example 2 into two fairly distinct blocs: the distribution of scale types strongly suggests that a dichotomy would be inappropriate. Quite the opposite situation obtains in Example 1, whose scale exhibits rather strong polarity among the members. To dichotomize between types 4 and 5 in Example 1 would, probably, erroneously categorize, at most, about five per cent of the members.[31]

Table 3—Scaling and the Dichotomy Problem

EXAMPLE 1		EXAMPLE 2	
Roll Call Percentages		Roll Call Percentages	
R.C. No.	% Pro-Labor	R.C. No.	% Pro-Labor
1	20	101	20
2	25	102	35
3	30	103	50
4	50	104	65
5	80	105	80

Expected Distribution of Scale Types		Expected Distribution of Scale Types	
Type	% of Members	Type	% of Members
6 (pro)	20	6 (pro)	20
5	5	5	15
4	5	4	15
3	20	3	15
2	30	2	15
1 (anti)	20	1 (anti)	20

In addition to its utility in solving selection problems, scaling also permits the analyst to make plausible inferences about the way in which some, if not all, members absent or undeclared on a roll call would have voted had they been present.[32] Consider, by way of illustration, the voting patterns shown in Table 4, where a "0" represents an absence or a general pair. One can plausibly argue that: Representatives 1 and 5 would have voted "—" on Roll Call 3; Representative 2 would have voted "+" on Roll Call 2; Representative 3 would have voted "+" on Roll Calls 3 and 4; and Representative 4 would have voted "—" on Roll Call 2. In the examples of Representatives 6 and 7, it would not be possible, of course, to make inferences or imputations with so much plausibility.[33]

It does not seem that any method of roll call analysis which takes as the basic element for analysis an individual roll call can systematically handle the problem of undeclared members. If the researcher is not interested in seeing the number of cases for analysis diminish, the utility of scaling in reducing the "shrinkage" due to undeclared positions is obvious.

The reliability problem in roll call analysis is, according to one viewpoint, no problem at all. When a legislator votes on a roll call, he performs a highly public and, presumably, a deliberate and conscious act. One would expect, if this argument were valid, that a legislator would usually vote as he "really" intended to vote, and that his vote on a "re-take" roll call identical with an earlier one would be the same as his vote on the earlier one.

A number of roll call analysts, however, seem to have felt that, by "summing" or percentaging a member's votes on several apparently related roll calls, they produced an index that "better" (i.e., more reliably) indicated his position than his vote on any single roll call.[34] This feeling, of course, is quite justifiable: five roll calls, say, obviously furnish more (and presumably "better") information about a member than one does. A scale also uses several roll calls to characterize the positions of individual members on the scale. Except by comparing the number of roll calls "summed" to make an index, one cannot say that a scale is either more or less reliable (in this "summational" sense) than any other "summational" technique.

There is another "summational" context, however, in which scaling is clearly superior to other methods. More rigorously than the usual "summational" method, scaling assures that, when a researcher "sums" a member's votes, he is "summing" similar, rather than disparate, sorts of things. The student of grade school arithmetic early learns (or used to learn, at least) that one "can't add apples and pears." The reason, of course, is that pears and apples do not share the same dimensionality.

As Gage and Shimberg have neatly shown,[35] the New Republic's conception of Senatorial "progressivism" in 1945-46, "measured" by "summing" senators' votes on "key" roll calls involving "progressive" issues that the editors selected, was not a uni-dimensional concept. The New Republic gave a Senator, a "progressive" credit, for example, when he voted pro-welfare-state, as well as when he voted pro-Negro, even though these two

Table 4—Scaling and the Absence Problem

Representative's Number	Roll Call Number				
	1	2	3	4	5
1	—	—	0	—	—
2	+	0	+	+	+
3	+	+	0	0	+
4	—	0	—	+	+
5	—	—	0	—	+
6	—	—	0	+	+
7	0	0	+	+	+

aspects of Senatorial "progressivism" can be shown to be distinguishably different.

From these considerations, it seems that any "aggregative" technique that fails to demonstrate the uni-dimensionality of the roll call votes it "sums" or "percentages" or "averages" is suspect —suspect of adding pounds and inches, or apples and pears. Moreover, if a researcher uses such "sums," varying as they do from member to member (or group to group), as indexes to rank or order members in respect of the variable "degree" of some characteristic which the index predicates, then the rank orders are also suspect. Grassmuck's "pro-Navy" or "pro-international organization" percentages, for example, Turner's and Rice's "averages" of indexes of cohesion or of likeness on a number of roll calls, Brimhall and Otis' "progressivism" scores—indexes such as these may be equivocal or multi-vocal, rather than uni-vocal.[36] Scale analysis, by contrast, copes explicitly with the dimensionality, "summational," and "ordinality" problems, and the scales which it produces are uni-dimensional and ordinal within the limits of specifiable amounts of error.

There is one concluding sense in which earlier techniques of roll call analysis seem inferior to Guttman scaling. Many of the earlier techniques have an *ad hoc* quality about them, which tends to restrict their applicability to one or two types of research operations. The situation with scale analysis is different. Once a scale analyst has spanned a heterogeneous aggregate of roll calls with a variety of uni-dimensional scales, he has not only successfully coped with the selection problems, the problem of absent or undeclared members, and the problems of reliability, "additivity," and ordinality. Using his scales, he is also prepared, with little or no further effort, to characterize individual members or aggregates of members, to compare the scale positions of members with others of their characteristics, to correlate one scale with others, and even (providing any of his scales contains "enough" roll calls) to isolate blocs in large, as well as in small, legislative bodies.[37]

For all these reasons, scale analysis seems clearly superior to any other technique of roll call analysis. The skeptic, of course, may still argue that scale analysis is, after all, a pretty high-powered technique to be used on such low-powered data as roll calls. Without admitting that scale analysis is necessarily "high-powered," one may point out that this putatively devastating witticism obscures the relationship between the quality of data and the complexity or sophistication of the methods by means of which one processes them. When a researcher can collect high-powered data

under conditions that he designs and in regard to matters that he wishes, the analysis of such data ordinarily can proceed along relatively simple, unsophisticated lines. Indeed, under such circumstances, sophisticated analytical techniques may be a wasteful luxury.

Roll call data, however, are relatively low-powered or crude. The researcher cannot control the conditions under which, or the issues on which, a legislative body will take the yeas and nays. He must, instead, take the data as they come to him. If scale analysis *is* a high-powered technique, then its high power should make it peculiarly appropriate to extracting all available information from crude, low-powered roll call data.[38]

Three criteria guided the selection of the particular scales (or issues) that were used to define ideological groupings in the House of the 79th Congress:

1. The issues which the selected scales embodied should be issues of mass concern or mass importance; so far as possible, they should be issues that can be made to arouse, in very large numbers of people, a considerable emotional voltage.

2. The selected scales ought to span a rather wide range of diverse issues; an ideology is a poor thing whose cardinal points of doctrine dictate a stand on only one or two questions.

3. The issues should be, so nearly as possible, "non-partisan": in operational terms, the members' stands on each selected issue should correlate to the least possible extent with the members' party affiliations.[39]

These criteria may be summarized in a verbal definition of an "ideology": a set of stands (pro or con) on a variety of "important," emotionally charged and (potentially) socially divisive issues over which the major "parliamentary" parties do not, as parties, oppose one another.[40] An ideological grouping is any number of members who, by their voting, show that they publicly share a common or similar "ideology."

The six issues selected for analysis come from among the 27 scales which Table 2 classifies into eight broad categories. All the issues in categories VII and VIII deal with complex or technical questions that seem either to have comparatively little mass appeal, or to concern pressure groups which, however efficiently organized as lobbies, are not mass organizations. The ten issues in these two categories, which include only about one-fifth of the scaled roll calls, thus fail to meet one of the three necessary criteria for selection. Accordingly, they do not appear in the analysis.

The remaining six categories meet all, or all

but one, of the criteria. Each set is, or can be made, a subject of mass concern. Each set but one (Foreign Policy) [41] contains at least one scale that correlates moderately or hardly at all with nominal party affiliation. And the number of issues is large enough to provide a fair test of the proposition that the federal House contained a rather small number of large ideological groupings, instead of a large number of splinter groups.

The scales included in the analysis were: foreign policy (1946); selective service (1946); labor (1946); Un-American activities; Negroes; immigration and naturalization. The analysis will show that it is possible to construct three-, four-, and five-position ideological groupings by cross-tabulating members' positions on the several analyzed issues.

Here is how the construction of several three-position ideological groupings proceeded. The scales on foreign policy, selective service, and labor were dichotomized. [42] Each member with a score on the scales was thus classified as tending to favor multi-lateralism or uni-lateralism in foreign relations; as tending to favor or oppose a peace-time draft; and as tending to favor or oppose the legislative demands of trade union organizations. Four hundred seven Representatives had scores on all three scales. The dichotomies yielded 271 "multi-lateralists" and 136 "uni-lateralists"; 311 supporters and 96 opponents of the draft; 138 "pro-laborites" and 269 "anti-laborites." There are eight possible ways in which the three dichotomies can be combined: These appear in Table 5.

Table 5—Major Ideological Groupings, U. S. House, 1945-1946

Foreign Policy	Draft	Labor	No. of Repr.	Ideological Designation
Multi	Vs	Pro	27	Liberal pacifists
Multi	Pro	Pro	97	Liberal internationalists
Multi	Vs	Vs	4*	Conservative pacifists
Multi	Pro	Vs	143	Conservative internationalists
Uni	Vs	Pro	8†	Liberal isolationists (LaFolletteites)
Uni	Pro	Pro	6‡	Liberal jingoes
Uni	Pro	Vs	65	Conservative jingoes
Uni	Vs	Vs	57	Conservative isolationists

* Barden (D-NCar), Boren (D-Okl), Folger (D-NCar), Russell (D-Tex).

† Bishop (R-Ill), Hull (Prog-Wisc), Lemke (R-ND), Mansfield (D-Mont), Murray (R-Wisc), Pittenger (R-Minn), Welch (R-Cal), White (D-Ida).

‡ Bender (R-Ohio), Butler (R-NY), Corbett (R-Pa), Engel (R-Mich), Kunkel (R-Pa), O'Konski (R-Wisc).

The following definitions appear in the names of the ideological groupings:

1. "Internationalists" means pro-draft multi-lateralists.

2. "Pacifists" means anti-draft multi-lateralists.

3. "Jingoes" means pro-draft uni-lateralists ("nationalists" might have been used in place of "jingoes").

4. "Isolationists" means anti-draft uni-lateralists.

5. "Liberal" means pro-labor, and "conservative" means anti-labor. [43]

Although there are eight logically possible categories, only five contain more than five per cent of the Representatives classified. The three smallest categories contain, altogether, less than five per cent of all the members with positions on all three scales.

A few speculative, non-assertive remarks about the ideological groupings may serve heuristic purposes. Conservative pacifism and liberal jingoism are apparently rather infrequently occurring ideological positions in the recent history of Western civilization. Liberal isolationism is, obviously, the traditional position of Wisconsin LaFolletteism, and it is arresting to note how small the Congressional representation of that position had become by 1946. Conservative isolationism may be a uniquely American phenomenon, although it may have counterparts in the national policies of some of the major Asiatic countries before they were "opened up" to the West. Liberal pacifism is—or was—the position of the American "left." Liberal internationalism would appear to correspond to the leadership position of the New Deal and Fair Deal after 1941. Conservative internationalism and conservative jingoism are positions espoused by many Western political movements during the 19th and 20th centuries.

A party-region breakdown of the ideological positions just defined, such as appears in Table 6, reveals some familiar facts in what may be a new guise. Liberalism, internationalism, and pacifism, as here defined, characterize much larger percentages of Democrats than of Republicans. Correspondingly, conservatism, jingoism, and isolationism characterize greater percentages of Republicans than of Democrats.

Within party groupings, the Democrats exhibit the long-familiar split between conservatives and liberals, as well as a less familiar and less severe split between internationalists and pacifists. [44] The Republican representatives were made up, for the most part, of three approximately equal groups of conservatives: internationalists, jingoes, and isolationists.

Regionally considered, the liberal-conservative split in the Democrats is the familiar South-non-South one. The pacifist group was concentrated mainly in the big cities of the Northeast, Midwest and Pacific areas. The Republicans' main supply of internationalists came from the Northeast, of jingoes from the Northeast and Midwest, and of isolationists from the Midwest.

The elements of the ideological positions just defined are the stands that Representatives took on only three major divisive issues. It can be argued, of course, that an ideology which takes stands on only three questions is rather unelaborate. To meet this objection, it is necessary to introduce additional issues into the analysis.

Bringing in new issues can have one of at least two possible consequences. The number of distinguishable ideological groupings in the House may become so large—the membership, that is to say, might become so fragmented into such a large number of splinter groups—that it would no longer make much political sense to think of Representatives in the groupings as leaders with a mass of followers. Conceivably, however, the number of major distinguishable groupings might continue to remain rather small, even as the number of

stands on issues in each grouping's ideology increased.

Table 7 shows the effect of introducing the Un-American Activities Committee as an additional issue. Of the five *major* groupings already defined, only the liberal internationalists are divided by this issue.

Table 8 shows the effect of introducing the Negro question as an issue in addition to the original three. Among the five *major* groupings already defined, the conservative internationalists split sharply,[45] and a small "anti-Negro" group splinters away from the conservative jingoes and the conservative isolationists.

The joint effects of introducing the Communist and Negro issues are shown in Table 9, along with the estimated number of Representatives, out of 435, who fall into each grouping. The significant thing about Table 9 is that, although there are 32 logically possible groupings of pro and con positions on five issues, only seven of the logically

Table 6—Regional-Partisan Correlates of Ideological Groupings, U. S. House, 1946

Nominal Party	Region	Lib. Pac.	Lib. Int.	Cons. Pac.	Cons. Int.	Lib. Iso.	Lib. Jingo	Cons. Jingo	Cons. Iso.	N
Demo.	Northeast	26%	74%	0	0	0	0	0	0	(47)
	South	0	8	3	81	0	0	8	0	(90)
	Border	0	43	4	54	0	0	0	0	(28)
	Midwest	21	79	0	0	0	0	0	0	(29)
	Rocky Mt.	14	43	0	14	29	0	0	0	(7)*
	Pacific	37	47	0	16	0	0	0	0	(19)
Repub.	Northeast	0	9	0	57	0	4	25	6	(69)
	South	0	0	0	0	0	0	100	0	(1)*
	Border	0	0	0	0	0	0	36	64	(11)*
	Midwest	0	1	0	7	5	4	35	48	(85)
	Rocky Mt.	0	0	0	0	0	0	50	50	(6)*
	Pacific	0	8	0	46	8	0	23	15	(13)*
Demo.	Total	12	40	2	42	1	0	3	0	(220)
Repub.	Total	0	4	0	28	3	3	31	31	(185)

* The percentages in these lines are unreliable for comparison purposes, since they are based on comparatively small N's.

Table 7—Attitudes Toward the Unamerican Activities Committee

Major Ideological Grouping	UNAMERICAN ACTIVITIES SCALE					
	1-2	3-4	5	6-7	8-9	N*
Liberal pacifists	4%	0%	8%	8%	81%	(26)
Liberal internationalists	4	17	6	30	42	(93)
Cons. internationalists	71	24	0	3	2	(131)
Cons. jingoes	90	10	0	0	0	(62)
Cons. isolationists	93	5	0	0	2	(56)
Total — all parties	55	16	2	9	17	(383)
Demo. — Non-So., Non-Border	2	6	8	29	55	(97)
Demo. — So.	65	28	0	6	1	(80)
Repub. — all	83	13	0	1	3	(179)

* Because the three smallest groupings have been omitted, the N's do not add to exactly 383.

Table 8—Attitudes Toward Federal Policy Re: Negoes

NEGRO SCALE

MAJOR IDEOLOGICAL GROUPING	1-2	5	6-7	8-9	N*
Liberal pacifists	0%	0%	0%	100%	(23)
Liberal internationalists	5	4	5	87	(84)
Cons. internationalists	58	5	10	24	(136)
Cons. jingoes	16	4	8	72	(61)
Cons. isolationists	13	10	19	58	(52)
Total — all parties	28	6	9	58	(372)
Demo. — Non-So.	0	1	5	94	(85)
Demo. — So.	96	3	1	0	(88)
Repub. — Non-So., Non-Border	6	6	15	73	(161)

* Because the three smallest groupings have been omitted, the N's do not add to exactly 372.

Table 9—Structure of Major and Minor Ideological Groupings, 1945-1946

Group No.	Foreign Policy	De-fense (Draft)	La-bor	Un-Am. Com.	Ne-groes (Fed.)	Esti-mated No.	Size* %
1	Major Multi	Vs	Pro	Vs	Pro	29	6.6
2	Major Multi	Pro	Pro	Vs	Pro	81	18.6
3	Major Multi	Pro	Pro	Pro	Pro	22	5.1
4	Major Multi	Pro	Vs	Pro	Pro	54	12.3
5	Major Multi	Pro	Vs	Pro	Vs	101	23.3
6	Major Uni	Pro	Vs	Pro	Pro	56	12.9
7	Major Uni	Vs	Vs	Pro	Pro	46	10.5
8	Minor Multi	Vs	Vs	—	—	4	0.9
9	Minor Uni	Pro	Pro	—	—	6	1.5
10	Minor Uni	Vs	Pro	—	—	8	2.0
11	Minor Uni	Pro	Vs	Pro	Vs	14	3.1
12	Minor Uni	Vs	Vs	Pro	Vs	14	3.1

* The percentages were obtained from the distribution of Representatives actually classified. These percentages, applied to the entire House, yielded the estimates in the "No." column.

possible groupings contain as many as five per cent of the members classified. Moreover, the members classified in the seven most numerous groupings comprise about 90 per cent of the entire House.[46]

Obviously, if attitudes toward aliens are introduced into the analysis, additional splinter groups and, conceivably, additional major groupings would result. This article includes no such analysis. Table 10, however, does display the divisive effects of variations in xenophobia on the simple, three-issue ideological groupings earlier defined. Of the five original major groupings, three are rather sharply split by the foreigner issue.[47]

It seems fair to conclude, then, that it is possible to construct a manageable number of ideological groupings in terms of Representatives' voting behavior on selected "major" issues. But are the selected issues the "right" ones—the only issues that "should" be used to define ideological group-

ings? Would the other, unselected scales in Table 2 "fit in with" the major groupings defined in this article, or would they, if included, have defined different groupings?

Part of the answers to these questions depends

Table 10—Attitudes Toward the Foreign-Born

Major Ideological Groupings	Immigration and Naturalization Scale 1	2	3	4	N*
Liberal pacifists	0%	0%	13%	87%	(24)
Liberal internationalists	3	1	9	87	(78)
Cons. internationalists	28	13	21	38	(106)
Cons. jingoes	48	4	20	28	(54)
Cons. isolationists	61	8	18	14	(51)
Total — all parties	29	6	17	48	(326)
All Democrats	20	8	14	58	(173)
All Republicans	38	5	20	37	(151)

* Because the three smallest groupings have been omitted, the N's do not add to exactly 326.

upon one's conception of an "ideological" issue. As political scientists, sociologists, and historians use it, the term "ideology" is not exactly a precise one.[48] This being so, a political scientist interested in "ideology" has available three alternative research strategies:

1. He can engage in verbalism about the meaning of the term.

2. He can postpone behavioral research on "ideology" until most members of the profession agree on what the word means.

3. He can propose, and, while he remains committed to them, he can consistently apply operational criteria for defining "ideology" and "ideological grouping." In so doing, he may possibly contribute both to the encouragement of his own and others' behavioral research, and to the systematization of political theory into researchable terms.

Since the third of these strategies obviously guided the research for this article, the unanswered portions of the questions recur. So far as categories V and VI in Table 2 are concerned, there was no selection problem, since there was only one issue or scale in each category. Categories I and IV, likewise, presented no real problem: the two foreign policy scales correlate fairly highly with each other ($\phi = .79$), and so do the two Un-American activities scales ($\phi = .80$). What these correlations mean is that it would have made rather little difference, so far as defining ideological groupings, which of the two scales in either category was selected.

There was a selection problem in categories II and III, whose solution the "non-partisanship" criterion facilitated. It is true that the selection, for analysis, of other scales than the draft and labor scales would have altered—in some cases, considerably—the groupings that emerged from the analysis. But the putative groupings that would have emerged, had other issues been selected, would have been divided (depending upon the degree of the selected scale's correlation with party affiliation) along Democratic-Republican lines, rather than along "liberal-conservative" or "pacifist-internationalist-jingoist-isolationist" lines.

To the apparently large number of people who are unable to see "real" differences between the major American parties, a demonstration that, on "selected" issues, the parties differ might have seemed a novel finding. It did not seem necessary, however, to write an article confirming Turner's work on the subject of party differences.

There was also a selection problem in categories VII and VIII. Some scales on both categories correlate moderately well with nominal party affiliation, and including them in the analysis would have led to the consequences described earlier. But there was a better reason for rejecting all issues in these two categories: it is difficult to see how they could be made to arouse much emotion or sense of commitment among any large number of people. But it is still true that such issues, if incorporated into the present ideological analysis, would have produced "ideological" groupings different from those already defined.

The process of making operational definitions is an end in itself for, possibly, only the professional specialist in methodology. Although the orientation of the present research report has been mainly methodological, the principal reason for showing that "ideological groupings" could be isolated and identified, even in an American context, was an heuristic one—to assist in, or to stimulate, further systematization of political theory into *researchable* terms.

Once the groupings have been defined, of course, the researcher can do many things by way of identifying the characteristics that discriminate, in a statistically significant sense, among the various groupings. Unless such research is to degenerate into, or never rise above, crude empiricism,[49] however, the researcher ought to be aware, in fairly broad terms, at least, of the types of characteristics he can reasonably attempt to relate to the ideological groupings and of the types of questions he ought to raise in his research.[50]

Among the types of questions, the following sorts seem relevant, in a specifically American context: biographical, situational, and developmental. Essentially, the biographical question is this: do the biographies of members differ significantly from one ideological grouping to another? Do the biographies differ only in respect of particular biographical traits, or can one line a number of different socio-biographical types whose incidences vary sharply from one ideological grouping to another?

There are problems in a biographical approach to ideology. Matthews, for example, has stressed the skimpiness of the biographical data available in the United States for such comparatively numerous and unimportant politicos as Representatives in Congress, but he, Lasswell, and the latter's associates have elaborated a fairly simple methodology, and have exploited some of the possibilities of the data available to them.[51] The researcher should obviously avoid using ideological data in constructing biographical types. And he should face up to the fact that, since biography and ideology are only two of the many variables in most political situations, he must be able to invent and apply relevant controls before he can show the plausibility of any connection between the two variables that interest him. Happily, because of the availability of some relatively simple techniques of multi-variate analysis,[52] the contemporary political scientist does not always need to feel impotent when confronted with a set of multiple, intricately interlocked variables.

The situational type of question is this: what sorts of constituencies, characterized in what ways, tend to send what sorts of "ideologues" to a legislative body? A similar type of question has been treated in much of the earlier work on roll call analysis, and a number of constituency typologies, based on a variety of constituency characteristics, is available. The relationship between constituency and ideology, like the biography-ideology relationship, exists, if it exists, in a multi-variate total context. Therefore, to demonstrate its existence will probably require the techniques of multivariate analysis.

The developmental problem is more complicated, since it concerns two very general sorts of questions: first, do the "same" ideological groupings persist from one session or term of a legislative body to another (are the groupings defined in this article, for example, peculiar to the 79th Congress); and second, under what historical conditions does membership in (recruitment into) an ideological grouping increase or decrease? The methodological problems in this area, though present, are susceptible of treatment in terms of an emerging codification of ways to analyze change through time.[53]

In addition to their usefulness in exploring these sorts of questions, which one may raise in a specifically American context, the concepts of ideology and ideological grouping seem of potential value in exploring some transnational, comparative aspects of political behavior. On the assumption that it would be possible to define—but not necessarily by the method used in this article—comparable ideological groupings for the legislative assemblies of a number of jurisdictions,[54] one could test the validity, in a variety of contexts, of proportions relating biographical, situational, and developmental variables to ideological ones.

Given the richness (despite its rather short duration) and the variety of the American political heritage, American political scientists may be pardoned for having possibly displayed an unconscious nationalistic bias—a bias that stressed the uniqueness and incomparability of American political phenomena.[55] Unfortunately, however, a political science based on American data and embodying propositions that hold only in the United States is a parochial political science, and parochial political science, like nationalistic physics and bourgeois genetics, is a contradiction in terms.

Notes

1. The substance of this article was presented as a paper, on November 9, 1956, at the meeting of the Southern Political Science Association at Gatlinburg, Tennessee. The comments of the panelists have helped me revise the paper. I have also received help from three other sources. Both the Research Committee and the Bureau of Public Administration of the University of Alabama have supplied financial support for the research on which the paper is based. My wife has served as an unpaid research associate.
2. *Cf.* DeAlva Stanwood Alexander, *History and Procedure of the House of Representatives* (Boston, 1916), pp. 155-179.
3. A minority of less than 10 per cent forces roll calls on a largely united legislative body; a constitution requires roll calls on certain types of questions, regardless of the lack of divided sentiment thereon; members, being "really" united on a question, are concerned to display their sentiments to a pressure group whose members are distributed throughout the country, or to force the hand of the other house of a legislative body when a conference committee is considering a bill. See A. Lawrence Lowell, "The Influence of Party upon Legislation in England and America," American Historical Association, *Annual Report, 1901*, 324-25; Stuart A. Rice, *Quantitative Methods in Politics* (New York, 1928), pp. 211-12; Julius Turner, *Party and Constituency: Pressures on Congress* (Johns Hopkins University Studies in Historical and Political Science, series LXIX, no. 1; Baltimore, 1952), pp. 14, 18; H. Bradford Westerfield, *Foreign Policy and Party Politics: Pearl Harbor to Korea* (New Haven, 1955), pp. 69, 338.
4. Lowell, *op. cit.*, p. 323.
5. Turner, *op. cit.*, pp. 23-24.
6. Westerfield, *op. cit.*, p. 24.
7. Guttman scale analysis has yielded a large methodological literature. Some references: Louis Guttman, "A Basis for Scaling Qualitative Data," *American Sociological Review*, IX (April, 1944), 139-50; Samuel A. Stouffer, "An Overview of the Contributions to Scaling and Scale Theory," in Samuel A. Stouffer *et al.*, *Measurement and Prediction*, vol. IV of *Studies in Social Psychology in World War II* (Princeton, 1950), pp. 3-19. For a good summary, critique, and bibliography, see Bert F. Green, "Attitude Measurement," in Gardner Lindzey, ed., *Handbook of Social Psychology* (Cambridge, Mass., 1954), I, 335-69.
8. George M. Belknap, "A Study of Senatorial Voting by Scale Analysis," unpublished Ph.D. dissertation, University of Chicago, 1951; N. L. Gage and Ben Shimberg, "Measuring Senatorial Progressivism," *Journal of Abnormal and Social Psychology*, XLIV (January, 1947), 112-17.
9. Charles D. Farris, "Scale Analysis of Roll Call Voting in the U. S. House of Representatives" [abstract], *Journal of the Alabama Academy of Sciences*, XXVI (December, 1954), 98. And see a forthcoming work by Duncan MacRae on the House of the 80th Congress, and work in progress by Hugh Price.
10. For the definition of "successful," see the works cited in note 7.
11. For the criteria, see the works cited in note 7.
12. Regardless of whether the "members" of the aggregate interact with each other or not. Turner makes a clear distinction between indexes of individual and of

aggregate behavior. Turner, *op. cit.*, p. 78. Frequently, the researcher who compares aggregates with one another is examining the aggregates for the existence of behavior from which interaction among the "members" of each aggregate may be plausibly or convincingly inferred.

13. Lowell, *op. cit.*; Turner, *op. cit.*, pp. 23-25.

14. Dichotomous characterizations different from and equally as useful as those mentioned in the text are readily imaginable. For an example of "summing" the votes both of an individual member, and of two or more members who, being of the same party, successively represent the same district, see George L. Grassmuck, *Sectional Biases in Congress on Foreign Policy* (Johns Hopkins University Studies in Historical and Political Science, series LXVIII, no. 3; Baltimore, 1951), pp. 20-29. For "summing" the votes of individuals, see Westerfield, *op. cit.*, pp. 25-29, and note also the summed "progressivism" scores used by Dean R. Brimhall and Arthur S. Otis, "Consistency of Voting by Our Congressmen," *Journal of Applied Psychology*, XXXII (February, 1948), 1-14.

15. Grassmuck, *op. cit.*

16. Westerfield, *op. cit.*

17. Rice, *op. cit.*, pp. 208-9, 212-18; Turner, *op. cit.*, pp. 26-29.

18. Rice, *op. cit.*, pp. 228-38. I use the term "duo" rather than "pair" to avoid confusion with "voting pairs" that absent legislators sometimes enter into.

19. Herman C. Beyle, *Identification and Analysis of Attribute-Cluster-Blocs: a Technique for Use in the Investigation of Behavior in Governance, Including Report on Identification and Analysis of Blocs in a Large Nonpartisan Legislative Body, the 1927 Session of the Minnesota State Senate* (Chicago, 1931); Samuel P. Hayes, Jr., "Probability and Beyle's 'Index of Cohesion,'" *Journal of Social Psychology*, IX (May, 1938), 161-67.

20. David B. Truman, "The State Delegations and the Structure of Party Voting in the United States House of Representatives," *American Political Science Review*, L (December, 1956), 1023-45.

21. *Cf.* C. Herman Pritchett, *The Roosevelt Court: a Study in Judicial Politics and Values, 1937-1947* (New York, 1948), especially Ch. II.

22. Rice, *op. cit.*, pp. 210-16.

23. Turner, *op. cit.*, pp. 29-33, and Ch. III.

24. Chester W. Harris, "A Factor Analysis of Selected Senate Roll Calls, 80th Congress," *Educational and Psychological Measurement*, VIII (1948), 582-91.

25. Brimhall and Otis, *op. cit.*

26. *Cf.* Grassmuck, *op. cit.*, pp. 23-24; Turner, *op. cit.*, p. 20; Westerfield, *op. cit.*, p. 27. Typically, the researcher resolves his problem by "weighting" all "relevant" roll calls equally. His critics continue to carp at the lack of a system of "weights."

27. I do not intend to assert that an operational definition of a "key" roll call is impossible to frame, but simply to point out that users of the adjective "key" seldom define it operationally. There are, indeed, some grounds to suspect that they sometimes give it a "persuasive" definition. On "persuasive" definitions, see Charles L. Stevenson, *Ethics and Language* (New Haven, 1944), pp. 206 *et seq.*

28. I am not now considering the exclusion of "unanimous" roll calls or "party votes" from analysis. There is a well-developed rationale for excluding the former, and, in terms of the working definition of "ideological grouping" in this paper, for excluding the latter as well.

29. I am indebted to Frank Munger for pointing out that coalition behavior may lead to scales. He has commented that scales based on roll calls may not be unidimensional in an attitudinal sense because of coalition behavior among differently motivated blocs. For example, administration supporters from "weak" labor districts and "laborites" from "strong" labor districts might both support a pro-labor bill and oppose anti-labor amendments to it. In terms of logic, Munger's point is well taken, and

a scale analyst's only chance to establish "real" uni-dimensionality in Munger's attitudinal sense would be to hope for a set of roll calls on a measure that sunders the coalition—for example, a bill, recommended by the President, providing for the military draft of strikers. If no such roll calls occur, the existence of the components of the coalition can not be inferred from the scale, but only from other sorts of behavioral data than roll call voting.

30. As examples, roll calls that are, possibly, bi-dimensional might be taken on the following questions: a farm surplus commodity dumping amendment to a mutual security authorization bill; a civil rights (anti-discrimination) amendment to a school lunch bill.

31. Readers familiar with the literature of Guttman scaling will recognize obvious connections between the argument in the text and Guttman's treatment of the "zero-point" problem by means of intensity analysis. I have been unable, so far, to devise an intensity scale or quasi-scale based on Congressmen's roll call voting. Assuming the validity of Guttman's solution of the "zero-point" problem, the solution that I propose in the text is obviously, therefore, something less than satisfactory. *Cf.* Louis Guttman and Edward A. Suchman, "Intensity and a Zero Point for Attitude Analysis," *American Sociological Review*, XII (February, 1947), 57-67; Edward A. Suchman and Louis Guttman, "A Solution to the Problem of Question 'Bias'," *Public Opinion Quarterly*, XI (1947), 445-55.

32. Rice (*op. cit.*, note, p. 231) has noted both the desirability and the difficulty of imputing positions to absent or undeclared members.

33. Inferences such as those in the text are possible because a scale not only makes possible, in Pepper's terms, "multiplicative corroboration" (consistent observations of the same "things" by different observers), but also exhibits "structural corroboration" as well. See Stephen C. Pepper, *World Hypotheses: a Study in Evidence* (Berkeley, 1942), pp. 47 *et seq.*

34. See Brimhall and Otis, *op. cit.*; Grassmuck, *op. cit.*; Westerfield, *op. cit.*

35. *Op. cit.*

36. These criticisms should be read subject to the qualifications that appear in the earlier treatment of unidimensionality and the selection problem.

37. The term "bloc" being defined in Rice's sense, it seems clear that members who occupy the same scale type, or two adjacent scale types, may be thought of as blocs.

38. W. Allen Wallis, "Statistics of the Kinsey Report," *Journal of the American Statistical Association*, XLIV (December, 1949), 463-84.

39. I do not intend to try to show that the "parliamentary" Democratic and Republican parties are "ideological" parties; rather, I am postulating that, in an American context, the (relative) absence of "partisanship" on an issue is a necessary, but not a sufficient, condition for that issue's being "ideological" in character.

40. I do not claim that this definition is applicable to the party politics of other countries. Whether it is, and whether "ideological groupings" as defined in this paper correspond to ideological groupings in other countries are questions for further research.

41. It would have been desirable for the foreign policy scales not to have correlated so highly with party affiliation. As noted above, however, the roll call researcher "must take the data as they come to him."

42. All dichotomies in Table 2 were made according to the principles discussed in the previous section and in Table 3.

43. Admittedly, I have selected these labels for their heuristic value. I put the reader on notice, however, that I have not intended to make any assertion in this article depend upon the rich, ambiguous, vague, or conflicting connotations of the labels. The definitions in the text

are intended to mean no more than what the text denotes them to mean.

44. Commenting on the 1946 draft roll calls, Westerfield argues that those whom I have called pacifist simply refused in an election year to vote for a "workable" draft bill. *Op. cit.*, pp. 199-200. This explanation may be correct, but it does not explain why 97 liberal internationalists "dared" vote in an election year for a "workable" draft.

45. As the reader may suspect, this issue splits the conservative internationalists into, approximately, Southern Democrats and non-Southern Republicans.

46. I have not been able to provide heuristic names for the groupings in Table 9.

47. Of the six scales selected for analysis, the one on immigration and naturalization is the weakest—weakest in terms of number of roll calls included, and weakest in terms of the high absence rates on all three roll calls included in the scale. In consequence, it proved possible to scale the votes of only about 325 members on the alien issue.

48. For some brilliant word-bandying, for example, see "Discussion," in *Totalitarianism:* Proceedings of a Conference Held at the American Academy of Arts and Sciences, ed. Carl J. Friedrich (Cambridge, Mass., 1954), pp. 129-37. The papers under discussion were: Alex Inkeles, "The Totalitarian Mystique: Some Impressions of the Dynamics of Totalitarian Society," *ibid.*, pp. 87-108; Franklin H. Littell, "The Protestant Churches and Totalitarianism (Germany 1933-1945)," *ibid.*, pp. 108-19;

Waldemar Gurian, "Totalitarianism as Political Religion," *ibid.*, pp. 119-29.

49. On "hyperfactualism" as an unfortunate characteristic of much American political research, see David Easton, *The Political System: an Inquiry into the State of Political Science* (New York, 1953), pp. 66-78.

50. What I am proposing is a simple "frame of reference," not a "miniature theory," to use Zetterberg's distinction. *Cf.* Hans Zetterberg, *On Theory and Verification in Sociology* (New York, 1954).

51. Donald R. Matthews, *The Social Background of Political Decision-Makers* (Doubleday Short Studies in Political Science, No. 8; Garden City, N. Y., 1954); Harold D. Lasswell, Daniel Lerner, and E. Easton Rothwell, *The Comparative Study of Elites: an Introduction and Bibliography* (Hoover Institute Studies, Series B, no. 1; Stanford, Cal., 1952); Daniel Lerner, *The Nazi Elite* (Hoover Institute Studies, Series B, no. 3; Stanford, Cal., 1951).

52. *The Language of Social Research:* a Reader in the Methodology of Social Research, ed. Paul F. Lazarsfeld and Morris Rosenberg (Glencoe, Ill., 1955), pp. 111-99.

53. *Ibid.*, pp. 203-83.

54. It does not seem reasonable to suppose that every possible grouping would appear in every jurisdiction. Poujadism, for example, may be unique in France.

55. Area research programs, like country desks in a foreign affairs department, may exhibit similar emphases in viewpoint, although not necessarily from a nationalistic bias in favor of a particular area or country.

DUE